INTRODUCTION TO
interpersonal relations

Clifford H. Swensen, Jr.
Purdue University

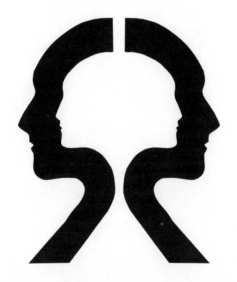

INTRODUCTION TO
interpersonal
relations

Scott, Foresman and Company
Glenview, Illinois   Brighton, England

Library of Congress Catalog Card Number: 72-96785
ISBN: 0-673-07597-4

Regional offices of Scott, Foresman and Company are located in Dallas, Texas;
Glenview, Illinois; Oakland, New Jersey; Palo Alto, California; Tucker,
Georgia; and Brighton, England.

To my father and mother,
whose ability to detect what
was going on between other people
was the wonder of my childhood.

Preface

The study of interpersonal relationships is a broad and complex undertaking that has its roots in disciplines ranging from theology to mathematics. People everywhere interact with one another; they form conclusions about the interpersonal interactions which they observe and in which they take part. I recall a real-estate agent once observing that he could always tell whether or not a prospect looking at a house was seriously interested in it. If the customer carefully noted things he did *not* like about the house, then he was interested; if the customer praised everything he saw in the house, then he was not likely to buy the house. Since the sales agent wants to sell his product, he studies the reactions of customers to his sales methods and learns which approach to use with which customer. He is a kind of applied researcher in a particular kind of interpersonal relations. The same can be said of adolescents who are beginning to date. Both boys and girls spend hours discussing the ways in which they interact with various members of the opposite sex, whom they like and why, who likes them and why, and the reasons for any conflicts.

This ubiquitous concern with interpersonal relations has spawned an industry of advice columns and advice books designed to improve the satisfaction people get from their interactions with each other. This concern has also resulted in a plethora of observation and research by psychiatrists, psychologists, sociologists, anthropologists, and other kinds of behavioral scientists — observation and research that have included almost every conceivable context within which people interact. Researchers have studied not only obvious situations, such as marriage and psychotherapy, but also less obvious settings, such as decision-making committees, navy combat information-center teams, and international diplomatic negotiations. If it is a situation within which people interact, almost certainly somebody has tried to study it, either as an observer or as a participant.

Since the study of interpersonal relationships covers such a wide range of topics and situations, a book dealing with the field must necessarily restrict the range of topics surveyed and focus on a particular approach so that the material produced can be contained within a single volume. This book focuses on the work done in specific areas by particular people or groups of people. Any study of an area, whether by observation or by laboratory research, implicitly or explicitly develops from and is organized around some particular point of view and some particular method of directing the search and organizing the information obtained from the search. This particular point of view is, by definition, a theory, whether or not it is formally acknowledged as such. Therefore, this book is probably more properly labeled a book of theories, although some of the material discussed is more empirical than theoretical. Since relationships do not occur in a vacuum, but rather between real people in real situations, much of the content of this book discusses specific kinds of relationships, such as those between two close friends, or between husbands and wives, or between psychotherapists and clients, or between parents and children. The dyadic, face-to-face relationship is basic, and ultimately it is the kind of relationship that is of most concern to people. The focus of INTRODUCTION TO INTERPERSONAL RELATIONS, then, is on the theories various people have proposed about the nature of relationships, including both the basic dimensions of these relationships and the ways in which these dimensions are involved in or relate to a relationship between two people. However, in studying interpersonal relations, it is not possible to completely confine the discussion to the two-person relationship, so some consideration of small groups enters into the material of this book.

The field of interpersonal relations has developed mainly out of three disciplines: psychiatry, psychology, and sociology. The psychiatric development has been based largely on clinical case studies, since psychiatrists treat people and draw conclusions from their experiences in psychotherapy. The psychological development of the field of interpersonal relations has been the most diverse of the disciplines, since psychologists come in various "models." Some psychologists also treat people, so some of their basic data are obtained from clinical case material. Psychologists also perform experiments, so some of their data come from laboratory observations of interpersonal interactions. These laboratory interactions are often carefully controlled experiments in which two or more people, often strangers to each other, interact under explicitly controlled conditions. Psychologists are also concerned with measuring behavior, so they have developed tests and other psychometric devices that measure or predict how a person will interact with other people. Therefore, some psychological data come from these psychometric devices. The psychometric approach has a method of thinking and a theoretical background which are its own and which have been applied to the study of interpersonal relationships to produce an ingenious way of viewing the topic. Finally, the sociological element of the field of interpersonal relations has its own special perspective to contribute. Sociologists study society and its institutions, such as marriage, and the roles people play in social settings.

The topics presented in INTRODUCTION TO INTERPERSONAL RELATIONS seem to fall into patterns that roughly correspond to the background training and experience of the people doing the studying and theorizing. The chapters are organized generally along these lines, with the psychiatric views coming first, followed by the psychological, and concluding with the sociological. Since psychiatrists tend to deal with people talking about themselves and about their experiences, while sociologists tend to deal with social statistics and the behavior of people as a function of the groups to which they belong or the roles they are playing, the organization of the book might also be viewed as progressing from the data obtained from individual persons involved in interactions to the data obtained from the external observation of the behavior of large groups of people. That is, the book moves in a sort of progression from an internal, close-up view to an external, long-distance view. However, people in the field of interpersonal relations tend to be curious and sociable—they exchange information and ideas with each other—so a certain amount of cross-fertilization has taken place.

However, not enough cross-fertilization has taken place, which brings me to a discussion of my objectives in writing this book. First, it has been my observation that people working in one area of interpersonal relations are frequently unaware of pertinent work or thinking taking place in another area. For example, one author writing about the application of attribution theory to emotional disturbance arrived at a hypothesis quite similar to Harry Stack Sullivan's concept of consensual validation. All this was done without any seeming awareness of Sullivan and his theories. I have repeatedly encountered instances of a similar vein. One objective of this book, then, has been to foster increased cross-fertilization by providing a single source which attempts to bring together, under one cover, the more pertinent approaches to the study of interpersonal relations.

A second objective has been to provide a survey of the field for students as they become more attracted to the study of interpersonal relationships. The very essence of the human race is a social and therefore an interpersonal one. This text, then, is designed for courses in Interpersonal Relations, Interpersonal Interaction, and Psychology of Human Relations. And some instructors may find it useful for Marriage and Counseling courses or Social Psychology courses. In addition, this text should be a valuable supplement to such courses as Personality, Communications, Sociology, Anthropology, Child Development, Abnormal Psychology, and Psychiatry. In short, students and instructors in any field that deals with the nature of human beings — their development, activities, and ideas — should find INTRODUCTION TO INTERPERSONAL RELATIONS a useful source for pursuing their studies.

Also, when I started this book, I had a third, personal objective — to inform myself in greater detail and depth.

In a way, writing a book is an act of arrogance, for one must assume that one has something to say which will be of importance to other people. And writing a book that presumes to describe the work and thinking of a large number of people who have devoted their lives to studying one particular aspect of a problem is probably an act of even greater arrogance. However, whatever arrogance may have prompted me to begin this task has long since been dissipated by the realization that interpersonal relations is a field growing far too rapidly for one person even to begin to account for the whole of it. In fact, some theories of this book might even now have been superseded, because the research and new discoveries in the field of interpersonal relations continue to progress at an accelerating rate of speed. However, to write this book I had to say to myself that I would stop at a certain point and do my best to give an account of the field as it appeared to me at that point. I cannot now assess how successful I have been at my first two objectives. That judgment is for others to make. But in terms of my third objective, the informing of myself, I can testify that the project has been highly successful. I have a much greater appreciation of how much there is to be learned, even in areas in which I initially considered myself to be rather well informed.

In writing a book of this sort, decisions must be made as to which areas to cover and which to leave out. Let me explain how I reached my decisions. When starting this project three years ago, I made an outline of the material I intended to cover. While reading each of the areas outlined, I made notes and followed up references until the area seemed to crystallize in my thinking. When this happened, I sat down and wrote. During this process, I often found myself leaving out or giving rather small mention to some authors whom I had originally thought would form a central part of a chapter, and conversely, I found myself devoting considerable space to authors whom I had thought peripheral.

Two people, in particular, received different amounts of space than I had anticipated at the time I began this project. They are Fritz Heider and Harry Stack Sullivan. Heider was the first author I read when I began investigating this field. I made more extensive notes on his *The Psychology of Interpersonal Relations* than on any other single book. His structure, which owes an intellectual debt to Kurt Lewin, was congenial to me, since Lewin was the theorist by whom I was most influenced as a graduate student. Heider's argument for a common-sense psychology also was a point of view for which I had sympathy. Therefore I expected Heider to occupy a much more prominent place in this book than he has. The reason he has not, I think, is that Heider was a stimulus to many other people, so his contribution does not appear as clearly as it might. His influence is there, but it is diffuse and not immediately apparent. Perhaps Heider would not be surprised by this, since he did not consider his book a theory so much as "work notes toward a pretheory of interpersonal relations." Sullivan, on the other hand, received more space than I had originally intended because the further I went in the project, the more I realized that practically every development that has taken place in the field of interpersonal relations in the past twenty years was anticipated and outlined by Sullivan.

✿   ✿   ✿

In the course of such a project, I have accumulated a large number of personal debts owed to people who have very generously aided me in the pursuit of this project, and to whom I wish to express my heartfelt thanks. The late John M. Hadley, formerly Chairman of the Psychology Department at Purdue, Marbury B. Ogle, Jr., formerly Dean of the School of Humanities, Social Science, and Education at Purdue, and James C. Naylor, current Chairman of the Department of Psychological Sciences at Purdue graciously allowed me to take a sabbatical year in which I started this project. Wilse B. Webb, former Chairman of the Psychology Department at the University of Florida, afforded me the hospitality of his department for a year, where this project was started. In addition, many colleagues have provided valuable discussion and stimulation. At the University of Florida these include Marvin Shaw, Irwin Silverman, and Franz Epting. I owe a special expression of thanks to my old friend, Sidney M. Jourard, who not only encouraged me in the project but also critically read parts of the manuscript. Many of my colleagues at Purdue have critically commented on the manuscript and provided materials for my use. These include Donn Byrne, Carl Castore, Kay Deaux, Richard Heslin, Fredic Weizmann, and Peter Schönemann. I owe extra thanks to Joseph Rychlak, who not only read the entire manuscript but also provided me with extensive useful comments on it. I also wish to thank Uriel G. Foa of Temple University, who provided valuable critical comments on parts of the manuscript.

I have attempted to have experts in each area discussed in this book read the manuscript, particularly to eliminate errors, which I hope I have kept to a minimum. But whatever errors remain are my fault for failing to learn as accurately as I could from those who were consistently generous in their attempts to correct me.

Finally, I would like to express my thanks to Harry Stack Sullivan and Fritz Heider. I never met either of these gentlemen, but I think it accurate to say that if it were not for them, the field of interpersonal relations would not have matured to the level it has reached today. Each in his own way was a pioneer whose seminal thoughts pointed the directions in which the field is now progressing.

An entirely different order of thanks is due to my secretaries, Gloria Fine, Lois Glotzbach, Marlene Airheart, and Carol Hopkins, who gave a variety of kinds of help, not the least of which was typing; Betsy Foote for drawing manuscript diagrams; my wife and children, who tried to stay out of my hair while I was working; and my students, who did not stay out of my hair, but who kept asking me if it wasn't finished yet, and if not, why not?

C. H. S.

Contents

Introduction

1

Selves can only exist in definite relationships to other selves. No hard-and-fast line can be drawn between our own selves and the selves of others, since our own selves exist and enter as such into our experience only insofar as the selves of others exist and enter as such into our experience also (1934, p. 164).

. . . human nature is something social through and through, and always presupposes the truly social individual (1934, p. 229).

—George Herbert Mead

People have been social beings from the beginning, and they have had problems in their social relationships from the beginning. The Bible tells us of how Adam and Eve had scarcely begotten two sons before sibling rivalry reared its ugly head, and their eldest son Cain slew his brother Abel, thus becoming the first elder brother on record to lose patience with a younger brother.

Any phenomenon which is as central to the being of people as interpersonal relationships and which produces the problems that interpersonal relationships have apparently produced is bound to be a topic of extensive observation and speculation. And in the writings of the ancients on this subject, we find that they observed, speculated, and instructed extensively.

The Book of Proverbs, for example, contains the instructions of a father to his son. It is full of observations on how to relate to various kinds of people, including rulers, beggars, the wise, the foolish, the righteous, the wicked, harlots, and other men's wives. To summarize, the instructions are to associate with the wise and the righteous; to avoid fools, the wicked, and harlots; to be generous and merciful to the weak and the poor; to deal circumspectly with the powerful. At a somewhat later date Jesus, the son of Sirach, made the observation that good interpersonal relationships preserve good health when he wrote, "A good wife makes a happy husband; / she doubles the length of his life."[1] With this statement, he anticipated the findings of psychosomatic medicine by some two thousand years.

Many of these observations concerning the relationships between people may be found in discussions of the topics of friendship and love. We find Cicero observing "that nature has so formed us that a certain tie unites us all, but that this tie becomes stronger from proximity."[2] This statement might be considered a hypothesis, which, as subsequent chapters will reveal, has been confirmed.

Yet however intensely the Ancients observed the interpersonal relationship and however many conclusions they reached, they were nonetheless confronted with some mysteries that neither they nor we have yet completely solved. The writer of Proverbs expresses the elusiveness of these mysteries in confessing:

> Three things are too wonderful for me;
>   four I do not understand:
> the way of an eagle in the sky,
>   the way of a serpent on a rock,
> the way of a ship on the high seas,
>   and the way of a man with a maiden.[3]

Background of the Modern Study of Interpersonal Relations

Until the beginning of the twentieth century, the study of interpersonal relationships continued to be the province of moral philosophers and essayists. We find such diverse spirits as St. Augustine, Montaigne, and

[1]From "Ecclesiasticus," *The Apocrypha, The New English Bible.* New York: Oxford University Press and Cambridge University Press, 1970, 26:1.
[2]From Cicero, "On Friendship." *Harvard Classics*, Vol. 9. New York: Collier & Son, 1909, p. 14.
[3]From "Proverbs," *The Oxford Annotated Bible, Revised Standard Version.* New York: Oxford University Press, 1965, 30:18–19.

Ralph Waldo Emerson discussing interpersonal relationships, usually, as did their predecessors, in the form of a discourse on friendship and love. Not until the twentieth century opened did social scientists begin to turn their attention toward interpersonal relationships. There is a good and sufficient reason for this lack, of course. Not until the twentieth century did such an animal as a social scientist exist.

The immediate forebear of the modern study of the interpersonal relationship was a psychiatrist named Harry Stack Sullivan. Sullivan completed medical school during World War I and, following the war, obtained a position as a psychiatrist working on a ward for schizophrenics. His unique contribution to the study and treatment of schizophrenia was the assertion that schizophrenia is primarily due to faulty experience in interpersonal relationships during the years of childhood and early adolescence. Since the schizophrenic disorder is primarily due to faulty interpersonal relationships, the cure is through the establishment of constructive, healing interpersonal relationships. Sullivan published his first papers on this topic during the 1920s and continued publishing journal articles and lecturing until his death in 1949. Perhaps he, more than any other single person, turned the attention of social and behavioral scientists toward the study of interpersonal relationships and, in his writings, anticipated many of the results of research conducted during the decades following his death.

Sullivan, however, did not invent his system out of whole cloth, nor did he envision it in a sudden flash of insight. He readily gave credit to others, notably Adolph Meyer, Charles Horton Cooley, and George Herbert Mead. As a psychiatrist Sullivan owed something to the psychiatric tradition and notably to the tradition in which he was trained — the psychobiological approach of the pioneering American psychiatrist, Adolph Meyer. Sullivan was also stimulated by and attempted to use the psychoanalytic approach developed by Sigmund Freud. But the greater part of his stimulation, as it pertained directly to the study of interpersonal relationships, came from Cooley and Mead.

Cooley, Mead, and Sullivan are fascinating individuals to study, particularly for a modern American university professor. All three were tremendously influential; they all held prestigious academic appointments, yet none of them published very much by current standards. Their chief influence came through teaching, lecturing, and giving seminars. They were men who had a tremendous impact through their direct, personal relationships with their students. And interestingly, the most significant books of Mead and Sullivan were not written by them at all. These books were compiled after their deaths by their students and were based on notes or recordings of their lectures and seminars.

Charles Horton Cooley was originally a professor of economics and later a professor of sociology at the University of Michigan. A child of the nineteenth century, his period of impact and productivity, like that of Mead, was during the first thirty years of the twentieth century. He died in 1929.

Cooley argued that there was no conflict between the individual and the society of which the individual was a part. He saw the two as being in an organic relationship to each other. He wrote that "the individual is not separable from the human whole, but a living member of it, deriving his life from the whole through social and hereditary transmission as truly as if men were literally one body. He cannot cut himself off. . . ." (1956, p. 35).

Cooley also asserted that all thought was, in effect, communication with another person who might be imaginary or real; he quoted essayists such as Montaigne, Goethe, and Thoreau in support of his argument. He felt that it was what a people held in common in their minds that formed the basis for a society. A person's self does not exist except in relationship with other people. "Only insofar as a man understands other people and thus enters into the life around him has he any effective existence . . ." (1956, p. 140). Ethics, he felt, is largely a matter of relationship to other people. He wrote, "What is to do good, in the ordinary sense? Is it not to help people to enjoy and to work, to fulfill the healthy and happy tendencies of human nature . . . ?" (1956, p. 143).

Cooley's most influential concept is that of the "looking-glass self." Basically, his idea is that our selves develop out of our perceptions of the reactions of others to us. We are what we perceive other people think we are. In this sense, of course, no self exists or could exist apart from other people. Our conceptions of ourselves are based on our selves as we see them mirrored in the reactions of other people to us. As we develop our perceptions of our physical appearance by looking in a real mirror, so we develop our perceptions of ourselves in the mirror of the reactions of other people to us. Cooley wrote that

> the social reference takes the form of a somewhat definite imagination of how one's self — that is any idea he appropriates — appears in a particular mind, and the kind of self-feeling one has is determined by the attitude toward this attributed to that other mind. A social self of this sort might be called the reflected or looking-glass self:
> > Each to each a looking glass
> > Reflects the other that doth pass (1956, pp. 183–84).

This kind of idea of the self is composed of three parts. These three components are our conception of how we appear to the other person, our conception of how the other person judges this appearance, and our own feeling about this appearance and judgment.

If our existence is so deeply bound up in our relationships, it follows that anyone's social situation is of crucial importance to his existence. A person with disturbed or unsatisfying relationships with others will unquestionably be a disturbed person. So Cooley argued that a social situation, and the social institutions that were an integral part of that situation, must meet a person's needs. If not, the person will be in trouble, and a person in trouble causes trouble. "Each man must have his 'I'; it is more necessary to him than bread; and if he does not find scope for it within the existing institutions he will be likely to make trouble" (1956, p. 258). From this basis Cooley argued for the necessity of changing the institutions of his time in order to more adequately meet the needs of those whom he saw at that time as being socially deprived: immigrants, children, blacks, and married women. To one reading him in the last third of the twentieth century, Cooley's manner of expression seems, sometimes, to be dated, but his topics are quite current.

George Herbert Mead was a professor of philosophy at the University of Chicago, but his influence has been primarily in sociology and social psychology. Perhaps some indication of the fruitfulness of his ideas is reflected in the amount of space devoted to him in two editions of the *Encyclopedia of the Social Sciences* published thirty-five years apart. The 1933 edition, published shortly after Mead's death, contained less than one page devoted to him, while the 1968 edition devoted almost five pages to him.

Mead probably had a greater influence on Sullivan and the subsequent development of the study of interpersonal relationships than did Cooley. In the writings of Mead we see the origins of some of the same concepts used by Sullivan, such as the function of communication, both verbal and nonverbal, and the processes of dissociation and prehension. He even discussed the structure of the interpersonal relationship within the paradigm of the game—anticipating and maybe even stimulating the subsequent observations and research of the game theorists and game psychiatrists (see Chapters 5 and 11).

Mead agreed with Cooley that the self develops out of interaction with other people, but disagreed with Cooley's location of this beginning in the person's feelings about the reactions of others to him. Mead felt that the essence of self was cognitive and that it lay in the internalized conversation a person carried on with himself which constituted thinking. This internal conversation takes place between the "me" and the "I." The "me" is that attitude of others toward a person that the person carries around within himself. My "me" is what I think others think about me. The "me" serves as a stimulus to the "I" which reacts to the "me." My "I" is what I think, feel, or do about what I think others think of me. It is this internal interactive process that constitutes a self. Mead wrote, "It is the social process of influencing others in a social act and then taking the attitude of the others aroused by the stimulus, and then reacting in turn to this response, which constitutes a self" (1934, p. 171). Literally, to exist as a person, to have a self, to be a personality, one must have others to interact with. If there is no one around to interact with, no self, no personality, no human being, as we usually think of the concept, can exist. And if the others who are around do not react to the embryo "person," then that embryo does not develop into a person. This assertion of Mead's and Cooley's (and somewhat later, Sullivan's) anticipated such later discoveries as that of Spitz that infants will not develop normally if they lack interaction with other human beings.

Mead called himself a social behaviorist. He felt that psychology was concerned with the experience of the individual in his relationship to the conditions under which the experience occurred. Psychology became social psychology when that condition was a social situation. He felt that his approach was behavioristic because he approached experience through conduct.

The social process begins with one person making a *gesture.* This gesture might be a movement, a facial expression, or a sound. If the sound or sounds made are words, then it becomes a vocal gesture. Although Mead does not deal with development, one might presume that this whole process begins with something like the first cry of hunger an infant makes after birth. This "gesture" is a communicative act. The meaning of the act is determined by the social situation within which the act occurs. If it is a baby crying, the probable interpretation of the mother, or whoever is around to take care of the baby, would be that something is wrong with the baby. Now everyone knows that newborn babies cry because they feel uncomfortable or in pain—and the causes of such distress are relatively finite: The baby is hungry, his diapers are in need of changing, a pin is sticking him, or he is in some sort of physical pain. If a quick check of the crying baby discloses no pin, clean diapers, and no indication of illness, the process of elimination then leaves hunger as the cause of crying. Mother then puts the baby to her breast to nurse, and the crying ceases. Thus the baby's gesture has communicated to another person; and the other person has responded, satisfying the need of the person, our baby, who initiated the whole process.

It is out of this process of interaction—started by a person through some sort of communicative act and followed by the response of another person to this act, the satisfaction or nonsatisfaction of a want, and the perception of the attitude of the other person toward him based on the behavior of the other toward him—that a person develops a conception of the attitude of other people toward him. The developing individual perceives the attitudes of others toward him from their response to him. These attitudes of various other people toward him crystallize into a single attitude, the attitude of the "generalized other." That is, as we go through life, we observe other people reacting to us.

From this perception of the reaction of others to us, we gradually develop a general idea, a kind of consensus, of what other people think of us and thus develop an idea of our selves. This "generalized other" is important, since it is the phenomenon which controls our behavior. That is, we anticipate how others will respond to us and what their attitude is toward us, and behave accordingly.

Mead observed that although we may have a general concept of what others think of us, and that this "generalized other" forms a basis for the unity of the self, we are nonetheless different selves to different people. We are one self to our parents, another self to our spouse, and still a third self to our children. In the normally functioning person living in a benign social environment, there is some communality among these three selves: If we have a quick temper, probably our parents, our spouse, our children, and our selves are all aware of it—although our best customer may never be exposed to it. Thus the self the customer knows and relates to is somewhat different from the self known to parents, spouse, and children. In this normally functioning person in a benign environment, these selves maintain a unity. They function, more or less, in harmony. However, in situations of emotional upheaval this unity of selves may break up; Mead called this breakup *dissociation*. The obvious implication of this conceptualization is that the prevention of dissociation (and subsequent disordered behavior) will be accomplished by a social situation that does not create emotional upheaval and does not require a person to produce selves that are too disparate. Benign social situations make for benign, functioning people.

In Mead's view, the whole fabric of society rests upon an individual's ability to "see" the attitude of other individuals. "The very organization of the self-conscious community is dependent upon individuals taking the attitude of other individuals" (1934, p. 256). Out of this process develops the sense of self and the relationship of selves to selves. To Mead the individual does not develop as an individual self and then relate to other selves, but rather the individual develops as a social being in a society and as such is not separable from other selves. "Selves can only exist in definite relationships to other selves. No hard-and-fast line can be drawn between our own selves and the selves of others, since our own selves exist and enter as such into our experience only insofar as the selves of others exist and enter as such into our experience also" (1934, p. 164). Quite literally, we do not exist except as we exist in relationship to other people.

All of society is built upon the relationships between individuals. The smallest unit, for Mead, was the family, which extended into the tribe, and from the tribe into the state or the nation. The basis for these relationships is individuals being able to understand the attitude of others. In any society, institutions such as schools, governments, industries, and so on are necessary for social functioning. These institutions come into existence as the result of individuals making common responses to particular situations.

Modern research and thinking about the interpersonal relationship has developed out of the groundwork laid by seminal thinkers such as Cooley and Mead, who saw human beings as being social in their basic nature and as having no existence apart from existence in relationship to other human beings.

Sources and Nature of the Study of Interpersonal Relations

A sensitive soul is bound to approach the writing of a chapter section such as this with feelings ranging somewhere between severe anxiety and extreme terror. The reason for this emotional state is the awareness that any statements made about the sources and nature of the study of interpersonal relationships can be nothing more than a basis for discussion (among kindly and moderate souls) or, more than likely, a basis for fervent argument (among most behavioral scientists).

The problem is this: How do we interpret, classify, and evaluate the various approaches to the study of interpersonal relations? This becomes a kind of problem in scientific theory or hypothesis building. As such, the effort should attempt to meet the values described as applying to the construction of scientific theories. That is, it should be simple, it should account for as much of the phenomena observed as possible, it should relate the phenomena to one another, and it should suggest potentially fruitful new areas of exploration. However, as Polanyi (1962), Kuhn (1969), and others have pointed out, it is also a personal enterprise, which reflects the peculiar personality, values, and interests of the person performing the task. Thus, what follow are (obviously) my own reflections on the nature of the study of the human relationship, and the organization of the book comes from the pattern of my reflections.

The Organization of This Book

The sources of current study of interpersonal relations are chiefly two: the clinic and the laboratory. Or if we wish to classify on the basis of disciplines, the two categories are the clinicians and the academicians. The party of the clinicians is composed mainly of psychiatrists, clinical psychologists, and social workers, while the party of the academicians is composed largely of social psychologists, sociologists, and anthropologists.

Both the clinicians and the academicians have one common source of information — libraries — but their main sources differ. The research data of the clinicians is derived largely from their experience with patients or clients with problems. People with problems are encountered in mental hospitals, mental health clinics, child guidance clinics, marriage counseling centers, and in private offices of professionals who counsel those who have problems. The academicians, on the other hand, obtain their data from different kinds of settings. They typically obtain their data either from laboratory experiments or from field observation of people behaving in their natural habitat.

The arrangement of the chapters which follow is based on this dichotomization of the study of interpersonal relationships. Chapter 2 discusses the work of Harry Stack Sullivan, who was a practicing psychiatrist during his entire professional life, obtaining his data from mental hospitals and the psychiatric counsulting office. In the four chapters which follow (Chapters 3, 4, 5, and 6), other theories developed out of the work of practicing clinicians are presented. The study of nonverbal communications (Chapter 4) was stimulated by, and its data largely obtained from, research on the interaction between the psychotherapist and the patient or client in the psychotherapy situation. The study of communications (Chapter 3) was derived from the study of the interactions among the members of the families of people who had become schizophrenic. Berne's "games" (Chapter 5) were also derived from observations of the interactions among the members of families that contained a member who exhibited deviant behavior of some kind. Laing's development of his existential phenomenological approach (Chapter 6) was stimulated first by his observations of his own interactions with psychiatric patients in the psychotherapy situation and his subsequent observations of the interaction of patients with the significant "other" people in their lives.

Chapter 7 presents a mixture of the clinical approach and the more precisely controlled observations of the experimenter. Essentially, this chapter describes an approach to the study of the interpersonal relationship that was derived from psychometrics and applied to clinical patients. The psychometric approach began with the search for a method for predicting those schoolchildren who would have trouble with their studies and those who would not. The development of psychometrics was also stimulated by the effort to classify soldiers for purposes of training during World War I. Subsequently, however, it became a serious research effort in its own right as psychologists sought to understand the nature of intelligence and abilities. Psychologists extended the development of measuring instruments into the realm of personality and the diagnosis of psychological disorders. Yet it awaited Timothy Leary to apply already developed psychometric instruments, such as the Minnesota Multiphasic Personality Inventory and the Thematic Apperception Test, to the problem of diagnosing psychiatric patients on the basis of the way the patients related to other people. Uriel Foa, also discussed in this chapter, took the results of empirical research conducted in other settings, including the social psychological laboratory, and combined both the clinical results and the laboratory results into a single system for studying and measuring interpersonal relationships. Thus the contents of Chapter 7 can be considered a bridge between the studies of the clinicians and the research of the academicians.

The contents of Chapters 8 through 13 reflect the results of the more academic efforts of behavioral scientists who derived their research from established psychological theory — much of which was based on laboratory research and all of which was based on empirical investigation outside of the consulting room and the mental hospital. Exchange theory (Chapter 8) and Byrne's interpersonal attraction theory (Chapter 9) are both behavioristic theories, derived directly from the well-established tradition of S–R research in psychology. Balance theory, also discussed in Chapter 9, derives from the Gestalt tradition in experimental psychology. The needs approach (Chapter 10) has a little closer relationship to clinical work, since both Murray and Maslow, originators of needs theories, spent their apprenticeship years studying within clinical settings. Their theories, however, really belong more within the tradition of research on the personality of the normal person than in the strictly clinical tradition which has been based largely on studying persons who were troubled. Chapter 11 presents game theory, which owes more to the experimental social psychology tradition and the study of the dynamics of conflict between competing parties than to any other investigative tradition. If there is a theory within the book that is related to political science, the games approach would be closest to it. The contents of Chapters 12 and 13, roles and the rules of the encounter, have developed from a fairly extensive tradition within sociology and social psychology, although Goffman's approach (Chapter 13) — postulating implicit rules for social relationships by observing regularities in interpersonal behavior displayed in public places — has a uniqueness of its own. Essentially, Goffman is a sensitive people-watcher who has developed a system from watching how people behave in public places.

Having thus classified the material to be covered, it should now be pointed out that these categories are anything but mutually exclusive. The people working in this field have cross-fertilized each other extensively and, in some cases, have productively collaborated. The earliest example of this cross-fertilization is that of Harry Stack Sullivan, who, in taking the work of two academic sociologists — Cooley and Mead — and applying it to an understanding of hospitalized mental patients, contributed substantially to the understanding and treatment of schizophrenia and a variety of psychoneurotic disorders. We find a similar phenomenon occurring at the opposite end of the spectrum. Goffman, a sociologist, began his work studying the behavior of people, both patients and staff, within a mental hospital. By observing people from the outside and systematizing his observations, Goffman, although his data were far removed from the inner turmoil of the schizophrenic, nonetheless contributed to understanding the nature of the schizophrenic's behavior. Such examples can be multiplied extensively.

Interpersonal Relations as a Field of Research

If interpersonal relations is considered to be a field of science, then it is now in the stage of development that Kuhn (1969) termed the "preparadigmatic" stage. That is, there does not exist within the field of interpersonal relations any generally accepted theory, any body of knowledge commonly accepted by all or most of the researchers, any generally accepted method of research, or any commonly accepted group of variables and measuring instruments. Nor does there exist any group of problems to be solved that are agreed upon and studied by the people in the field; rather, the field is characterized by an array of individual practitioners and small groups, all pursuing their own research problems, very often using their own instruments which they share with few other people, and adopting their own theoretical orientation as a basis for designing their study. In some areas, as in the area of research on interpersonal attraction (see Chapter 9), there are directly competing theories (e.g., balance theory and reinforcement theory). In other areas the research is mainly empirical, with the scientists collecting facts and trying to fit them together into some sort of meaningful scheme. This characterizes, fairly I think, the study of nonverbal communications (see Chapter 4). There is no commonly accepted theory in this field. In still other areas, such as role theory, there is really no general system that could be characterized as a "theory." Rather, role theory is a rather loose collection of hypotheses that have been grouped together, in one fashion or another, by one scholar or another. To put it simply, the field of interpersonal relations is now characterized by widely diverse groups of people from varying disciplines, working as individuals or as small groups, all pursuing their own problems in their own way, with occasional and sometimes extensive interaction between two or more groups, but with no generally agreed upon theory or research strategy for the field.

The actual research methodologies used range from the rather loose empiricism of the practicing clinician (e.g., Sullivan) to the rather rigorous experimental methodology of Donn Byrne (described in Chapter 9). Yet in spite of this rather wide range of diversity in research methodology, it seems to me that I can detect a thread of consensus as to how research in this field should be conducted. This consensus seems to be expressed (perhaps unwittingly) by Robert Carson (1969, Ch. 1), who argues that research in interpersonal relationships should include data which is both behavioral and introspectional, and that this research should strive to relate the two to each other.

Carson argues that the purely behaviorist approach, in which the researcher studies only the overt behavior of people interacting with each other, is basically sterile. The reason it is sterile is because it is impossible to understand why a person behaves in a certain way in a certain situation unless you understand how he perceives that situation. Behavior by itself explains nothing. If you observe a little boy hitting a little girl, the behavior means nothing—or perhaps it would be more correct to say that the behavior is likely to be misunderstood—unless you realize that he thinks the little girl is about to steal his favorite red truck. For this reason Carson argues that it is important to obtain a person's reflections upon his own behavior. Carson adds, however, that a person's self-report of his experience should be coupled with behavioral observation of the subject by another, because "a person's behavior in any situation is jointly determined by the characteristics of that situation, as he perceives them, and by the particular behavioral dispositions of which he is possessed at that time" (1969, p. 9).

Of course, practicing clinicians have always used self-report as a main source of data. In the typical psychotherapy situation the therapist and the patient talk to each other, with the patient reporting how he acted or felt in the various kinds of situations he has encountered. From the patient's report of his experiences and behavior, the clinician draws conclusions. But any shrewd clinician learns to detect behavioral clues that can be related to the patient's report of his behavior or experience. Sullivan, for example, instructed the clinician to be alert for signs of anxiety, which would indicate areas of problems. Sullivan suggested that when the patient veered off from a topic, misunderstood, or forgot, these behavioral cues suggested that the topic avoided was one that aroused anxiety.

If we turn to the behavioristic investigators, we find that they, too, utilize self-report techniques. Byrne, who is a rigorous behaviorist in his research, has used as one of his main research instruments a scale, the "liking" scale, which is basically a self-report instrument. It is a device through which a person states how much he likes another person. Further, Byrne's basis for pairing people in his early research was a series of scales on which people reported their attitudes on a variety of topics, such as politics and religion. This, too, was a self-report instrument.

In my opinion, the most interesting case of the evolution of the self-report research technique is that of Longabaugh (see Chapter 8). Beginning from a theoretical orientation based on exchange theory—a rigorously behavioristic approach to interpersonal relations—Longabaugh developed a system for measuring the interpersonal relationship based on the introspection not only of the subjects, but also of the experimenter. He introduced not only the personal experience of the subject into the research procedure, but also the personal experience of the experimenter into the experimental procedure. Longabaugh argued that it is both permissible and desirable for the experimenter to rate and categorize the behavior of an experimental subject on the basis of what the experimenter thinks the subject was trying to do. Longabaugh argued that it is permissible for the experimenter to make assumptions as to what the subject is trying to do because the experimenter himself has had experience in interpersonal relationships. Starting from a rigorously behavioristic foundation, Longabaugh ended up with a research methodology that introduced directly into the research situation the purpose of the subject, the inferred experience of the subject, and the experience of the experimenter.

To summarize, by their actions as well as by their statements, both clinical and behavioral researchers in the field of interpersonal relations seem to have reached an unacknowledged consensus that self-reported experience and observed behavior are both essential parts of the research enterprise.

As a research enterprise, the study of interpersonal relationships is a field with rather peculiar opportunities stemming from the rather peculiar problem of Longabaugh's insertion of the experimenter and the experimenter's experience into the research enterprise. Rather than being an undesirable contamination of the research procedure, this insertion was a creative step forward. In recent years researchers such as Percy Bridgman (1961), who have reflected on the processes of science, have been pointing out that the researcher is an integral part of the experiment. The experimenter decides what data to collect and how and where to collect it; he is directly involved in the data-collecting process and decides what interpretation to place upon the data after it is collected. In any sort of behavior-observation method, be it counting responses or rating behavior, it is the data collector who decides what responses to count and what ratings to give. Further, recent research indicates that the experimenter has a direct effect on the outcome of the experiment. Rosenthal (1966) has demonstrated that the expectations of the experimenter affect the results obtained in the experiment, and Jourard (1969) has shown that the way the experimenter relates to the subject affects how the subject performs in the experiment. In short, the experimenter is, whether he acknowledges it or not, an integral part of the research procedure and the research results. Thus, Longabaugh's tactic may be considered a step forward, since he has more explicitly described the experimenter's role in the research process and has incorporated it more explicitly into the measurement procedure.

The researcher as a part of the research system, however, creates ultimate problems for the interpersonal relationship enterprise, for as Bridgman (1961) points out, in order to prove a system you must go outside the system. Yet in the study of any scientific problem, the researcher is an integral part of the research system, and perhaps in no area is this so clearly the case as it is in research on interpersonal relationships. If, as Cooley, Mead, and Sullivan suggest, a person's very existence is composed of his relationships with other people, and if, as the research of Rosenthal and Jourard indicates, the researcher affects the outcome of his research, then the researcher himself is an integral part of and an important variable in the research. This puts the researcher in something of the same bind as a surgeon trying to do an appendectomy on himself. All findings become tentative and variable, depending on who is doing the research, and we are forced to conclude, like Bridgman, that "certainty is not possible."

Having thus destroyed the worth and meaning of the whole enterprise before even getting into it, I wish to assure the reader that though certainty is not possible, at least some probabilities are probable. It is the collection of some of these probabilities that the remainder of this book attempts to describe.

A Basis for Comparing and Assessing Approaches

In a field as diverse as interpersonal relations, it is desirable to have some sort of framework in which to compare the many approaches. The dimensions that suggest themselves as bases for comparing the various ways of studying interpersonal relations are derived from those methods of study themselves. The views described in this book vary along five main dimensions:

1. The kind of subjects studied;
2. The situation within which the data are obtained;
3. The level at which the subjects are studied;
4. The kind of data obtained from the subjects;
5. The kind of theoretical structure within which the data are organized.

These dimensions will be discussed in the paragraphs that follow.

1. Thus far in the progress of the field there seem to be two broad categories of subjects who have been studied. These are patients, who are studied in clinics, hospitals, or the consulting office, and normal people, who are studied in laboratories or natural-life settings. There is no good reason to assume that the data obtained from "normals" are in any qualitative way different from data obtained from patients because of supposed differences in the ways "normals" or patients relate to other people; but there are differences in the motivation of the two groups. "Normals" presumably allow themselves to be studied because they want to aid the cause of science, while patients

find themselves in positions where they are studied because they have problems which are causing them serious distress and which they very much wish to solve. Thus it is conceivable that what we learn from one group may differ from what we learn from the other group because of very real differences in the kind and amount of motivation of the two groups.

2. There are three primary kinds of situations within which interpersonal relations are studied. These are the clinical situation, the laboratory, and real life. Psychiatrists and clinical psychologists commonly draw their conclusions from observing how people interact with each other within individual or group psychotherapy or from listening to how people in psychotherapy *say* they interact with other people in real life. Social psychologists usually draw most of their conclusions from behavior observed in carefully controlled experimental laboratory situations. Sociologists and anthropologists are more likely to base their conclusions on observations they have made of people behaving in real-life settings or on data (e.g., marriage and divorce statistics) obtained from real life.

3. The level at which the subjects are studied and the data obtained may range from very small segments of behavior to behavior that occurs only in a group. Those who study nonverbal communications are often concerned with very small segments of behavior exhibited in a small portion of the body (e.g., the raised-and-lowered eyebrow), while studies of marriage interaction are at the level of the dyad, or two-person group. A person studying mob behavior would use data obtained from an even larger group. Those who study the behavior of people in roles are studying, essentially, at the level of the person, although the performance of some roles requires more than one person (e.g., husband/father).

4. The kind of data obtained and studied range from introspection, or self-report, to observed, overt behavior. The phenomenologist is primarily interested in the interpersonal relationship as the person in the relationship experiences it. Since no one but the person himself knows what he experiences, the phenomenologist depends on introspective report. On the other hand, those studying the behavior of people in public places depend entirely on what they observe people doing in public places. Most of those studying interpersonal relations use both kinds of data. The psychotherapist, for example, bases his conclusions, in part, on how he observes a patient interacting with himself and with other people, but also on the large amount of information obtained from what the patient tells him about his interactions with people outside of the psychotherapy situation.

5. Finally, the data may be organized within theoretical structures that vary greatly in their comprehensiveness and complexity. The study of nonverbal communication is, to a large extent, an empirical

enterprise. Those studying nonverbal communication stay rather close to their data and develop explanations that are directly related to the data. For example, Goffman's studies of the behavior of people in public places is essentially an orderly description of what he observed. Social-exchange theory, on the other hand, is a comprehensive and complex theory that attempts to explain all of interpersonal behavior.

Ideally, a theory should account for all of the data that are pertinent to it, should be logically consistent, should explain the phenomena that have been observed, should suggest and stimulate new areas of research, and should be simple. This, of course, is the description of an ideal, an ideal that no theory of interpersonal relations yet reaches. Any theoretical approach should be evaluated by these criteria. However, no one studying a phenomenon should be criticized for failing to achieve what he did not set out to do in the first place. For example, an attempt made to account for the observable behavior of people in public places should not be criticized for failing to account for the personal experiences of people in public places. In such a study, behavior—not personal experience—would be the object of study. However, such an account should be responsible for adequately describing, explaining, and predicting the behavior of people in public places; in addition, it should stimulate others to do worthwhile research on public behavior.

As we discuss each of the areas of study presented within this book, then, we shall also assess them in terms of the kinds of people they study, the situation within which they study people, the level of study, the kinds of data obtained, and the theoretical structures within which the data are organized.

Summary

Interpersonal relationships have been a topic of concern to people since the beginning of history. Discussion about this concern was largely conducted by essayists and moral philosophers until the beginning of the twentieth century.

The modern study of interpersonal relationships was given its first push largely by two sociologists, C. H. Cooley and G. H. Mead. Cooley and Mead stressed the fact that one exists as a human being only in relationship with other people, and that one's self develops out of interaction with other people. Harry Stack Sullivan, a psychiatrist, applied the concepts of Cooley and Mead to his work with mental patients and, out of this experience, developed a theory of interpersonal relations which has served as a basis for and an anticipation of much subsequent research.

The field of interpersonal relations might be roughly divided into two categories: one stemming from the clinical tradition of the mental

hospital and psychological clinic, and the other deriving from the research tradition of the academic, behavioral scientist. However, these
two streams have interacted and combined.

An implicit consensus for research procedure seems to have
emerged in this field. It is the procedure that relates the reported experience of the subject to the behavior of the subject and includes data
from both introspection and observed behavior as a basis for knowledge
in the field.

The process of research in this field is complicated, however, by
the fact that the experimenter is an unavoidable and usually unassessed
variable in the research process. Thus, certainty in the study of interpersonal relationships is impossible, but probability is possible.

The various methods for studying interpersonal relations may be
ordered along five basic dimensions: the kind of subjects studied, the
situation within which the data are obtained, the level at which the subjects are studied, the kind of data obtained, and the kind of theoretical
structure within which the data are organized.

References

Bridgman, P. W. *The way things are.* New York: Viking Press, 1961.

Carson, R. C. *Interaction concepts of personality.* Chicago: Aldine,
1969.

Cooley, C. H. *Human nature and the social order.* Glencoe, Ill.: The
Free Press, 1956.

Jourard, S. M. Project replication: experimenter-subject acquaintance
and outcome in psychological research. In C. Spielberger (Ed.),
Current topics in community psychology. New York: Academic
Press, 1969.

Kuhn, T. S. *The structure of scientific revolutions.* (2nd ed.) Chicago:
University of Chicago Press, 1969.

Mead, G. H. *Mind, self and society.* Chicago: University of Chicago
Press, 1934.

Polanyi, M. *Personal knowledge.* New York: Harper & Row, 1962.

Rosenthal, R. *Experimenter effects in behavioral research.* New York:
Appleton-Century-Crofts, 1966.

Shibutani, T. Mead, George Herbert, in *Encyclopedia of the Social
Sciences,* 1933, Vol. 10, 241–42.

Smith, T. V. Mead, George Herbert, in *Encyclopedia of the Social
Sciences,* 1968, Vol. 10, 83–87.

The Psychiatry of Interpersonal Relationships

2

People are decidedly the hardest things we have to deal with. Not only does this task require a great amount of skill learning, but also the full value of achievement at this task does not begin clearly to appear to the individual until he is in the second decade of life (1962, p. 248).

—Harry Stack Sullivan

The modern study of interpersonal relationships is rooted, to a substantial extent, in the work of Harry Stack Sullivan. Much of the research and theory described in the chapters to follow was clearly foreshadowed in the observations Sullivan made and described a generation earlier. Sullivan asserted that schizophrenia, as well as other forms of deviant behavior, was the consequence of disordered interpersonal relationships. He described various kinds of interpersonal communications and emphasized that these were nonverbal as well as verbal. To Sullivan, the various patterns of interpersonal interactions were aimed toward the twin goals of personal satisfaction and security. One who reads Sullivan today, after reading descriptions of current research and thinking in interpersonal relationships, is struck by the extent to which this research has followed furrows first plowed by Sullivan.

Sullivan was a psychiatrist who began his career using Freudian concepts in therapy with schizophrenics, but gradually developed his own theoretical system. This system was derived from the psychiatry of Adolf Meyer and the social psychology of C. H. Cooley and G. H. Mead. Sullivan came to see schizophrenia and all other kinds of psychopathology (in fact, all of personality) as rooted in interpersonal relationships. He wrote that "Personality is manifest . . . in interpersonal situations, only" (1964, p. 64). He defined personality as "the relatively enduring pattern of recurrent interpersonal situations which characterize a human life" (1953a, p. xi). For Sullivan, personality did not exist except within interpersonal relationships, and he argued against the concept of individuality. He felt the concept of the individual apart from other people to be an essentially misleading falsehood perpetuated by the peculiarities of our culture.

Sullivan gave some thought to organizing the universe in interpersonal terms. He suggested that the universe presented three aspects: the impersonal, the personal (or subjective), and the interpersonal (1964, p. 61). Within this scheme, psychiatry was a branch of social science; more specifically, psychiatry was that branch of social science which was concerned with interpersonal relationships. Sullivan made the assumption, based on his observations of mental patients, that all people are "much more simply human than otherwise" (1953b, p. 32). Or to put it another way, if a person behaves in a crazy manner, there must be something in his relationships with other people that makes it sensible for him to act crazy.

Most of the data from which Sullivan derived his ideas were obtained by using a type of self-report research technique which he called "participant observation." In this method, the researcher acquires data by interacting with the subject and observing both himself and the subject in the interaction. Sullivan believed that only in this way could valid data be obtained, since "psychiatric data arise from participation in the situation that is observed . . ." (1954, p. 57). For the psychiatrist, or other interpersonal researcher, this method would be primarily applied in the interview, a method to which Sullivan (1954) applied a great deal of creative thought.

Perhaps the most impressive aspect of Sullivan's achievement is that, though he wrote relatively little during his life, his ideas have become well known. For the most part he practiced psychiatry in the Baltimore-Washington area and in New York, and he taught and supervised students in psychiatry. He communicated largely through lectures and seminars. This was not the most efficient method for wide communication of ideas, yet the impact of his teaching was such that his lectures were published after his death in 1949 as books written by his students from their recordings and lecture notes. It is a rare teacher whose impact is such that his students publish his lectures posthumously.

Personality Development

Sullivan looked at people from the point of view of development. A human being is born into the world with certain needs. He needs oxygen, he needs water, he needs food, he needs to eliminate waste products from his body, he needs contact with other human beings. For the newborn, all of these needs require the cooperation of another person, if they are to be met. Therefore, the study of the development of the human personality is essentially the study of the growing infant and child in interaction with other people. If this interaction with other people satisfies the needs and is satisfying, human development takes a benign and constructive path. If this interaction is fraught with fear and anxiety, development takes a less constructive path—one determined by the timing and the location of fear or anxiety.

Modes of Experience

From the time of conception, the organism interacts with his environment of the physical and the social world. It is in this interaction that "experience" occurs. Sullivan calls the point of interaction between the person and his environment the "nexus," and says of it, "The nexus of all this experience by which we form views of the world, the universe, our place in it, and so on, is always in the experience of me-and-my-mind . . ." (1964, p. 202). By "mind," Sullivan means consciousness. Or to oversimplify, what we have in our minds is our experience of interaction with the world. This experience is important because it interpenetrates all behavior and all interaction with other people. The manner in which Sullivan outlines experience is shown in Figure 1.

Experience may be of *tensions* or of *energy transformations* which may occur in any of three modes—the *prototaxic*, the *parataxic*, and the *syntaxic*. The prototaxic mode is the mode of the newborn, in which an experience is not related to other experiences. The parataxic mode is the mode of the growing infant and child, in which experiences are associated with other experiences, and with causation, but in a rather illogical fashion. The syntaxic mode is the mode of the adult, in which experiences are logically related to one another. These modes will be discussed in greater detail later in the chapter.

The first category of experience, *tensions*, is a kind of "state-of-being," or feeling. Tensions may be of two types: of needs or of anxiety. To dissipate the experience of tension, the second category of experience, *energy transformation*, must take place. Sullivan uses the term *energy* in the sense that something happens. That is, if the experience is an *overt energy transformation*, the person does something or acts in some manner; if the experience is a *covert energy transformation*, the

FIGURE 1. **SULLIVAN'S OUTLINE OF EXPERIENCE**

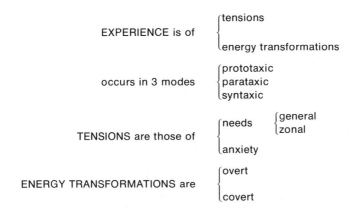

person does not perform an overt action, but rather performs some covert action, such as a fantasy or a dream. In either case, the experience is of the person doing something, either overtly or covertly; and this action relieves the tension.

A person's behavior is motivated by his tensions which are, in turn, motivated by two main drives: the drive for satisfaction and the drive for security. The tensions of needs are basic, biologically rooted needs; they are motivated by the drive for satisfaction. These needs may be either general or zonal. Sullivan (1953a, Ch. 3) lists the basic zones involved as the oral, retinal, auditory, tactile, vestibulo-kines-thetic, genital, and anal. For example, everybody needs to eat and to drink, and these needs are focalized around the oral zone. A zonal need is one that is satisfied by the interaction of a particular part of the body with the environment. A more general need is not localized in a specific part of the body—for example, the need to maintain a stable body temperature. Self-satisfaction comes when a need, either general or zonal, is met. In most cases, the fulfillment of a tension of need is dependent on interaction with other people.

Tensions of anxiety are feelings of uneasiness; they are motivated by the drive for security. They are quite different from tensions of needs since they are directly related to other people. Quite early in life, an infant meets anxiety, often coming from his mother. Anxious mothers often produce anxious infants, because an infant is likely to acquire his mother's anxiety through empathy. However, even if the mother is not anxious, the infant will eventually encounter anxiety. For example, anything that threatens self-esteem or security produces anxiety. As an infant grows, certain things are expected of him. Among other things, his parents begin to expect him to eliminate waste products from his body in certain ways and at certain times. If he fails to do so, he will find his parents both look and sound quite disapproving. This disapproval threatens the infant's self-esteem and security and, thus, produces anxiety.

In Sullivan's view, tension is at the opposite end of a continuum from euphoria. Euphoria is a state of blissful satisfaction, perhaps best illustrated by a sleeping infant. Tension is a state of insecurity (anxiety) or unsatisfied need. Of the two, unsatisfied need and anxiety, anxiety is the more powerful motivator. Anxiety is in opposition to the satisfaction of any other need, because it interferes with effective behavior. When anxiety is present, behavior designed to satisfy another need is rendered relatively ineffective by the interference of anxiety. And anxiety always has to do with relationships to other people. Sullivan states that "the role of anxiety in interpersonal relations is so profoundly important that its differentiation from all other tensions is vital" (1953b, p. 44). We will have much more to say about anxiety throughout the chapter. Let it suffice, for now, to say that anxiety begins with disapproval from significant other people and is so powerful that it interferes with all other kinds of behavior.

The earliest experience the infant has is with the person who has the role of mother. As needs arise in the infant, he expresses them in a generalized sort of way. That is, he cries and thrashes about. This loud expression of need from the infant induces tension in the mother. This baby-need-tension induced in the mother is usually experienced by the mother as tenderness; that is, she discharges the tension by taking care of the infant. Among other things, the baby needs tenderness from his mother, because if he doesn't get it, he isn't taken care of. However, if the mother is anxious, her anxiety interferes with the perception and behavior by which she would normally discharge her tension—that is, with tenderness. In this case, the baby's needs are not taken care of, and he gets anxious. And an anxious baby makes an even more anxious mother, who in turn makes an even more anxious baby, thus producing a vicious circle in which both the baby and the mother are miserable. Such a situation creates long-range difficulties for the interpersonal relationships of both.

To summarize, what people have in their heads is experience, which is tied up with interactions with other people. This experience is either of tensions or of energy transformations (overt or covert). Tensions come from either needs that must be satisfied or from anxiety. Anxiety comes from insecurity in relationship with other people. The satisfaction of needs or the reduction of anxiety and increase in security are the goals toward which behavior (energy transformation) is aimed.

At the beginning of this section it was stated that experience occurs in three modes, the prototaxic, the parataxic, and the syntaxic. We will now turn to a discussion of these modes of experience.

Prototaxic Mode. Experience in the prototaxic mode might be considered to be raw experience, not related to any other experiences, not evaluated, and not represented by any symbols. The alternation between tension and euphoria is experienced in this mode. For example, a hungry baby is in tension, while a just-fed baby who is quietly nodding off to sleep is in euphoria. This baby, once he awakens, will again be in tension because of wet diapers and hunger, but will slip back into euphoria as soon as his needs are satisfied. In the prototaxic mode there is no discrimination between what is self and not-self. And since experience in the prototaxic mode is not represented by symbols, it cannot be discussed with other people.

Parataxic Mode. Experience in the parataxic mode is experience that has begun to be associated with other experiences. These associations might not be logical. For example, an infant might have been pinched by a man wearing glasses, and thus associate pinching with people who wear glasses. An association is made, but it is not a logical one. When the infant begins to generalize among experiences, the parataxic mode of experience has begun. Although in the parataxic mode experiences are connected with symbols also known to other people, such as words, it is still a mode of experience that is peculiar to a specific person. Thus, the parataxic mode is of particular applicability to the study of the interpersonal relationship because we each experience other people in a specific way that is peculiar to ourselves. In a relationship I not only relate to the "real" other person with whom I am interacting, but I also interact with the image of that person (or personifications of that person, as Sullivan would term it) that I carry around in my head, and some of these images are peculiar to me alone. For example, my sister and I both experienced our mother. We have personifications of her that we share. That is, my sister has personifications of my mother that are quite similar to my personifications of my mother. These we share, and these are consensually validated, and thus in the syntaxic mode. But my sister has images of my mother that I don't share, and I have images of my mother that my sister does not share — and nobody else who knows my mother shares them either. These are peculiar to me alone, and are, therefore, parataxic. In the parataxic mode the infant begins to discriminate between what is self and what is not-self and to make some discrimination among experiences. The parataxic mode might be considered a primitive stage of assimilation of experience. The experience is related to other experiences and is symbolized, but the relationships and the symbols are peculiar to the person doing the symbolizing—they are not shared with others.

Syntaxic Mode. The discussion in the previous paragraph gives some idea of the nature of the syntaxic mode. Experience in the syntaxic mode can be shared with other people. We can talk to other people about this experience and come to an agreement about the experience. This kind of experience can be precisely symbolized, which means that it can be described fairly accurately in words that another person can understand. This sort of experience is quite common in interpersonal relationships. We meet a person for the first time, we cast about for some common topic of conversation, and we discover that we both know a third party. We have, at different times in our careers, worked with him. So we discuss him and discover that we both agree that he tends to be slow in his work, but quite thorough, that his understanding of his field is extensive, that he is easy to get along with, and that he is generous to a fault. We have each consensually validated our interpersonal experience with this third person. This is experience in the syntaxic mode. For experience to be in the syntaxic mode, it must be precisely communicable to other people, and for it to be communicable, the person must have the necessary language skill to communicate precisely. Therefore, experience in the syntaxic mode tends to be delayed until the person has developed to the level of maturity that makes it possible for him to develop the necessary precision of communication, and also the necessary relationship with another person with whom he may communicate.

As we indicated earlier, Sullivan's view of interpersonal relationships was a developmental one. These various kinds of experience just described do not occur in a developmental vacuum. As the person grows, he progresses through certain stages of life; and in these different stages, he is open to and affected differentially by the different kinds of experience discussed above. Let us now move on to a description of these stages of development.

Stages of Development

Sullivan (1954, Ch. 7) found two gross categories of personality development: first, the interaction between serial maturation of ability and opportunities for experience during the first twenty-six or twenty-seven years of life; and second, the signs of "personality warp," which is the result of deficiencies in experience, and the security operations, which are a person's attempts to cover deficiencies in experience. Sullivan felt that for a person to relate constructively to others in adult life, it was essential to have the right kinds of experiences at the right stages of life. He wrote that "unfortunate experience at any developmental phase may do great damage to one's possibilities of future interpersonal relations and . . . very fortunate experience at any developmental stage may do much to remedy the limitations already introduced by previous developmental misfortunes" (1964, p. 266).

The actual stages of development in Western European societies are listed by Sullivan as being *infancy, childhood, the juvenile era, preadolescence, early adolescence,* and *late adolescence.* In the following discussion we will consider each of these stages in turn.

Infancy. Infancy lasts from birth until the appearance of articulate speech. (Sullivan, 1953b, Chs. 4–8). The newborn infant has needs, but no means by which to satisfy them. So when he is hungry, he cries. He cries until he receives a nipple, which provides the milk that satisfies his hunger, or else he cries until fear sets in. This fear is mitigated by apathy, which is followed by sleep. When he wakes up, he cries again. The infant's first power comes through the power of the cry.

If the cry of the hungry baby arouses the mother, she produces a nipple for the baby to suck on. If the nipple produces milk, then the baby is satisfied and goes to sleep. If the nipple is produced by a mother who is anxious, however, this anxiety interferes with the baby's obtaining satisfaction of his need. Such a nipple is not a "good" nipple, but rather, it is a "bad" nipple. The "bad" nipple does not produce satisfaction, it produces anxiety.

This experience of the "good" and the "bad" nipple leads to a categorization of the mother who has produced the nipple. That is, a mother who induces anxiety is a "bad" mother, while a mother who produces satisfaction and security is a "good" mother. These different perceptions of the mother are termed *personifications,* which will be discussed in greater detail later. The infant does not perceive the "good" mother and the "bad" mother as being the same person, but rather perceives them as being two different persons. One, the "good," produces pleasant experiences, and the other, the "bad," produces dissatisfaction and anxiety. These personifications provide the basis for relating to other people later in life.

For the infant to discriminate a "good" mother from a "bad" mother, he must first discriminate a mother. The process of learning to discriminate himself from others takes place during infancy.

The infant first encounters anxiety during infancy. As has already been suggested, this experience probably comes through an anxious mother. In Sullivan's view, anxiety has its source in insecurity, and insecurity comes primarily from disapproval, or anticipated disapproval from another person. "Anxiety . . . can often be explained plausibly as anticipated unfavorable appraisal of one's current activity by someone whose opinion is significant" (1953b, p. 113). Since anxiety is unpleasant, the infant develops means to deal with it. The *self-system* is the primary mechanism developed to deal with anxiety. It promotes what is "good" for the individual and gets rid of what is "bad," or anxiety-arousing.

The infant incurs disapproval (which results in anxiety) from a mother (or other significant adult) who is trying to make him fit to live with other people. The unconditional acceptance the infant may have received from birth gives way to a state of affairs in which approval is conditional upon the infant's changing some of his behavior. Thus, learning enters the picture.

The infant learns a variety of things. Toward the end of the period of infancy he begins to coordinate different zones of interaction. For example, when he has learned to pick up an object and put it in his mouth, he has succeeded in coordinating the oral and the tactile zones of interaction. Also, he begins to learn the elements of speech from his parents, through a process Sullivan labeled trial-and-error learning by example. When the infant begins to utter his first words, infancy has come to an end, and childhood has begun.

Childhood. Childhood begins with the development of speech and lasts until the child begins to need playmates (Sullivan, 1953b, Chs. 11–14). That is, the childhood stage starts when the child begins to be able to communicate with other people, and ends when he begins to need to interact with people his own age.

With the development of speech, the child's world begins to change. First, because of speech, the process of acculturation can be speeded up. Second, with the development of language skills, the child becomes able to manipulate experiences intellectually. Personifications can be fused into the perception of a single person. The "bad" mother and the "good" mother become fused into the conception of a single person, Mother, who has her virtues and her deficiencies. During this stage syntaxic language begins to develop. The child begins to develop language through which he communicates and consensually validates experience with other people. If the child says "good," Mother knows what he means; if Mother says "hot," the child knows what she means.

During this stage the child also develops a sense of gender. He knows a boy from a girl, associates certain kinds of clothes or other peripheral details to the sexes, and learns to which sex he belongs.

The process of socialization continues during this stage, so the child often experiences anxiety, and the self-system develops more intricate means of handling anxiety. Changes in the self-system of the child become more difficult, since the self avoids any experience that threatens to produce anxiety. The self confines itself to experiences that experience has taught will not produce anxiety, and thus avoids new experiences that might produce a change in the structure of the self.

One maneuver that the self-system introduces in this stage of life is the substitution of anger for anxiety. Since anger is not as painful an emotion as anxiety, anxiety may be converted into anger. However, parents tend to become upset at displays of anger, so they may punish the expression of anger. If this occurs, the anxiety which was expressed in anger is suppressed and becomes resentment.

The encounter with parental disapproval at this stage may produce an even more malignant development. If the child exhibits behavior that earlier in life elicited tenderness from the parent, but now, in childhood, elicits punishment and anxiety, the child develops what Sullivan termed "malevolence." That behavior which earlier brought tenderness now brings pain, so the child develops the feeling that he lives among enemies. This produces a generalized attitude of malevolence, or the feeling that "People are no good." Sullivan states that for the malevolent person, this attitude is "Once upon a time everything was lovely, but that was before I had to deal with people" (1953b, p. 216).

During this stage of life, the child is learning a great deal about the world in general and about himself in particular. Most of what he learns is through interaction with his parents, so they, obviously, are exceedingly important for his development. The child develops a view of the world he acquires from his parents, and he develops his basic view of himself from his perception of his parents' view of him. This learning colors all subsequent learning. For this reason, Sullivan (1962, Ch. 7) concluded that a person could not grow up to develop constructive relationships with other people unless he had an interaction during childhood with significant adults who were free from destructive attitudes and beliefs.

The Juvenile Era. The juvenile period begins when the child seeks interaction with people his own age (Sullivan, 1953b, Chs. 14–15). At this stage he is living a significant portion of his life outside of the home, and he is beginning to interact with people he has not known before. This stage of development ends when the juvenile begins to seek an intimate relationship with one specific person his own age and his own sex.

Since the child is now beginning to interact with people he has not interacted with earlier in life, it is important for him to be able to communicate with them. If the child lives a lonely life, in which he does not have the opportunity to interact with and communicate with other people, he will fail to develop consensual validation for his experiences and will be handicapped in his ability to communicate with and interact with new people outside of home. It is through consensual validation that the child learns to discriminate his private fantasies from public fact. If he is deprived of the opportunity of learning to communicate in ways that make sense to other people, he will run the risk of rejection or ridicule when he begins to interact with other children. If these other children do ridicule him, his likely reaction to this unpleasant experience will be withdrawal, which will further arrest his personality development and deprive him of the experience with other people that corrects the inaccuracies of his own cognitive processes.

The juvenile era is an era of widening acquaintanceship and development of interpersonal skills. Every home has its own eccentricities. When the child moves out into the wider world, he learns that other children have homes that are not like his own home, and that other parents do not behave exactly like his own parents. Further, when he goes to school he meets other adults, teachers, and by comparing his parents to them, the child becomes able to see his parents as people.

Juveniles are a remarkably insensitive lot, so the child now is exposed to a give-and-take with other children in which the other children tell him the crude truth about himself. The chief kinds of interaction to which the child is exposed are compromise and competition. In competition with other children he learns his ability and worth relative to other children. He observes how fast they can run, or how well they can read, and can compare his own performance with theirs, thus getting a general idea of where he stands relative to them. Children of this age fight much like kittens or puppies, and thus the child gains an idea of his strength relative to other children.

The child also learns the necessity of compromise, in order to accomplish the satisfactions that come with interacting with others. For example, if a ball game is to be played, a group of children must come to some mutual decision as to who bats first.

Sullivan makes the point that competition is typical of this stage of development. He adds that the adult who is overly competitive in all activities is one who has failed, to some degree, to mature beyond the juvenile stage of development. The person who has suffered a "malevolent" transformation not only seeks to defeat his opponent—he seeks to put them down.

The juvenile era is a stage of extensive experience in interacting with other people. This stage comes to a close when the growing juvenile becomes more descriminating and seeks to develop a more intimate relationship with one other person.

Preadolescence. This stage begins with the formation of an intimate relationship with another person of the same sex, a "chum" (Sullivan, 1953b, Ch.16). In this stage the person first finds himself in a relationship in which the needs or desires of another person become as important to him as his own needs. The other person's triumphs are felt as his own triumphs, and his own triumphs are shared with the other.

This stage is particularly important because it is in the close relationship with another person that one can first consensually validate one's own conception of oneself. It is in this stage that a person gets a first glimpse of himself through another person's eyes. It is because of this aspect of the relationship between close friends that this stage is particularly important for making changes in the self-system. Through consensual validation with another person it becomes possible to correct autistic views of oneself and of others. In this stage the opportunity for consensual validation of self-worth occurs.

Preadolescence is the first stage of life in which intense loneliness can be recalled. Loneliness is felt in the infant as a need for contact; in the child, as a need for adult participation in activities; and in the juvenile, as a need for compeers and acceptance. But in the preadolescent, loneliness is felt as a need for intimate exchange with a fellow human being. Loneliness is so terrible an experience that it will drive a person to face anxiety in order to make contact with a fellow being. Thus, intimacy with a friend becomes a very powerful need for the preadolescent.

Having the experience of a close friend during this period was considered by Sullivan to be so important that he asserted that a person who did not have a fortunate experience with another person of the same sex during this period was never able to maintain good relationships with peers in later life or to feel at ease among strangers.

Although the primary relationship during this stage is the two-person relationship between chums, these "chumships" tend to overlap, so that the preadolescent dyads tend to merge into gangs. This relationship, in addition to providing for consensual validation of the self, also provides the final binding agent between the growing person and his culture.

With the dawn of puberty, preadolescence draws to a close.

Early Adolescence. This stage of development begins with puberty, and ends with the patterning of some kind of behavior which satisfies lust (Sullivan, 1953b, Ch. 17). Sullivan calls lust a need which is "the felt component of integrating tendencies pertaining to the genital zone of interaction . . ." (1953b, p. 263).

In adolescence the need for intimacy with a person of the same sex changes to the need for intimacy with a person of the opposite sex. The adolescent is faced with the problem of working out some sort of a viable relationship among three needs: the need for intimacy with a person of the opposite sex, the need for satisfaction of lust, and the need to avoid anxiety. The lust dynamism (or pattern of lust behavior) serves as an integrating tendency which integrates the person in his relationship with persons of the opposite sex or, as Sullivan says, "which get[s] us involved with others or lead[s] us to avoid them" (1953b, p. 288).

Sullivan observed that the pattern of sexual behavior that develops may not have anything to do with sex, per se. Sexual behavior may merely serve as a channel through which other unsatisfied impulses may get expressed. In dealing with people who complained of sexual problems, Sullivan asserted that the sexual problems were not basically problems with sex, but rather problems in living with people.

The person who suffers unfortunate experiences in this stage of development is never able to feel at ease with strangers of the opposite sex, and encounters difficulty in establishing relationships with the opposite sex.

Late Adolescence. This stage begins when the person discovers what he prefers in genital behavior and how he can fit it into his life; it ends when the person has established an enduring intimate relationship with a person of the opposite sex (Sullivan, 1953b, Ch. 18).

This is a stage of development in which there is a great growth of experience in the syntaxic mode. Some people do not progress very far in this stage of development because of anxiety which causes a malfunctioning of their self-system. This malfunctioning has its source in inadequate personifications of the self and of other people. Because of anxiety, these inadequate personifications are not corrected and lead to conflicting relationships with other people. Instead of relating to the other person, one relates to the inaccurate personification of the other. Or, to put it simply, one does not relate to the other. One relates to an imaginary person carried around in one's head. To say the least, this leads to difficult interpersonal relationships.

Ideally, late adolescence comes to an end when the person establishes an intimate relationship with another person of the opposite sex, in which the two collaborate with each other in a relationship in which each is highly sensitive to the needs of the other and to the interpersonal security of the other.

The developing person changes, and hopefully matures, as he progresses through these stages, ending up at age twenty-six or twenty-seven as an adult personality. In discussing this course of development we have, of necessity, referred to some features of the personality structure that have been only briefly described. In the next section we will describe the personality structure and its components somewhat more fully.

Personality Structure

The discussion which follows will center on the dynamisms and the self-system. Since these patterns of the functioning personality develop and are modified through experience, or learning, we will also summarize Sullivan's views of the processes of learning.

Dynamisms and Needs

Sullivan calls a *dynamism* "the relatively enduring pattern of energy transformations which recurrently characterize the organism in its duration as a living organism" (1953b, p. 103). In their discussion of dynamisms, Hall and Lindzey (1957, p. 138) characterize Sullivan's concept of the dynamism as being very much like a habit. This characterization, however, seems a little too simple a behavior pattern to cover what Sullivan includes in the concept of the dynamism.

A dynamism is a complex pattern of behavior that satisfies a need[1] (and thereby discharges a tension) of some sort. This pattern of behavior may be overt, but it may also be covert, such as a fantasy. It might be as simple as the oral dynamism, by which a baby satisfies his need for oral activity by sucking his thumb; or it might be as complex as the self-dynamism, by which a person maintains his self-esteem and security by avoiding anxiety through all the intricate maneuvers he engages in as a means of protecting himself from threat.

There are two kinds of dynamisms. One kind is closely associated with a particular zone of the body in interaction with the environment and is concerned with satisfying the simple, biological needs of the body. Dynamisms of this sort might well resemble habits, although the oral dynamism can also develop into some rather complex eating rituals. The second kind of dynamism relates to the recurring tensions which are instigated by such experiences as fear, lust, and the self-system, all of which are forms of anxiety. The first kind of dynamism might be conceived of as that which is involved in satisfying the basic physical needs of the person; the second kind, as that which is involved in satisfying those needs that are more directly related to maintaining fulfilling, nonanxiety-arousing relationships with other people.

Dynamisms are modified by experience, which is to say that the specific pattern of behavior by which a dynamism manifests itself is a function of learning.

The dynamism exists to meet a need. The needs are the motivators of behavior. If the needs are for physiological satisfaction through eating, drinking, elimination, or physical movement of some kind, they can be generally labeled as *needs for self-satisfaction*. If the needs refer to interpersonal relationships and include the need to alleviate or avoid anxiety and the need to maintain self-esteem, they can be labeled as *needs for security*.

Needs exhibit a hierarchy. If a person is satisfying one need through some activity, but another, stronger need is activated, the person stops the activity that satisfies his first need and turns to an activity

[1]In discussing dynamisms, Sullivan uses the term "need" in the more general sense, rather than the more specific one of "need" as one of two types of tension, used earlier in his outline of experience.

that will satisfy the second, more powerful need. For example, a hungry man who is eating a meal may stop to slap at a mosquito that is buzzing around his head. When the mosquito is slapped the man returns to eating. To illustrate this point, Sullivan used the example of a baby who is developing eye-hand coordination through some activity such as picking up objects and sticking them in his mouth. The baby will stop this activity when his mother comes to feed him. When the feeding is finished the baby will return to his original activity. The fact that the first activity is interrupted in order to engage in the second activity indicates that there exists a hierarchy of needs. Hunger is more powerful than the development of eye-hand coordination. The fact that the person returns to the original, interrupted activity after satisfying the more powerful need indicated to Sullivan that there is covert as well as overt activity. Overt activity is overt behavior, of course, but covert activity is what goes on while a person is overtly doing something else. Sullivan asked himself the question, Why does the baby return to practicing eye-hand coordination when he has finished eating? It must be because some covert process has been going on, undetected by the observer, during the eating period. When eating is finished the covert becomes overt, and the baby returns to exploring nonedible objects by sticking them into and pulling them out of his mouth.

Some needs change as life progresses. The need for contact with other people is continous throughout life, but the way in which this need manifests itself changes with each stage of life. In infancy this is the simple need for physical contact with another person; in childhood, the need for adult participation in activities; in the juvenile era, the need for compeers; in the preadolescent era, the need for an intimate chum of the same sex; and in adolescence, the need for an intimate companion of the opposite sex.

Some needs potentially collide with other needs creating the necessity of developing some rather delicate coordination in order to avoid serious problems. In adolescence, for example, lust collides with the need for security. Adolescence is spent in working out this problem.

Sullivan sees the last development in the growth of personality as the emergence of the need for intimacy — "for collaboration with at least one other . . ." (1953b, p. 310). The ultimate need is the need for intimacy with another person, and in a sense, all that has preceded eventuates in failure if this need is not met.

The Self-System

The personality is composed of two parts, the *self-system* and the *not-self*. That part which is within the self is more-or-less available to awareness. That part which is in the not-self is there because it arouses anxiety, and thus has been shunted, or dissociated, into unawareness.

Though the not-self still has its effect, through dreams or through un-witting behavior, it is not available to awareness.

The self-system develops to avoid, evade, or eliminate anxiety. Sullivan defines the self as a "system within a personality, built up from innumerable experiences from early life, the central notion of which is that we satisfy the people that matter to us and therefore satis-fy ourselves, and are spared the experience of anxiety" (1964, p. 218). The self-system develops entirely out of the effect of others on a per-son's sense of well-being. To put it simply, other people make us anx-ious, anxiety is exceedingly unpleasant, so we develop a self-system to deal with this anxiety.

As was mentioned earlier, this anxiety is first met in infancy. At first the mother is a source of satisfaction to the infant. However, as the infant grows, his mother begins to withhold approval and express dis-approval in order to teach the infant the things that are necessary for social survival. Sullivan makes a point of this training and concomitant disapproval, particularly in connection with elimination and the sexual parts of the body. The mother disapproves of the infant's eliminating whenever and wherever he wishes. She disapproves of his messing his diapers. Even more, she disapproves, and may even be horrified, to discover that the infant is playing in the feces he has produced. Also, a mother is likely to disapprove of the infant's playing with his genitals. Although Sullivan does not mention it, it seems to me, from my own experience with infants, that the infant is likely to encounter a great deal of disapproval from the mother when he reaches a stage of de-velopment when he is able to pick up objects and put them into his mouth, and when he is able to crawl around and get into mischief on his own. The infant is ignorant and curious. He learns by exploring, and two of his chief tactics of exploration are putting his fingers onto objects and putting objects into his mouth. This exploration is likely to lead him into situations that are dangerous, or to lead things that are dangerous into him. In any case, the net effect is that the infant who earlier was an object of continuous concern, care, and approval now finds his pleasant world rudely shattered by frequent shouts of "No! No!" This disapproval from the mother produces anxiety in the infant. Anxi-ety is unpleasant, so he develops the self-system as a way of dealing with it.

Sullivan calls this self-system a secondary dynamism. It develops entirely out of interactions with other people, and its contents are expe-riences with other people. This experience teaches the developing in-fant to be highly sensitive to signs of increasing and decreasing anxiety, and to take actions which will decrease anxiety. This anxiety has large-ly to do with anxiety about security, and security is bound up with rela-tionships to other people. That is, when other people approve, we feel secure; when others disapprove, we feel insecure.

The self-system tends to be resistant to change. It is resistant to change because it tends to avoid situations or experiences which threaten security and thus raise anxiety. The self detects increases in anxiety and tends to move in directions away from this increase and toward security. However, movements toward security are not movements toward change, but rather movements that will avoid change.

Nonetheless, the self-system does change during life. It does so because it has a tendency toward growth, and growth brings about change. Further, the self-system is particularly open to change at stages of life in which a person is especially open to experiences with other people. One such stage is preadolescence, when the main need of the person is for an intimate relationship with another person of the same sex. In this intimate relationship with another person, the child's self-system is open to appraisals from the other person that may well be different from the self-appraisals received from parents earlier in life. Thus, many distorted views the child might have of himself are open to correction by the views of the new friend he has acquired. From preadolescence onward, the growing person is also open to the experience of loneliness. Loneliness is even more distressing an experience than anxiety, so the person may be driven to closer relationships with others, and to the possibility of a change in his self-system, in spite of the anxiety such a change brings with it.

In adult life the self-system serves chiefly to protect self-esteem and prestige. Since our esteem is built upon our perceptions of that in our personality in which we can take some pride, and upon our rationalizations of that which is not so admirable, any new information is likely to upset this *modus vivendi* and thus be rejected. Experiences which upset our view of ourselves are traumatic, and therefore resisted.

That which arouses anxiety is shunted into the not-self, and into unawareness. The process by which this occurs is called *selective inattention*. That is, the self chooses not to attend to certain things, and those things it chooses not to attend to are those things that arouse anxiety. However, there are other kinds of experiences that are also selectively not attended to. Sullivan cites the case of the child who cries for the moon. He does not receive the moon, so he gradually tends to treat the moon as if it does not exist. Through the process of selective inattention, the child becomes unaware of the moon.

Personifications. The self-system contains the personifications. They are the elaborate organization of the experience of the other person (or of the self) within the person's own experience.

The first personification, hopefully, is the personification of the "good" mother. The good mother is the one who brings satisfaction to the infant, although the infant does not personify the good mother until he has encountered a bad mother with whom to contrast her. The "bad" mother is the mother who produces anxiety. At first the infant does not experience the good mother and the bad mother as the same person. They are two different people. With the development of linguistic ability and the attachment of one word, "Mama," to both the good mother and the bad mother, the two merge into one person. Sullivan points out that the separate personifications of the good and the bad mother may persist into adulthood, although they may remain out of awareness. Most likely, the joint identity of good mother and bad mother does not become really firm until well into the juvenile era. As an experiment, tell a child you know (who is around three years old) that you are a lion and are going to eat him up. Then growl loudly and thrash about. Chances are he will show some fright, or at least serious uncertainty about the situation, suggesting that he is not certain of the continuous identity of you and the lion you are pretending to be. Perhaps tales of the werewolf and the story of *Dr. Jekyll and Mr. Hyde* are also indications of the persistence of the concept of discrete personifications that merely happen to inhabit the same body. In any case, the infant develops his first two personifications in the concepts of the good mother and the bad mother.

The infant also begins to develop personifications of himself. The first is the *"good-me,"* who gains satisfaction and is approved of by his mother. The second is the *"bad-me,"* who is disapproved of by his mother. It is the bad-me that is associated with anxiety. Beyond personification is the *"not-me,"* which is associated with severe anxiety. The anxiety in connection with the not-me is so severe that the whole experience is dissociated from the self, and the experience is described by Sullivan as "uncanny" or awe-producing. That is, it is an experience that is outside of usual or understandable experience. This kind of experience is not of the world we ordinarily inhabit.

As the child develops, he also develops a concept of "I." "I," like "Mama," is formed of a fusion of the good-me and the bad-me. This "I" is the personified self, and the personified self is composed of all the self we know about. If someone asked us to tell all there was for us to tell about ourselves, the personified self would be what we would describe. This is the self that is measured by self-concept questionnaires.

The not-me persists into adulthood. It is the "me" that does the things I do that are not like me. It is the John who does the things that we say are "not like John." And that which is "not like John" is not a part of the personified self—the self we all know and love.

The relationship between the personifications and that which is personified is not exact. Our personifications of ourselves or of another person are not identical with either ourselves or that other person. To the extent that our personifications of others and of ourselves are inadequate or inaccurate, we are likely to have difficulty in our relationships with other people. We may respond to the other as though he is a person whom he cannot recognize — and we are likely to proceed as though the personification we have of ourselves is a reasonable facsimile of the personification the other has of us. Only when our relationships go awry are we likely to realize that our personification of ourselves, or of the other person, has been somewhat removed from the actuality of that other person. And if we are going to predict accurately the reaction of other people to us, we had better have a personification of ourselves that corresponds somewhat to the selves that other people encounter.

Sullivan (1964, p. 246) notes that anxiety in an interpersonal situation is always traceable back to the good mother and the bad mother and is tied into the concepts of the good-me, bad-me, and not-me. To generalize the proposition, our current relationships with people are, in part, a function both of our past relationships with significant others and of our personifications developed from our experience with those significant others in the past.

Communications. Since the development of the personality is a function of relationships between people, and since the relationships between people are carried on through communications, it seems desirable to discuss briefly interpersonal communications as they were viewed by Sullivan. Sullivan (1954) was acutely aware of the fact that communications between people are not exclusively, or even primarily, verbal. He divided communications into two "grand divisions," gesture and verbal. Within the category of gesture he included all nonverbal communications.

Language is learned in interaction with others and serves as the medium through which consensual validation with others is developed. The corrections that take place in the self-system, and in the personifications of the self and others, take place through communications. Carson (1969, Ch. 2) suggests that "digital" language serves as the means by which consensual validation and the development of experience in the syntaxic mode is brought about. By digital language, Carson means language which is precise and which communicates accurately the experience of the one person to the other.

To repeat a point, however, it should be noted that Sullivan was well aware of the importance of communication in the process of personality development and took pains to emphasize that communications are both verbal and nonverbal.

Learning. Learning was a topic to which Sullivan attached a great deal of importance, though he never felt he had completely grasped its essence and its implications. No doubt learning theorists would agree with him, although he did pretty well for an amateur in attacking the topic.

For learning to take place, Sullivan felt that two things were necessary: the organism had to have matured so that it had the capability to learn, and it had to be exposed to the necessary experience for learning. Repeatedly in discussing interpersonal relationships, Sullivan stressed the necessity of a person having the right kind of experience at the appropriate period in life for normal development to take place.

Sullivan listed four kinds of learning. The first and most important learning comes by or from *anxiety.* He was not very clear as to how anxiety is a learning experience — in fact, one might argue that as Sullivan presented it, anxiety is an unlearning experience, since he stated that severe anxiety is like a blow on the head — it wipes out everything that is proximal to its occurrence. However, less severe anxiety teaches the growing infant to detect the anxiety gradient. The infant learns to detect increasing and decreasing anxiety, and to behave in ways that move him down the gradient, away from anxiety. The infant learns to gain satisfaction in ways that do not stir up intolerable amounts of anxiety. This process Sullivan termed *sublimation.* That is, the infant learns to detect anxiety and to avoid satisfying needs in ways that increase anxiety; he develops methods that satisfy needs without unduly incurring the cost of anxiety. Apparently this is, from Sullivan's point of view, the most important kind of learning that takes place.

A second kind of learning comes through *trial-and-success,* in which the infant randomly tries various methods, then strikes a method that works, and continues to use it to satisfy needs. As Sullivan described it, it seems to be similar to Skinner's concept of training through reinforcing desired behavior.

A third kind of learning comes through *rewards and punishments.* The infant is rewarded for the desired behavior through fondling or through some other expression of approval, and he is punished for forbidden behavior, through the induction of pain or some other behavior that produces anxiety in the infant.

The fourth kind of learning comes through *trial-and-error by human example.* In this learning the infant tries to, and gradually becomes able to, imitate his elders. This kind of learning is particularly important in the development of the ability to communicate through language and facial expressions.

The last kind of learning is *education,* which is learning the relationships among various phenomena.

Carson (1969, Ch. 3), who is considerably more sophisticated than Sullivan on the topic of learning, has related various Sullivanian concepts to modern concepts of learning. He divides learning into two categories, action learning and cognitive learning. According to Carson there are three types of action learning: cognitive learning, instrumental behavior, and prompted behavior. Instrumental behavior is learning to do that which brings pleasure, and this has been termed the "Law of Effect." Carson feels that Sullivan's categories of learning by anxiety, learning by trial-and-success, and learning by rewards and punishments are all examples of the Law of Effect. Sullivan's trial-and-error learning by example is a case of prompted learning, in which the person is given prebehavior guidance in learning. Carson feels that by far the most important kind of learning for interpersonal relationships is cognitive learning, and he discusses interpersonal behavior, the development of the self-system, and other Sullivanian concepts in terms of cognitive learning. Cognitive learning is learning which affects how a person sees his environment, which will determine how he will act in order to bring about desired conditions or relationships.

Personality Dynamics

The human personality is not a static thing — or even a thing at all. It is dynamic, which is to say that it is always in action. According to Sullivan the action of the personality is directed toward gaining satisfactions or gaining and preserving security. In this section we will consider the processes by which these desirable ends are brought about.

Sullivan drew a diagram which illustrated the general pattern of all interpersonal processes. This diagram is presented in Figure 2.

The "situation integrated by any dynamism" could be any interpersonal situation moving toward a goal determined by the dynamisms operating within two people interacting with each other. If the situation is resolved or if it disintegrates, then in either case, it ceases to exist, and no more action goes on. However, if the tension continues or increases, and/or if supplementary processes are brought into play, then some action goes on. And action is what we are interested in when we discuss personality dynamics.

By "personality dynamics" we mean the things going on within a person during the process of an interaction. These might be termed "intrapersonal" processes. In the next section of the chapter "interpersonal" processes, or what goes on between people, will be discussed.

Behavior is driven or motivated to achieve satisfactions and security. Satisfactions have to do largely with satisfying the physical needs of a person, while security has to do with securing his relationships with other people. Satisfying the physical needs, however, is bound up with relationships to other people, since the chief problem with which people have to contend is the maintenance of security. Inasmuch as this is true, most of what occupies the personality — or to be more accurate, that which defines the personality — is determined by relationships with other people.

Anything that threatens approval or prestige or esteem from other people is a threat to security, and a threat to security leads to anxiety. Anxiety disrupts the satisfaction of a need. Therefore, what goes

FIGURE 2. **GENERAL PATTERN OF INTERPERSONAL PROCESSES**

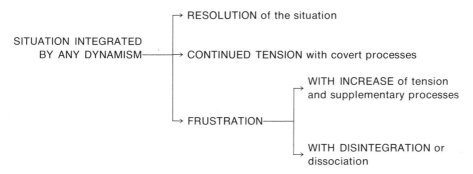

on within the inner regions of the personality of a person is designed to evade, avoid, eliminate, or otherwise deal with anxiety so that the person can satisfy his needs, whether they be physical or social. Further, anxiety itself is unpleasant, so that one of the aims of the personality process is to eliminate the experience of anxiety itself. In the remainder of this section, we will consider some of the tactics used to deal with anxiety.

Anger. Sullivan states that "anger, in either its mild or severe grades, is one of the most common masking operations for anxiety" (1954, p. 135). Anxiety is converted into anger because it is easier on a person to feel anger than to feel anxiety. Since anger, or rage, is observed quite early in infancy, it might be considered the first "defense mechanism" to appear in life. A person who becomes angry ceases to feel anxious, and even though the anger may not remove the source of anxiety, it does remove the experience of anxiety.

Selective Inattention. This is a rather remarkable process whereby a person is not made anxious by something because he refuses to recognize that it exists. In this process the person avoids attending to the anxiety-arousing situation by attending to other things. Since the anxiety-arousing situation does not get attended to, it does not get solved. Sullivan (1953b, p. 319) suggests that selective inattention is particularly impressive in that one must pay close but unacknowledged attention to some aspects of oneself or one's relationships with others in order to make sure that one never becomes aware of them. It takes an alert person to remain ignorant of the more important things in his life.

Dissociation.[2] In dissociation, anxiety-arousing material is kept out of awareness by the use of selective inattention. The person just does not pay any attention to the material (Sullivan, 1956, Ch. 3). This tactic is accomplished by carrying on within awareness processes that make it practically impossible for the dissociated material to be brought into awareness. However, dissociated material may be contained in dreams or represented in awareness by the memory of fragments of dreams within which the dissociated material is contained. Dissociation, as described by Sullivan, is very much like the Freudian process of repression.

Sublimation. As an infant develops, he encounters anxiety. This usually occurs when a behavior that earlier brought the baby satisfaction is now disapproved of by significant others—namely parents. To resolve the anxiety, the infant unwittingly substitutes for the behavior that stirs up anxiety another, nonanxiety-arousing behavior which more or less satisfies the original need (Sullivan, 1953b, p. 139). This pattern of substitution is called sublimation. The new overt behavior may not completely satisfy the need, but it does avoid paying the price of anxiety; the remainder of the need may be taken care of through covert, symbolic processes in sleep.

Obsessionalism. Obsessionalism is a kind of smoke screen that people put up to hide their own vulnerability from others and themselves. This vulnerability, Sullivan (1956, Ch. 2) says, is based on the rather deep-seated feeling of the individuals that they are not very good. In order to keep awareness of this vulnerability from themselves and from other people, they spew out verbal additions and revisions to anything that is going on, so that they can avoid revealing their inadequacy to themselves and to other people. The best example of this defensive process that I have ever encountered was with a client with whom I engaged in psychotherapy for three years, three times a week, before he would allow me to make any comment beyond "uh-huh," "hello," and "good-by." His obsessive talk allowed him to prevent the discussion from entering into anxiety-arousing topics.

Other Personality Processes. Sullivan had valuable insight on many other aspects of the functioning personality, particularly in the

[2]Though there seems to be little difference between dissociation and selective inattention, Sullivan does make a distinction. Dissociation is *what happens* to material when it has been subjected to selective inattention. Selective inattention is the *process* by which this happens.

seminars he conducted, which were published in his book entitled *Clinical Studies in Psychiatry.* He observed that one way a person may get rid of an anxiety-arousing part of his self-system is to develop "specious ideals." With specious ideals he becomes very sensitive to and critical of the characteristics in others that he fears he himself possesses. My favorite example of this phenomenon is a middle-aged school-teacher I know who has become quite critical of the scandalous behavior of young people these days. She fails to recall that when she and I were young, she was the most scandalous young woman in our social group. When she got older, she became respectable; that is, she repressed, or selectively inattended to, whatever inner impulses motivated her to outrage the sensibilities of the keepers of the moral order of our youth.

Guilt is often a rationalization for anxiety. Guilt develops from the failure of a person to live up to the expectations of his ideal self. The reason a person fails to live up to these expectations is because of something in his personality of which he is unaware, which, if it were brought to awareness, would arouse deep anxiety.

Pride is a cover for insecurity. Sullivan felt that people are often proud of things that aren't true. Conceit, however, is based upon real qualities of a person that are overvalued.

Envy occurs in a person who is not able to form adequate interpersonal relationships, and thus tries to bolster his security by achieving high positions or acquiring prestigious material possessions. The jealous person has a deep feeling of unworthiness; he feels incapable of achieving the level of intimacy other people are capable of achieving.

The above tactics used to reduce anxiety are all within the range of the "normal" person. Later in the chapter we will briefly describe some tactics that exceed normal limits and become pathological. But now let us turn to a consideration of interpersonal processes.

Interpersonal Processes

In the last section we considered what might be termed "intrapersonal processes"—those processes taking place within the personality of a person in order to maintain security and reduce anxiety. Now let us turn to a consideration of the interaction between people.

Whenever two people are collaborating toward the achievement of some common goal, they become integrated into an interpersonal situation. Factors that increase the likelihood that they will achieve that goal are constructive and integrative for the interpersonal situation, while factors that impede the achievement of that goal are destructive or disintegrative. The chief disintegrative factor, of course, is anxiety, which derives from insecurity. Sullivan (1954) stated a concept of integration in his Theorem of Reciprocal Emotion.

> Integration in an interpersonal situation is a process in which (1) comple-
> mentary needs are resolved (or aggravated); (2) reciprocal patterns of
> activity are developed (or disintegrated); and (3) foresight of satisfaction
> (or rebuff) of similar needs is facilitated (p. 129).

In short, the interpersonal process follows the pattern outlined in Figure 2, page 39. The situation is integrated and leads to satisfaction and security; or it is somewhere in the process of achieving those two ends; or it fails to achieve these ends and disintegrates.

It would probably be impossible to overstate the extent to which Sullivan stressed the importance of anxiety, and its polar opposite, security, in relationships between people. In the integration of an interpersonal situation, it is essential that those participating should feel secure. That is, if two people are going to achieve whatever it is they want to achieve, the probability that they will achieve that goal is much greater if both feel secure in their relationship with each other. Not only does anxiety interfere with the achievement of interpersonal goals; more often than not, it leads to the disintegration of interpersonal situations.

Quite early in his career, when he was devising treatment methods for schizophrenics, Sullivan (1962, p. 224) stressed the importance of hiring aides who were understanding of, or sensitive to, the schizophrenics as people. In writing about the ordinary interview situation, Sullivan (1954, Ch. 2) discussed the importance of "understanding" in bringing about a satisfactory end result to that very common kind of interpersonal situation. He felt that a person you consider as understanding you is one who shows, by various kinds of consideration, that he feels that you are a worthwhile person. He does not jolt you when he tells you unsettling facts about yourself or your situation; he prepares you for these jolts by giving you hints that make it possible for you to prepare yourself to receive them; he also comes to your rescue by helping you find ways of dealing with these jolts. The understanding person provides you with information that he knows you don't have, but will need for making decisions in your life; he is one who respects your worth, is sensitive to what will threaten your security, and takes care to guard that security. It is this security that increases the probability that any given interpersonal situation will achieve its goals — and indeed this security is, in itself, one of the main goals of the interpersonal relationship.

Any interaction between any two people is a function of their past experiences in interpersonal interactions, and their past experiences with each other in interacting. An interpersonal interaction, at any given time, is a complex phenomenon, which reflects not only the immediate situation, but the past interpersonal history of both of the participants. Consequently, making a person feel secure in an interpersonal situation may not be a simple matter. We carry around with us tendencies to react to other people which we have developed out of our experience with others in the past. Thus, we might feel anxious in a present relationship, not because of anything the other person is doing, but because of what some other person did at some time in the past. To give a rather extreme example, I once knew a man who had spent several years in a Nazi concentration camp. For many years afterward he reacted to anyone in a position of authority with extreme anxiety and went to great lengths to avoid having to deal with any people of this type.

In fact, any interpersonal relationship is a very complex process. Sullivan writes:

> When one has regard for the multiple me-you patterns that complicate interpersonal relations, for the possible differences in individual prehension of events, and for the peculiarities of language behavior which characterize each of us . . . the practical impossibility of one-to-one correspondence of mental states of the observer and the observed person should be evident. We never know all about another, we are fortunate when we achieve an approximate consensus and can carry on meaningful communication about relatively simple contexts of experience. Most of us spend the greater part of our social life in much less adequate contact with our interlocutors, with whom we manifest considerable skill at avoiding frank misunderstanding, with whom in fact we agree and disagree quite often with very little consensus as to subject of discussion (1964, p. 55).

To understand the interaction between two people, you must know the history of their own past interactions, including their interactions with each other. Because of parataxic distortion, an interaction between two people may become quite a complex process. Instead of one me-you pattern there may be several me-you patterns in the interaction. Between a husband and wife, for example, the husband carries on an interaction between himself and his wife as he perceives her. Likewise, the wife carries on an interaction between herself and her husband as she sees him. However, there may be little identity at all between the husband as he sees himself and the husband as seen by the wife. Likewise, there may be little identity between the wife as she sees herself and the wife as seen by the husband. Thus there may be two people, a husband and wife, interacting with each other, yet in no sense *simply* interacting with each other. Their interaction is between themselves and their personifications of the other. To illustrate this point, I once counseled a man and a wife who battled continuously, to their own misery and to the detriment of the happiness of their children. As the counseling progressed, it became apparent that one personification the husband had of his wife was as a kind of witch who was trying to consume and control him totally, while the wife viewed her husband as a totally self-centered man who refused to give any affection or consideration to her or to the children. The wife's efforts to gain attention and affection were experienced by the husband as attempts to consume and control. The husband's efforts to protect himself from total control by his wife were experienced by the wife as a self-centered withdrawal from the family. The perception of each by the other contained an element of truth, but the correspondence between the views each had of the other and each had of himself was quite slight. Obviously, in such a situation the interpersonal relationship is likely to be difficult and complicated, since neither person in the interaction is interacting with a person perceived or recognized by the other person in the interaction. Instead of a two-person interaction it becomes a four-person interaction, but it is a four-person interaction in which two of the interactors are invisible to the other two interactors.

Ordinarily in an interaction, if the two people are reasonably mature and if the anxiety level is not so high that perception of the other is distorted, the attitude and behavior of each toward the other changes. This change is generally in the direction of consensual validation. That is, each corrects the view the other has of him, until, assuming the relationship becomes intimate, each develops a view of the other that is in reasonable harmony with the other's view of himself.

When a relationship begins, both persons usually tend to feel ill-at-ease and anxious with the other, because they do not know what the other thinks of them. As the relationship proceeds, both persons gain some idea of the other person's attitude, and security in the relationship grows. With this growth in security, security operations decline, and the two people develop a consensually validated view of each other. Thus, the personifications one has of the other tend to come into correspondence with the personifications the other has of himself.

Of course, the phenomenon that interferes with this development of the interpersonal relationship is anxiety, or that which produces anxiety, insecurity. In discussing the interview, Sullivan (1964) described how he dealt with anxiety when he developed a relationship with a person with whom he wished to do psychotherapeutic work. His formula could apply, as well, to the development of any interpersonal relationship:

> My work with a stranger soon becomes a mapping of the areas in interpersonal fields in which he becomes anxious—which can be said to mean that he there tends to "pull away"; to explore many leads as to the historic why and distorted present that account for these incidents of anxiety; to elevate what I observe to lucid attention, when and if that can be done without a defeating degree of anxiety; and only then, by stating

the problem as I have surmised it, to establish a beginning collaboration for its remedy (1964, p. 331).

To establish an intimate relationship with another person one must learn the areas of his sensitivity and anxiety, and one must learn to deal with these areas in a way that helps the other person.

The main process by which an interpersonal relationship is carried on is through communication. The chief disruption of communication is anxiety. Anxiety is chiefly the result of lowered self-esteem or anticipated threats to self-esteem. Lowered self-esteem, of course, threatens security. Therefore, the tactic to follow in promoting the development of an interpersonal relationship is to avoid threats to the self-esteem of the other, and thus avoid arousing anxiety in the relationship; if anxiety is aroused, one must seek to restrain its development. Sullivan suggests that communications with another person are so important that "one has information about one's own experience only to the extent that one has tended to communicate it to another . . ."(1953a, p. 185).

Psychopathology

Before ending this chapter, a short section should be devoted to summarizing Sullivan's view of some of the more prominent forms of deviant behavior. Sullivan was, after all, a psychiatrist who developed his theory of interpersonal relationships from his experience with mental patients.

Underlying all deviant behavior is the feeling that the person feels unworthy and incompetent in his relationships with other people. His deviant behavior and symptoms are designed to compensate for this incompetence. Sullivan (1953a, Ch. 4) describes this process as occurring in the following way: Early in life, threatening experience creates a negative view of the self. This negative personification of the self produces a projected low estimate of other people and results in unsatisfying relationships with other people. These unsatisfying relationships lead to despair, result in a cessation of efforts to relate to other people, and interrupt the process of consensual validation. With consensual validation suspended, autistic material becomes more and more a part of the person's reveries. In these reveries the person regresses until he comes upon reveries of a more satisfactory and happy time in the past. The reveries of bygone bliss, uncorrected by consensual validation, may become part of expressions of behavior disorder. When reverie includes so much energy that it cannot be dissociated, it is then resymbolized by the self. It may then be expressed in the form of a symptom, which makes no obvious sense to other people, but which does serve to ward off the person's awareness and anxiety.

In the most severe of the mental disorders, schizophrenia, the resymbolization fails, and there is "literally a fragmentation of the mind" (Sullivan, 1953a, p. 142). The schizophrenic accepts the terrors of schizophrenia rather than integrating the dissociated tendencies into the self, because to accept the dissociated material would be equivalent to undergoing extensive changes in personality and in interpersonal relations—changes that would bring too much anxiety to the schizophrenic. The schizophrenic is a person who has suffered a disastrous loss in self-esteem—so much so that, for him, the universe has lost its integrity and become unpredictable. To escape anxiety, he retreats into a dreamlike state, building a barrier between himself and other people. Since this barrier deprives him of consensual validation, he becomes interpersonally incompetent. As his interpersonal behavior becomes increasingly inappropriate, he may begin to feel persecuted, and his behavior will gradually deteriorate. Sullivan prescribed a sympathetic environment as the cure.

The obsessive person is one who feels deeply insecure. To maintain his tenuous security, he must maintain control over the details of his environment. The obsessive person has come to believe, at some primitive level, that words have some type of magical power to undo the threatened harm incurred by an inappropriate previous action. To him, words can ward off evil or achieve desired ends, even though the words themselves don't necessarily make any sense. He suffers from a deep-seated, life-long sense of insecurity.

The hysteric person is one who has missed the basic interaction with other people in the juvenile era—interaction that usually defines a person for life. He is usually one who had a parent who used him as an audience to the parent's own personality. As a consequence, the hysteric has a rather shadowy personification of other people as existing chiefly to serve as an audience to his performance. He does not interact with other people so much as he performs for them. He has an active fantasy life that began developing in childhood, and he has continued to elaborate on these fantasies throughout life. He tends to gravitate toward people who have as little ability as he does to interact with others on a real, intimate basis.

The hypochondriacal person is one who uses his physical problems for two purposes. First, they give him something to talk about with other people. Second, they serve a security function by providing an excuse for his past failures.

As this rather abbreviated description of some of the more prominent examples of behavior pathology demonstrates, Sullivan viewed behavior disorders as having their roots in the interpersonal relationship.

Discussion

Perhaps the best way to evaluate the contribution of Harry Stack Sullivan is to review his description of the interpersonal relationship against the background of work produced in the field in the more than twenty years that have elapsed since his death. This comparison is even more impressive when it is realized that some of Sullivan's observations anticipated recent work by as much as forty years.

By tracing the source of schizophrenia to the relationships between the schizophrenic and significant other people, Sullivan clearly anticipated not only the work of Bateson, Jackson, and the communication theorists (see Chapter 3), but also the work of Laing (see Chapter 6) and his phenomenological approach to interpersonal relations. In addition, Sullivan anticipated Laing's complex "refraction of refractions of refractions" when he observed that there is a process of complex interaction between two people who are in interrelationship. That is, Sullivan anticipated the observation that as people interact, their views of each other and of themselves change as a function of the interaction.

Sullivan anticipated the work on communications and the "double-bind" described in Chapter 3; in addition, he emphasized that communication was nonverbal as well as verbal, a topic discussed at length in Chapter 4. Sullivan's descriptions of some of the habitual kinds of interactions that go on between people, particularly those that are conducted for purposes of maintaining security, anticipated the more detailed descriptions of security interactions between people described by Berne. Sullivan's emphasis on needs and on the function of needs, anticipated the needs view of interpersonal relationships, although Sullivan's elaboration of needs in the interpersonal context is somewhat more primitive than that of Winch and Maslow (see Chapter 10).

Perhaps the best indication of the prescience of Sullivan's observations is the fact that Robert Carson (1969), in writing a book that attempted to integrate most of the known data about interpersonal relationships, chose Sullivan's theory as the organizing scheme around which he structured his book. He took the two main needs, for satisfaction and for security, as the basis for payoff or reward in exchange theory (see Chapter 8), and organized habitual styles of relating to other people around the scheme developed by Leary and Foa (see Chapter 7). In short, Carson found that most of what has been happening recently in interpersonal relations could be fit within the Sullivanian scheme, with some revisions, of course. Perhaps nothing could be more laudatory than to say that after almost thirty years, Sullivan's theoretical scheme is still able to accommodate most of the facts accumulated in the study of interpersonal relationships within that time.

As for Sullivan's method, the method of participant observation, it is perhaps as sophisticated as we are likely to get with purely clinical methods. He did provide a manual by which one might learn the method, and the scheme he developed through the use of it has withstood the test of time well enough to provide some sort of recommendation for it. But it still suffers the weaknesses of the clinical method. However, Sullivan repeatedly stressed that a phenomenon detected by clinical observation should always be viewed as a hypothesis, subject to further test. In this sense, the method of participant observation becomes a process of hypothesis generation as much as a process of hypothesis confirmation. Sullivan was not naive about the possible pitfalls inherent in the method of participant observation. He just felt it was the best, and perhaps only, way to obtain the necessary information for developing a science of interpersonal relations.

Let us now turn to a consideration of where Sullivan stands on the dimensions proposed in Chapter 1 as a basis for comparing the various approaches to the study of interpersonal relations.

The people Sullivan studied were clinical patients encountered either in a hospital or in a consulting office. The situation in which he studied them was psychotherapy. He studied them at the level of dyadic interaction. That is, he studied them as they engaged in an interaction with him as the participant observer. However, the concepts he used were both intrapersonal and interpersonal, so Sullivan was actually studying his patients at both the personal and the dyadic level. The kind of data he obtained was both self-report and behavior observation. The behavior he observed was the patient's behavior in the psychotherapy interaction. Sullivan's "theory" is a comprehensive one that attempts to include the whole process of interpersonal interaction, including the processes by which it develops.

When viewed in contrast with the other approaches to be discussed in this book, Sullivan's is the most comprehensive. In some aspects, his ideas are dated, his conceptualizations having been superseded by research that more precisely accounts for some of the processes he describes. This is particularly true of his conceptualizations of learning, self-processes, and the cognitive processes that are relevant to learning and the functioning of the self.

As a theory, Sullivan's is closer to the center of our dimension (or we might say, the mainstream of the study of interpersonal relations) than most of the others presented in this book. This "centrality" is illustrated in Chapter 14. The chief potential weakness of Sullivan's work lies in the fact that it is based entirely upon a particular kind of data obtained from a "non-normal" population in a particular kind of situation. This weakness is offset by the fact that many of his concepts have been confirmed by data obtained from other kinds of people, by other methods, and in other settings.

Summary

Sullivan developed his theory of interpersonal relationships out of his experience as a psychiatrist and his knowledge of the psychiatric tradition of Adolf Meyer and the social psychology of C. H. Cooley and G. H. Mead.

Sullivan saw the individual as motivated by two main needs: satisfaction of physical needs and maintenance of security, which come primarily from relationships with other people. He saw the individual personality as being composed primarily of the person's experiences with other people. Experience itself is organized in three modes: prototaxic, parataxic, and syntaxic. The *prototaxic* is raw experience; the *parataxic* is experience that is connected with persons or other experiences in a nonlogical manner; and the *syntaxic* is experience that is logically related to other experiences and is communicable to other people.

The growing person goes through six stages of development until reaching maturity. These are infancy, childhood, the juvenile era, preadolescence, early adolescence, late adolescence. The most important thing that happens to a person as he progresses through these stages is his development of relationships with other people, culminating in his capacity for intimacy with another person when he reaches adulthood. One of the key processes in developing constructive relationships with others is consensual validation. Through consensual validation a person validates his views of himself and of other people by communication with another person with whom he is intimate.

In the course of development the individual encounters anxiety, which is very unpleasant. To cope with anxiety a person develops the self-system, a dynamism designed to avoid, evade, eliminate, or otherwise deal with anxiety. A dynamism is a complex pattern of behavior by which needs are satisfied. Anxiety-arousing material is shunted out of consciousness and out of the self-system, through dissociation or other means, but it continues to exert an effect in dreams and unwitting behavior.

Interpersonal relations have the satisfaction of needs and the maintenance of security as their aim. In the process of meeting these goals, relationships between people become quite complex. To meet the goals, the secret is for the persons engaged in an interpersonal relationship to protect and maintain each other's security.

References

Carson, R. C. *Interaction concepts of personality.* Chicago: Aldine, 1969.

Hall, C. S., & Lindzey, G. *Theories of personality.* New York: Wiley, 1957.

Sullivan, H. S. *Conceptions of modern psychiatry.* New York: Norton, 1953. (a)

Sullivan, H. S. *The interpersonal theory of psychiatry.* New York: Norton, 1953. (b)

Sullivan, H. S. *The psychiatric interview.* New York: Norton, 1954.

Sullivan, H. S. *Clinical studies in psychiatry.* New York: Norton, 1956.

Sullivan, H. S. *Schizophrenia as a human process.* New York: Norton, 1962.

Sullivan, H. S. *The fusion of psychiatry and social science.* New York: Norton, 1964.

Additional Sources

For an extended description of Sullivan's system, see the following:

Mullahy, P. *Psychoanalysis and interpersonal psychiatry.* New York: Science House, 1970.

For shorter summaries of Sullivan's system, see the following:

Carson, R. C. *Interaction concepts of personality.* Chicago: Aldine, 1969, Chapter 2.

Ford, D. H., & Urban, H. B. *Systems of psychotherapy.* New York: Wiley, 1963, Chapter 14.

Hall, C. S., & Lindzey, G. *Theories of personality.* New York: Wiley, 1957, Chapter 4.

Communications and the Double Bind

Each individual in a relationship is constantly commenting on his definition of the relationship implicitly or explicitly. Every message exchanged (including silence) defines the relationship implicitly since it expresses the idea, "this is the sort of relationship where this sort of message may be given" (1959, p. 129).

—Don Jackson

The approach to interpersonal relations as a process of communications was stimulated by the problems of schizophrenia. People working with schizophrenics have long noted peculiarities in the way schizophrenics express themselves. Their speech is *circumstantial*, that is, it wanders from topic to topic without ever arriving at a destination. It is often characterized by *delusions* (tales that no one in his right mind would believe), by *neologisms* (invented words whose meanings are unknown), or by *"word salad"* (jumbled words which communicate little or nothing to the hearer).

Those who have studied the families of schizophrenics have observed certain characteristics of those families. Among these recurring patterns of behavior they have noticed are the rejection of the child by the mother (although she may express a superficial affection and concern), the detachment of the father, who lacks involvement in the family, and the emotional estrangement between the mother and the father.

Researchers observing the relationships between the peculiar family interactions and the peculiarities of schizophrenic communication have brought two advances: an approach to the study of interpersonal relations which stresses analysis of communications, and a theory of schizophrenia based upon the peculiar kind of communications that go on in the family of the schizophrenic. This particular communication situation has been labeled the "double bind." In the double-bind situation, the schizophrenic learns from his parents to communicate in an abnormal manner. It is this pathology of communications that is the source of his schizophrenia.

The Structure and Dynamics of the Family of the Schizophrenic

Clinical research on the schizophrenic's family experience first focused on the relationship between the mother and child. What the researchers thought they observed was that the child who later became schizophrenic had been rejected by his mother.

The observation of this mother-child relationship stimulated more intensive observation of the family of the schizophrenic, which led to the conclusion that the abnormal mother-child relationship did not exist in a vacuum—that it was rather just one relationship in a constellation of interrelated and interacting relationships which tend to encourage schizophrenia. Further observation disclosed certain similarities among families of schizophrenics and thus suggested a theory of schizophrenia based upon family dynamics.

The families of schizophrenics are characterized by mothers who are dominating and overprotective, fathers who are weak and passive, and a deep division between the parents. The parents may be actually estranged from each other, or the estrangement may be psychological. The parents may live in the same house, but as strangers to each other (see Bateson, Jackson, Haley, & Weakland, 1956; Fleck, Lindz, Cornelison, Schafer, & Terry, 1959).

Communications between the members of these families are unclear. No one seems able to make and stick to a single declarative statement. It is as though no one has the right to assert anything; and if a person does make an assertion, either he disqualifies it, or the statement is disqualified by another person in the family. The result is a constant confusion among the members of the family as to what is being communicated. This disqualification might be illustrated by the following example:

Daughter: Dad, please be quiet. I'm trying to do my homework.
Father: Well, I never realized you thought I was a bother.
Daughter: I didn't really mean that. You aren't a bother.

In this example the daughter makes an assertion, which she really means. She is trying to concentrate on her work, but her father is distracting her. He really is, at that moment, a bother. But when he reacts to her statement with emotional hurt, she immediately disqualifies her original assertion. She clearly asserted in her first statement that he was a bother, but to mollify him, she disqualifies the statement. What is she communicating? The communication is unclear, so both are confused and unhappy over themselves and the relationship.

This same example could be changed slightly, so that the disqualification comes not from the daughter, who initiated the exchange, but from the father who received it:

Daughter: Dad, please be quiet. I'm trying to do my homework.
Father: I'm not making very much noise. I couldn't be bothering you. I'm not distracting you a bit.

Again the original message is disqualified. The daughter asks her father to be quiet so she can do her work, clearly implying that he is distracting her. But her father immediately disqualifies her message, telling her that she is not experiencing what she says she is experiencing.

Recently I was describing the process of disqualification to a class, and one of the students, who worked in a mental hospital with psychotic children, observed that this was how people always reacted to these confused children. If a child asked for a drink of water when it was inconvenient for the attendant to get him a drink, the child was told "You aren't thirsty. You don't need a drink right now."

In that situation, the child's testimony to his own feelings was disqualified. The attendant was telling the child that he didn't mean what he said. If the child didn't mean what he said, what did he mean? Actually, in this example, confusion occurred on both sides. What the child really meant was "I am thirsty and want a drink." What the attendant really meant was "I can't get you a drink right now. You'll have to wait." But instead of meeting the issue squarely—or instead of communicating clearly—the attendant evaded the potential issue by disqualifying the communication. Disqualification may be the discretion that avoids trouble for an adult, but it can block communication among adults and often causes confusion for a child.

Communications are confused, apparently, because of a need to avoid unpleasant emotional conflicts. It is easier to refuse to confirm a communication than to risk a fight in which one person may be emotionally hurt or may reject the other person. It is as though the relationships among the members of the family are so fragile that the slightest jolt will destroy them. So, confusion is introduced and maintained to prevent something worse from happening. Haley (1959a) points out that the families of schizophrenics can go on for hours without a single member affirming a single statement. It is as though the family has enacted rules forbidding anyone from clearly making and affirming any assertion.

These observations led Haley to conclude that there are several aspects of importance to communications:

1. Communications can be classified into the levels of message. Verbally I may say, "I really like you." But if I say it in a sarcastic tone, the emotional message communicated is "You are a pain in the backside." There may be more than two levels to communication, and the messages being communicated at these various levels may be *congruent*—that is, they may confirm each other; or they may be *contradictory*—denying each other as in the preceding example; or they may be *unrelated* to each other. A boy and a girl may earnestly discuss the dialogues of Plato, verbally, but what he really communicates to her is "I find you fascinating." And what she communicates back to him is "I am fascinated with your fascination."

2. Communication is a cybernetic, or self-corrective, system. I tell you something. You react, and by your reaction you tell me the message you received from me. I then react to your statement, correcting it if necessary. Thus we correct each other's communications and should improve the precision with which we communicate to each other. My wife may ask, "Would you like another cup of coffee?" I reply "No." To which she responds, "What's wrong with the coffee?" All I said was that I didn't want any more coffee, but the message she got was "The coffee is lousy." Now if her interpretation is correct (which it usually is) I will say, "It's too weak" or "It's stale." But let's assume that this is one of those rare occasions when she misreads me. Then I would say "It's not the coffee. I've been drinking coffee all afternoon, and I'm tired of it." In the constant round of disqualifications the schizophrenic faces in his family, he never learns how to correct either his own communications or his perception of the communications of others.

3. When people interact, they establish the rules by which they interact. In communications this may be termed *metacommunications,* that is, communications about communications. There are certain things we do or don't do in certain relationships, and there are certain things we may say or not say in certain relationships. Let's suppose my good friend has a dog that is a constant pest. Every time we visit, the dog barks and jumps all over me with his dirty paws; until he is put out in the backyard, it is impossible for us to talk. Now I know that my friend loves his dog as much as I love my children. To fail to endure

this hazing would be, in effect, to place a limit on my affection for my friend. Or to put it another way, this mongrel bitch is my friend's eccentricity, so to maintain my relationship with him, I endure the dog. The rule is "Love me, love my dog." In normal relationships, one of the unstated rules is "Don't say anything derogatory about another person's spouse." If you want to make a man your enemy, tell him something nasty about his wife. He may already know it; that is not the point. The point is that in a relationship there are rules which are unstated, but ironclad, which govern what you can and can't say to another person. In the schizophrenic's family, the rule is "No one ever says anything definite."

Before ending this section, I would like to describe an interesting hypothesis proposed by Bowen (1960) explaining how the particular pattern of interaction develops in the family of the schizophrenic. Bowen participated in a project studying fourteen families containing schizophrenic members. Seven of these families were asked to come into the hospital to live, so the way the members related to one another could be studied intensively. Seven additional families were studied outside of the hospital.

The families in both situations were studied in depth; that is, not only was the immediate family studied, but also the grandparents and the great-grandparents. Bowen concluded from these studies that it takes three generations to produce a schizophrenic. In one family he studied, the schizophrenic's grandparents on both sides were mature, stable people. His parents, however, were the weakest members from each of the families. The schizophrenic was, in turn, the weakest member of his already weak immediate family. (The weakest member is the child who has had the closest, most intense relationship with the mother, and who has remained dependent on the mother for the longest period of time. The "weakness" of the weakest child is equal to the sum of the weaknesses of the two parents. Thus, the "weak" child is weaker than either of the parents or any of the other children in the family.)

When people marry, they tend to marry mates who are as mature or as neurotic or as "weak" as themselves. The weak child seeks a mate who is as weak as he is. They in turn have children, and the weakest child in this family has a weakness that is equivalent to the sum of the weaknesses of his two parents. Thus, through successive generations increasingly weak children are produced, until one of them becomes too weak to function.

According to Bowen, the pattern in the schizophrenic family is one in which the weaknesses of the parents complement each other. That is, one parent, usually the mother, is overcompetent and runs the family, while the other member, usually the father, is undercompetent and passive. The parents may fluctuate, with one being the dominant one and the other the dependent one, but the parents are never able to achieve a relationship that is a happy medium between these extremes. There is also a vast psychological distance between the two parents. Often there is an inability within the family to make decisions, with the mother usually having this task thrust upon her. The pattern Bowen describes is one in which an inadequate woman, who hides her sense of inadequacy behind a vivacious exterior, marries an inadequate man who hides his inadequacy behind a shy, quiet exterior. The man sees strength in his wife's social poise, while the woman sees kindness and reliability behind the husband's quiet exterior. In the early months of marriage the two come into conflict over making decisions; they soon develop an emotional distance from each other in order to avoid conflict. Then when a child is born, the mother is in a securely overadequate position with the child, so she develops an intense relationship with the child, and the father becomes a peripheral figure in the family. The mother has her feelings of inadequacy, which she projects onto the child. What she is afraid of in herself, she sees in and fears for the child. Thus the mother's fears are projected onto the child and become a reality in the child. As the child grows, he is too close to the mother and has too many of the mother's feelings and perceptions projected onto him, so that he does not develop a strong, stable self of his own. He is not prepared to live by himself in the world. When he first faces the realities of the outside world, being ill-equipped to meet these challenges, he collapses. He becomes schizophrenic.

Others (Fleck et al., 1959; Lindz & Fleck, 1960) who have studied the family of the schizophrenic have made similar observations, noting that the mothers of schizophrenics project their own needs onto the children, and fail to make clear distinctions between the generations (parents and children) and between the sexes, so that the children do not have an opportunity to develop clear ego boundaries or a strong sense of the self.

According to Bowen, the solution to the problem is first to help the patient become emotionally untangled from his mother, which is best accomplished by arranging to have the mother and father become more emotionally invested in each other.

The Analysis of Communications Between People

The communications between people are on at least two levels and have four elements (Haley, 1959b). The levels of communication are:

1. The direct communication, and
2. The qualification of that communication by tone of voice, gestures, behavior, etc.

In a communication between two people there are four elements:

1. The person communicating;
2. What the person is communicating;
3. The person communicated to; and
4. The situation in which the communication takes place.

For example, (1) I (2) am saying something (3) to you (4) in this situation. Thus, in any communication there are at least two levels and four elements. Any one of the four elements may be stated at the first level and either affirmed or disqualified at the second level.

Let's consider an example to illustrate the point of levels, elements, and affirmation or disqualification. I once had an opportunity to observe a rather touching scene between a husband and wife. It was Christmas, so as a present for his wife, the husband had found an old snapshot of his wife's father, who had recently died. On one or two occasions the wife had expressed regret that she owned no portrait of her father. When her husband presented her with the package containing an enlargement of the photograph of her father, she opened it, and when she saw what it was, she burst into tears and exclaimed, "Oh you stinker, you!" At the verbal level she was saying:

"(1) I (2) think badly (3) of you (4) for giving me this present."

But by her behavior she was disqualifying this overt, verbal statement and "saying":

"(1) I (2) think you must love me and be very sensitive to me (3) for you (4) to have brought me this present."

The disqualification, in this case, comes in the second element of the communication.

The second-level revision of the communication may, of course, affect any or all of the four elements of the communication, and it may affirm or disqualify the overt, verbal communication. The wife in the previous illustration might have told her husband, "(1) I (2) love (3) you [(4) now]." And the expression on her face and the tone of her voice certainly would also have said, "(1) I (2) love (3) you [(4) now]."

Haley presents the above structure for classifying communications as a step toward an explanation of schizophrenia. He describes the communication of the schizophrenic as usually being characterized by one communication at the overt level and a disqualification at the lower level, so that no clear message is ever sent.

The Double-Bind Hypothesis

Haley's ideas derive from an earlier, classic paper (Bateson et al., 1956) written in collaboration with Bateson, Jackson, and Weakland. In it they present what has come to be known as the "double-bind" theory of schizophrenia. To oversimplify, the double-bind hypothesis is that the schizophrenic grows up in a family in which the messages he receives from his parents are always telling him to do one thing on the overt, verbal level and another and contradictory thing at the second level. If he obeys the message at one level, then he will be disobeying the message at the second level. He is damned if he does and damned if he doesn't.

The result of this constant diet of confusing and upsetting messages is that the schizophrenic is never able to develop a clear idea of who he is, who his parents are, or what is going on. This has been called by some a "weak-ego function." The schizophrenic has a "weak" ego in three areas of functioning: (1) he has trouble assigning the correct communicational mode to messages he receives from others—he's not sure what they mean; (2) he has trouble assigning the correct communicational mode to messages he gives nonverbally—he's not sure what his own gestures, expressions, etc., mean; (3) he has trouble assigning the correct communicational mode to his own thoughts, feelings, etc.—he's not sure what to make of what he observes going on inside himself. He is confused not only about what is happening within himself, but also about what others are telling him. This confusion over communications, learned over a long period of time beginning with infancy, is fostered by his parents. Confused and ambiguous parents produce a confused and ambiguous young person, who, in his confusion and ambiguity, is unable to meet the demands of life.

The necessary conditions producing the double bind are: (1) two persons, one of whom is the victim; (2) repeated experience, so that the double bind becomes a habitual expectation; (3) a primary negative injunction which may have two forms: (a) Do not do so and so, or I will punish you, or (b) If you do not do so and so, I will punish you; (4) a secondary injunction conflicting with the first injunction, but at a more abstract level, and like the primary injunction threatening punishment, and usually communicated by nonverbal means; (5) a tertiary negative injunction prohibiting the victim from escaping from the field; and finally (6) a victim who learns the lesson so well that he continues to see the universe in double-bind terms, even when the first five ingredients are no longer present.

The consequence of this learned way of perceiving is that the schizophrenic is constantly in an inescapable situation that threatens him with punishment, and he is constantly confused as to who he is and what the situation is, so that disorientation becomes not only a consequence of his confused learning experience, but also a way out of a miserable situation. Even his symptoms become a way of escape. In normal relationships it is necessary for people to be able to discriminate accurately what people are really expressing, and to do this they must be able to evaluate what is communicated. The schizophrenic cannot do this because for him it is too dangerous.

Bateson et al. illustrate the above point with a transaction between a schizophrenic patient and his mother. This young man had been hospitalized for a schizophrenic episode, but was well on his way toward recovery. Following a visit by his mother he relapsed. During his mother's visit, the following sequence had been observed: When she walked into the room, the young man impulsively put his arm around his mother's shoulders. The mother visibly stiffened at this contact. He then withdrew his arm. When he withdrew his arm, his mother said, "Don't you love me any more?" He blushed at this comment, and she told him that he mustn't be afraid of his feelings. A few minutes later he assaulted an aide on the ward.

Communications and Types of Relationships

The original observations of the communications within the families of schizophrenics stimulated Jackson (1959) and his colleagues to cast a wider net. To analyze the communications within a variety of families, they tape-recorded the interactions among the members of several families and analyzed these tapes. They worked on the hypothesis that a family is a system which tries to maintain a particular balance. Jackson called this hypothesis a "control theory." This theory grows from "the belief that all persons implicitly or explicitly are constantly attempting to define the nature of their relationships" (1959, p. 126).

Every communication can be viewed as a report and a command, and the command may be a message that holds higher priority than the explicit verbal communication. Thus one person may, on the overt, verbal level, defer to the other person, but on the higher priority level, he is in fact commanding him. When a general says to his aide, "Lieutenant, could you come here for a minute?" he is really saying "Lieutenant, get down here immediately." If the lieutenant doubts this, just let him say "No, I'm busy right now" and then observe the consequences. I had an opportunity to observe these high-priority, lower-level communications in a research project done by some of my graduate students (Gold, DeLeon, & Swensen, 1966). To study dominance and submission in a decision-making situation, the students first tested subjects to determine whether they were dominant or submissive. Then they presented the individual subjects with two advertisements and asked each subject to decide which ad would more effectively induce people to buy a product. Subjects were then paired with other subjects who held an opposite opinion and who were also known to be of the opposite character type—that is, a dominant subject was paired with a submissive one. Again they were asked to decide which ad would be more effective. Since the paired subjects were known to disagree, their final decision would necessarily represent the judgment of one winning out over the judgment of the other. Predictably, the more dominant member of the pair usually decided which ad was selected as the best. But every once in a while the dominant member apparently gave way to the submissive member, telling him, "Go ahead. You make the decision this time." In fact, the dominant member was continuing to dominate, but he was exerting his dominance at a higher level. Instead of making the decision, he made the decision as to who would make the decision.

In communications between two people, the two are constantly engaged in defining the relationship in one of two ways: either the relationship is (1) complementary or it is (2) symmetric. A *complementary relationship* is one in which one person gives and the other receives, or one person is dominant and the other is submissive. The members are of unequal status. The relationship between a parent and a child is complementary. Also the relationship between a teacher and a student or an officer and an enlisted man is complementary. A *symmetric relationship* is one between two people who behave as if they have equal status. It is a give-and-take relationship between peers. In a complementary relationship the dominant member usually initiates activity and defines the relationship. In a symmetric relationship each has the right to initiate an exchange of communications, and each has the right to define the relationship through comment, criticism, advice, and so on.

Mature relationships are of a kind labeled "parallel" by Jackson (1959). By "parallel" he means that the relationship oscillates, or changes from time to time from symmetric to complementary and back to symmetric again. In a healthy marriage, for example, the husband and wife define who will dominate in which areas, and which areas they will share. One study (Blood & Wolfe, 1960), for example, has found that wives tend to dominate in such things as buying the food and caring for the house, while husbands dominate in deciding where to live and what kind of car to drive. In the case of buying food, the wife plays the role of the mother who decides what is bought, and if the husband is involved, it is as the boy who goes to the store with a shopping list. In deciding where to live, the decision is made by the husband when he decides which job he will take. His wife goes along, just as the daughters in the family do. In deciding which house to buy, however, the husband and wife cooperatively make the decision by mutual discussion. In the area of food purchase, the relationship is complementary with the wife dominant; in the area of deciding where to live, the relationship is complementary with the husband dominant; and in the choice of a house, the relationship is symmetric. Who makes the decision is determined by who is most competent to make the decision, or who is most concerned with and involved in the matter to be decided. Healthy relationships are characterized by such an oscillation.

In unhealthy relationships, however, rather than areas of control, the attempts of one member of the relationship to define the relationship are sabotaged by the other member. The sabotage may be as obvious as a simple, direct "no," or as devious as a well-concealed, covert, emotional disqualification which, when it is called to the attention of the disqualifier, is then in turn disqualified. The disqualification can be through a constant battle for dominance, or a steady, subtle undermining of one member of the pair by the other. The healthy situation is characterized by an oscillation, a healthy give-and-take, while the unhealthy situation, rather than oscillating, has a tendency or a direction.

The way a person relates to others is learned from his parents. Jackson says that "a child not only learns to respond to his parents, but learns to use them as a model for how to respond" (1959, p. 129). In a relationship, each person is constantly commenting on his definition of the relationship, either implicitly or explicitly:

> Every message exchanged (including silence) defines the relationship implicitly since it expresses the idea, "this is the sort of relationship where this sort of message may be given." There are also relationship messages (or maneuvers, or ploys) in which the purpose of the message is to test the other's acceptance of one's definition of the relationship (Jackson, 1959, p. 129).

On the basis of the maneuvers used to maintain the balance of the family relationship, Jackson classified families into four categories. In a book written in collaboration with William Lederer, *The Mirages of Marriage* (1968), he applied these categories to different types of marriages. These four types of families and marriages are:

1. Stable-satisfactory;
2. Unstable-satisfactory;
3. Unstable-unsatisfactory; and
4. Stable-unsatisfactory.

1. The *stable-satisfactory relationship* is one in which both parties can explicitly reach agreement that one or the other is in control of the relationship at a given time, or in control of given areas of the relationship. The person in control initiates action, or establishes which areas will be controlled by the other person. This action is explicit, and it is possible for the participants to discuss the relationship and the effect each person has on the other's behavior. Thus, the stability of the relationship is maintained by the possibility of reestablishing a stable state after a period of instability due to disagreement. "Stable" does not mean that the relationship is completely trouble free, but rather that it

is trouble free most of the time. The stable-satisfactory marriage is one which Jackson was only able to observe between couples who had been married for many years. Lederer and Jackson stated that they had never observed a genuinely collaborative union between spouses during the period they were raising children. In a stable-satisfactory marriage the couple sometimes disagree, but when they do, the disagreement is a comfortable, nonthreatening disagreement. They can agree to disagree. There are two subcategories in this kind of marriage.

1. The "Heavenly Twins," who seem to have been "born for each other." This couple comes from similar social, educational, and ethnic backgrounds.
2. The "Collaborative Geniuses," who do not have extremely similar backgrounds, but nonetheless seem to be more similar to each other than the average couple.

For these couples, basic, shared experiences occur before marriage begins. There is agreement as to who is in charge of what and when. An example of this kind of marriage might be one in which the husband keeps the books and pays most of the bills, but gives his wife a regular amount of money each week or each month for the expenditures she must make. The wife might be in charge of planning the meals, shopping for groceries, decorating the house, and purchasing the furniture and housewares, while the husband might be responsible for the area around the house and the purchase and maintenance of the automobile. They jointly make decisions about where and when they will take vacations. They agree on the rearing and disciplining of the children. They would probably have mutual interests outside the home, so that they might collaborate in their religious or political activities. They might disagree over a religious or political issue, but the disagreement would not be disagreeable, but rather a difference that added spice to their relationship.

2. The *unstable-satisfactory relationship* is one in which two people are in the process of working out their definition of a new or changed relationship. The change might come from external stress or changes in the circumstances in which the couple lives. Lederer and Jackson felt that most marriages that had lasted for more than five or ten years would fall into this category. Occasional resentment or hostility emerge in this relationship, resulting in periodic battles, after which the issues are resolved and the relationship lapses into a tranquil phase. There are two subcategories of this kind of marriage.

1. The "Spare-Time Battlers," who show hostile competitiveness from time to time, but beneath the surface of the relationship have an underlying network of agreement between them about

who is responsible for what. They are capable of working out their disagreements, although some "tears and blood" are shed from time to time in the process.

2. The "Pawnbrokers," who realize that their relationship is not perfect, but feel that on the whole the satisfactions in the relationship outweigh the dissatisfactions, so that breaking up the relationship and trying to find a hypothetically more satisfying one does not seem to be worth the cost or the trouble involved.

3. The *unstable-unsatisfactory relationship* is one where no implicit or explicit agreement is reached on the question of who is in control of which areas of the relationship, and any attempt at definition of the relationship by one member of the relationship is sabotaged by the other member. This kind of relationship is characterized by the need of one party to redefine the relationship the moment the other party tries to define it, so that the periods of stability are relatively short compared to the periods of instability. Each party tends to take any behavior of the other party as a challenge at the relationship level, without the relationship or the challenge ever being discussed. Neither can decide who is boss of what, so the transactions are apt to be complementary maneuvers that are redefined by the other person as soon as the message is received. Actual messages are apt to be quarrels over concrete items, rather than over basic issues. For example, a husband may decide to buy a new car but his wife demurs, claiming she doesn't like the make or the color of the car he proposes to buy, rather than admitting that she resents his claim of dominance over the car-buying area. So he forgoes buying the car, and criticizes her for spending money on a new dress. Neither can communicate directly with the other about what is going on in the relationship. Neither can explicitly take responsibility for defining or setting the limits to the relationship. Like two married porcupines, the pair in an unstable-unsatisfactory relationship relate to each other very carefully. Cultural, social, and religious rules are very important to these kinds of families, since these forces are an external source for the rules that the members of the family are unwilling to promulgate. Such couples may engage in some joint enterprise like political activities or church activities or some social cause, and thus mask the fundamental lack of communication between them. Jackson's observation of these families has led him to conclude that there is "a virtual absence of completed transactions in the unstable-unsatisfactory family" (1959, p. 133). Treatment of these families is very difficult, since no member of the family is willing or able to comment on the behavior of another member. It is as though their relationships are so fragile that they would shatter under the slightest stress.

Lederer and Jackson (1968) define two kinds of marriages that are unstable-unsatisfactory.

1. The "Weary Wranglers," who battle for years to reach their position. They get comfort from their battle, since each can shift the blame to the other.
2. The "Psychosomatic Avoiders," who wage their battles covertly by expressing their anger and disappointment through subtle sarcasm, through indirect and nonverbal means, through physical symptoms such as chronic headaches or backaches, or through excessive use of alcohol.

4. The *stable-unsatisfactory relationship* suffers more pain and inflicts more trouble on other people than the other three kinds of relationships, but people in this type of relationship are not aware of their behavior. There are two kinds of marriages falling under this classification.

1. The "Gruesome Twosome," who are quite stable in their relationship because they are unable to recognize the conflict between them. If they seek help it is because their children are having problems rather than because they are having problems. Neither partner dares comment on the behavior of the other because people in glass houses dare not cast stones. These are couples growing old together in a stable but unsatisfactory marriage because neither is able or willing to acknowledge his or her dissatisfaction. One partner may take excessively considerate care of the other, and thus bully the other into an unhappy, compliant passivity. Still another kind of stable-unsatisfactory marriage is one in which a dependent, demanding person is served by a spouse who serves as a loyal, but quietly resentful servant.
2. The "Paranoid Predators," who exist by avoiding each other without this avoidance being immediately obvious. They make a stand together to fight against a hostile world. There is virtually no relationship information exchanged between the couple. They live separate, distant lives. Their problems are manifested in the problems of their children. No new information is introduced into the pair's relationship unless it is introduced by their children, in which case it may disrupt the marriage.

An Example of the Analysis of Communications

An example of analyzing communications in a family was presented by Jackson, Riskin, and Satir (1961). Their analysis is in terms of the theory and categories described in the preceding section.

As explained earlier, the purpose of communications within the family is to maintain some kind of homeostasis, or balance, in the family, and the individuals communicating are attempting to define the relationship. These definitions may indicate whether the relationship is symmetric or complementary. The communications are on at least two levels, the overt, verbal level and a covert, nonverbal level. The covert communication may affirm, or qualify, or contradict the overt communication. This affirmation or disqualification may be conveyed in many ways. It may be in *the sequence of the communications* — that is, the last part of the sentence may contradict the beginning of the sentence ("Go away closer"). This is a disqualification that is sequential in time. Or the disqualification may be in *the tone of voice* (saying "That was a *great* job you did" in a sarcastic tone). Or the disqualification may be in *the contradiction between the words and the context* (A person who has a good job saying he can't afford to buy his son a pair of shoes). Troubled families have a much higher proportion of disqualified statements in their communications than do stable families, so that troubled families have a lot of incomplete transactions and much unfinished business.

The transcript beginning on the next page is presented by Jackson, Riskin, and Satir (1961) to demonstrate how they analyze the communications among the members of a family. This segment is from a family that included a father, a mother, and a son. They analyzed the communications from a tape recording, and had no knowledge of the family prior to hearing the recording.

The left-hand column, entitled "Transcript," records the actual conversation among the members of the family; the center column, entitled "Interactional Dynamics Analysis," describes the dynamics of the interaction among the members of the family; and the right-hand column, entitled "Communication Analysis," analyzes what is being communicated — that is, how each person is defining the existing relationship.

The most obvious fact about the relationship between this husband and wife is that they cannot agree. They cannot agree on who is allowed to do what, or on the meaning of the statements one makes to the other, or on the nature of the relationships within the family. Scarcely a single statement uttered by one was confirmed, either by the person who uttered it or by the other person. Further, the attempts by one person to define the relationship as either symmetric or complementary are contradicted by the response of the other person. The result is labeled by the authors as something like Eric Berne's game of "Uproar" which will be discussed in Chapter 5.

Another interesting feature of this relationship is that both husband and wife allow the interaction to proceed only a few steps toward an irrevocable explosion before stepping in to dampen the conflict. Both are exerting effort to maintain the relationship within certain bounds of conflict. Conflict continues, but thus far has not been allowed to reach the point of destroying the relationship.

Transcript	Interactional Dynamics Analysis	Communication Analysis
1. *Husband* Well, last time we were together Mrs. Bryant gave a very . . . well a rather (Pause) dissertation, and one of the things I got out of it was she said that uh if I seem to make up my mind sometime and go ahead and do something I want to do and have the courage to do it, or something of that sort (evidently turns to wife) you remember that? (hedging – slightly whining)	1. Husband reminds therapist that last week wife said "I should do what I wanted to do." (Husband is saying "last week wife gave me permission to please myself and indicated by so doing I would please her.")‡ (Does this complaining tone mean wife doesn't keep promises?) *(I am a little boy who must ask permission from mother.)*	1. (CD)° The message "I should be more assertive" is framed by: (a) My wife told me to, and (b) you therapists are responsible – isn't that right? Thus, the interview begins with the husband's difficulty in making a symmetrical statement because it would raise the question with his wife, "Who has what rights in our relationship." Anything that is further stated must be viewed in the framework of "she told me to" and "you said it was all right."
2. *Therapist* Uh-huh.	2. Therapist makes affirming response indicating husband should continue.	2. Therapist makes a neutral comment which in this context means go ahead.
3. *Husband* Well so when I tried a little sample of that Saturday, she just *raised* hell. (mimics, with raising voice) (he laughs) (evidently turns to wife) Your reaction was interesting. I just said that I was going to play . . . this was Friday, wasn't it? (tries to sound factual)	3. Husband tells therapist he tried to please himself but wife objected. ("Wife doesn't mean what she says. She gives permission but takes it away, and this is what I expected. As usual I can't please her.") (Husband's comments are indirect criticism of wife and at the same time a plea for understanding from her.) *(You must never make women angry. Women don't like grown-up men. I resent this.)*	3. (Sym‡to CD) Husband starts again with a symmetrical statement "My wife is like this." He almost immediately disqualifies himself by "little sample" and by using an exaggerated tone, for example on the word "raised," thus criticizing her without risking being overt about it. He does not state "I am critical of my wife." Instead, by mimicking her, he implies "this is what she sounds like."
4. *Therapist* You were what?	4. Therapist asks for more information.	4. Therapist asks for more information.
	‡Statements range from those being of low inference (having no parentheses), through those of medium inference (having parentheses), to those being highly inferential (having parentheses and italicized).	°CD – Complementary one-down comment. ‡Sym – Symmetrical comment.

Transcript is from D. D. Jackson, J. Riskin, & V. Satir, "A method of analysis of a family interview," in *Archives of General Psychiatry*, 1961, XX, 5, 326–33. Copyright © 1961, American Medical Association, and reproduced by permission.

5. *Husband*
This was Friday (sounds factual) I'd been away on this trip. Didn't have any vacation Friday. Thought I was going to play golf, (pause) and so made this statement, I was going to play golf, and she started in (apparently mimics her complaining tone) well, Dick wanted some kids to go swimming and one thing and another. And she had to do some shopping because Pete was coming over, bringing his friends over. And immediately got *angry* about this. (someone coughs) At one point, it involved things about (mimicking) I was selfish and I wasn't thinking about anybody else and all this sort of thing. (back to reportorial tone) Meanwhile I had arrived at the suggestion that part of this was because Pete had to have the car over here. That, I imagine Pete had nothing to do Friday morning and he could solve this whole thing extremely simply by just coming home and taking his mother shopping. (sounds heroic) And I would call him up and ask him to do this. At which point (mimics) *don't you dare* – all that sort of thing, (suffering, complaining) I mean everything here was pinning this whole business on what Dick wanted to do with his little children, what Pete might be just inconvenienced one way, slightly one way or another. And you were just going to see by God if you could not keep me from, if you could keep me *from* playing golf, I *do believe*. (pause) But I did. . . .

5. Husband says "after working hard, I wanted to enjoy myself." ("I had justification for enjoying myself but my wife says children's needs come first. Wife criticizes me for not dropping my needs and meeting children's needs, but I saw a reasonable way that both my needs and theirs could be met.") ("Wife refused to accept this way, but continued to favor the kids. My wife is unreasonable. You, wife, lie when you say you want me to do what I want to do.") ("If I want to do what I want I have to defy you, wife. Doing what I want to do can only be an act of rebellion.") (*You always have to defy mothers to get what you want. If you rebel you make them angry, but if you don't rebel they think you are weak and you remain a little boy.*)

5. (Sym to CD) Again he starts out with a symmetrical statement but again disqualifies himself in two ways: (*a*) He gives up his reportorial tone and factual reporting and then mimics his wife again, implying that she is unreasonable and she will not let him determine what goes on in the house; (*b*) he then adopts a suffering, complaining tone during which he apparently turns to his wife and addresses her directly in a challenging way. In addition, he seems to be indicating to the therapist what he has to put up with.

6. *Wife*
(Overlaps husband's statement) The way you take it. (quietly determined)

6. Wife denies husband's accusation. ("I am not bad, you are. You are misunderstanding me.") (Wife feels that men are really just little boys, they are to be humored,

6. (Sym) The wife's statement, "The way you take it," is said in a quietly determined voice, indicating all too clearly "you are unreasonable and I have to put

7. **Husband**
And I called up your son and he was glad to come over and help you and all this and that. So this was your reaction to me deciding I wanted to do something and meaning it. (more tentatively) Wasn't it?

7. Husband says ("I proved to you that I had a reasonable idea but you won't accept proof. You just want to deprive me. You are unreasonable.") (*Mothers lie when they say they want to be accepting. They are always depriving, Men have no way of influencing women.*) ("You want the children on your side and are against me. You make me feel that my children and I are rivals: When I try to be the father, I am left out. You don't really want a man.") ("Isn't it true that you are unreasonable? If you can admit to being unreasonable, then we both can feel equal. How I feel depends on how you feel.")

7. (Sym to CD) Husband ignores the challenge apparently, and resorts again to an attempt at a symmetrical statement. Again he backs down by ending on a question "Wasn't it?" This is an invitation to being cut down. (Note that so far there have been no completed transactions.)

8. **Wife**
(With a sigh—icy) That's the way you like to take it. You must remember when you left (deadly, bitter) you said (mimics) that you *may* not be here. . . .

8. Wife says "I am justified in criticizing you because you are so unreasonable." (*You can't count on men.*)

8. (Sym to CD) Wife repeats her statement with greater emphasis, for example the sigh implying his unreasonableness. Although the statement is uttered generally in a deadly bitter, icy tone and she continues in the symmetrical position, she disqualifies it slightly by mimicking him in the words, "May not be here." She ends in a one-down position as she appeals to the therapist, "Listen how unreasonable he sounds."

9. **Husband**
(Filling in her last statement) Thursday. And you know my custom is I would let you. (injured innocence) (Wife murmurs) So what's the difference? (loudly)

9. Husband says "You are unreasonable for labeling me as unreasonable.") (*Men can't please women.*)

9. (Sym to CD) Husband again resorts to making a symmetrical maneuver by simply reporting the facts, but ends again on a question "What is the difference?" which obviously calls for a response from her, thus putting him in a complementary one-down position.

not to be taken seriously.) (*Father was ineffectual and treated by mother as a little boy.*)

up with you." The measured tone is an appropriate qualification of the content.)

10. *Wife*
What's the difference? (exaggeratedly factual) Because Pete had called up very nicely and asked if you were back yet or if I knew and I said—No, I didn't. So he said he'd like, he'd bring the car back but I couldn't as I explained to you, (slightly faltering) get the car and drive Pete back to the hospital because he had booked up the evening, because that was the night that Dick had a baseball game which you simply accepted. And I, I uh, (exaggeratedly factual) we had made our plans because we hadn't heard you'd come back or not. Dick invited some boys over there and when you came back and you were sore at me. It wasn't that . . . (mimics) you just came out and said (mimicking—slightly faltering) by God, I'm home, by golly I'm going to have the car by golly, I'm going . . . the hell with—(Wife gets increasingly louder) (factual tone—mimicking attitude)

10. (Wife says "How can I help but criticize you when you are so unreasonable; you are just a blustery little boy." (*Men cannot be counted upon.* Men are unreasonable. *Father was an unreasonable, unpredictable, unreasonable man who couldn't be counted on either.*) (Wife has a need for a husband who will confirm her expectation that men are unreliable, but on the other hand desperately hopes they won't turn out that way.)

10. (CU $ to CD) Wife responds to his one-down position by taking the complementary one-up position, stating by her tone and her factual content "I am reasonable; you are unreasonable." She then weakens her position when she uses his technique of mimicking again, again asking for his support.

11. *Husband*
(Interrupting) (sounds very defensive) I wasn't saying anything like that. (loud) I just said I was going to play golf.

11. Husband rejects wife's accusation. By defending himself husband automatically denies wife's plea for a strong man who will understand her. (He comments instead—"I didn't mean to hurt you, I just wanted to do something for myself.")

11. (Sym to CD) Husband responds to first part of wife's message by attacking. He becomes literal "I just said I was going to play golf" rather than dealing explicitly with her message that he is unreasonable. He thus invites a reiteration from her. His defensive tone (hurt?) is perhaps a comment on her using the one-up position to criticize him.

12. *Wife*
(Mock horror) *Oh-h-h* you just when I said—

12. (Wife attacks him for being a little boy.)

12. (Not determined) Her exaggerated mock horror is a comment on his being a child, but she is utilizing a child-like technique and it is thus not a strong ploy. She does not continue to usurp the one-up position, perhaps because she recognizes that

§CU—Complementary one-up comment.

she has gone too far in criticizing him. This pattern would suggest that apparently they have an inflexible set of rules as to how far they can go in devastating each other. Wife attacks husband for being a little boy, which makes her seem like an evil mother because husband cannot better tolerate her criticism. She is hurt by his being hurt. And this circularity seems to serve as a governor on the extent of their relatedness.

13. (Sym to CD) The governor now in effect, husband returns to the starting statement. Even the content of his statement says clearly "You went too far and now let's start over." He is back to his original position.

14. (CU to Sym) In the absence of an intervention by the therapist, wife responds to husband by asking a therapist-like question, thus switching the context from their private circular interaction. Wife's attempt to get out of the rut misfires because she frames it with a superior tone, thus baiting him; so he must reattack instead of responding helpfully.

13. (Husband says "I am not a bad little boy, you are the unreasonable one.") (If this interaction continued, their mutual hurt would show. In order to avoid this, husband joins in setting the automatic governor in motion and returns to opening gambit saying—"I don't want to hurt you, I am only trying to do what you want me to do. Damn you. Please let me!")

14. Wife changes subject ostensibly. (Wife implies she is speaking to a little boy who is bad—she therefore acts ostensibly like a solicitous mother. Wife is wanting to give by being mothering to husband even though critical. The tone is softer—making a bid for closeness—conciliation to husband.) (Wife, if denied gratification of her needs to be given to further denies them by defensively taking the role of mother.)

13. *Husband*
(Sharply interrupting) It was not until you started (she interrupts, some overlapping) (fast, sharp interaction, each being exaggeratedly factual), not until you started.

13a. *Wife*
I said . . .

13b. *Husband*
. . . yelping about it. This seems almost petty of me to bring a thing like this in here but it goes back to this point that you were saying (mimicking) by golly you would like to see me make up my mind some time or other what I wanted to do and do it.

14. *Wife*
What did you learn that week end, John? (quietly determined, matronizing)

15. *Husband*
Hm?

15. (Since this mothering is seen by husband as defensive, as a disguise for the lack of gratification of her needs, it is not possible for him to fully respond to it. Husband seems taken aback and behaves as though he doesn't hear.) (Mothering probably feels phony to him.)

15. Husband is unclear which message to respond to, therefore he stalls.

16. *Wife*
What did you learn (pause) after all that snorting around? (more critical and with slight edge)

16. Wife initially repeats mothering tone, but changes to critical one in tone and word after being denied any response to her offering. (*Wife feels confirmation of her expectation that men will not accept any giving from women, therefore women are useless in the eyes of men.*) (Wife denies being put in this position by accusing husband of being incapable of giving or receiving.)

16. (CU to Sym) Wife interprets husband's stalling as a lack of response to the helpful aspect of her statement and reinforces the superior aspect in order to punish him. This is not being a "good therapist" and invites attack from husband by her failure.

17. *Husband*
I learned that you just do a lot of yelping no matter what. (sharply critical) Another thing is yesterday was another example. (Wife – "um hum") Uh, *you* wanted to go swimming. (gentle, definitive, teaching quality) And because Dick –

17. Husband denies wife's accusation ("I am not ungiving; your demands are insatiable.") (*Your needs, like those of all women are so great that they are incapable of satiation.*) (Wife says apprehensively—"Go ahead. I know you are going to blame me but you are not going to get away with it." (Husband continues . . . "You say you want to do something for yourself, but you let the kids interfere just as they interfere with my pleasures. You blame me for not pleasing you when you really won't let yourself be pleased.")

17. (Sym to CU) Husband responds with the expected attack, using "yelping" instead of "snorting." As soon as he is critical, he attempts conciliation by being solicitous in the manner of a therapist. However this effort on husband's part to become a therapist, although conciliatory, labels her a patient and will bring forth a rebuttal, which will lead to a symmetrical relationship such as these two have.

18. *Wife*
(Interrupts) I *didn't* say I *wanted* to go swimming. I said I *may* go swimming. But I didn't want to rush. (edgy, exasperated) And we were going out at four o'clock. (Defensively starts to get legalistic)

18. (Wife denies she desires pleasures. "My concern is for you and the children. My pleasures are only secondary to yours and the childrens'.") (*Women dare not expect pleasure or gratification. Wife's mother was a martyr, thus she expects it is woman's role to suffer.*)

18. (Sym to CD) The expected rebuttal occurs but with a revealing edge to it. By denying husband's implication that she is entitled to want for herself, she indicates that their relationship is one in which wanting is bad. However, her defensive tone disqualifies this definition and invites the husband to pursue his attack. They have now reversed roles. He is telling her she

should be more assertive, and she is denying it as he was doing earlier. It is as if each had told the other: "If you would get more for yourself, I could too." Although husband has her on the defensive, it is the same old issue; there has been no progress toward clarification.

19. **Husband**
(Interrupting) But you hinged all this around Dick not liking to do something or other. (Patient, patronizing—trying to be factual)

19. (Husband says, "You, wife, can't openly ask to have pleasure though you really want to. You can only attain it under the guise of doing it for the children." (*Husband's mother would have used him against his father as wife uses Dick against him.*) (Husband feels competitive with son and at the same time critical of wife for using Dick.) (It could additionally be that husband suspects women can ask for what they want, but they consciously deny this. Husband is attempting to get wife to acknowledge this.)

19. (Sym) This again is a symmetrical statement in which he accuses her of taking second place to the children. At the same time in this context he removes himself from the charge of being a spoiled child since he, too, is put in second position.

20. **Wife**
Well, I didn't want to go swimming by myself. (defensive) (faster) You were (quite fast, almost stumbling) I was half planning on doing something like that and I (defensively)

20. (Wife denies that she can't ask for pleasures. "It appears that I can't because you desert me and I have to turn to Dick. It really is your fault since you don't give to me. I'd really want to receive.")

20. (Attempts CU but settles for CD) She again switches context by ignoring the "Dick" charge. This may have been partly caused by his ignoring her statement "and we were going to go out at four o'clock." Her content is disqualified, however, by her fast, defensive vocalization. She again uses a similar type of message to his—an apparently factual statement disqualified by hurt defensiveness and inviting further movement from the spouse. Wife has ignored husband's implication that when she puts children first, he suffers.

21. **Husband**
(Interrupting) Then you couldn't. (indignantly) You had to rush back to cook him his supper and the other night you cooked him his supper and he didn't even eat it. (pause) I mean all this stuff starts

21. (Husband says "I don't believe you want to give me anything. You don't give me anything. The children get more than I do and they are not as appreciative as I would be." (*Husband feels unloved and that his mother was depriving in a man-*

21. (Sym to CD) Here he nearly reaches his finest hour. "You sacrifice me for the kids and it doesn't pay off." But on the threshold of becoming one-up, he backs down and asks: "Is it necessary?" which is an invitation for wife to take a CU.

22. (Sym) She doesn't immediately respond to his invitation to take the one-up position, perhaps because she is still caught by the first part of his message.

23. (CU to Sym) Her refusal to accept his message that "we are both losing out to the kids" leads to further attack, in which he overgeneralizes and thus leaves himself open.

24. (Strong Sym) Again as in sequence 14, she nails him with a "therapeutic" interpretation, which fails for the same reason (Cf. 14).

---

ner that prevented overt labeling by him. Thus it is important that he get his wife to openly acknowledge her deprivation of him.)

22. Wife is taken aback by the extent of husband's accusation that children come first, especially since wife views him as one of the children. She views his accusation of partiality as a comment on her being a bad mother. (Her need to maintain a good-mother image might also relate to her not perceiving illness in Pete until external factors force it to her attention.)

23. In order to avoid a direct frontal attack on wife for not caring about him, husband points to the children as the reason for his being left out, inferring that wife would care for him very much if she were able to, that is, the children prevent her from doing this. It would be dangerous openly to accuse wife of not caring lest he receive concrete evidence of her not caring, that is, his own unworthiness. *(His mother's preferential treatment of Pete, much like his wife's treatment of Pete, resulted in feelings of privilege, and, at the same time an inadequacy to live up to them. He repeats this pattern with his wife.) (Husband's preferential position with his mother makes him a hopeless competitor with his father and denies him an identification which would enable him to carry out his fathering role. Thus fathers can't help their sons because they are rivals. They can only look out for themselves.)*

24. (Wife says "I knew you always felt like a rival with your children. Which means that you make me a mother instead of a wife. Thus I am deprived of a husband.")

---

hinging around what do these little *rascals* want to *do* (mimicking) all the time (pause) and are they absolutely first?

22. *Wife*
Well I always (quieter—regaining her composure)

23. *Husband*
(Interrupting)—interfere with you and interfere with me and interfere with everything else. (Indignant and angry)

24. *Wife*
I always knew you were jealous of your children. (contemptuous, cold, critical, definite, sounds almost triumphant)

25. *(Her cutting tone indicates the attitude, "You aren't a man.") (Since wife married such a "man," she has no expectations of being treated as a wife.) (Her mother did not openly label her father as "no good" but implied men are ungiving and women must be the responsive ones. Wife's father cooperated in this attitude by being dead tired, too busy. Thus she was denied an opportunity of being a Daddy's girl and thus was not prepared to be given to by a husband.)*

25. Husband denies rivalry with children. *("It's your fault that I am not a man. It is not the children but your preferential treatment of the children that makes me feel deprived. Why do you treat yourself this way? I could help you if you would let me.") (This man needs the evidence of external validation from wife to give him feelings of self-esteem.)*

26. *(Wife says "I almost believe you would like to be a man, which means I could be a wife, but I know really you want me to be a mother to you. I can't even be a mother to you because your picture of a mother is unacceptable to me and I can see what your mother did to you. I deny that she and I have anything in common. Your attitude prevents me from having anything to offer.") (Thus wife expects external validation is necessary for her own feeling of worth as a wife or mother.)*

25. Husband
I (only mildly defensive) am not jealous of them.

25a. Wife
Yes you are (as he says)

25b. Husband
I just expect equal *rights*. (long pause) You do all this self-sacrificing all the time and what does it get you? (righteously indignant)

26. Wife
I am not self-sacrificing, John. (pause) (soft) You think so . . . (mimicking through phony toughness) you want me, it's like the last time, you want me to treat your children the way your mother treated you. (bitter contempt) She ran her little roost over there and this thing was done this way. You liked it. (biting)

25. (Sym to CD) He attempts to escape a damning charge by restating his message, "Don't put them in front of us." As usual, however, his bid is double-edged and difficult to respond to. His major message is, "Why can't we get together?" but it is disqualified by his angry tone and the label, "You are bad" attached to being self-sacrificing.

26. (Starts Sym and ends CU) She responds to his implicit charge rather than to his attempts to get together. Again she outmaneuvers-him by switching the context to "You loved your mother and she was wrong so I won't be like her." This is a double-leveled message that is difficult to respond to. If he accepts the "You liked it," he accepts a damning charge as well. If he agrees mother was wrong, he is ignoring the charge "you loved her," and may step into further difficulties, namely "You don't love me any more than you loved your mother." If he could rise to a new level, namely, "I care for you as much as I did my mother," he could handle her message.

Research on Communications and the Double-Bind Hypothesis

Any view of a phenomenon provides not only a hypothesis (or several hypotheses) to be tested, but also a way of studying problems that can be applied in many different contexts. This is true of the ideas discussed in this chapter. But since a definitive review of the literature on the double-bind hypothesis is beyond the scope of this book, three studies will be briefly discussed to give some idea of the kinds of research that this approach has stimulated.

First, let us consider the method of communications analysis as a way of studying what goes on between people. If a method of study is of any value, it will discover differences that make a difference. In studying the application of the method, we are trying to find out whether or not it finds any differences. When we test a method, we are trying to find out whether or not the differences we have observed make a difference.

The method of communications analysis has been applied in a rather imaginative way by Sluzki, Beavin, Tanopolsky, and Veron (1967) in classifying methods of disqualification. Essentially, they developed a taxonomy of transactional disqualifications. That is, they classified the tactics used by one person to disqualify the statements made by another. This study is an interesting example of the general applicability of the method, since the data were obtained in Buenos Aires — a culture quite different from that where the method originated.

One type of disqualification Sluzki et al. noted is "Evasion — Change of Subject." In this disqualification one person makes a statement, but the other person switches the topic, and thus fails to affirm the statement made by the first person.

A second type of disqualification they observed is "Sleight-of-Hand." In this disqualification, the first person makes a statement, and the second person responds with a statement that is confusing. An example of this given by Sluzki et al. is the following:

> Son: Then, you say it is exactly the opposite of what I say.
> Father: No, no, no, no. I say that you say . . . let . . . say whatever you want.

What did the father say? There are many "sleight-of-hand" tactics, with new ones probably being invented every day.

A third type of disqualification is "Status Disqualification." This is a case of one person making a statement, but the other disqualifying that statement because he is in a position of superior knowledge or wisdom. Most families encounter this regularly at bedtime:

> Son: I'm not sleepy. I don't want to go to bed.
> Mother: I can tell when you're sleepy. You are yawning. To bed!

In addition to these three forms of verbal disqualification used by the listeners, the authors list such nonverbal forms of disqualification as facial expression and silence.

This study is an example of the kinds of taxonomic research that remain to be done with the communications approach, and of the kinds of transactions that may be observed. While the study does not conclusively prove the validity of the communications analysis method, it does show that communications analysis can be a useful research tool in a field not directly related to schizophrenia.

As explained earlier, the original experiments in communications analysis provide not only a research tool, but also a hypothesis about the causes of schizophrenia. If this double-bind hypothesis has validity, communications analysis should detect some significant differences between the communication patterns of apparently normal families, on the one hand, and families of schizophrenics on the other.

The following two studies provide evidence to support the original double-bind hypothesis. This is not all the evidence that is available, nor would these studies necessarily lead to the irrevocable conclusion that the hypothesis were "true" even if no contradictory studies existed. But the data presented do indicate that this hypothesis is worth pursuing further.

One of the authors of the original article putting forth the double-bind hypothesis, Jay Haley (1962), compared the communications among members of families containing a schizophrenic with families in which none of the members was deviant in any obvious way. He devised an experiment in which the mother, father, and one child sat around a round table. Each of the three participants had buttons in front of him for each of the other two participants. They were to play a simple game in which, if one member pushed a button and another member also pushed the corresponding button, then both received a score. The object was to obtain as many scores as possible. All the game required was simple cooperation among two members of the family at a time.

Haley did two experiments with this game. In the first game he compared twenty families containing a schizophrenic member with twenty normal families. In this experiment the players could push the buttons any way they chose. In the second experiment there were ten families in each group, and the players could only push one button at a time. The game consisted of three rounds of two minutes each. He found that among the normal families the members spent a significantly greater amount of time with one member in coalition with one other member of the family, and the schizophrenic families had greater amounts of time in which no member was in any coalition with any other member. The normal families ended up with the members having approximately equal scores, while in the schizophrenic family one member tended to win most. After the regular three rounds of the game, a fourth round was played in which the families were to decide in advance who was to win. The normal families were more successful in making the final score of the game come out the way they wanted it than were the schizophrenic families. The authors observed that the normal families tended to operate pretty much alike, while the schizophrenic families displayed a wide variety of ways to play the game. The essential result seems to be that, as would be hypothesized from communications theory, the schizophrenic families are unable to get together, even in a simple situation in which they have agreed in advance on what it is they want to accomplish.

Berger (1965) made a more direct test of the double-bind hypothesis itself. He composed a list of double-bind statements and compared four groups on the extent to which the members of the groups said that their mothers typically made such kinds of statements. The four groups included a group of hospitalized schizophrenics, a group of hospitalized mental patients who were not schizophrenic, a group of ward attendants, and a group of college students. He found that the schizophrenics gave their mothers higher double-bind scores than any of the other groups. The statements that showed the most difference among the groups were: "You really hate me—you're just pretending you love me"; "You can always talk to me, but don't bother me with unimportant problems"; "I saw you hugging your father yesterday, and I know you never come to me like that"; "You don't deserve to have a mother like me"; and "If you do it your father won't like it, and if you don't do it, I won't like it."

These studies are merely illustrative, but they do suggest the value of the basic communications approach and are evidence for its heuristic value.

Discussion

This chapter describes a line of investigation that started with the study of one phenomenon—schizophrenia—but produced information about another phenomenon—communications between people. Although the study of communications among schizophrenics disclosed differences between schizophrenics and normals in the way they communicate and in the kinds of families in which they grew up, the data and theory should not be taken as definitive. The voluminous literature on schizophrenia has demonstrated differences between schizophrenics and normals on many variables, and the theories of schizophrenia are both numerous and various, with all theories presenting data of some kind in their support.

The chief importance of the material presented in this chapter lies in the fact that these studies have opened up a new area of re-search—the communications between people—and have outlined some of the main dimensions of this area. Certainly the communications between people are a matter of central concern to the study of the inter-action between people, and, as much clinical information suggests, communications are a matter of central concern in the development of emotional problems.

The studies in this chapter form the core of a new area of re-search, but the information presents merely an outline of the study of interpersonal communications. Thus far the study has merely scratched the surface, so it seems safe to predict that many of the conclusions suggested thus far will be refined and revised in the light of subse-quent data.

The subjects originally studied were abnormals—schizophre-nics—but the study broadened to include normal subjects as well. One of the objectives of this line of research has been to describe the ways in which schizophrenics differ from normals in their communications. The situations within which communications have been studied have been all three of the kinds we have outlined: the clinic, the research laboratory, and real life. Having been studied with various kinds of subjects in a variety of situations, the conclusions suggested by commu-nications theorists are somewhat more reliable than if they had been based only on clinical observation. The level of study has been essen-tially that of the dyad, since any communication must be from one per-son to another. However, the person himself has also been included in the study, since what one communicates to himself is considered as part of the phenomenon. The data on which the study has been based have been obtained from the external observation of overt behavior. Who said what to whom is what is studied. How the participants felt about what was communicated must be inferred from what was said. The experience of the subjects has not been elicited as a basis for drawing conclusions. However, since this line of research has been pursued, in part, in the clinical setting and had its origin in clinical practice, it nec-essarily follows that the researchers have based part of their conclu-sions on what their patients told them they thought or felt while en-gaged in interaction with other people. The personal experiences of the patient form a substantial portion of the discussion in most forms of psychotherapy.

In terms of generality, this theory is a rather narrow one. It is concerned with one aspect of the interpersonal interaction process: the communications process. However, communications are at the heart of the interpersonal interaction, so although the theory is a narrow one, its content is of central importance.

One final word should be said about the relationship between the study of communications and the study of linguistics. Communications, as discussed in this chapter, is confined to one line of endeavor, the study of communications between small numbers of people. Linguistics, the study of language, is a broad, rapidly developing field in itself. Obviously the study of linguistics is directly applicable to the study of communications between people. We have avoided that topic here because it is another book in itself. I mention it here to emphasize the fact that this chapter merely scratches the surface of a line of inquiry still in its infancy.

Summary

This chapter has described an approach to interpersonal relationships that is based on an analysis of the communications between people who are relating to each other. The approach was stimulated by the communications observed among the members of families that contained at least one member who was schizophrenic. These observations led to the *double-bind hypothesis*, which states that the schizophrenic receives messages from his parents which, in effect, tell him that if he does something he will be condemned, but that if he doesn't do it he will also be condemned. He is constantly caught on the horns of a communicational dilemma.

The basic nature of communications is such that there are two levels of communications: the *overt, verbal level* and the *nonverbal level*. The information communicated on the latter level may confirm the verbal communication, qualify it, or disqualify it.

Communications between people are designed to define the relationship between them. This relationship may be one between equals—that is, a *symmetric relationship*—or it may be one in which each is in some way superior to the other—that is, a *complementary relationship*. In a relationship between normal, mature adults, one person's definition is accepted and reinforced by the other person. The relationship usually tends to oscillate; that is, at one time it is symmetric, and at other times it is complementary, with first one and then the other of the pair in the superior position. Pathological relationships tend to proceed in a particular direction rather than oscillating like the normal relationship.

The way we communicate, and thus the way we relate to others, is largely learned in childhood from our parents.

References

Bateson, B., Jackson, D. D., Haley, J., & Weakland, J. Toward a theory of schizophrenia. *Behavioral Science,* 1956, 1, 251–64.

Berger, A. A test of the double-bind hypothesis of schizophrenia. *Family Process*, 1965, 4, 198–205.

Blood, R. O., & Wolfe, D. M. *Husbands and wives.* New York: The Free Press, 1960.

Bowen, M. A family concept of schizophrenia. In D. D. Jackson (Ed.), *The etiology of schizophrenia.* New York: Basic Books, 1960.

Fleck, S., Lindz, T., Cornelison, A., Schafer, S., & Terry, D. The intrafamilial environment of the schizophrenic patient. In J. H. Masserman (Ed.), *Individual and familial dynamics.* New York: Grune & Stratton, 1959.

Gold, S., DeLeon, P., & Swensen, C. H. The construction and validation of a scale for measuring dominance-submission. *Psychological Reports*, 1966, 19, 735–39.

Haley, J. The family of the schizophrenic: a model system. *Journal of Nervous and Mental Disease*, 1959, 129, 357–74. (a)

Haley, J. An interactional description of schizophrenia. *Psychiatry*, 1959, 22, 321–32. (b)

Haley, J. Family experiments: a new type of experiment. *Family Process*, 1962, 1, 265–93.

Jackson, D. D. Family interaction, family homeostasis and some implications for conjoint family psychotherapy. In J. H. Masserman (Ed.), *Individual and familial dynamics.* New York: Grune & Stratton, 1959.

Jackson, D. D., Riskin, J., & Satir, V. A method of analysis of a family interview. *Archives of General Psychiatry*, 1961, 5, 321–86.

Lederer, W. J., & Jackson, D. D. *The mirages of marriage.* New York: Norton, 1968.

Lindz, T., & Fleck, S. Schizophrenia, human integration and the role of the family. In D. D. Jackson (Ed.), *The etiology of schizophrenia.* New York: Basic Books, 1960.

Sluzki, C. E., Beavin, J., Tanopolsky, A., & Veron, E. Transactional disqualification: Research on the double bind. *Archives of General Psychiatry*, 1967, 16, 494–504.

Additional Sources

Jackson, D. D. (Ed.) *Communications, family and marriage.* Palo Alto, Calif: Science and Behavior Books, 1968.

Schuham, A. I. The double-bind hypothesis a decade later. *Psychological Bulletin*, 1967, 68, 409–16.

Watzlowick, P., Beavin, J. H., & Jackson, D. D. *Pragmatics of human communication.* New York: Norton, 1967.

Proxemics, Kinesics, and Paralanguage

Nonverbal behavior can be considered a *relationship language,*
sensitive to, and the primary means of, signaling changes in the quality
of an ongoing interpersonal relationship. While conceivably the verbal
discourse may duplicate this information, usually such matters are too
direct or too embarrassing to be easily stated (1968, p. 180).

—P. Ekman and W. V. Friesen

Literary and artistic productions from antiquity clearly demonstrate that
men have long been aware that much can be learned about the relationship between two people by observing how they stand or sit in relationship to each other, or by observing how they look at each other, or
by listening to the tones of their voices as they talk to each other.
Therefore it seems rather surprising that it has been only in relatively
recent years that serious scientific efforts have been directed toward the
study of nonverbal communications.

The study of nonverbal communications is largely an area of
empirical endeavor. Strictly speaking, there is no such thing as a theory
of nonverbal communications. Rather, various people working within
various contexts have studied nonverbal communications within the
theoretical context familar to them, ranging from a behavioral context to

a psychoanalytic one and even to a linguistic one. To a large extent this research has been carried on within the context of psychotherapy, since psychotherapists quite early in their careers try to learn how to read all of the signals, behavioral as well as verbal, transmitted by their clients. Psychoanalytical writings are full of references to the revelation of unconscious phenomena through the observation of behavior, gestures, choice of words, and so on. Freud (1938, p. 138), for example, was quick to point out that in a popular play of his time, a married woman who was having an affair was unconsciously emitting nonverbal communication when she played with her wedding ring, finally taking it off her finger before going to meet her lover.

Although popular publications (e.g., Fast, 1970) tend to emphasize the meaning of a particular stance, facial expression, or gesture (e.g., they often say that a woman who wants to indicate "hands off" stands rigid, crosses her arms over her breasts, or, if sitting, crosses her legs demurely), researchers in the field emphasize that no particular nonverbal signal can be taken as having a particular meaning. The meaning of any nonverbal cue depends on the culture, the situation, and other such factors. The popularizers, however, know that people who are interested in reading about gestures, expressions, and body movements are primarily motivated by a desire to find out what it means when another person scratches his nose, or frowns, or kicks his foot in the dirt. And as we progress through this chapter, we shall find that those engaged in serious research are no less motivated to find out what specific nonverbal acts mean, but they recognize that this meaning must come within a particular context. After all, the term "nonverbal communication" itself implies that something is communicated through nonverbal means, and if something is communicated, that something must be something specific. People interested in nonverbal communications don't study nose scratching with the expectation that they will discover that people who scratch their noses frequently do it primarily because their noses itch.

Classes and Dimensions
of Nonverbal Phenomena

Scheflen (1967) has categorized the channels of face-to-face communications into two main classes: the *language modalities* and the *nonlanguage modalities*. The language modalities include linguistics and paralanguage. The nonlanguage modalities include the following: kinesic, tactile, odorific, territorial, and artifactual.

Of the language modalities, linguistics is concerned with language itself; that is, it is verbal (as distinct from nonverbal) and, therefore, does not concern us in this chapter. *Paralanguage* does concern us, however, since it includes all the aspects of sound production that are vocal but not verbal; that is, it includes voice quality, ways of verbal expression, and various sounds that are not verbal (such as laughing and crying). Paralanguage is what one person communicates to another through sounds that are not contained within the words themselves. Any experienced husband (or wife) can tell if his (or her) spouse is angry from the tone of voice, regardless of the words mouthed. That is paralanguage.

The nonlanguage modalities include the kinesic, tactile, odorific, territorial, and artifactual. *Kinesics* is concerned with communication through body movement, body stance, gestures, and facial expressions. The *tactile* is concerned with communication through touch. *Odorifics* is concerned with communication through smell. The *territorial* is concerned with communication through space and is also labeled *proxemics*. The *artifactual* is concerned with communication through dress, decorations, and props.

Of the various kinds of nonverbal communications listed in the previous paragraphs, those that have been the object of the most research attention are paralanguage, kinesics, and proxemics. Later in this chapter we shall be concerned primarily with these three areas of study. For now, we shall devote a few lines to the other three nonlanguage modalities. Although none of these modalities has been the object of extensive empirical research, there has been some study that would suggest that these areas are worthy of more attention than they have received.

Hall (1966) suggests that other cultures use the sense of smell (odorifics) as a means of communication more than do the northern European and American cultures. On the basis of his own observation, he concludes that smell is an important part of the Arab culture: For example, the intermediaries arranging a marriage will sometimes ask to smell the prospective bride, rejecting her if she "does not smell nice." I can recall reading once, several years ago, of a research project on mate selection that obtained results suggesting that men and women select mates whose body odor is pleasing to them.

Jourard (1971), one of the very few to do any research on touch (the tactile), reports that women tend to touch others more than men, and to be touched more by others. Both men and women are more likely to touch or to be touched by opposite-sex friends or spouses than by any other person. Self-disclosure of intimate facts about oneself tends to be independent of touching another person, although for women there is a slight relationship between touching another person and disclosing something to that person. Jourard suggests that in our culture, touching carries a sexual connotation, so that touching tends to be restricted to relationships that have a sexual element to them.

Knapp (1958) delved into the artifactual when he studied the kinds of Scotch tartans preferred by people who had different levels of need for achievement. He found that those subjects who had a high need for achievement preferred tartans that contained somber colors, while those subjects with a low need for achievement preferred tartans containing bright colors. He concluded that people with a high need for achievement will prefer more conservative and subdued dress, while persons with a low need for achievement will prefer bright and striking forms of dress.

Dimensions of Nonverbal Behavior

One of the basic questions to be asked of any area of research is What are the basic parameters or dimensions of the phenomena to be studied? For example, the basic spatial dimensions of any physical object are height, width, and length. In reviewing the research on the basic dimensions of nonverbal behavior, Mehrabian (1970) concluded that they consist of three: evaluation, potency or status, and responsiveness. That is, he concluded that these three dimensions are the main kinds of information conveyed by nonverbal behavior.

The first dimension, evaluation, reveals how well one person likes another. The second dimension, potency or status, reveals how two people rank on a status hierarchy. Finally, the third dimension, responsiveness, reveals how much one person is interested in and involved with another person.

Mehrabian derived the above dimensions primarily from surveying three studies. The earliest was by Schlosberg (1954), who concluded that there were three dimensions to facial expression: pleasant-unpleasant, attention-rejection, and activation. The second study, by Williams and Sundene (1965), detected emotion through visual and vocal modalities. The subjects either saw or heard (or both saw and heard) the expression of twelve different emotions; they then rated those emotions on sixty-four different rating scales. These data were factor-analyzed, and the factor analysis produced three factors: general evaluation, social control, and activity. The third study, by Osgood (1966), was one in which some subjects mimicked emotional expressions, while other subjects judged the emotions being expressed. These data were also factor-analyzed, and the analysis produced three factors that could be interpreted: pleasantness, control, and intensity or activation.

Mehrabian reviewed the three studies cited above and concluded that although the different researchers labeled the dimensions of nonverbal behavior differently, there were nonetheless no more than three basic dimensions. The way in which Mehrabian equated the dimensions of the above studies with his own is shown in Table 1.

TABLE 1. **DIMENSIONS OF NONVERBAL BEHAVIOR**

Mehrabian		Schlosberg		Williams & Sundene		Osgood
evaluation	↔	pleasant-unpleasant	↔	evaluation	↔	pleasantness
potency	↔	attention-rejection	↔	social control	↔	control
responsiveness	↔	activation	↔	activity	↔	intensity

Kinds of Information Derived from Nonverbal Communication

This section might also be labeled "Relationship of nonverbal communications to verbal communications." Since the most obvious kind of communication is verbal, the study of nonverbal communication necessarily raises the question of what is learned through nonverbal channels that is not learned through verbal channels. Perhaps the first point that should be made is suggested by Birdwhistell, who asserts that communications is "a system which makes use of the channels of all of the sensory modalities" (1970, p. 70). That is, the process of communications is one that includes words, inflections, gestures, posture, facial expressions, and anything else that the senses can detect. The nonverbal channels are as much a part of the communication process as the verbal channels.

However, those studying the topic suggest that there are relationships between the verbal and nonverbal channels. Mahl (1968) suggested that these relationships were of four basic kinds. Ekman and Friesen (1968) added five more, to bring the total to nine kinds of relationship between verbal and nonverbal communications. They are as follows:

1. The nonverbal act can express the same meaning as the verbal act. A person says he is angry, and he looks angry. His brows are knit, his chin is thrust forward, his face is red, and so on.
2. The nonverbal act can anticipate future amplification of the concurrent verbal content. That is, the nonverbal act gives a preview of what is to come in the verbal communication. (Mahl elaborated this function of nonverbal communication in a model, which will be discussed later in this section.)
3. The nonverbal act can convey meaning that is contradictory to the verbal material. A person says he is not angry, but he looks and acts angry.
4. The nonverbal act can be related to the more global aspects of the interaction, rather than to the specific part of the verbal message. Two people may be having a verbal disagreement, but their nonverbal actions toward each other indicate that their relationship is still a solid and satisfying one.

5. The nonverbal act can accent a specific part of the verbal act.
6. The nonverbal act can fill or explain silences, communicating that a person has not finished speaking or is reaching for words.
7. The nonverbal act can function to maintain or to regulate the communicative flow, indicating that one is listening, bored, ready to speak, etc.
8. The nonverbal act can be a substitute for a word or phrase in a verbal message.
9. The nonverbal act can be a delayed registration of content that has already been expressed verbally. This is the stuff of which sight comedy is made. There is the well-known scene in which a wife and husband are discussing some mundane topic, such as their next vacation, while the wife is calmly trying to tell her husband that she is pregnant. The husband continues talking in a normal conversational tone until the message sinks in; then he stops in the middle of a sentence and registers astonishment, amazement, glee, or dismay, depending on how he views the advent of a new progeny.

It was mentioned in the second relationship that Mahl had developed a model of nonverbal communication as an anticipation of the verbal content of an interpersonal interaction. Mahl had noted in psychotherapy interviews that it was often possible to anticipate what the client thought or felt about a topic before the client broached the subject. He observed that while one client talked about her marital life and discussed her feelings of inferiority toward her husband, she briefly placed her fingers to her mouth. A little later she said that her feelings of inferiority began in her childhood when she felt she was not as pretty as her sister because she had two buckteeth. Mahl cited several other instances from psychotherapy interviews in which the movements, gestures, or other nonverbal behavior of the client anticipated the content of verbal discussion that came later. Mahl's model, which diagrams this phenomenon, is presented in Figure 1.

In the diagram, the box labeled "Manifest verbal content" under A represents the words the person is saying. Associated with these words are feelings, represented by the broken-lined box below. These feelings stimulate an action, represented by the box labeled "Overt action." These feelings, which stimulate the overt action, are later expressed verbally; the later verbal expression is represented by the box under B in the diagram. In the example just given, the woman felt inferior when she talked about her relationship with her husband. This inferiority feeling originated with her feeling less attractive than her sister because of her buckteeth, so the feeling stimulated her to touch her two front teeth. This overt action foreshadowed her discussion of feeling inferior to her sister.

FIGURE 1.   **MAHL'S MODEL OF NONVERBAL BEHAVIOR AS AN
ANTICIPATION OF LATER VERBAL CONTENT IN COMMUNICATIONS**

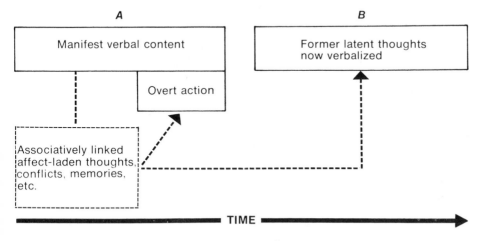

From G. Mahl, "Gestures and body movements in interviews," in J. M. Shlien (Ed.), *Research in Psychotherapy*, Vol. 3, 1968, p. 323. Copyright © 1968 by the American Psychological Association, and reproduced by permission.

One final note on general considerations in the study of nonverbal communications. Birdwhistell (1970) emphasizes that communication is a complex system that engages all the senses and activities of a human being. Communication is not a case of John communicating to Mary or Mary communicating to John. Rather, it is a case of John and Mary jointly engaged in communications. These communications are a total process that includes all of the things that go into communications, including words, gestures, facial expressions, vocal tones, posture, and all of the other means by which two people tell each other something. Birdwhistell takes what might be considered a holistic view of the communications process: To understand the meaning of any particular aspect of the nonverbal process, it is necessary to study it within the context within which the nonverbal activity occurs. Yet as we shall see, much of the study of nonverbal communications is directed toward discovering the meaning of various positions, expressions, or movements in and of themselves, with little regard for the particular contexts within which they occur.

Proxemics

Proxemics is the study of personal and social space and of man's perception of it. Considering the fact that everything that goes on between people goes on within space, and in view of the fact that countless wars, large and small, have been fought over territory, it is strange that so little research has been done on how people arrange themselves in space and on the effect spatial arrangements have on the ways in which people interact. E. T. Hall has noted that we seem to have suppressed or repressed all discussion of man as a spatial being. "Man has developed his territoriality to an almost unbelievable extent . . . . For some unknown reason, our culture has tended to play down or cause us to repress and dissociate the feelings we have about space" (1959, p. 157).

As this section will demonstrate, a start has been made in the study of space as it affects or reflects how people interact with each other. However, the more remarkable aspect of proxemics is that so little has been done in this area. It would seem both logical and desirable for every school of architecture and city planning to have a department concerned with studying the effect of spatial arrangements on the behavior of people.

Hall (1966, Ch. 2), in reviewing ethological research, points out that territory is not only a concept that affects man, but one that affects animals too. All creatures within a species carry a bubble of space around them. When this space is violated, the animal either fights or flees. Dominant animals maintain greater space around them than submissive animals, who will give ground to larger animals. Some animals are social, or contact, animals. They belong to a social group of their own kind, and the total group, herd, pride, or whatever, is contained within a bubble of space. Animals will fight to defend their own territory if it is invaded; they recognize and usually respect the territory of each other. Violation of the territory of one animal by another animal means a fight until one of the animals has either been killed or driven off. Anyone who has owned a cat or dog has probably observed this phenomenon. Usually a growl suffices to drive off the invading animal, but if the growl does not suffice, then a fight ensues. I recall a time when we built a new house on what had been a vacant lot. We moved into the house with our cat, who, at the time, was mothering a litter of kittens. Our cat was particularly touchy about the invasion of her space when she had kittens. Apparently this lot had been used as a rabbit-hunting ground by the neighborhood dogs prior to our moving in. For weeks after we had moved into the house, our cat was engaged in fighting off the dogs that continued to invade the territory. Eventually, however, she drove them all off, and thereafter, a dog roaming through our yard took a long, circuitous route around our house, along the edges of the lot.

Hall (1966, Chs. 2 & 3) points out that when crowding among animals reaches the point at which it is no longer physically possible for them to maintain their usual distance from each other, both a behavioral and physical breakdown occurs. Physical disease and death rates increase. The organized social life breaks down, so that the young are abandoned, ignored, and sometimes eaten. Various kinds of deviant sexual behavior appear, and the females have difficulty carrying their young to term.

People also have a personal space around them, which varies with the situation and the relationship; when this space is violated, people react with avoidance, embarrassment, and bewilderment, and sometimes by flight from the scene (Sommer, 1967). When others get too close to us, given the situation and the relationship, we become uncomfortable.

People perceive space through all of the senses. The "distance" receptors of sight and sound are perhaps the most important to the perception of space. However, smell is also a distance receptor and is very important in the perception of space for animals, although some people also use it. Hall (1966, Ch. 4) reports a psychiatrist who was able to smell anger in a patient at a distance of more than six feet. Different cultures use different senses for defining space: The Japanese apparently use vision as a primary space sensor; the Germans use sound. Space is also perceived through touch and the sense of heat. Hall notes that language is full of expressions describing interactions between people in terms of heat—"a heated argument" and a "cold stare" being but two examples. Further, Hall notes that we hate to sit in a chair or climb into a bed that still contains the body heat left by someone else. The remaining heat seems to leave some lingering claim of the other person upon the space.

The distance at which people stand from each other is an indication of their relationship to each other. After study, Hall (1966, Ch. 10) concluded that there are four categories of distance that are of importance for people: *intimate, personal, social,* and *public.* The first category is obviously for those who are intimate. In the close phase of intimate distance, the two people are in physical contact with each other. They can smell each other and feel heat from each others' body. The muscles and the skin communicate. Vision is blurred because of the closeness, and vocal communication is muted and involuntary. In the far phase of intimate distance, the two people are 6 to 18 inches apart. At this distance, vision is still distorted, heat and smell are still perceptible, and the voice level is kept to a whisper. The use of intimate distance is not considered proper in public in American culture, so if crowding is forced by a situation, certain other compensatory behavior becomes necessary. In a crowded situation, people typically stand or walk rather rigidly, keep their hands close at their sides, gaze off into the distance rather than focusing on anything or anybody close at hand, and ignore the people pressing in upon them.

The close phase of personal distance is from 1½ to 2 feet. This is the distance at which only those people who have a close personal relationship stand relative to each other. The far phase of personal distance is from 2½ to 4 feet. This distance extends from the point a person may reach at arm's length to the distance at which two people can touch fingers if they both extend their arms toward each other. No smells or heat can be detected, and the voice level is moderate.

The close phase of social distance ranges from 4 to 7 feet. This is the distance at which impersonal business is conducted and is the usual distance maintained between people who work together. The far phase of social distance is 7 to 12 feet. The business and social interaction at this distance is more formal. At the far boundary of this distance, you can see the whole person, and the voice level is louder than in the close phase. At this distance, two people can engage in independent activities and ignore each other.

The close phase of the public distance is 12 to 25 feet. The voice is loud at this distance, but not at full volume. The choice of words and phrases becomes more formal at this distance. The far phase of public distance is 25 feet or more. Thirty feet is the distance automatically set around important public figures. The subtle shades of vocal expression, facial expression, and gesture are lost at this distance, so that all must be exaggerated or dramatized in order to be perceived by an audience. The tempo of the voice drops, and words are enunciated loudly and clearly. Much of the nonverbal communication at this distance must be through body stance and gestures.

It should be emphasized that these distances are typical for American culture. Hall notes that the distances vary for other cultures. He has particularly studied the Arabs, noting that they prefer much closer distances than are normal for Americans. As a consequence, Americans often feel they are being constantly crowded by Arabs. Because Americans have a tendency to remain at a distance or to move back, they are likely to be perceived as cool or "stand-offish" (literally) by Arabs. Hall's observation had particular meaning for me when first I read it, because at that time I had an Arab student who frequently came to me to discuss various aspects of his work. He always seemed to me to be crowding me, which resulted in my compensating by trying to avoid him whenever possible. The distance that was comfortable for him was too close for me.

Variables Related to Physical Proximity

Physical closeness has been found to be a function of several pertinent variables. When two people are relatively close to each other, they are obviously in a much better position to have some effect on each other. If they are quite close, they can embrace or attack each other, and they can smell and feel each other. Hall suggests that "the influence of two bodies on each other is inversely proportional not only to the square of the distance but possibly even the cube of the distance between them" (1966, p. 121). This observation would suggest the obvious, namely that people will approach closer to those whom they want to influence and by whom they wish to be influenced, and will maintain their distance from those they are not sure about.

Some research evidence fits this hypothesis. People do tend to stand or sit closer to those they like than to those they dislike; they lean toward people they like (Mehrabian, 1969, 1970). Also, people tend to come closer to other people who are of the same status than to people of a higher or lower status. Status differences are positively correlated with the distance people put between themselves and another person. Introverts tend to maintain a greater distance from others than extroverts (Sommer, 1967).

Women tolerate greater physical closeness than do men, generally approaching closer to other people than men do in similar situations. Normal conversational distance varies, depending upon the situation, with 5 feet seeming to be a comfortable conversational distance in a large lounge, but 8 to 10 feet being the normal conversational distance in a private home (Sommer, 1967).

One thing that seems to emerge clearly from both observations and experimental studies of distance is that there is an appropriate distance between people which is determined by the situation and the relationship. Violation of this distance by another person results in tension, discomfort, embarrassment, and avoidance (Hall, 1966; Mehrabian, 1969, 1970; Sommer, 1967).

Seating Arrangements and Behavior

Seating arrangements affect who talks to whom, and also who is likely to dominate the conversation. Hall (1966, Ch. 9) points out that space can be arranged so that it encourages people to interact or discourages them from interacting (what he terms "sociofugal and sociopetal space"). People are most likely to converse with those who are seated at right angles to them, and next most likely to talk with those seated beside them. In one study of people seated at tables, it was observed that people sitting across a corner from each other were twice as likely to talk to each other as people sitting side-by-side, and people sitting side-by-side talk to each other three times as often as to people seated across the table.

In discussions, leaders tend to gravitate to the head of the table, and those who sit at the head of the table do more of the talking and have a greater influence on the outcome of the discussion (Sommer, 1967).

In placing themselves at a table, men are more likely to sit across from each other, while women are more likely to sit side-by-side. Studies have found that people who are cooperating with each other are more likely to sit side-by-side, while those who are competing are more likely to sit at opposite sides of the table. This finding might suggest that women are more cooperative and men more competitive with each other; however, it also fits in with the observation that women seem to seek greater physical closeness than do men (Sommer, 1967). These results do suggest that if you want people to talk to each other, arrange the room so that you have chairs sitting at right angles to each other.

These few pages summarizing the findings of proxemics leave one with a sense of unfulfillment. They demonstrate that here is a phenomenon of tremendous impact upon human behavior that has been relatively ignored until recently. The spatial arrangements within which we live have substantial, and often unsuspected, effects upon how we interact with each other. Thus far we know very little about this effect.

Kinesics

Kinesics is the study of body language. This includes facial expressions, gestures, posture, and any other movement of parts of the body from which some sort of message might be deduced. The terms "kinesics," "body language," and "nonverbal behavior" are used synonymously in this section.

The earliest studies (see Allport, 1961, Ch. 19) were of body language as an "expressive" medium, but more recent research, beginning with Birdwhistell's pioneering effort (1952), has emphasized body movement as a medium of communications. By "expressive" medium is meant that body movements, facial expressions, and gestures are expressive of the personality of the person being studied. The movements are not meant to convey any information to another person—they are just expressive of the kind of person the person doing the gesturing is. Mahl (1968) refers to such gestures as "autistic" gestures, by which he means that they only have meaning to the person exhibiting them. Such things as scratching the head, or picking the nose, or folding the hands behind the head are not generally meant to convey any information to another person. Pointing, nodding, and similar gestures convey information to another person, and are so intended.

Mahl (1968) did a study in which he had subjects interviewed in two different conditions. In the first condition, the subject was face-to-face with the interviewer, and in the second, the subject was back-to-back to the interviewer. When the subjects shifted from the face-to-face to the back-to-back situation, Mahl found that the number of communicative gestures made by the subjects decreased and that the number of autistic, or expressive, gestures increased. He suggested that people tend to suppress autistic gestures when they are talking to another person, but increase the communicative gestures since they convey information. It would be worthwhile to study the difference in the body behavior of people when they are talking to another person face-to-face and when they are talking over a telephone. In any case, Mahl's study indicates that some kinds of nonverbal behavior seem to be more "expressive" than communicative.

Although behavior may not be intended to communicate anything to another person, it may nonetheless carry a message. The original research on nonverbal behavior was designed to discover which personality characteristics were revealed by which kinds of behavior. If folding the fingers at the tips means that a person is suspicious, and the other person knows this, then this gesture is communicating something from one person to the other, even though the finger-folder does not intend to convey this message. Birdwhistell (1952, Ch. 7) suggests that much of the nonverbal communication that takes place between two people is unconscious. That is, each is reading the nonverbal signals of the other, even though neither may be aware of it. Perhaps it would be more accurate to talk of "intentional" and "unintentional" nonverbal behavior rather than expressive and communicative nonverbal behavior.

Birdwhistell (1952, Ch. 8) illustrated the unintentional, communicational function of nonverbal behavior by telling a story of the visit of one of his brother's girlfriends to his family home. First, the fact that a boy brings a girl home to visit his parents suggests that the relationship between the boy and the girl is one that may well blossom into marriage. That is, "bringing-home" behavior is a gesture that communicates something. Birdwhistell was not at home at the time of the visit, so he wrote his mother asking her how the visit had gone. His mother answered with a letter that was devoted to various other topics, but which contained the following description of the visit: "You ask about the visit of Miss Withers. I think some people would think she is very pretty . . . . She spent the entire time blowing smoke in your father's face and flushing the toilet." In a family in which smoking is not an approved activity for women and water is viewed as a precious commodity not to be wasted, Miss Withers had communicated unintentionally, through her behavior, that she was not acceptable as a daughter-in-law to the Birdwhistell family.

Birdwhistell feels that communication also serves an integrational function, in addition to its function as a process of information exchange. Communication serves to keep the body's systems in operation, regulates the interactional process, cross-references particular messages to the context within which they are to be understood, and relates a particular context to some larger context of which the present interaction is just a part. To illustrate it simply, a teacher in a classroom maintains order among the student speakers by pointing first to one and then to another to speak. Thus each gets an opportunity to speak, and pandemonium is averted.

Although nonverbal behavior may serve as an intentional or unintentional communication system, it is not assumed that the kinds of information conveyed by nonverbal behavior are the same as those conveyed by verbal behavior. Ekman and Friesen (1968) make five assumptions about the kinds of information conveyed by nonverbal communications:

1. Nonverbal behavior is primarily a relationship language. Verbal behavior may convey the same information, but usually such matters are too embarrassing or too difficult to state directly.
2. Nonverbal behavior has a special symbolic language for expressing emotion.
3. Nonverbal behavior has a special symbolic language for expressing unconscious and semiconscious attitudes toward the self or the body image.
4. Nonverbal behavior is metacommunicative, serving to qualify verbal behavior.
5. Nonverbal behavior is less subject to censorship than verbal behavior. It serves as a channel of leakage of communications.

Although the study of nonverbal behavior is largely an inductive endeavor, proceeding from observation to conclusions rather than testing hypotheses derived from any general theoretical structure, the five assumptions listed above are hypotheses that come close to stating a theory of nonverbal behavior. That is, nonverbal behavior is primarily a channel for expressing emotions. From a survey of research, Ekman and Friesen conclude that nonverbal communications also provide information about on-going interpersonal relationships, psychodynamics, and ego defenses. Expressed emotions can, of course, be a reflection of all of these functions; or it could be said that conclusions about interpersonal relationships, ego defenses, and psychodynamics can be derived from the expression of emotions.

Ekman and Friesen hypothesize that the main-effect display system is focalized in facial expressions and that concurrent nonverbal behavior does not necessarily express the same emotions. That is, more than one emotion can be expressed at the same time. The face, for example, can display fear while the hands express anger. Ekman and Friesen (1967) report a study in which they had judges judge emotions of the head (face) and the body separately. They found that the judges agreed more on which emotion was being expressed by the head than by the body. But perhaps more interesting is that in only thirteen out of sixty different stimuli pictures did the judges conclude that the body was expressing the same emotion as the head.

Another general conclusion about nonverbal communications, based on empirical observation, is that they are, to a large extent, learned behaviors. Birdwhistell (1952, p. 190) does not deny that there is a biological base to kinesic behavior, but concludes that the main source lies in learning, and that much of this learning may well be unconscious.

Let us summarize this introduction to the section on kinesics. Kinesics is the study of body language. This language includes such things as facial expressions, posture, and gestures. This language serves the function of communicating information, expressing the personality of the communicator, and integrating the ongoing communication process. The main kind of information carried through nonverbal behavior is the expression of emotions. Perhaps much of this communication is below the level of awareness of the person behaving, and it may be that the person getting the message is also unaware of the message he is receiving, although he may react to the message in a way that indicates that he received it. More than one message may be transmitted at the same time through different parts of the body. Body language is largely learned, and this learning is at least partially unconscious. Data suggests that the kind of information obtained from nonverbal behavior is an accurate reflection of the personality and emotions of the person being observed.

Finally, a repeat of an earlier note of caution before we plunge ahead to a description of some of the specific issues and findings of research on kinesics: No facial expression, posture, or gesture has a universal meaning. The meaning of any kind of nonverbal behavior must be deduced from the context within which it occurs.

Methods of Research and Measurement

Any relatively new area of research spawns a series of discussions about matters that have direct bearing on the area of study. These discussions center around disagreement over methods of research and measurement, units of measurement, and similar issues. Everybody agrees, more or less, on where they are trying to go, but since no one has been there yet, there is little consensus on the best way to get there. To some extent, this is the situation in kinesics research today. In this section we will describe different strategies and methods of research, as well as an example of a research study of nonverbal behavior.

Research Strategies. Three basic research strategies have been used in the study of kinesics, or body language. These three are the natural-history method and two experimental methods, which might be termed the "simulated-emotion" experiment and the "natural-emotion" experiment.

The *natural-history method* is a method in which a person who is interacting in a normal interpersonal situation is either observed or, more likely, filmed, with the various expressions, postures, and movements being observed and scored. The natural-history method requires studying behavior in the context within which it occurs, and thus provides data that is closest to real life. Body-language research of this kind has usually been done within the setting of psychotherapy. Most data has been obtained by filming the patient during a psychotherapy interview and analyzing it intensively after the interview. This method is used by Birdwhistell, Scheflen, and their colleagues. The argument in its favor is that it catches nonverbal behavior in a natural situation— thus conclusions can be drawn taking into account all of the variables affecting a real-life situation. Those who use this method use what has been termed the "structural approach" to nonverbal communication (Duncan, 1969). That is, they study nonverbal communication as a social system and try, through their research, to determine the rules by which the social system operates.

Both of the experimental methods used in the study of body language seek to relate the occurrence of specific nonverbal behavior to other variables. The experimental approaches make extensive use of statistical analysis of data, while the natural-history method is much less inclined to rely upon such analysis. In the *simulated-emotion experiment*, two basic methods, the encoding method and the decoding method, have been used. In the encoding method the subject is asked to simulate a particular emotion, say fear or joy, and the researcher notes the subject's various movements, gestures, postures, and facial expressions. In the decoding method the subject is asked to observe people taking certain positions and postures and to judge which emotions are being portrayed (Mehrabian, 1969). Osgood (1966) did a study which is a good example of both the decoding and the encoding method, in which he studied facial expressions by having part of his subjects portray certain emotions and having the remainder of his subjects judge which emotions had been portrayed.

In the *natural-emotion experiment* some variable is manipulated, and the subjects, in reaction to this manipulation, exhibit an emotion which is then analyzed. An example of this kind of study is one by Ekman (1965) in which the subjects were interviewed in three phases. The first phase was a neutral warm-up phase; the second phase, an unpleasant, stress phase; the third phase, a relaxed, joking, catharsis stage. Pictures were taken of the subjects during the last two phases. These photographs were shown to a group of judges who then determined which emotions were being expressed in each of the various pictures.

Both the natural-history method and the experimental methods of study require judges to decide what movements are made, what postures taken, what gestures used, and what facial expressions displayed. This can sometimes be a rather tricky problem: If an observed subject makes a movement, such as moving his hand and arm, the judge must determine what he was doing with this motion. He may have been waving or pointing or merely exercising. The judgment as to exactly what the movement was may be a rather difficult one. If there are several judges, they may have trouble agreeing on whether the subject pointed with his finger or not. In the case of judging which emotion was expressed, the problem may be even more difficult.

In any kind of behavioral research, some reliable method of measurement is essential if reliable results are to be obtained. When the measurement method consists of several judges' judgments as to whether something did or did not occur, it becomes essential to have judges who are in agreement a high proportion of the time. Very often it is necessary to give the judges a rather extensive training session before they reach an acceptable level of agreement. For this reason, Birdwhistell argues that it is necessary to use highly trained observers. He writes, "I am highly suspicious of categories which elicit high agreement among naive observers (and by naive I mean not specifically trained in observation techniques)" (1952, p. 153). Ekman and others, however, have used naive observers. Their use of naive observers is based on the rationale that for a nonverbal behavior to be communicative it must be observable by the relatively naive man in the street, and it must communicate something to this ordinary, untrained human being. Further, many clinical studies in various areas of research have produced results that seem to suggest that the untrained observer is just as sensitive to various kinds of emotional behavior as the professionally trained observer. Of course, Birdwhistell does not mean that we must have professional, clinical-study observers; rather, he means that the observers used should have some prior knowledge of and training in observing the many types of body language. In any case, the use of trained versus untrained observers is an issue in kinesics research.

Contextual Variables. Representatives of both the natural-history and the experimental schools of research stress the importance of considering the context within which a behavior occurs in interpreting its meaning. Birdwhistell stresses that "we must know a great deal about the nature of the social context within which the particular communicative acts take place" (1952, p. 50). To illustrate the wide variations in expressive behavior from one culture to another, Birdwhistell reports the results of his study on smiling. He observed the frequency of smiling in various parts of the United States and discovered that Southerners smiled the most, Middle-Westerners next most frequently, New

Englanders next, and New Yorkers the least of all. Though these subjects were observed within the same country, smiling behavior varied widely from one area to another. I can recall that during my many years living in the South, newcomers would initially comment about how friendly people were, but after having lived in the area for some time they would comment that although people were friendly, they seemed to have great difficulty in getting to know any of the natives more intimately than they had early in their acquaintance. Apparently in some sections of the country, a friendly initial encounter carries with it the promise of a developing relationship. In the South, a friendly encounter merely means that the person encountered is a friendly person. It is not intended to convey the message that "I want to get to know you better."

Ekman and Friesen (1968) list five variables in the context of a nonverbal act that may serve to qualify or revise its meaning:

1. Other simultaneous body behavior. A smile from a person who is approaching may mean friendliness or joy at seeing you. A smile from a person who is backing away from you is more likely designed to hide fear.
2. Any concomitant verbal behavior. That famous old line from *The Virginian* — "Smile when you say that" — demonstrates exactly this point.
3. The setting within which the behavior occurs. Smiling at another person at a party probably conveys nothing more than mildly convivial spirits. Smiling at a person at a funeral home may convey sympathy or perhaps something even deeper.
4. The physical characteristics of the sender. If a very small person challenges a very large person to a fight, the large person will probably take the challenge as a joke and the small person most likely intended it that way. On the other hand, if the challenger is of approximately the same size as the challengee, then the challenge is more likely to be taken seriously.
5. The verbal and nonverbal behavior of the other person. If the other person is behaving in a friendly manner, a smile may indicate friendliness toward the other. If the other is menacing, then a smile by the person responding to him is more likely to be a cover for fear and/or hostility.

Mahl (1968) suggests that scratching is an indication of hostility, but if the other person is observed tickling the subject, then scratching is much more likely to an indicator of itching. (We will ignore the question of tickling as a cause of hostility.)

In sum, the meaning of any nonverbal behavior depends on the context within which the behavior occurs. No movement, gesture, facial expression, or physical stance has universal meaning.

The Basic Units of Nonverbal Behavior. Before beginning a research study, one must determine what is to be studied; that is, one
must know the basic unit of the phenomenon to be studied. In nonverbal communication, the basic unit to be studied is *movement*. Yet researchers still disagree about what type of movement composes the
basic unit of nonverbal communication.

There are two approaches to this problem. One approach is to
use as the basic unit fairly large, broad movements that are easily detected by the untrained observer in the ordinary, everyday, social situation. The other approach is to use as the basic unit the slightest movements that trained observers can detect in slow-motion pictures.

Ekman and Friesen (1968) use the first approach. The unit they
use is the *nonverbal act/position* which is based on easily observable,
visually distinct patterns of movement. The beginning and end of this
unit are determined by the neutral start and stop points. The unit
begins when a person begins a movement with a specific part of his
body and ends when the body either returns to its normal rest position
or when another movement is begun with another part of the body. A
wink, for example, would begin when the eyelid started to move and
end when the eyelid had returned to its normal position. Head scratching would begin when the hand began to move toward the head and
end when the hand returned to the side. Each body act is one that is
visually distinct from another act. Ekman and Friesen use this as the
unit because they feel that for a nonverbal act to communicate to another person it must be the sort of act which is ordinarily observable to
another person.

Birdwhistell (1952) uses the second approach. He and his associates adapted the theory and the research of the structural linguist to
the study of nonverbal behavior. Roughly speaking, they translated the
units of verbal behavior into approximately equivalent units of nonverbal behavior. As structural linguistics has units such as the phoneme
and the morpheme, so kinesics has the units of *kineme* and *kinemorph*.
In linguistics the phoneme is the smallest basic unit of sound that is
ordinarily used in a language (e.g., "s," "t," "sh," "ch"). The morpheme is the smallest collection of sounds that has a meaning. A word
is a morpheme (e.g., "back"); but a word may also be composed of a
group of morphemes (e.g., "quarterback"). Researchers in linguistics
have developed a highly refined ability to detect the differences in
sounds, both as they are produced by people from different subcultures
and as they are produced by different people within a subculture. Since
Birdwhistell was trying to develop an approach to nonverbal communications in which slight differences in movements would be equivalent
to the slight differences in sound for the linguist, it follows that he
stressed the importance of having well-trained observers.

Birdwhistell's basic units are the kine, the allokine, the kineme, the kinemorph, and the kinemorphic construction. The *kine* is the least detectable body movement which may or may not have meaning. The kine is a movement of split-second duration that is detectable only on slow-motion film. If a second movement, equivalent to a kine, occurs in a different body part at the same time as an already-located kine is occurring, the second movement is called an *allokine*.

The basic unit, the *kineme*, is the least movement that has some meaning. A kine may be a kineme. Typical kinemes are such movements as the head nod, the lifted brow, and closed eyes. Structural linguistics has determined that each language has a certain number of basic sounds, or phonemes, out of which the thousands of words in the language are constructed. In English there are about forty-five phonemes. Likewise, the nonverbal language of a culture has a certain number of kinemes out of which the body language is constructed. Birdwhistell counts about fifty to sixty kinemes in the American culture. He points out that as the number and kind of basic sounds differ from one language to another, so the number and kind of basic movements in the body language of one culture differ from that of another culture. He reports a study of Fiorello LaGuardia, the late mayor of New York, in which it was observed that the gestures and body movements he made changed when he spoke different languages. From silent film it was possible to tell whether LaGuardia was speaking English, Italian, or Yiddish, thus demonstrating that as the verbal language changed the nonverbal language also changed.

Kinemes combine into kinemorphs. A *kinemorph* is composed of a series of motions in one area of the body (left arm, face, etc.). Birdwhistell's kinemorph is approximately equivalent to Ekman and Friesen's "act/position." The kinemorph begins with the start of the body movement and ends either with the body part returned to its original position or with the beginning of a movement in another part of the body. Kinemorphs combine into *kinemorphic constructions*, which are a series of body movements. Birdwhistell believes that nonverbal communications combine with and interact with the verbal communications to produce one communicational process. When two people run into each other and begin to communicate, the total communication process becomes an interaction. To be understood, the interaction must be a meaningful, structured whole composed of many different basic units.

Perhaps a house might be used as a rough analogy. To understand what a house is, you must understand that it is a place designed for people to live in. They will eat, sleep, wash, play, and interact there. To understand a house, you must take into account the house as a totality. However, that house is built out of basic units such as bricks, nails, pipes, glass, and so on. The communications process is also a whole, and to be understood it must be viewed as a whole, or as a continuing stream; but that stream is composed of many discriminable parts, and among these parts are blinks, nods, wiggles, and pointings. The sounds and movements organize into a whole that carries on the communication process.

In the approach to nonverbal communications that Birdwhistell uses, there are two kinesic streams. One stream is the *macrokinesic,* which is composed of the body movements that convey information. The second stream is the *parakinesic,* which is composed of the movements that amplify, emphasize, or qualify the basic verbal communications. Just as Bateson, Jackson, Haley, and the others studying the verbal communications in the interpersonal interaction describe two levels of communication, so Birdwhistell describes two levels of nonverbal communications.

An example of how this process is recorded is contained in Figure 2. On the top line of the figure the researcher records the time, progressing from left to right, during which an observation occurs. On the second line, the parakinesic behavior is recorded, serving to modify or emphasize the basic message which is conveyed by the kinesic behavior and/or the audible speech behavior. On the third line, the kinesic behavior, or communicational body movements are noted. The last line contains the audible speech behavior. From this record, it is possible to see what movements occurred at the time each word was spoken.

An Example of Kinesics Research. A good example of the way researchers studying nonverbal behavior go about their work is provided in a study by Ekman and Friesen (1958). They were interested in finding out whether or not nonverbal behavior would reveal changes in psychological functioning. By "psychological functioning," they meant the patient's reactions to various experiences, types of interpersonal relationships, and attitudes toward self and other people. They wanted to discover whether or not these changes, if they were found to exist, would be reflected by the movements of specific body parts, such as the feet or the hands.

To begin their study, Ekman and Friesen took eight-minute sound films of psychiatric patients being interviewed at the time they

FIGURE 2. **MODEL OF CONTINUOUS, PATTERNED SPEECH AND MOVEMENT**

Observational time	T^1	T^2	T^3	T^4	T^5	T^6	T^N
Parakinesic behavior							
Kinesic behavior							
Audible speech behavior							

were admitted to the hospital. Later, they took eight-minute sound films of these same patients as they were being interviewed just prior to their discharge from the hospital. By studying these films, Ekman and Friesen hoped to see whether or not psychological changes in the patients were revealed by changes in the movements they made during the two interviews. Since the patients were not discharged from the hospital until they had improved, it was expected that the changes revealed by the nonverbal behavior would be in the direction of improved psychological functioning.

To determine whether changes in psychological functioning occurred, Ekman and Friesen used six groups of naive judges (college sophomores). This was in accordance with their feeling that for movements to communicate, they should be movements that are noticeable by other people. (However, they later concluded that perhaps some movements would have been more noticeable to judges who were trained and experienced at observing body movements.)

In this experiment, Gough's Adjective Checklist (ACL) was the measuring instrument used. This is a list of adjectives such as "pessimistic," "tense," "fearful," "friendly," "sociable," and "cheerful" used to describe a person. Each judge viewed the eight-minute films (without the sound portion) of the patients—both as they were entering and as they were leaving the hospital. None of the judges knew anything about the patients or when the films had been taken. For each film viewed, each judge filled out the ACL, selecting adjectives that he felt described the person seen in the film.

In addition to the checklists of the judges, Ekman and Friesen had the ward psychiatrist fill out a checklist on the patient; and finally, the patient filled out a checklist on himself. Both the doctor and the patient filled out these checklists twice—as the patient entered the hospital and as he (or she) left. Thus the researchers had adjective descriptions of each patient which had been made by the patient, by the psychiatrist, and by the judges watching the silent film of the patient.

The judges' evaluations revealed differences in the patients between the film taken at the time of admission to the hospital and the film taken at the time of discharge. One patient, Mrs. A, was judged as "pessimistic," "suspicious," "bitter," "gloomy," and "hostile" at the time she was admitted to the hospital. At the time of discharge, Mrs. A was judged to be "cooperative," "calm," "gentle," and "kind." Another patient, Mrs. B, was judged to be "tense," "confused," "nervous," "dissatisfied," and "inhibited" at the time she entered the hospital. When she left, Mrs. B was judged to be "talkative," "restless," "sociable," and "complaining." A third patient, Mrs. C, was judged to be "despondent," "worrying," "fearful," and "self-pitying" at the time she was admitted, but when she was discharged, she was judged to be "talkative," "active," and "impulsive."

These results seem to indicate that the patients did show changes in their nonverbal behavior between the time they entered and the time they left the hospital. They also indicate individual differences among the patients. In comparing the adjectives chosen by the judges (who saw only the silent motion picture) and those chosen by the psychiatrist and the patient (who did not see the motion picture, but did know things that could not be revealed in a silent movie), Ekman and Friesen did find differences. These differences should indicate that there are some aspects of psychological functioning that are revealed by body movement and some that are not. To illustrate these differences, those adjectives chosen by the psychiatrist and the patient but usually not listed by the judges included, at the time of admission to the hospital, adjectives such as "dissatisfied" and "worrying," while at the time of discharge the doctor and the patient listed "anxious," "emotional," "friendly," "talkative," "cheerful," and "cooperative."

Next, Ekman and Friesen wanted to find out what individual body acts might mean, so they took the sound transcription of the film to find out if certain topics were being discussed at the time the patient made a particular body motion. They also had a group of judges observe the film with the face of the patient blocked out. They then asked these judges to list the adjectives that were descriptive of the psychological meaning of the body movements. They had a second group of judges view the movie of the body movement and describe what they thought the movement meant. Finally, they asked the patient one year later to give free associations about what the particular body movement under consideration meant.

To illustrate the results obtained by this method of investigation, we will list the verbal content, judges' judgments, and patient's free associations to three different kinds of hand movement made by one patient. These three kinds of hand movements are illustrated in Figure 3. The "hand-toss" is a movement in which both hands are on the armrests of a chair; then they are moved rather rapidly straight up into the air until they are about level with the shoulders; then they are dropped down to the armrests again. The "chair-arm rub" starts with both hands resting on the arms of a chair; then the hands are moved forward over the front ends of the armrests and then back again over the armrests. The "hand-shrug rotation" begins with the hands resting on the arms of a chair; then the shoulders are shrugged, and the hands are rotated outward (with the palms showing face upward) and then back down to rest on the armrests.

What do these movements mean? Let us discuss each in turn. When the hand-toss was exhibited, the topic being discussed by the patient was usually one of lack of control. That is, Mrs. C was expressing an inability to stop crying, or an inability to articulate, or an inability to accept responsibilities. Twice the verbal theme was ambivalent

FIGURE 3. **THREE KINDS OF HAND MOVEMENTS**

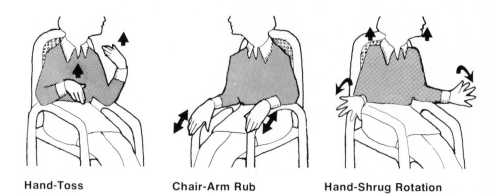

Hand-Toss   **Chair-Arm Rub**   **Hand-Shrug Rotation**

From P. Ekman & W. V. Friesen, "Nonverbal behavior in psychotherapy research," in J. M. Shlien (Ed.), *Research in Psychotherapy*, Vol. 3, 1968, p. 180. Copyright © 1968 by the American Psychological Association, and reproduced by permission.

feelings the patient had for members of her family. The adjectives chosen by the first group of judges for the patient when she made the hand-toss were "argumentative," "emotional," and "excitable." The second group of judges suggested that the hand-toss meant frustration or exasperated anger. When interviewed, the patient thought that the hand-toss meant frustrated anger and was expressed when she was talking about loss of control or ambivalence toward the members of her family. Ekman and Friesen concluded that the hand-toss meant frustrated anger that was directed by the patient mostly toward herself, and that the hands were not repeating the verbal theme but rather expressing the feelings stirred up in the patient by the topic discussed verbally.

There was no consistent verbal theme expressed when the patient made the chair-arm rub. The first group of judges chose the adjectives "fearful," "withdrawn," "restless," and "emotional" as descriptive of the patient's psychological state. The second group of judges did not evaluate this hand movement. The patient felt that the chair-arm rub indicated agitated restlessness and that the act served as a partial soothing reassurance. Ekman and Friesen noted that this act occurred so frequently at the time the patient was admitted to the hospital that it was impossible to tie it to any verbal theme. This act was probably indicative of the patient's general emotional state at the time.

The verbal theme when the patient made the hand-shrug rotation was either uncertainty or confusion. The first group of judges chose no consistent set of adjectives as descriptive of the patient's psychological functioning. The second group of judges thought that the gesture indicated uncertainty, defensiveness, and helplessness. The patient associated helpless uncertainty with the hand-shrug rotation. Ekman and Friesen concluded that this movement indicated uncertainty and confusion and was physically communicating the same content as the theme that was being verbalized by the patient at the time.

The Meaning of Body Movements

We have already emphasized that no body movement, gesture, posture, or facial expression has meaning in and of itself. Each nonverbal act must be interpreted in the context within which it occurs and the subcultural group within which it occurs. However, people who study nonverbal behavior are ultimately interested in learning how to read the language universally. Therefore, it follows that they try to find out what a particular motion or facial expression is communicating most of the time. The discussion contained in this section will describe the meanings deduced from different kinds of nonverbal acts. Since the research was conducted largely on the populations most readily available (middle-class Americans) to the researchers, it follows that these results are largely applicable to that group.

The Head. Nodding the head would seem to indicate that the one doing the nodding is paying attention to the speaker and is active (Mehrabian, 1970). Different numbers of nods, however, have different effects upon the person doing the speaking. One nod sustains the verbal interaction without affecting the flow of communication. Two nods either stimulate an elaboration by the speaker of his previously established point or are followed by either an increased or decreased rate of verbal flow from the speaker. That is, two nods have a discernable effect upon the verbal interaction. Three nods usually result in the speaker hesitating, changing the subject, or fading into silence. Three nods interrupt the verbal flow from the speaker. Repeated rhythmic nods of the head seem to communicate to the speaker that the listener is not paying attention, and result in the speaker searching around for a way of catching the listener's attention (Birdwhistell, 1952, Ch. 22).

Facial Expressions. The face is the chief nonverbal vehicle through which emotions are expressed. In fact, it may be considered the *main* way of expressing emotion, verbal or nonverbal (Ekman and Friesen, 1968; Davitz, 1964). Davitz suggests that the face expresses gross categories of emotions such as positive versus negative and active versus passive, but that the situation provides those cues that determine more precisely exactly which emotion is being expressed. There is some disagreement as to whether or not there are any facial expressions which have the same meaning the world over. It is suggested that such expressions as crying when in pain and laughing when happy are universal. But there is also general agreement that facial expressions vary a great deal from one culture to another; and even within a culture, there is variation in the emotional meaning of a given facial expression (Birdwhistell, 1952, Ch. 5).

Haggard and Isaacs (1966) accidentally discovered a phenomenon of facial expressions which they called "micromomentary expressions" (MME). These are facial expressions that are so short in time duration that they are almost quicker than the eye can see. They last about one-fifth of a second and can be seen in motion pictures run at one-sixth of normal speed. Haggard and Isaacs first noticed MME's while they were scanning slow-motion movies of psychotherapy, looking for indications of nonverbal communications between the therapist and the client. These rapid facial expressions were not apparent when the motion picture was run at normal speed. They found that MME's were most likely to occur when the patient was making statements of denial or was blocking verbally. The MME's were incongruent both with the verbal content of what the patient was saying and with the facial expressions that preceded and followed the MME. For example, the patient might be talking about how he liked another person and, during this discussion, exhibit a pleasant facial expression, but the MME was an expression of anger. Haggard and Isaacs cite the case of one patient who displayed few MME's when talking about his wife and children, but displayed many MME's when talking about blonds and sensuality. Haggard and Isaacs think that MME's "may serve as a safety valve to permit at least the very brief expression of unacceptable impulses and affects" (1966, p. 165).

The results of studies of eye contact, or looking directly into another person's eyes, have been fairly consistent. People are more likely to look at another person when they are listening than when they are talking. Women look directly at others more often than men. Both sexes look directly at the other person less frequently when the interaction is unpleasant than when the interaction is pleasant. People more frequently look directly at those with whom they have had previous friendly interactions than they do at people with whom they have had neutral or unfriendly interactions. People look directly at others less often when discussing embarrassing topics, or when they are being deceitful (thus suggesting some truth to the old adage that you can't trust a person who won't look you in the eye). Eye contact seems also to serve as a signal in conversations. People usually look directly at the person to whom they are speaking when they begin to speak, and again when they are finished speaking. The direct glance seems to signal that the speaker has said what he had to say. If the person speaking does not glance directly at the other person when he pauses in his speech, the

other person tends to delay in responding, waiting for the speaker to
continue talking (Duncan, 1969; Ekman & Friesen, 1968; Exline, Gray,
& Schuette, 1965; Mehrabian, 1969, 1970; Sommer, 1967).

Posture. Body posture does not seem to communicate the same
content as facial expressions. Ekman and Friesen found that "the emotion judged from the face usually differs from the emotion judged from
the body" (1967, p. 722). Posture seems to indicate the posturer's state
of relaxation or tension and his attitude toward the person with whom
he is interacting. A person who is relaxed is more likely to have his
arms and legs arranged in assymmetrical positions, to be leaning back if
seated, and to have his arms and legs arranged in open positions. People tend to be most relaxed around other people of low status and, sur-
prisingly, are often quite relaxed around those they dislike. People are
somewhat less relaxed around people of high status and people they
like. Leaning forward indicates liking for the other, and a sidewise lean
indicates that the leaner has some feeling for the other person. A high
rate of leg movements, while seated, seems to indicate a slightly negative attitude toward the person being addressed. Body orientation (the
degree to which the communicator's shoulder and legs are turned toward the person to whom he is talking) seems to be related to how well
the communicator is esteemed and liked. Orientation is more direct
with high-status than with low-status persons who are being addressed.
For people who are seated, men use a less direct body orientation toward people they like very much; women, on the other hand, use very
indirect body orientation toward people whom they dislike very much
and the most direct body orientation toward people toward whom they
are neutral, with an intermediate body orientation toward people they
like (Mehrabian, 1970). When a person shifts posture it seems to indicate an attempt at establishing rapport with the person with whom he is
talking (Scheflen, 1966). The general level of body activity, moving
around, shifting, and so on, seems to indicate that the person doing the
moving is responsive to the person with whom he is interacting. Movement is related to how much one person is trying to persuade another,
and is related to how persuasive he is perceived as being (Mehrabian,
1970).
Men and women differ in the kinds of postures they assume and
in the kinds of movements they make. Men are more likely to point,
while women are more frequently observed shrugging their shoulders,
shaking their heads, patting their hair and turning their palms up and
out. Men cross their legs with an open cross, while women more frequently cross their legs with a tight cross (Mahl, 1968). Women usually
stand with their legs together, while men stand with their legs separated at a 10 to 15 degree angle. Women keep their arms beside their
bodies, while men have their arms hanging at a 5 to 10 degree angle from

the trunk of their bodies. Women tend to move their bodies as a whole, while men move their arms independently of their bodies. Women generally sway their pelvises slightly toward the front, while men sway their pelvises slightly toward the rear (Birdwhistell, 1952, Ch. 6).

This summary of some of the findings of research on nonverbal behavior suggests that gestures, movements, postures, and facial expressions do communicate meaning that has some generality, within one culture or subculture at least. A review of the basic data obtained in these studies also indicates, however, that one had best progress cautiously in drawing any profound conclusions about another person's attitude, personality, or general state of psychological functioning purely upon the basis of one facial expression, gesture, or posture. The individual variations in the expression of a particular act of nonverbal behavior are substantial.

Paralanguage

Paralanguage is communication through the vocal apparatus, carried not via the words spoken, but rather via the way in which the words are spoken. Consider the simple exclamation "Oh!" It may be said quickly in a high pitch that indicates surprise; or it may be said in a slow, drawn-out, dropping inflection that communicates disappointment: "Oooooh"; or it may be said with a rising inflection that indicates a question: "Oh?" In each case the same word is spoken, but the message communicated is quite different. It is the communication through the manner of speaking rather than through the content of speech with which paralanguage is concerned.

Trager (1958) has classified paralanguage into two main categories, vocalizations and voice qualities. Vocalizations are noises and sounds. He classifies these sounds into vocal characterizers, vocal qualifiers, and vocal segregates. Vocal characterizers are recognizable sounds such as laughing, crying, moaning, belching, and yawning. Vocal qualifiers are characteristics of sounds such as intensity (loud-soft), pitch (high-low), and extent (drawl-clipping). Vocal segregates are sounds that, strictly speaking, are not words, but communicate something. These include sounds such as "sh," "uh," and "uh-huh." The voice qualities are the qualities of a person's speech and include the pitch range and control, the vocal lip control, the glottal control, the articulation control, rhythm control, resonance, and tempo. To some extent the voice qualities overlap with the vocal qualifiers since both have to do with the characteristics of the sounds emitted by the person speaking.

Those doing research on paralanguage assume that the quality of speech is a method of expressing emotion, and have primarily concerned themselves with relating various emotions to the various qualities of speech. The kinds of emotions studied have usually been disruptive emotions (Mahl & Schulze, 1964). Since studies in this area, as in the other areas discussed in this chapter, have been carried out mostly by people interested in psychotherapy, it is natural that disruptive emotional states would be studied, since those are the kinds of emotional states often dealt with by psychotherapists.

The basic dimensions of emotional expression through vocal means seem to be similar to the basic dimensions of emotional expression through facial expression. Williams and Sundene (1965), in a study in which they related the expression of twelve emotions to judges' evaluations of facial expressions and of vocal qualities on sixty-four scales of Osgood's semantic differential, factor-analyzed the data and found three factors of vocal expression of emotion. These factors were general evaluation (pleasure-pain, pleasant-unpleasant), social control (stable-changeable), and activity (fast-slow, active-passive). In this same study, they found that the same dimensions accounted for the facial expression of emotion.

Active emotions tend to be expressed by a fast rate of speech, loud volume, high pitch, and a "blaring" timbre. Anger is an active emotion. People who are angry talk faster, louder, and at a higher pitch than they do when they are not angry. Passive emotions are expressed by the reverse: slower rate of speech, lower volume, lower pitch, and a more resonant timbre. Sadness is a passive emotion that is expressed through slow speech, low volume, and a low pitch. Davitz (1964) speculates that the other two dimensions derived from Osgood's semantic differential are probably accounted for by more subtle aspects of speech such as changes in rhythm, inflection, and enunciation. Grief is expressed by a high ratio of pause time to speaking time, and fear is reflected by a high pitch. Happiness is expressed by a higher pitch than sadness. Anxiety is expressed by nonfluency or blockages in speech (Mahl & Schulze, 1964).

Perhaps one of the most interesting discoveries in this area of research is that people differ greatly in their ability to detect emotional expression in speech. Those who are more accurate in expressing emotion are also more sensitive in judging the expression of emotions in others. Those who are accurate in detecting emotions in others seem to have a set of cognitive abilities that are a kind of intelligence. Davitz (1964) found that those who are sensitive to emotional expression in others are also able to discriminate pitch, loudness, time, and timbre of sounds; in addition, they are high in verbal intelligence and abstract, symbolic ability, have a knowledge of vocal characteristics of emotional expression, and are able to distinguish figure from ground in perception tasks. Davitz suggests that the ability to be sensitive to the emotions of others is based on a kind of intelligence and is improved with practice at sending and receiving emotions. That is, Davitz' results suggest there is a basic aptitude for detecting and expressing emotions through nonverbal behavior.

Discussion

The material cited in this chapter does not seem, at first glance, to discuss the interpersonal interaction, at least in the sense that the interpersonal interaction is discussed in the other chapters of this book. There is a reason for this: The other chapters of this book deal with the interpersonal interaction largely at the level of the dyad or the small group, while this chapter discusses specific acts by which the interpersonal interaction is carried on. Interpersonal communication must be carried on by two or more people if it is to be interpersonal communication, but in discussing the nuts and bolts of interpersonal communication, the "interpersonal" part of it tends to get short shrift.

The research discussed in this chapter indicates that nonverbal communications do go on between people; that some of the information conveyed by nonverbal means is information about emotions; that various emotions are expressed through nonverbal means. However, what the research has not yet produced is a clear study of the interpersonal interaction at the nonverbal level. The data reviewed have largely been data about single individuals reacting to particular situations. There has been little research on the process of nonverbal interaction between two or more people. Or perhaps even more to the point, there has been little research on the whole vast complex of interpersonal interaction, including both the verbal and the nonverbal channels of communication. The study of the whole complex process, as outlined by Birdwhistell, remains to be done. There are good and sufficient reasons for this. Such study requires the expenditure of exhorbitant amounts of time. It also requires expensive equipment, although the equipment is available. Probably the one thing that would advance the field most rapidly would be the development of research methods that make it possible to collect and analyze large amounts of data efficiently. But even so, the field is inching along steadily, and with great promise.

Thus far the study of nonverbal communications has largely been a process of collecting data and arriving at conclusions through the inductive process. Such theoretical structure as exists has been borrowed from other areas. Birdwhistell borrowed the framework of structural linguistics; most of the other researchers have started from the basic theoretical structures of psychiatry and psychology. There are mini-theories, however, or perhaps they might be called hypotheses, which are largely empirical in origin. First, there seems to be general agreement that nonverbal communications are largely the channel through which emotional information is communicated. Ekman and Friesen suggest that this is because this information is too sensitive to be communicated verbally or is perhaps beyond being adequately expressed verbally. This is a tantalizing hypothesis in itself. Is it possible that some emotions, if they are truly to be communicated to another person, must be expressed through a nonverbal channel? Certainly tears in the eyes or a smile on the lips do convey something that cannot be conveyed by words alone. Then there is the hypothesis that nonverbal communications serve as a kind of safety valve for the expression of feelings that for reasons of tact, safety, or whatever, cannot safely be expressed directly through words. This suggests that nonverbal communications serve an expressive function that is both essential to the healthy functioning of human beings, but also is an expression of the functioning of a person.

Finally we have the three-factor idea cropping up again. There are three factors in Bales' theory of interpersonal interaction (Chapter 7). There are three facets to Foa's system (Chapter 7). There are three dimensions to Osgood's semantic differential. Now we find three factors of vocal and facial expression. Are these three factors basic to the human personality, and also to nonverbal communications, and thus to interpersonal interaction? Or are these three factors an artifact, a function of the methods of research used? And if we assume that these three factors are basic to personality, interpersonal relations, and nonverbal behavior, then how do they fit together? These questions pose substantial research projects.

When compared with the other approaches to the study of interpersonal relationships presented within this book, the study of nonverbal communications is in some dimensions broader than the others, and in other dimensions more narrow. (See Chapter 1, pp. 14–16 for a description of the five basic dimensions of the study of interpersonal relations.) The study of nonverbal communications has included the study of both normal people and psychiatric patients behaving within all the kinds of situations within which interpersonal interaction has been studied. Nonverbal communications have been studied in psychotherapy, in the experimental laboratory, and in real-life settings. This variety of kinds of subjects and kinds of settings is a reflection of the fact that the phenomenon being studied is a subtle one, which may be easily misinterpreted. Those doing research in this area have, from the first, been sensitive to the fact that nonverbal communications must be considered within the situation within which they occur. Thus, those doing research in this area have been sensitive to the necessity of taking into account the effect of the setting within which the research is conducted on the results obtained by that research.

However, when viewed from the other three dimensions of the study of interpersonal relations, the study of nonverbal communications is quite narrow. First, the level of behavior studied is that of the behavior segment. There are no grand views of "love," "hate," or "conflict." The topic of study is grunts and shrugs. Second, the kind of data is almost entirely behavioral. Little research, such as that of Ekman and Friesen, has attempted to relate gestures to what a person was experiencing at the time of that gesture; rather, research has concentrated upon small segments of behavior and, in the case of Birdwhistell, has used segments of behavior that are too small to be seen by the naked eye. This comparative dearth of studies relating a subject's intent or feelings to the nonverbal portions of his communications is a neglect of what could be a rich source of highly useful information. Third, when the breadth of theoretical view is considered, the study of nonverbal communications again appears to be very narrow — or perhaps the more accurate description is that it is almost atheoretical. There are no true theories of nonverbal communications. There are hypotheses, such as the hypothesis that nonverbal communications are the main channel for the expression of the emotions. Any theory in nonverbal communications is still quite narrow, or partial, dealing only with specific kinds of behavior. To the extent that nonverbal communications are related to more general theories, most of the limited theories of nonverbal communications have developed in other areas of study, such as linguistics and personality.

Summary

That human beings communicate with each other nonverbally has been known since the dawn of history, but the systematic study of nonverbal communications has a fairly short history. Those areas that have received the most attention have been proxemics, kinesics, and paralanguage. *Proxemics* is the study of the effect of spatial arrangement on the interaction between people. *Kinesics* is the study of communications through gestures, posture, facial expressions, and body movement. *Paralanguage* is the study of the nonverbal aspects of vocalization. Other areas of nonverbal interaction that have received relatively little attention include the tactile (touch), odorifics (smell), and the artifactual.

The results of research suggest that nonverbal communications serve as a channel for communicating emotion. Nonverbal communications may also serve as a safety valve through which emotions may be expressed that cannot otherwise be safely or tactfully expressed.

The ways in which emotions are expressed nonverbally vary greatly from one subculture to another, so that the interpretation of the meaning of any given nonverbal act must be made within the context of the culture and the context of the situation within which the act occurs.

The ability to read nonverbal communications appears to be a form of cognitive ability. People who are most skilled at expressing emotions nonverbally are also most skilled at detecting the emotions expressed nonverbally by other people.

References

Allport, G. W. *Pattern and growth in personality.* New York: Holt, Rinehart & Winston, 1961.

Birdwhistell, R. L. *Introduction to kinesics.* Louisville: University of Louisville Press, 1952.

Birdwhistell, R. L. *Kinesics and context.* Philadelphia: University of Pennsylvania Press, 1970.

Davitz, J. P. *The communication of emotional meaning.* New York: McGraw-Hill, 1964.

Duncan, S. Nonverbal communication. *Psychological Bulletin,* 1969, 72, 118–37.

Ekman, P. Communication through nonverbal behavior: a source of information about an interpersonal relationship. In S. S. Tomkins & C. E. Izard (Eds.), *Affect, cognition and personality.* New York: Springer, 1965.

Ekman, P., & Friesen, W. V. Head and body cues in the judgment of emotion: A reformulation. *Perceptual and Motor Skills,* 1967, 24, 711–24.

Ekman, P., & Friesen, W. V. Nonverbal behavior in psychotherapy research. In J. M. Shlien (Ed.), *Research in psychotherapy* (Vol. 3). Washington, D.C.: American Psychological Association, 1968.

Exline, R., Gray, D., & Schuette, D. Visual behavior in a dyad as affected by interview content and sex of respondent. *Journal of Personality and Social Psychology,* 1965, 1, 201–209.

Fast, J. *Body language.* New York: M. Evans & Co., 1970.

Freud, S. The psychopathology of everyday life. In *The basic writings of Sigmund Freud.* New York: Random House, 1938.

Haggard, E. A., & Isaacs, K. S. Micromomentary facial expressions as indicators of ego mechanisms in psychotherapy. In L. A. Gottschalk & A. H. Auerbach (Eds.), *Methods of research in psychotherapy.* New York: Meredith, 1966.

Hall, E. T. *The silent language.* New York: Fawcett, 1959.

Hall, E. T. *The hidden dimension.* New York: Doubleday, 1966.

Jourard, S. M. *Self-disclosure.* New York: Wiley, 1971.

Knapp, R. H. n Achievement and aesthetic preference. In J. W. Atkinson (Ed.), *Motives in fantasy, action, and society.* Princeton, N.J.: D. Van Nostrand, 1958.

Mahl, G. F. Gestures and body movements in interviews. In J. M. Shlien (Ed.), *Research in psychotherapy* (Vol. 3). Washington, D.C.: American Psychological Association, 1968.

Mahl, G. F., & Schulze, G. Psychological research in the extralinguistic area. In T. A. Sebeok, A. S. Hayes, & M. C. Bateson (Eds.), *Approaches to semiotics*. The Hague: Mouton & Co., 1964.

Mehrabian, A. Significance of posture and position in the communication of attitude and status relationships. *Psychological Bulletin*, 1969, 71, 359–72.

Mehrabian, A. A semantic space for nonverbal behavior. *Journal of Consulting and Clinical Psychology*, 1970, 35, 248–57.

Osgood, C. E. Dimensionality of semantic space for communication via facial expressions. *Scandinavian Journal of Psychology*, 1966, 7, 1–30.

Scheflen, A. E. Natural history method in psychotherapy: communicational research. In L. A. Gottschalk & A. H. Auerbach (Eds.), *Methods of research in psychotherapy*. New York: Meredith 1966.

Scheflen, A. E. On the structuring of human communication. *American Behavioral Scientist*, 1967, 10(8), 8–12.

Schlosberg, H. Three dimensions of emotion. *Psychological Review*, 1954, 61, 81–88.

Sommer, R. Small group ecology. *Psychological Bulletin*, 1967, 67, 145–52.

Trager, G. L. Paralanguage: a first approximation. *Studies in Linguistics*, 1958, 13, 1–12.

Williams, F., & Sundene, B. Dimensions of recognition: visual vs. vocal expression of emotion. *AV Communication Review*, 1965, 13, 44–52.

Transactional Analysis and Games

Qualitatively, there are at least four possibilities in "a relationship": some people get along "well" together; some enjoy fighting or arguing with each other; some cannot stand each other; and some just have nothing to say to each other. These alternatives may be characterized respectively as *sympathy, antagonism, antipathy,* and *indifference . . .* (1961, p. 133).

— Eric Berne

Eric Berne was a psychiatrist who practiced in California for years. During this time, he developed a theory of interpersonal relations which he used to analyze and treat his clients. Transactional analysis is probably best known among the public because of his very popular book, *Games People Play.* In many respects, Berne's approach to interpersonal relations is closely related to that of the communications theory discussed in Chapter 3. Both approaches stress the interaction between people as a symptom and a cause of emotional distress; both analyze and categorize the various kinds of interactions that go on; both see a revision of the interpersonal interaction as the means of correcting emotional difficulties. However, Berne extends his theory in two directions, creating a personality theory that is integrated with his theory of interpersonal relations and including the kinds of reactions that typically go on between "normal" people.

Although Berne is best known for his description and classification of the "games" that people play among themselves, his theory is more extensive than a mere cataloging of interpersonal gambits and ploys. The theory that he used in his practice really includes two kinds of analysis: structural and transactional. *Structural analysis* is the analysis of the personality structure of the individual, while *transactional analysis* is the analysis of the interaction between two people. The kinds of interactions that go on between people include not just "games," but also interactions Berne classifies as strokes, rituals, and pastimes, which are all lower-order kinds of interactions. Beyond these, "intimacy," is an interaction in which two people are realistic and constructive; there is openness, honesty, support, concern, and encouragement in the relationship. The "script," according to Berne, is a chain of interpersonal interactions which may take a lifetime to complete.

Although Berne gives his theory a separate name—transactional analysis—it would probably not be too misleading to describe it as a translation of Freudian personality theory, revised (in the light of the work of Alfred Adler) into terms and structures that are somewhat more relevant to modern life and cast in a way that makes it useful for extension into the interpersonal realm. Freud's description of the personality structure included three structures: the id, the ego, and the superego. Berne's equivalent structures are the Child, the Adult, and the Parent. Using these structures, Berne developed his concept of games and the "script" of life, echoing Adler's emphasis on the preeminence of the social side of people and the concept of a life style.

Structural Analysis

Structural analysis is Berne's term for what, in his system, corresponds to personality assessment. It is an evaluation and description of the personality structure, or the "psychic apparatus" (1961, p. 238), which is composed of three "instances": determinants, organizers, and phenomena. We shall briefly discuss the first two instances and then concentrate on the third and most important, the phenomena.

The *determinants* are the forces which provide the source for the content of the organizers and phenomena and determine the development and the quality of their structure. The determinants might be considered the raw material out of which the others are formed. Berne calls this process of formation the establishment of the programming. "Internal" programming arises from indigenous biological forces; "probability" programming arises from a person's past experience; and external" programming arises from external rules a person has incorporated.

The *organizers* are the "psychic organs" of the personality structure. The three organizers are the archaeopsyche, the neopsyche, and the exteropsyche. These three organs approximately correspond to the Freudian id, ego, and superego.[1] The *archaeopsyche* is characteristic of the Freudian primary process, that is, basic impulse seeking immediate gratification. In other personality theories this might be called the primary drive or need. The archaeopsyche is the home of simple need or impulse seeking immediate satisfaction and is formed by internal programming. The *neopsyche* is similar to the Freudian secondary process, or a consideration for the demands of reality. Since it is based on experience, it is affected by learning and based on probability programming. The *exteropsyche* is characterized by identification, and contains external rules and values acquired from the environment or, more specifically, acquired from the parents. It derives from external programming.

The *phenomena* are "ego states," and from the point of view of transactional analysis, they are the most important "instance." The ego states are those aspects of a person that are most directly accessible to the person himself and to an observer. The ego states are the person's feelings and behavior — or more explicitly, the ego state that is dominant at a particular time is inferred from the person's behavior and report of his feelings at that time. The three ego states are the *Child*, the *Adult*, and the *Parent*. Most of our discussion of structural analysis and its use in analyzing the transactions among people will be based on the three ego states of Parent, Adult, and Child. Figure 1 is Berne's diagram of the personality structure, showing the relationship of the organizers to the phenomena.

Berne arrived at the idea of three existing ego states from a patient who could clearly label the source of his behavior as coming from his Child, his Parent, or his Adult. The Child is the innocent, spontaneous, fun-loving, responsibility-evading part of a person. Every person was once a child, and that child, although it becomes submerged as the person grows to adulthood, still remains buried within the person's personality, emerging from time to time. The Parent is the surviving image a person has of his parents within his own personality structure. The Adult is the mature, reality-oriented adult within a person; it is the accumulated wisdom and know-how a person has developed from his experiences in life. Regarding the three ego states, Berne terms some "pragmatic absolutes":

1. That every grown-up individual was once a child.
2. That every human being with sufficient functioning brain-tissue is potentially capable of reality-testing.

---

[1]The organizers also seem to correspond to Berne's Child, Adult, and Parent. Operationally, there is little difference. For example, the archaeopsyche is the organizer, or "organ," while the Child is the phenomenon, or what we observe. Berne's distinction here is, practically speaking, an artificial one.

3. That every individual who survives into adult life has had either functioning parents or someone *in loco parentis* (1961, p. 35).

Berne (1961, p. 60) characterizes the Parent as the weakest member, the Adult as the least easily decommissioned, and the Child as almost indefatigable. These ego states might be characterized by certain occupations. Parent, for example, might be the judge or the school principal or (as Berne suggests) the clergyman; the Adult might be the scientist or the accountant or the lawyer; the Child might be the clown or the student or the patient in the doctor's office.

If we reflect, we might recall observing these different states within ourselves. We are most likely to be aware of them at the times when we shift from one state to another. For example, sometimes I play ball with my son. When I am hitting and he is pitching, we are two kids playing ball. I try to hit the ball over the fence and out of the yard if I can, and my feeling is one of absolute glee if I manage to whack it over the roof of the house next door. However, my son has more stamina

FIGURE 1. **THE PSYCHIC ORGANS AND EGO STATES**

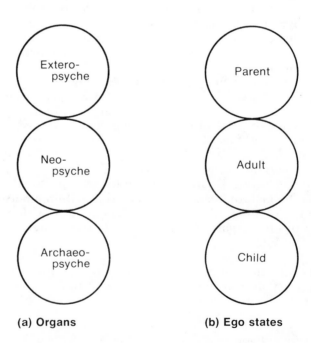

(a) **Organs**   (b) **Ego states**

From E. Berne, *Transactional analysis in psychotherapy.* New York: Grove Press, 1961, p. 31. Reprinted by permission of Grove Press, Inc. Copyright © 1961 by Eric Berne.

than I do, so when I become tired, my realistic Adult takes over, and I say something like "That's about all, son. I'm tired." Then dinner time arrives, my Parent takes over, and I tell my son to put the bat and ball away and to come into the house to wash his hands.

Detecting which ego state is in control at the moment may be deduced from several kinds of clues. These clues are behavioral, social, historical, and phenomenological. The behavioral clues include the person's demeanor, gestures, voice, vocabulary, and other kinds of behavior that are overtly observable by another person. The social clues are the social situation within which a person is behaving. If, for example, a person whose ego state we are evaluating is behaving, we think, like a Parent, and the person with whom he is interacting is behaving like a Child, then the social situation corroborates the conclusion suggested by the behavioral observation. The historical clues refer to the behavior of the person's own parent in a similar situation. The ego state would be judged to be that of the Parent if the person's behavior was similar to the behavior of the person's own parent in a similar situation. This kind of information would most likely be obtained from life-history data supplied by the person we were studying, although it would be more reliable and valid if we had an opportunity to observe the person's own parent in a similar situation. The phenomenological clues are obtained from the person's description of his own feelings at the time of the observation. If he says that he felt like a parent in the situation being studied, this would be additional evidence supporting the conclusion that he was in the ego state of Parent.

To recapitulate, the diagnosis of the ego state of a person is determined by four factors. These factors include the way he behaves, the situation in which he is behaving, the correspondence between this behavior and the behavior either he or his parent exhibited in the past, and the person's feelings and experiences during the incident being studied.

The Parent ego state is characterized by evaluation and support. The Parent may criticize, for example, and this behavior would include the gestures, facial expressions, and language of the critic. A person whose Parent is in control at the moment would feel critical during this phase. Yet the Parent may also be supportive and sympathetic. In any case, a person who is in the Parent ego state experiences himself as being in a superordinate role to the person with whom he is interacting.

Since the Parent ego state is learned by a person from his own parents during his childhood, it is to a certain extent, a reproduction of the person's perception of his own parents, expressed during a present situation. Most parents have had this experience at some time in their relationship with their own children. It has been my own experience, both as a parent, and as a clinician counseling parents, to observe myself and my clients doing the very things we had seen our parents do, which we had vowed we would never do when we became parents. One particular gambit my father used to use has, I have found, turned out to be especially effective with my own children. When, as a boy, I asked my father if I could go someplace, he usually asked me who else was going. I would reply, in the manner of all boys, "Everybody is going." To which my father replied, "No, everybody is not going. I am not going. Now, specifically, who is going?" I have found myself spontaneously using the same words with my own children. If we could watch television tapes of ourselves with our own children, we would probably recognize a great deal more of our parents in ourselves than we ever suspected.

The Adult ego state is characterized by a set of autonomous feelings, attitudes, and behavior patterns which a person has learned or developed to deal with current reality. A person whose Adult is in control relates as a peer to others and behaves in a manner intended to solve current problems or achieve current goals. The Adult is organized, adaptable, and intelligent. As I sit here writing, my Adult is in control. As I relate to my colleagues, let us say in a staff meeting, I am one of many Adult ego states interacting with each other.

The Child ego state is composed of the feelings, attitudes, and behaviors that are left over from childhood. The Child is exhibited in two forms, the "adapted" Child, who is under the dominance of parental influence, and the "natural" Child, who is self-indulgent and rebellious. Most people when they are sick and visit a physician are in the Child ego state to the physician, who is most likely in the Parent ego state. If they are what physicians term "good" patients and do what the doctor tells them to, they are in the adapted Child state. If they are "bad" patients, they are in the natural Child state and might spit out the medicine or refuse to allow the physician to jam a needle into their arm or elsewhere.

Each of the ego states has its useful function in the life of the person who is living a full life. The function of the Adult is the most obvious. The Adult plans, solves problems, and generally takes care of the ongoing requirements of life. The Parent serves as an actual parent to the literal or figurative children a person has to care for. The values and restrictions of the Parent also serve to conserve energy, since the Parent determines how things are done or should be done, thus eliminating the necessity of making decisions for every aspect of life and leaving the Adult free to confine itself to life's more important aspects. Finally, the Child is the repository of intuition, creativity, and spontaneous drive.

Berne has a great deal more to say about the signs by which the various ego states may be determined. Perhaps one of the more interesting of the criteria he lists are the words typical of the various ego states. Berne writes:

Typical Parental words are: cute, sonny, naughty, low, vulgar, disgusting, ridiculous, and many of their synonyms. Adult words are: unconstructive, apt, parsimonious, desirable. Oaths, expletives, and epithets are usually manifestations of the Child. Substantives and verbs are intrinsically Adult, since they refer without prejudice, distortion, or exaggeration to objective reality. . . . Diagnosis of the word "good" is a simple and gratifying exercise in intuition. With an implicit capital G it is Parental. When its application is realistically defensible, it is Adult. When it denotes instinctual gratification, and is essentially an exclamation, it comes from the Child, being then an educated synonym for something like "Nyum nyum!" (1961, p. 73).

Second-Order Structural Analysis

The structure of the personality has a second order, the understanding of which Berne often found to be important for understanding a particular person. This second-order structure is shown in Figure 2.

FIGURE 2. **BERNE'S SECOND-ORDER STRUCTURAL ANALYSIS**

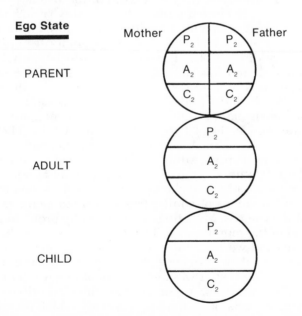

Adapted from E. Berne, *Transactional analysis in psychotherapy*. New York: Grove Press, 1961, p. 193. Reprinted by permission of Grove Press, Inc. Copyright © 1961 by Eric Berne.

The Parent is learned by a person from his own parents. It is his parents still living within his own feelings, values, perceptions, and behavior. But most people have two parents. Therefore, the Parent is not a unitary structure, but rather is composed of two parts, the mother part and the father part. This division is reflected in the diagram for the Parent in Figure 2. Ideally these two parts are in harmony with each other. That is, the two parts will be in harmony if a person's parents were more or less in agreement with each other. However, if his parents were in conflict, then his Parent will contain conflict which usually will be reflected in his own values, feelings, and behavior when the Parent is the dominant ego state.

This unhappy state was the topic of Peter DeVries's novel, *Let Me Count the Ways*. In this novel, the unhappy hero, who was trying to rebel against his parents, had a father who was an iconoclast, a high-liver, and an atheist and a mother who was a quiet and devout believer. When he wished to rebel against his mother on Saturday night, he would go out to a party, get roaring drunk, and generally raise hell. Unfortunately, his pleasure in rebelling against his mother was not complete, since he realized he was doing just what his father wanted him to do. So, on Sunday morning after a Saturday night carouse, he dragged himself out of bed and went off to church to rebel against his father. Unfortunately his joy at church was also flawed once he realized that by going to church he was doing just what his mother wanted him to do. His parents' conflict made it impossible for him either to rebel or to conform with satisfaction, as a result of a rift in his Parent ego state.

In addition to the Parent being split laterally by the mother and the father, there is also a horizontal split of each Parent into three parts. Each parent is himself (or herself) a person with the three ego states of Parent, Adult, and Child. The Parent in a person is acquired from that person's own parents, and those parents contained within themselves the three ego states of Parent, Adult, and Child. Therefore, within the Parent of the person being studied will be the representation of his parents' own Parent, Adult, and Child. That is, some of the time that I act like my father I am really acting like my father's Child. My father, for example, had a few choice expletives he used on appropriate occasions. In situations of similar frustration I sometimes find myself using my father's words. My father was especially prone to use these words at the end of the month when it came time to pay the bills. I use the same emotions and words at these times. It was many years before I realized that my verbal performance was more a repetition of a ritual learned from my father than it was a reflection of my own feelings.

The Adult of a person has three subdivisions, representing the three aspects of dealing with reality which ideally should be present. Since the Adult is concerned with planning and solving problems in the real world, these subdivisions represent aspects of importance to real-world problem solving. The Child part of the Adult has to do with the personal qualities a person exhibits in his interaction with others. The charm, spontaneity, and creativity of the Child are often of importance in solving real problems. In many situations it is constructive to be warm and charming or to exhibit a creativity that is focused on a problem. The Adult part of the Adult is concerned with the objective analysis of a situation and the planning of rational means to deal with that situation. Finally, the Parent part of the Adult of the personality is concerned with considering the ethical aspects of a problem being solved. This Parent in the Adult is focused on ethical considerations as they affect solving a particular problem.

The Child is also split into three parts. The Child contains the archaic leftovers from a person's childhood. This includes the child's perception of the parent. This is not a mature parent, but rather the child's view of the parent during childhood. My father can still speak sharply to me in a way that makes me anxious. My father is in no position to harm me. I am now stronger than he is, and I am completely independent of him. He can't spank me or turn me out of the house to starve, and after all these years of enduring my impertinence, it hardly seems likely that he would forbid me to darken his door. The response he stirs in me with his criticism comes from the representation of my father in my Child. Likewise, the Child is able to perceive, learn from, and react to reality, and the remnants of that reality coping in childhood remain within the Child.

In addition to the second-order analysis, it may even be possible or desirable to do a third-order structural analysis, although this would be more difficult. For example, my father's Parent contains remnants of his parents. How much of my fatherly behavior is fatherly behavior which I learned from my father, and which he, in turn, learned from his parents, or my grandparents? I may, without knowing it, be using many of the same values, attitudes, and behaviors with my children that my great-grandparents used with their children. This same general thought is reflected by Bowen (1960) in his theory of schizophrenia (described in Chapter 3), in which he suggests that it takes three generations to produce a schizophrenic.

Transactional Analysis

Transactional analysis is the analysis of the transactions between people. The transactions with which we will be concerned include procedures, rituals, pastimes, and games.

A *procedure* is a reality-oriented transaction designed to manipulate reality. A clerk and a customer go through a procedure:

Customer: I'd like a chocolate ice-cream cone.
Clerk: OK. (He then constructs the cone—with the proper number of dips of ice cream.) There you are.
Customer: Here (hands the clerk the money).
Clerk: Thank you.

A *ritual* is an interaction, such as an exchange of greetings, that is usually prescribed by culture. When I arrive at the office in the morning and first see my colleague, I say, "Good morning, Bill." And Bill says, "Good morning, Cliff." If one of us has been out of town for a few days the prescribed ritual may require a somewhat more extensive series of interchanges in which the one who has been gone describes his trip. If I have just returned from a trip and Bill neglects to ask me about it, I will proceed to describe it to him anyway. If he fails to show the amount of interest that the culture has taught us to expect, I will wonder about Bill, concluding that perhaps he is worried about something.

A *pastime* is a transaction that focuses on a particular subject. A pastime is small talk at a party, or discussion of a subject that has been in the news recently, or the discussion of a topic that is of particular interest to the group with which one is currently associated. Examples of pastimes among mothers are discussions of children, grocery prices, fashions, and so on. Among fathers, common pastimes are discussions of children, sports, and automobiles. During a national political campaign a common pastime is talking about politics.

Games are ongoing series of cooperative transactions progressing toward a well-defined outcome. The real purpose of the game is the final outcome, although this may be well hidden from the participants while the game is underway. Further, a game is characterized by particular kinds of transactions, which are classified as complementary and ulterior. The types of transactions will be discussed in the next section, and then we will return to a more detailed discussion of games.

Levels of Transactions

Berne (1964) sees the roots of transactions as lying in basic human need. The human infant needs physical contact with another human being—he needs to be stroked physically or he will "shrivel" (1964, p. 14). As the child matures, this stimulus-hunger is sublimated into recognition-hunger. The adult needs to have other people recognize the fact that he exists by reacting to him. After stimulus-hunger and recognition-hunger, comes structure-hunger. People have to pass time, and to pass time they need to have something to do. The kinds of transactions we have discussed serve the function of providing for the need to be recognized and the need to structure time. Rituals are culturally prescribed ways for people to recognize each other. Pastimes and games are designed to structure time. People who spend an evening together have to have some way of passing the time, or structuring the time, and the pastime serves this function. People who have a lifetime to spend together have to have some way to pass that time, so they devise games for structuring the time. Yet most games serve a further function of preventing real intimacy, which might be too dangerous, from developing.

The smallest unit in a transaction is a "stroke." For a transaction to begin, someone must start it. The first stimulus in a transaction might be the statement "Hello." That is one stroke. Then the other person responds, "Hello." That is the second stroke. A typical early morning transaction between two colleagues might then progress into a ritual, in which the first person responds to the second stroke by saying, "Are you going to the staff meeting today?" And the second person responds by saying, "Yes. Are you?" "Yes, if I can cancel another appointment I had scheduled for that time." Thus the ritual is completed in five strokes.

The five-stroke ritual described in the previous paragraph is an interaction between the Adult of the two people involved in a transaction. The Adult of the first person (the "agent") addressed the Adult of the second person, and the Adult of the second person (the "respondent") responded by addressing the Adult of the first person. This kind of interaction—in which the ego state of the respondent which was addressed by the agent responds, and in its response addresses the ego state of the agent which initiated the ritual—is called a *complementary transaction.* In a complementary transaction the two people are cooperating, so the person addressed accepts the conditions of the relationship implicit in the first remark of the person initiating the interchange.

There are two kinds of complementary transactions, which Berne terms Types I and II. Examples of both types are diagrammed in Figure 3. In both, the person initiating the interchange is labeled the "Agent," and the person responding is the "Respondent." That first kind of complementary transaction, Type I, is a transaction between the same ego state in each of the two people participating. The transaction between two colleagues described earlier was an example of a Type I complementary transaction between the Adults of the two people involved. Type I complementary transactions could also take place between the two Parents of the two people, or between the Childs (or Children?). An example of Type I complementary transaction between the Parents might be:

Agent: Isn't it awful the way college students carry on these days? Something ought to be done about it.

Respondent: Yes it is. I think the trouble is that they don't have enough to do. Their professors should give them more work.

FIGURE 3. **TYPES OF COMPLEMENTARY TRANSACTIONS**

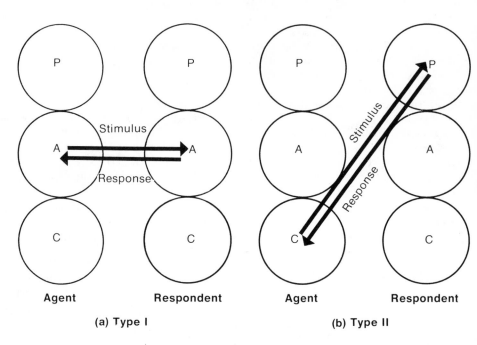

| (a) Type I | (b) Type II |

From E. Berne, *Games people play.* New York: Grove Press, 1964, p. 30. Reprinted by permission of Grove Press, Inc. Copyright © 1964 by Eric Berne.

And an example of a complementary transaction between the Child of each of the people involved might be:

> Agent: I bought my son a toy rocket for his birthday. How about coming over Saturday to help me shoot it off?
> Respondent: That sounds like fun. I wouldn't miss it.

Type I complementary relationships are relationships in which two people address each other as equals, regardless of the ego state involved. The Parent of the one addresses the Parent of the other, the Adult of one addresses the Adult of the other, or the Child of one addresses the Child of the other.

Type II complementary relationships are those in which the two participants are not equals. For example, either the Parent of the agent addresses the Child of the respondent, or, as in Figure 3b, the Child of the agent addresses the Parent of the respondent. In any case, that ego state which is addressed is the ego state which responds. An example of a Type II complementary transaction in which the Parent of the agent addresses and is responded to by the Child of the respondent might be the following:

> Agent (Parent): You've spent too much money out of the budget again this month.
> Respondent (Child): I'm sorry. I thought I would have enough left over to buy a new outfit, but I discovered we needed more money for the electricity bill before the end of the month.

A Type II complementary transaction in which the Child of the agent addresses the Parent of the respondent would be the following:

> Agent (Child): Can I take some money out of the checking account to buy a new outfit?
> Respondent (Parent): No. We have to pay the taxes this month, so there won't be any money left over.

Type II complementary transactions are usual in the relationship between a professional and his client, such as a lawyer and a client, or a mechanic and the owner of a troubled car.

A second kind of transaction is a *crossed transaction*, in which the respondent does not respond with the ego state addressed by the initiator of the transaction. In a crossed transaction, communication is broken off—there is no attempt to cooperate. Though there are many kinds, crossed transactions are most often found to be of two types, which Berne labeled Types I and II. They are diagrammed in Figure 4. A Type I crossed transaction occurs when the Adult of the agent addresses the Adult of the respondent, but the Child of the respondent replies to the Parent of the agent. An example of a Type I crossed transaction is the following:

> Agent (Adult): Mary, could you bring me a clean white shirt?
> Respondent (Child): I can't keep up with your shirts, and take care of the kids, and cook the meals, and do everything else I'm supposed to do. It's too much for me.

A Type II crossed transaction occurs when the Adult of the agent addresses the Adult of the respondent, but the Parent of the respondent replies to the Child of the agent. An example of a Type II crossed transaction is the following:

> Agent (Adult): Mary, could you bring me a clean white shirt?
> Respondent (Parent): Why can't you keep track of your own shirts? You're grown-up, aren't you?

FIGURE 4. **TYPES OF CROSSED TRANSACTIONS**

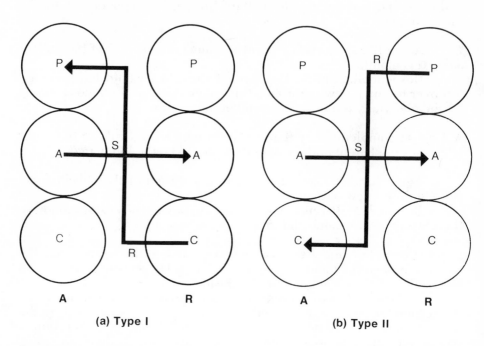

(a) Type I   (b) Type II

The transactions, complementary and crossed, that have been described above are the two basic levels of transactions. The examples we have used to describe them have all been simple, social transactions. As one can easily see, in the crossed transaction, communication is broken off because there is no attempt to cooperate. In complementary transactions, there is an attempt to cooperate, so the transaction can continue. Since we are here concerned with interaction between people, we will now leave crossed transactions, with their ineffective interaction, and proceed to examine complementary transactions in greater detail.

Complementary transactions can be more complicated than those examples shown above. They can proceed at two levels, an *overt, social level* and a *covert, psychological level*. Such two-layered transactions are called *ulterior transactions*. Ulterior transactions are transactions that proceed at two levels at the same time; though these levels are different, each is still complementary. There are two types of ulterior transactions, *angular* and *duplex*. Examples of both are diagrammed in

FIGURE 5. **TYPES OF ULTERIOR TRANSACTIONS**

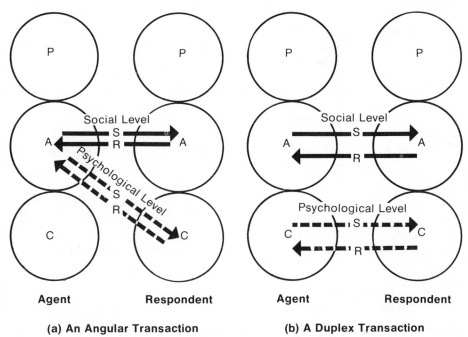

Agent   **Respondent**   **Agent**   **Respondent**

(a) An Angular Transaction   **(b) A Duplex Transaction**

Figure 5. Angular transactions involve three ego states, while duplex transactions involve four ego states.

An angular transaction is one in which an ego state of the agent is overtly addressing the same ego state of the respondent, but on a covert, psychological level a different ego state of the respondent is really being addressed. Angular transactions are ascribed by Berne as common to salespersons who ostensibly address the Adult of the customer, but in fact appeal to the Child of the customer. An example of an angular transaction is the following:

Social Level

Agent-salesperson (Adult): This red convertible is just what you need for your short business trips. It is a compact car, gives good mileage, and handles well on the highway. And, of course, the top comes down for nice weather.

Respondent-customer (Adult): Yes, I think the convertible is what I need for my purposes. It should be economical to drive, and yet provide the handling I'll need for the highway.

Psychological Level

Agent-salesperson (Adult): This job is what a sport like you needs to give the image you want to convey.

Respondent-customer (Child): Oh goody! I can hardly wait to hear what they say down at the office when they see me in this!

A duplex transaction is carried on at two levels at once, typically with the social transaction taking place at the Adult level, but the psychological transaction going on at the Child level. An example of a duplex ulterior transaction is the following:

Social Level

Agent (Adult): My, but that is an attractive outfit you're wearing. Did you make it yourself?

Respondent (Adult): Thanks very much. Yes, I did make it. I needed somthing in a hurry so I whipped it together last night. It saved me some money.

Psychological Level

Agent (Child): What a crummy outfit that is. No store would have sold it. You must have made it yourself.

Respondent (Child): So it isn't much, but I didn't have much time to put it together, and at least I'm not running my family to the poorhouse spending money on clothes the way you are.

Games

Complementary transactions proceed in series, with the response to one stroke also serving as the stimulus to the next stroke. These series of transactions form procedures, rituals, pastimes, and games. Ideally they may result in intimacy. In this section we shall discuss games in greater detail.

Berne defines a *game* as "an ongoing series of complementary ulterior transactions progressing toward a well-defined, predictable outcome" (1964, p. 48). Rituals and pastimes differ from a game in that they merely structure time while a game has a predetermined outcome. The players in a game may not be consciously aware of the outcome toward which they are progressing, but the outcome lurks there in the future nonetheless.

Games have several features. They are described as follows:

1. Thesis: a description of the sequence of events in the game (social level) and the psychological dynamics of the game (psychological level).

2. Antithesis: a description of the tactics by which one can undercut or frustrate a game; it results in the initiator of the game becoming frustrated or despairing.

3. Aim: the general purpose, or payoff, of the game.

4. Roles: the positions that must be filled if the game is to be played.

5. Dynamics: the psychological motivations that drive the game.

6. Examples: the prototypes of the game, rooted in childhood experience.

7. Transactional paradigm: the transactional analysis diagram of the game.

8. Moves in the game: the steps of the game, similar to the strokes in a ritual.

9. The advantages of the game: a description of the advantages the players obtain from playing the game. The main kinds of advantages are internal social, external social, internal psychological and external psychological, biological, and existential.

These aspects or features of games will be illustrated in the description of a specific game later in the chapter.

Games are taught to children by their parents. They serve a time-structuring function, and since they provide social payoff, they also serve a social function. That is, a person can get "one-up" on another by playing a game successfully. Games also provide people with something to do with their time and as a way of avoiding more intimate personal contact than some people might feel capable of managing.

Games vary in the flexibility, tenacity, and intensity with which they are played. A game may be played with a rigid format or a flexible one. Some people cling tenaciously to the game they are playing, while others give their game up rather easily. And some people play their game for pennies and others for life itself. Berne (1964, p. 64) classifies the intensity with which games are played into three levels: (1) A first-degree game, which is socially acceptable in the agent's social circle; (2) a second-degree game, which causes no serious or permanent damage, but which the participants would rather keep concealed, if possible; and (3) a third-degree game, which is played for keeps, and may result in death, divorce, or some other serious and permanent payoff.

An Example of a Game

One of the first games identified by Berne and his co-workers was "If It Weren't For You." This game is considered to be the most common game played by married couples and was used by Berne

(1964, pp. 50–58) to illustrate the general characteristics of games in his book, *Games People Play.*

The game, "If It Weren't For You" (abbreviated IFWY), requires one passive player and one dominant player. Usually the players are a dominant husband and a submissive wife, though it could be the reverse. In the game described by Berne, Mrs. White complained that her husband severely restricted her social activities and that she had never learned to dance because her husband wouldn't let her take lessons. Mrs. White entered psychotherapy, and as a result of some changes wrought by the therapy, she became more assertive, while her husband became more indulgent. This gave her the incentive to sign up for dancing classes, but she then discovered that she had an overwhelming fear of dance floors, so she was forced to abandon the project.

Mrs. White's revealed fear of the dance floor uncovered the nature of her relationship with her husband. She had chosen a man who would dominate her and forbid her to become involved in various activities. Further, she had developed a circle of women friends who had similar relationships with their own husbands.

The dance floor fiasco revealed that Mrs. White had a fear of social relationships, so she married a man who would prevent her from being exposed to that which she feared and who would also provide her with an excuse for not facing her fears. She had two advantages: She did not have to become involved in feared social situations, and she could avoid the blame for this—it was her husband's fault.

This game had additional advantages. Mr. White's prohibitions led to frequent fights at home. Because Mr. White felt guilty about these fights, he frequently brought Mrs. White gifts. The Whites had little in common outside of their household and children, so their fights provided a way of passing the time and kept them from having to come intimately face-to-face with each other. In addition, Mrs. White gained the material advantage of the presents Mr. White brought her.

The following analysis of the game illustrates the process of game analysis within the framework of the features of the game that were listed earlier. The game is analyzed from the point of view of the person who is "It,"—that is, Mrs. White—since she is the one who gets to say "If It Weren't For You."

Thesis. The sequence of events is one person forbidding the other to do something, with the forbidden one being able to say that if it weren't for the prohibitions of the dominant member, one could do this, that, or something else. This game, incidentally, can be played in many kinds of relationships other than the marital one. College students often play the game, with the revision that if it weren't for their parents they could paint, play football, or work in the slums.

Antithesis. The antithesis to IFWY is permissiveness. The wife who would take dancing lessons if only her husband would let her is told by her husband, "Go ahead. Dance away." I once knew a husband who was forever propositioning other men's wives, but only provisionally, since his own wife wouldn't allow him to dally. When, on one occasion, his wife told him to go ahead and dally, he begged off on the plea that he was busy with other things. Undercutting the IFWY game may lead into another game called "Yes, But," in which the person then lists eighty-three other reasons why he can't do what he said he wanted to do.

Aim. The aim of IFWY may be either reassurance ("It's not that I'm afraid, but that I'm not allowed") or vindication ("It's not that I'm not trying, but he keeps me from it").

Roles. IFWY is a two-handed game, calling for one player who is domineering and a second player who is submissive.

Dynamics. IFWY most likely derives from fears or phobias. It protects the person who is "It" from having to face the thing he fears.

Examples. The game probably has its prototype in childhood, where the parent substitutes for the dominant player. In fact, it has been recognized that children and adolescents often welcome parental restrictions, even though they protest against them publicly, because they protect children from having to face situations they fear.

Transactional Paradigm. A game is a complementary ulterior transaction. The overt, social interaction in IFWY is most likely between the Parent of the dominant player ("You can't") and the Child of the submissive player ("If it weren't for you"). On the covert, psychological level, the interaction is probably between the Child of each of the participants. In the case of the Whites, Mr. White most likely is dominant as a cover for his own insecurity, so his demand that his wife stay home is really a plea for her to keep him company because he is afraid when he is left by himself. The response by Mrs. White is "I'll keep you company if you'll protect me from having to face situations I fear." The transactional diagram is presented in Figure 6.

Moves. The moves in a game correspond roughly to the strokes in a ritual. With practice the players may become quite proficient in their performance. The movie *Who's Afraid of Virginia Woolf?* beautifully illustrated a couple who had not only perfected the moves of the game, but added many creative embellishments to the performance. In

FIGURE 6.   **TRANSACTION DIAGRAM OF THE GAME "IF IT WEREN'T FOR YOU"**

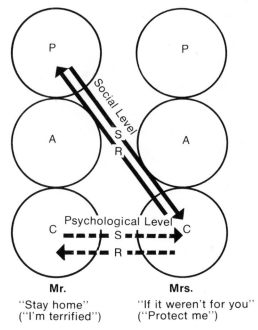

Mr.   **Mrs.**

"Stay home"   "If it weren't for you"
("I'm terrified")   ("Protect me")

the IFWY game of the Whites, the moves are essentially two: instruction-compliance ("You stay home" — "All right") and instruction-protest ("You stay home" — "If It Weren't For You").

Advantages. In IFWY the internal social advantage of the game is that it allows the players to structure the time they spend together. They don't have to face the problem of intimately interacting with each other while they are playing the game. The external social advantage is that it gives Mrs. White an excuse she can give to her friends for not becoming involved in various social activities; in addition, it gives her something to talk about with her friends. It is a kind of ticket of admission to the *kaffee klatsch* in which the game "If It Weren't For You" is the main topic of conversation. The internal psychological advantage is that surrender to the husband keeps Mrs. White from experiencing neurotic fears. The external psychological advantage is that the game keeps Mrs. White from having to face the feared situation. The biological advantage, that is the advantage of having external stimuli to attend to, is provided by the exciting verbal exchanges that take place in the game. The existential advantage is that each match played confirms the wife's existential view that "all men are tyrants."

Taxonomy of Games

There are several families of games, with the classification based on the situations in which the games are found. Berne (1964) lists the following categories of games: Life Games, Marital Games, Party Games, Sexual Games, Underworld Games, Consulting Room Games, and Good Games. Most games are not desirable, but Good Games are the exception to this rule. Actually, the families of games listed by Berne are probably limited to the areas of life to which he and his co-workers have been exposed. Had Berne been a teacher, he probably could have listed classroom games, student games, and teaching-staff games. Other games could, no doubt, be listed by people in other walks of life. Probably there are a finite number of types of games, with variations on the main theme of the game to be found in different environments. We shall discuss a few of these.

Life Games are games that form a way of life. These games often require several players. Among the Life Games listed by Berne is "Alcoholic" which requires five players, although the roles may be condensed so that one person may play more than one role. "Alcoholic" requires a central player, who is "It" (or the alcoholic), a persecutor who is usually the spouse, a rescuer who may be a close friend or the family doctor, a patsy who gives the alcoholic money to buy his liquor and who sympathizes with him, and a connection who is the source of liquor supply. In this game the alcoholic gets his liquor from the connection, gets drunk, is berated by the persecuter, is helped out of his messes by the rescuer, and is given small supplies and support by the patsy. The payoff in the game comes during the hangover, when the alcoholic is most miserable. Berne points out that among alcoholics the topic they are most likely to discuss is the suffering they endure subsequent to a drinking bout. Actually, my own experience with alcoholics suggests that there are several different kinds of "Alcoholic" games (Swensen & Davis, 1959), of which the game Berne describes is just one version.

There are many other Life Games. "Debtor" is one in which a person gets into debt and then uses various strategies for dealing with the debt. "Kick Me" is a game in which a person seeks out others to reject him or punish him. These people are the perennial losers in life. "Now I've Got You, You Son of a Bitch" is a game in which the instigator seeks to have another person shortchange him or gyp him so he can catch the culprit. The payoff is not in the prevention of fraud, but in the indignation the man who is "It" is allowed to express when he catches the other person. "See What You Made Me Do" is a family game, which may be played between mates or between parents and children. The object is to foul up some project in such a way that another person can be blamed for your foul-up. The main purpose of this game is to give the one who is "It" an acceptable excuse for unloading irritation on the one who is blamed for causing the foul-up. This game is often played by husbands engaged in repair work around the house and by children engaged in chores for which they have been involuntarily drafted.

Marital Games are played between husbands and wives. "Corner" is a game in which one person slickly refuses to play the game of the other. In this game one person suggests they do something, such as go to the movies. The other agrees. Then the instigator lets "slip" the fact that there is something else that needs to be done, such as buying a new washing machine. If the instigator is the wife, the husband then becomes angry about being reminded of this expediture, since the budget is strained at the moment. The wife then takes offense at the husband's anger and says she won't go. The husband then stomps out of the house and goes to the movies alone. "Courtroom" requires three players, a husband, a wife, and a third party who plays the part of the judge. In this game, the couple recite their grievances against each other, with the third party apparently providing the judgment. This game is also played frequently between two fighting siblings and a parent. "Frigid Woman" is a game in which the wife rebuffs her husband's advances until he gives up making advances; she then starts making seductive movements toward him until he starts making advances again, at which point she resumes her rejection. When the game is played by unmarried women it is called "Rapo," and the payoff comes when the woman has seduced the man into making an overt advance which she can then reject with vehemence. With single women who play a hard game, the conclusion to this game may come in court. "Harried" is a game played by housewives, and the objective is that they have ten or twelve different roles, but time and energy to fulfill only three or four of them. "Look How Hard I've Tried" is a game played by a married couple and a marriage counselor. In this game one partner wants to continue the marriage, but the other partner wants to dissolve the marriage—but only after being able to say that he has tried everything to save it. The object of the game is for the partner who wants to end the marriage to be able to say after it is all over that he has tried everything before giving up. Finally, "Sweetheart" is a game in which one marital partner criticizes the other, but in such a sweet and understanding way that it would seem bad form for the criticized partner to demur or argue.

The taxonomy of games, of course, is a task that can be extended to every realm of human endeavor. It might make an interesting project for people in a particular occupation to describe and list the kinds of games that go on around them. For example, a common graduate-student game might be "But I'm Just a Little Boy (Girl)" in which the professor encourages the graduate student to undertake a particular project, to which the graduate student, in effect, responds "But I don't know how to do it." The object of this game is to minimize work and win sympathy.

Beyond Games

Although Berne lists some games as "Good Games," he feels that the objective of human development should be to progress beyond games to genuine intimacy between persons, in which interaction is honest. In an honest interaction there are no ulterior components which are hidden from the pair. As Berne writes, "For certain fortunate people there is something which transcends all classifications of behavior, and that is awareness; something which rises above the programming of the past, and that is spontaneity; and something that is more rewarding than games, and that is intimacy" (1964, p. 184).

Research

Though Berne has used transactional analysis with his patients, he has reported little research on the success of his method. He published one study (1957; 1961, p. 244) on the effectiveness of transactional analysis in which he reported that 78 percent of twenty-three psychotic patients and 67 percent of forty-two neurotic patients improved when treated with transactional analysis.

However, he later indicated (Berne, 1966) that this research was undertaken only at the insistence of his publisher, and he expressed doubt at the value of research, at least as it is currently conducted, for contributing much of value to understanding the interaction between people. In fact, he suggested that by conducting an experiment, the researcher may not only *not* be helping his patient to become more game-free, but may in fact be teaching the patient a new game, which might be called the "Research Game."

Discussion

Berne's theory has received more popular attention than any of the other views of interpersonal relationships discussed in this book. There is good reason for this. He and his colleagues have written books about the interpersonal interaction for the general public. At a time when many people have problems in their relationships with other people,

Berne has provided an understandable explanation of what is going wrong when people have trouble with each other.

However great an impact Berne has had on the general public, he has had relatively little impact upon serious students of interpersonal interaction. There are probably two main reasons for this state of affairs. One is that his ideas are not particularly new, although he did organize his ideas uniquely and present them in a form that made them easily applicable to life as most people observe it today. The more serious lack in his work is the lack of research. Because of the clear, well-structured manner in which these ideas are presented, they should easily be subject to a variety of kinds of research, including laboratory research. But Berne resisted the idea of research because he felt research distorted the phenomenon being studied. Although it is certainly true that the method by which interpersonal relations is studied affects the phenomenon being observed, this fact is not a bar to research, but rather a barrier to be overcome. It is through research that the validity of ideas is tested. The validity of a concept is much greater if that concept has been observed in the clinical setting and confirmed in the laboratory, and still explains interactions people have noticed in real life. If people who seek the help of psychotherapists because they feel ill-at-ease in talking to other people are observed by that therapist to fidget more in his office; if laboratory observations confirm the observation that people who feel uncomfortable with other people make more body movements in a given period of time when another person is present; and if the "man-in-the-street" notices that shy people seem to be nervous at parties, then the concept of "people anxiety" being related to increased body movement is more firmly established than if the psychotherapist were the only one to make the observation. Berne resisted this kind of investigation.

As a consequence, Berne's game theory is based almost entirely on patients observed in group and individual psychotherapy. Thus the data base for Berne is quite narrow. The level from which Berne obtained his data is the level of the individual person and the level of the dyad. Structural analysis is at the individual level, while transactional analysis is at the dyadic level. The "games" part of this approach is a conceptualization that is genuinely at the level of the interacting couple (or group). The kinds of data used are almost entirely obtained from group and individual psychotherapy and are based on either the self-report of the patients or the observation of the behavior of the patients in the psychotherapeutic situation.

As a theory, transactional analysis is broad but shallow. It is broad in that it includes not only the internal personality functioning of the people involved in an interaction, but also the couple interacting as a unit. It includes the processes by which they interact—the communications between them—and also the processes by which these patterns of interaction develop. Berne describes how people function and how they got that way. But the theory is narrow, compared with Sullivan (see Chapter 2), since Berne does not attempt to describe the processes through which people *learn* patterns of interaction from their parents, nor does he delve with any depth into the mental processes by which people communicate with each other.

Unfortunately, the development of transactional analysis has led to the establishment of institutes and workshops for the teaching of transactional analysis rather than toward the development of research that would correct, refine, and extend these views. The development of institutes is not necessarily undesirable, but when it is done in the absence of research designed to establish more firmly the concepts taught, it is more likely to result in the establishment of a cult than the development of a maturing field of study.

Summary

Transactional analysis is composed of two components, structural analysis and transactional analysis. *Structural analysis* is the analysis of the personality structure of the individual. *Transactional analysis* is the analysis of the interaction between people.

The personality of an individual is composed of determinants, organizers, and phenomena. The *determinants* are the biological processes of the body, the person's past experience, and the value systems acquired from the parents. The *organizers* are the "psychic organs" and include the *archaeopsyche*, the *neopsyche*, and the *exteropsyche*. The *phenomena* are "ego states" and are the *Child*, *Adult*, and *Parent*. In therapy, most emphasis is placed upon the ego states. The Child in a person is composed of remnants of childhood which a person carries around within himself. The Adult is the mature, practical, realistic part of the person that conducts transactions with the environment. The Parent within the person contains the remnants of the person's own parent, which include values and attitudes. These three ego states determine the person's behavior and feelings.

Transactional analysis analyzes the interactions between people and is based on analyzing these transactions into the ego states involved in each transaction. There are two basic levels of transactions: complementary and crossed. *Complementary transactions* are those in which the same ego state in the respondent which is addressed by the agent, or instigator, replies to the agent. A complementary transaction is one in which the two persons involved cooperate with each other. There are two kinds of complementary transactions: Type I and Type II. A *Type I complementary transaction* is one in which the ego states of the two people involved are the same. For example, the Adult of the agent addresses and is responded to by the Adult of the respondent, or the Child of the agent addresses and is responded to by the Child of the respondent. A *Type II complementary transaction* is one in which one ego state of the agent *addresses and is responded to* by a different ego state of the respondent. For example, the Child of the agent addresses and is responded to by the Parent of the respondent.

Crossed transactions are those in which the agent addresses one ego state of the respondent, but the respondent replies with a different ego state. In these transactions, communication is broken off. There are two common types of crossed transactions: Type I and Type II. A *Type I crossed transaction* is one in which the Adult of the agent addresses the Adult of the respondent, but the Child of the respondent replies to the Parent of the agent. A *Type II crossed transaction* is one in which the Adult of the agent addresses the Adult of the respondent, but the Parent of the respondent replies to the Child of the agent.

Complementary transactions may involve more than one level of interaction. The two levels of interaction are the *overt, social level* and the *covert, psychological level.* These are called *ulterior transactions.* An ulterior transaction may be angular or duplex. An *angular ulterior transaction* is one which on the social level the Adult of the agent addresses the Adult of the respondent, while on the psychological level the Adult of the agent addresses and is responded to by the Child of the respondent. A *duplex ulterior transaction* is one which on the social level the Adult of the agent addresses the Adult of the respondent, while on the psychological level the Child of the agent addresses the Child of the respondent.

Among the various kinds of transactions are rituals, procedures, pastimes, games, intimacy, and scripts. A *ritual* is a short interchange between people which is usually prescribed by the culture. It is not much more than a formalized greeting. A *procedure* is a transaction between people to accomplish some specific purpose or task. A *pastime* is designed to structure time and is usually a discussion of some topic of mutual interest. A *game* is a complementary ulterior transaction designed to structure time between people who are involved in some close, continuing relationship. *Intimacy* is an honest interchange in which people become genuinely close to each other. A *script* is a complex, long-term series of transactions that may take a lifetime to complete.

References

Berne, E. Ego states in psychotherapy. *American Journal of Psychotherapy,* 1957, 11, 293.

Berne, E. *Transactional analysis in psychotherapy.* New York: Grove Press, 1961.

Berne, E. *Games people play.* New York: Grove Press, 1964.
Berne, E. *Principles of group treatment.* New York: Oxford University Press, 1966.
Bowen, M. A family concept of schizophrenia. In D. D. Jackson, (Ed.), *The etiology of schizophrenia.* New York: Basic Books, 1960.
Swensen, C. H., & Davis, H. C. Types of workhouse inmate alcoholics. *Quarterly Journal of Studies on Alcohol,* 1959, 22, 757–66.

Additional Sources

Berne, E. Concerning the nature of communication. *Psychiatric Quarterly,* 1953, 27, 185–98.
Berne, E. Primal images and primal judgment. *Psychiatric Quarterly,* 1955, 29, 634–58.
Berne, E. The psychodynamics of intuition. *Psychiatric Quarterly,* 1962, 36, 294–300.
Berne, E. *The structure and dynamics of organizations and groups.* Philadelphia: Lippincott, 1963.
Harris, T. A. *I'm OK—you're OK: a practical guide to transactional analysis.* New York: Harper & Row, 1967.

Existential Phenomenology and the Experiencing Person

6

The human race is a myriad of refractive surfaces staining the white radiance of eternity. Each surface refracts the refraction of refractions of refractions. Each self refracts the refractions of others' refractions of self's refractions of others' refractions . . . (1966, p. 3).

—Ronald Laing

The term "existential phenomenology" conjures the image of a rather grim, intellectual, esoteric approach, shrouded in ambiguity and mystical overtones, devoid of any substantial, factual basis. One psychologist (Koch, 1965) expressed his uneasiness with the existential approach in psychology with the observation that it seemed to him that it was a revolt against arid behaviorism supplying "opaque" answers to suit personal desires, given to "ardent association-chasing," and characterized by "wooly revivalist overtones."

Existentialism generally refers to a broad philosophical approach that in psychology has been characterized by a concern with the person from the point of view of the person's own experience. The origins are generally traced back to the nineteenth-century Danish philosopher, Sören Kierkegaard, but the views discussed in this chapter have Jean-Paul Sartre as a more recent ancestor (see Laing, 1964).

As it has been expressed in modern psychology, existentialism has been a response to what social philosophers have seen happening to people in a modern, mechanized, urbanized, technological society. As they see it, we have been cut off from ourselves, from our fellow beings, and from our physical environment (see May, Angel, & Ellenberger, 1958). We are no longer open to our own inner experiences, feelings, attitudes, or body sensations. We have been told, through the massive armamentarium of modern communications, what we should feel or think or experience, so that we no longer trust our own experience. We ignore and repress our own experience of ourselves, to the extent that we are not consciously aware of what we really feel or of the sensations of our own bodies. We have been cut off from others by being trained to perform certain functions and fill certain roles, so that we do not interact with our fellow beings as one person relating to another person but as one role relating to another role: as teacher to student, as clerk to customer, or as doctor to patient. The person has been lost. The most important element of the relationship, the relationship of one person to another person, has been repressed. Instead, the person has become "doctor" acting out the role "doctor" to the patient who is not a person, but rather the "pneumonia case" in Room 188.

We have become cut off from, or alienated from, the physical world within which we live. We are no longer people living in the world and experiencing and interacting with the world—with the wind, the rain, the earth, the insects. Rather, we live in an artificial urban environment that is warmed in the winter and cooled in the summer. We do not travel through the countryside, but are whisked over it in an aluminum tube, so that we have been almost literally translated from one city to another, say from New York to Chicago, with little sense of any countryside between the two cities. When we arrive in the second city, we eat and sleep in rooms that are scarcely distinguishable from those of the first city. If we travel on the ground, we are in a metal box, moving rapidly over a four-lane freeway, with limited access to the countryside we are traversing. The ground itself has been covered with pavement.

The existentialists see much of our modern torment as rooted in our alienation from ourselves, from our fellow beings, and from nature. They seek to put us back into contact with that from which we are alienated—particularly with our own experience.

The Phenomenological Approach of Laing

Phenomenology has a long history in psychology. It might even be considered the first method of psychological research. Phenomenology is an attempt to understand people from the point of view of their own experience. It seeks to understand pain by asking people to describe how their pain feels. Phenomenology fell into scientific disrepute because it seemed to many to be too subjective to provide data that would be the basis of a scientific—that is an objective and general—psychology. It gave way to behaviorism, seeking to overcome the problems of subjectivity by studying only overt behavior, that two or more observers could observe independently and yet be in agreement about what it was that they had observed. Behavior was public, but experience was private, and science was concerned with public matters.

Phenomenology is the study of human behavior and experience from the standpoint of the person experiencing. It is the study of human existence from where each one of us lives it. While a behaviorist would try to predict what course a person will take in college by observing what he had been rewarded for doing in the past, the phenomenologist would try to predict and explain a person's choice of a course by asking him what he planned to take and why he planned to take it.[1]

In this chapter we will focus on the work of Ronald D. Laing, a Scottish psychiatrist who has written extensively and creatively about the interpersonal relationship from the existential point of view. He has used phenomenological methods to understand the behavior of people in relationships, basing his views on data he has collected from psychiatric clinic patients. His ideas have been further validated by data from a psychological inventory which he and his co-workers constructed to analyze interpersonal relationships.

Laing started out to be a conventional psychiatrist, working within the framework of the standard psychiatric-diagnostic categories based on the work of Kraepelin and Bleuler. But when he interviewed chronic schizophrenics, he did not observe the classical symptoms of schizophrenia as they were described in the standard psychiatric textbooks. At first, Laing attributed this inability to observe the classical signs to some deficiency within himself. Then Laing realized that the interviewing psychiatrist was a part of the behavioral field of the patient. The things the patient says and does are not only a function of the person the patient is, but are also a function of the person the psychiatrist is. "The standard psychiatric patient is a function of the standard psychiatrist, and of the standard mental hospital" (1965, p. 28). The classical, psychiatric approach of viewing the patient with detached scientific objectivity and curiosity was as much a cause of the schizophrenic's symptoms as was the process of schizophrenia within the person who was labeled "schizophrenic." Since Laing did not observe the schizophrenic with quite the same detachment and noninvolvement as a Bleuler to whom the schizophrenic was "stranger than the birds in his own garden," Laing did not observe the typical signs of schizophrenia in the persons he interviewed in the hospital.

---

[1]For a more thorough discussion about the differences between behaviorism and phenomenology, see MacLeod, R. B., 1965.

If the psychiatrist changes his point of view from that of the detached, objective scientist, who observes the patient as an object to be studied, and instead tries to get inside the skin of the patient so he can grasp and understand the schizophrenic's own experience of the world and of himself, then a new view of the process of schizophrenia emerges. Viewed objectively, from the outside, the patient's behavior is seen as the sign of "disease," but viewed phenomenologically, from the inside, the patient's behavior expresses his existence.

The difference between the two approaches may be illustrated by the behavior of a schizophrenic patient I once encountered in a psychiatric hospital. This young man had been arrested by the police for dancing nude on the street of his hometown one warm autumn evening. The police wrestled him into a straitjacket and carried him to the hospital. At the hospital the attendants tried to process him through the usual admission procedures of the hospital, which included measuring his height and weight. The patient violently resisted their measuring efforts, smashing a window and chair in the process. The attendants called for reinforcements and finally subdued him by taking a mattress, which they used as a shield, forcing him up against a wall, and having the physician on duty inject a sedative while the attendants held him immobile. The behavior of the man was clearly psychotic and suggested that he was potentially dangerous. From the objective point of view his behavior made no sense. He was psychotic. Several days after this man's violent introduction to psychotic life, I had an opportunity to talk with him about himself. He explained his behavior from his own point of view. While reading some books on perception, it occurred to him that people see what they expect to see. He decided to test this insight. He reasoned that since people would not expect to see a man walking nude on the street, it would be possible for him to stroll down the street naked and unnoticed. So he took off his clothes and walked down the street. While he was walking down the street, he felt as though his self were breaking into fragments and floating out around the universe. As these fragments circumnavigated the universe, floating by him as they started their second lap around, he leaped about trying to recapture them and stuff them back into his body. It was at this point that his endeavors were interrupted by the police. When he was brought to the hospital, he thought that the scale, with the height measure attached to it, was electrically wired and that the attendants planned to electrocute him. He had no intention of submitting passively to his own execution, so he resisted with all the strength he could muster.

Viewed from the outside, this man's behavior made no sense at all. It was objectively psychotic. Viewed from the point of view of his own experience—of his experience of himself and the world at that moment—his behavior was understandable. The way he was experiencing himself and the world at the time was still quite eccentric, but given his experience, his behavior made sense.

But understanding the sense that this man's behavior made from the point of view of his experience of himself and his world at that time is just a start. It still remains to be explained how he developed such an unusual view of himself in the world. It was to understand the transition from a sane to an insane being-in-the-world that Laing developed his system.

Laing reasoned that to understand persons, it is necessary to develop a science that deals with persons as persons, and not as an abstract system of reflexes or biochemical processes, or as an interacting network of traits, or as some other, nonpersonal kind of process. To analyze a person with such objective concepts can be quite useful, but the person is lost in the process. To develop a science of persons, it is necessary to construct a science that deals with the person as a person and begins with the relationship of one person to another person. To study the other person as a person means seeing him as being responsible, capable of choice, and self-initiating, and as having plans, hopes, fears, and all the other experiences that we all experience as persons. To develop a science of persons it is necessary to study persons as persons, and not as machines or biochemical processes or some other nonpersonal process. It might be argued that any theory is an analogy or perhaps a metaphor. Yet persons are less precise than machines, more complex than the most intricate chemical reaction—there is no adequate metaphor for the person.

The argument is not that the phenomenological point of view is right and the objective view is wrong, but rather that persons, including schizophrenic persons, can be looked at in more than one way, and that from the standpoint of developing a science of persons, the most useful method for understanding persons is the phenomenological. Laing illustrates this with the vase-face figure below. The figure can be seen as either a vase, or as two profiles. Which is correct? Either can be correct. It all depends on which you see as figure and which you see as ground.

How this method is applied by Laing to understanding the schizo-phrenic process is illustrated in the following case from *The Divided Self.*[2]

The Case of Peter

Peter was a large man of twenty-five, and he looked the picture of health. He came to see me complaining that there was a constant un-pleasant smell coming from him. He could smell it clearly, but he was not too sure whether it was the sort of smell that others could smell. He thought that it came particularly from the lower part of his body and the genital region. In the fresh air, it was like the smell of burning, but usu-ally it was a smell of something sour, rancid, old, decayed. He likened it to the sooty, gritty, musty smell of a railway waiting-room; or the smell that comes from the broken-down "closets" of the slum tenements of the district in which he grew up. He could not get away from this smell although he had taken to having several baths a day.

The following information about his life was given by his father's brother:

His parents were not happy people but they stuck close to each other. They had been married ten years before he was born. They were insep-arable. The baby, the only child, made no difference to their life. He slept in the same room as his parents from birth until he left school. His parents were never openly unkind to him and he seemed to be with them all the time and yet they simply *treated him as though he wasn't there.*

His mother, his uncle went on, never could give him affection since she had never had any herself. He was bottle-fed and put on weight well, but he was never cuddled or played with. As a baby, he was always crying. His mother, however, did not openly reject him or neglect him. He was adequately fed and clothed. He passed through his subsequent child-hood and adolescence without any noticeable peculiarities. His mother, however, his uncle said, hardly noticed him at all. She was a pretty woman, and was always fond of dressing up and admiring herself. His father liked to see this, bought her clothes when he could, and was very proud to be seen with his attractive wife.

The uncle thought that though the father was very fond of the boy in his way, something seemed to stop him from being able to show his affec-tion to him. He tended to be gruff, to pick on faults, occasionally to thrash him for no good reason, and to belittle him with such remarks as, "Useless Eustace," "You're just a big lump of dough." The uncle

2The following excerpt is from *The divided self,* by R. D. Laing. New York: Pan-theon Books, 1969, pp. 129–35. Copyright © 1960 by Tavistock Publications, © 1969 by R. D. Laing. Reprinted by permission of Pantheon Books/A Division of Random House, Inc., and Tavistock Publications, Ltd.

thought this was a pity because when he did well at school and later when he got a job in an office, which was a big step-up socially for this very poor family, he really was "terribly proud of that boy"; it was "a terrible blow to him" when his son seemed later just not to want to make anything of himself.

He was a lonely child, and he was always very good. When he was nine, a little girl of his own age who lived beside him was blinded in an air-raid in which both her parents were killed. For several years he spent most of his time with this little girl; he had inexhaustible patience and kindness, he taught her how to get around the district, took her to pictures, sat with her, and talked with her. This girl later partially recovered her sight. She told his uncle that she owed her life to the little boy of nine, because he was the only person who had really had time for her when she was blind, helpless, and friendless, with no one who either could or would step into the place of her dead parents.

In his last years of school, his uncle took a special interest in him and with his prompting, and through arrangements he made, he went into a solicitor's office. The boy left this office after a few months because of lack of interest but, again through his uncle, he obtained work in a shipping office. He stayed with this firm till his call-up to the Army. In the Army, at his own wish, he looked after patrol dogs and when he left, after serving his two years without incident, he "broke his father's heart" by, literally, "going to the dogs," in that he obtained a job as a kennel-man at a dog track. He left this, however, after a year, and after five months doing various unskilled odd jobs he simply did nothing for the seven months before he went to his general practitioner complaining of smell. There was, in fact, no smell from him so his G.P. referred him for psychiatric help.

The patient described his life in the following way:

His own feeling about his birth was that neither his father nor his mother had wanted him and, indeed, that they had never forgiven him for being born. His mother, he felt, resented his presence in the world because he had messed up her figure and damaged and hurt her in being born. He maintained that she had cast this up to him frequently during his childhood. His father, he felt, resented him simply for existing at all, "He never gave me any place in the world . . ." He thought too that his father probably hated him because the damage and pain he had caused his mother by his birth had put her against having sexual intercourse. He entered life, he felt, as a thief and criminal.

. . .

He said he was not lonely as a child although he was on his own a good deal, but "lonely is not the same as being alone."

He had what was probably a "screen" memory from about four or five years of his mother telling him, when she caught him playing with his penis, that it wouldn't grow if he did that; when he was about seven or eight there were a few episodes of a sexual nature with a girl of his own age, but he did not start masturbating until the age of about fourteen. All this was of major importance to him and served to intensify his self-consciousness. The only early memories he told me to begin with were of these sexual incidents. They were told without any warmth. It was many months before he mentioned, in a casual way, the blind little girl, Jean.

At secondary school his feelings about himself were becoming more definitely crystallized. As far as it is now possible to reconstruct them, he was beginning to have a growing sense that he was being put by everyone in a false position. He felt under an obligation to his teacher and his parents to be somebody and to make something of himself, whereas all the time he felt that this was on the one hand impossible and on the other hand unfair. He felt that he had to spend all his time and energy in being a credit to his father, his mother, his uncle, or his teacher. However, he was convinced in himself that he was nobody and worthless, that all this effort to be somebody was a deception and a pretense. His teacher, for instance, wanted him to "speak properly" and to wear "middle-class clothes." But all this was trying to make him be what he was not. She had him, the secret masturbator, reading Bible lessons to the other children at school and held him up as a paragon. When people said how good he must be to be able to read the Bible so well he laughed sardonically to himself. "It just showed what a good actor I was." Yet he himself, beyond feeling that he was not the person he was playing at being, did not know what he wanted to be. Alongside the feeling that he was worthless, there was also the growing impression that he was someone very special, sent by God for a special mission, but who, or what . . . he could not say. In the meantime, he deeply resented what he felt were everybody's efforts to make him into a saint, which were "more or less just for credit to themselves." It was without joy, therefore, that he worked in his office job. He came to hate more and more, and women in particular. He was aware of hating others, but it had not occurred to him that he feared them. Why should he, when "they couldn't stop me thinking what I liked"? This, of course, implies that "they" had some power to coerce him to do what "they" wanted, but as long as he was outwardly compliant to "their" wishes, he avoided experiencing the anxiety which we must suppose led him to conform to others and hardly ever reveal himself to them.

It was at the second office that he first experienced attacks of anxiety. By then, the central issue for him had crystallized in terms of being sincere or being a hypocrite; being genuine or playing a part. For himself, he knew he was a hypocrite, a liar, a sham, a pretense, and it was largely a matter of how long he could kid people before he would be found out.

At school, he had believed that he had been able, to a large extent, to get away with it. But the more he dissembled what he regarded as his real feelings and did things and had thoughts that had to be kept hidden and secret from every other, the more he began to scan people's faces in order to try to make out, from what he could read in them, what he imagined they either thought about him or knew about him. At the office what he regarded as his "real feelings" were largely sadistic sexual fantasies about his female colleagues, particularly one woman there who, he thought, looked respectable enough but who, he imagined, was probably a hypocrite like himself. He used to masturbate in the office lavatory while evoking these fantasies and once, as had previously happened with his mother, just after he had been doing this, he emerged and encountered the very woman whom he had been raping in his mind. She was looking directly at him so that she seemed to look straight through him into his secret self and to see there what he had been doing to her. He was filled with panic. He now could no longer believe with any assurance that he could conceal his actions and his thoughts from other people. In particular, as he said, he could no longer feel confidence that his face would not "give him away." At the same time, he became frightened lest a smell of semen should betray him.

He was in this state when he entered the Army. He completed his service, however, without exhibiting outward signs of his inner distress. Indeed, he seems to have achieved an outward appearance of normality and a measure of freedom from anxiety. His sense of achieving this was most interesting and important. His apparent normality was the consequence of a deliberate intensification of the split between his inner "true" self and outer "false" self in a quite calculated way. This was expressed by a dream he had at that time. He was in a fast-moving car: he jumped off, hurting himself but not seriously, while the car went on to crash. He thus took to the logical but disastrous conclusion the game that he had been playing with himself for some while. *He finally opted out as completely as he knew how: he dissociated himself both from himself and from other people.* The immediate effect of this was to lessen his anxiety and to allow him to appear normal. But this was not all he did and these were not the only consequences.

His sense of pointlessness, of lack of direction, of futility, was enhanced, as was his conviction that he was nobody "really." He felt that it was pointless to pretend any more. He formulated this to himself in these words: "I am nobody, so I'll do nothing." He was now bent not only on dissociating himself from his false self but on destroying everything he seemed to be. "I derived," as he said, "a certain sardonic satisfaction out of becoming even less than I had thought I was or they had thought me to be. . . ."

He had all along felt that he was, in his own words, . . . "on the fringe of being," with only one foot in life and with no right even to that. He felt that he was not really alive and that anyway he was of no value and had hardly the right to the pretension of having life. He imagined himself to be outside it all, yet he cherished for a while one shred of hope. Women might still have the secret. If he could somehow be loved by a woman, then he felt he might be able to overcome his sense of worthlessness. But this possible avenue was blocked for him by his conviction that any woman who had anything to do with him could only be as empty as he was, and that anything that he might be able to get from women, whether he took it or whether they gave it to him, could only be as worthless as the stuff of which he himself was made. Any woman who was not as futile as he was could, therefore, never have anything to do with him, least of all in a sexual sense. All his actual sexual relationships with women were entirely promiscuous and through them he was never able to break through his "shut-upness." With the one girl whom he regarded as "pure," he maintained a tenuous and platonic relationship for some years. But he was unable to translate his relationship with this girl into anything more than this . . . (Laing, 1969, pp. 129–35).

From the standard psychiatric point of view, Peter's symptom—his complaint that an unpleasant smell was coming from his genitals—was probably an hallucination and a sign of schizophrenia. We could continue in a psychoanalytic vein and make much of several items in his case history. He slept in the same room as his parents for the first ten years of his life. This might suggest Oedipal problems, the trauma of witnessing sexual intercourse between his parents, and thus be connected to his current inability to form a close relationship with a woman, his preoccupation with the smell of his genitals, and his general sense of guilt. Since all of these psychodynamics are unconscious, we would not expect Peter to be aware of them. We would arrive at these conclusions through interpretations based on some variant of psychoanalytic theory. Trying to understand Peter via any other psychiatric theory would proceed in the same way. We would take the overt facts of his behavior and his case history, insert them into some theoretical scheme, and come up with a conclusion as to what was bothering him. The terms of the theory would be abstract (such as ego, superego, and id) and have nothing to do with Peter as Peter experienced himself.

Trying to understand Peter from the existential-phenomenological framework, Laing used Peter's own experience of himself and his world. The important facts are that Peter was not wanted by his parents, so they treated him as though he wasn't there; therefore he experienced himself as not deserving to exist. This feeling was reinforced by his father who called him "useless Eustace" and "a big lump of dough." Since he was ignored, he experienced himself as being "nobody"—that is, having no body—as not really being there. His only tactic for being accepted was to behave in the ways he thought others expected him to behave. He could not be himself, but must try to present to others the self that they expected him to be. The discrepancy between his real self and the self he presented to the world became crystallized in secondary school, where his family saw him as a credit to them and his teacher saw him as a paragon, while he saw himself as a worthless nobody. To complicate his earlier feelings of having no body, he was now agitated by sexual feelings that intruded and impelled him either to masturbate or to have sexual intercourse with promiscuous girls. This behavior was at variance with his public reputation, and the sexual feelings themselves—that is, the sensations of his own body whose real existence he could not grant—were alien to his real self. Peter's real self was split from the false self other people saw. Further, his real self was split from his body.

This analysis of Peter's problem was based on Peter's experience of himself in the world and illustrates Laing's analysis of the process of schizophrenia. The schizophrenic keeps his real self split off from other people and from the world, in order to protect it from being overwhelmed and/or destroyed by the world. To protect the real self the schizophrenic presents a false self. So the schizophrenic is, in a sense, a phony putting on an act—an act that is a desperate attempt at self-preservation. The schizophrenic is also split off from his own body. He relates to his body as he relates to the world—as a foreign body that is not himself. Laing illustrates it thus: For the normal the experience is self/body—world; but for the schizophrenic the experience is self—body/world.

The Self in Relationship to Others

There are two aspects to note about the discussion of Peter. The first is that Peter's "schizophrenia" was analyzed from the point of view of Peter's own experience. This illustrates the existential-phenomenological approach to the problem. The second is that Peter's problem had its roots in the discrepancy between his experience of himself (his real self) and the self he presented to other people, and that this discrepancy developed because of Peter's early relationship to his family. He was treated as a nobody, so he felt like a nobody who had no right to be his real self; therefore he had to present to other people the self he thought they wanted him to be.

The self grows out of our relationship to others and, in part, is created and defined by the other people to whom we relate. As my self is created and developed by the selves of those people with whom I associate, so their selves are created and developed, in part, by my self. The study of interpersonal relationships, from this point of view, is the study of what happens when the selves of two people interact; or in other words, it is the existential-phenomenological study of the process and praxis of interacting selves.

"Process" and "praxis" are terms Laing (1964, p. 8) borrows from Jean-Paul Sartre. *Process* refers to events that are the outcome of the on-going interaction between people, while *praxis* refers to events that are the result of an intentional action by a person. Process refers to what happens as a consequence of what has been going on, while praxis is a deed done by a doer.

The importance of other people to the developing self was forcefully brought home to me, before I had encountered Laing's writing, by a man I was counseling who was agitated and depressed. His main problem, as he saw it, was figuring out who he was. He said that he could not be sure of himself until and unless he had a relationship with another person who saw in him aspects of his self that he could recognize. Unless he had a relationship with another who saw himself as he saw himself, it was as though his self did not really exist. His life was a search for people who would confirm him. If other people did not corroborate what he was in himself, then he was uncertain about his own existence.

The idea of the self being a function of the reaction of others to us is not new. Cooley's concept of the "looking-glass self" was introduced almost three-quarters of a century ago (see Chapter 1). But Laing has developed a concept of the self as an integral part of the interpersonal relationship that is an extension of the original idea of self as a function of others' reactions to it; this extension provides a system for analyzing and studying the interpersonal relationship, and also for understanding phenomena such as the schizophrenic experience.

Laing believes that to understand the dyad, it is necessary to study the dyad at the level of the dyad, rather than at the level of the individual person within the dyad. The dyad is not one person interacting with another person; it is a process going on between two people. What goes on between any two people is different from what would go on "between" either person of the dyad by himself, or between one person of that dyad and a different person. I am one person when I am by myself; I am another person when I am alone with my wife; I am still another person when I am alone with my father; I am a still different person when I am alone with my friend, Don. What makes the difference? The difference is made by the different ingredients. There is a part of myself that remains much the same from one situation to another. I have a sense of continuity—that is, I am still myself from one situation to another—but still I am not quite the same person in each situation. I don't behave in quite the same way. There are words and phrases that I use with my wife, and that carry a great deal of meaning to her, which would be meaningless to Don—or perhaps worse, would carry an unintended meaning to Don. And if I kissed Don on the nose, he would be both surprised and mildly frightened. So I am not quite the same person in each situation. And the others to whom I relate are also not the same with me as they are with the other people in their lives.

The paragraph above illustrates the nature of the situation to be studied—two selves interacting—and suggests the basic elements to be studied: the self of each of the members of the dyad.

In a dyad, then, there are two selves. In a dyad of which I am a part there are two selves: my self and the other person's self. I perceive my self. The other person perceives his self. I perceive the other person's self. The other person perceives my self. I perceive the other person perceiving my self, and the other perceives me perceiving his self. That is, I have an idea of what he thinks of me, and he has an idea of what I think of him. These perceptions provide the basis of the interpersonal interaction.

Laing takes it as axiomatic that behavior is a function of experience, and that experience and behavior are in relation to someone or something other than the self. The way we experience another is a function of our past experience, and the way he experiences us is a function of his past experience. What the other person considers in himself to be courage, we may see as foolish impetuosity, and what we see in ourselves as prudence, he may consider cowardice. If I pat my teen-age daughter on the back, intending to convey affectionate concern at a moment when she is agitated about a difficult algebra problem, she might interpret my gesture as a kind of kidding condescension and derision. The reason her interpretation might be such would be that, feeling inadequate herself, she would expect me to see her as she sees herself—as inadequate.

So the interaction between two people is a function of the way they perceive themselves, the way they perceive the other person, and the way they see the other person perceiving them. Our perceptions are a function of our past experience with other people; they affect the way we react to them.

Some behavioral interactions are prescribed by the society we live in and are called roles. To be a particular kind of person, it is necessary to have another person who helps us play the role. If I want to see myself as a father figure, I must have some cooperation from my children or students, who will play the child to my father.

The necessity of another person to the self, if the self is to be the self it wants to be, is clearly illustrated by roles, but the necessity of the other is basic, regardless of roles. We each have a "basic human need to make a difference to another person" (Laing, 1962, p. 73). Our own identities—what we think our selves are—depend, in part, on what other people think of us. Therefore, to confirm ourselves, we tend to seek out other people who will see us as we see ourselves. The view we have of ourselves Laing terms (as do many others) "identity," and what we think others think of us he calls "metaidentity." We seek to bring the two into harmony."I therefore tend to select others for whom I can be the other that I wish to be, so that I may then reappropriate the sort of metaidentity I want" (Laing, Phillipson, & Lee, 1966, p. 15).

Because what others think of us is important to us and affects the way we look at ourselves, one of the most powerful ways another person can affect us is to tell us what he thinks of us; and one of the most powerful ways we can affect another person is to tell him what we think of him. Since we tend to seek out other people who confirm our own view of ourselves, one of the most powerful devices we have for attracting another person is to tell him we think of him what he would like to have us think of him—and which, incidentally, he would also like to think of himself—which is a complex way of saying that appropriate flattery is powerful.

Obviously, honest, open communications between two people, in which there is agreement on their views of themselves and of each other, make for good relationships. But in the harsh realities of life such happy events don't always happen, so we try to make them happy anyway. We pretend in order to keep things happy. Two pretending devices are called "elusion" and "collusion."

Elusion is when we pretend to be something that we really are. Laing (1962, p. 28) suggests the following exercise for eliciting the experience of elusion:

1. You are sitting in a room.
2. Now, pretend that you are not sitting in the room, but sitting someplace else—on the beach, or in a park.
3. Now, while you are, in your mind's eye, in the park, pretend that you are sitting in a room.
4. Now you end up, not experiencing yourself sitting in a room (which is what you are really doing), but rather experiencing yourself *pretending* you are sitting in a room.

Through the device of elusion we are pretending we are doing what we *actually* are doing, so we have subtly removed ourselves from experiencing the real situation. In this way we are not quite real, and not quite experiencing the situation we really are in. This is a maneuver that makes us a little false, less than our true selves, and sneaks up on us rather easily. I think, in my own experience, that I am most aware of elusion when marching in an academic procession. I *really* am a professor, but when I am marching slowly in an academic procession, with stately tread and academic robes and hood, I feel slightly false—as though I were playing a part, when in fact what I am "playing" is what I really am.

Collusion is the more serious of pretenses, since it is an act carried out by both members of a dyad to preserve the illusion of a particular kind of relationship. Collusion occurs when two people cooperatively delude each other. In collusion one member plays the identity he would like to assume, and the other partner cooperates in supporting the deception. Jean Genet's play, *The Balcony*, illustrates this process. *The Balcony* is set in a brothel where the customers play any role they like, and the prostitutes accept and play the complement to the customer's role. Collusive dyads tend to be unstable.

Collusion is a case of one member of a dyad confirming the other member's illusions about himself. If a person interacted with only one other person who supported the collusive dyad, he might live a long and happy deluded life. But we all require confirmation of our conception of ourselves from other people, too, and it will be quite probable that the delusions a person holds in a collusive dyad will be disconfirmed in his interactions with others. Laing sees the lack of confirmation as the chief factor in the development of schizophrenia. That is, the family of the schizophrenic either confirms nothing about him or disconfirms his own developing conception of himself. Laing concludes that "what the schizophrenic requires of us, as much as anything, is uncorrupted spontaneity and honesty (1962, p. 97).

One member of the dyad can induce insanity in the other, and the basic tactic is to produce confusion. Laing (1962, p. 131) lists six basic ways one person can drive another person crazy:

1. One person repeatedly calls the attention of the other to areas of the other's personality of which the other is only dimly aware, and which are at variance with the other's view of himself.
2. One person stimulates the other sexually in a situation in which it would be disastrous for the other to seek satisfaction.
3. One person simultaneously exposes the other to stimulation and frustration.
4. One person relates to the other simultaneously on two unrelated levels (e.g., intellectually and sexually).
5. One person switches from one emotional wavelength to another while on the same topic (e.g., from being serious to being funny).
6. One person switches from one topic to another while remaining on the same emotional wavelength (e.g., from discussing life-and-death matters to discussing trivia in the same emotional vein).

For one person to produce psychosis in the other, the essential ingredient is confusion, and in this respect Laing enunciates a principle similar to the principle of the "double bind," in which one person communicates to the other, simultaneously, two contradictory messages.

However, it should be mentioned here that the above six ways will be successful only if the person ("victim") has no other people to whom he refers for consensual validation or if he relies heavily on the validation of the person confusing him. The requirement is that the person who is driving the other crazy is in an intimate relationship, and that there is no other, competing relationship that is so intimate or so important to the one being driven crazy.

The Interpersonal Perception Method

Although the dyad starts out with two simple elements, two selves, the interaction between the two quickly escalates into a complex and confusing phenomenon. As a way of systematizing and analyzing the dyadic interaction, Laing et al. (1966) developed the Interpersonal Perception Method. This section describes the method and presents some examples of its use.

For the purpose of this illustration we will use the relationship between a husband (H) and wife (W).

The husband has a view of himself.	$H \rightarrow H$
The husband has a view of his wife.	$H \rightarrow W$
The wife has a view of herself.	$W \rightarrow W$
The wife has a view of her husband.	$W \rightarrow H$

The above views are called direct perspectives. However, since we are studying relationships, the symbols are changed slightly to represent relationships. The symbol for the husband's relationship to himself is (HH), and the symbol for the husband's relationship to his wife is (HW), and so on. Since the approach is phenomenological, the view of these relationships that is examined is the relationship as it is experienced by the persons involved in the relationship. Therefore, the data that are studied are not the relationships themselves, but the relationships as viewed by the participants in them. Thus the direct perspectives on the relationship would not be the husband's relationship with himself, (HH), but rather the husband's view of his relationship with himself, $H \rightarrow (HH)$.

For the husband-wife relationship, there are four phases. These phases are:

1. Husband's relationship with himself.   (HH)
2. Husband's relationship with wife.   (HW)
3. Wife's relationship with herself.   (WW)
4. Wife's relationship with husband.   (WH)

Each person in the dyad has a view of each one of these phases. This view is the person's direct perspective on the relationship. Since there are two persons involved in the relationship and each has a view of the four phases of the relationship, there are eight elements of the direct perspective. These eight elements are:

1.	Husband's view of his relationship with himself.	$H \rightarrow (HH)$
2.	Husband's view of his relationship with wife.	$H \rightarrow (HW)$
3.	Husband's view of wife's relationship with herself.	$H \rightarrow (WW)$
4.	Husband's view of wife's relationship with husband.	$H \rightarrow (WH)$
5.	Wife's view of husband's relationship with himself.	$W \rightarrow (HH)$
6.	Wife's view of husband's relationship with wife.	$W \rightarrow (HW)$
7.	Wife's view of her relationship with herself.	$W \rightarrow (WW)$
8.	Wife's view of her relationship with husband.	$W \rightarrow (WH)$

These eight different direct perspectives can be diagrammed as follows:

$$H \rightarrow (HH) \leftarrow W$$
$$H \rightarrow (HW) \leftarrow W$$
$$H \rightarrow (WW) \leftarrow W$$
$$H \rightarrow (WH) \leftarrow W$$

In addition to the direct perspective, there are two other levels of perspective that are included in Laing's scheme. These are the *meta-perspective* and the *meta-metaperspective*. An example of the meta-perspective is the husband's view of the wife's view of the husband's relationship with himself. The meta-metaperspective adds one more layer to the cake. A meta-metaperspective would be the wife's view of the husband's view of her view of his relationship with himself. The following example illustrates the relationship among the various perspectives:

Direct Perspective:	$H \rightarrow (HH)$	Husband's view of his relationship with himself.
Metaperspective:	$W \rightarrow H \rightarrow (HH)$	Wife's view of husband's view of his relationship with himself.
Meta-metaperspective:	$H \rightarrow W \rightarrow H \rightarrow (HH)$	Husband's view of wife's view of husband's view of his relationship with himself.

The direct perspective is easy to see, but as we add additional levels of perspective, the whole thing becomes difficult to follow. Therefore, let's try to illustrate it in still another way. America has a view of France. That's direct perspective. France has a view of America. That's also direct perspective. Now there is a journal entitled *Atlas* that reprints for an American audience articles from foreign journals. Some of these articles are about America. The content of one of these articles, let us say an article from a French journal, would contain a French view of America. That would be direct perspective. I, an American, read the article and gain an American view of the French view of America. That is metaperspective. Now I write an article for a journal in which I describe what I learned from the article in the French journal. That is, I write my view of the French view of America. This is metaperspective. Now a Frenchman reads my article, so that he gets his own view of my view of the French view of America. That's meta-metaperspective.

Let us try still another example. I feel good about myself as a teacher. That is direct perspective. My wife knows that I feel I am a good teacher. That is metaperspective. I know that my wife knows that I think I am a good teacher. That is meta-metaperspective.

The metaperspective and the meta-metaperspective can be represented in the following fashion, using the same basic scheme that we used to represent direct perspective:

Metaperspective: $W \rightarrow H \rightarrow (HH) \leftarrow W \leftarrow H$
$W \rightarrow H \rightarrow (HW) \leftarrow W \leftarrow H$
$W \rightarrow H \rightarrow (WW) \leftarrow W \leftarrow H$
$W \rightarrow H \rightarrow (WH) \leftarrow W \leftarrow H$

Meta-metaperspective: $H \rightarrow W \rightarrow H \rightarrow (HH) \leftarrow W \leftarrow H \leftarrow W$
$H \rightarrow W \rightarrow H \rightarrow (HW) \leftarrow W \leftarrow H \leftarrow W$
$H \rightarrow W \rightarrow H \rightarrow (WW) \leftarrow W \leftarrow H \leftarrow W$
$H \rightarrow W \rightarrow H \rightarrow (WH) \leftarrow W \leftarrow H \leftarrow W$

This game of added levels could go on forever, and in reality it probably does approach infinity (particularly as these views are reflected in the views of other people), but for the purpose of studying a particular dyadic relationship, it is necessary to stop somewhere, and it is at this point that Laing stops.

The meta-metaperspective level gives us what Laing describes as "a spiral of reciprocal perspectives carried to third-level perspectives on both sides" (1966, p. 59). The different perspectives on these three levels may be compared to obtain information about a relationship. The direct view of one person may be compared with the direct view of the other person to determine if they *agree* or *disagree*. If $H \rightarrow (HH) = W \rightarrow (HH)$, then they agree; if not, they disagree.

If one person is aware of the other person's point of view, then the first person *understands* the second; if not, he misunderstands. Understanding and misunderstanding involve comparing the meta-perspective of one person with the direct perspective of the other person. That is, if the wife understands the husband, then $W \rightarrow H \rightarrow (HH) = H \rightarrow (HH)$, and if the wife's metaperspective does not equal the husband's direct perspective, she misunderstands.

If one person thinks that the other person has the same view of his relationship to himself as he has of his own relationship with himself, then he *feels understood*. That is, if a person's direct perspective agrees with his own meta-metaperspective, then he feels understood, otherwise he *feels misunderstood*. This has nothing to do with the accuracy of the perception of the first person. He may correctly or incorrectly feel understood or misunderstood. The feeling of being understood or misunderstood involves the comparison of one person's direct perspective with that same person's meta-metaperspective. That is, if $H \rightarrow (HH) = H \rightarrow W \rightarrow H \rightarrow (HH)$ the person *feels understood,* otherwise he feels misunderstood.

If the first person understands the second person (that is, the first person's metaperspective equals the second person's direct perspective), and the second person *realizes* that the first person understands him, then the first person's metaperspective equals the second person's meta-metaperspective. If the husband realizes that his wife understands him, then $W \rightarrow H \rightarrow (HH) = H \rightarrow W \rightarrow H \rightarrow (HH)$. If the metaperspective of the one does not equal the meta-metaperspective of the other, there is a *failure of realization*.

To recapitulate, there are three levels of perspective:

1. Direct perspective: $\qquad\qquad\qquad$ $H \rightarrow (HH) \leftarrow W$
2. Metaperspective: $\qquad\qquad\quad$ $W \rightarrow H \rightarrow (HH) \leftarrow W \leftarrow H$
3. Meta-metaperspective: $\quad$ $H \rightarrow W \rightarrow H \rightarrow (HH) \leftarrow W \leftarrow H \leftarrow W$

And there are four kinds of comparison which are useful in understanding the interpersonal relationship:

1. Agreement: $\qquad\qquad\qquad\qquad$ $H \rightarrow (HH) = W \rightarrow (HH)$
   or disagreement: $\qquad\qquad\quad$ $H \rightarrow (HH) \neq W \rightarrow (HH)$
2. Understanding: $\qquad\qquad\qquad$ $W \rightarrow H \rightarrow (HH) = H \rightarrow (HH)$
   or misunderstanding: $\qquad\quad$ $W \rightarrow H \rightarrow (HH) \neq H \rightarrow (HH)$
3. Feeling understood: $\qquad\qquad$ $H \rightarrow (HH) = H \rightarrow W \rightarrow H \rightarrow (HH)$
   or feeling misunderstood: $\quad$ $H \rightarrow (HH) \neq H \rightarrow W \rightarrow H \rightarrow (HH)$
4. Realization
   of understanding: $\qquad$ $W \rightarrow H \rightarrow (HH) = H \rightarrow W \rightarrow H \rightarrow (HH)$
   or of failure
   of realization: $\qquad\quad$ $W \rightarrow H \rightarrow (HH) \neq H \rightarrow W \rightarrow H \rightarrow (HH)$

It should be noted for the fourth item, realization, that if the me-taperspective of the one person agrees with the meta-metaperspective of the other person, then there is realization of understanding. How-ever, if the metaperspective of the one does *not* agree with the meta-metaperspective of the other person, it is possible for the person to feel understood, when in fact he is not understood. To determine this, it is necessary to compare all three levels.

The basic scheme of the entire Interpersonal Perception Method of studying dyads may be schematically represented as follows:

Meta-meta		*Meta*		*Direct*				*Direct*		*Meta*		*Meta-meta*
3		2		1		(X)		1		2		3
H	→	W	→	H	→	(HH)	←	W	←	H	←	W
H	→	W	→	H	→	(HW)	←	W	←	H	←	W
H	→	W	→	H	→	(WW)	←	W	←	H	←	W
H	→	W	→	H	→	(WH)	←	W	←	H	←	W

In comparing these various levels, there are several possibilities in the spiral of the interaction. There may be (1) agreement or disagreement; (2) understanding or misunderstanding; (3) understanding and a reali-zation of understanding; (4) understanding and a failure to realize un-derstanding; (5) misunderstanding and a realization of misunderstand-ing; or (6) misunderstanding and a failure to realize misunderstanding.

An analysis of the spiral may be represented by a series of sym-bols used for the various relationships:

A = agreement
D = disagreement
U = understanding
M = misunderstanding
R = realization
F = failure of realization

If we took the schematization of the spiral H W H (X) W H W and compared the three levels in order, starting with the first level which tells us whether the two agree or disagree, we would get several repre-sentations. For example, R U A U R would tell us that the husband and wife agree on the relationship, that each understands the other on that relationship, and that each realizes that he is understood. Or, for anoth-er example, F U A M R would indicate that they agree, that the hus-band understands but the wife fails to understand, that the husband fails to realize that he is misunderstood but the wife realizes that she is understood.

This rather complex scheme of comparison is applied to each of the four relationships: the husband's relationship to himself, the husband's relationship to the wife, the wife's relationship to herself, and the wife's relationship to the husband. In the scale Laing has developed for studying the interpersonal perception of the members of the dyad, he studies the perceptions of the pairs in six areas: (1) interdependence and autonomy; (2) warm concern and support; (3) disparagement and disappointment; (4) contentions: fight/flight; (5) contradictions and confusion; and (6) extreme denial of autonomy.

Laing illustrated the usefulness of the system for studying the interpersonal relationship with two studies, one a comparison of disturbed married couples with nondisturbed married couples, and the other a case study of a single married couple.

In the first study, Laing et al. (1966, pp. 73–91) compared twelve disturbed married couples with ten nondisturbed married couples and found that the nondisturbed couples agreed on more of the items on the scale, understood on more items, and had realization of understanding on more of the items than did the disturbed couples. They found that the agreement was higher for all couples on the items having to do with their relationship with each other (HW and WH items) than it was for the items having to do with their relationship with themselves (HH and WW items). Understanding and the realization of understanding was more frequent on items on which each couple agreed than on items on which they disagreed. (One must keep in mind, though, that people are more aware of being in agreement than they are aware of being in disagreement.) Laing concluded that "To be in disagreement, to recognize the disagreement, to be misunderstood and to realize that one is misunderstood is presumably the most exacting of unilateral accomplishments" (p. 86).

In the second study (Laing et al., 1966, pp. 92–130), this method of analyzing the dyad is illustrated in the case of a married couple, Mr. and Mrs. Jones. They had been married ten years and had four children, all boys. Mrs. Jones sought help for their marriage because her husband was "greedy, lacked consideration, and had a violent temper." Although disagreements between them were frequent, the crisis was precipitated when Mr. Jones took a short business trip and stayed away from home overnight without informing his wife. Mrs. Jones assumed he had slept with another woman, so she withdrew from their bedroom. When Mr. Jones failed to try to reestablish their former sleeping arrangement, Mrs. Jones felt that her suspicion was confirmed.

Mrs. Jones came from a working-class family, whereas Mr. Jones came from a middle-class family. Mrs. Jones felt that Mr. Jones' family belittled her, and that Mr. Jones spent too much money and time on the purchase and upkeep of a house and not enough on the entertainment of her and the children. Mrs. Jones also felt that Mr. Jones was critical of the way she ran the house.

In individual therapy interviews with the Joneses, it became apparent that Mrs. Jones felt that she was the "giver" in the family and that Mr. Jones had no real interest in her and the children. It became apparent, however, that she could not really give very much to Mr. Jones for fear he would gain control over her. It also became apparent that the more Mrs. Jones gave things to the children and fussed over them, the more Mr. Jones withdrew from the children because he felt there was nothing he could give.

Mr. Jones appeared surprised at all of the things Mrs. Jones was concerned about. He had not noticed incidents she complained about, and he protested that she was touchy, while he was more detached. He had no complaints about his wife, but he did express anger at his wife's continual demands for attention and consideration. He also resented her apparent lack of concern for him and for what he did for the family. He also felt she was too indulgent with the children.

The Interpersonal Perception Method analysis of the interaction between Mr. and Mrs. Jones revealed that Mrs. Jones generally had a higher understanding (U) than her husband over all areas of their relationship. The lowest agreement (A), and therefore highest disagreement (D), between the two came in how the husband saw his relationship to his wife (HW). It was in the area of the way the husband saw his relationship to his wife that the discrepancy between the understanding of Mr. Jones and Mrs. Jones was the greatest, with Mrs. Jones having the greater understanding.

After the Joneses had had some marriage counseling, the case was again analyzed by this method. The second analysis indicated that overall understanding (U) and realization of understanding (R) had increased, even though there was not much change from disagreement (D) to agreement (A). The agreement between the metaperspectives and meta-metaperspectives of the pair had increased, even though there was little improvement in their agreement on the level of the direct perspective.

Laing summarized the results, writing "that in spite of the persistence of a large measure of more surface disagreement, both partners have increased their awareness of the attitudes and responses of the other and are able to work on their disagreements more effectively at those levels of perspective that help to cement their experience as a dyad" (1966, p. 125).

This analysis is particularly interesting because it demonstrates, with a quantitative method, a phenomenon often noted in marriage relationships; that is, that although the overt disagreement between a couple does not change, or even increases, the relationship improves because they are relating to each other more realistically. They are relating to each other as they really are, rather than relating to the false images they have of each other.

The Interpersonal Perception Method is a promising tool for analyzing interaction in intimate, permanent dyads. For troubled dyads (e.g., miserable married couples) it appears useful for identifying the sources of stress.

Discussion

The most obviously unique contribution Laing's existential phenomenology makes is that it contributes a different dimension to the study of the interpersonal relationship. That dimension is the experiences of the people in a relationship.

In adding this dimension, however, Laing does more than merely add more kinds of data to the data others have accumulated. He really tries to found a new science, bringing within the domain of study a whole range of phenomena that have been either left out or left on the fringe of psychology. Laing promotes a science of persons — not a science of behavior or a science of the mind — and a science of persons must study persons. For Laing the person may be defined in two ways. In terms of experience, the person is the center of orientation; in terms of behavior, the person is the initiator, or origin of actions. Persons must not be studied as objects, but as persons. This means that researchers must study persons not as inert, physical objects, but rather as experiencing beings; in behavior this means studying their behavior not as reactions to stimuli, but as actions initiated by the persons. What Laing proposes is a science of people as people actually experience their own existence — a science that studies people where people really live.

When studying people where they really live, we are faced with phenomena that have had little or no respectable place within the behavioral sciences. People itch; they perspire and feel the sweat run down into and burn their eyes; they hope; they fear; they have experiences of being at one with the infinite; they forget simple and immediate things but remember remote and complex experiences. People don't experience life the way psychology texts describe it. Therefore a science of persons introduces for study troublesome phenomena that the behavioral scientists of a generation ago thought they had eliminated. Laing drags old issues back into psychology.

Bringing back old issues, preferably labeled with new names, is often a successful path to fame. But Laing has reintroduced old issues because they could not be dismissed by fiat. An older generation of behavioral scientists might dismiss them and then proceed to act as though they no longer existed, but as Feigl (1959) has pointed out, such issues don't disappear — they are merely repressed — and like all repressions they return in new guise to cause problems. Laing has dragged them out into the open and has done it in the nexus of what seems to many to be the essence of the human phenomenon: the inter-personal relationship.

Laing seeks to study persons—the essence of human beings—and for him the ground of all beings is the relationship between them. "Behavior is a function of experience; and both experience and behavior are always in relation to someone or something other than self" (1967, p. 9). He tries to understand and develop a science that encom-passes the relationship between experience and behavior.

A science of persons that attempts to understand and describe the relationship between experience and behavior opens up for study the vast realm of human experience, and perhaps more importantly, raises questions about the experiences to which people no longer seem open. This means studying, in all seriousness and reverence, those ex-treme kinds of experience that in times past have been taken to have profound significance for people, but in the modern era have been dis-missed as psychopathological phenomena. This means studying, from the point of view of the experiencer, psychosis, religious experience, mystical experience, and so on.

In *The Politics of Experience,* Laing argues that we of today are cut off from much of our own experience—it has been suppressed and repressed so that we scarcely can believe that we had it—and thus we are cut off from much of ourselves. If our experiences are destroyed, then we are destroyed. And if our experience is destroyed, then we will be destructive. Thus we must be reopened to our experiences from which we have been cut off.

In this insistence on the inclusion of experiential data as central to the study of persons, Laing is pushing for the inclusion of kinds of data that have often been excluded from the study of the interpersonal relationship. But Laing is doing more than that. He is placing experien-tial data in the central position—these are primary data, and behavioral data are secondary. However, in doing this he has powerful support from other sources. Percy Bridgman (1961) and Michael Polanyi (1959; 1962; 1966), philosophers of science and scientists of eminence, have argued persuasively that knowledge is essentially personal—that is, it is an ac-tion and experience of persons—and that therefore science itself is basi-cally a personal enterprise.

There seem to me to be two basic shortcomings in Laing's ap-proach, which result in a very small data base. First, Laing has obtained all of his data from the self-reports of the persons he has studied. Most of the data come from their reports on themselves in psychotherapy inter-views, while some data come from their reports on themselves as given in response to questionnaires. Of course, the emphasis Laing places up-on self-report data is dictated by his phenomenological approach. The only way you can find out what a person's experience is, is to ask him to report it. Thus, if you start with the assumption that the important data are the phenomenological, then you must use self-report data. Laing further argues that these are the important data because a psychology of persons must be based on data obtained at the level of the person. So this procedure is consistent with his argument, and there can be no argument with Laing doing what he set out to do. However, the value of his work would be enhanced if he could integrate the self-reports of the subjects with the actual behaviors of the subjects. That is, the emphasis could continue to be on the experiences of the subjects, which are derived from their self-reports, but it would be strengthened by relating these experiences to what the subjects were observed doing at the time of reported experiences. The second shortcoming is that Laing has obtained his data from subjects who were either patients in psychotherapy or marriage counseling. No data were obtained from normal people—clerks, lawyers, teen-agers, and so on. That is, Laing based his theory on a small data base: (1) small because he only uses self-report data, and (2) small because he has only one kind of subject—clients in either psychotherapy or marriage counseling.

The level from which Laing obtained his data is the level of the person. Essentially, Laing analyzes the individual experience of the two people involved in an interaction and relates this to the quality of the interaction, or the satisfaction of each of the people involved in the interaction. There is no extensive description of patterns of interaction. Although Laing discusses process and praxis (which are phenomena occurring at the level of the dyad), he does not develop, or has not yet developed, this theme. His view is not that of the interpersonal interaction itself, but rather a view of the interpersonal interaction as it is experienced by the individual people involved in the interaction.

As a theory, Laing's is really the outline for the development of a more extensive theory. When one reads Laing in conjunction with reading Sullivan, one is struck by the many similarities and communalities between their two theories. For example, both maintain that the person or self only exists in interaction with other selves; that schizophrenics are schizophrenic because of their interaction with other people, and that by changing the interaction, you change the schizophrenia; that abnormal behavior is a consequence of abnormal relationships with other people. The most obvious differences between them are that Laing emphasizes the experience of the individual in the interaction, while Sullivan does not, and that Sullivan goes into much greater depth and breadth in his theory, while Laing does not. Laing has made a contribution, but it is not of the same level as that of Sullivan. However, Sullivan's contribution has been made, while Laing's is still in process. By emphasizing the importance of the experience of the person involved in the interpersonal interaction and by developing methods for assessing that experience, Laing is making a contribution that is unique.

Summary

Laing was stimulated to study the schizophrenic by his failure to observe the same symptoms that other psychiatrists had reported. He concluded that schizophrenic symptoms were a function of the schizophrenic interacting with a particular kind of psychiatrist.

He concluded that the schizophrenic was split off from other people, that he had a real self which was split off from the public self he presented to others, and that he was split off from his own body.

Laing feels that it is necessary to study the person from the point of view of the person's experience, and that the most important part of his experience is his interaction with other people. People do not exist as separate entities, but in interaction with other selves.

He developed a method for measuring the interpersonal relationship which includes the person's view of his relationship to himself, the other person's relationship to himself, his own relationship to the other, and the other's relationship to him. These relationships can be viewed directly, or from direct perspective, metaperspective, and meta-metaperspective. The direct perspective is the person's view of himself or the other, the metaperspective is the person's view of the other's view of himself, and the meta-metaperspective is the person's view of the other's view of himself. Combining these various perspectives makes it possible to measure the agreement between a pair, the understanding between them, and the realization of understanding between them. Laing has found that happily married couples have more agreement, more understanding, and more realization of understanding than unhappy couples.

References

Bridgman, P. W. *The way things are.* New York: Viking Press, 1961.

Feigl, H. Philosophical embarrassments in psychology. *American Psychologist*, 1959, 14, pp. 115–28.

Koch, S. Psychology and emerging conceptions of knowledge as unitary. In T. W. Wann (Ed.), *Behaviorism and phenomenology.* Chicago: University of Chicago Press, 1965.

Laing, R. D. *The self and others.* Chicago: Quadrangle Press, 1962.

Laing, R. D. *Reason and violence.* New York: Humanities Press, 1964.

Laing, R. D. *The divided self.* New York: Pantheon Books, 1969.

Laing, R. D. *The politics of experience.* New York: Pantheon Books, 1967.

Laing, R. D., Phillipson, H., and Lee, A. R. *Interpersonal perception.* New York: Springer, 1966.

MacLeod, R. B. Phenomenology: A challenge to experimental psychology. In T. W. Wann (Ed.), *Behaviorism and phenomenology.* Chicago: University of Chicago Press, 1965.

May, R., Angel, E., & Ellenberg, H. S. *Existence: a new dimension in psychiatry & psychology.* New York: Basic Books, 1958.

Polanyi, M. *The study of man.* Chicago: University of Chicago Press, 1959.

Polanyi, M. *Personal knowledge.* New York: Harper & Row, 1962.

Polanyi, M. *The tacit dimension.* New York: Doubleday, 1966.

Additional Sources

Laing, R. D. Mystification, confusion and conflict. In I. Boszormenyi-Nagy & J. L. Framo (Eds.), *Intensive family therapy.* New York: Harper & Row, 1965.

Laing, R. D. Family and individual structure. In P. Loman (Ed.), *Psychoanalytic approaches to the family.* London: Hogarth Press, 1966.

Laing, R. D., & Esterson, A. *Sanity, madness and the family.* New York: Basic Books, 1964.

Psychological Measurement and Interpersonal Behavior

7

Measurement of interpersonal behavior requires a broad collection of simple, specific variables which are systematically related to each other, and which are applicable to the study of adjustive or maladjustive responses. (1957, p. 39).

—Timothy Leary

Measurement has a long history in psychology and the social sciences which can be traced back to Alfred Binet and his desire to measure intelligence, and beyond Binet to Sir Francis Galton and his attempts to study genius. The approach to the study of interpersonal behavior described in this chapter is a lineal descendant of the work of both men.

Once social scientists had developed measurement methods that seemed to have some value, it was only a matter of time until these methods would be applied to a wide variety of matters of interest to the social scientist, and among these matters is the study of the interpersonal relationship. The process of the study of the interpersonal relationship can be viewed just as Timothy Leary described it in the quote at the beginning of the chapter. It is a matter of determining which specific variables will be measured, devising reliable methods of measuring these variables, and then determining the relationships among these variables. The impetus to this kind of approach to the interpersonal relationship might well be credited to Leary (1957), since he published the first technique to receive fairly general recognition for such measurement.

In this chapter two psychometrically derived theories of the interpersonal relationship will be described. The first is that developed by Uriel G. Foa. Foa analyzes the interpersonal relationship using a psychometric method of fairly recent origin: facet analysis. This approach is derived directly from research on intelligence and its measurement. The second approach is that of Robert F. Bales; it was derived from the utilization of factor analysis, a method of analysis developed originally for research on intelligence. Bales' system was based on the study of individuals interacting in small groups. However, it will be apparent that his theoretical system is similar and related to other systems presented in this chapter.

Finally, one word of advance caution. Since this chapter describes approaches to the interpersonal relationship that developed out of the measurement tradition in psychology, the chapter must, of necessity, include reference to the psychometric techniques from which these views of the interpersonal relationship proceed. Psychometric techniques have, in recent years, become quite complex. To present the techniques in detail would require an additional book and would have to assume a certain amount of mathematical background on the part of the reader. Since I am not qualified to write that book (relatively few people really are) and since psychometrics is not the primary topic of this book, I shall attempt to give only a brief description of psychometric techniques and their intended use and purpose, leaving interested readers with the necessary references to pursue the matter further, if they so wish.

An Attempt to Encompass Converging Research on Interpersonal Behavior in a Single System: The Ringex

Foa (1961) wrote a paper entitled "Convergences in the Analysis of the Structure of Interpersonal Behavior." In this paper he described four different lines of research on the interpersonal relationship, noted the similarities of their results, and proposed a system which he felt explained those results. First, to more clearly present the development of Foa's thought, we will examine some of the research he reviewed in his paper.

Converging Lines
of Interpersonal Research

Timothy Leary and his co-workers at the Kaiser Foundation in California were interested in developing a system for classifying personality that would be more useful than the systems available at the time they began their research. Since they were working within the context of a psychiatric clinic and hospital, they were interested in developing a diagnostic scheme that would be useful in diagnosing psychiatric cases. Also, this setting provided many of the subjects they studied in developing their system.

They brought "several scores" of individuals into a small-group situation in which the people interacted with one another. These people included both males and females with neurotic problems, psychosomatic problems, and no problems at all. Some of the groups were psychotherapy groups, and some were ordinary discussion groups. The interactions were observed, recorded, and studied. Also, the subjects were asked to give verbal descriptions of themselves and other people. They contributed their autobiographies, fantasies, and dreams, and they answered a variety of psychological inventories.

After accumulating this large amount of data, Leary (1957, p. 64) studied it to see if some pattern emerged. He noticed that the descriptions given by the subjects seemed to be related in some way to either power or affiliation. The descriptions seemed to have four nodal points—*dominance, submission, hostility,* and *affection.* All of the descriptions seemed to reflect either one of these four kinds of interaction or some combination of two of these four kinds. Leary organized these four points into two dimensions, illustrating the two dimensions as lines at right angles to each other and forming the axes for a circle around which the various personality types could be arranged. The two axes were *dominance-submission* and *love-hate.* The personality types arrayed themselves in a circle around these two axes. This classification system is illustrated in Figure 1.

A totally different line of research conducted by Launor Carter (1954) produced similar results. Carter was primarily interested in determining the factors involved in leadership. He observed college men interacting in groups of four to eight men each. These men were involved in a variety of tasks, including a reasoning task, a mechanical assembly task, and a discussion. In some groups Carter allowed the leader to emerge during the interaction, while in other groups the leader was appointed. He had two judges observe each group and judge each member on nineteen different variables. These ratings were intercorrelated, and the correlation matrices were factor-analyzed. At this point we will make a brief detour to give a basic explanation of factor analysis.

FIGURE 1. **LEARY INTERPERSONAL BEHAVIOR CLASSIFICATION SYSTEM**

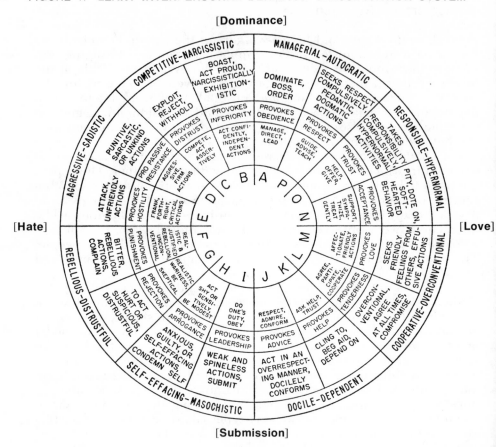

FIGURE 1. Classification of Interpersonal Behavior into Sixteen Mechanisms or Reflexes. Each of the sixteen interpersonal variables is illustrated by sample behaviors. The inner circle presents illustrations of adaptive reflexes, e.g., for the variable A, *manage*. The center ring indicates the type of behavior that this interpersonal reflex tends to "pull" from the other one. Thus we see that the person who uses the reflex A tends to provoke others to *obedience*, etc. These findings involve two-way interpersonal phenomena (what the subject does and what the "Other" does back) and are therefore less reliable than the other interpersonal codes presented in this figure. The next circle illustrates extreme or rigid reflexes, e.g., *dominates*. The perimeter of the circle is divided into eight general categories employed in *interpersonal diagnosis*. Each category has a moderate (adaptive) and an extreme (pathological) intensity, e.g., *Managerial-Autocratic*.

Adapted from T. Leary, *Interpersonal diagnosis of personality.* New York: The Ronald Press Company, 1957, p. 65. Copyright © 1957, The Ronald Press Company, New York, and reproduced by permission.

Factor Analysis

Factor analysis is a technique whereby the basic factors underlying a series of measures may be determined.[1] For example, suppose we were to take a series of measures of intelligence, or ability. Further, let us suppose that these measures included tests of the following abilities: (1) vocabulary, (2) grammar, (3) number of four-letter words beginning with the letter c that can be written in five minutes, (4) synonyms for a list of fifty words, (5) addition, (6) fractions, and (7) long division. Next, suppose that we gave this test to one hundred people and correlated their scores. The correlation coefficient[2] shows how highly two measures are related to each other and ranges from +1.00 to −1.00. A correlation of 1.00 would mean that the two measures were perfectly related to each other, a correlation of .00 would mean that there was no relationship at all between the two measures, and a correlation of −1.00 would mean that the two measures had a perfectly inverse relationship (when one went up, the other went down, or when a person received a high score on one, he would receive a low score on the other). Now, suppose that for the seven tests described above we obtained the correlations indicated in Table 1.

If we want to find the correlation between any two tests, we merely look down the column for the first test and find the cell in the table where that column intersects the row for the second test. For example, if we want to know the correlation between vocabulary (1) and synonyms (4), we simply look down column 1 for the cell where

TABLE 1. **HYPOTHETICAL CORRELATIONS BETWEEN SEVEN ABILITY MEASURES**

Test	1	2	3	4	5	6	7
1	1.00	.76	.93	.91	.32	.25	.24
2	.76	1.00	.79	.84	.24	.29	.30
3	.93	.79	1.00	.89	.29	.27	.30
4	.91	.84	.89	1.00	.19	.24	.26
5	.32	.24	.29	.19	1.00	.85	.89
6	.25	.29	.27	.24	.85	1.00	.95
7	.24	.30	.30	.26	.89	.95	1.00

[1]For a brief description of factor analysis, see Cronbach, L. J. *Essentials of Psychological Testing*. New York: Harper & Row, 1970, Chapter 10. More extensive, authoritative discussions may be found in Horst, P. *Factor Analysis of Data Matrices*. New York: Holt, Rinehart & Winston, 1965; or in Harman, H. *Modern Factor Analysis*, Chicago: University of Chicago Press, 1967.

[2]A description of the correlation coefficient can be found in any elementary statistics textbook. One such book is Downie, N. M., & Heath, R. W. *Basic Statistical Methods*. New York: Harper & Row, 1965, Chapter 7.

column 1 intersects row 4 and find ".91," which means that scores on vocabulary tests for this sample correlate .91 with scores on the synonyms test. Examining this table, we notice that tests 1, 2, 3, and 4 all correlate highly with each other. Test 1 correlates .76 with test 2, .93 with test 3, and .91 with test 4. The other three tests in this group are also highly correlated with each other. On the other hand, these tests have a low correlation with tests 5, 6, and 7. Test 1 correlates .32 with test 5, .25 with test 6, and .24 with test 7. Tests 2, 3, and 4 also have low correlations with tests 5, 6, and 7. However, tests 5, 6, and 7 all correlate highly with each other. Test 5 correlates .85 with test 6 and .89 with test 7. Tests 6 and 7 correlate .95 with each other. In short, examination of this table of correlations suggests that we have two groups of tests that correlate highly among themselves. One group is composed of tests that measure verbal abilities, and the other group is composed of tests that measure mathematical abilities. This pattern of correlations suggests that although we have seven tests in this group, these tests are, in fact, measuring only two abilities, verbal and mathematical.

Factor analysis is a statistical technique designed to determine the dimensions, or factors, that underly a series of measures of some sort. If we factor-analyzed the matrix of correlations in Table 1, we would surely find that this table has two factors, with one factor containing the verbal tests and the other factor containing the mathematical tests.

Factor analysis was originally developed to deal with the same task we have described here—that is, to determine the basic factors underlying intelligence. Those who devised the technique of factor analysis hoped to make it possible to determine the basic elements that make up some mental function, such as intelligence, much in the same manner that a chemist analyzes a substance to determine the chemical elements that make up the substance. A chemist might analyze water, for example, and discover that it is composed of the elements hydrogen and oxygen. Early factor analysts wanted to determine the basic elements in psychological functioning. However, the results of many years of experience with factor analysis have shown that what comes from the factor analysis of a batch of data depends on what is put into the batch and how the analysis is performed. Most psychometricians now feel that factor analysis provides one way of looking at data that may well suggest the basic dimensions that underly a series of measures, but does not detect the basic psychological "elements" in the sense that a chemical analysis does. Cronbach (1970) suggests that factor analysis helps clarify how a group of measures relates much in the same way that a series of photographs taken from different angles helps clarify the structure of an object. Perhaps a psychologist doing a factor analysis is somewhat analogous to a surgeon taking X rays from different angles to discover what is going on inside a patient.

A Return to Converging Lines
of Interpersonal Research

And now back to Carter's research on men interacting in groups. When we left it we were about to factor-analyze a matrix of intercorrelations among the judgments of nineteen variables. In the factor analysis of these data, three factors emerged. These three factors were: (1) Factor I — *individual prominence* — the degree to which a person stood out from the group; (2) Factor II — *group goal facilitation* — the degree to which an individual helped the group reach its goal; (3) Factor III — *group sociability* — the positive social interaction a person had with the other members of the group. Carter reviewed other studies of group interaction and concluded that these had reached approximately the same conclusions. Therefore, the three factors seemed to account for the variance observed in people interacting in a group.

Carter's study produced three factors instead of the two factors described by Leary, but two of Carter's factors seem to be quite similar to Leary's. Carter's Factor I, individual prominence, seems similar to Leary's dominance-submission axis, and Carter's Factor III, group sociability, seems similar to Leary's affection-hostility, or love-hate, axis. Factor II obtained by Carter, group facilitation, seems more a function of the task of the group than a function of the relationships among the members in the group.

Borgatta, Cottrell, and Mann (1958) did another study, attempting to replicate Carter's research. They used forty-seven graduate students who met as a group for a two-hour discussion once a week. After meeting nine weeks, they were studied. Each student ranked each other student in the group on sixteen personality traits and twenty-four behavior-descriptive categories. The variables studied were selected for their relevance to the factors described by Carter and included those described by Bales (1951) which are presented later in this chapter. The groups were also observed in action, and the members of the groups were rated with the Bales system.

All of these measures were intercorrelated and factor-analyzed. The factor analysis produced two large factors and three small factors. The two large factors were the same as Carter's Factor I, individual prominence, and Factor III, sociability. One of the three small factors they obtained was similar to Carter's Factor II, group facilitation. The other two small factors were "manifest emotionality" and "named-task interest." These two factors describe subjects who overtly expressed emotion and showed interest in the task they were performing.

A third kind of research was reviewed by Schaefer (1959) and included three studies of the interaction between mother and child. These studies were confined to the direct social and emotional behavior of a mother toward her child. This included direct observation of mothers in interaction with their children and interviews with them about their behavior toward their children.

Some of the data were factor-analyzed, but Schaefer was more interested in analyzing the data from the point of view of Guttman's radex theory (1954a), which will be described later in the chapter. Analyzing the data from the circumplex (a part of the radex) point of view, Schaefer concluded that maternal behavior consisted of two major dimensions. These two dimensions were love versus hostility and autonomy versus control.

Schaefer's two dimensions appear to be quite similar to the dimensions described by Leary, Carter, and Borgatta, Cottrell, and Mann. Schaefer's love versus hostility can be likened to sociability and attraction-hostility, and his autonomy versus control seems similar to individual prominence and dominance-submission.

The four studies described above stimulated Foa to conclude that some basic dimensions of the interpersonal relationship were beginning to emerge. But before commencing a description of Foa's attempt to develop an interpersonal system, still another program of research on the interpersonal relationship, that was conducted at the same time as the research already described and produced similar results, should be described.

William Schutz (1958) first began to speculate about the interaction among people while conducting research on groups in the navy. Reviewing a variety of studies, including those by Leary and Carter and also many psychoanalysts, he applied the thinking of some social science methodologists, especially Guttman (whose applicability will be described shortly). The resultant product was his own system for analyzing the interpersonal relationship, which he then tested in a series of studies. This system is of interest, since Schutz reached conclusions that are somewhat similar to those of Foa.

Schutz concluded that the interpersonal interaction can be accounted for by three dimensions. These three dimensions are (1) inclusion, (2) control, and (3) affection. *Inclusion* typically concerns the feelings and behavior of one person toward a group, *affection* is always confined to the one-to-one relationship, and *control* is concerned with who bosses whom, and may operate in either the one-to-one or the group situation.

Schutz applied his system to the study of different kinds of people in a variety of situations and found his hypotheses confirmed. Of primary interest here is that by deduction from a review of many sources, Schutz concluded that three dimensions accounted for what happened in an interpersonal relationship. His "control" is quite similar to the individual prominence or dominance-submission dimensions, and his "affection" is similar to the love-hate or sociability dimensions.

Thus Foa began analyzing the interpersonal relationship against a background of research from a variety of sources studying different kinds of subjects. The data, although analyzed by differing methods, seemed to point toward the conclusion that the interpersonal relationship could be explained by two or perhaps three basic dimensions. It may be of some importance to note that two of these dimensions seemed to apply to the dyadic, or one-to-one relationship, while the third dimension seemed to be confined to relationships within groups.

Guttman's Radex and Facet Analysis

Foa was exposed to the thinking Louis Guttman had applied to the problem of measurement in the social sciences. Upon examination of his own data presented in the last section, Foa concluded that the results could all be accounted for with three facets which produce Guttman's circumplex. Before describing Foa's system, it is first necessary to define Guttman's concept of the circumplex and his system of facet analysis (see Guttman, 1954a, 1954b, 1958).

In studying matrices of correlation coefficients, Guttman observed certain patterns among the correlations between certain variables. The correlation coefficient is a measure of the relationship between two variables. When a group of variables are correlated with each other, they are arranged in a table in which it is possible to find the correlation between any two variables. This table is, in mathematical terms, a matrix.

Guttman was studying the correlations between different variables used to measure intelligence. He noticed that when the various tests he used were correlated, if the tests varied in the *degree* of complexity but not in the *kind* of complexity, the correlations arranged themselves in a pattern that he called a *simplex;* if the tests differed among themselves in the *kind* of complexity, the correlations arranged themselves in a pattern he called a *circumplex.*

One of the patterns of intercorrelation Guttman studied which produced a simplex pattern was computed from a series of tests of verbal ability. These tests included letter grouping, letter series, sentences, vocabulary, four-letter words, and so on. He found that if these tests were arranged in order of complexity, from the least complex task (letter grouping) to the most complex task (four-letter words), the correlation of any given test was highest with the tests that were next to it in complexity and located immediately adjacent to it in the matrix. Table 2 presents Guttman's example of a simplex.

A perfect correlation is 1.0, and no correlation at all is .00. It may be seen from the simplex in Table 2 that test 1 (t_1) correlates perfectly with itself, and correlates less with the tests located at a greater distance from it in the table. Starting with the diagonal, which contains the correlation of each test with itself, and working out either along the rows or up and down the columns, the correlations become progressively lower. These tests seem to arrange themselves in an order such

TABLE 2. **TEST INTERCORRELATIONS FOR A HYPOTHETICAL, EQUALLY SPACED, PERFECT SIMPLEX**

Test	t_1	t_2	t_3	t_4	t_5
t_1	1.0	.6	.36	.216	.1296
t_2	.6	1.0	.6	.36	.216
t_3	.36	.6	1.0	.6	.36
t_4	.216	.36	.6	1.0	.6
t_5	.1296	.216	.36	.6	1.0

Reprinted with permission of The Macmillan Company from L. Guttman, "A new approach to factor analysis: the radex." In P. Lazarsfeld (Ed.), *Mathematical thinking in the social sciences*, p. 271. Copyright 1954 by The Free Press.

that any given test correlates most highly with the tests adjacent to it and progressively less with tests farther removed from it. If we were to arrange the tests in order so that tests with the highest correlations were located spatially closest to each other, the tests would order themselves in a line, with test 1 at one end of the line and test 5 at the opposite end of the line. The tests would be arranged as follows: $t_1\, t_2\, t_3\, t_4\, t_5$. The correlation between any two adjacent tests (say t_1 and t_2 or t_3 and t_4) would be .6. The correlation between any two tests that were two steps removed (t_1 and t_3) would be .36; between tests three steps removed (t_1 and t_4), .216; and between tests four steps removed (t_1 and t_5), .1296. Thus, the farther apart the tests, the lower the correlation, and the tests arrange themselves in a straight line if they are placed so that the distance between them is inverse to the size of the correlation between them.

The simplex occurs when the tests measure essentially the same variable, but differ on the degree of complexity of that variable. But suppose the tests are measuring different *kinds* of complexity. Suppose that instead of measuring verbal abilities, the different tests are measuring verbal ability, mathematical ability, mechanical ability, and so on. If these tests are then intercorrelated, it seems likely that their correlation coefficients will not be such that they will be arranged in any pattern as simple as a straight line. Guttman proposed that the next order of arrangement of correlation coefficients would be such that the variables, if spatially arranged in accordance with the size of the correlation coefficients, would be a circle, and if the variables were ordered, the matrix of the correlation coefficients would arrange itself so that the correlations would first decline as you moved out the columns and rows from the diagonal and then would increase again. Table 3 illustrates the matrix of correlations for a circumplex.

If we look at Table 3, we notice that for test 1 (t_1), as we move to tests farther removed from it in the table, the correlation coefficients progressively decline from .75 with t_2 to .25 with t_4; but then as we move farther down the row, the correlations then increase to .50 with t_5

TABLE 3. **THE INTERCORRELATIONS FOR AN EQUALLY SPACED, UNIFORM, PERFECT, ADDITIVE CIRCUMPLEX**

Test	t_1	t_2	t_3	t_4	t_5	t_6
t_1	1.00	.75	.50	.25	.50	.75
t_2	.75	1.00	.75	.50	.25	.50
t_3	.50	.75	1.00	.75	.50	.25
t_4	.25	.50	.75	1.00	.75	.50
t_5	.50	.25	.50	.75	1.00	.75
t_6	.75	.50	.25	.50	.75	1.00

Reprinted with permission of The Macmillan Company from L. Guttman, "A new approach to factor analysis: the radex." In P. Lazarsfeld (Ed.), *Mathematical thinking in the social sciences*, p. 329. Copyright 1954 by The Free Press.

and .75 with t_6. If we arrange these tests spatially so that the distance between them is the inverse of the size of their correlation coefficients, they arrange themselves in a circle. The arrangement looks something like the following:

$$t_1 \quad t_2$$
$$t_6 \qquad t_3$$
$$t_5 \quad t_4$$

Thus, any two adjacent tests (e.g., t_1 with t_2 or t_6) will be correlated .75, any tests two steps removed from each other (e.g., t_1 with t_3 or t_5) will be correlated .50, and any two tests opposite to each other on the circle (e.g., t_1 with t_4) will be correlated .25 with each other.

The correlation coefficient is a measure of the degree to which two variables relate to each other. If the correlation is high, the two variables vary together, and thus they are presumably impelled in some way to vary by some common underlying factor or variable. These underlying variables are called by many names, but Foa borrowed from Guttman (1958; 1965) the term "facet." The more facets any two measures share in common, the higher their correlation coefficient will be. To give a simple example of the use of the facet approach to analyze the relationship between variables, let us now consider the following expression of affection which might be exchanged between a husband and wife: "I love you." This simple sentence might be said by either one to the other, but for the purposes of illustration let us assume that the husband has said this to his wife. This sentence can be considered to be a piece of behavior in the interpersonal relationship between the husband and the wife. What are the basic elements, or facets, contained within it? Let us consider the sentence again. Rewording it slightly, it reads "I do love you." We can break it down into the following facets:

1	2	3	4
I (the actor)	do (action)	love (mode)	you (object).

Thus, in this sentence we find four facets. They are: (1) the actor, which in the case of a two-person interpersonal relationship can be either oneself or the other person; (2) the action, which can be either acceptance or rejection of the other person; (3) the mode, which can be either emotional or social; and (4) the object, which in the case of the two-person interpersonal relationship can be either the self or the other person. Thus in this simple sentence we have four facets, each facet having one of two possible elements.

If we take the four facets with two alternatives for each facet in the sentence outlined above, we can produce 2^4 different sentences describing an interpersonal behavior. We have the following possibilities:

1. a) self   3. a) emotional
    b) other   b) social
2. a) acceptance   4. a) self
    b) rejection   b) other

As we have said, this gives us 2^4 possible behaviors, or sixteen altogether. What are the possibilities? We have already presented one of them, which is a combination of 1a, 2a, 3a, 4b. Now suppose we change just one element, 4b to 4a. What is the result? We would then have a sentence reading "I do love myself." The following sentences are examples of the sixteen possibilities produced by the four facets we have described.

1.	1a, 2a, 3a, 4b:	I do love you.
2.	1a, 2a, 3a, 4a:	I do love myself.
3.	1a, 2a, 3b, 4a:	I do respect myself.
4.	1a, 2a, 3b, 4b:	I do respect you.
5.	1a, 2b, 3a, 4a:	I don't love myself.
6.	1a, 2b, 3a, 4b:	I don't love you.
7.	1a, 2b, 3b, 4a:	I don't respect myself.
8.	1a, 2b, 3b, 4b:	I don't respect you.
9.	1b, 2a, 3a, 4a:	You do love me.
10.	1b, 2a, 3a, 4b:	You do love yourself.
11.	1b, 2a, 3b, 4a:	You do respect me.
12.	1b, 2a, 3b, 4b:	You do respect yourself.
13.	1b, 2b, 3a, 4a:	You don't love me.
14.	1b, 2b, 3a, 4b:	You don't love yourself.
15.	1b, 2b, 3b, 4a:	You don't respect me.
16.	1b, 2b, 3b, 4b:	You don't respect yourself.

Thus, out of these four facets with two elements to each facet we have derived sixteen statements about interpersonal behavior (and also about the behavior of a person toward himself).

Now, according to the theory, the more facets two variables have in common, the higher the correlation between them. Thus, if we took the statements above as an example, we would expect sentences 3 and 4 to be more highly correlated than sentences 3 and 16, since sentences 3 and 4 have three facets (facets 1, 2, and 3) in common, while sentences 3 and 16 have only one facet (facet 3) in common. Sentences 2 and 16 would have an even lower correlation, since they have no facets in common.

One aspect of our example that should be noted is that the behaviors, or verbal expressions of feeling, contained within those sixteen sentences could be expressed in a variety of ways. Because of error or slight variation in expression, any two sentences that were the expression of the same behavior or feeling would probably not correlate perfectly, but could be expected to correlate quite highly.

And finally, if we used these sentences as examples of behavior, the actual behavior measured would almost certainly be verbal behavior. That is, individuals would be asked if such a statement was one they had expressed to the other person with whom they had a relationship and they would answer "yes" or "no," the yeses and noes being correlated in some fashion. These sentences could, however, be converted into some sort of a behavioral rating scale, by which a judge could observe the persons in interaction and rate the extent to which they expressed a given behavior toward each other. If, for example, the behavior was emotional acceptance of the other (expressed in the sentence "I do love you"), this rating could be based on observation of how the one acted toward the other.

With this background discussion of the circumplex and facet analysis, we now move to Foa's application of it to the analysis of interpersonal relationship research.

Foa's Application of Facet Analysis to the Interpersonal Relationship

Foa felt that the research summarized earlier in the chapter clearly suggested that interpersonal relationships could be defined by the two dimensions, dominance-submission and love-hostility. Further, Leary's ordering of his variables in a circle and Schaefer's analysis of his mother-child research as a circumplex suggested that the variables in the interpersonal relationship should order themselves in a circumplex. Foa, then, sought to discover an appropriate underlying facet structure that would produce a circumplex.

Variables are defined as the Cartesian products of the elements taken from each facet that make up the variable. If we return to our earlier example of the statement, "I do love you," which we defined as a variable (or behavior), then it would be the Cartesian product of the elements from each facet that go to make it up and would be mathematically represented by the following formula: $a_1 \times a_2 \times a_3 \times b_4$. A representation of a tabular arrangement of four facets with two elements to each facet is shown in Table 4. In this table a column is assigned to each facet and a row to each of four variables. (For Foa these four variables are the four definition points of the two dimensions, love—hostility and dominance—submission.) The cell at the crossing of a given row with a given column contains the element of a particular facet that is appropriate to the given variable. Thus, variable 1 is determined by the elements a_1, b_1, c_2, and d_2 of the facets A, B, C, and D.

For a circumplex to exist, two conditions are necessary. The first is that it is possible to arrange the table in such a way that by drawing lines parallel to certain diagonals, the table is divided into sectors so that all of the facet elements in a given sector have the same position in the ordering of the elements. This is possible in the ordering presented in Table 4. It should be noted that the facet elements in the segment of the table in the upper left-hand corner are all the first element in their facets. That is, they all have "1" as a subscript. The elements in the next sector in the table all have "2" for a subscript, so they are all from the second element of their facets. The third sector elements are composed of the first element of their facets. The fourth sector is composed of only one element which is taken from the second element of its facet. Thus, in this example the first condition for a circumplex is met.

The second condition for a circumplex is that the *contiguity principle* will operate. This principle holds that the more similar two variables are in their facet structure, the higher the correlation between them will be. In the section of this chapter that immediately precedes this section, it was stated that the more facets two variables have in common, the higher the correlation between them should be. This, however, may not always work out to be so in practice, and certainly will not be true if only the number of facets in common is considered. This may come about because one facet describes a dimension that is particularly potent. The relationship provided by two variables sharing the same element of a facet which is highly potent may be greater than

TABLE 4. **THE SIMPLEST HYPOTHETICAL EXAMPLE OF A CIRCUMPLEX ORDERING**

Variable	Facet			
	A	*B*	*C*	*D*
1	a_1	b_1	c_2	d_2
2	a_1	b_2	c_2	d_1
3	a_2	b_2	c_1	d_1
4	a_2	b_1	c_1	d_2

the relationship between two other variables that share two or three less-potent facet elements. It seems reasonable to say, however, that if the facet concept has any validity at all, then two variables that share the same element of a facet should certainly have some relationship to each other, and that the more facet elements they share, the higher that relationship should be.

If we return to Table 4 we find that variable 1 shares two facet elements with variable 2, but variable 1 shares no facet elements with variable 3; therefore, variable 1 should have a higher relationship with variable 2 than with variable 3. Variable 1 also has two facet elements in common with variable 4, so variable 1 should have a higher relationship with variable 4 than with variable 3. Similar relationships appear in the pairings of the other variables (e.g., variable 3 has two facets in common with variables 2 and 4, etc.). This same kind of ordering holds for the facets as it does for the variables. That is, if we look down the columns for the facets A, B, C, and D we find that facet A shares two facet element subscripts with facets B and D, and shares no facet subscripts with facet C.

Thus, Foa concluded that in the case of the interpersonal-relationship variables love, hate, dominance, and submission, the necessary conditions for a circumplex order exist.

First, Foa reasoned that the two dimensions (or facets, as he refers to them), love-hostility and dominance-submission, can be split in two, giving four "values": love, hostility, dominance, and submission. Next, he concluded that any action that is meaningful toward another person can also be meaningful toward the self. That is, if we can love another, then we can also love ourselves. And of course the language is full of "self" kinds of expressions, such as self-confidant, self-denial, self-respecting, and so on. By introducing the self-other distinction, the original four behaviors have now been expanded into the following eight:

1. Hostility to self
2. Submission to self
3. Dominance of other
4. Hostility to other
5. Love of self
6. Dominance of self
7. Submission to other
8. Love of other

Looking at these eight, which Foa calls *profiles*, he concluded that the first four, which include hostility to both self and other, and dominance of the other and submission to self all look like some kind of rejection. The last four, which include love of self and other, and dominance of self but submission to the other all look like acceptance. The two dimensions dominance-submission and love-hate can likewise be interpreted in other terms. Love, either of self or the other, is essentially an emotional matter, while dominance and submission are more social matters. Thus, Foa decided that the eight profiles could be defined as the Cartesian product of three facets, or components. These three facets are: (1) the content of the action (acceptance or rejection); (2) the object of the action (the self or the other); and (3) the mode of the action (emotional or social). The eight profiles listed above could be described in terms of the elements they obtain from each of the three facets in the following manner:

1. Rejection of self, emotional
2. Rejection of self, social
3. Rejection of other, social
4. Rejection of other, emotional
5. Acceptance of self, emotional
6. Acceptance of self, social
7. Acceptance of other, social
8. Acceptance of other, emotional

In the paper in which this system was first presented, Foa (1961) argued for the addition of a fourth facet, or component, which he called *intensity*. This argument was based on mathematical considerations derived from Guttman (1954b). With the inclusion of this additional component, Foa produced a table of components and profiles that looked like Table 5.

Foa presented a system that accounted for the two main dimensions of interpersonal interaction in terms of three facets (the additional component, intensity, does not add any profiles or variables), and these three facets result in a pattern of intercorrelations among the profiles that is a circumplex. However, nothing stays this simple, particularly in a phenomenon as complex as the interpersonal relationship. So, as Foa proceeded with his investigations his system became more complex.

Foa progressed, following lines prefigured by the example of facets described earlier in the chapter. Recalling the sentence "I do love you," we note that one of the four facets is the pronoun "I." In the

TABLE 5. **FOA'S TABLE OF COMPONENTS AND PROFILES**

Fourth component	Emotional	Social	Social	Emotional	Emotional	Social	Social	Emotional
Third component	Self		Other		Self		Other	
Second component	High intensity		Low intensity				High intensity	
First component	Rejection				Acceptance			
Order of profiles	A	B	C	D	E	F	G	H

From U. G. Foa, "Convergences in the analysis of the structure of interpersonal behavior," in *Psychological Review*, 1961, 68, p. 349. Copyright © 1961 by the American Psychological Association, and reproduced by permission.

analysis by Foa just described, there were facets that accounted for acceptance and rejection, social and emotional, and self and other, but there was no facet for the "I." That is, Foa's system contained facets 2, 3, and 4 from the "I do love you" example, but it provided no facet 1 for the "I," or the actor who was doing the loving. So Foa (1966) expanded his system to include a facet for the person doing the acting. He also added two more facets: the level of the action (whether the action was what was actually done or what ought to have been done), and the person from whose point of view the action was being observed.

Foa called these three new facets *perceptual facets,* and the three original facets he labeled *behavioral facets.* Each of the six facets has two alternatives, or elements.

The Perceptual Facets

Facet *A.* The person doing the action, or actor: (1) the other (nonobserver) and (2) the self (observer).

Facet *B.* The level: (1) actual (what is done) and (2) ideal (what ought to be done).

Facet *C.* The person from whose point of view the action of the actor is perceived, or alias: (1) the other (nonactor) and (2) the self (actor).

The Behavioral Facets

Facet *D.* Content of behavior: (1) acceptance, or giving, and (2) rejection, or taking away.

Facet *E.* Object of behavior: (1) the other (nonactor) and (2) the self (actor).

Facet *F.* Mode of behavior: (1) social, or status, and (2) emotional, or love.

The last three facets, *D, E,* and *F,* each have two elements and produce the eight behavior types, or patterns, that we have already described. However, for the sake of clarity, we will reproduce these eight types again. They are:

1. Rejection of self, emotional (facet elements D_2, E_2, F_2)
2. Rejection of self, social (facet elements D_2, E_2, F_1)
3. Rejection of other, social (facet elements D_2, E_1, F_1)
4. Rejection of other, emotional (facet elements D_2, E_1, F_2)
5. Acceptance of self, emotional (facet elements D_1, E_2, F_2)
6. Acceptance of self, social (facet elements D_1, E_2, F_1)
7. Acceptance of other, social (facet elements D_1, E_1, F_1)
8. Acceptance of other, emotional (facet elements D_1, E_1, F_2)

These eight behavior patterns are derived from the behavioral facets. And as has already been demonstrated, if they are measured in some way and intercorrelated, they should form a circumplex.

The three perceptual facets should also produce eight perceptual patterns which should look something like the following (although Foa doesn't list them in this way):

1. The other acting, actual action, observed by other (A_1, B_1, C_1)
2. The other acting, actual action, observed by self (A_1, B_1, C_2)
3. The other acting, ideal action, observed by self (A_1, B_2, C_2)
4. The other acting, ideal action, observed by other (A_1, B_2, C_1)
5. The self acting, ideal action, observed by other (A_2, B_2, C_1)
6. The self acting, ideal action, observed by self (A_2, B_2, C_2)
7. The self acting, actual action, observed by self (A_2, B_1, C_2)
8. The self acting, actual action, observed by other (A_2, B_1, C_1)

This second set of three perceptual facets with its eight perceptual types should also produce a circumplex. Assuming that it does produce a circumplex, how does one go about putting two circumplexes together? How can two circles be fit into one system?

Foa's solution to this question was to place the circles at right angles to each other, producing what he termed a *ringex*. The ringex is shaped like the inner tubes that are put inside automobile tires. Or if you prefer a different analogy, the ringex is shaped like a life preserver. Figure 2 contains a diagram of the ringex.

FIGURE 2. **A REPRESENTATION OF THE RINGEX MODEL**

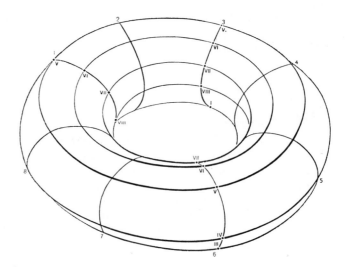

An examination of the ringex presents several interesting aspects. It contains two kinds of circles, small and large ones. The small circles form cross-sections of the inner tube, or lifesaver, while the large ones follow the rim. There are eight circles running in each direction, with eight circles making cross-sections of the inner tube and eight running around the rim. We will return to these circles later in our discussion of the ringex.

On the ringex there are both roman numerals, I to VIII, and arabic numerals, 1 to 8. The roman numerals stand for the perceptual types, of which there are eight, and the arabic numerals stand for the behavioral types, of which there are also eight. The types for which these numerals stand are presented in Table 6. Each row of the table (roman numerals) represents a perceptual type, while each column of the table (arabic numerals) represents a behavioral type. The intersection point of each row and column in the table corresponds to an intersection between two of the circles on the ringex.

Let us consider some examples taken from Foa (1966). At the intersection of I and 1 (on the underside of the left side of the diagram), the variable is "To what degree does the observer perceive, from his point of view, that the other (nonobserver) accepts him socially?" or

TABLE 6. **FACET DEFINITION OF THE VARIABLES OF AN OBSERVER**

Perceptual Type			Content	Behavioral Type							
				Acceptance				Rejection			
			Object	Other		Self		Self		Other	
Actor	Level	Alias	Mode	Social	Emotional	Emotional	Social	Social	Emotional	Emotional	Social
			Type	1	2	3	4	5	6	7	8
Nonobserver or other	Actual	Nonactor	I								
		Actor	II								
	Ideal	Actor	III								
		Nonactor	IV								
Observer or self	Ideal	Nonactor	V								
		Actor	VI								
	Actual	Actor	VII								
		Nonactor	VIII								

"To what extent does the observer perceive he is receiving status from the other?" Other examples Foa gives are variable V, 2 (upper-left section of the diagram), "To what degree, according to the observer, does the other think that he (the observer) ought to accept the other emotionally?" and variable VII, 5 (inside the left side of the diagram), "To what degree does the observer feel that he is rejecting himself socially (taking status away from himself)?"

This table and the ringex diagram are somewhat confusing until you have worked with them for a while. Then the meaning begins to come through, although even then it is rather complex. The thing to remember is that the self is always the observer. Then the next step becomes a little easier. The actor who is doing whatever is being done can be either the self (who is the observer) or the other person (who is the nonobserver). What is perceived can either be the actual behavior or what is felt to be the ideal behavior (what the actor ought to do rather than what he actually did or did not do). Finally, this action or ideal can be seen from the point of view of either the person doing the acting (the actor) or the person being acted upon (the nonactor). That takes care of the perceptual types.

The behavioral types describe the action that actually took place or the action that ought to have taken place. Thus, the action can be described from the point of view of the person who is doing the observing or from the point of view of the other person. Of course, the person who is observing can be acting or being acted upon, and he can be observing his own perceptions, or he can be presuming the perceptions of the other person. However, if you start with the understanding that the original observation is always from the point of view of the self (the observer), it makes tracking through the complex maze a little easier.

The next thing to notice about the ringex diagram is that the perceptual circles (which cut cross-sections of the ringex) are smaller than the behavioral circles (which go around the ringex), and that the behavioral circles going around the inside of the ringex are smaller than those going around the outside. The relative sizes of these circles have significance, which we shall discuss after one short, but important, digression.

At this point you may be confused about which circles are perceptual and which are behavioral, so I will endeavor to explain. The perceptual circles include all the types produced by the perceptual facets. These facets were lettered A, B, and C, and they produced the eight perceptual variables, I, II, III, IV, V, VI, VII, and VIII. To be a perceptual circle, it must include each of these eight perceptual variables. To get a perceptual circle, you would start at a particular point and follow the circle around through I–VIII, including all the perceptual types for that section of the ringex.

The behavioral circles include all the types produced by behavioral facets. These facets were labeled D, E, and F, and they produced the eight behavioral variables 1, 2, 3, 4, 5, 6, 7, and 8. To be a behavioral circle, it must include each of these eight behavioral variables. To get a behavioral circle, then, you would start at a particular point and follow the circle around, taking in all the behavioral types 1–8 on the ringex.

What all the above amounts to is that for each perceptual point of view, you may observe all of the eight possible behaviors, which include acceptance or rejection of the self or the other, either emotionally or socially. All of these may be observed from any particular perceptual point of view; in fact, any time these behaviors are described, they must be described from a particular point of view. And any one of these specific behaviors may be perceived from several points of view. In this system, they may be observed from eight points of view—these being either the self or the other, who may be either the actor or the nonactor, and the action being either the ideal action or the actual action.

Now, having waded through that mass of complexity, let us return to the size of the circles. You will recall that the closer two variables are to each other spatially, the higher the intercorrelations between them. This means that the circles that are located on the inside of the ringex contain variables that are more highly correlated with each other than the circles located on the outside of the ringex. It also means that the variables that cut across the ringex (the perceptual variables) are more highly correlated with each other than the variables that run around the ringex (the behavioral variables). This is precisely the significance of the difference in the sizes of the circles.

Foa found that in computing the multiple correlations among the variables, the interpersonal variables had higher correlations than those that were not interpersonal; that is, the variables that include the other, the social, and acceptance correlate more highly than variables that do not require an interpersonal relationship. The noninterpersonal variables include the self, rejection, the emotional, and the ideal. Looking at circle VIII, which is on the inside of the ringex, we observe that this includes the actual behavior of the self who is the observer and is interacting with the other (nonactor). This is clearly an interpersonal interaction. Circle IV, which is larger than circle VII and is on the outside of the ringex, is the self's perception of what the other ought to do. This is a kind of speculative operation about what another person ought to do and is not at all interpersonal.

A point that should be noted is that some of these interpersonal variables fall within the perceptual facets (other and ideal), while others fall within the behavioral facets (other, social, acceptance), so that if the ringex accurately reflects the size of the correlations, it seems that it ought to be a little lumpy. It should look more like an inner tube with some weak places in it.

Foa (1966, p. 4) speculates that the development of these facets should correspond to stages in the development of the child. He suggests that in the perceptual facets, the child first differentiates between himself and other people (that is, between actors). This distinction should take place quite early in the life of the infant, when he first realizes that some behavior is initiated by himself and some by another person who is not himself. The next differentiation in the perceptual facets would be between actual behavior and ideal behavior. This should take place when the child realizes that some of his behavior is accepted and approved by the other (usually the mother) while other behavior is disapproved. Finally, the child learns to distinguish between perceptual points of view—that is, to differentiate between what the child wants to do and what the child thinks the mother thinks he ought to do. This requires the child to have some idea of what another person thinks as distinct from what he himself thinks about an action.

Of the behavioral facets, Foa speculates that the first differentiation is in the content of behavior, between acceptance and rejection. The child first learns to perceive acceptance or rejection, either done to him by another person or done by him to either another person or object. Next, he learns to differentiate what is rejected—that is, the object or person rejected. Finally comes the differentiation in the mode—that is, the child begins to distinguish whether the acceptance or rejection is a social or emotional one. Actually, clinical experience would suggest that some adults have trouble differentiating between social and emotional acceptance or rejection. I once knew a man who always analyzed his chances of being accepted for a job in terms of whether or not the person doing the hiring liked him or not. Ordinarily, hiring a person for a job first requires that the applicant be competent for the job, and assessing a person as being vocationally competent is social acceptance. Whether or not the person doing the hiring likes him is likely to be irrelevant if he is not competent. Conversely, it is not uncommon for a person to feel that he did not get a job because he did something to anger the person doing the hiring. Of course, people hiring may also confuse emotional considerations with social ones. This provides the setting for jokes about hiring secretaries for looks rather than ability.

Foa did not develop this system in a vacuum. Rather, it was logically developed from the earlier research of others, then tested on a rather large sample of subjects. Foa composed a scale with a series of hypothetical situations and then asked his subjects to answer how they would react in a particular situation or how they thought the other person with whom they had an interpersonal relationship would react in the situation described. His subjects were 633 married couples in Jerusalem, Israel. Since they were married, they were asked to give their responses in terms of either their own reaction or what they thought their spouse's reaction would be. The situations were appropriate to a marital relationship. The questionnaire was designed to test each of the sixty-four variables provided by the six perceptual and behavioral facets.

For each one of the eight types of behavior, and for each of the two actors, three brief story situations were prepared. For example, the three stories referring to a husband's social acceptance of his wife are the following:

> 1.   Abraham has consideration for his wife and displays toward her respect and esteem.
> 2.   Isaac thinks his wife is very successful and especially esteems her personality and her actions.
> 3.   Jacob is sure that everything his wife does is important and good, and there is no limit to the esteem and importance that he attributes to her (Foa, 1966, p. 6).

Examples of some of the other stories follow.

Social acceptance of the self: "Abraham is a husband who esteems himself and relies on himself and on his decisions."

Emotional acceptance of self: "Isaac is a husband who is satisfied with his actions and feels very much at peace with himself."

Social rejection of wife: "Abraham slightly criticizes his wife's behavior and thinks that she makes a few mistakes."

Emotional rejection of self: "Jacob is a husband very dissatisfied with himself and with his behavior toward his wife, rejects and blames himself."

Similar stories were also used for the behavior of the wife.

After each story the subject was asked four questions to differentiate between the perceptual types. The perceptual types and the questions asked to get at these perceptual types follow.

Actual level, alias of the actor: "Do you behave toward your wife as does the husband in the story?"

Ideal level, alias of the actor: "Do you think that a husband should behave as does the husband in the story in relation to his wife?"

Actual level, alias of the nonactor: "Would your wife say that you resemble the husband in the story?"

Ideal level, alias of the nonactor: "Would your wife say that a husband should behave thusly?"

Thus, each situation provided a specification of the three behavioral facets and the actor facet of the perceptual facets, while the questions provided a specification for the other two facets of the perceptual type, level and alias.

The same four questions were asked after each of the three stories for each of the behavioral variables, so that three measures were obtained for each of the behavioral variables. These answers were then quantified, with the totals for each question and each behavioral type correlated with all of the other answers for every other behavioral type. The intercorrelations for any eight variables belonging to any row (perceptual types) or column (behavioral types) can be arranged in an 8 × 8 table. These intercorrelations, whether among either a perceptual or behavioral type, should arrange themselves in a circumplex, since the perceptual types and the behavioral types each form a circle when spatially placed in accordance with the size of their intercorrelation. If you recall the earlier description of a circumplex, when these intercorrelations are entered in a table, the correlations should be highest along the diagonal of the table, should decline in size moving out from the diagonal along the rows and the column, and should rise again near the outer edge of the table. Table 7 presents the intercorrelations Foa obtained among the behavioral types for perceptual type VII in which the wife is the observer.

Selecting one row from the table, let us say row 4, you will notice that the correlation coefficients immediately before and after the diagonal are .52 and .31. Moving to the left and right along Row 4, the correlations drop to a low of .16 on the left and a low of −.11 on the right. Then the correlations rise again at the edges of the table, with a correlation of .24 on the left and a correlation of −.01 on the right. Notice that the pattern of the other correlations also follows this general trend. In this paper, Foa presents several other tables indicating the same trend, with the sizes of the correlations and the patterns of the correlations approximately fitting the pattern predicted by his model. Thus, he presents some empirical evidence to support his very complex scheme.

TABLE 7. **AN EXAMPLE OF BEHAVIORAL CIRCUMPLEX; CONSTANT PERCEPTUAL TYPE VII; OBSERVER: WIFE**

Type	1	2	3	4	5	6	7	8
1	—	.65	.27	.24	.06	.20	.35	.45
2	.65	—	.28	.16	.09	.20	.36	.40
3	.27	.28	—	.52	.28	.17	.01	.07
4	.24	.16	.52	—	.31	.17	−.11	−.01
5	.06	.09	.28	.31	—	.39	.18	.24
6	.20	.20	.17	.17	.39	—	.34	.35
7	.35	.36	.01	−.11	.18	.34	—	.53
8	.45	.40	.07	−.01	.24	.35	.53	—

In a later paper Foa (1969) progresses toward an integration of his own approach to interpersonal interaction with other approaches, notably exchange theory and needs. This integration will be discussed in the last chapter, which deals with conflict and congruence among various approaches to interpersonal relations.

Bales and the Rating of Group Interaction

Another approach to interpersonal interaction that derives from the measurement tradition is that of Robert F. Bales (1951). Bales' method for interaction process analysis was developed originally to measure the interaction of people in small groups and has been used in research on the interpersonal interaction for over twenty years. This method is also described in Chapter 8 in relation to exchange theory.

Although Bales' approach derives from the application of measurement methods and the analysis of data through complex statistical means, it differs from Foa's in three main ways. First and most obviously, Bales was primarily interested in studying the way people interacted in small groups, rather than studying people interacting in pairs. Second, Bales' measurement method was based on the observation of people actually interacting, rather than on their statements as to how they would interact, obtained from paper-and-pencil questionnaires. In Bales' research, "emphasis is laid upon firsthand observation in natural situations as the starting point for understanding personalities, rather than upon tests, questionnaires, or experimental situations" (1970, p.v). Finally, Bales analyzed his data by factor analysis rather than by facet analysis, which Foa used. It should be noted that both facet analysis and factor analysis rely on the correlation coefficient as a basic statistical tool. Factor analysis is performed on the matrices of correlation coefficients, while in facet analysis the correlation matrices are used as the method by which to confirm the hypotheses derived from facet analysis.

In this section two measurement methods will be described. The first is *Interaction Process Analysis*. This is a measurement of the interaction among members of a group. The second measurement device is *Interpersonal Ratings*. These ratings classify the personality of each individual, based on his behavior within the group. The first device might be considered a method for measuring group interaction, while the second is based on the way a person behaves in interaction with other people. Bales states that there are two determinants of behavior in a group situation: (1) the personality of the individual and (2) the situation, or group role. The first device is a method for determining the group role of an individual, while the second device is a method for determining his personality. The two functions are interrelated.

Interaction Process Analysis

Before describing Bales' current theory and the research that produced it, a short explanation of his interaction process analysis would seem to be in order. This method was one of the first to be applied to the measurement of the interpersonal interaction and might well be considered classical. A variety of methods have been derived from it for measuring interpersonal interaction in small groups.

The original interest in developing the method was stimulated by "general and theoretical" concerns rather than any practical concern with small group interaction per se. Bales was interested in using small groups as a means to investigate the dynamics of larger social systems. Further, he wanted to develop a method that would be applicable to all kinds of groups, two-person groups as well as larger groups. When he first described the method, he speculated that it might be more useful as a conceptual and operational model for the analysis of interaction systems than as a measuring device for use in experimental studies. His concerns were theoretical rather than practical.

The first step toward the development of the method foreshadowed the subsequent development of Bales' research. He had observers sit in on the meetings of some staff members of the Harvard Psychological Clinic who were conducting a study of several subjects. On the basis of what the observers noted, categories were developed in accordance with theoretical principles derived from a variety of sources, including those of a psychological, psychoanalytic, anthropological, and sociological nature. These categories were then tested empirically on interacting groups and corrected, so that the method evolved in an ongoing interaction between theoretical considerations and empirical observation of actual groups in operation. This process continued for several years, even after the publication of *Interaction Process Analysis* (1951), with a variety of groups serving as subjects.

The set of categories used in the first presentation of the method are described by Bales as

> a kind of practical compromise between the demands of theoretical adequacy, the curbs introduced by the number and kinds of distinctions moderately trained observers can make in actual scoring situations, and the demand for a reasonable simplicity in the processing of data and the interpretation of results to subjects for feedback and training purposes (1951, p. viii).

The method comprises a way of "classifying direct, face-to-face interaction as it takes place, act by act, and a series of ways of summarizing and analyzing the resulting data so that they yield useful information" (1951, p. 5). Basically, this method classifies into twelve categories the action or statement one person makes to another within the social situation. These twelve categories of statements are further categorized into three kinds of categories. The categories of categories, which we might call "metacategories," are categories of (1) problems, (2) questions and answers and positive and negative reactions, and (3) social-emotional and task areas.

In this method the observer watches the group interacting, records the amount of time each person speaks, and categorizes the statement the person makes into one of the twelve categories. The categories are shown in Table 8. As can be seen, these categories are in turn classified into the three kinds of metacategories. Categories 1, 2, and 3 are classified as positive statements in the social-emotional area, while statements 10, 11, and 12 are negative statements in the social-emotional area. Statements 4, 5, 6, 7, 8, and 9 are classified as falling in the task area and as being socially and emotionally neutral.

Statements 6 and 7 are classified as indicating problems of communication. Statements 5 and 8 indicate problems of evaluation. Statements 4 and 9 indicate problems of control. Statements 3 and 10 indicate problems of decision, statements 2 and 11 indicate problems of tension reduction, and statements 1 and 12 indicate problems of reintegration.

Finally, statements 1, 2, and 3 are classified as positive reactions, statements 4, 5, and 6 are attempted answers, statements 7, 8, and 9 are questions, and statements 10, 11, and 12 are negative reactions.

Any action is by a person toward another within a situation. The action proceeds from the past and moves toward some future goal. If an act is oriented toward the past, it is *expressive;* if it is oriented toward the future, it is *instrumental.* In the process of interaction, each of the problem areas must be solved in consecutive order. The first problem area is communication, so problems of communication in an interaction must be solved before the interaction can progress to solving the problems of evaluation. The problems of evaluation must be solved before the people involved in the interaction can proceed to the problems of control, and so on. The solving of problems is the social process.

The Three-Dimensional Model of Interpersonal Behavior

Bales' scheme is rooted in the observation of actual, functioning groups of people, with the data obtained from the observations subjected to the discipline of statistical analysis and theoretical organization. Bales believes that "to be of any practical use a theory has to start with something you can observe, and must enable you to predict something else you can observe" (1970, p. 174).

The observations of individuals interacting in a group provided

TABLE 8.   **THE SYSTEM OF CATEGORIES USED IN OBSERVATION AND THEIR MAJOR RELATIONS**

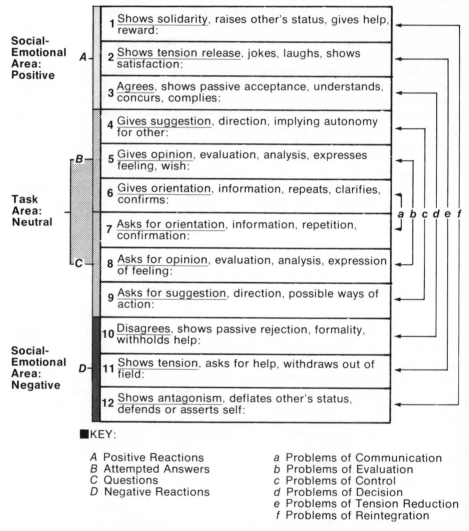

Social-Emotional Area: Positive   A

1 <u>Shows solidarity</u>, raises other's status, gives help, reward:

2 <u>Shows tension release</u>, jokes, laughs, shows satisfaction:

3 <u>Agrees</u>, shows passive acceptance, understands, concurs, complies:

Task Area: Neutral   B

4 <u>Gives suggestion</u>, direction, implying autonomy for other:

5 <u>Gives opinion</u>, evaluation, analysis, expresses feeling, wish:

6 <u>Gives orientation</u>, information, repeats, clarifies, confirms:

7 <u>Asks for orientation</u>, information, repetition, confirmation:

C

8 <u>Asks for opinion</u>, evaluation, analysis, expression of feeling:

9 <u>Asks for suggestion</u>, direction, possible ways of action:

Social-Emotional Area: Negative   D

10 <u>Disagrees</u>, shows passive rejection, formality, withholds help:

11 <u>Shows tension</u>, asks for help, withdraws out of field:

12 <u>Shows antagonism</u>, deflates other's status, defends or asserts self:

a b c d e f

■KEY:

A Positive Reactions
B Attempted Answers
C Questions
D Negative Reactions

a Problems of Communication
b Problems of Evaluation
c Problems of Control
d Problems of Decision
e Problems of Tension Reduction
f Problems of Reintegration

Bales with the basis for categorizing each person into one of twenty-six basic personality types. These types are really theoretical abstractions which tie together many inferences and theories as to what things go together psychologically and sociologically. "A type description is simply a way of saying that some given aspect of interpersonal behavior observable in a group is likely to be associated with something else not yet observed" (Bales, 1970, p. 4). The type system also provides a basis for predicting how people of different types are likely to interact with each other.

The type system is based on a three-dimensional spatial model of interpersonal types. This system is diagramed in Figure 3. The self is located in the middle. The person may try to move himself, and also the group, in any of the six directions or in some combination of the six directions. The six directions and their combinations provide twenty-six different interpersonal behavior types. These directions are: (1) Up, (2) Down, (3) Forward, (4) Backward, (5) Positive, and (6) Negative.

Each of these directions has a meaning and/or a value. To put something upward means to give it power, to put it downward is to reduce its power. To put something forward in a group context means to offer it for group acceptance, while to put something backward is to disassociate it from authority. To make something negative is to asso-

FIGURE 3. **A SCHEMATIC DIAGRAM OF BALES' THREE-DIMENSIONAL MODEL OF INTERPERSONAL BEHAVIOR**

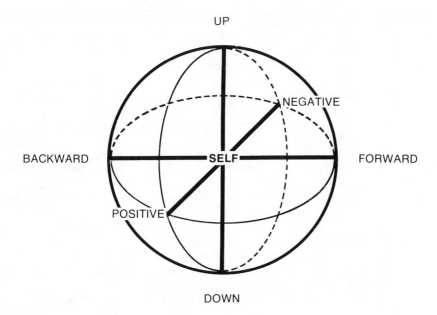

ciate it with other negative things, such as anxiety and hostility, while to make it positive is to associate it with positive things, such as love and gratification.

The three factors (Up/Down, Forward/Backward, Positive/Negative) used in the spatial model were derived from both theoretical considerations and the factor analysis of a large amount of different kinds of data. But Bales arrived at the value meaning of the directions while mapping the value statements into the factor space of the model. He classified together those things that had like consequences.

As a way of understanding the system, Bales suggests observing a real group in interaction and evaluating the behavior of a particular group member. He recommends the selection of a group that has some authority-oriented task as a part of its regular activity. This group should be observed during its task-oriented phase. After observing the interaction of a particular person within the group, Bales provides a series of questions to ask about that person's behavior within the group. He has provided three forms of these questions, Forms A, B, and C, but we will study only one, Form A, which is as follows:

1. Does he (or she) seem to *receive a lot of interaction* from others?
2. Does he seem *personally involved in the group?*
3. Does he seem *valuable for a logical task?*
4. Does he *assume responsibility for task leadership?*
5. Does he *speak like an autocratic authority?*
6. Does he seem *dominating?*
7. Does he seem to *demand pleasure and gratification?*
8. Does he seem to *think of himself as entertaining?*
9. Does he seem *warm and personal?*
10. Does he *arouse your admiration?*
11. Does he seem especially to be *addressed when others have serious opinions* about which they want confirmation?
12. Does he seem to stand for the most *conservative ideas and beliefs of the group?*
13. Does he always seem to try to speak *objectively?*
14. Does he seem to feel that his *individual independence* is very important?
15. Does he seem to *feel that others are generally too conforming* to conventional social expectations?
16. Does he seem to *reject religious belief generally?*
17. Do you feel *liking* for him or her?
18. Does he seem to *make others feel he admires them?*
19. Does he seem to believe that *equality and humanitarian concern* for others is important?
20. Does he seem very *introverted,* serious, shy, introspective?

21. Does he seem to believe that it is necessary to *sacrifice the self* for higher values?
22. Does he seem *resentful?*
23. Does he seem to accept *failure and withdrawal* for himself?
24. Does he seem to *withhold cooperation passively?*
25. Does he seem to *identify with some group of underprivileged persons?*
26. Does he tend to *devaluate himself?*[3]

Each of these questions about the person is answered either "yes" or "no" by the rater. The yesses and noes are then analyzed according to the following key in Table 9. The score for the person is found by adding up the total number of answers tallied for each of the six categories "Up" *(U),* "Down" *(D),* "Positive" *(P),* "Negative" *(N),* "Forward" *(F),* and "Backward" *(B).* You will note that some of the answers are coded for more than one of the six categories. For example, an answer "no" to question 2 is scored *"DN,"* so tallies would be entered in both the *D* and the *N* category. If the answer for the subject is "no" to question 3, that answer is scored *"DNB,"* and tallies are entered in the *D,* the *N,* and the *B* categories.

After all the questions have been scored and all the tallies entered in the appropriate categories, the following is done: (1) The absolute difference between the *U* tallies and the *D* tallies is determined, and the one with the larger number of tallies is retained, along with the difference. For example, if 10 *U* tallies were made and only 8 *D* tallies, 10−8 = 2, and *U* has the larger number of tallies, so 2*U* would be retained. (2) The absolute difference between the *P* tallies and the *N* tallies is determined, and the category with the larger number of tallies and the difference between the number of tallies for the two categories are retained. For example, if the subject had scored 13 *P* tallies and 5 *N* tallies, 13−5 = 8, and *P* has the larger number of tallies, so 8*P* is retained. (3) The absolute difference between the *F* tallies and the *B* tallies is determined, and the category with the larger number of tallies and the number of the difference between the tallies are retained. For example, if *F* received 14 tallies and *B* received 4 tallies, 14−4 = 10, and *F* received the larger number of tallies, so 10*F* would be retained.

Finally, the categories with numbers below 3 are dropped. In our example we have 2*U,* 8*P,* and 10*F.* Since *U* has a number below 3, it is dropped, leaving us with *P* and *F.* The subject studied would then be classified as *PF.* That is, this subject would tend to move in the positive and the forward directions within the group. A schematic diagram of this scoring system is presented in Figure 4.

TABLE 9. **KEY TO INTERPERSONAL RATING FORMS**

	(This key is used for Forms A, B, C.)	
1.	No = D	Yes = U
2.	No = DN	Yes = UP
3.	No = DNB	Yes = UPF
4.	No = DB	Yes = UF
5.	No = DPB	Yes = UNF
6.	No = DP	Yes = UN
7.	No = DPF	Yes = UNB
8.	No = DF	Yes = UB
9.	No = DNF	Yes = UPB
10.	No = N	Yes = P
11.	No = NB	Yes = PF
12.	No = B	Yes = F
13.	No = PB	Yes = NF
14.	No = P	Yes = N
15.	No = PF	Yes = NB
16.	No = F	Yes = B
17.	No = NF	Yes = PB
18.	No = UN	Yes = DP
19.	No = UNB	Yes = DPF
20.	No = UB	Yes = DF
21.	No = UPB	Yes = DNF
22.	No = UP	Yes = DN
23.	No = UPF	Yes = DNB
24.	No = UF	Yes = DB
25.	No = UNF	Yes = DPB
26.	No = U	Yes = D

From *Personality and interpersonal behavior* by Robert Freed Bales, p. 7. Copyright © 1970 by Holt, Rinehart and Winston, Inc. Reprinted by permission of Holt, Rinehart and Winston, Inc.

With these measuring devices based on the observation of a person's behavior in a group, it is possible to classify the person being observed into one of twenty-six different types—or into a twenty-seventh type labeled "Average." The following describes the twenty-seven different types and locates them on the diagram in Figure 3.

Average (Ave.): People of this type are hard to describe, since they, by definition, deviate in no noteworthy way. Basically, they are residual types who cannot be classified in any of the other twenty-six ways.

Type U: People of this type are located in the upward part of the group space and are active, talkative, and powerful, but not unusually friendly or unfriendly. They seem to move toward material success and power.

FIGURE 4. **SCORING PROCEDURE FOR INTERPERSONAL RATINGS**

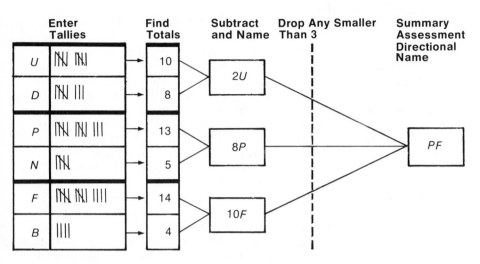

From *Personality and Interpersonal behavior* by Robert Freed Bales, p. 9. Copyright © 1970 by Holt, Rinehart and Winston, Inc. Reprinted by permission of Holt, Rinehart and Winston, Inc.

Type UP: People of this type are located in the upward-positive section of the group space. They are socially extroverted and ascendant, but also open and friendly. They seem to move toward social success and popularity.

Type UPF: People of this type are located in the upward-positive-forward section of the group space. They are ascendant and friendly, but also take the lead in moving the group toward completing its tasks. They seem to move simultaneously toward social solidarity and progress.

Type UF: People of this type are located in the upward-forward part of the group space. They take the lead in giving suggestions to the group and are ascendant, task-oriented, and impersonal. They seem to move toward group loyalty and cooperation.

Type UNF: People of this type are located in the upward-negative-forward part of the group space. They take the initiative in the task-oriented direction. They are dominating and unfriendly and regard themselves as morally superior to the others. They seem to move toward autocratic authority.

Type UN: People of this type are located in the upward-negative sector. They are dominating, self-confident, aggressive, hostile, and unfriendly. They are not concerned about morality, values, or the group task and take pleasure in their power over others. They seem to move toward tough-minded assertiveness.

Type UNB: People of this type are located in the upward-negative-backward sector. They are dominating, self-confident, and rebellious toward authority and hostile toward others. They appear self-centered, deviant, exhibitionistic, and exploitative. They seem to move toward rugged individualism and the gratification of themselves alone.

Type UB: People of this type are located in the upward-backward sector. They seem ascendant, expressive, nontask-oriented, and perhaps unconventional or deviant. They are entertaining, joking, dramatic, and take pleasure in play and novelty. They seem to move toward value-relativism and the expression of underlying emotions.

Type UPB: People of this type are located in the upward-positive-backward sector. They are ascendant and expressive, open, warm, friendly, affectionate, nurturing, permissive, and rewarding to others. They are free to give unconditional love and praise. They seem to move toward emotional supportiveness and warmth.

Type P: People of this type are located in the positive part of the group space. They are friendly, sociable, and informal. They approach others as equals. They are interested in others as individual persons with needs as important as their own. They seem to move toward equalitarianism.

Type PF: People of this type are located in the positive-forward part of the group space. They are friendly and agreeable, task- and value-oriented. They do not take the initiative, but they are not submissive; rather, they are equalitarian. They are serious about group agreements. They seem to move toward a quiet, dedicated, altruistic love.

Type F: People of this type are located in the forward sector. They are primarily task- and value-oriented. They are directly to the point and oriented toward problem solving. They are strictly impersonal, but seriously searching for solutions. They seem to move toward the conservation of the best in group beliefs and precedents.

Type NF: People of this type are located in the negative-forward sector. They are value- and task-oriented. They always try to be objective. They are so persistent in their insistence on always doing the right thing that they seem unfriendly and inhibiting. They seem to move toward the acceptance of all the restraints necessary to realize values — that is, they accept certain inhibitions in order to meet the demands of, or goals of, certain values.

Type N: People of this type are located in the negative sector. They are unfriendly and disagreeable. They are self-concerned and isolated, detached, unsocial, and negativistic. They seem to move toward personal isolation.

Type NB: People of this type are located in the negative-backward sector. They are autonomous and resistant to authority and unfriendly toward others. They are evasive, stubborn, obstinate, cynical, and radically unconforming. They seem to move toward the rejection of social conformity.

Type B: People of this type are located in the backward section of the group space. They are heretical and disbelieving. They wish to install another mode of existence, a fantasy mode, in another place and time. They tend to be poised, lost in the fantasy of wildly improbable ambitions, unable to decide anything or to actually strive for anything far in the future. They seem to move toward the rejection of all conservative group belief.

Type PB: People of this type are located in the positive-backward sector. They are friendly and receptive to jokes and stories and are equalitarian. They are ready to share and enjoy sociability. They want everybody to have what he needs without complications. They are concerned about persons and their growth. They seem to move toward permissive liberalism.

Type DP: People of this type are located in the downward-positive sector. They are friendly and nonassertive, calm and ready to admire others. They are responsive to others as individuals. They tend to trust and identify with others. They seem to move toward a trust in the goodness of others.

Type DPF: People of this type are located in the downward-positive-forward sector. They are friendly, submissive, and task- and value-oriented. They are ready to follow, obey, and conform. They are respectful, loving, gentle, idealistic, and altruistic. They seem to move toward "salvation" through the giving and receiving of love.

Type DF: People of this type are located in the downward-forward sector. They are submissive, dutiful, and conventional, wishing to follow a task- and value-oriented leader. They are impersonal, cautious, hardworking, and fearful of disapproval. They seem to move toward more complete knowledge of themselves and more subjective completeness.

Type DNF: People of this type are located in the downward-negative-forward sector. They are submissive, conventional, dutiful, self-sacrificing, and self-pitying. They sometimes make themselves the object of the aggression of others and may seek to martyr themselves so they can blame others. They seem to move toward some sort of self-sacrifice in order to preserve some higher set of values.

Type DN: People of this type are located in the downward-negative sector. They are self-conscious and unresponsive, unfriendly and resentful, and passively reject the overtures of others. They seem to wish to be left alone. They are indifferent to the value and task orientation of the group. They seem to move away from social attachment of any kind.

Type DNB: People of this type are located in the downward-negative-backward sector. They are passively alienated and unfriendly toward persons and cynical toward values. They are discouraged, dejected, and ready to quit if possible. They seem to be trying to confirm their own failures and to move toward withdrawal from life and active effort.

Type DB: People of this type are located in the downward-backward sector. They are passively anxious, tense, and negative to the demands of authority and forward group leadership. They are primarily oriented toward the repression of negative feelings about the requirements of convention and the value and task demands of the group. They seem to move toward withholding cooperation.

Type DPB: People of this type are located in the downward-positive-backward sector. They are friendly and nonassertive, passive, and wishing to receive acceptance from the others. They are not at all value- or task-oriented, but they are responsive to the nurture of others and expect to receive what they need without achievement. They seem to move toward identification with the underprivileged.

Type D: People of this type are located in the downward sector of the group space. They are self-effacing and nonassertive, passive and powerless. They accept things as they are without enthusiasm. They are simply inactive and inert in their adaptation to all influences. They seem to move toward a devaluation of themselves.

These different types interact within the group. Each type appears to be trying to move the group in his own value direction. In order to move the group, it is necessary for the individual members to form coalitions with other members of the group. The coalitions tend to form among the members of the group who share the same value directions and the same power positions, each person in a group tends to unite with the person who is nearest to him in the group in power and values. These coalitions lead to the formation of subnetworks within the group structure.

Generally speaking, the possession of power in the group is located in the upward and forward sector of the sphere. Possession of power is in the upward portion, legitimate status is in the upward and forward sector, and the forward sector is the area of legitimacy, conformity, and orthodoxy. However, a person may be quite influential within a group, not because he has power but because he is strategically located at the intersection of subnetworks within the group. Located here, he is important for the same reason that a small nation such as Israel may be of crucial international importance, not because of power but because of strategic location.

Inferences about relative power in a group may be deduced by observing who speaks to whom and how much. People tend to address those who are higher than themselves on the power structure, so those high in the power structure receive more direct messages than they send. A person who is active in a group tries to exercise power. And high initiators of action tend to receive as much action as they send.

However, the need for agreement within a group seems to be more basic than the need for power. Therefore, if a member of a group is deviant, the group tends to concentrate on trying to either win over or defeat the deviant one before returning to matters of power.

Power is important in a group, since the persons who possess it directly affect group activity and direction. Ideas are important to any group that is trying to solve a problem, but whether or not an idea is adopted depends on who suggests it. Therefore, for an idea or suggestion to be accepted it must be sponsored by a member of the group who has status. If I suggest a policy, that's one thing. If the President of the United States suggests it, that is something quite different.

Dyads, or two-person groups, function differently than larger groups. In a group, one person talks to another person, and the other members of the group serve as judges of what happens. In a dyad there is no other person, so there is no impartial or impersonal judge. Therefore,

> if a two-person group cannot run on the assumption of "love" it cannot run, since neither norms nor coalitions have their usual representation in actual third persons. Individuals in two-person groups tend to adjust to their problem of having no third person, or judge, to appeal to by being very careful to maintain the appearance, at least, of solidarity. They tend to have high rates of agreeing, and low rates of disagreeing, but they also have high rates of showing tension—all indications that they tend to suppress disagreement and negative feeling (Bales, 1951, p. 79).

Bales hypothesizes that people develop their tendency to interact with others in a particular manner because of their previous interaction with others. These past experiences are the determining factors. He states that no test is as important for understanding a person as knowing the experiences which that person has had. "In general, one supposes the critical and emotionally significant relations with others experienced in the person's life history are retained in his memory in a way that tends to leave his preferred picture of himself as strong, secure and triumphant as possible" (Bales, 1951, p. 16).

Of course, the most significant others in the past history of most people are their parents. So Bales relates his types to the way each of the types describes his parents. For example, Type U, who is active, talkative, and powerful, describes his father as high on discipline but also high on emotional supportiveness and warmth. Apparently the active and dominant Type U had a father who was also active and dominant. Bales noted that "the average tendency is for subjects to describe their parents in much the same way that they themselves are described by other group members" (1970, p. 198). Type *U* also reports that his mother was high on inhibitory demands and high on emotional supportiveness. Type *D*, who is passive and nonassertive, gives the impression that he had little interaction with his parents and that they were low on both inhibitory demands and emotional supportiveness.

As was stated at the beginning of this section, this theoretical structure was based on the application of extensive measurement techniques subjected to statistical analysis and interacting with theory. The basic empirical data upon which Bales' structure rests were obtained from sixty subjects who were studied extensively by a variety of methods. These subjects met in twelve groups of five for a series of five two-hour meetings in which they were faced with a variety of tasks. These included interviewing and inference tasks, a self-analytic task, and value-dilemma tasks based on cases. The data from these meetings were combined for every subject.

The kinds of measurement obtained from these subjects included written personality tests, observation of their behavior in group meetings, classification of value statements they made during group meetings, ratings of the individual made by other group members, and estimations by the individual of how the other members of the group would rate him.

The data obtained from this final group were factor-analyzed, forming the main basis for the Bales structure. However, he notes that actually six different factor analyses were performed, including three on data obtained from subjects who were not a part of his main study.[4] These factor analyses provided differing numbers of factors (for example, one [Bales & Couch, 1970] produced four factors), but Bales decided to restrict the model to three factors. Three factors seemed to account for the largest part of the variance in the data, and it seemed more manageable to restrict the model to three factors, or dimensions. Bales argued that

> the restriction to three dimensions does not necessarily mean that some types of value-statements are completely disregarded. It means they are less-exactly defined and located than they might be. But the gain in exactness may not be worth the cost in complication. The restriction to three dimensions for the present system is a restriction for the sake of practical manageability (1970, p. 52).

[4]Bales cites three other studies from which he obtained data. These included Bales, R. F., & Couch, A. S. The value-profile: A factor analytic study of value statements. In R. F. Bales, *Personality and interpersonal behavior.* New York: Holt, Rinehart & Winston, 1970, pp. 492–510; and Couch, A. S. Factors of group satisfaction. Paper read at American Sociological Association Convention, 1956; and Melvin, D. An experimental and statistical study of two primary social attitudes. Unpublished doctoral thesis, University of London, 1953.

Bales notes that his system has produced dimensions that are similar to those presented by other systems. Bales' Up and Down are similar to Leary's dominance versus submission, and his positive and negative are similar to Leary's love versus hate. He also relates his dimensions to Osgood's analysis (1957) of the meanings people assign to objects and people. Bales likens Osgood's dimension of good versus bad to positive versus negative, his fast versus slow to the upward-backward versus downward-forward sectors, and his powerful versus weak to the upward-forward versus downward-backward sectors.

A Desultory Discussion

At this point I feel fatigued and brain-weary. I trust the reader feels likewise. In this chapter I have attempted to give some inkling of some rather complex measurement techniques and methods for data analysis and theory construction that have produced two noteworthy approaches to the study of the interpersonal relationship.

Foa's six-facet system is confusing to describe and no doubt confusing to read as well. In using his system to analyze data, it seems that his facets are not independent. That is, the actor and the observer facets of the perceptual facets are not necessarily independent of the person who is acted upon in the behavioral facets. For example, if we take Type I, 1, in which the variable is "To what degree does the observer perceive, from his point of view, that the other (nonobserver) accepts him socially?" are not the perceiver and the one acted upon the same person? It seems to me that the confusion in distinguishing the actor, the alias, and the one acted upon is not just a result of the complexity of the system. In attempting to teach this system, I have repeatedly found that students find it almost impossible to grasp these distinctions, and I think this difficulty may well be rooted in the fact that the distinctions are more semantic than real. To put it simply, it seems that the system is more complicated than is desirable, useful, or actual.

Another problem with the Foa system is that it is based largely on verbal statements made by people as to what they would do or ought to do. This is one kind of data that has a long and honorable history in personality research, but it is also a method that long experience suggests is something less than completely valid. Some people accurately report what they did do and with reasonable accurateness predict what they will do, but many people do neither with accuracy. How does this effect the validity of the system? There is no way of telling, although it is an empirical question that can be tested.

Generally speaking, the facet analysis system is highly regarded by methodologists in the area, so that the application of it to the study of the interpersonal relationship is to be applauded. Foa is a diligent worker who is well aware of the research that needs to be done, so it can be expected that he will continue to expand and improve his theory.

The problems with Bales' system that seem most obvious are two, and both of them are methodological. First is his use of factor analysis. Guttman developed his facet analysis approach because of dissatisfaction with factor analysis. Disillusionment with factor analysis has increased since that time, although the method does have its proponents and its opponents. I suppose, therefore, one could raise the question of whether Bales should have used factor analysis, or some other method, instead. However, the obvious defense is that factor analysis, while not necessarily the best or only synthesizer of basic psychological elements, is still a useful method for organizing and viewing data.

The second criticism regards the size of the sample. Bales' system is based on data obtained largely from only sixty subjects. Not only the generality of the findings but also the extensive statistical analysis of large amounts of data from such a relatively small sample is questionable. Bales used over one hundred measures in his research. The chances for error in obtaining significant findings are quite substantial with a sample of this size.

However, Bales was well aware of the problems and pitfalls he faced. His use of the factor analysis data within the framework of the theory that developed out of more than twenty-five years of research provided safeguards against erroneous theorizing. His obtained factors were used to the extent that they appeared useful and in agreement with the theory developed in interaction with other data. He was aware of the problem of the small sample. Any errors that derive from that can be corrected by further research, and there can be no doubt that the system will get a rigorous test from many social scientists.

On the other hand, there is something to be said in favor of exhaustive research on a relatively small panel of subjects. Any researcher who is studying human beings in human kinds of situations is usually faced with limitations on the amount and kinds of data he can obtain. If he elects to obtain data from a large number of subjects, he is generally limited in the kind of data he can collect. Large amounts of information cannot be obtained from each subject if a large number of subjects is to be studied. Conversely, if the researcher hopes to obtain extensive data from each subject, then practicality limits him to a relatively small number of subjects. Obviously, some kinds of problems cannot be studied effectively unless they include large numbers of subjects. Any reliable assessment of the political opinion of the nation requires several hundred subjects. On the other hand, an attempt to determine the in-depth determinants of a political opinion require rather extensive data obtained from each subject. Bales elected to study a relatively small number of subjects intensively, and that particular option has its uses and its justifications.

In the approaches of both men, the ultimate evaluation rests on how useful their systems prove to be in explaining and predicting the behavior of people interacting with each other.

It should be noted that the theories of Bales and Foa can be related to each other. It will be recalled that one of the studies Foa used as a basis for his original facet analysis of interpersonal behavior was Leary's two-factor theory. Bales also related his theory to Leary's two factors of love-hate and dominance-submission. Foa added a third dimension of self-other to develop his three behavioral facets, while Bales added the dimension of forward-backward to provide a third dimension. It might be argued that Bales is primarily concerned with group interaction rather than dyadic interaction, so that his three factors are applicable only to groups. But his third dimension is a conservative-iconoclastic dimension, so it would seem to be applicable to the dyad as well as to the group. It would be an interesting exercise to translate Bales' three factors into facets. This could be done rather easily by applying facet analysis to the questions (Forms A, B, and C) describing a person's interaction in a group.

This chapter began with an examination of Leary's development of a scheme for diagnosing psychiatric patients on the basis of how they related to other people. Thus, at least a part of the original impetus for this whole line of research developed out of a study of the interaction of patients in psychotherapy. Since that beginning, this area of research has involved a wide variety of subjects in a variety of relationships that were observed in a variety of situations. None of the research reported the experimental manipulation of subjects in a laboratory, but almost every other conceivable situation and relationship has been studied.

Foa and Bales obtained different kinds of data. Foa based his research on self-report, while Bales based his on observed behavior. The fact that both self-report and observed behavior result in similar kinds of dimensions suggests that there is substantial validity to the conclusion that the way a person relates to another is a function of at least two dimensions, acceptance-rejection and dominance-submission.

This whole line of endeavor can be commended for its large amount of data obtained from many different kinds of people behaving in many different kinds of situations. What it lacks is integration of theories and research, and more extended, detailed investigation of both the dyadic and group levels. To some extent Bales undertakes this task, but it needs to be pursued. What are the different types of group or dyadic interaction? What happens when a *UPF* finds himself in an intimate situation with a girl who is a *DNB?* How many basic patterns of dyadic interaction are there? What is the relationship between how one of these types observes himself behaving and how another person describes his behavior? When members of different types exhibit the same kind of behavior (e.g., withdrawal, boredom, aggressiveness) what kinds of experiences do they report? Do some feel more comfortable with one kind of behavior (e.g., aggressive self-assertion) and tense, anxious, or resentful when the other person insists on doing all of the talking? How much variety does one type exhibit in his behavior compared with other types? Are some types more "interpersonally versatile" than others? These kinds of questions could be multiplied, and they need to be answered. However, it is to the credit of those laboring in this area that the answers to such pertinent questions are being sought.

As theories these are relatively narrow. They are really empirical studies of interpersonal interaction, and the theoretical background from which they develop is more that of psychological measurement than that of personality theory or interpersonal relations theory. However, both Foa and Bales are working toward integrating the content of their own work with the content of broader theories. Assuming that their efforts succeed, the results should produce a theory of interpersonal relations for which there are reliable and valid methods of measurement. The measurement contribution would come, of course, from those people whose work we have described in this chapter.

Summary

This chapter has presented approaches to the interpersonal relationship based on methods of measuring the way people interact with each other. The two theorists described are Uriel G. Foa and Robert F. Bales.

Foa's system involves the *facet analysis method* developed by Louis Guttman. Foa analyzes the interpersonal relationship into six facets, of which three facets are *perceptual facets* and three are *behavioral facets*. The perceptual facets deal with who is observing whom doing what, and the behavioral facets deal with what is done and to whom. The three perceptual facets are (1) the observer (self) or the nonobserver (other), (2) whether the action observed is actual behavior or ideal behavior, and (3) the actor or the nonactor. The behavioral facets deal with what is done (actually or ideally); these three facets are (1) acceptance or rejection, (2) in the emotional or social area, and (3) done to the self or to the other. Data obtained from married couples tended to support Foa's structure.

Bales based his method on the *factor analysis* of data obtained from personality tests, questionnaires, and especially from extensive observation and rating of people actually interacting in groups. His system uses three dimensions, *Up* and *Down, Forward* and *Backward,* and *Positive* and *Negative.* Up has to do with obtaining power; Down, with losing power. Positive has to do with positive things such as love and gratification, while Negative has to do with negative things such as anxiety and hostility. To put something Forward means to offer it for group acceptance, while to put something Backward is to dissociate it from authority.

References

Bales, R. F. *Interaction process analysis*. Reading, Mass.: Addison-Wesley, 1951.

Bales, R. F. *Personality and interpersonal behavior*. New York: Holt, Rinehart & Winston, 1970.

Bales, R.F., & Couch, A. S. The value-profile: a factor analytic study of value statements. In R. F. Bales, *Personality and interpersonal behavior*. New York: Holt, Rinehart & Winston, 1970.

Borgatta, E. F., Cottrell, L. S., & Mann, J. M. The spectrum of individual interaction characteristics: an interdimensional analysis. *Psychological Reports*, 1958, 4, 279–319.

Carter, L. F. Evaluating the performance of individuals as members of small groups. *Personnel Psychology*, 1954, 7, 477–84.

Couch, A. S. Factors of group satisfaction. Paper read at American Sociological Association Convention, 1956.

Cronbach, L. J. *Essentials of psychological testing*. New York: Harper & Row, 1970.

Foa, U. G. Convergences in the analysis of the structure of interpersonal behavior, *Psychological Review*, 1961, 68, 341–53.

Foa, U. G. New developments in facet design and analysis. *Psychological Review*, 1965, 72, 262–74.

Foa, U. G. Perception of behavior in reciprocal roles: the ringex model. *Psychological Monographs: General and Applied*, 1966, 80(Whole No. 623).

Foa, U. G., & Foa, E. Resource exchange: toward a structural theory of interpersonal communication. In A. W. Siegman & B. Pope (Eds.), *Studies in dyadic communication*. Long Island City, New York: Pergamon Press, 1969.

Guttman, L. A new approach to factor analysis: the radex. In P. Lazarsfeld (Ed.), *Mathematical thinking in the social sciences*. Glencoe, Ill.: The Free Press, 1954. (a)

Guttman, L. The principle components of scalable attitudes. In P. Lazarsfeld (Ed.), *Mathematical thinking in the social sciences*. Glencoe, Ill.: The Free Press, 1954. (b)

Guttman, L. Introduction to facet design and analysis. In *Proceedings of the fifteenth international congress of psychology*. Amsterdam: North Holland, 1958.

Guttman, L. A faceted definition of intelligence. Dittoed paper, University of Michigan, 1965.

Leary, T. *Interpersonal diagnosis of personality.* New York: The Ronald Press, 1957.

Melvin, D. An experimental and statistical study of two primary social attitudes. Unpublished doctoral thesis, University of London, 1953.

Osgood, C. E., Suci, G. J., & Tannenbaum, P. H. *The measurement of meaning.* Urbana, Ill.: University of Illinois Press, 1957.

Schaefer, E. S. A circumplex model for maternal behavior. *Journal of Abnormal and Social Psychology,* 1959, 59, 226–35.

Schutz, W. C. *FIRO: a three-dimensional theory of interpersonal behavior.* New York: Holt, Rinehart & Winston, 1958.

Social Exchange

8

The point should be made, however, that whatever the gratifications achieved in dyads, however lofty or fine the motives satisfied may be, the relationship may be viewed as a trading or bargaining one. The basic assumption running throughout our analysis is that every individual voluntarily enters and stays in any relationship only as long as it is adequately satisfactory in terms of his rewards and costs (1959, p. 37).

—J. W. Thibaut and H. H. Kelley

The open secret of human exchange is to give the other man behavior that is more valuable to him than it is costly to you and to get from him behavior that is more valuable to you than it is costly to him (1961, p. 62).

—G. C. Homans

Since World War I the dominant theoretical and research orientation in psychology has been "behaviorism." Behaviorism and its variants have been defined in many different ways, but one main feature of this point of view has been the emphasis on the actual, observed behavior of the persons or the animals studied. This approach to research in psychology led to a great emphasis on the study of the process of learning, since it was through learning that an organism acquired specific kinds of behavior or changed its behavior. The most salient feature of learning is that people or animals learn behavior that is rewarded, avoid behavior that is punished, and change their behavior from that which is not rewarded to that which is rewarded. The observation of the effect of reward on behavior is not a particularly unique one, since parents, teachers, and animal trainers throughout recorded history have observed and used the techniques of reward. Such techniques are evident in every human realm, from the friendly pat of the master's hand on the obedient dog's head to the theological concepts of heaven and hell.

The application of the behavioristic approach to the study of interpersonal relationships has had its most fruitful flowering in exchange theory. The main statements in exchange theory are by the psychologists John Thibaut and H. H. Kelley and the sociologist G. C. Homans.

Thibaut and Kelley (1959) characterize their approach as a "point of view" or a "framework" rather than a theory. By this they presumably mean that what they present is more a way of looking at the material of the field of interpersonal relationships, rather than a thoroughly articulated theoretical system. This way of looking at the phenomenon of interpersonal relationships is characterized by certain restrictions and assumptions. As outlined by Homans (1961) they are: (1) social behavior is rewarded or punished by the behavior of another person; (2) when a person acts in a certain way toward another person, he is punished or rewarded by that person; (3) the behavior must be actual behavior and not a norm of behavior. The basic subject matter, as Homans describes it, is "the actual social behavior of individuals in direct contact with one another (1961, p. 3). For Homans, elementary social behavior is face-to-face behavior. The basic assumption as described by Thibaut and Kelley is that "most socially significant behavior will not be repeated unless it is reinforced, rewarded in some way" (1959, p. 5).

In addition to the concepts of behavioristic psychology, Homans borrows from elementary economics the concept of the exchange of goods for money in the marketplace. In his view "both behavioral psychology and elementary economics envisage human behavior as a function of its payoff; in amount and kind it depends on the amount and kind of reward and punishment it fetches" (1961, p. 12).

To put it simply, exchange theory sees the interaction between two people as a function of what each person gets out of the relationship: no payoff in the relationship, no relationship. Or if there has been payoff, when the payoff stops, the relationship stops. Love and stock manipulation, altruism and huckstering, all are at base motivated by the same force: profit.

This theory has, in my opinion, two advantages. First, it is simple and partakes of whatever righteousness accrues to the theorist who honors the principle of parsimony. It starts with simple concepts and tries to keep them simple. Second, it integrates the study of the inter-personal relationship with what has been the mainstream of behavioral science—the behavioristic approach and the function of reward in human behavior.

Exchange theory is heir to all of the criticisms that have been leveled at behaviorism in recent years, but we shall leave a discussion of these criticisms for later. An additional criticism, which is not scien-tific, is that an approach of this kind explains some of the most sublime human actions in the crassest of terms. To describe the sacrifice of a loving mother in terms of profit and loss seems to border on sacrilege. Homans has anticipated this criticism by pointing out that the only profit in interpersonal relationships does not have to come from materi-al gain or hedonistic pleasure. The greatest payoff may come from doing good to another person. As Homans puts it, "So long as men's values are altruistic, they can take a profit in altruism too. Some of the greatest profiteers we know are altruists" (1961, p. 79).

Theoretical Basis
in Behavioristic Psychology

Exchange theory grows out of a long tradition of research in behavioris-tic psychology, which has devoted itself, to a large extent, to the pro-cess of learning. The basic idea is that any organism learns to repeat behavior that is rewarded, ceases to behave in ways that are not re-warded, and suppresses behavior that is punished.

Thibaut and Kelley (1959, Ch. 1) derive their approach from the history of this point of view as it has been applied to problems in social psychology. Social psychology has typically studied situations in which the social situation is seen as the stimulus and the behavior of the per-son in the situation is seen as the response. It has, for example, studied the effect of the opinion of a group on the opinion of an experimental subject, or the effect of the behavior of a leader on some variable, such as the productivity of the group. To Thibaut and Kelley, the individual person can be substituted for the group as both a stimulus and a reward-er of the other person in the dyad, or two-person group. When two people relate, each person is rewarding or not rewarding, or perhaps punishing, the behavior of the other person. In a dyad, each person has some control over what goes on, since each has the power to reward the other. A basic premise is that behavior will not be repeated unless it is rewarded in some way. This means that if a person in a dyad behaves in a certain way, he must have been rewarded for that behavior; and if he continues to behave in this way, he must be continuing to receive reward from the other person in the dyad.

Homans is more explicit in the theoretical sources of his approach, which he derives from the psychologist B. F. Skinner,[1] who is even more rigorous than the typical behaviorist in his analysis of behavior and its stimuli. Defining the stimulus of a behavior has proven to be a sticky problem in psychology. What is a stimulus? It can be anything that stimulates a person to behave. But this raises problems in the form of inferences, since if a person fails to behave in some overt way after he has been stimulated, the obvious conclusion would seem to be that he has not been stimulated. Therefore you cannot be sure he has been stimulated unless he behaves. If you wave your hand in front of a blind man and he fails to blink, you conclude he cannot see, that is, he has not been stimulated. Thus the stimulus has come to be defined in terms of the way a person behaves in reaction to it: no response behavior, no stimulus.[2]

Skinner avoids the stimulus problem by dealing only with "operants." An operant is behavior that a person emits. When dealing with operants, the experimenter makes no assumptions as to what stimulated the behavior in the first place. The stimulation may have been some internal physiological state, such as an empty stomach, or it may have been some external situation, such as a person asking a question. In any case, the only thing the experimenter notes is that the behavior occurred. Reward, or reinforcement, is basic to this system. If a person behaves in a certain way and this behavior is reinforced, then in similar situations in the future this person will emit the same behavior for which he received reinforcement in the past.

The emission of behavior is a function of the state of the organism, the rate of reinforcement, be it positive or negative, and the withdrawal of reinforcement. The more an organism is reinforced for a particular behavior, the more likely it is to emit that behavior. However, the state of the organism affects the behavior that is emitted. A hungry person is more likely to go into a restaurant if he has been satisfactorily fed in restaurants in the past, but a person who has just eaten is not likely to go into a restaurant because he is satiated. That is, the state of the organism has changed. Negative reinforcements such as punishment or fatigue also effect behavior. If a person has found that restaurants usually charge higher prices than he is able to pay, he is not likely to go into a restaurant even though he is hungry. Or if an activity is satisfying, but after a while the experimental subject becomes fatigued, he is likely to stop emitting the behavior. Adults don't often get so tired while eating that they have to stop because of fatigue, but hungry babies have been observed to fall asleep at their mother's breast, particularly if the mother wasn't able to feed them on time and they had to cry for some time before being fed. Finally, if a person has been reinforced

---

[1] For example, Skinner, 1938, 1953, 1957, 1959.

[2] For a discussion of S – R psychology and some of the problems with it, see Koch, 1964.

for emitting a behavior in the past, but now emits the behavior and is not reinforced, he becomes frustrated and may release aggressive behavior. A man who has usually been well fed at a restaurant in the past but who on the current occasion finds that the service in the restaurant is poor and the food is scarcely edible is likely to be irritated and may well express this irritation by leaving a small tip or complaining to the waiter.

There are many refinements to the basic concepts that have evolved from the extensive research conducted within this system. For example, the rate of reinforcement affects the emission of behavior and the resistance to the extinction of behavior when the reinforcement is no longer supplied. However, we need not go into the complexities of the Skinnerian system here.

In addition to the concepts of behavioristic psychology, Homans also includes the basic concept of the marketplace from elementary economics (1961, p. 12). Elementary economics, as Homans utilizes it, is concerned with the exchange of goods for money. A person does not spend himself; that is, he does not behave in a certain way unless he is paid for it in some way. From both sources, psychology and economics, the basic concept that is derived is that of the *payoff*. If a person behaves toward another person in a certain way, it is because he expects to gain from the other person some profit from the transaction.

Basic Concepts in Exchange Theory

There are four basic concepts in exchange theory: (1) rewards, (2) costs, (3) outcome, and (4) comparison level. Also, there is the idea of the interaction itself. These concepts will be discussed in this section.

According to Homans (1961, Ch. 3), each concept has two classes, descriptive terms and variables. *Descriptive terms* are the names for the different kinds of activity. Reward, for example, may be in the form of food, or a vacation trip to Hawaii, or a smile, or a pat on the back. An activity can be any kind of behavior, including the verbal expression of feeling or sentiment. Telling another person "I love you" is an activity.

Variables are the properties of behavior that vary in quantity or in value. *Quantity* deals with how frequently a particular behavior is emitted over a given period of time; as the amount of emitted behavior increases, so does the quantity. *Value* is the worth the person receiving the behavior places on the behavior. The more a person has been deprived of a particular kind of behavior, the more he values it. A person who is constantly being told that he is loved is not likely to value the statement "I love you" nearly as much as a person to whom little positive feeling has been expressed. A wife who has just been told by her husband that he loves her is not likely to value an immediate repetition of the statement nearly as much as a wife who has not heard the words "I love you" for a month. Value is value per each unit of behavior emitted.

Value changes as the behavior is emitted. The more the behavior is emitted, the less the value per unit of emitted behavior. The more a person receives of a particular kind of behavior, the more satiated he becomes, and the value declines. Value is determined by the past history of a person. If he hasn't received much of the behavior recently, the value will be higher; if he has received a lot of it, the value will be lower.

There are two components which determine a behavior's value: (1) whether a person likes the behavior and (2) whether he has been the target of much of it lately. Since value is particular to a person and his state at the time, it naturally follows that values will vary from person to person, with one person valuing a particular kind of behavior more than the next person.

Interaction

In the actual interaction between two people, the basic unit is the behavior sequence or set (Thibaut & Kelley, 1959, Ch. 2). An interaction has taken place when the behavior of one person has been rewarded or punished by the other person (Homans, 1961, Ch. 3). Any given person has a repertoire which includes all of the possible behaviors he could emit. However, in an actual interaction, a person will emit only certain selected behaviors. The behavior in an interaction is highly selective, and the behavior which is selected is behavior which has been rewarded in the past. That is, the behavior in an interaction depends on the outcomes the person has experienced.

The elements of a given behavior sequence tend to follow a certain order; that is, a given person in similar situations will tend to follow much the same sequence of actions from one situation to another. The fact that a given person tends to maintain the same sequence of actions in his behavior toward another suggests that people tend to maintain the same orientation toward relationships with others from one situation to another and from one person to another.

Jones and Gerard (1967, Ch. 13) classify the dyadic interaction into four types: (1) pseudocontingency; (2) asymmetrical contingency; (3) reactive contingency; and (4) mutual contingency. Figure 1 presents a diagram of these four contingencies.

Any interaction is determined by two sources: what goes on within each of the participants and what goes on between them. Jones and Gerard classify interactions according to whether or not the interaction is governed by what is going on within the participants or between them.

Pseudocontingency occurs when each person's responses in the interaction are determined entirely by each person's own internal, preestablished plan which unwinds to its predetermined end. This type of interaction is not determined in any way by what goes on between the pair. Two patients talking about their operations are engaged in a pseudocontingency interaction. Their only response to each other is to wait until the other stops talking.

Asymmetrical contingency occurs when one of the members of a pair is preprogrammed to emit a certain series of behaviors, while the other member of the pair responds spontaneously to what the first member is saying or doing. In this situation the first member is behaving entirely according to what is going on within himself, while the other member of the pair is behaving in accordance with what is going on within himself and also with what is going on in the interaction between the pair. An example of this might be a recently trained vacuum cleaner salesperson and his first customer. The salesperson concentrates on his sales talk, while the customer attends both to the talk and to his own internal responses to the talk.

Reactive contingency occurs in a panic situation in which each

FIGURE 1. **CLASSES OF INTERACTION IN TERMS OF CONTINGENCY**

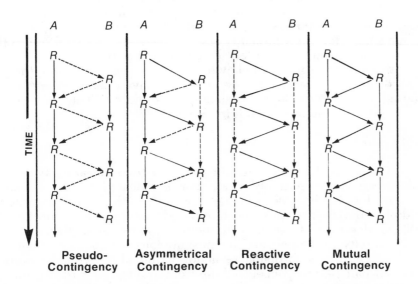

A and B are the two people participating in the interaction. R is the response of each. The solid black line indicates the main determinant of the person's behavior, while the dotted line indicates that a determiner is of minor or no importance to the person's behavior.

person reacts spontaneously without thought to the consequences of what the other does. In this situation each person is reacting to what is going on in the interaction and neither is reacting in terms of what is in the best interests of himself. Perhaps two children in a fight would be an example of reactive contingency.

Mutual contingency occurs when each participant in an interaction contributes something to and takes something away from the exchange. In this exchange the behavior is determined by what goes on within each person and also by what goes on between them. Two people engaged in a genuine conversation are an example of mutual contingency.

Rewards

Reward is anything that meets a person's needs. How rewarding a particular behavior is to another person is a function of both the behavior emitted and the person receiving the behavior. Much of our previous discussion of value applies to reward, since the value determines how rewarding a particular behavior is to the person receiving it. The more often a person is rewarded for a particular behavior, the more he will emit that behavior, and the more likely he is to emit that specific behavior in similar situations in the future. However, as was pointed out in the case of value, the more of a particular reward a person has received recently, the less the value of that particular reward, since the person's need for it has probably been satiated. The general rule is that the more a person is rewarded for emitting a particular behavior and the more value per unit of behavior the reward has, the more the person will emit that behavior. Any kind of behavior can be a reward, including such diverse items as money or a smile. Whatever a person needs or wants, the receipt of it is a reward.

Costs

Costs are the other side of the coin from rewards. If rewards make a behavior more likely to occur or be repeated, then costs make a behavior less likely to occur or be repeated. As the cost of a particular kind of behavior increases, the likelihood that a person will emit that behavior decreases. Costs may be incurred from sources that are either inside or outside the person. The most obvious source of cost is punishment for emitting a particular behavior. Criminal justice has long been based in part on the concept of the "deterrant." That is, presumably people are less likely to rob banks or commit any other crime if they know that the punishment is likely to be greater than is warranted by the amount of money they can steal.

In the interpersonal relationship the deterring aspect of potential costs is often illustrated by one person hesitating to ask another person a question for fear that the cost will be too high. Children are often afraid to ask questions of their parents for fear they might think them stupid for not knowing the answer. Or perhaps children are afraid they will be laughed at for asking such a question.

Costs may be incurred in other ways. A cost may be any alternative activity that is given up in order to participate in a current activity. When Tom and Beth decide to marry, they both incur the cost of giving up the advantages of being single. In any relationship part of the cost is the other alternative relationships that have been given up in order to engage in the current relationship. An additional source of cost may be within the person himself. Any activity, carried on long enough, causes fatigue. So the continuation of a particular behavior over a period of time results in fatigue which is a rising cost in a relationship. The old love song that contains the line about two sleepy people too much in love to say good-night is an example of the relationship triumphing over the cost of fatigue. Probably most of us know people whom we like, but with whom the relationship invariably incurs the cost of fatigue because we don't know when to quit. I recall having a friend whom I visited overnight occasionally. I enjoyed his company greatly, but any visit meant an all-night session of conversation. The fatigue cost was high.

Still another source of cost within a person may be conflict. A person may have a set to produce two different behavior sequences, so that one sequence conflicts with or interferes with the other sequence. This conflict is a cost, and since it probably causes the behavior to be less efficient, the rewards that are obtained are probably less. An example of this conflict, often seen in persons who are being counseled, is called ambivalence. *Ambivalence* is the presence of both love and hate toward the same person. I once saw this demonstrated by a mother toward her little boy. The mother was standing on a bank that stood about ten feet above a busy street. Her little boy wandered across the street, heedless of the traffic that was whizzing by. The mother looked up and was paralyzed by the sight of her son wandering across the street with cars screeching to panic stops and swerving to avoid hitting him. The boy made it safely across the street, where a man picked him up and brought him back to his mother, who was obviously torn between a desire to hug and kiss him and an overwhelming urge to give him a thorough whipping. What she did was an ineffectual combination of the two.

With the repetition of any behavior over a period of time, the costs tend to rise, because of fatigue factors if for nothing else. Also, the repetition of a behavior over a period of time tends to reduce the rewards obtained from that behavior. Secord and Backman (1964, p. 262) list what they consider to be the five sources of changes in the values of rewards and costs over a period of time. First, they suggest that changes in value may take place as a function of past exchanges. That is, fatigue may increase the costs, and satiation may decrease the reward value. Second, a change in value may come about as a result of changes within the members of the dyad. These changes may occur because one or both members of the dyad have changed in response to other relationships. Married people who are in psychotherapy and who change as a consequence of therapy generally produce a change in their relationship with their spouses. A third source of change may be a change in the external situation. For a paroled convict, the probation officer may be a powerful source of reward, but after his parole period is over, the convict will find that the officer no longer has this power. Likewise, the reward value of a pat on the back from a proud parent declines as a child grows up. A fourth source of change may be within the relationship itself. When a relationship is rewarding to a person, he will want to continue the relationship and will try to increase the amount of reward he gives to the other. Two people involved in a new romance are likely to give each other presents, pay each other compliments, and fulfill each other's wishes. This same internal dynamic of the relationship may also work in the opposite direction. A warm smile from a lover is quite rewarding. That same smile from the irascible old spouse to whom one has been married for twenty years has lost some of its reward value. A fifth source of change may come about through the association of a particular behavior with another rewarding behavior. We may initially dislike playing bridge, but if we must play bridge in order to associate with a person from whom we get other kinds of rewards, perhaps in time playing bridge will in itself become a rewarding behavior. Likewise, behavior that is associated with behavior that is costly may come to be experienced as increasing in cost.

Outcomes and Profit

The essence of the exchange theory view of interpersonal relations lies in the outcome, or the profit. The outcome, or profit, is the rewards minus the costs. The formula is: Profit = Rewards − Costs. As Homans puts it, "The open secret of human exchange is to give the other man behavior that is more valuable to him than it is costly to you and to get from him behavior that is more valuable to you than it is costly to him" (1961, p. 62). When the profit in a relationship drops down to or near zero, a person will begin looking for another relationship that promises more profit. There is nothing to be gained in perpetuating an unprofitable relationship.

It will be remembered that part of the cost of a relationship is the reward that could have been obtained from an alternative relationship. If the potential rewards in an alternative relationship go up and/or its costs go down, while the costs in the present relationship go up and/or its rewards go down, then the cost of giving up the alternative relationship goes up, thus reducing the profit in the current relationship and increasing the likelihood that the current relationship will be dropped and a new relationship will be formed. Or it may even be that when the profit drops to zero in a relationship, a person will not seek a relationship with another person, but rather a solitary activity. A person engaged in a solitary activity might be considered engaged in a relationship with himself, although this has not been proposed by exchange theorists.

The fluctuation in the profit in relationships has not been charted, but if it were, the chart, maintained for a particular relationship on an hourly basis, would probably reveal fluctuations by the hour, by the day, by the week, by the month, and by the year. It would probably look something like a chart of the value of a particular stock on the stock market. For example, at this moment I am engaged in a solitary activity, writing. A couple of hours ago I left one of my children, with whom my relationship is generally profitable. However, from the exchange theory point of view, a couple of hours ago the profit in my relationship with my child approached zero, given my scale of values. I sought out an alternative, which was discussing some work with a colleague; then having exhausted the immediate profit in that relationship, I sought solitary endeavor, or a relationship with myself, namely writing.

Since any person is seeking to maximize profit in a relationship, it naturally follows that he is going to seek, as has been pointed out, relationships that bring him maximum profits at minimum costs. It would seem that certain kinds of people are more likely to reward others at less cost to the others and thus to be much sought after for relationships with other people. Studies of who chooses whom to relate to have been analyzed by exchange theorists in these terms.

A study that has perhaps become a classic, since it is cited so frequently in the literature, is one by Helen Jennings (1943). She studied the girls in a school for delinquent girls to find out which girls were most chosen by the other girls for various kinds of relationships, which girls were not chosen, and what the difference was between the two groups. Jennings discovered that the girls frequently chosen were girls who: sought out situations which would give them an opportunity to interact with other people; initiated activities and showed ingenuity in solving problems; cooperated with others; had even dispositions; voluntarily did more than their share of the chores; were successful at planning and organizing activities; were willing to accept minor roles in activities; were solicitous of the welfare of new girls; were more likely to seek fairness by the authorities in the treatment of the other girls; were rebellious; and were reticent about their own affairs.

In analyzing these characteristics about the girls with whom others sought relationships, it would appear that these were girls who gave greater rewards to the others at a relatively low cost. By being solicitous of the welfare of the others and taking the initiative and showing ingenuity in the solution of problems, these girls would raise the rewards others could get from a relationship with them. Even their rebelliousness toward authority was probably a way of increasing rewards for the other inmates. On the other hand, their even dispositions and their keeping their own problems to themselves would reduce the cost others had to pay for maintaining a relationship with them.

The underchosen girls exhibited different characteristics, which can be seen as producing little reward for others while exacting a relatively high cost from them. These underchosen girls were quarrelsome and irritable, nervous, aggressive, and dominant; they nagged and whined, sought praise from others, and interfered with or interrupted the activities of the group.

In this list of characteristics we see little that would reward others and much that would exact a cost from them. As any parent knows, a relationship with a whining, complaining child is a trying thing. And as anybody knows, a relationship with an irritable, quarrelsome, aggressive, domineering person who seeks solely to interfere with and interrupt the activities of the group is something to be avoided.

Jennings found that the leaders in the group tended to be girls who seemed to have a greater ability to see and to meet the needs of others. They were able to differentiate between others and see how they needed to be treated. They seemed to lift the others and to give them a view of themselves that was beyond what the others had accomplished. She also found that these characteristics seemed to be stable over a period of several months, which suggests that personal attractiveness, or the ability to maximize the rewards of others in a relationship and to minimize the costs, is a fairly stable personality characteristic.

The concept of profit can also be used to explain other aspects of the choice of relationship. It has been observed, for example, that we tend to choose to relate to others who agree with us in attitudes and opinions. A person who agrees with us provides us with reward by giving us consensual validation for our opinions, and he does not exact from us the cost of a disagreement. People who have outstanding abilities are able to provide more rewards than people who lack abilities; thus they should be more attractive to others. And obviously, a person who is nearby can be related to at less cost than one who lives at a distance, since we don't have to pay the cost of traveling to relate to him. We will discuss some of these topics in more detail later in the chapter, as well as in other chapters in this book.

Jones and Gerard (1967, Ch. 13) revised the basic concept of outcome in exchange theory by separating "cue control" from simple outcome. In their view, it is because of the socialization process that people develop rather complex patterns of behavior that occur when certain cues are given by the other person. Much of the behavior between two people who have had a great deal of previous interaction with each other is determined not by outcome, but by cue control. That is, one person gives a cue, and the other person then goes into a well-rehearsed sequence of behaviors, which becomes the cue for the first person to go into his behavior, and so on. Outcome or profit, however, is of importance in new situations where the person carefully monitors the outcomes of his behavior and repeats that behavior which brings a positive outcome and avoids that which produces an unhappy outcome. Assessment of the outcome, then, is essential when a new pattern of behavior is first learned in an interpersonal interaction; but after people become well acquainted, much of the behavior between them is the result of one giving the other cues which produce behavior that has been well practiced.

This idea of cue control has much common-sense observation to support it. Anyone who has watched a pair of people who are close to each other can usually predict what one will do when the other says something. I have two daughters who are constantly predictable in this way. If one of them says "How do you like my new dress?" the other is sure to say something like "Are you going to wear that thing in public?" To which the first will say "Why? What's wrong with it?" No matter who starts the contretemps, it always plays out the same tune. The games described by Berne (1964) and described in Chapter 5 are examples of cue control in operation, usually to the detriment of the people involved.

Matrix Representation of Rewards and Costs

Thibaut and Kelley (1959, Ch. 2) suggest using the matrix as a way of representing and studying the possible interactions and outcomes between the members of a pair. Their basic matrix is presented in Table 1. It is a chart of possible outcomes or profits for each person. Across the horizontal axis are the possible behaviors for partner A; down the vertical axis are listed the possible behaviors for partner B. Within the entries in the matrix itself are listed the outcomes or profits (these being, of course, equal to rewards minus costs, or $r-c$) for both A and B, if each enacts the behavior listed for the column or row appropriate for each. The outcome for A is listed in the upper part of the cell, and the outcome for B is listed in the lower part of the cell.

The way the matrix works can perhaps be better illustrated by another sample matrix, which is presented in Table 2. The behaviors in the repertoire of A are listed across the top of the table, and the behaviors in B's repertoire are listed down the left side of the table. If A en-

TABLE 1. **MATRIX OF POSSIBLE INTERACTIONS AND OUTCOMES**

		A's Repertoire							
		a_1	a_2	$\cdots$	a_n	a_1a_2	a_1a_3		$a_1a_2\cdots a_n$
	b_1	r_A, c_A / r_B, c_B	etc.	$\cdots$					
	b_2	etc.							
	$\vdots$	$\vdots$							
B's Repertoire	b_n								
	b_1b_2								
	b_1b_3								
	$\vdots$								
	$b_1b_2\cdots b_n$								

acts behavior a_1 and if B enacts behavior b_1, then the payoff (listed in the cell in the extreme upper lefthand corner of the table) would be 6 for A and 2 for B. (The payoff comes in whatever units might be available for quantifying payoff in an interpersonal situation.) A might be a wife who really wants to see a particular movie, and B might be her husband who doesn't particularly care about the movie, but knows that his wife does want to see it. So he says, "Let's go to the movies," and she says "Oh good," for which she gets a lot of payoff and he gets a little payoff from her appreciation. If A emits behavior a_2 and B emits behavior b_1 in response, then A receives a unit of 1 in payoff while B receives no payoff at all. Since this particular sequence does not particularly reward either one, it would seem probable that neither would choose that particular combination.

Generally speaking, the members of a pair will emit the behavior that is likely to provide the greatest payoff, so that if the matrix in Table 2 represented the payoffs for this pair, we would expect them to settle into the behavior represented by the cell for a_2b_2. The reason for this is that each would be seeking to maximize his payoff. If B starts the se-

TABLE 2.   **MATRIX OF POSSIBLE OUTCOMES, SCALED ACCORDING TO
OVERALL GOODNESS OF OUTCOMES**

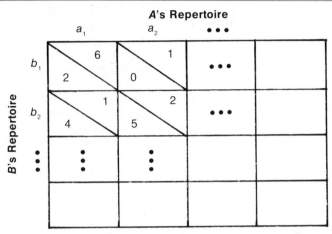

quence of behavior, he would most likely emit behavior b_2, since this
row gives him the highest payoff. A would respond by emitting behavior a_2 since it gives him greater payoff when B emits b_2. If A starts off
the sequence we might at first glance expect him to emit behavior a_1
since his highest payoff (6) comes in the a_1 column. However, if we
look down the column we will notice that when A emits behavior a_1, B
gets his highest payoff (4) by emitting behavior b_2. However, when B
emits behavior b_2, then A gets a payoff of only 1. Therefore, A should
expect B to emit b_2 every time he emits a_1, and as a consequence he
will learn to emit a_2 since this will give him a higher payoff. In this relationship B has more power than A, since he gets a high payoff every
time he emits b_2, regardless of what A does either before or after this.

It should be emphasized that this matrix used by Thibaut and
Kelley is not a matrix of the probability of the emission of a particular
behavior. It is a matrix of the payoff (or outcome or profit) for each person. A separate matrix presenting the probability of any two people
emitting a particular combination of behaviors could be constructed,
however. It should also be noted that the values in the cells of the matrix would change after every sequence of behaviors. A and B might
tend to emit the combination a_2b_2 until it becomes nonrewarding for
both of them. Then they would shift to another cell, say a_1b_1, or they
might each shift to another relationship, if the other relationship presented a matrix of outcomes that contained potentially greater payoffs.

Comparison Level

Comparison level is a kind of standard against which a person evaluates his present relationship (Thibaut & Kelley, 1959, Chs. 2 and 6). There are two kinds of comparison levels. The first is composed of all other relationships a person has experienced. It is a kind of distribution of the payoffs a person has received in his relationships with others. The mean, or average, of this comparison level might be considered the zero point. If the current relationship is providing payoffs that are greater than the zero point or mean of the comparison level, then the person should be satisfied with the relationship. If the payoff for the current relationship is below the mean comparison level for all relationships, then the person will be dissatisfied with the relationship. The comparison level may be affected not only by the person's own relationship, but also by his observation of the relationships of others. A person who is satisfied with his automobile may visit a friend and come home dissatisfied because the friend's car is newer, more attractive, and has more comfort and safety features. Comparison level is affected by comparing notes with the Joneses.

The second comparison level is the comparison level for alternatives. In this comparison, the person contrasts the payoff of his present relationship with the possible payoff in other relationships available to him. If the person receives much more payoff from his current relationship than he could from any of the possible alternative relationships or from the payoff he could get by being alone, then he is dependent on the current relationship. Being by himself or relating to anyone else who is available to him is less satisfactory than the relationship in which he is now engaged. On the other hand, if the comparison level for alternatives is higher than the payoff in his current relationship, then he will drop the current relationship and transfer his relationship to another person who promises higher payoff. If the payoff for the current relationship is approximately equal to the payoff in the comparison level for alternatives, the person will presumably show no great attachment to the current relationship.

The two comparison levels produce four possible kinds of relationships depending on how the payoffs with the current relationship compare with the general comparison level and the comparison level for alternatives. The four possibilities are:

1. *The payoff in the current relationship is higher than the general comparison level and higher than the comparison level for alternatives.* This would produce a relationship that is stable and satisfying. An example of this would be a happy marriage in which each partner is satisfied and neither partner can see any possible other partner who would be as satisfying to live with. Each

would be dependent on the relationship, since there are no comparable alternatives available.

2. *The payoff in the current relationship is higher than the general comparison level but lower than the comparison level for alternatives.* This would be a satisfying relationship, but it would not be a stable relationship, since the alternatives would provide a higher payoff. Perhaps an example of this would be two friends preparing to part from each other.

3. *The payoff in the current relationship is lower than the general comparison level and higher than the comparison level for alternatives.* This would be an unsatisfying relationship, but it would be a stable one, since the person has no better or equivalent alternative. The person would be dependent on this relationship. An example of this might be an unhappy marriage that endures over a period of time. This relationship would also be a nonvoluntary relationship, since the only reason the person stays in it is because the alternatives are worse.

4. *The payoff in the current relationship is lower than the general comparison level and lower than the comparison level for alternatives.* This would be an unsatisfactory relationship that is about to end.

The comparison level changes over time. As a person experiences satisfying relationships, his comparison level rises; as he experiences poor relationships, his comparison level drops. Also, certain aspects of the behavior of the other person are more or less salient, or important, as the situation changes. That is, I might find that, generally speaking, the most satisfying relationship I have is with my wife, since my relationship with her is satisfying and better than any alternatives I can see on the horizon. However, if I am taking a trip, I would much rather have any of ten friends reading the maps for me, since my wife is incapable of navigating any course that is beyond her eyesight. If the situation changes, the matrix changes for each of my possible partners, and therefore the comparison level changes. There are as many comparison levels as there are situations a person habitually encounters in life, and there are as many comparison levels for alternatives as there are alternative partners in a person's life.

Thibaut and Kelley suggest that comparison levels vary from person to person depending on the extent to which the person feels he has control over his own fate. A person who feels he has a great degree of control over his fate will be more aware of the possible rewards in a situation than of the costs and will have a relatively high comparison level; a person who feels he has relatively little control over his fate will be more concerned with costs than with rewards and will have a low comparison level.

Secord and Backman (1964, p. 264) suggest that changes in comparison levels may tend to produce a relatively stable amount of satisfaction in a relationship, regardless of what goes on. If the relationship is a good one, the comparison level rises so that the difference between the payoff and the comparison level declines. Secord and Backman suggest that this may explain why the first glow disappears from a relationship after it has been carried on for a period of time. Conversely, as an unsatisfactory relationship continues, the comparison level drops, so that the relative dissatisfaction declines as the comparison level drops to near the payoff level for the relationship. This would suggest that any relationship can become tolerable if somehow it can be kept in existence long enough for the comparison level to drop. Even an unsatisfactory nonvoluntary relationship, which continues only because there are no better alternative relationships available, would in time become less unsatisfying, and possibly even satisfying, if the comparison level could be dropped below the payoff level by some other factor, such as observing other people who have even worse relationships.

The Development of a Relationship

There are certain stages through which a relationship passes (Thibaut & Kelley, 1959, Ch. 5; Secord & Backman, 1964, Ch. 7). These stages are labeled *sampling, bargaining, commitment,* and *institutionalization.* Obviously, not every relationship will pass through all four of these stages.

Sampling is a kind of sifting or selection process by which a person selects those people with whom he will choose to have a more involved relationship. Probably most relationships never get past the sampling stage. After a person has decided on the basis of sampling that the person is someone with whom he would like to have a closer relationship, the relationship moves into the bargaining stage, in which the people get to know each other better—or in exchange theory metaphor, they bargain to see if a more permanent trading arrangement would be to their mutual advantage. If the bargaining goes successfully, and presumably most bargaining doesn't since most people have few intimate relationships, then the pair moves on to commitments in which the relationship becomes an intimate one. If the commitment is a deep one and an appropriate one for institutionalization, then the pair formally ratifies the commitment to the relationship and institutionalizes it by getting married or forming a partnership or signing a mutual contract, or signing the adoption papers, or entering whatever form of institutionalization is appropriate for their relationship.

With that brief description behind us, we shall now examine the four stages in more depth.

Sampling

Sampling is the process by which we decide whom among the people who are available to us we will seek out for a relationship. As the term "sampling" implies, we try out some of the interpersonal rewards that these other people have to offer to see whether or not they seem promising. Those people that are the most promising are pursued, while the others are ignored.

However, before any sampling can take place we must first meet another person. It follows that the first requirement for the formation of any relationship is that the two people meet. For sampling to occur there must be propinquity. Studies have shown that propinquity, or physical closeness, is related to the formation of friendships and that people who live close to each other are more likely to become friends than people who live at a distance from each other (Homans, 1961, p. 208). There would appear to be at least two reasons for this. First, people who are close to each other are statistically more likely to run into each other. Second, it costs less to form a relationship with a person close at hand than with one who is at a distance. As Thibaut and Kelley write, ". . . a relationship voluntarily maintained over great distances would have to provide some sort of compensation for the high cost" (1959, p. 41). For people near at hand, the costs are lower. We are far more likely to try to form a relationship with a pretty girl we see across the room at a party than with one we see in the window of a building across the street.

Other factors enter into the sampling procedure. We tend to seek out other people on the basis of their appearance, or their manner, or perhaps something we have heard about them from another person. A young man with whom I became acquainted pointed out to me that long hair and a beard were a kind of badge by which one could immediately gain acceptance and help from other long-haired and bearded people anywhere. Appearance guaranteed immediate acceptance.

Similarity of background is another factor that leads to acceptance in the sampling background. When two people first meet, the first thing they usually do is ask where the other comes from, what he does for a living, where he went to school, and so on. The pair searches for some mutual connection, experience, or acquaintance as a basis for relating. Each person also seeks this information about another as a basis for forming some judgment as to what the other person's opinions and attitudes are likely to be.

Finally it should be pointed out, as Jennings (1943) discovered, that people who seek out situations where they are likely to meet other people are more likely to be chosen by others for social relationships than people who do not. The more sampling, the more opportunities for relationship.

Bargaining

People start bargaining the moment they begin to interact. They are receiving rewards from the other person, they are paying costs in whatever the appropriate "coin" may be, and they are giving rewards to the other person. They are finding out whether or not the rewards received are great enough to outweigh the costs incurred.

As Secord and Backman (1964, Ch. 7) point out, interaction itself enters into the payoff picture. Two people who interact with each other are likely to grow to like one another and to seek to continue the relationship simply because they have been rewarding one another and are likely to repeat in the future the responses that have been rewarded in the past. Ease of continued interaction is itself a factor in the bargaining process, since ease of interaction means lower costs for the interaction; even though the reward is not in itself high, the cost is relatively low, and therefore the ratio of reward to cost makes for a good payoff figure.

Ease of interaction enters into consideration in other aspects of the bargaining situation as well. People who come from a particular background are likely to find that the costs of relating to others from the same background are low, since they speak the same language, have similar values and attitudes, and are likely to be located geographically in the same area.

People who have the same values and attitudes are more likely to find a satisfactory reward-cost ratio in their relationship. The consensual validation they receive from another person who confirms their own attitudes is rewarding to them, and the fact that the other is likely to act in ways that are expected and anticipated lowers the chances for misunderstanding and conflict, thus lowering the costs of the relationship.

It may be that complementary needs are also a factor in the reward-cost ratio. The complementary-needs hypothesis (Winch, 1958) will be discussed in greater detail in Chapter 10. Briefly, the idea is that people whose needs complement each other are more likely to seek and maintain relationships with each other than people whose needs are not complementary. A person who needs to be dominated by another is more likely to have this need satisfied by a dominant person; therefore, he will find a relationship with a dominant person more rewarding than a relationship with a person who is not dominant. Thus, if the needs of the two are complementary, their mutual payoffs are likely to be higher, and they will seek to maintain the relationship.

In bargaining, the two people enter into a provisional relationship in which they trade payoffs to find out whether or not it will be profitable to enter into a deeper relationship. This giving and receiving of rewards continues in a kind of spiral until some maximum level of rewards is reached. For most relationships this will not progress beyond the level of rather superficial relationships. For others it will progress to a deeper level of intimacy. And for a few the spiral will progress to a level of deep intimacy.

Commitment

Commitment occurs when a person foregoes his relationships with other people in order to engage in a relationship with one person — as the line in the marriage ceremony goes, "forsaking all others." In exchange theory terms, this means that the payoff for the current relationship is significantly higher than the payoff (comparison level for alternatives) for any other relationship that might be available. Or it might even be that the pair is stranded on a desert island, so that no alternative relationship is available — it is this relationship or none.

Relationships that involve some degree of commitment — that is, relationships which are maintained over a period of time and in which each person is emotionally involved to some extent — tend to be relationships between equals. The Jennings study indicated that girls who chose each other for purely social relationships were girls who were approximately equal in popularity. Homans (1961, Ch. 15) analyzes this matter of choice and concludes that other things being approximately equal, people will choose for close friends (and presumably for spouses) others who are about equal to them in status. The reason for this is that the cost is lower than it would be for other relationships, so the reward-cost ratio is relatively high.

Relationships of commitment tend to be highly reciprocal. Jennings found that if girl A chose girl B for a close friend, girl B tended to choose girl A. Also, the rewards the participants in close relationships provide for each other tend to be approximately equal. In studies of love relationships, I found that the total number of behaviors in which a person manifested his love for another person were reciprocated by an equal number of behaviors by the other person, although the behaviors might not be exactly the same for each person (Swensen, 1972).

Institutionalization

Finally, if a relationship has become one in which the two people involved have become committed to each other, and if it is appropriate for this kind of relationship, the relationship is institutionalized. The most obvious example is marriage, where two people institutionalize their relationship by going through a ceremony and taking certain legal steps by which their relationship becomes publicly acknowledged and registered and subject to certain laws. However, a relationship may become institutionalized without going through a formal legal process.

During wartime, buddies have institutionalized their relationship themselves by splitting a dollar bill and each taking half, or some adolescents institutionalize their friendship by cutting their fingers and mingling their blood. Institutionalization is a sort of symbolic ratification and mutual acknowledgement of the commitment of two (or more) people to each other.

Factors Within a Relationship

Within any relationship there are a variety of factors that affect the course the relationship takes. Within the exchange theory framework several factors have been considered, four of which will be discussed in this section. These four factors are power and authority, norms and conformity, justice, and status and esteem.

Power and Authority

According to Chairman Mao, all power flows from the barrel of a gun, but in terms of exchange theory, Chairman Mao is only half right. As Homans describes it, "a man's authority finally rests on his ability to reward and punish" (1961, p. 292; see also Adams & Romney, 1962).

Thibaut and Kelley (1959, Ch. 7) divide the power in relationships into two kinds, *fate control* and *behavior control*. In fate control one person has the power to determine the outcome for the other regardless of what the other does—the other has no control over his outcome. If, for example, A has money and B has none, A can enrich B regardless of what B does, if A so wishes. In behavior control the first person has the power to affect the outcome of the other, depending on the other's behavior; B can affect how A pays off by his own behavior. If it is a marketplace in which B is selling watches, A may tell B that he will give him $50 for a silver watch or $75 for a gold watch. B can determine whether he gets $50 or $75 or nothing at all by deciding which watch (or no watch) he will give for the offered money. The first person, who has fate control, can convert his fate control into behavior control. In the previous example, A has money which he can convert into behavior control by offering so much money for a particular kind of behavior from B.

Power in a relationship rests on the capacity of one person to determine the costs and rewards incurred or achieved by the other person. However, power is valuable only to the extent that a person can use it without high cost to himself. I, for example, could force my wife to keep the family books (probably). However, my wife is incapable of adding and subtracting correctly for any sustained period of time, so this power would most likely be exercised at the cost of a confused checkbook, and eventually, an overdrawn bank account.

Thibaut and Kelley (1959, p. 114) point out that two people who have a close relationship each have a great deal of power over the other, since each has great capacity to reward or extract costs from the other. In a marriage, ill temper in one person can make life a constant chore for the other. On the other hand, no one has a better opportunity to express affection to an individual than his spouse, and no one has a better opportunity to reciprocate his appreciation than that individual.

For power to be maintained at its maximum, it must be used sparingly. If one person exercises too much fate control over another, he reduces the other's ability to obtain rewards through his own behavior. The other has no incentive to behave in any particular way toward the first person, since his behavior has no effect on his outcomes. Thus the first person loses his power over the second. If the first person raises the costs of the second, then the second most likely will seek another relationship which gives a better payoff, so the first person again loses power. The use of power affects the payoffs, thereby affecting the comparison levels for the other person, so that if it is used to the detriment of the other, the other will soon be looking for a way out.

Homans (1961, p. 14) points out that any person with high power in a relationship has the capacity to give great rewards to the other person and also to exact high costs from the other person. This leads the other to feel ambivalence toward the one with power. He is loving for the rewards he gets and hostile for the costs that may be exacted from him. This is one explanation for the attitude of the son toward the powerful mother, or the nation toward the powerful leader. Britain may appreciate a Churchill, but the country can also throw him out of office when threat is gone and the need for a strong leader is no longer felt.

Jones and Gerard (1967, Ch. 14) list seven ways people may increase their power in a relationship. First, they may increase the attractiveness of their own alternatives. A girl who despairs of attracting a boy who is interested but not willing to commit himself may do this by dating other attractive boys. Second, they can minimize the rewards the other gives them. A man can do this by responding to his wife's best efforts at cooking with faint praise, or making remarks about how his mother made it. Third, they can minimize the hurt of the punishment they have received from the other. Children do this by refusing to cry when they have been spanked. (Of course, they run the risk of a harder spanking the next time.) Fourth, they can exaggerate the hurt incurred by the punishment. Children also use this gambit by howling loudly when being punished, especially when the punishment is inflicted by indulgent parents. Fifth, they may build up the value of their behavior in the eyes of the other by propaganda. Both husbands and wives utilize this gambit by reporting the compliments paid them by other people's spouses at parties. Sixth, they may increase their own value by increasing their skills. Husbands or wives might accomplish this by learning elementary plumbing skills. And finally, they may increase their power to reward by using ingratiation. By being ingratiating they can increase their attractiveness to the other, and thus their power to reward the other. Of course, the ingratiation must be appropriate. Jones and Gerard suggest that "the research thus far suggests that the more obvious the dependence of one person is on another, the more subtle his ingratiation tactics must be in order to be effective" (1967, p. 589).

Thibaut and Kelley suggest that a person may increase the impression of power he gives, whether or not he possesses actual power, by giving the impression that "he undergoes little variation in outcomes as a consequence of the actions of others and that his behaviors are largely internally rather than externally caused" (1959, p. 125).

Norms and Conformity

Any relationship that continues over any period of time and becomes relatively stable develops rules or norms. These norms may not be formally enacted or even overtly stated, but both members of the pair abide by them. Norms are a substitute for informal influence. They develop because they make a relationship simpler and reduce the amount of conflict that the members of the pair have to contend with. Without rules every situation would require the pair to go through a new bargaining phase in their relationship, and this would increase the costs in the relationship. Norms develop because they reduce the costs for both of the members of the pair.

Norms may cover any aspect of a relationship. They may determine who does what. For example, in many families the husband earns the money and the wife keeps the house, but this is a norm that is becoming less rigid. Norms may prescribe the way conflicts are to be resolved. My two youngest children fight over who is to take the first bath. The one who takes the first bath has to come in from play earlier than the other. This conflict was resolved by having them take turns, with one taking the first bath on one night and the other taking the first bath the next night. Now they fight over who took the first bath the night before. Any established dyad develops rules for resolving conflicts because it makes life simpler—that is, it reduces the costs for both.

A norm is defined by Thibaut and Kelley as a "behavioral rule that is accepted, at least to some degree, by both members of the dyad" (1959, p. 129). They list three items that are evidence of a norm: (1) there is some observable regularity in the behavior of the members of a dyad; (2) when a norm is broken, the one who lost out is likely to appeal to the rule; and (3) the one who has broken the rule is apt to exhibit some feeling of guilt and show some obligation to adhere to the agreement.

The rules in a relationship may have been worked out deliberately and overtly, such as deciding who takes the first bath. Or they may have developed more or less covertly by trial-and-error, such as deciding who sleeps on which side of the bed, with the first one to bed climbing in on the far side and this developing into each person sleeping on a particular side of the bed because he or she is always first or last into bed. Or norms may be imported from other relationships, such as the wife keeping the checkbook because both her mother and her husband's mother kept the checkbook.

The more agreed-upon the norms are, the better the cost-reward ratio in the relationship and the more cohesive the dyad. Lest this seem to suggest that the more regulated and thus the more dull the relationship, the more cohesive the relationship, it should be pointed out that even spontaneous fun, if it is to be successful, will follow norms. Woe betide the husband who suggests to his wife that they stop at a formal restaurant when returning from the beach.

Just as organizations that have large numbers of committees find it necessary to establish committees on committees, so dyads often find it necessary to establish norms about how they will establish norms. These are called *metanorms*. In some dyads these are arrived at by fiat (so I have been told), but in most dyads they are worked out in the same ways that norms are.

The topic of rules and norms raises the question of conformity to the norms. In highly cohesive groups the members conform to the norms, while in groups of low cohesion conformity tends to be low (Homans, 1961, Ch. 6). Status and esteem also affect the degree to which a person conforms to the rules. High-status people gain their status by their assumed ability to reward other people. Having high status, they can afford to spend some of it by not adhering to the norms of the group, and they have little in the way of status to gain by conforming. On the other hand, they must conform to the most valued rules of the group in order to maintain membership in the group. Low-status people have little with which to reward others, thus they have low status; they have little reason to conform to the norms of the group, since they have little to gain by it. This would lead one to reason that in a highly cohesive dyad, if either one of the members of the dyad changed status markedly, the dyad would become less cohesive. The observed break-up of the marriages of people who suddenly become rich or famous would seem to confirm this observation. Homans (1961, Ch. 16) cites research which confirms his assertion that high- and low-status people tend to be nonconformists.

Justice

In any relationship among men, the question of what is fair comes up sooner or later. Homans (1961, Chs. 4 & 12) discusses this topic in the context of the small group, but it is also applicable to the dyad. The basic rule is that in a relationship, each person's profits (rewards — costs) should be equal. However, since one person's costs may be higher than another person's costs, it follows that if the total profit is to be equal, the person who has incurred the higher costs should also reap greater rewards. The more difficult and the more responsible the role, the higher the costs, and therefore the higher the rewards should be if the profits are to be equal.

Homans lists four rules which assure that profits will be equal for each member of the group:

Rule 1: The value of what a member receives should be proportional to what he contributes.

Rule 2: The value of what a member receives in rewards should be proportional to his investments. (His investments may be in time spent, in money, or in any other "coin." This rule would be the basis for the seniority rule in some organizations and most families.)

Rule 3: What a member gets should be proportional to what he gives up—his costs.

Rule 4: If one person is better than another in investments, he should also be better in his contribution, and therefore should receive greater rewards.

Of course not every relationship results in equal profits for all the participants. So, a person who receives lower profits than the other member in the relationship is likely to feel put upon, or perhaps frustrated and angry. He will certainly feel that he has been treated unfairly. Conversely, the person who receives more profits than the other is likely to feel guilty about it. If the relationship is to remain stable, some effort must be made to redress the balance of profits, or the losing partner is likely to start eyeing his comparison level for alternatives.

Justice in a relationship is also a function of past rewards. A person who has been rewarded for an activity in the past is likely to feel that similar behavior in the future should be similarly rewarded. If it is not, he feels cheated and becomes angry. Aggressive behavior over failure to be rewarded by another for activity that has been rewarded in the past can be observed in animals who have pressed the lever but have failed to receive the expected food. Such behavior can also be seen in a person standing before a vending machine into which he has dropped a coin but has failed to receive his reward. The moral is that when your friend does a special favor for you, praise him lest you be confronted with an angry friend.

Status and Esteem

People generally seek relationships with other people who are equal to them in status or esteem. The Jennings study found that although delinquent girls were more attracted to the others who had high status, for social relationships they chose girls who were equal to them in status. Homans (1961, Ch. 15) suggests that the reason for this is that relationships with others of equal esteem cost less, so although rewards are also likely to be less, the overall profit is greater because of lower cost.

Homans analyzed data from several studies which showed that people tended to choose and prefer relationships with others who were equal or near to them in status. Actually, since the higher status person has the greater power to reward, the expectation would be that a person would choose to relate to another of approximately equivalent status, but given a choice between two people of slightly different status, the one chosen would be the one with the higher status. The reward-cost ratio in a relationship is maximized in the relationship with a person just above you in the status hierarchy.

Obviously the costs related to status are intertwined with all kinds of other costs. People of equal status are more likely to live in the same neighborhoods, to have similar interests, to have similar attitudes, and so on, so that the reduction of costs that accrues from these factors would overlap a great deal with the reduction of cost that comes from little difference in status. Obviously, if everyone sought to have a relationship with the person next above him in the status hierarchy, most relationships would be unstable because none would last beyond the time a person with slightly higher status appeared. Let us be thankful that status is only one factor contributing to the payoff matrix.

Measurement and Research

No other approach to the interpersonal interaction has generated more research than the exchange theory approach. This situation might well have been expected, since exchange theory derives directly from the tradition of experimental psychology, and therefore is well designed to generate research that lends itself rather easily to being studied by experimental methods. There are many ways in which an experimenter can set up a situation in which two players each have a finite number of responses and each gets a certain payoff which depends on which response each of the partners chooses.

Jones and Gerard (1967, Ch. 14) have reviewed this research. In general, as might be expected, the behavior a person emits tends to drift toward those responses that are rewarded. However, when the reward of one person depends not only on his own response but also on the response of another person, the situation becomes more complicated. In this situation the two players might cooperate, and under some circumstances they do cooperate. However, a cooperative exchange of rewards does not appear to happen under some conditions of timing, nor does it happen when fate control and behavior control are included in figuring the payoff.

If cooperation does not occur in the relationship, competition then becomes the strategy people follow. The research suggests that creating situations of mutual trust—and therefore, of cooperation—is rather difficult. Generally, it appears that when the situation is an ambiguous one, the participants tend to compete rather than cooperate. Also, when cooperation rests on mutual trust in a situation in which each might stand to gain by competing instead, the cooperation strategy rests on what Jones and Gerard term a "shaky base." Cooperation is much more likely to occur in a situation in which there are high incentives to maximize absolute individual outcomes.

Measurement

Experimental research depends on measuring behavior that is prescribed in advance by the experimenter. However, most people are primarily interested in the interaction of people in natural situations. Interpersonal interaction between people in normal situations is not accounted for within the narrow confines of a game devised by research psychologists. People interacting in their normal habitat emit a wide variety of behaviors. Research requires some method for measuring the behavior being studied. Ways of measuring what goes on between people in natural situations have been devised, the well-known ones being developed by Bales (1951) and Longabaugh (1963). Bales' system is described in Chapter 7, but we will review it briefly here.

Bales' system was not originally designed to provide a way for measuring the interaction between people within the exchange theory system. In fact, it was developed before the theorizing of either Homans or Thibaut and Kelley. However, this system has appeared to be useful for measuring interaction because it is oriented toward the way people behave toward each other as a function of what has happened to them in the past; that is, as a function of their past rewards and costs. Bales states that "both the remembered consequences and the expected consequences can become a part of the effective causation of action" (1951, p. 50).

Homans, in particular, has referred to Bales' system because it has produced research that is applicable to exchange theory. Bales' approach was originally designed for measuring what goes on within small groups rather than specifically within dyads, but it is applicable to the dyad.

The responses of one person to another within Bales' system are presented in Table 8 of Chapter 7. This system is divided into two main categories: (1) responses toward tasks or solving problems, labeled the "Task Area" in the table, and (2) responses which express feelings or attitudes toward the other person, labeled the "Social-Emotional Area" in the table. Each of these two categories is further divided into two categories. Responses toward solving problems are divided into questions and answers, and responses that express feelings or attitudes toward the other person are divided into positive reactions and negative reactions. Within each one of these categories are three classes of responses to the other person, so that three responses in each of four areas make twelve possible ways a response can be scored or categorized.

An example of how a simple interaction might be scored is the following:

Person A: What time is it? (scored category 7, asks for information)
Person B: It is nine o'clock. (scored category 6, gives information)

Still another example of a different kind of interaction would be:

Person A: Do you still love me? (scored category 8, asks for expression of feeling)
Person B: Yes, I love you. (scored category 1, shows solidarity, given reward)

With this method of scoring it is possible to sum up the total number of behaviors and which kind of behaviors one person emits to another. Some of this research is cited in support of the concepts contained within exchange theory, particularly by Homans (1961, Ch. 10).

Lest the inexperienced leader be led to feel that rating behavior by the Bales system—or by any other system for that matter—is a simple thing, let me assure you that classifying what two people say to each other is anything but simple. The Bales system is much more complicated than the brief discussion above indicates. Many responses are difficult to classify, so that two people rating the same interaction are likely to come up with somewhat different results unless they have been trained together to rate the interactions they observe. Further, anyone who has used a rating scale developed by another person for any length of time is likely to begin to feel that he could make some improvements in it, or even develop a better rating scale.

Longabaugh (1963) did invent another rating scale, which was specifically designed to measure the interaction between people within the framework of exchange theory. He feels that it is better than the Bales system because it attempts to rate behavior from the point of view of the relationship between the two people rather than on the basis of the meaning of the act for the actor or for the person who is the target of the behavior. That is, he is concerned with what a person is trying to do within the relationship, rather than what the behavior amounts to by itself. As Longabaugh writes, "With research on people, however, to ignore purpose is to ignore a great deal of meaning—perhaps the most significant variable in behavior" (1963, p. 327). He goes on to state that it is possible for the rater to infer the meaning of a particular behavior in a relationship, since the rater himself has had some experience in relationships and in observing the relationships of other people. In fact, for the rater to fail to do this in his evaluation and scoring of a relationship would be to exclude a great deal of relevant information.

Longabaugh proposes two categories, *resources* and *modality*. Resources are anything one person can give to another person that is of value to the other person. Resources are what rewards the other person. There are theoretically an unlimited number of resources, although within any given relationship the number of resources that would be exchanged is limited. No doubt the kinds of resources given from one relationship to another would be very similar, although not identical. In a sample study of the interaction between mothers and children, Longabaugh scored for the resources of information, freedom, and support. A resource should include only items of behavior that the other person really values and that can be measured.

Modality, or interaction modes, is the actual method of exchange. The modes indicate what the person does in the exchange. Longabaugh lists five modes: (1) seeking or asking; (2) offering; (3) depriving, which is subdivided into (a) taking away and (b) withholding; (4) accepting; (5) not accepting, which is subdivided into (a) ignoring and (b) rejecting.

Longabaugh demonstrates the usefulness of his system by using it to measure the interaction between mothers and children. With this system he can measure the total amount of interaction that takes place and the categories of behavior emitted by each mother and child. Then he may correlate the various categories of behavior with other variables, such as the life situation of the family, the personality characteristics of the pair, the child-rearing techniques used by the mother, or anything else that might be of significance. For example, one item of interest that Longabaugh found was that in homes in which the father was absent, there was more intense interaction between mothers and their sons.

A student of mine used the Longabaugh system to analyze psychotherapy sessions between clients in a clinic and therapists who were experienced as compared with therapists who were inexperienced. These same therapy sessions, which had been tape-recorded, were analyzed by another system for measuring the interaction between people, but no differences were found between the experienced therapists and the inexperienced therapists. Analyzing the tapes with the Longabaugh system, researchers found that there was a significant difference between the two kinds of therapists in the amount of exchange in resources that took place in the therapy sessions. With the experienced therapists there was a greater equality between the therapist and the client in the resources possessed and a greater amount of resource exchange between the two than for the pairs that contained an inexperienced therapist. There seemed to be more actually going on between the experienced therapists and their clients than between the inexperienced therapists and their clients (Casagrande, 1969).

These two measurement systems have been described primarily because they have either been referred to by exchange theorists (in the case of Bales' system) or were designed specifically for use within the exchange theory approach (Longabaugh's system). Actually, any system designed to measure what goes on between people could probably be translated into exchange theory terms, but these two are more clearly applicable. Other measurement systems are described in other chapters in the book.

Discussion

Exchange theory has much to recommend it as a way of looking at the interpersonal relationship. It stresses the behavior that is exchanged between two people who are relating to each other, and thus it fits within behaviorism, which has been the mainstream, or at least one of the main currents, in psychology for the past fifty years. Exchange theory places great stress on reward causing behavior to be repeated, which ties the interpersonal relationship to the vast store of data obtained from the study of learning, which has been at the heart of the research enterprise in psychology over this same fifty years. Exchange theory produces many hypotheses that are testable by experiment, which has inevitably meant that it has stimulated a substantial amount of research, and thereby given itself great heuristic value, whatever the merits of the theory itself may be. Further, much of what exchange theory suggests about the relationships between people agrees with what common sense tells us about why two people relate to each other.

Exchange theory is a reasonable theory in a hard-headed sort of way. In most everyday relationships, it seems obvious to most anyone that he relates to other people because he stands to get something from it. Our cultural heritage is full of stories about schoolchildren who take an apple to the teacher as a way of winning favor and perhaps gaining a higher mark. Business abounds with variations on the story about the employee who always loses golf matches with the boss as a way of smoothing the way to a promotion or a raise in pay. And of course the husband who has offended his wife comes home with a box of candy or a bouquet of flowers to soothe her temper. So most anyone who has casually observed how people get along with each other is bound to grant that there is some truth in exchange theory.

However, even though many grant that there is some truth to the exchange theory contention that people relate to other people because they gain a net profit from the encounter, a very large number of these same people boggle at the thought that *all* human relationships are governed by the profit motive. How about the person who sacrifices his own life in order to save the lives of his friends? Or parents who slave so that their children might go to school? Or the pilot who purposely crashes in a safe place rather than save his own life at the risk of killing a playground full of children by bailing out of his disabled plane? Our newspapers are full of stories of parents who enter burning houses to try to save their children, or of soldiers who throw their bodies over a hand grenade to save their buddies. How do people who sacrifice, especially those who sacrifice everything, profit from such an interaction?

Homans recognizes these objections and tries to deal with them by pointing out that there are many kinds of profit. What profits people, depends on what they value, and the things they value are not necessarily position, money, material possessions, power, or sensual pleasure. They may value the success of another person. They may value their view of themselves as loving parents or gallant humanitarians. In a sense, by stressing the fact that people may profit in ways other than the material, Homans places exchange theory and the profit motive squarely in line with some of the highest values in western civilization, for it was Jesus Christ who said, "What will it *profit* a man if he should gain the whole world but lose his own soul?" (Matthew 16:26).

The profit-motive objection can be dealt with in the exchange theory framework. So the question is not Can it be accounted for? but rather Does the profit motive give us the most satisfactory way of explaining it? Or are altruistic motives more usefully (or should we say, profitably) viewed from some other point of view? Are their two kinds of relationships or two kinds of motives operating within human relationships, or is one kind of motive inclusive of all interaction between people? The law of parsimony, which suggests that the simplest answer is the best and that mechanisms or factors or motives should not be increased beyond the absolute number necessary, would lead us to conclude that the profit motive should be enough until someone clearly demonstrates that it is not adequate to account for all of the things that go on between people. From the strictly scientific point of view, it seems to me that Homans's answer sufficiently deals with that particular objection. However, from a strictly human point of view (and I suspect that includes most ordinary humble human beings who have not been corrupted by sophistication in the methodology and thought of social science), I find it quite difficult to accept the idea that one human being sacrifices for another purely because of what he hopes to gain from it. Indeed, to account for this kind of behavior one cannot really keep his concepts simple and small in number, anyway. Since it is necessary to introduce such ideas as the self-concept, value, etc., in order to fit the behavior within the framework, we might well ask if it is not really simpler and more parsimonious to introduce another motive. But that is a matter of personal taste, so that the hard-headed will no doubt be satisfied with the profit motive, while the tender-minded will introduce soft-hearted motives such as love and altruism.

It is intriguing to me that a theory which in part derives from the Skinnerian background should end up by producing a measuring system like that of Longabaugh's. Skinner (1964) places a great emphasis on connecting behavior with reinforcement, holding strictly to what can be observed, and eschewing all truck with such things as purpose, while Longabaugh explicitly introduces the idea of purpose in interpersonal behavior and even includes the measurer's own experience as a basis for making inferences about what people are trying to do in their relationships. Although Skinner lets phenomenological-like statements creep into his writing occasionally, he certainly leaves no doubt that the inferences drawn by the observer in an experiment have no place in the measurement of what goes on in the experiment. And yet Longabaugh explicitly recognizes that without drawing inferences about what people are trying to do in a relationship, much that is significant is left out. What is to be made of such a situation?

It seems to me that Longabaugh is correct in his assertion that it is possible for a trained observer to infer what people are trying to do in a relationship and that to exclude this information is to leave out a great deal that is significant—in fact, this would unnecessarily and unprofitably hobble the person doing research on interpersonal relationships. Writing as one who has spent hundreds of hours observing people interact and participating as an observer in dyadic interactions, it seems to me that Longabaugh is not only correct, but that it is a fiction for the observer to assert that he does not make inferences about what is going on in a relationship based on his own experience in human relationships. Indeed, most of the other points of view described in this book take this position implicitly. Longabaugh's attitude will no doubt be taken by some as an unnecessary and undesirable departure from the rigorous measurement of overt behavior, but it seems that it is more accurately viewed as a sign that understanding behavior requires something more than just observing and tallying the overt behavior that goes on between two people. This topic will be discussed further in the last chapter of the book.

In comparison with the other theories discussed in this book, exchange theory has a rather broad data base. The subjects have included both patients and mentally healthy individuals in a variety of different kinds of situations, including psychotherapy, the experimental laboratory, and observation in real-life settings. The level at which exchange theory studies the interpersonal relationship is the level of the behavior segment. In this sense, exchange theory is based on data from a level "lower" than that of Sullivan or existential theory. The kind of data obtained are overtly observed behavior. Longabaugh inserts introspection, but it is the introspection of the observer, not the subject. As a theory it is fairly broad, in that it attempts to embrace all kinds of behavior that can be observed being exchanged between two (or more) people.

It seems that the chief weaknesses of this approach lie in its emphasis on the behavior segment and on overtly observed behavior. The level of explanation is at the level of behavior segments. Exchange theory makes a contribution, but this contribution would be enhanced by integrating study of behavior segments with study at the level of the person and the dyad. Patterns of behavior at the dyadic level are, after all, composed of sequences of behavior segments. However, this would require study at a "higher" level — at the level of the pattern rather than at the level of the single act. Another weakness of exchange theory is the failure to relate overtly observed behavior to the experience of the subject. Perhaps the work of Longabaugh represents an attempt to remedy this situation.

Yet another problem with exchange theory is that, although its attempt to represent the process of behavior exchange through values entered in matrices represents an interesting illustration, as an actual method for quantification, it is hopeless. The values in the cells of the matrix change every time behavior is emitted by one person and received by another person. This presents a situation that seems practically impossible to implement. No doubt computers could compute the values quickly enough, but no one has yet worked out methods for measuring all the values of the behaviors emitted or the complex relationships among them to program into the computer.

Summary

Exchange theory asserts that people relate to each other because they profit from the encounter: If there is no profit, there is no relationship. In a relationship people exchange behavior. They are rewarded for the behavior they emit, and emitting behavior costs them something. The *profit* is equal to the *rewards* they receive *minus the costs* they incur in the relationship.

Each person has a *comparison level*, which consists of the average of the profits he has received from relationships in the past. There are two comparison levels, a *general comparison level*, which is the average of all of a person's relationships, and a *comparison level for alternatives*, which is the profit a person could receive from the other relationships that are available to him compared with the profit he is receiving from his current relationship. If the profit a person receives from his current relationship drops lower than his comparison level for alternative relationships, he will drop his current relationship and turn to the alternative relationship that offers him the highest profit. If his profit from a current relationship is higher than his general comparison level, he will be satisfied in his current relationship. If his profit from his current relationship is lower than his general comparison level, he will be dissatisfied with his current relationship. If the profit from his current relationship is much higher than the comparison level for alternative relationships, he will be dependent on the current relationship.

A person who is able to control the rewards received and costs incurred by another person has power over the other person. The two kinds of control are *fate control* and *behavior control*. A person who is high in status and esteem is seen as one who is high in the capacity to reward others. A person may increase his power in a relationship by increasing his ability to give rewards and exact costs from others.

Techniques have been devised to measure the behaviors exchanged by persons relating to each other. Two of these, the Bales system and the Longabaugh system, were described in this chapter.

Exchange theory refers to anything of value that is exchanged between two people who relate to each other. Things that are valued may not only be material, but may also be altruistic values, so that the sacrifices one person makes for another may be accounted for within exchange theory.

References

Adams, J. S., & Romney, A. K. The determinants of authority interactions. In M. F. Washburne (Ed.), *Decisions, values and groups.* New York: Pergamon, 1962.

Bales, R. F. *Interaction process analysis.* Cambridge, Mass.: Addison-Wesley, 1951.

Casagrande, J. J. The coding of interaction in psychotherapy as a process of social exchange. Unpublished M.S. thesis, Purdue University, 1969.

Homans, G. C. *Social behavior: its elementary form.* New York: Harcourt, Brace, 1961.

Jennings, H. H. *Leadership and isolation.* New York: Longmans, Green & Co., 1943.

Jones, E. E., & Gerard, H. B. *Foundations of social psychology.* New York: Wiley, 1967.

Koch, S. Psychology and emerging conceptions of knowledge as unitary. In T. W. Wann (Ed.), *Behaviorism and phenomenology.* Chicago: University of Chicago Press, 1964.

Longabaugh, R. A category system for coding interpersonal behavior as social exchange. *Sociometry,* 1963, 26, 319–43.

Secord, P. F., & Backman, C. W. *Social psychology.* New York: McGraw-Hill, 1964.

Skinner, B. F. *The behavior of organisms.* New York: Appleton-Century-Crofts, 1938.

Skinner, B. F. *Science and human behavior.* New York: Macmillan, 1953.

Skinner, B. F. *Verbal behavior.* New York: Appleton-Century-Crofts, 1957.

Skinner, B. F. *Cumulative record.* New York: Appleton-Century-Crofts, 1959.

Skinner, B. F. Behaviorism at fifty. In T. W. Wann (Ed.), *Behaviorism and phenomenology.* Chicago: University of Chicago Press, 1964.

Swensen, C. H. The behavior of love. In H. Otto (Ed.), *Love today: a new exploration.* New York: Association Press, 1972.

Thibaut, J. W., & Kelley, H. H. *The social psychology of groups.* New York: Wiley, 1959.

Winch, R. *Mate-selection: a study of complementary needs.* New York: Harper & Row, 1958.

Additional Sources

Adams, J. S., & Romney, A. K. A functional analysis of authority. *Psychological Review,* 1959, 66, 234–51.

Shaw, M. E., & Costanzo, P. R. *Theories of social psychology.* New York: McGraw-Hill, 1969. (Chapter 4 contains an excellent description of exchange theory.)

Attitudes, Attribution, and Attraction

. . . the stronger an individual's attraction to another person, the greater the likelihood that he will perceive agreement with that other person concerning objects important and relevant to him (1961, p. 70).

—T. M. Newcomb

Why is one person attracted to another? The first and most obvious answer is simple opportunity. Meeting and marrying the girl next door is an old and repeated story. Propinquity leads to interaction between people. As one research summary states, "people tend to choose others as friends on the basis of the physical distance between them" (Berelson & Steiner, 1964, p. 328).

But even the most casual observation leads us to conclude that there is more to being attracted to a person than just being near them. A popular song lampoons this idea with the statement that when I'm not near the one I love, I love the one I'm near. It is fairly safe to state that only a person who lives in a sparsely settled wilderness interacts mostly with the people nearest to him. Those of us who live in more settled areas generally find that our closest friends do not live next door to us.

For example, some of my closest friends live hundreds and even thousands of miles away. I sometimes make considerable effort to visit these people who are located hundreds of miles from me, while there are other people living less than a mile from me with whom I would not spend five minutes, unless it was to serve a particular purpose. So, simple observation suggests that physical proximity, in itself, is not what attracts one person to another. Obviously, it is a necessary prerequisite. I cannot be friends with a person I've never encountered, but my attraction to another person must be something more than our occupying contiguous geographical space.

The attraction between people may be the function of many unsuspected factors. Various sources have attributed this attraction to things as diverse as the smell of one person pleasing another to the belief that one person was extensively involved with the other person in a previous incarnation. However, little research is available, and little attention has been paid to the effect of either smell or reincarnation on the attraction of one person to another.

Most of the research on attraction has focused on two people sharing similar attitudes or having needs that mesh. In this chapter we will discuss the more prominent approaches to similarity in attitudes as a basis of interpersonal attraction. We will also present some of the hypotheses of how we attribute attitudes to other people. In Chapter 10 needs as a basis of mutual attraction will be discussed.

A Brief Historical Background

The observation that people who agree are attracted to each other is not a new insight. For example, Western civilization is generally seen as springing from two ancient cultures, the Greek and the Hebrew. We will cite an example from each to illustrate the antiquity of this observation. From the Greek source, Aristotle, we have:

> Those, then, are friends to whom the same things are good and evil; and those who are, moreover, friendly or unfriendly to the same people; for in that case they must have the same wishes, and thus by wishing for each other what they wish for themselves, they show themselves each other's friends. . . . For all such persons think the things good which we think good . . . .[1]

And from the Hebrew prophet, Amos, we have "Can two walk together, except they be agreed?" (Amos 3 : 3).

[1] From Aristotle, *Rhetoric* (trans. by W. R. Roberts), New York: Modern Library, 1954, p. 100.

Empirical evidence supports the conclusions of the sages. Berelson and Steiner summarized a wide variety of empirical studies of marriage choice, and concluded:

> People tend to marry people who are in various social ways like themselves, rather than to marry people with differing characteristics. The similarities include, in rough order of importance (mainly in the United States), these social characteristics: race, religion, socioeconomic and educational status, age, previous marital status, residential propinquity (1964, p. 304).

Further, they presented a table summarizing studies correlating husbands and wives on a variety of characteristics. This table contains positive correlations between husbands and wives for age, stature, eye color, weight, memory, intelligence, word association, neurotic tendency, dominance, religious affiliation, drinking habits, number of children desired, years of education, and number of siblings. In summarizing the research on the formation of small groups, Berelson and Steiner concluded that the evidence indicates "there is a tendency for people to gravitate into groups or subgroups with the effect of maximizing their shared values" (1964, p. 328). To summarize, empirical studies have repeatedly demonstrated that husbands and wives and friends are people who are similar to each other in respect to many variables, including attitudes and values.

Most of the research on similarity as a basis for attraction has concentrated on similarity in attitudes, although other variables, especially personality, have been included. Many different theoretical approaches have been suggested as a basis for explaining how it comes about that those who are similar are attracted to each other. The two approaches that have received the most notice and have generated the most research are balance theory and reinforcement theory. We will first discuss attraction within the structure of balance theory, particularly as it has been studied by Heider and Newcomb. We will then discuss some of the work that has been done on how we attribute attitudes or actions to others and ourselves. Attribution theory derives particularly from the work of Heider and Kelley. This will be followed by a presentation of attraction within the framework of the reinforcement theory approach of Byrne and Clore.

Balance Theory

Balance theory might be considered to have, if not two fathers, then at least a father and an uncle. Fritz Heider is generally recognized as the originator of balance theory, but certainly much credit for the elaboration, empirical investigation, and demonstration of the effect of balance in the interaction between people must go to Theodore Newcomb.

Development of Balance Theory

Heider's original concern, which led to the development of balance theory, was the attitude of one person toward another. This concern grew out of the field theory of Lewin (1935) which states that the behavior of a person is a function of the person and his environment, and that the person lives within a psychological "life space." In the psychological life space are many objects or persons, and these objects or persons have valence, that is, a force which attracts or repels. This valence may be positive or negative. If the valence is positive, then the person we are studying will be attracted toward the object, but if the valence is negative, the person will avoid the object. Valence may attach to persons as well as to objects, so that we are attracted to people who have positive valence and repelled by those who have negative valence.

Heider (1944, 1945) was first concerned with attitudes toward persons. He observed that an attitude toward a person and the attitude toward an act by that person were interrelated, and that these attitudes influenced each other. An attitude toward an event can alter the attitude toward a person who caused that event. The attitudes toward the person and toward the event form a cognitive configuration. This configuration is in balance if the attitude toward the person and the attitude toward the event are similar, or if the event and the person are segregated from each other. If the attitude toward the event and the attitude toward the person are not similar, then an imbalance exists. The imbalance produces tension, which the person then tends to reduce by changing his cognitive structure to reestablish balance.

The statement of the situation implicitly suggests the kinds of changes that will restore balance. If a person toward whom we have positive feelings acts in a way of which we disapprove, we are in a state of imbalance. We can change our attitude toward our friend, in which case we like him less; or we can change our attitude toward the act, in which case we decide that the act wasn't so bad after all; or we can divorce the two, in which case we decide that he wasn't really himself at the time.

Heider's more extensive and formal description of balance is contained in his original book, *The Psychology of Interpersonal Relations*, in which he defines balance in the following words:

> The concept of balanced state designates a situation in which the perceived units and the experienced sentiments co-exist without stress; there is thus no pressure toward change, either in the cognitive organi-

zation or in the sentiment. . . . By a balanced state (or situation) is meant a harmonious state, one in which the entities comprising the situation and the feelings about them fit together without stress (1958, pp. 176, 180).

Stated in its simplest form when applied to the interpersonal situation, balance exists if a person likes another and is near that other person, or if a person dislikes another and is removed from that other person. This is a simple statement of the obvious, but it does not appear to be very helpful. However, Heider is presenting what he calls a common-sense psychology, so by common sense the balance idea may easily be extended a little. A common folk observation is "Like me, like my dog (or car or etchings or whatever)"; that is, if you like me, then you will like that which goes with me, in which case a state of balance exists. If you like me, but don't like what goes with me, then imbalance is created. This state is illustrated in a television commercial in which a lovely, charming woman who has just eaten an onion circulates through a party-crowded room. As people see her approach, their faces light up in anticipation of an enjoyable social encounter. But then they catch a whiff of her breath and imbalance sets in, which rapidly registers on their faces. The point to this particular commercial is that a particular breath sweetener rapidly restores balance to the social occasion—or to the woman's acquaintances.

The formal statement of this situation is: If a person likes another person (p L o); if a person likes an object, attitude, behavior, or personality trait (p L x); and if the other person is connected with or possesses this object, attitude, or trait ($o \cup x$); then a state of balance exists. If, however, any of the signs change, then imbalance results. If one person likes another person (p L o); if this person dislikes a particular attitude (p DL x); and if this other person has this attitude ($o \cup x$); then imbalance exists and tension will arise.

Since the tendency is toward balance and the reduction of tension, it then follows that a person will tend to gravitate toward those who hold attitudes of which he approves, and away from those who hold attitudes of which he disapproves. Heider points out that even the language seems to recognize the relationship between sentiment and similarity: ". . . the word 'like,' as a verb, refers to a positive sentiment; as an adjective, it means 'similar' " (1958, p. 184).

Since the x in the formulation described above can stand for anything, it opens the way for considering all kinds of interesting interrelationships. For example, x can stand for another person's personality characteristics. If I like the personality characteristics of another person (p L x), and if that other person likes his own personality characteristics (o L x), then a state of balance would exist if I also liked that other person (p L o), or if that other person liked me (o L p). From this it would seem to follow that the pressures toward balance would tend to create situations in which a person is liked by those other people whom he likes. This situation is called *symmetry*. The fact that one person likes another does not necessarily imply that this liking is reciprocal, but balance considerations would suggest that if these two people have much interaction with each other, then symmetry would tend to develop.

However, symmetry does not always exist. Among adolescents it is not uncommon for John to "love" Mary, but Mary to dislike John — she "loves" Dick. Dick can scarcely tolerate being in the same room with Mary — he "loves" Betty. But Betty is indifferent to Dick — she "loves" John. This phenomenon is obviously, within balance theory structure, a state of imbalance. Heider pointed out that it is in the state of imbalance that some of the most interesting aspects of life and drama are revealed. Balance can be bland and uninteresting and a "finality of superficial self-evidence." On the other hand,

> unbalanced situations stimulate us to further thinking; they have the character of interesting puzzles, problems which make us suspect of depth of interesting background. Sometimes they evoke, like other patterns with unsolved ambiguities, powerful aesthetic forces of a tragic or comic nature. . . . Stories in which the stress is laid on unbalanced situations are felt to have a deep psychological meaning (Heider, 1958, pp. 180–81).

Balance lacks tension, and thus creates no action; imbalance creates tension, and thus action. And action seizes our attention. The working out of this tension is the substance of which drama is made.

The working out, or reduction, of tension is the process of restoring balance, so we now turn to a consideration of how an upset balance can be restored. There are two main aspects to an interpersonal situation, units and sentiments. *Units* are any two entities that are seen as belonging together. This could include two people, a person and an attitude, or a person and an act. *Sentiments* are the feelings that go with or are attached to a person, an act, or an attitude. If the sentiments are not all the same — that is, if they are both positive and negative in a unit — then a state of imbalance exists. Balance may be restored by a change in either sentiment or unit.

To illustrate the point, let's consider an example. I have a friend for whom I have very high regard. Let us give him the fictional name of John. In my experience, he is honest in his dealings with others, and he is considerate of the welfare of others. John sold his house to a second friend. Let us give this second friend the fictional name of Myron. After moving into the house, Myron discovered that there was a crack in the foundation of the basement. The basement wall was slowly caving in. Myron, who had had only a slight acquaintance with John, assumed that John surely must have known about the crack in the basement, and therefore that he had purposely concealed this defect in the house at the time he sold it to Myron. Myron concluded, in short, that John was something less than honest. Myron complained to me about what he saw as a piece of business chicanery. Now let us represent my cognitive state of affairs. I like John (person likes the other, or p L o), and I also like and approve of honesty in business dealings and disapprove of dishonesty (person dislikes dishonesty, p DL x); but I was presented with a bit of information that suggested that John might have committed a shady act (other united with a disapproved of act, or o ∪ x). I like a person who is connected or associated with an act which I dislike. In Heider's symbolization this would be represented by the following: p L o, p DL x, o ∪ x. Thus my sentiments were positive toward the person and negative toward the act, and the person and the act combined in a unit. Since the signs of the sentiments of the two elements (the person and the act) of the unit were not identical, I was in a state of imbalance. How was I to resolve this imbalance?

This imbalance might have been resolved into a state of balance by a change in the sentiment relations (Heider, 1958, p. 207). I could change my sentiment toward the person involved, my friend John, and conclude that he was perhaps not so honest and considerate as I had thought him to be. Or I could decide that insofar as real-estate transactions are concerned, all is fair, and not telling the prospective buyer of your house about the major flaws in the house is, after all, not such a reprehensible thing to do. Or I could make a change in the unit relations involved. I could conclude that John is not really responsible for selling as sound a house that contained a major flaw. After all, his wife had recently died, so he may have been emotionally upset and not really consciously thinking about the crack in his basement. Or, since the crack was covered by wallboard, it may have been that John was not even aware that the crack existed. Finally, I could gain a more differentiated picture of John. I could conclude that, although he is generally a trustworthy and considerate fellow, in business transactions he sometimes shaves the truth a bit in order to make a little, or even much more, profit.

In this case I was inclined to conclude that John probably was not aware of the crack in the basement, since this particular act seemed so out of character for him. That is, I resolved my imbalance by changing unit relations.

The Acquaintance Process

So far in this chapter we have devoted little space to the topic of attraction. Theodore Newcomb (1961) developed his own approach to balance theory and set up an experimental situation within which he could demonstrate and study its applicability to the attraction between people.

Newcomb (1953b) observed that people who associated with each other tended to agree on things, and that the amount of agreement within a group varied directly with the frequency of communication about the thing on which they agreed. The more people talk to each other about something, the more they will agree about it.

To create a formal structure, Newcomb (1953a) described what he termed the *A-B-X system*. In this system one person (*A*) communicates to another (*B*) about something (*X*). A communication is any observable behavior by which information is transmitted from one person to another person. If the attitudes of the two people (*A* and *B*) are the same toward the object (*X*), the relationship is symmetrical.

The *A-B-X* system is characterized by a balance of forces. A change in any part of the system will lead to a change in the other parts of the system to restore a balance. Further, forces outside of the system affect the system, so that there are strains toward preferred states of equilibrium. There are advantages in symmetry. The more similar *A* and *B* are in orientation toward *X*, the less they have to communicate in order to predict and understand the other's reaction to *X*, and if the other person agrees, then one's own attitude is validated. These advantages are such that communications that lead to greater symmetry are rewarded.

Newcomb postulated that "The stronger the forces toward *A*'s co-orientation in respect to *B* and *X*, (a) the greater *A*'s strain toward symmetry with *B* in respect to *X*, and (b) the greater the likelihood of increased symmetry as a consequence of one or more communicative acts" (1953a, p. 395). That is, the stronger a person's attraction toward another person and the stronger his attitude toward the object, the more likely communication with the other person will lead to symmetry. The more I am attracted to another person and the stronger my attitude toward a particular topic, the more likely that talking to this other person about the topic is going to lead us to agreement. Newcomb hypothesized that if the attraction between the two people is not so great, then the strain toward symmetry will be limited to a particular topic. Finally, there may be some external constraints. I may not particularly like my boss, but my job pays well, so external forces may impel me to improve my agreement with him on a topic on which we disagree – or perhaps better worded, I will be more highly motivated to find ways in which we can arrive at an agreement in order to restore balance to my system.

Newcomb's whole formulation, when applied to attraction between people, centers on the concept of *orientation* (1961, Ch. 2). In the *A-B-X* system, *A* has an orientation toward *B* and *X*, and *B* has an orientation toward *A* and *X*. It should be kept in mind that *X* can stand for anything toward which the two people can have an orientation. In an interpersonal relationship all kinds of *X*s may be of great importance. *X* could be an attitude toward a particular topic, such as religion or politics. *X* could be the personality characteristics, or a particular characteristic, of either of the people, *A* or *B*. *X* could be moral or ethical values. Or *X* could be another person, say the mother of either *A* or *B*. Finally, *X* could be a *perceived* attitude of either *A* or *B*. Some of the most interesting interpersonal contretemps occur when two people do not agree on what the attitude of one of them is toward something (e.g., "I love you." "You do not! If you do, why did you forget our anniversary?").

Orientation has three main characteristics—*direction, sign,* and *intensity.* Orientation is directed toward something or somebody. The sign of an orientation may be positive or negative. The intensity of an orientation may be strong or weak or somewhere in between. Categories of orientations include *attraction,* which may be described in terms of sign and intensity; *attitude,* which is any orientation of one person to another; and the *perceived orientation* of other people. Attraction is the direct component of interpersonal orientation, and attitudes are the indirect components. Both affect interpersonal relationships.

An *individual system* is composed of three orientations: *A*'s orientation toward *B*; *A*'s orientation toward a third person or object, *X*; and *A*'s perception of *B*'s orientation toward *X*. The third orientation can also include *A*'s perception of *B*'s orientation toward *A* himself, since as Newcomb deals with it, *X* can stand for anything, including *A*. All these orientations are interrelated, and a change in one of them affects the others in the system. A system exists only if *A* has an attitude, either positive or negative, toward *X*, *A* attributes an attitude, either positive or negative, of *B* toward *X*, and *A* has some degree of attraction, either positive or negative, toward *B*. The *components* of an individual's system are his own orientations and the orientations he attributes to another, while the *properties* are the relationships among these components, which include the similarities or differences between the individual's perception of the other's orientations and the actual orientations of the other.

A *collective system* is one in which the same systems in each of two people have been activated, and each person assumes the same system has been activated in the other. In a collective system it is necessary that there be some degree of attraction between the two, and that they each have some attitude toward the same *X*.

The schematic representation of the systems of orientation is illustrated in Figure 1. In the figure, arrows point from the orienting person to the person or object of orientation. The broken lines in (a), the individual system, refer to the orientations attributed by *A* to *B*, while the solid lines refer to the orientations of the person from whom the arrows stem. The broad bands in (b), the collective system, refer to the relationships between orientations connected by the bands.

FIGURE 1. **SYSTEMS OF ORIENTATION**

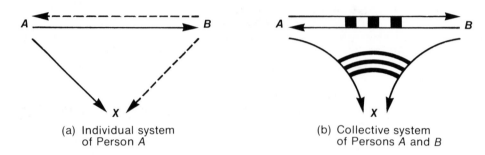

(a) Individual system
of Person *A*

(b) Collective system
of Persons *A* and *B*

From *The acquaintance process* by Theodore M. Newcomb, p. 9. Copyright © 1961, by Holt, Rinehart and Winston, Inc. Reprinted by permission of Holt, Rinehart and Winston, Inc.

In a collective system the problem is to find stability in the relationships among orientations. In such a system, if *A* has a positive attitude toward *B* and toward *X*, and if he does not perceive a similar positive attitude by *B* toward *X*, he will feel strain. Strain is more likely to occur if there is a common relevance of an *X* to the two. Newcomb (1961) illustrates the point of common relevance with an example of the coffee preferences of *A* and *B*. If *A* likes sugar in his coffee but *B* likes coffee black, there will ordinarily be no problem. *A* just puts some sugar in his coffee cup. If they are going to a football game and taking the coffee in one thermos bottle, however, the difference in their attitude develops common relevance. Do they sweeten the coffee they put in the bottle or do they leave the coffee black? This is a situation that calls for some discussion between *A* and *B*.

The postulated force of the strain caused when imbalance occurs has the quality of a psychological drive, and its force is a function of the relevance of the object and the strength of the attitudes toward the object. The stronger the attitudes and the more important or relevant the object, the greater the strain and the greater the drive toward restoring balance.

Imbalance is a force toward the reduction of strain. Imbalance may be of different importance to the two people in a relationship. To return to Newcomb's example of the coffee, the person who likes his coffee black may not be able to stand sweetened coffee and may drink a substantial amount of coffee, while the person who prefers sugar may not drink much coffee, and when he does, is not unduly upset by the fact that it has not been sweetened.

Strain in an individual system (let us say *A*'s system) may be reduced by any of the following: (1) a change in *A*'s attitude toward *X*;

(2) a change in the perception of B's attitude toward X; (3) a reduction in the importance assigned to X; (4) a reduction in the positive attraction of A for B; or (5) a reduction of the common relevance assigned to X for A and B. These five kinds of changes may be brought about by an internal organization within A or by new information from the outside. If new information comes from the outside, two things may happen: (a) either the attitude is changed, or (b) the new information is discredited.

This organization and presentation of balance theory is quite similar to that of Heider, which Newcomb fully recognizes. To illustrate how this approach works, let us return to the example of my friend, John, who sold a house with a cracked foundation wall to my other friend, Myron. You will recall that my system was unbalanced when Myron told me of the real-estate transaction. I rebalanced the situation and reduced the strain by choosing alternative (3) listed above. That is, I assumed that John was not aware of the state of his basement wall at the time he sold the house; thus, his selling a house with a cracked basement wall was not of importance to my evaluation of him or my valuing of honesty in business transactions. Actually, my mild state of imbalance was induced in the first place by new information being taken into my system, and with regard to this new information, I utilized alternative (b) cited above—that is, I discredited the information I had received.

To recapitulate, several things should be kept in mind. First, a system is contained within an individual person, and this system includes the person's attitude toward another person, his attitude toward an object, and his perception of the other person's attitude toward that object. When two people are in interaction, each person has these elements contained within his own personal system, and these two systems are in interaction with each other. This is a collective system. The tendency of this collective system is toward balance, or the reduction of strain. Balance in this collective system means that a person, A, has an attitude toward another person, B. A also has an attitude toward an object, X, and A has a perception of B's attitude toward X. Also, B has an attitude toward A, B has an attitude toward X, and B has a perception of A's attitude toward X. If this collective system is in balance, then the signs of A's attitude toward B, A's attitude toward X, and A's perception of B's attitude toward X will be in balance. Likewise, B's sentiments toward A, B's attitude toward X, and B's perception of A's attitude toward X will be in balance.

The important wrinkle to note in Newcomb's systems of orientation is that for balance to exist it is necessary only for A to have an attitude toward X and for A to perceive B as having the same attitude toward X. Likewise, it is necessary only for B to have an attitude toward X and to perceive A as having that same attitude toward X for the system to be in balance, assuming that A and B like each other. This may mean that balance may exist, when, in reality, there is no balance. Research (e.g., Levinger & Breedlove, 1966) has demonstrated this point by the finding that among happily married couples the important fact was the similarity in attitudes each of the pair *assumed* they had with their mate, rather than actual agreement in attitudes. This point was illustrated rather graphically to me one time when I discovered, to my very great surprise, that my wife disliked a person whom I had assumed she liked. I was quite fond of the husband of this person, so naturally enjoyed spending social occasions with the couple. Since I liked the husband very much, in accordance with good balance principles I also liked that which was connected with him, namely his wife. Since I also liked my wife very much, again in accordance with good balance principles and my own desires for socializing, I assumed that my wife had the same attitude toward his wife as I had—that is, she liked his wife. I went happily along in my balanced way, assuming that my wife liked his wife, as I liked his wife. However, my wife was in a state of imbalance, since she liked me but she didn't like what I liked, this other man's wife. My wife then spread around her imbalance by introducing some new information into my system by informing me that she did not like this other man's wife. Balance was restored by continued interaction with the other woman whom, in time, my wife came to like.

The Observed Interaction

Newcomb (1961) conceived a research project by which he could test his hypotheses on the interaction between people. He obtained a house near the University of Michigan campus, and arranged to have seventeen new male transfer students live there. He wanted new students who were complete strangers, so he could watch the development of the acquaintance process from the beginning.

The project ran for two years, with a different group of students participating each year. After each group had established residence in the house, regular meetings were held, both for the purpose of gathering data and encouraging the men to become acquainted with each other.

Each year the researchers measured the liking of each member of the house for every other member of the house. They also had the subjects describe the cliques or small groups that had formed, and compared the liking or attraction ratings between and among members of these groups.

At the start of the study, each subject answered a variety of attitude and personality inventories. Originally the subjects were asked to describe their attitudes in seven general areas: house policies, university practices, public affairs, racial and ethnic relations, religion, family, and interpersonal relationships. However, the researchers did not find enough diversity among the subjects on these topics, so they decided that there might be more variability among the subjects on basic values than on attitudes toward the seven basic subject areas. Therefore, the researchers developed a list of ten values and had each of the subjects arrange these values in order of personal importance. These ten values were: (1) being successful in financial arrangements; (2) being well liked by others; (3) being successful in family life; (4) being successful in an occupation; (5) being intellectually capable; (6) living in accordance with religious principles; (7) being able to help other persons; (8) being a normal, well-adjusted person; (9) working cooperatively with people; (10) doing a thorough and careful job. Each subject was correlated with every other subject on his rank ordering of these values.

The subjects were also rank-ordered according to the importance they attached to the values on the Allport-Vernon-Lindzey Scale of values. The six values on this scale are (1) theoretical—interested primarily in empirical, critical, or rational matters; (2) economic—interested primarily in that which is useful and practical, especially of the business world; (3) aesthetic—interested primarily in beauty, in form and harmony for its own sake; (4) social—interested primarily in other human beings; (5) political—interested primarily in power and influence; and (6) religious—interested primarily in the satisfaction and the meaning derived from religious experiences.

Finally, the subjects were measured on five personality variables. These were: (1) authoritarianism, measured by the thirty-item F-scale; (2) conformity, measured by twenty-seven items from the Minnesota Multiphasic Personality Inventory; (3) projection, measured by eighteen items from the Minnesota Multiphasic Personality Inventory; (4) need achievement, measured by stories told in response to four pictures from the Thematic Apperception Test; and (5) need affiliation, measured by stories told in response to four pictures of the Thematic Apperception Test.

In addition to these various attitude, personality, and liking measures of the subjects themselves, Newcomb also obtained, at varied intervals during the study, the subjects' estimates of the attitudes of the other subjects,[2] frequency of communication among subjects, sociometric measures of attraction, the common relevance of an attitude object, relationships with the staff running the research project, relationships

---

[2]The method by which liking was measured was revised, so that the measures were not exactly the same for each of the two years; they both include, however, a general rating of each man (using a general, standardized scale) and a second, specific rating, showing where each man ranked in the group. The method and timing for ranking the others in the group on how well they were liked varied from the first year to the second year, but in both years estimates were taken at both the beginning and the end of the term, as well as during the term. Thus, an evaluation could be obtained of how much each man was attracted to the other men at the beginning; shifts in preferences during the year could also be noted.

with outside groups, demographic measures, and so on. In short, Newcomb obtained the data necessary to determine who was attracted to whom, how long the attraction lasted, and how this attraction related to things like attitudes, values, personal background, attraction to third persons, involvement with outside groups, and the amount of communication among the subjects. Thus, considerable data was available for testing a variety of hypotheses about the attraction between people suggested by balance theory.

The first hypothesis was that the more one person, A, was attracted to another person, B, the less would be the discrepancy A perceived between his own attitude toward a third object, X, and B's attitude toward X. That is, it was predicted that a person who was attracted to another person would perceive this other person as agreeing with him about some particular topic or person. The researchers found this hypothesis confirmed for the Allport-Vernon-Lindzey values. That is, subjects were attracted to others whom they saw valuing the same kinds of things. Since the third object, X, can also stand for a person, this hypothesis would predict that a person would be attracted to another person who liked the same people, and this was confirmed. Since a person's attitude toward himself can also be an X, it followed that a person would be attracted to other people whom he saw as liking himself, and this was also confirmed.

Balance theory would predict that if one person is attracted to another person, the strain toward balance would lead him to agree with the point of view of the person to whom he is attracted. To test this hypothesis, an experiment was performed in which a speaker was to present a point of view on a topic. It then followed that those subjects who found a speaker highly attractive would agree with what the speaker said. In this experiment the researchers had a speaker present himself to the group in a highly attractive manner, speaking affably and convincingly. He talked about juvenile delinquency, blaming it primarily on the environment. An intermission occurred following the speech. During and following this break the speaker behaved in an obnoxious manner, getting into an argument with the project director and berating the subjects for their docility. The attitude of the subjects toward juvenile delinquency was measured before the speech, after the speech, and after the speaker's display of irascibility. The changes that occurred in the subjects' attitudes were in the directions predicted, first toward agreeing with the speaker when he was likable, and toward disagreement with the speaker when he became obnoxious. On the basis of this segment of the research, it was concluded that "the stronger an individual's attraction to another person, the greater the likelihood that he will perceive agreement with that other person concerning objects important and relevant to him" (Newcomb, 1961, p. 70).

The important variables in predicting the above outcome are the importance of the topic to the person and the degree to which that person is attracted to another person. Strain occurs only if one person is attracted to the other, but perceives that the other disagrees with him on a topic that is important. Strain does not occur if the topic or the person is unimportant. This aspect of the theory would suggest that there should be no particular relationship between a subject's estimate of the attraction between two other people, B and C, and of their agreement on some subject, X. When the subject's own self is not involved, there should be no drive toward seeing agreement on an important topic. Newcomb found that the empirical results supported this hypothesis. That is, the subjects' estimate of the attraction between two other people, B and C, and their estimate of the agreement between B and C on some third topic, X, were not related.

Another hypothesis that was tested was that similarity in attitudes is the basis for attraction. When the house members were compared for their attraction to each other and the similarity in their attitudes, this hypothesis was found to be true. Pairs of subjects who agreed highly with each other in attitudes became highly attracted to each other after they became acquainted. This high attraction did not occur early in the subjects' acquaintanceship, but developed later as the subjects discovered their close agreement on attitudes. The evidence also indicated that as pairs became increasingly acquainted with each other, they also developed closer agreement on the attractiveness of other house members. Estimates of the popularity of the subjects were also obtained, and it was found that popular subjects were attracted to each other. (This result is in agreement with the results Jennings [1943] obtained in her study of girls in a detention home, reported in Chapter 8.)

Yet another hypothesis that balance theory would predict is that subjects will interact in balance-promoting ways, which would suggest that subjects who agree will be attracted to each other and that subjects who are attracted to each other will develop agreement with each other. That is, agreement and attraction will interact so that in an intimate pair, both liking and agreement should increase. This is what Newcomb found. He concluded that similarity of attitude is the basis of attraction, and the more attitudes two subjects share, the greater will be their attraction to each other. Later in the chapter we shall report data obtained by Byrne which confirm and quantify this relationship between attraction and agreement.

Newcomb and his associates next turned to a consideration of the differences among individuals in their sensitivity to agreement and to strain. To demonstrate that within a group, people who agree are attracted to each other is one thing, but it is quite a different matter to assert that this is a truth that is applicable to all people. In studying the evaluations of the subjects, the researchers concluded that all were aware of reality—that is, the subjects showed some degree of accuracy in estimating the attitudes of the other subjects—and that all subjects showed some sensitivity to strain. In both years of the experiment Newcomb found results that were similar and concluded that "while sensitivity to strain varies with the nature of objects of orientations and with stages of acquaintance, and while individuals vary in degree and manner of showing the effects of such sensitivity, its effects were observable in virtually all of our subjects" (1961, p. 121). In short, practically everybody responded to reality and to strain or imbalance, but the degree to which these phenomena occurred varied from person to person, depending on how long the people had known each other and on the topics that were under consideration.

When a psychologist discovers that people differ along some dimension that he is interested in studying, one of the questions he is likely to ask is What kind of people behave in what kinds of ways? Or to be more specific, Do people with certain kinds of personality behave one way, while people with other kinds of personality behave differently? If there are differences among the subjects in the accuracy with which they estimate reality and in their sensitivity to strain, are there personality factors that are related to these differences?

To determine the answers to these questions, Newcomb and his associates investigated the relationship between authoritarianism and accuracy in estimating reality and in sensitivity to strain. The authoritarian personality is supposed to be a person who is rigid, who defers to the authority of persons over him, and who exercises his own authority over those beneath him. He is a person who sees things in terms of his own preconceived notions, rather than one who views events or people accurately. Therefore, it would be predicted that authoritarians would be less accurate in their perception of other people than nonauthoritarians. Although this prediction was not confirmed in the first year's study, it was found to be true in the second year. The nonauthoritarians were more accurate than the authoritarians early in the term because the authoritarians projected; that is, they saw other people as sharing their own attitudes. Late in the semester the authoritarians were still less accurate than the nonauthoritarians, but then it was because the nonauthoritarians were just more sensitive to other people and thus more accurate in their estimate of the opinions of others. Both groups were equally likely to achieve balance in their relationships with other people, but the authoritarians did it by distorting their perception of the attitudes of other people, while the nonauthoritarians achieved balance by becoming more attracted to people who agreed with them. Nonauthoritarians achieved balance by changing friends, while authoritarians achieved balance by changing their perception of their friends' opinions. The moral of these data is probably that if you are going to disagree with someone, it is safer to disagree with an authoritarian because he won't perceive you as disagreeing; if you disagree with a nonauthoritarian, you may lose a friend. Newcomb summarized this particular piece of research, stating that "the nonauthoritarians' solution to threat of imbalance is to perceive those with whom they are in agreement and to form closer relationships with them, while the authoritarians tend to achieve balance by seeing agreement with others to whom they are already attracted when agreement does not exist" (1961, p. 136).

No relationship was found between the need for affiliation with others and authoritarianism, except among those people who were on extreme ends of the distribution. In the population studied, extreme authoritarianism, an extreme tendency to keep to oneself, and a lack of sensitivity to strain occurred in the same persons.

During the research study, Newcomb and his associates noticed that as people became attracted to each other, they tended to form highly stable pairs within a relatively short period of time. These pairs were usually formed and stabilized within the first three weeks of acquaintance. As might be expected, it was found that early acquaintance was based on propinquity, balance considerations weighed in, and high attraction pairs formed on the basis of similarity of attitudes. In the first year of the study roommates were assigned randomly, but in the second year Newcomb decided to study the effect of propinquity and agreement by determining the attitudes of the subjects beforehand, and assigning sets of roommates who had high agreement with each other and others who had high disagreement with each other. In four out of five cases the roommates ended up being highly attracted to each other regardless of their agreement or disagreement in attitudes. This result was somewhat confusing, since it did not fit in with the predictions of the theory. Newcomb (1961) presents the case histories of these pairs, giving the reader an opportunity to develop a theory of his own as to why roommates usually end up liking each other even if they do disagree about things. One important fact should be noted, however. The data indicate that there is more to the development of an intimate and satisfying relationship than mere agreement on values.

Over a period of time the two-person groups tended to attract third and fourth persons to the group, developing consensus in opinions among the members of the group and high attraction for one another. Such changes within groups were in balance-promoting directions, with the groups developing a high degree of consensus over a period of time.

In the second year two kinds of groups developed. One group was composed of conformers, while the other group was composed of nonconformers. These two groups perceived each other as being groups that were different from one another. Each group estimated its differences in relation to the other group as being greater than they actually were. Or to put it another way, there was more agreement between the groups on issues than the members of either group perceived. Among the conformers, who would presumably be expected to have a high degree of agreement, it was found that there was more disagreement than the members of either group realized. Both groups overestimated the agreement among the conformers. The nonconformers, on the other hand, disagreed with each other much less than the members of the nonconformist group themselves thought, but they disagreed with each other more than the conformers thought they did. The nonconformers underestimated their own agreement, thus preserving for themselves their image as nonconformers. The conformers were not as conformist as they appeared, and the nonconformers were not as nonconformist, at least within the group, as they thought.

Over the period of the two studies Newcomb found little change in the attitudes or values of the subjects. The attitudes a subject came with, he left with. Thus, the inescapable conclusion seemed to be that among the three components of the balance system—attitudes, attraction, and the perception of the attitudes of the other—only the last two changed to produce balance. Some achieved balance by becoming more accurately aware of the attitudes of others and by forming acquaintance with those with whom they agreed, while others achieved balance by distorting their own perception of the attitudes of the other people. A very few subjects seemed to be immune to considerations of balance. Newcomb concluded that "the most stable of interpersonal relationships, in short, are those characterized by both system balance and high attraction—a combination that presupposes an area of mutually shared orientations of importance to system members" (1961, p. 261).

This extensive study by Newcomb and his associates should be rated a classic in its field. They took a carefully developed theory about what attracts one person to another, then put a group of strangers together for a year and predicted with a rather commendable degree of accuracy who would be attracted to whom. For centuries people had noted that friends tend to agree with each other, and in more recent years social scientists had demonstrated that those who share intimate relationships correlate positively with one another on a variety of factors. But Newcomb demonstrated that the agreement precedes the attraction. Newcomb also demonstrated, without intending to, that in enforced propinquity, something besides agreement operates in promoting attraction between people.

Attribution Theory

Directly related to attraction as a function of balance is the process of attribution. Balance theory holds that if person A is attracted to an attitude X, and if person B is attracted to that same attitude X, then A and B will be attracted to each other. However, before A and B can be attracted to each other, they must attribute X to each other. Attribution theory deals with the processes by which people attribute actions or attitudes to each other.

We draw inferences about people from what they say and what they do. However, we do not always assume that what a person says or does really reveals anything basic about him. I well remember a friend describing the agonies he endured eating a sweet-potato pie. This trauma came about when he was visiting the home of a girl he liked. The girl's mother baked and was especially proud of her sweet-potato pie. When the mother asked my friend if he liked sweet-potato pie, he, eager to make a good impression, said "I love it." In order to confirm his statement, he found himself faced with the necessity of eating large quantities of sweet-potato pie. In the cause of love, he enthusiastically ate the pie and suppressed his nausea until he was safely away from the mother. In this case the mother inferred that he loved sweet-potato pie because (a) he said he did and (b) he consumed large quantities of it. However, her attribution was false. His words and actions should not have been attributed to a fondness for sweet-potato pie but to a fondness for her daughter.

If we turn to the earlier example of my friends, John and Myron, who engaged in a real-estate transaction, you will recall that Myron concluded that John had been dishonest in selling him a house with a cracked foundation. Myron and I attributed John's behavior to different causes. Myron attributed John's behavior to dishonesty, while I attributed John's behavior to unawareness. The essential difference is that Myron held John personally responsible for having sold him a house with a cracked foundation. Myron assumed that John knew about the crack in the foundation and could have told him about it, but failed to do so. I, on the other hand, concluded that John did not know about the crack in the foundation; therefore, he could not have told Myron about it. This story illustrates one of the primary dimensions of attribution theory: *personal causation* versus *situational causation*. Myron assumed that the cause of John's behavior lay in John, who could have told but didn't. I assumed that the cause lay in the situation, which John did not know and therefore could not tell.

The process of attribution is central to the connection of people with their behavior or statements and to the attribution of attitudes or personality characteristics to people. A friend may make a statement that indicates that he holds an attitude that is repugnant to us. However, rather than disrupt the relationship, we may conclude, "He didn't mean what he said." We attribute his statement not to a stable attitude he holds but to the pressure he is under at the moment. That is, we make an attribution of his behavior to the situation rather than to him.

Attribution theory was originated by Fritz Heider, who wrote that ". . . we find ourselves in a certain situation, and something happens which has to be fitted into the situation—it has to be attributed to one or the other of the contents of the environment" (1958, p. 296). In-

cluded in that environment is the other person with whom we are interacting, so that the event, whether it be a behavior or a statement, must
be attributed to something or somebody in the environment. We must
assign some cause for what happens. Heider felt that we must assign
some cause because we need to make sense out of our environment—or
in the case of interpersonal relations, we need to make sense out of
what happens between us and the other person. For example, if a
friend of mine says something that is repugnant to me, I might ask
myself, "Did he make the statement because he hates me, because he
is tired and overwrought, or because he genuinely believes what he
said?" The attribution of the statement will effect whether I am, in the
future, attracted to him or repelled by him. If, on the other hand, a person makes a statement with which I passionately agree, I might wonder, "Did he make it because he genuinely means it, or because he
wants to influence me in some way and feels that the expression of this
opinion will induce me to like him, making me more amenable to his
influence?" If I think he was sincere in the statement, then I am likely to
be amenable, but if I attribute his statement to ulterior motives, I will
probably resist his influence.

A more recent statement of attribution theory that has stimulated
much research is that of Kelley (1967, 1971). He credits the attribution
process to much the same motivation as Heider, stating that "the attribution processes are to be understood, not only as a means of providing
the individual with a veridical view of his world, but as a means of
encouraging and maintaining his effective exercise of control in that
world" (1971, p. 23). People attribute the sources of statements or behavior of other people in order to adapt themselves in their relationships with other people.

We may attribute our own behavior and the behavior of other
people either to the person involved or to the situation in which we
find ourselves. If we attribute a person's behavior or attitudes to the
situation, we are not so likely to hold him responsible. If, for example,
we find that a friend holds an attitude that we consider reprehensible,
we consider his situation and his experiences. If he has lived most of
his life in an environment in which this attitude is common, we are not
nearly as likely to reject him as we would if we thought he had arrived
at this attitude after much careful thought and reflection.

Kelley (1967) lists four criteria for concluding that a person's
behavior or attitudes develop from the situation or external factors the
person is exposed to:

1. The person behaves this way when a particular situation occurs,
    but does not behave this way when the situation does not occur.
2. The person is consistent in his behavior—he always behaves this
    way in this situation.

3. The person is consistent over modalities—he always behaves this way, regardless of the senses through which the situation is communicated.
4. Other people react this way when they are placed in the situation.

Let us look at an example demonstrating these four criteria. Suppose we notice that a person always reacts with anger when he is accused of doing something for personal gain. Is this anger caused because he is an angry, contentious person? If so, we would probably conclude that he is a person we would prefer not to associate with. On the other hand suppose we notice that : (1) he always acts with anger when he is accused of acting for personal advantage; (2) he always acts this way when the accusation is made; (3) he acts this way whether the accusation is made in person, through letters, or is suggested by a raised eyebrow; and (4) most people we know also react with anger when they are accused of acting for personal profit. If these four conditions are met (or for that matter, only one of them is met), we would conclude that he is not an angry, contentious person, but rather that his anger is in response to a particular situation. If, for example, the first three criteria are met—for example, we never observe him reacting with anger at any time other than when his motives are questioned—we would not conclude that he is an angry man, but rather that he reacts to one particular situation with anger.

Kelley also lists criteria for deciding that a person acted because of personal characteristics or personal motivation:

1. The person's action was not what most people would have done in that situation.
2. The person was not limited in his action—that is, he could have taken several other courses of action—but still he took a particular action (or made a particular statement).
3. The action taken or statement made cannot be attributed to any external pressure on the person.
4. The action was not taken because of any particular view the actor has toward himself.

In addition to these criteria, Kelley lists several others for attributing an action or attitude to the person rather than the situation: There is no strong reward for the action; there are no particular forces either inducing or preventing the action; all of the actions that are possible are equally attractive or unattractive; the person gave much thought to the action before taking it; and the person seemed to go through much conflict before finally taking the action.

If a person is considered to have taken an action or adopted an attitude because of external forces, he is generally not held responsible for what he did or said, and the attitude or action will have little effect on how other people view him and are attracted to or repelled by him. On the other hand, if he is judged to have taken the action because of his personal characteristics—if the action or attitude is attributed to him rather than to the situation—then the action or attitude will have a powerful effect on whether others are attracted to or repelled by him.

Sometimes the adopted attitude is not one on which a person has any strong opinion. If A has no strong opinion, but would like to develop some view on the topic, he may turn to B for help. What does B think about the topic? Is B's opinion trustworthy? The evaluation of the opinion will depend on whether or not B's opinion is judged to have been developed from his interaction with the environment, or from his personal peculiarities or motivations. If A and B are in the same environment and A judges B to have arrived at his opinion from his interaction with this environment, A is likely to take B's opinion seriously. If, on the other hand, A judges B to have arrived at his opinion because of B's own personal peculiarities or motivations, that opinion will be discounted. If, for example, B holds the opinion while nobody else holds the same opinion—that is, B's opinion is not related to any particular situation in the environment and is one of many possible and plausible opinions—then the opinion is likely to be a function of B's personal peculiarities or motivations. If, on the other hand, other people hold the same opinion, B always forms that same opinion about similar situations, B always forms that opinion when a particular situation occurs and does not form the opinion when the situation is not present, and B forms that opinion regardless of the modality through which he becomes aware of the situation, then B's opinion is likely due to the situation rather than to B's personal peculiarities. To summarize, if B forms an opinion that is consistent and seems to agree with what A observes in the environment and the opinions of other people, then A is likely to conclude that B's opinion has some validity. If, on the other hand, B's opinion does not agree with the opinions of others and seems to be due to B's personal proclivities, A will be inclined to doubt the validity of B's opinion. When it comes down to the criteria for the validity of an opinion based on external situations, physical reality takes precedence over consensus. That is, we are more likely to accept a person's opinion if it agrees with what we have observed happening in the environment than if the opinion is merely in agreement with the opinions of other people.

Jones and Nisbett (1971) argue that we tend to attribute our own actions differently from the way we attribute the actions of the other people we observe or interact with. We have a tendency to attribute our own actions to the situation in which we find ourselves, while we attribute the actions of others to their own personal proclivities. Jones and Nisbett suggest that this occurs because the person acting has a different view of the situation than the view of the person observing the interaction. They argue that for the person taking an action or forming an opinion, the attention is focused on the situation. If a woman, let us say, observes an attractive man across the room and walks over to meet him, the woman's attention is focused on the man and his physical attractiveness. She acts because of what she observes in the situation. Her attention is focused on the man, not on her own action. Thus, she sees her action as being a function of the situation. Another person observing her, however, focuses his attention on the woman's movement, so that he sees the woman's action as being a function of the woman, rather than the environment. The man she approaches, of course, does not see his own handsomeness. He sees a strange woman approaching him, and wonders what she has in mind. Thus he sees her action as a function of her, rather than a function of himself. After all, he did nothing to invite her over.

Some research, however, suggests exceptions to the findings of Jones and Nisbett. It has been shown that people who are high in motivation to achieve tend to see the results of situations in which they are successful as being due to themselves, while people who are low in motivation to achieve tend to see the outcome of a situation as being the result of the situation rather than themselves (Weiner, Frieze, Kukla, Reed, Rest, & Rosenbaum, 1971). Almost certainly, additional research will indicate that there are many situational and personality variables that affect how people attribute the sources of actions and opinions.

People in conflict with another person tend to see this conflict as coming from the other person. Kelley suggests that "interacting persons in conflict tend to underestimate the degree to which the conflict they experience is due to the common external situation . . ." (1971, p. 19). In a bargaining situation, as the bargaining becomes more difficult, the source of difficulty tends to be seen as being within the other person rather than in the situation. However, if the other person begins to become reasonable and pleasant, the person doing the attributing tends to attribute the improvement in relations to himself. To state it simply, when other people become difficult to get along with, we blame the trouble on them, but when they become easy to get along with, we attribute it to the way we handled them. We are not too inclined to think that the other person's irascibility or pleasantness is due to the situation.

There appears to be a primacy effect in making attributions. That is, we form a conclusion as to the cause of a person's behavior on the basis of the first information we receive and are not likely to change that opinion unless something happens to make it very difficult to maintain. Kanouse (1971) suggests that this is because we are motivated to make sense out of the world around us; once we have arrived at what seems to be a satisfactory explanation for how another person behaved, we are not likely to change that opinion unless something happens that we cannot ignore because it does not fit in with the attribution we have made. Kanouse writes, "It is as if individuals in their attributional endeavors are satisfied with sufficient explanations and do not require explanations to be necessary as well" (1971, p. 14).

Judgment of guilt is also a function of the location of the attribution. We generally judge a person guilty if we believe an action of his that is harmful to others came about because of his personal action, while we do not hold him responsible if we believe that his action was caused by the situation (Kelley, 1971). We are more likely to feel pride in success or shame in failure if we feel that the success or failure is due to ourselves rather than to the situation, and we will usually attribute success or failure to ourselves on the basis of how much effort we made. Our perception of the amount of effort we put forth is a function of both our personality and the situation we are in (Weiner et al., 1971). Both clinical and experimental evidence suggest that we often blame ourselves or praise ourselves for outcomes that, in effect, we would neither have prevented nor brought about no matter how much or how little effort we made.

Attribution theory is an area of research in its infant stage, but it makes a substantial contribution to understanding the interaction between people. Just one area, the attribution of conflict, suggests that much conflict between people is exacerbated by the fact that people blame each other for the conflict rather than seeing that it is the product of the situation they are in. Football players knock each other to the ground regularly without becoming angry because they see their conflict as a function of the situation they are in, namely a football game. There can be little doubt that there are many other situations in which people find themselves in conflict without realizing that their conflict is not due to the hostility or unreasonableness of the other, but rather to the situation. Greater precision of attribution would increase the constructiveness of relationships.

Now, after this excursion into some of the processes by which people attribute attitudes to each other, let us return to a different line of research relating attitudes to attraction.

Reinforcement Theory

Although Newcomb designed and executed his study of the acquaintance process as a validation of balance theory, he left the door open for a different theoretical approach when he wrote "that we acquire favorable or unfavorable attitudes toward persons as we are rewarded or punished by them, and that the principles of contiguity, or reciprocal reward, and of complimentarity have to do with the conditions under which rewards are most probable" (1956, p. 577). We now turn to a description of the work that most thoroughly develops and demonstrates the usefulness of the reward, or reinforcement, point of view.

Donn Byrne has devoted more than a decade to empirically demonstrating the validity of the idea that attraction between people is a function of the attitudes they share, to showing the generality of this conclusion, and to working out the precise mathematical relationships between attraction and similarity. However, he has been interested not only in demonstrating that people are attracted to those who agree with them, but also in determining the principles that lay behind this observation. He has been interested in answering the question, How does agreement lead to attraction? His conclusion is that the basic principle underlying this phenomenon is reinforcement. We are attracted to those who agree with us because people who agree with us are more likely to reinforce or reward us. And conversely, those who disagree with us are more likely to punish us.

The first paper Byrne (1961) published to initiate this research campaign reported a study designed to demonstrate that people will be more attracted to those who agree with them. He reasoned that people would be more attracted to those who agree because agreement is rewarding, while disagreement is punishing. Agreement is rewarding because in our culture people have learned to be logical, and agreement is confirmation that one has been logical.

In this study Byrne set out to prove three hypotheses. They are that (1) a stranger who has similar attitudes will be better liked; (2) a stranger with similar attitudes will be judged more intelligent, better informed, more moral, and better adjusted; (3) a stranger who has attitudes that agree on issues important to the subject and dissimilar attitudes on topics unimportant to the subject will be judged higher on intelligence, general information, morality, and adjustment.

The study was performed with sixty-four college students. These students first answered a scale which required them to state their attitudes on twenty-six different subjects. These included such items as a belief in God, preference for political parties, interest in sports, and so on. The students were also asked to designate which of these topics were most important to them and which were least important.

After this initial task, the subjects were divided into four groups. Each group member was given a copy of an attitude scale which was purported to have been filled out by a stranger. The members of the first group were given attitude scales that had been filled out exactly as the subjects had answered their own attitude scales, while the second group received scales with answers opposite to their own. The third group received scales answered the same for the important attitudes and the opposite for the unimportant attitudes, and the fourth group received scales answered the opposite for the important attitudes and the same for the unimportant attitudes.

The students were then asked to rate this "stranger" who had the attitudes described in the scale. They were to rate him on two variables: how much they thought they would like the stranger if they met him, and whether they would enjoy or dislike working with him. These two ratings were each on a seven-point scale, which ranged from liking the stranger very much to disliking him very much, and from greatly enjoying working with him to greatly disliking working with him. These two scale scores were combined into a single "liking" score for the stranger.

The results confirmed the first two hypotheses and partially confirmed the third. The students said they would like the stranger who shared their attitudes significantly more than they would like the stranger who disagreed with them. They also judged the agreeing stranger as significantly more intelligent, better informed, and more moral than the disagreeing stranger. The stranger who agreed with the students only on the important issues was judged by the students to be significantly more moral and better adjusted, and their personal feelings toward him were somewhat more positive, but no other significant differences were obtained.

Byrne's first experiment is described for three reasons. The first and most obvious reason is that it demonstrated empirically that people at least say they like and have a higher opinion of a stranger who agrees with them on a variety of attitudes. Second, it was designed to demonstrate the validity of conclusions that would be deduced from a reinforcement theory approach to attraction, although it must be admitted that the study doesn't show that the reinforcement approach has any more to recommend it than balance theory or some other theory that asserts that people are attracted to each other because they agree with each other. Third, this study was conceived within the framework of a research paradigm, which we will now describe.

Byrne's research on attraction is unique in that it was conceived and carried out within the framework of a particular research paradigm. Basically, Byrne chose a particular variable to serve as the dependent variable and designed his research to demonstrate how other variables related to it. This dependent variable was the two-item "liking" measure. These two items, whether the subject would like or dislike the stranger and whether the subject would enjoy or dislike working with this stranger, were each scored on a seven-point scale on which the score could range from 1 (dislike) to 7 (like). Thus, the subject's combined two-item rating of his liking for the stranger whose attitudes were described could range from 2 (extreme dislike) to 14 (extreme liking). The reliability of this scale was .85, as measured by correlating the score of the first item with the score of the second item.

In designing this paradigm, Byrne made three assumptions:

1. An increase in knowledge is possible only if the same operations or empirical equivalents serve as connecting links across the experiments.
2. The theoretical constructs refer to experimental variables rather than real-life variables.
3. The initial theoretical model is broadly based on behavior theory and utilizes stimulus-response language.

In this series of experiments the same general design and dependent variable were used, thus providing a connecting link across the experiments. The theory which developed from the research was derived from the relationships observed within the experiments themselves, without consideration of what might appear to be happening in real life outside the laboratory. And finally, Byrne began with and tried to fit his results into a stimulus-response (S−R), behavioristic theoretical structure.

At this point we might pause briefly to consider Byrne's three assumptions. They, like any other assumptions, are taken on faith — which is to say that we just take them to be true without any conclusive demonstration that they are. But then, any research begins with some assumptions, so the choice of assumptions is purely a personal matter, based on the proclivities of the person making them. The question is How does it all work out in the end? or more specifically, Does the research based on the assumption lead to any results that are useful? By useful is meant, Do we feel we know any more about the phenomenon than we did before the research was executed? Can we predict anything we could not have predicted previously? Can we explain phenomena that were previously puzzling? The answers to these questions are left to those who are interested in research on the phenomenon in question. If a large proportion of those recognized experts on the phenomenon agree that the answers to the questions are affirmative, then the research providing these answers is judged to have been useful; by implication the assumptions are taken to have some validity, until someone else comes along with some extensive objections that are accepted as valid by a large proportion of the current panel of publicly accepted experts.

Insofar as Byrne's assumptions are concerned, the results suggest that they have some validity. Certainly designing the research so that there are connecting links across the experiments is a tactic that is to be recommended. It makes it possible to present some definitive statements about what kinds of variables dispose a person to conclude that he would like another person if he were to meet this other person. Tying the theoretical constructs to the experimental variables makes it possible to construct a theory that has some identifiable referents and avoids the unproductive kinds of arguments that arise when these constructs are referred to real-life variables that may or may not be approximately equivalent to the experimental variables. Real life is notoriously full of personality variables that are not what they seem or what a prudent man would expect them to be. Finally, Byrne's choice of S – R theory is a matter of personal preference. The deficiencies (and advantages) of this theory have been discussed extensively enough in other contexts (e.g., Wann, 1964) so they need not be described here. My own conclusion is that Byrne has performed a signal service to the field of interpersonal relations by demonstrating how a predetermined paradigm can contribute substantial and valid knowledge to understanding the interaction between people.

Now to return to the research. In Byrne's first study the students agreed with each other on most of the issues. Therefore, a stranger who disagreed with them on many of the attitudes was not just a person who disagreed, but a person who was markedly deviant from the student group. Furthermore, the stranger either agreed completely with the student subject or disagreed completely with the student subject on either all attitudes or on the important attitudes. Therefore, Byrne (1962) designed a second study in which the stranger would not be an outcast from the student group because of his attitudes, and in which there would be gradations of differences between the student subjects and the hypothetical stranger to whom they were reacting.

In this study Byrne chose those seven items out of the original twenty-six-item scale on which the students had expressed the most diversity of opinion. These would be topics on which the students would normally expect to discover disagreement with other students. These topics were: undergraduates getting married, smoking, racial integration in the public schools, drinking, money as a goal in life, the university grading system, and political parties. To provide degrees of disagreement, the student subjects for this new study were given the scales of strangers who ranged from complete agreement to complete disagreement and all the various degrees between these two poles. The results were the same as for the first study. Strangers who agreed were judged more intelligent, better informed about current affairs, more moral, and better adjusted than disagreeing strangers. The correlation between attraction to the stranger and amount of agreement with the stranger was .64, which led Byrne (data summarized in 1969) to conclude that similarity in attitude accounted for 41 percent of the variance in interpersonal attraction.

In the research just described, there were actually three independent variables: the number of similar attitudes, the number of dissimilar attitudes, and the proportion between the two. Since there were only seven attitudes, these three variables were interrelated. If the hypothetical stranger agreed on six attitudes, he must necessarily disagree on one attitude, and the ratio between the two would be six to one. If he agreed on four attitudes, he must necessarily disagree on the other three, and the ratio would be four to three. Therefore, the question raised was Is the significant variable the number of attitudes on which the stranger agrees, or is it the proportion of total attitudes expressed on which he agrees?

Another experiment by Byrne and Nelson (1965) was performed in which the number of attitudes on which the subjects agreed with the stranger and the proportion of attitudes on which they agreed were varied independently. This was accomplished by having the subjects express themselves on a varying number of topics. If the subject expressed himself on four attitudes, and the stranger expressed himself on four attitudes, and they agreed on all four, the proportion of agreement was 100 percent. If eight attitudes were used, and the subject and the stranger agreed on only four of them, the proportion of agreement dropped to 50 percent. If sixteen attitudes were expressed, and they agreed on four of them, the proportion of agreement would decline still further to 25 percent.

Byrne and Nelson found that the important variable was the proportion of attitudes on which the subjects agreed with the stranger, and not the number of attitudes on which they agreed. Using this data as a base, they fit a straight line to the data, using the least-squares method, and derived a formula describing the relationship between liking and the proportion of similar attitudes expressed. This formula was: $Y = 5.44X + 6.62$. In this formula Y stands for the liking score (which could range from 2 to 14), and X stands for the proportion of similar attitudes expressed. For example, if a subject agreed with a stranger on 50 percent of the attitudes expressed, the liking score that subject could be expected to express for that stranger would be calculated as follows: $Y = 5.44(.50) + 6.62$, or $Y = 2.72 + 6.62$, or $Y = 9.34$. Thus, expressed liking, as measured by this two-item scale, is quantified as a definite function of the proportion of similar attitudes.

Further research (Nelson, 1965), in which the degree of disagreement in attitude was varied (from slight to extreme disagreement on the topics), indicated that the important variable was not just simple disagreement, but also the amount of disagreement. Not only is the proportion of attitudes on which they disagree important, but the extent to which they disagree on these attitudes is also an important variable.

The result of Nelson's study led to the speculation that the importance of the attitude might also be of significance. It seemed reasonable to expect that a person would dislike a stranger more if he disagreed on a topic considered to be highly important than if the disagreement were over a trivial topic. However, several studies failed to find such a result. Instead, it seems to be the proportion of topics on which the subjects disagree and not the importance of the topics that is the significant variable.

Up to this point, the research done by Byrne and his colleagues raised several questions and objections. First, the method of presenting the stranger had been consistently the same: The experimental subject was presented with a mimeographed attitude inventory on which the attitudes had been checked. The subject was told that a stranger, a person whom he did not know, had answered this attitude inventory. The subject was then asked to look over the stranger's opinions and evaluate the stranger, expressing how well the stranger would be liked as a person and how well the subject would enjoy working with him. The obvious objection to this procedure was that it was highly impersonal. Would different results be obtained if a more personal method were used?

To overcome this objection, Byrne and Clore (1966) tested several different methods of presenting the stranger to see if this would affect the expressed liking for him. The stranger was presented on a tape recording answering the items on the attitude inventory, he was presented in a movie, and finally the subject and the stranger met face-to-face and gave their opinions on the topics contained in the attitude inventory. In every case the results came out the same. Proportion of similar attitudes was significantly related to expressed liking for the stranger. In the course of these studies a new formula for attraction was derived, $Y = 6.47X + 5.06$, but this slight change did not mitigate the basic principle that attraction was a positive, linear function of the proportion of expressed similar attitudes.

Next came the question of the representativeness of the subjects. All of the subjects thus far had been college students. Psychological experimenters have often been criticized for confining their research to two main kinds of experimental animals: white rats and college sophomores. How representative are college students? Are they real people, or are they a deviant breed of human being? Is being a college student an aberrant state? To answer this question Byrne (1969) repeated the research with clerical workers, schoolchildren, job corps trainees, and hospitalized schizophrenics. All were more attracted to the stranger as a positive, linear function of the proportion of similar attitudes expressed. Next, to extend the research even further, the study was repeated using as subjects Indians from India, Japanese, Mexicans, and Hawaiians with an oriental background (Byrne, Gouaux, Griffitt, Lamberth, Muruakawa, Prasad, Prasad, & Ramirez, 1970). The results were the same. The principle seems to hold for human beings ranging from children to adults, from normals to hospitalized schizophrenics, and from Western culture to Eastern culture.

Finally, the ultimate question arises: What does the research by Byrne and his colleagues have to do with real life? Byrne could retort that he did not start out to do research on real life. Rather, he started out to do a series of experiments within a theoretical paradigm, and whether or not the results have anything to do with real life is a matter of no direct importance to him. However, sooner or later the moment of truth comes. If it works in the laboratory, then it should work in real life, if it is to be of any general significance. So Byrne, Ervin, and Lamberth (1970) – perhaps with hearts palpitating in trepidation – tried the principle in real life. They had college students answer a fifty-item attitude questionnaire and, with a computer (of course), they matched the students for agreement on expressed attitudes. They chose the twenty-four best matched pairs and the twenty worst matched pairs, called them in, gave them fifty cents, and sent them off for a thirty-minute coke date. The experimenters also rated each member of each couple for physical attractiveness. When the pair came back they were asked to rate each other on a ten-item scale. The experimenters had also slyly calibrated the front of their desk so they could measure how closely the couple stood together when they returned from the date.

As it turned out, both physical attractiveness and similarity in attitudes were significantly related to how well the couple liked each other and to how close they stood to each other when they returned. Physical attractiveness was also significantly related to ratings of desirability as a date, desirability as a spouse, and to sexual attractiveness. The subjects were asked at the end of the semester if they could remember their date's name, if they had talked to one another in the interim, and if they desired to date each other in the future. All behavioral measures were significantly related to similarity in attitudes and physical attractiveness. When the subjects were asked to verbalize the factors that attracted them (or did not attract them) to their computer-arranged date, the men usually mentioned physical attractiveness, while the women mentioned attitudes.

Although attitudes have provided the main independent variable for investigating the relationship between similarity and attraction, studies in this series have extended the principle into socioeconomic and personality variables as well, using the same research paradigm Byrne followed. Subjects were found to be more attracted to strangers who came from the same economic level, who were similar in answering a repression-sensitization scale, and who were similar in answering a self-concept scale (Byrne, 1969, pp. 35–89).

Efficacy of Reinforcement Theory

The research just described was not designed apart from a theoretical scheme. From the beginning, reinforcement was seen as the principle underlying the attraction between people who agreed in their attitudes. Yet none of the research described thus far demonstrates the operation of reinforcement in attraction. Granted, it has been demonstrated that people are attracted to those with whom they agree, that the strength of this attraction is a positive, linear function of the proportion of attitudes on which they agree, and that the phenomenon holds over wide varieties of people, over several different modes of presentation, and actually predicts how well people will like those whom they actually meet. However, none of this data requires a reinforcement explanation. To demonstrate the validity of reinforcement as a theoretical explanation, the next study was performed.

Byrne and Rhamey (1965) hypothesized that the crucial element in attraction was reinforcement that the subject received from the other person, and that similarity in attitudes would be relatively less powerful than direct reward in inducing liking. They asserted that positive and negative reinforcement would have greater weight than similarity in attitudes in attraction between pairs of people. They derived this hypothesis by reasoning that those who are similar in attitudes are more likely to reward us, so that the crucial element in attraction is not similarity in attitude per se, but rather similarity in attitude as the sign or cue of a person from whom reward is likely to be obtained.

The subjects in this experiment were 180 students. These students were given material that was supposed to have been obtained from another person, including what were purported to be this other person's attitudes. The subjects received attitude statements that agreed with the subjects' own attitudes 100 percent, 67 percent, 33 percent, and 0 percent. The subjects were also told either (a) that the other person had expressed a positive evaluation of the subject or (b) that the other person had expressed negative evaluation of the subject; in the control situation, no mention was made of an evaluation of the subject by the stranger.

The results indicated that liking was significantly related to similarity in attitude and to positive reinforcement (being told that the other person liked and approved of them). Positive reinforcement was three times as powerful as agreement in its effect on the attitudes of the subjects. A positive, linear relationship was found between both positive reinforcement and similarity in attitudes and liking.

Another experiment (McDonald, 1963) demonstrated the effect of reinforcement alone on liking another person. In this study the subjects were asked to invent stories for Thematic Apperception Test pictures. A stooge was to listen to the story and rate it for creativity on a scale from one to ten. Actually the subjects were rated on a prearranged schedule that had nothing to do with the quality of their stories, so that they would receive a certain amount of positive reinforcement through positive ratings for their stories. Afterward the subjects were to rate the stooge. The subjects' expressed liking for the stooge was found to be a function of the number of positive ratings the stooge gave them for their stories.

Still another study (Byrne, 1969) had the subjects rate their subjective feelings in connection with attitudes, and it was found that positive feelings accompanied attitudes with which the subjects agreed and negative feelings accompanied attitudes with which the subjects disagreed.

The studies cited in this section were conducted to demonstrate the power of positive reinforcement in inducing liking or in being associated with liking. They have demonstrated that being told you are liked or having your stories approved does induce liking, and also that positive feelings, which should be rewarding, go with being exposed to opinions with which you agree.

Byrne (1969) in conjunction with G. L. Clore, has developed a theory and formula for liking and attraction based on reinforcement. The underlying assumption of the research is that attraction toward any X, including a person, is a function of the number of positive rewards associated with X. This attraction is a positive, linear function expressed by the formula $A_x = mPR_x + k$. The reinforcement model is based on classical conditioning principles. The basic idea is that any stimulus, if associated with reward, will in itself gain secondary reward value. Thus, similar opinions can gain reward value in two ways. First, it is assumed that in our culture people have a need to be logical, so the expression of an opinion that is similar to our own opinion confirms us as being logical or sensible. Second, an opinion can have secondary reward value. If an opinion has been associated with a person whom we like and who has rewarded us, then this opinion is one about which we will have positive feelings. If another person expressed this opinion, the positive feelings that go with that opinion will be attached to the person expressing it. Presumably the mediation of this transfer of liking takes place through the positive feelings that the expression of the opinion evokes. These positive feelings are a cue that stimulates the expectancy of reward, since in the past they have been associated with reward. For example, my father was a graduate of the University of Minnesota, and he strongly supported the Golden Gophers in their athletic endeavors. Since he supported Minnesota, as a boy I also supported Minnesota, and I continue to have warm feelings toward the University of Minnesota, although I have never been a student there. Suppose I now meet a stranger who makes an off-hand comment that is favorable to the University of Minnesota. This approval stirs up positive feelings within me. These positive feelings are associated with the opinion the stranger expressed, so these positive feelings become associated with the stranger, and I like him.

Of course, in everyday life the people you meet don't exclusively reward you or punish you. Most acquaintances, friends, and close relatives give off both positive and negative reinforcements. My father, who rewarded me often, also punished me. To take into account the realities of life, Clore and Byrne (in press) formulated attraction in terms of both rewards and punishments. The following formula expresses the relationship:

$$\underline{A}_x = \underline{m}\left(\frac{\Sigma(\underline{PR}_x \times \underline{M})}{\Sigma(\underline{PR}_x \times \underline{M}) + \Sigma(\underline{NR}_x + \underline{M})}\right) + \underline{k}.$$

This formula states that "attraction toward X is a positive linear function of the sum of the weighted positive reinforcements (Number × Magnitude) received from X divided by the total number of weighted positive and negative reinforcements received from X" (Byrne, 1969, p. 76). This formula would imply that unless there were *no* positive reinforcements at all, there would be some positive attraction to another person, although this attraction might be very slight.

Byrne prefers the reinforcement model to other models, in part, because he feels that the weight of evidence favors it over other models, but also because a wide variety of seemingly different stimulus conditions can be conceptualized in terms of reinforcement theory and because the reinforcement concept suggests the possibility of relating the attraction paradigm to learning theory. The reinforcement paradigm makes it possible to fit the attraction data within the broad net of behavior theory.

Discussion: Balance and Reward

In this chapter, we have described a substantial amount of research which clearly demonstrates in a variety of ways that people are attracted to others who are similar and with whom they share attitudes. However, the research described was stimulated by and designed within different theoretical models. Which model is the most adequate explanation of the interpersonal attraction between people who are similar?

Several studies have been cited demonstrating the positive effect reward has on attraction. Clore and Byrne (in press) cite a study by Stapert and Clore which, in their opinion, supports the contention that the basic principle underlying attraction between those who are similar is reinforcement and not balance. In this study the subjects were first exposed to disagreement and then to agreement. Their argument is that if balance is the primary principle, then the tension aroused by disagreement would be reduced by rejecting the stranger. Thus, presumably an agreeing stranger would be liked if he were encountered after the encounter with the disagreeing stranger, but no more than if the encounter with the disagreeing stranger had not occurred. That is, rejecting the disagreeing stranger solves the balance problem. However, they argue that within reinforcement theory the stranger is rejected because of his *association* with the arousal, and the rejection of the stranger merely gets rid of a disagreeable cue but does not dissipate the arousal. In the Stapert and Clore study it was found that the agreeing stranger was liked more when encountered after a disagreeing stranger than when no disagreement preceded the agreeable encounter.

However, this experiment does not settle the issue, nor is any experiment likely to settle the issue. After all, it might be argued that a disturbed balance does not necessarily return to normal immediately after the rejection of the source of disagreement. Perhaps balance has a certain inertia, like the pendulum on a clock, and once a person's balance is disturbed it takes a while to settle down, even when the original source of the disturbance has been geographically and/or temporally removed. Thus an agreeing stranger supplies that extra element, which operates like a shock absorber, that speeds up the process of balance restoration, and therefore is better liked after an encounter with another who disagreed. (Of course, in introducing this argument we have introduced a new model — either a hydraulic or mechanical model, depending on which kind of shock absorber you prefer — and have argued for balance, and then completed it with a reward.) One thing that seems fairly certain is that most all of us have experienced continuing an argument in our heads for days after an encounter with a person who has disagreed with us, thus demonstrating phenomenologically that mere removal from the source of disagreement does not restore balance.

Of course, this argument could be carried on indefinitely and to little profit. It seems beyond dispute that those who reward us are liked and sought while those who punish us are disliked and avoided. The evidence is overwhelming. The question is, Is reinforcement the basic and the totally sufficient explanation? In considering reinforcement theory in this light, some objections from the contaminated and contaminating real outside world can be introduced; in fact, they can scarcely be avoided.

Byrne and his co-workers demonstrated that attraction is a function of the proportion of attitudes on which the subject agreed with the stranger. However, in real life two people may agree on practically everything they discuss, yet disagreement on a single issue may severely disrupt the relationship. Indeed, the most bitter quarrels have been fought between people who are ideologically quite close to one another but disagree over what seems to outsiders to be a trivial point. Of course, other kinds of personality theory would suggest that hidden and unconscious factors explain what seems to be one small attitude difference. But the point is that real life provides many examples that seem to clearly contradict the conclusion that attraction is a function of proportion of similar attitudes shared, or of simple reinforcement alone. In a situation of disagreement between those who by experience or circumstance are closely bound to one another, one area of disagreement can outweigh one hundred areas of agreement, and the proportion formula becomes meaningless. The emphasis of balance theory on common relevance seems more appropriate. When a person who is close to you becomes associated with an attitude or an act which is reprehensible to you, an imbalance occurs. Imbalance creates strain. This balance must be restored in some way that directly relates to the topic of disagreement and the other person involved. In this kind of situation balance theory seems more persuasive and closer to the reality of the phenomenon.

The argument presented above does not necessarily eliminate the sufficiency of reinforcement theory, however. It may be reintroduced in a variety of ways, such as the reward value of tension reduction through restoring balance, through introducing new levels at which reinforcement occurs in the guise of restored balance, or through introducing hierarchies of topics and fluctuating reward values among them, and so on. Of such stuff is made the arguments by which psychologists while away the long winter nights.

The differences between the research approaches should not be overlooked in considering their significance. Byrne and his co-workers were, to a large extent, asking subjects how they *thought* they would like a stranger who was described to them. In most of the research the subjects never met anyone. In the research in which they actually met another person, the other person was a real stranger so that the liking was for a person who was a new acquaintance. Balance theory also predicted that agreeing strangers would be preferred, but Newcomb's research observed closer relationships that extended over a school year. In this longitudinal research he found that it took a period of time, approximately three weeks, for relationships to settle down. In any case, the argument presented in support of balance theory upheld the persuasiveness of balance theory as the explanation for agreement in an intimate relationship that has existed over a long period of time. A long term acquaintanceship is different from a new acquaintanceship, both in time and in degree of intimacy. It may well be that different principles apply to different stages of a relationship.

Finally, it should be pointed out that both life and research have provided examples that appear to be exceptions to the principles of both balance and reinforcement theory. As Heider pointed out, drama is full of situations in which lack of balance seems to provide the interest in the story—and it might be added that drama is full of examples of couples who did not remain in close relationship with each other because of the ratio of reward to punishment that they received from each other. *Who's Afraid of Virginia Woolf?* might be considered Edward Albee's refutation of both Newcomb and Byrne.

Empirical evidence also contradicts both theories. Newcomb cites the observation that roommates who disagreed in attitudes, values, and socioeconomic background nonetheless, in an unexplained fashion, came to like and prefer each other. And Swensen and Nelson (1967) performed a study in which they matched pairs of subjects on the basis of personality variables and the attitude variables used by Byrne, had the subjects interact for an hour, and failed to find a consistent liking (using Byrne's liking measure) or a consistent amount of self-disclosure related to similarity.

Thus, both theoretical approaches have much data to support them, as well as unexplained, contradictory data to contend with. Objections can be raised for each explanation. Each explanation seems to account better for some of the observed attraction between people who agree with one another. Byrne, of course, is aware of this and has argued for the value of both the reinforcement and cognitive, or balance, approaches (Byrne & Lamberth, 1971). What is perhaps more important, both have demonstrated a heuristic value in the research they have stimulated, in which those stimulated researchers have clearly demonstrated that people are attracted to those with whom they agree. As Byrne concludes,

> Whether this particular paradigm directed at this specific research problem will prove to be of such general utility is an open question. The necessity for paradigmatic research in personality and social psychology, whatever the initial orienting theory, should be self-evident (1969, p. 85).

When compared with the other theories we have discussed, balance theory and reinforcement theory have a relatively deep, but narrow data base. Most of the subjects studied in the research reported here have been college students. However, there have been enough studies using other kinds of subjects to suggest that the conclusions are founded on substantial amounts of reliable data. Further, the conclusions are in harmony with observations made in everyday life. People do seem to prefer the company of other people who agree with them. The situation in which attraction has been studied is largely the experimental laboratory, although there has been some real-life observation. There has been little application of these findings to the clinic. This is rather surprising, since the conclusions would seem to be of value to psychotherapists. One obvious application that suggests itself is that patients might progress faster and be more satisfied with a therapist who agrees with them on basic attitudes than with a therapist who disagrees. There is some evidence to suggest that this is true, but it would be worthwhile to make a more extensive test of this hypothesis. If a simple attitude survey helps improve the match between therapist and patient, this device would be of value in every clinic and counseling center.

For these theories, the data obtained are at the level of the person and the level of the behavior segment. It could be argued that specific attitudes are behavior segments, but the liking of one person for another is at the level of the person. This would suggest that there is room for extension of both balance theory and reinforcement theory into the level of patterns of interaction between people. Certain specific kinds of reinforcement must combine into different patterns of interaction. There are, after all, many different kinds of reinforcement. One spouse might be useless doing household chores, but very good at giving verbal reinforcement. Another might be relatively taciturn, yet quite good at fixing the washing machine and taking out the garbage. These are different kinds of reinforcement and must surely be a part of a different pattern of interpersonal interaction. Both theoretical approaches should extend their research into patterns of interaction.

The kinds of data used by both approaches are behavioral observation and introspection, since both have observed the behavior of individuals and also used self-report as basic data. The major criterion of these studies, how well one person likes another, is self-report data. As theories, they are really parts of larger theories applied to one aspect of the interpersonal interaction—the factors that attract one person to another.

All of the material discussed in this chapter derives from the empirical tradition of psychology. These theories have been derived from research and have stimulated research. They represent a part of the psychological tradition in which there is constant interaction between empirical research and theory, with theory constantly being revised in the light of new data. As a consequence, it can confidently be foretold that both approaches will continue to progress, adding more explicit and broader explanations and developing more accurate predictions. The balance and reinforcement investigations, in addition to the research on attribution, have just begun to contribute to the understanding of interpersonal interaction.

Summary

That people are attracted to those to whom they are similar has been observed by sages throughout the centuries and in more recent years has been demonstrated by empirical research. Friends and husbands and wives are similar to each other with respect to a wide variety of variables, including attitudes, values, personality characteristics, socioeconomic status, and level of education.

A variety of explanations have attempted to account for the phenomenon of attraction, but the two theories that have received the most attention and stimulated the most research are balance theory and reinforcement theory. In addition, attribution theory, though not directly concerned with what accounts for attraction, does deal with the processes by which a person attributes a particular attitude to another, and so is an important theory to consider in any discussion of balance and reinforcement as factors determining attraction.

In *balance theory* there are three main elements. These are a person, A, another person, B, and an object X (which may be anything, including a third person). A and B have some relationship to each other, and they each have an attitude toward the third object or person, X. For each person, A or B, the essential elements are his attitude toward the other person, his attitude toward the third object, and his perception of the other person's attitude toward the third object. If A is attracted to B, if A feels positively toward X, and if A perceives B as feeling positive toward X, then balance exists. All the signs are positive. If, however, A has a positive feeling toward B and toward X, but perceives B as having a negative attitude toward X, then imbalance exists, and strain occurs. The A-B-X system tends toward balance, so the imbalance must be corrected. This can be done by changing the sentiments (attitudes toward X and the other person) or changing the unit (the connection between the other person and X or the subject's own connection with either the other person or X). Since the tendency is toward balance, it follows that any person will be attracted toward those with whom he agrees and will avoid those with whom he disagrees.

Attribution theory describes how we attribute attitudes or causes to other people. We attribute the attitudes or actions of another either to the situation in which the person finds himself or to the person himself. We tend to hold people responsible for those effects that are not due to the environment. In conflict the people involved tend to blame each other, rather than the situation, for the conflict. We tend to attribute the attitudes and actions of others to the other person, while we tend to attribute our own attitudes and actions to the situation.

Reinforcement theory holds that a person is attracted to those with whom he agrees because, in his past experience, reward has been associated with agreement and punishment with disagreement. Thus, an attitude with which one agrees stimulates implicit, positive, affective states within the person; these become associated with the person expressing the agreeable attitude, and the agreeing person becomes attractive. The agreeing person implicitly induces an expectancy of reward.

References

Albee, E. *Who's afraid of Virginia Woolf?* New York: Atheneum, 1962.

Aristotle. *Rhetoric* (trans. by W. R. Roberts). New York: Modern Library, 1954.

Berelson, B., & Steiner, G. A. *Human behavior.* New York: Harcourt, Brace & World, 1964.

Byrne, D. Interpersonal attraction and attitude similarity. *Journal of Abnormal and Social Psychology,* 1961, 62, 713–15.

Byrne, D. Response to attitude similarity-dissimilarity as a function of affiliation need. *Journal of Personality,* 1962, 30, 164–77.

Byrne, D. Attitudes and attraction. In L. Berkowitz (Ed.), *Advances in experimental social psychology.* Vol. 4. New York: Academic Press, 1969.

Byrne, D., & Clore, G. L. Predicting interpersonal attraction toward strangers presented in three different stimulus modes. *Psychonomic Science,* 1966, 4, 239–40.

Byrne, D., Ervin, C. R., & Lamberth, J. The continuity between the experimental study of attraction and "real life" computer dating. Unpublished manuscript, Purdue University, 1970.

Byrne, D., Gouaux, C., Griffitt, W., Lamberth, J., Muruakawa, N., Prasad, M. B., Prasad, A., & Ramirez, M. The ubiquitous relationship: attitude similarity and attraction. Unpublished manuscript, Purdue University, 1970.

Byrne, D., & Lamberth, J. Cognitive and reinforcement theories as complementary approaches to the study of attraction. In B. Murstein (Ed.), *Theories of attraction and love.* New York: Springer, 1971.

Byrne, D., & Nelson, D. Attraction as a linear function of proportion of positive reinforcements. *Journal of Personality and Social Psychology,* 1965, 1, 659–63.

Byrne, D., & Rhamey, R. Magnitude of positive and negative reinforcements as a determinant of attraction. *Journal of Personality and Social Psychology,* 1965, 2, 884–89.

Clore, G. L., & Byrne, D. The process of personality interaction. In R. B. Cattell & R. M. Dreger (Eds.), *Handbook of modern personality theory.* New York: Appleton-Century-Crofts, 1973, in press.

Heider, F. Social perception and phenomenal causality. *Psychological Review,* 1944, 51, 358–74.

Heider, F. Attitudes and cognitive organization. *Journal of Psychology,* 1945, 21, 107–12.

Heider, F. *The psychology of interpersonal relations.* New York: John Wiley & Sons, 1958.

Jennings, H. H., *Leadership and isolation.* New York: Longmans, Green, 1943.

Jones, E. E., & Nisbett, R. E. *The actor and the observer: divergent perceptions of the causes of behavior.* New York: General Learning Press, 1971.

Kanouse, D. E. *Language, labeling, and attribution.* New York: General Learning Press, 1971.

Kelley, H. H. Attribution theory in social psychology. In D. Levine (Ed.), *Nebraska symposium on motivation, 1967.* Lincoln, Nebr.: University of Nebraska Press, 1967.

Kelley, H. H. *Attribution in social interaction.* New York: General Learning Press, 1971.

Levinger, G., & Breedlove, J. Interpersonal attraction and agreement: a study of marriage partners. *Journal of Personality and Social Psychology,* 1966, 3, 367–72.

Lewin, K. *A dynamic theory of personality.* New York: McGraw-Hill, 1935.

McDonald, R. D. The effect of reward-punishment and affiliation need on interpersonal attraction. *Dissertation Abstracts,* 1963, 23, 3967–8.

Nelson, D. The effect of differential magnitude of reinforcement on interpersonal attraction. Unpublished doctoral dissertation, University of Texas, 1965.

Newcomb, T. M. An approach to the study of communicative acts. *Psychological Review,* 1953, 60, 393–404. (a)

Newcomb, T. M. Motivation in social behavior. In *Current theory and research in motivation.* Lincoln, Nebr.: University of Nebraska Press, 1953. (b)

Newcomb, T. M. The prediction of interpersonal attraction. *American Psychologist,* 1956, 11, 577.

Newcomb, T. M. *The acquaintance process,* New York: Holt, Rinehart, & Winston, 1961.

Stapert, J. C., & Clore, G. L. Attraction and disagreement-produced arousal. *Journal of Personality and Social Psychology,* 1969, 13, 64–69.

Swensen, C. H., & Nelson, D. Interpersonal attraction as a function of attitude and personality. Paper presented at the convention of the Midwestern Psychological Association, 1967.

Wann, T. W. (Ed.) *Behaviorism and phenomenology.* Chicago: University of Chicago Press, 1964.

Weiner, B., Frieze, I., Kukla, A., Reed, L., Rest, S., & Rosenbaum, R. M. *Perceiving the causes of success and failure.* New York: General Learning Press, 1971.

Additional Sources

Byrne, D., & Clore, G. L. Effectance arousal and attraction. *Journal of Personality and Social Psychology,* 1967, 6(4, Whole No. 638).

Jones, E. E. *Ingratiation.* New York: Appleton-Century-Crofts, 1964.

Lott, B., & Lott, A. J. The formation of positive attitudes toward group members. *Journal of Abnormal and Social Psychology,* 1960, 61, 297–300.

Newcomb, T. M. Individual systems of orientation. In S. Koch (Ed.), *Psychology: a study of a science.* Vol. 3. New York: McGraw-Hill, 1959.

Schachter, S. *The psychology of affiliation.* Palo Alto, Calif.: Stanford University Press, 1959.

Needs and the Interpersonal Relationship

10

Our way of proceeding is to rephrase the question "What does he see in her?" into several questions: What are his more important needs? What sorts of gratification does he seek? What sort of rewards can she provide him with? And then we ask the corresponding questions about her needs and rewards. And on both sides, to what degree are these needs conscious? To what extent is there unconscious collusion? What are the reciprocal rewards? In formulating and answering these questions we are then proceeding to describe the love of two people on a meaningful, working basis. And that, very simply, is what the theory of complementary needs is about (1958, p. 289).

—R. F. Winch

Implicitly or explicitly, all psychological theory begins with the assumption that people have needs. The origin of the concept might be traced to psychoanalysis, to common sense, or like every other idea, to the Greeks. The concept of needs is implicit in most of our common-sense, everyday discussion of the behavior of ourselves and of other people. The detective who is trying to solve a murder case wonders what the motive was. The parent trying to cope with a difficult child wonders why he behaves the way he does. And the psychologist trying to diagnose a case asks what needs his client is trying to satisfy by his behavior.

We assume needs because most of the time people do things in order to satisfy some need. We drink in order to slake our thirst. We eat in order to satisfy our hunger. We might call the "need" by some other name, such as "drive" or "motive," but the underlying assumption is the same: The organism behaves in order to satisfy a need.

People being what they are, generalizers, it follows that they would generalize the concept of need to relationships between people. Why do people socialize with other people? Because "people need people." Why do people choose to socialize with some people and avoid other people? The answer seems obvious. Because people need what certain other people have to give — and they avoid other people because what those other people have to give is not needed. As the saying goes, "Who needs it?"

As you might suspect, needs have been studied and organized into systems. In modern psychology two widely used elaborations of the need concept are those of H. A. Murray (1938) and A. H. Maslow (1970). The need theory of both has been applied to the study of the interpersonal relationship. Murray's theory has been applied to the study of mate-selection by R. F. Winch (1958), who asserts that people are attracted to others who will meet their needs, and therefore people who choose to pair with each other are complementary in their needs. Maslow has studied intimate interpersonal relationships and concluded that the way two people relate to each other is a function of their level of self-actualization, or self-development, which is, in turn, a function of the kinds of needs which motivate them. In this chapter we will discuss both views of needs as they operate in the relationships between people.

Complementary Needs in Mate-Selection

R. F. Winch (1958) hypothesized that people marry whom they do because they have needs that are complementary. He conducted intensive studies that produced data he interpreted as supporting his hypothesis, and thereby set off a debate that raged in sociological and psychological literature for years. The debate has not yet been settled.

Winch did not arrive at his hypothesis lightly, nor by spontaneous inspiration. Rather, he thoroughly reviewed psychological and sociological research and then derived a hypothesis that seemed to fit both the data and the history of the topic. The question of why people marry whom they marry is not a recent one. The debate over whether like attracts like or opposite attracts opposite has gone on for a long time. The data that sociologists had accumulated before Winch presented his hypothesis seemed to support the "like attracts like" side of the controversy (as does the material discussed in Chapter 9). Therefore, to suggest that opposites in needs are attracted to each other was to paddle upstream against the prevailing currents of both data and conventional wisdom.

Winch's stimulation and support for going against the current came from psychoanalysis. Those who had counseled married couples with problems or who had done psychotherapy with married people had noticed that neurotic people seemed to marry spouses who had neuroses that complemented their own. One of the rules of the trade among clinicians has long been the observation that people don't marry the people they marry by accident. Therefore if a husband complains that his wife is a harridan, the clinician begins to wonder why he wanted to marry a harridan.

Further, clinicians noticed that certain kinds of people tend to be attracted to certain other kinds of people — some kinds of men prefer certain kinds of women and vice versa — whose personality dynamics fit in with their own. They meet each others' needs. An example of these kinds of observations is stated by the psychoanalyst, Lawrence Kubie, who advanced the thesis that "a major source of unhappiness between husband and wife is to be found in the discrepancies between their conscious and unconscious demands on each other and on the marriage, as these are expressed first in the choosing of a mate and then in the subsequent evolution of their relationship" (1956, p. 14). Kubie concluded that in marriage, people are driven to fulfill a need that is rooted in some past lack or fixation.

Kubie (1956) illustrated the origin of these needs and the way they operate in relationships with other people by describing several cases. One of the cases was that of a young woman who had been left fatherless at an early age. Over a number of years she was driven to find a man who would serve as a substitute father and would also be her ally in her conflicts with her mother. This need was apparently obvious to the young woman's friends, although the woman herself was not aware of it. She broke engagements with several older men before she finally married a man who was approximately her own father's age. Unfortunately, she discovered that a substitute is never more than a substitute, and that despite the age difference, her husband was looking for a mother as much as she was hunting for a father. Since both were disappointed and frustrated in their relationship, the marriage ended in bitter recriminations.

Another psychoanalyst, Bela Mittelmann (1956), observed the interactions of twenty-eight couples and concluded that the interactions could be classified into complementary patterns. Mittelmann wrote that "the emotional patterns of the mates complement each other in such a way as to perpetuate their pathological reactions through an intrapsychic vicious circle of reactions. . . . Complementary patterns between marriage partners . . . may be found in combination" (1956, p. 82). Mittelmann described five kinds of complementary patterns in marriage:

1. One partner is aggressive and sadistic, seeking to humiliate and hurt the other and thus relieve his own anxiety which is aroused by the relationship, while the other partner is dependent, submissive, and enduring.

2. One partner attempts to be self-sufficient through emotional detachment (usually the man), while the other partner makes intense, open demands for love (usually the woman). This kind of marriage often occurs because the woman interprets the man's detachment as strength, while the man feels that the woman's vivacity is a sign of independence.

3. Each partner attempts to dominate, and each defends violently against being dominated. This pattern is characterized by frequent major quarrels. (This type is described as being complementary because what each does, in part, feeds the other's needs. Each wants to win a complete victory over the other, but because of strong dependency needs, each is terrified at the possibility that the other may leave. Thus they stay locked in a struggle.)

4. One partner is neurotically ill and pleas helplessness, while the other partner attempts to be extremely considerate to the "ill" partner.

5. One partner alternates periods of helplessness and suffering with periods of intense self-assertion, while the other partner provides support and assumes responsibility during the helpless periods and feels a disappointed desire for love and support during the self-assertive periods. This is a more complex complementary pattern.

The problem Winch faced was how to square the numerous sociological studies that demonstrated that like marry like with the clinical observation that people seem to marry those who complement them in their needs. He resolved the problem with the explanation that similarity in background, religion, and socioeconomic status bring people into contact with each other, while complementary needs keep them together.

Winch reasoned that before two people can form a relationship, they must meet. If they are similar in interests, values, education, religion, and so on, they are much more likely to meet each other. As the saying goes, "Birds of a feather flock together." Thus similarity in background makes the probability that two people will meet and get to know each other higher than if they had little or nothing in common. "To make the point tediously clear, if a young man habituates the corner tavern, it seems unlikely that he will meet there very many female teetotalers; and an habitue of the Wednesday night prayer meeting runs little risk of encountering the Bohemian atheist" (Winch, 1958, p. 13). Any correlation between similarity in background and marriage or any other permanent relationship is likely to be positive and significant because people who have dissimilar backgrounds just don't have nearly as much opportunity to meet each other.

Yet even people from similar backgrounds, though they may meet, do not always form relationships. Any observer who has casually watched a church picnic for teenagers has observed that there are members of the group who have little regard for each other—and conversely, that some are highly attracted to each other. The same can be said for college students, members of a political club, or any other activity that brings similar people together. Therefore the question becomes one of determining what it is that attracts the members of these homogamous groups to each other.

Winch's hypothesis is that the attraction is a function of complementary needs. However, before one can go off and do research on needs one must first define what it is that he is doing research on. What is a need? Winch (1958, p. 71) used H. A. Murray's definition of needs. To perhaps oversimplify, Murray defines a need as a lack of satisfaction within the person that impels him to do something that will provide that which is lacking. It is "a construct which stands for a force . . . which organizes perception, intellection, conation, and action in such a way as to transform in a certain direction an existing, unsatisfying situation" (Murray, 1938, p. 123).[1]

In his original book, *Explorations in Personality,* Murray wrote several rather extensive definitions of a "need." These definitions would be worthwhile to examine briefly. One of the most obvious aspects of Murray's definition of a need is that it is a hypothetical construct. That is, a person is observed to behave in certain ways, and these ways of behaving have a trend; it is inferred that this trend is produced by some state within the person that motivates him to behave the way he does. Murray wrote:

> A behavioral trend may be attributed to a hypothetical force (a drive, need, or propensity) within the organism. The proper way of conceptualizing this force which (if uninhibited) promotes activity which (if competent) brings about a situation that is opposite (as regards its relevant properties) to the one that aroused it. Frequently, an innumerable number of subneeds (producing subeffects) are temporally organized so as to promote the course of a major need (1938, p. 42).

[1]This and the following quotations dealing with Murray's definition of "need" are from H. A. Murray, *Explorations in personality.* New York: Oxford University Press, 1938. Copyright 1938 by Oxford University Press, Inc., renewed 1966 by Henry A. Murray, and reprinted with permission.

Murray also suggested that a need is latent force within people, or other organisms, which predisposes them to behave in certain ways if certain circumstances occur. In this vein Murray wrote:

> Strictly speaking, a need is the immediate outcome of certain internal and external occurrences. . . . we may loosely use the term "need" to refer to an organic potentiality or readiness to respond in a certain way under given conditions. In this sense a need is a latent attribute of an organism. More strictly, it is a noun which stands for the fact that a certain trend is apt to recur. . . . A need is, by definition, the force within the organism which determines a certain trend or major effect (1938, p. 60).

Murray located needs in the body, or more specifically in the brain, but they may be stimulated by physiological factors within the body.

> A need is a construct (a convenient fiction or hypothetical concept) which stands for a force (the physicochemical nature of which is unknown) in the brain region, a force which organizes perception, apperception, intellection, conation, and action in such a way as to transform in a certain direction an existing, unsatisfying situation. A need is sometimes provoked directly by internal processes of a certain kind (viscerogenic, endocrinogenic, thalamicogenic) arising in the course of vital sequences, but, more frequently (when in a state of readiness) by the occurrence of one of a few commonly effective press (or by anticipatory images of such press). Thus it manifests itself by leading the organism to search for or to avoid encountering or, when encountered, to attend and respond to certain kinds of press . . . . Each need is characteristically accompanied by a particular feeling or emotion and tends to use certain modes (subneeds and actones) to further its trend. It may be weak or intense, momentary or enduring. But usually it persists and gives rise to a certain course of overt behavior (or fantasy), which (if the organism is competent and external opposition not insurmountable) changes the initiating circumstance in such a way as to bring about an end situation which stills, appeases, or satisfies the organism. . . . It is not possible to confine oneself to a single operational definition. It seems that the best objective basis is the behavioral attainment of an apparently satisfying effect, an effect which brings the activity to a halt (usually by facilitating a vital process). The best subjective criterion is the occurrence of a wish or resolution to do a certain thing . . . (Murray, 1938, p. 123).

Thus a need is something that is inferred to exist from observing the trends in the behavior or the thoughts of a person. A need stimulates a person to behave in a certain way. A need has its source in some unsatisfying situation. This unsatisfying situation may be physiological, or it may be social.

Where do needs come from? Obviously, if they are at least partially physiological, they have their source in the organism and are present at birth. The need for food, water, and oxygen are examples of needs that a person is born with. However, needs may also be learned, and they may have their source in a person's culture. In this regard, Murray wrote:

> Some needs may become established because of their success in furthering other more elementary needs. . . . A need may also become established by repetition, due to the frequent occurrence of specific press. . . . Certain cultures and subcultures to which an individual is exposed may be characterized by a predominance of certain needs (1938, p. 129).

And finally, the strength of needs vary from one person to another. This variation may be due to differences in strength at birth—some babies eat more than others from the time they are born—or it may be due to learning or differential reinforcement that takes place after birth.

All of these definitions and elaborations of need may be somewhat confusing, but there are certain points which they make clear: A need is inferred from a behavioral trend. It is something within the organism which motivates it to behave in certain ways. This something is some lack or dissatisfaction or frustration, and the behavior motivated is meant to provide that which is lacking or to remove the frustration. It is important to note here that the "behavior" exhibited by the organism can be any kind of behavior, including dreams, fantasies, wishes, or feelings, as well as overt behavior. This point is important, since one of the main methods of determining needs has been the assessment of a person's fantasies or other imaginative productions.

Murray's definition of needs is one that is widely used, and it is the definition on which Winch based his work. But it should be noted here that Murray's definition is not the only definition of need. A somewhat different definition of need, that of A. H. Maslow, will be discussed later in the chapter.

The Research on Needs and Mate-Selection

When the concept of needs is applied to mate-selection, or any other aspect of interpersonal behavior, it implies that both parties involved in the interaction are seeking to supply some deficiency or remove some frustration. Each has a need that the other can satisfy. Winch (1958) hypothesized that these needs must complement each other, and that when the needs of two people do complement each other, they lead to the establishment of "love," which is defined by Winch as a state of complementary needs satisfaction.

> Love is the positive emotion experienced by one person (the person lov-ing, or the lover) in an interpersonal relationship in which the second person (the person loved, or love-object) either (1) meets certain impor-tant needs of the first or (2) manifests or appears (to the first) to mani-fest personal attributes (e.g., beauty, skills, or status) highly prized by the first, or both. . . . In mate-selection each individual seeks within his or her field of eligibles for that person who gives the greatest promise of providing him or her with maximum need gratification (Winch, 1958, p. 88).

However, stating that people relate to other people because the other people satisfy their needs does not specify the nature of the rela-tionship between or among the needs. The needs met by a pair for each other could be the same needs or different needs. For example, if you have money and I have skill, we might trade, with you paying me your money and me supplying you with my skill. In this case we would complement each other. But if we both have itchy backs, we might scratch each other's back. In this case we would have the same needs, and they would not be complementary to each other. The question is Which needs *must* be complementary in the attraction between two people?

Winch addressed himself to this question. He examined the many needs listed by Murray and simplified and reduced the list to those needs that looked like they might be pertinent to mate-selection. He ended up with twelve needs that looked promising. He also added three general personality "traits" listed by Murray. The twelve needs chosen by Winch (1958, p. 89) for investigation were (1) abasement; (2) achievement; (3) approach; (4) autonomy; (5) deference; (6) dominance; (7) hostility; (8) nurturance; (9) recognition; (10) status aspiration; (11) status striving; (12) succorance. He also included as variables the gen-eral personality traits of anxiety, emotionality, and vicariousness.

In looking over this list of needs, it becomes apparent that to sat-isfy some of them, the relationship between two people would have to be complementary. Winch cites the need to express hostility as an ex-ample. What kind of a wife would give a man who needs to express hostility the opportunity to express that hostility? Obviously a woman who enjoys receiving expressions of hostility. And what kind of need would such a woman have? She would be a woman who is masochistic and turns her own hostility toward herself; she would have the need termed *abasement*. Thus a man who is high in need *hostility* would be expected to be attracted to a woman who is high in need *abasement*, and vice versa. It seems fairly obvious that a man who needs to express hostility will not long be able to keep a woman who does not need to be abased. She will cut off the relationship rather quickly.

If we consider another need, dominance, it seems rather obvious that two people who need to dominate will probably end up quarreling about who is the boss. It seems very probable that a person who has a high need to dominate will more likely be attracted to another person who has a low need to dominate. Thus, it appears that trying to match people so that they will meet each others' needs, for at least some of the needs on the list, requires that they have different needs.

In the examples described above, two kinds of complementariness are described. Winch (1958, pp. 94–95) categorized these two kinds of complementariness as Type I and Type II. *Type I complementariness* exists when one partner is high on a need and the other partner is low on that need (+X and −X). An example of this kind of complementariness is when one mate is high on *dominance* and the other low on *dominance*. *Type II complementariness* exists when one partner is high on one need and the other partner is high on a different, complementary need (+X and +Y). The example of the man who was high on *hostility* who had a wife who was high on *abasement* is an example of this kind of complementariness. If *dominance* were to be paired in a Type II complementariness with another need, *deference* would seem to be a likely candidate for the complementary need. That is, a dominant person would seem to be most likely complemented by a deferent person.

Since Winch intended to use extensive, time-consuming methods of measuring the needs described above, he decided that the sample he studied should be small. He chose twenty-five married couples, of which at least one member of each pair was an undergraduate student at Northwestern University. These twenty-five couples were composed of individuals who were white, middle-class, native-born, childless, married less than two years, and between nineteen and twenty-six years of age (Winch, 1958, p. 107).

The subjects' needs were measured through information obtained from the subjects in two kinds of interviews, and from the subjects' responses to eight cards of the Thematic Apperception Test. The Thematic Apperception Test (TAT) is a test designed by Murray to measure the basic needs he felt existed. The test is composed of cards which contain a variety of different kinds of pictures. The subject is supposed to make up a story about what is going on in the picture and tell how it all comes out. The stories are then scored for the several variables in Murray's personality system, including needs.

The two interviews were designed to elicit different kinds of information from the subjects. The first interview, called a "need interview" was one in which the subjects were asked forty-five open-ended questions. These questions were designed to elicit responses that would, hopefully, reveal their needs. They were asked questions about such topics as how they felt when someone stepped in front of them in a line at a restaurant, and how they felt when they saw their names in print. The second interview was a case history interview, which included inquiries about such things as their earliest memories, their relationships with other members of their families, and their development in various areas of their lives. A third method, which has already been mentioned, was having the subjects make up stories for eight cards of the TAT. Another test, the Cattell 16 P.F. Test was given, but it yielded largely negative results, so it was discarded.

For each subject, two raters rated each of the variables for each of the measures, and a final global rating was derived on each of the variables at a case conference composed of five people who analyzed as a group all of the information about each subject.

It should be added at this point that Winch realized that a need might be clearly apparent and overt, or it might be covert, hidden behind personality defenses. He also recognized that a need might be satisfied in the relationship with the spouse, but that it might also be satisfied outside the marriage. He suggested that the need "achievement," for example, might well be expected to be satisfied outside the marriage rather than inside the marriage. Thus for each of the twelve needs and three traits, it might be possible for each of them to be composed of four subneeds, which would include the overt, the covert, inside the marriage, and outside the marriage. Theoretically, this would leave sixty total variables ($15 \times 4 = 60$). However, Winch judged that some of the variables would not necessarily be covert or outside, and he arrived at a total of forty-four total variables to rate.

With forty-four variables and three sets of ratings, Winch had a total of 5,808 correlations to examine for some sort of order or meaning. The first analysis he did was to take 344 of these correlations — correlations that he thought would be particularly meaningful — and examine them. Winch concluded that the data indicated a tendency toward complementariness in needs between married couples, although this was not a strong tendency. He also examined the need scores of each of the men and women in his sample and attempted to match each man with the appropriate woman on the basis of these need scores. He correctly matched twenty out of the twenty-five pairs of husbands and wives.

Winch then moved on to an analysis of all of the 5,808 correlations. He first looked for some pattern or regularity among these correlation coefficients, and he found one. This regularity is that there is a bipolar dimension of mate-selection which is characterized by needs and traits which are assertive and receptive, and that persons who are assertive tend to marry receptive persons, and vice versa.

Winch also factor analyzed the matrix of intercorrelations (see Chapter 7 for a brief description of factor analysis) and obtained six factors. These factors were (1) achievement-oriented independence versus succorance; (2) anxious succorance versus secure nurturance; (3) strong need approval; (4) submissiveness versus dominance; (5) instrumental deference; (6) neurotic self-deprecation versus status-oriented dominance. These six factors were obtained from an R-type of factor analysis,[2] in which the various measures or tests were correlated with each other. Winch also performed a Q-type factor analysis, in which each person studied was correlated with each other person studied. Q-type factor analysis produces types of people rather than test factors. In this analysis Winch obtained four factors, or perhaps it might be more accurate to say he obtained four types of mates. These four were (1) yielding dependency; (2) hostile dominance; (3) mature nurturance; (4) neurotic self-deprecation.

Winch concluded that the factor analysis "suggest[s] that complementariness may be stated in part at least in terms of achievement and passivity, of nurturance and dependence, of dominance and deference" (1958, p. 130).

Types of Marriage

Having concluded that people who marry each other are complementary, and that what they are complementary on is some dimension that partakes of achievement and passivity, nurturance and dependence, and dominance and deference, Winch (1958) next described what might be termed a taxonomy of marriages. This was a taxonomy of types of marriages derived, of course, from the twenty-five married couples he had interviewed and studied intensively. Winch believed he observed four different types of marriages: Mothers and Sons, Ibsenian, Masters and Servant Girls, and Thurberian.

1. Mothers and Sons. This is a marriage in which the wife is nurturant and the husband seeks succorance. Winch (1958, pp. 135–39) illustrated this type of marriage with the case of Alice and Adam. Adam grew up with a mother who was very affectionate with her son. When he was a little boy he would curl up on his mother's lap, and they would talk for hours. Adam's father not only worked during the day, but often worked evenings at another job. His father was usually under his mother's control, and on the only occasion when his father had a strong disagreement with his mother, Adam's mother took Adam and left his father for several months, until his father humbly begged her to come home.

[2]Described in Cattell, R. B. *Factor analysis.* New York: Harper & Row, 1952, Ch. 7.

There were few children in the neighborhood in which Adam grew up, so he had little opportunity to play with children his own age. Most of his social experience was with adults rather than with other children. He had friends after he entered high school, but these friendships were apparently not very deep. He dated occasionally.

When Adam was sixteen, his mother died. The center of his life disappeared with her death. He said, "Months afterward I was just in a daze. I was really a lost soul."

Alice was also an only child. Her father was an attorney and her mother a legal secretary, but from Alice's earliest memory, her father had been a semi-invalid. He was hospitalized for protracted periods of time. During the times he was at home, he carried on a partial legal practice from his home. Because of her father's inability to work, it was necessary for her mother to work to support the family. Her mother both directed the home and earned most of the money to support the family.

While her mother was at work, Alice was often at home, where she not only performed what chores she could, but also nurtured her father—an activity which she enjoyed, since she both loved and idolized him. Alice saw her father as kind, generous, attractive, warm and friendly, and close and loving. She perceived her mother, on the other hand, as dominating, aggressive, a leader, vain, and liking material things rather than people. Alice did not feel particularly liked by her mother and had many disagreements with her. When Alice was sixteen her father died.

When they were seventeen, Alice and Adam met each other. They had both just lost parents who had been the center of their lives. When they found each other, they each found another person who was able to fill the center that had been taken from them by death. Adam's ideal for a woman was someone who was like his mother, while Alice admired older men like her father. Alice saw Adam as being like her father in his personality, mannerisms, and values. After dating for four years, Alice and Adam were married.

At the time they were studied by Winch, Adam was going to college after serving in the Army, while Alice was teaching kindergarten. During their interviews, several details were revealed, some of which follow. Alice has two places in which she is dominant: her home and her schoolroom. Adam enjoys Alice's competence and provides an appreciative audience for her performance. Adam does not perceive his wife as a good listener, since she does not listen to his answer when she asks him a question. They do not have arguments, because Adam is an easy person to get along with. Alice does criticize Adam, but Adam sees her criticism as coming only when it is justified.

This case seems to be a very neat example of two people with needs finding in each other a person who is trained, experienced, and more than anxious to supply what the other needs. Adam needed a competent woman to look after him, and Alice needed a man to take care of, so they found what they were looking for in each other. In this case the husband is passive and receptive, while the wife is dominant and nurturing.

2. *Ibsenian Complementariness.* In Ibsenian complementariness the husband is the protector and caretaker of his wife, who plays the role of a doll-child. Winch adds the hunch that in this type of marriage the husband seeks to control and mold his wife into the kind of woman he wants her to be. Winch derived the name for this type from Henrik Ibsen's play, *A Doll's House.* In this play the husband, Torvald Helmer, treats his wife, Nora, as though she were a child who is incompetent to do anything without his help and guidance. (Perhaps it should be added that Ibsen's play might not be a very good source for a type of stable marriage, since at the end of the play Nora leaves Torvald, which was no trivial step for a woman to take in nineteenth century Norway.)

Winch (1958, pp. 148–56) cited Carl and Clare to illustrate this kind of marriage. Carl was the second son of parents who ran a family grocery store. His father ran the store while his mother ran the home, although his mother did keep the books for the store. His parents were sober, thrifty, industrious, and capable.

Carl had an older brother who, it was planned, would help his father around the store; when his mother became pregnant with Carl, she hoped the child would be a girl who could help her around the house. Despite his sex, Carl did end up helping his mother around the house while his brother worked with his father in the store. Carl dusted, cleaned, washed dishes, and cooked. Carl admired both of his parents, but he was closer to his mother, and came to see himself as being more like his mother than his father.

In addition to his domestic chores, Carl was active in athletics and became a star high school athlete. In the army Carl became the cook and enjoyed feeding his men well. After the service, Carl resumed his habit of spending his evenings with the fellows. These fellows congregated around the drug store, and it was there that Carl first met Clare, who worked at the soda fountain.

Carl described his ideal wife as one who would be similar to his mother—that is, she would be neat and a good cook, take care of his clothes, and run the house well. He also wanted an attractive, affectionate wife with whom he could sit and talk.

Clare was the eighth child in a family of twelve. Her mother always appeared overworked, while her father was quiet, unobtrusive, nurturant, and the one who tried to keep peace in the family. Since the family was large, Clare received very little attention from either her mother or father; her older sister did most of the actual supervising of the younger children. Clare came to see this older sister as rather harsh and forbidding.

Clare did not have a happy childhood. Favoritism was shown to her brothers just because they were boys. In addition, Clare was treated as a scapegoat by her older sister. Her brothers and sisters, knowing she was afraid of dark rooms, would lock her in one just to hear her scream. Clare also lost out on the few toys and other goodies that were distributed in the family because she talked back to her sister. (Clare sounds like the Cinderella of the family.)

Clare had wanted to escape from her family for a long time. But she did not, or could not, go off on her own, so she worked at the soda fountain waiting for someone to rescue her from her situation.

While being interviewed, Clare revealed that she feels no one else in her family is as easily frightened as she. She still fears darkness and being left alone at night. When Carl does have to be gone from home at night, he arranges to have someone stay with her. Although they live in the suburb of a large city, Clare has never been to the city alone.

When asked what kind of man attracted her, Clare said a man who would not "fall all over her." When they were dating, she liked the fact that when Carl asked her to go some place, he would ask her in a way that implied she could go or not go as she pleased; she also liked the fact that Carl was not interested in other women. Carl doesn't notice the kinds of clothes she wears, but this doesn't bother her. Carl is quiet and gives Clare a chance to talk, which is a change from her brothers and sisters who constantly told her to shut up. At home, if Clare said something the older brothers did not like, she was apt to be on the receiving end of some kind of reprisal, but Carl doesn't seem to pay much attention to what she says, so she feels she can talk freely without having to worry about any untoward consequences.

Winch concluded that Clare seemed to be a girl who had the nipple removed from her mouth before "she could begin to suck," and who was a waif looking for a maternal husband who would help her mature emotionally, and that Carl, on the other hand, seemed to have served an apprenticeship for just such a role, first at home with his mother, then later in the army.

Winch noted that Carl was closer to his mother and identified with her, so that the role he would be likely to play would be one similar to that played by his mother. Carl's mother ran the house and took care of Carl when he was young, teaching him the things he learned. Now Carl is recreating his mother's role, and Clare is playing in relationship to Carl the same role Carl played in relationship to his mother when he was a boy.

Still another complementary aspect of this marriage is that Clare is attractive and much more socially adept and motivated than Carl, so that she carries the main burden of the couple's relationship with the outside world. She can serve as a kind of foreign minister for the family. Also Clare encourages Carl when he gets depressed about school.

3. *Masters and Servant Girls.* In this kind of marriage the wife is much more competent than the Ibsenian wife. The husband is the head of the house, and the wife is the servant, but a capable and worthy servant. There are two levels of complementariness in this kind of marriage. On the overt, public level, the man is dominating, self-assured, and somewhat frosty, while the wife is compliant, active, nurturing, and outgoing. The husband is the master, and the wife is the servant girl who is destined to become the breeder and governess of the children. On a deeper level, however, the wife is a nurturing, accepting, and emotionally strong supporter of her husband who has a streak of dependency in his personality. In this kind of marriage the husband typically comes from a higher social level than his wife.

Winch (1958, pp. 167–76) used Earl and Edith as an example of this kind of marriage. Earl was the older of two sons. Neither his father nor his mother were educated beyond high school, but his father had succeeded in business and was determined to provide for all of the education his sons would take. When Earl was a child, his mother administered the spankings that were given, but he feared his father's verbal disapproval more than his mother's physical punishment.

In the interview, Earl described his father as an impressive and successful man who is liked and respected by all of his associates. He described his mother as being attractive, but limited in her education (although she had had more education than his father), nervous, overly concerned about her housekeeping and the affairs of the other members of the family, and overprotective of her sons. Earl respects his father more than his mother, and he feels that he resembles his father more than his mother.

At the time of the study Earl planned to pursue a rather lengthy education, getting first an M.D. degree, then a Ph.D. in physics so he could work with isotopes in medicine.

Winch speculated that the kind of wife Earl would look for would be one who could render all the services he wanted "with the decor and quality of service of one of the best clubs" (1958, p. 171), which would require that she be someone he could look down upon. To meet these qualifications, she would have to be a competent woman who had less education, or came from a lower social class, or was inferior to Earl in some respect. However, since she would become the mother of his children, it would be necessary for her to come from "good stock." Presumably this would mean an intelligent, capable woman from a good, stable family of lower social class than his own family. And, of course, she should be a woman of such background and characteristics that she would be happy with such a relationship as Earl wished to establish.

Edith was the next to youngest child of a father who was an active and attractive man who managed a large farm. Her mother died when she was young. As the older children left home, Edith took over running the home and raising her younger brother. Edith was her "father's girl" so she spent all the time she could with him. Because of her mother's death, Edith was called upon to assume two roles: a wife substitute for her father and a mother substitute for her younger brother. Edith had always wanted to be a nurse, and she spent much of her childhood taking care of other living things. Later she became a nurse and functioned well in the role.

In her interview, Edith described herself as being like her father—that is, aggressive, decisive, and liking responsibility. She described her ideal husband as a man who is able to help, and who she does not have to "carry along." The things she liked about Earl were that he took her to parties and formal dances, which she had not been able to attend as a working girl or a farmer's daughter. He had beautiful manners and was enjoyable to be with. (Winch interpreted Edith's perception of Earl's beautiful manners as a misperception brought about by his having developed the social behaviors of a higher social stratum than her own.) Edith feels that Earl places her on a pedestal, and she likes that.

Although Edith feels that Earl has placed her on a pedestal, when Earl described Edith, he said that she is understanding and will be a good mother because she is good both morally and ethically and will instill these qualities in the children, and that she is sociable and more than adequate in meeting and entertaining his friends. Earl feels that she is not quite as reserved as she should be and needs to develop more social poise, but that she has good manners. (Winch likened Earl's description of his wife to that of an employer giving an employee good references.)

Winch noted two conspicuous differences between this kind of marriage and the Ibsenian marriage. First, in this marriage the woman is seen more as a servant who is expected to provide good service rather than as a doll to be taken care of. Second, the woman in this kind of marriage is much more competent than the woman in the Ibsenian marriage. These women are capable of making their own way in the world. Edith brings money into the family, thus providing part of the help for Earl's schooling, and she also encourages him in his school work, presumably much as she did her younger brother when she was at home. She is willing to accept a subordinate role since she was reared in a family in which the man was the head of the house, and for her own career, although she had thought of medicine, she chose nursing, since nursing seemed more appropriate for a woman.

4. Thurberian Complementariness. In this kind of marraige the wife is a dominant, active woman, while the husband is a passive man who has a passive hostility that is expressed only under great provocation. The name for this marriage was derived from the drawings of James Thurber. The relationship between Charley Brown and Lucy in Charles Schulz's "Peanuts" comic strip would perhaps be an example of a Thurberian man-woman (or boy-girl) relationship.

Winch (1958, pp. 187–93) used Grace and George as an example of this kind of marriage. George's mother was a short, slender, attractive blond who was always busy doing something. She was generous and had a good sense of humor, but when she was angry she expressed her anger immediately and directly. When she wanted something she insisted on having it. She did not give George suggestions as a boy—she gave him orders. If George resisted, she talked him down until he saw things her way. When George was in high school, his mother didn't want George to play baseball, so she asked the coach to cut him from the squad, which the coach did. George did not find out about this until years later.

George's father died when George was two years old. His mother remarried a man who was pleasant and athletic. George was very fond of him and thought of him as his real father.

George stated that he hates to be pushed around. He said he developed, in his relationship with his mother, the technique of avoiding being pushed around by giving the appearance of complying with her demands, then doing what he pleased. George sees himself as being somewhat shy, as wanting to be left alone when he is sick, and as being quiet when he is angry. When he is nervous he lets off steam by talking a lot.

Grace's father gave her anything she wanted. He would go out at night and get her an ice-cream cone if she wanted it. She saw him as an attractive, sociable, affectionate man who liked to have a good time. He was probably more affectionate to Grace than to Grace's mother. Also, Grace said that people could walk all over him without his knowing it.

Grace's mother was the boss in the family. She made the family decisions and disciplined Grace. When Grace began to assert her independence in high school, she had many fights with her mother. Grace's mother was a conscientious and meticulous housekeeper, and Grace sees herself as being like her mother in this regard.

Grace has a brother who is several years older. When they were children, her brother teased her a great deal. As a girl Grace played all kinds of "boys' games." During adolescence Grace dated many different boys and had many crushes, including some that both her family and friends disapproved of because the boys were daredevils and show-offs.

Grace says she is the sort of person that all kinds of people bring their troubles to. She likes to help people and feels that she must have a strong maternal instinct. She describes George as sympathetic, understanding, and perhaps allowing people to take advantage of him as her father did. In their marriage George apparently worries about things, but Grace feels that she has been able to help him lead a little more relaxed and less worrisome life than he had.

George had sometimes found, in dating girls, that he had difficulty keeping the conversation going, but when he dated Grace he found that he did not have to talk. They could be comfortable walking together in silence.

One thing that Grace complains about in George is his dependence on his mother. George isn't quite so sure about what he doesn't like about Grace, but did mention her tendency to lose her temper easily. However, he said he would not want to change that in her since he gets "a kick out of it." After Grace has expressed her anger she forgets about it.

Winch noted that Grace expressed the feeling that although George was easy-going on the surface, deep down she did not feel he was that way, so Winch speculated that in Grace's temper outbursts, George gained vicarious satisfaction of his own suppressed temper by watching Grace blow off steam.

In the case of both Grace and George we can see a clear similarity between the person they married and their parent of the opposite sex.

Having described four different types of marriages that he had observed in his sample, Winch then faced the question of how to order these four types. Recall Winch's conclusion earlier in the chapter that patterns in his correlational data suggested that in any marriage relationship one person is active or assertive while the other person is receptive or passive. In all of the marriages described, one person is passive and the other receptive, so the question that arises is What are the dimensions along which these types might be passive or assertive? Since Winch derived four types of marriages, it would seem promising to pursue the thought that perhaps there are two dimensions involved. This is what Winch did.

Winch suggests that two dimensions underlie these four types of marriages. One dimension is *dominant-submissive* and the other dimension is *nurturant-receptive*. Since there are a husband and a wife in each marriage, it follows that there could be types of marriages in which the husband is dominant and the wife submissive, or vice versa, and marriages in which the husband is nurturant and the wife receptive, or vice versa. Arranging these dimensions in a table, Winch arrived at a schematization of the four types of marriage which is presented in Table 1.

TABLE 1. **DIMENSIONS AND TYPES OF COMPLEMENTARY MARRIAGES**

Dominant-Submissive	Nurturant-Receptive	
	Husband-nurturant Wife-receptive	Wife-nurturant Husband-receptive
Husband-dominant Wife-submissive	*Ibsenian* *Carl-Clare*	*Master-Servant Girl* *Earl-Edith*
Wife-dominant Husband-submissive	*Thurberian* *George-Grace*	*Mother-Son* *Adam-Alice*

From R. F. Winch, *Mate-selection: a study of complementary needs*, p. 214. New York: Harper & Row, 1958. Copyright © 1958 by Robert F. Winch, and reprinted with permission.

Winch listed sixteen hypotheses[3] about marriage derived from these dimensions and types. The first two hypotheses deal with the dimensions of marriages:

1. If a person (either a man or woman) is highly nurturant, it is probable that the person will marry someone who is highly receptive and relatively nonnurturant.

2. If a person is highly dominant, it is probable that the person will marry someone who is highly submissive and relatively nondominant.

The next two hypotheses concern dominance, hostility, and socioeconomic status as they relate to mate-selection and marriage interaction:

3. Irrespective of the gender of the spouse, the more dominant tends to come from the family of higher socioeconomic status.

4. The more dominant spouse tends to be the more overtly hostile spouse.

In describing the cases that illustrated his marriage types, Winch noted that some of the spouses tended to be "Pygmalions" (the name derived from George Bernard Shaw's play of the same name) who tried to shape their spouse into a particular kind of person. In the cases we have described, Carl and Earl seemed to try to shape their mates to some extent. Of all the cases Winch discussed in his book, five were Pygmalions. He noted that all the Pygmalions were dominant, but that not all the dominant spouses were Pygmalions. He noted that the non-Pygmalion dominant spouses married people who were similar to their opposite-sex parent. This observation led to the following hypothesis:

[3]The sixteen hypotheses that follow are from R. F. Winch, *Mate-selection: a study of complementary needs*, pp. 214–19. New York: Harper & Row, 1958. Copyright © 1958 by Robert F. Winch, and reprinted with permission.

5. When a spouse is a Pygmalion, (a) that spouse is the more dominant spouse; (b) that spouse is trying to mold the mate into his or her own likeness; (c) that spouse is trying to mold the mate into the likeness of the spouse's own opposite-sex parent; and (d) the mate is very different from the spouse's own opposite-sex parent.

To hypothesis 5, Winch added its converse, although he admitted he was not ready to propose it in all seriousness: "A non-Pygmalionizing spouse is either a non-dominant spouse or a dominant spouse whose mate is rather similar to the opposite-sex parent" (1958, p. 217).

Next, Winch proposed two hypotheses concerning the Ibsenian and Mother-Son types:

6. Persons who assume the parental role in marriage tend not to explore the field of eligibles very widely.

7. Husbands who assume the role of son in marriage tend not to explore the field of eligibles very widely.

And, finally, Winch formulated nine hypotheses concerning the Thurberian and Mother-Son types of marriages:

8. Wives of these two types tend to have mothers who are aggressive, assertive, expressive, and dominant.

9. Wives of these two types tend to have negative attitudes toward their mothers.

10. Wives of these two types tend to have some conflict about their own behavior which is overtly aggressive, assertive, expressive, and dominant.

11. Husbands of these two types tend to have mothers who are aggressive, assertive, expressive, and dominant.

12. For husbands of these two types wives tend to fill the dominant role vacated by their mothers.

13. The vigorous expressiveness of these wives makes them attractive to their husbands.

14. Wives of these two types are attracted to their husbands, in part at least on the ground that they see these men as relaxing and tranquilizing.

15. Thurberian and Mother-Son wives tend to appear more "intelligent" than their husbands.

16. Thurberian husbands exceed husbands of other types in wanting to be liked and in making strenuous efforts to achieve acceptance.

Winch conceded that these four types of marriage do not account for all of the different kinds of marriage that might be encountered.

Anyone who has ever attempted to classify people according to any classification scheme has experienced the kind of problem Winch observed with his marriage types. All classification systems leave some cases that do not seem to fit into any of the available categories. Winch concluded, however, that those marriages that do not fit into his four types are composed of husbands and wives who are complementary on either dominance or nurturance, but not on both.

Several problems with Winch's types of marriages may have occurred to the reader at this point. Earlier in the chapter it was noted that Winch described needs as existing on both the overt and the covert level. What if the needs on one level are different from the needs on the other level? Also, it was noted that needs might be satisfied within or outside of a marriage. Which of these needs can be happily satisfied outside of a marriage, and what effect does this have on the marriage? And finally, the system has been presented as though the needs remain constant throughout a marriage. The types Winch described were based on couples who had been married two years or less. What happens to the needs and the interaction between the husband and the wife if their needs change, or if they have children, or if some other external event changes their situation?

Winch recognized these problems and acknowledged that he did not have the answers to them. However, he described a case in which the couple had two sets of needs, one overt and the other covert. The overt needs seemed to be the basis of the couple's initial attraction to each other, but after marriage the covert needs came into play, and one mate attempted to change the other mate. Early in this relationship the wife appeared to be the dominant member of the pair, but after marriage the husband became more dominant. Winch (1958, pp. 234–45) cites the Lloyd and Laura case to illustrate this pattern.

Lloyd was the second child in a family of three boys. His older brother was handsome, intelligent, and a good athlete. By comparison to his older brother Lloyd did not come off so well, since he was smaller and not so adept an athlete. Both parents were concerned about Lloyd developing into a man, so his father spent long hours with him helping him develop his athletic skills. Due mostly to hard work, Lloyd became a successful high school baseball player.

Lloyd's mother was an attractive, sociable woman who had a temper and taught her boys to be aggressive. On one occasion when two other boys were waiting outside to fight with Lloyd, Lloyd, who was content to stay in the house until they left, was forced by his mother to go outside and fight. The mother taught her boys not to allow others to take advantage of them or to push them around. Lloyd saw his mother as not being particularly affectionate, and as a meticulous housekeeper. When she was angered by her sons, she lost her temper quickly and expressed it by hitting them with a strap or with her hand.

Lloyd's father was more easy going than his mother; he was slow to anger and affectionate. Lloyd saw his father's affectionateness as being a masculine trait. His father was more likely to give the boys permission to do things than his mother. Also, his father was an accountant who was more oriented toward details than his mother.

Lloyd sees himself as being more like his mother than his father in that he tends to be aggressive, which he feels he developed as a consequence of his mother's training. Lloyd's mother felt that his father took too much from other people and should have been more insistent on his own rights.

Winch noted that Lloyd sees his father as being more likeable and passive than his mother, that he can describe his father only in comparison with his mother, which suggests that his mother was the more powerful figure in the family. Winch added that Lloyd is more like his mother than his father in his aggressiveness, but that this is largely due to his mother's training, which infers that his natural bent is toward being passive like his father. Lloyd sees aggressiveness as being more a feminine than a masculine trait.

Laura is quite similar to her mother, whom she describes as being quite sociable and active, belonging to many organizations and holding offices in all of them. Laura's mother is the boss in the family. Laura's father is a mild-mannered man.

Both of Laura's parents had been excellent students in school, so they expected Laura to be a good student also. In adolescence Laura began to rebel, and this rebellion centered around education. She dropped out of college and moved to New York where she took a job with a newspaper, a job at which she was successful, moving quickly up to the post of an assistant editor.

When Lloyd and Laura first met, she was attracted to his casual air, his conversational ability, and his intelligence. Although Laura enjoyed her job, after she and Lloyd married she quit because he wished it, and she changed her goals to being a "perfect wife." When asked how she made decisions, Laura replied that "I decide what I want to do and I do it. If he doesn't want me to do it, then I don't do it." She sees Lloyd as very charming and as being decisive like his mother. Laura says she feels like she is an entirely different person at home with Lloyd than she is at work. Without Lloyd she goes for what she wants, but when he is around it becomes "our" way, which, in her description, sounds like a euphemism for Lloyd's way. After Laura quit her newspaper job, she took a less demanding clerical job, but she plans to quit this job as soon as she can. Although the job is less demanding than the newspaper job, Laura reported that she seems to tire more easily than she used to.

Lloyd sees Laura as being aggressive and extroverted. She cannot be pushed around by other people, although she is not as openly aggressive as Lloyd's mother. Laura is witty, intelligent, sociable, and self-contained. Lloyd feels she is more trusting of other people than he is, but he thinks he may tend to be too suspicious of others. He object- ed to her working for the newspaper because he felt that it would make her rough and coarse.

Winch noted that Lloyd seems to feel that his own natural ten- dency is to be quiet and passive, but that he was taught to be aggres- sive by his mother. This suggests that he has two levels to his personal- ity, a surface aggressiveness and a covert passivity. Lloyd was attracted to the active, outgoing Laura, but after they were married he exerted pressure on her to give up her job, stay at home, and live a more pas- sive life. Laura also exhibited two different selves, the active, outgoing newspaperwoman and the different, more passive woman she is at home with Lloyd.

Winch suggested that their original attraction to each other was based on the passivity of Lloyd and the activity of Laura, and that origi- nally Laura was the dominant member of the pair, but that after mar- riage Lloyd began pressuring Laura to be more passive, and Laura complied. When they first married, Lloyd was a college student, but after he moved into the world of work he began pressuring his wife to conform more to the model of the wife in the middle class, and Lloyd exerted more effort to live according to the role he was taught by his mother.

If we were to base our expectancy of Laura and Lloyd's marriage pattern on the experience of each in his or her own family, we would expect Laura to be the more assertive member of the pair and Lloyd to be the more passive, since each came from a family in which the moth- er was assertive and the father relatively easygoing. Whatever their cur- rent efforts to meet what they feel to be the proper role for husband and wife in their own social group, or in the verbally stated expectancies of their parents, it would seem likely, to this writer at least, that they will eventually revert to the pattern of interaction that is the more natural to both of them. No doubt Lloyd will continue to work and earn the family living, but Laura's fatigue, despite a less demanding pace, suggests that eventually she will have to find an outlet for her own outgoing and ag- gressive nature, perhaps in the kinds of organizations in which her mother was so active, and which abound everywhere.

Winch theorized about this case along lines that are somewhat different from those I have described above. He saw Lloyd's attempt at being active and aggressive and his desire to have Laura remain at home as attempts to grow or develop from a dependent boy into a more assertive, independent man. This situation required Laura to grow in sensitivity and flexibility into the roles required of her in this change process. However, it should be pointed out that the parents of both Lloyd and Laura seem to have had reasonably stable, happy homes, and both sets of parents seem to have met their responsibilities as fathers and mothers in a reasonably satisfactory, adult fashion. In fact, Lloyd seems to have seen being a man as a more passive role than that of being a woman. Therefore, maturity would suggest to this writer that when maturity is achieved by Lloyd he will feel more secure, and thus more able to be his natural self, which is somewhat passive, and also feel secure enough to allow Laura to be her more natural self, which is an active woman. One not uncommon marriage interaction that can be observed is that of the husband who is the dominant member of the pair in the early years of the marriage but becomes relatively less so as time passes.

In any case, Lloyd and Laura present one example of a pattern of interaction that changes after marriage from what it was during the earlier days of the relationship.

However, the questions about what happens over many years of marriage and what happens when the circumstances change, as with the birth of children, are questions that are not answered by Winch's research. These await inquiries that cover a longer time span.

Criticisms of Winch

Winch's need theory has, as might well be expected, stimulated much research and much critical comment. This was bound to occur since he stated such an explicit theory from which testable hypotheses are easily derivable. Winch himself stated sixteen explicit hypotheses. The net result of all this research and discussion seems to be a certain amount of confusion, and the conclusion by some is that Winch's theory is not very useful.

Let us first review some of the research that failed to confirm Winch. This research generally has either failed to find any relationship between needs and interpersonal attraction, or it has found that similarity in needs, rather than complementarity, leads to interpersonal attraction.

The first study purporting to test the complementariness hypothesis was that of Bowerman and Day (1956), who studied the relationship among needs between pairs of dating couples. They found no significant relationship between dating and complementary needs. Winch denied that this study was really a test of his hypothesis, since (a) Bowerman and Day used dating couples rather than married couples; (b) many of the needs they correlated were not the same needs as Winch studied; (c) they used the Edwards Personal Preference Schedule (EPPS) to measure needs, which is a different method of measurement from that used by Winch, and which Winch stated had no known validity for measuring needs; (d) in this study they measured for complementariness on every need measured, which is not Winch's hypothesis.

Two other studies, also using the Edwards Personal Preference Schedule as the measuring device, failed to find a relationship between complementary needs and marriage satisfaction (Katz, Glucksberg, & Krauss, 1960) or between complementary needs and friendship choice (Reilly, Commins, & Stefic, 1960).

A series of other studies reported tend to give some support for similarity in needs as being the basis for attraction, rather than complementariness of needs. Izard (1960) studied liking in a college class. He had forty-seven college students pick out the three other students in the class they liked most and the three they liked least. He used the Edwards Personality Preference Schedule as the measuring device. He found that those most liked tended to have personality profiles similar to those of the chooser. Two other studies, also comparing subjects on all scales of the Edwards, found similarity in mate-selection (Schellenberg & Bee, 1960) and among pairs who were friends or fiances (Banta & Hetherington, 1963).

Murstein (1961) studied both newlyweds and veteran married couples for complementariness. He also used the Edwards as the measuring device. He found little relationship for needs among newlyweds, but he found complementariness on one need and similarity on four needs for the couples that had been married more than two years. He concluded that successful marriage probably depends on similarity on some needs and complementarity on other needs. Katz, Cohen, and Castiglione (1963) were even more sophisticated. They studied the influence of one mate on the other as a function of complementariness and found that in marriages where the husband was high on need "succorance" and the wives were high on need "nurturance" the wife had a significant influence on judgments. However, they found no relationship between complementarity and marriage satisfaction.

Negative evidence produced by these studies, plus his own intensive review of Winch's research led Roland Tharp (1963) to conclude that the complementary-need hypothesis as Winch had presented it was not tenable. Tharp leveled six main criticisms at Winch's research: (1) the sample—twenty-five undergraduates married less than two years is not a sample that is representative of the population; (2) ratings of the material upon which strength of need was assessed—the raters may have been influenced by their own biases in rating this material; (3) statistics—the various measures that were correlated with each other were not independent; (4) results—the three kinds of measurement that supported the conclusions were highly correlated with each other so they were, in effect, measuring the same thing and did not constitute three kinds of support for the hypothesis, but only one kind of support for it; (5) research philosophy—Tharp felt that with all the data collected and all the correlations computed, the investigator was almost bound to come up with some data supporting his idea; and finally, (6) other research—the studies producing negative evidence were many.

Tharp's review of Winch's theory and research did not exactly promote its popularity. In fact, one reviewer (Barry, 1970) concluded that Tharp had "sharply and decisively" demolished Winch. However, even this conclusion is not final, since there is evidence supporting Winch's hypothesis.

But before turning to that evidence, some characteristics of the research that did not support him should be noted. First, it should be noted that the studies contradicting Winch were based almost entirely on data obtained from the Edwards Personal Preference Schedule. Winch himself raised a question about the validity of the Edwards as a measure of needs. Others (Katzell & Katzell, 1959) have also raised questions about the adequacy of the Edwards as a measuring device, and one study (Fiske, 1966) indicates that a very high proportion of the variance of scores on the Edwards comes from error variance, which would indicate that it is rather inadequate as a measuring device. Many negative studies that have used the same measuring instrument may just indicate that the measuring instrument is flawed, rather than that the hypothesis is flawed. A second aspect of these studies is that they have tended to correlate relationships between the members of couples on all of the scales, rather than just on the scales purporting to measure the needs that Winch hypothesizes as being important to mate-selection. In short, the negative results reported cannot be taken as decisive. And finally, there are the studies reporting positive evidence, to which we shall now turn.

William Schutz (1958) developed a measuring device to measure what he called "Fundamental Interpersonal Relations Orientation." This device contains three scales: a scale measuring "control" or dominance, a scale measuring "inclusion" or the desire to include others and be included in a group, and a scale measuring "affection" or the tendency to express and receive affection from another person. He found that within small groups in the Navy, men tended to choose as friends other men who were opposite to them on the "control" and "affection" measures. These two measures are quite similar to the dominance-submission and nurturance-receptance needs that Winch studied.

In addition to the Schutz study, there are several others which confirm Winch. Hilkevitch (1960), using the Rorschach and other techniques, found that schoolboys tended to choose friends who were complementary on a variety of variables. Kerchoff and Davis (1962) measured the degree to which dating couples move toward making their relationship permanent and found that those dating couples who were complementary to each other on Schutz's scale were the ones who moved toward a more permanent relationship over a seven-month period. Rychlak (1965), using the Edwards Personal Preference Schedule found that similarity was not related to men in a work situation choosing each other as either next-door neighbors or as superiors or subordinates, but that those who were complementary on nurturance and succorance did choose each other as desirable next-door neighbors. Sapolsky (1965) found that, in a hospital, if a psychiatrist and a patient were complementary on Schutz's scale, the patient tended to improve with treatment. Swensen (1967) studied psychotherapists and clients and found that clients tended to improve if they were complementary to their therapist in dominance, and further that in therapy responses, well-known therapists were complementary to their clients on both dominance and interpersonal approach (which is similar to nurturance). Finally, a carefully done study by Bermann and Miller (1967) found that among student nurses, those who formed stable, satisfying roommate pairs were complementary to each other in dominance.

By now the reader may well be confused. Has Winch's hypothesis been confirmed or denied? Or perhaps just revised? Probably the best answer is "yes and no," which isn't very satisfactory. Let's consider some of the issues and see where they lead.

First, needs are not unitary. Winch himself divides needs into those that are overt and those that are covert, suggesting that there may be different needs at different levels of personality. To take the Master-Servant Girl relationship as an example, we would say that the husband has a need to appear to the public (at the overt level) as though he is the lord and master in the family. At the covert level, however, he is dependent and needs a wife who will give him emotional support. Thus he has different needs at different levels. He needs to make one kind of appearance to the world, and probably to himself, but unconsciously he has quite a different need. Winch also points out that needs may be satisfied both within and outside the marriage relationship. A common cultural stereotype is that of the boss who is domineering at the office, but passive and compliant with his wife. If he has a need to be dominant, it is presumably satisfied at the office, and not in his relationship with his wife.

Actually, the satisfaction of needs and the interaction of needs between a married couple may be even more complex. Rosow (1957) suggested four kinds of complementariness that may operate. The first kind of complementariness is that which Winch studied—complementariness within the marriage relationship. A second kind of complementariness is one in which the strengths of one member of the pair may compensate for the weaknesses in the other member. The couple operates something like a modern football team—the large, strong player, who is not too maneuverable, plays in the line, while the lighter and more agile player becomes a flanker back. A third kind of complementariness is one in which the needs of the couple complement each other in their relationships with other people. This might involve child-rearing practices, in which one is the disciplinarian and the other the comforter. Finally, a fourth kind of complementariness, not unlike that already described by Winch, is one in which the mate provides satisfactions that are not obtainable outside the relationship—that is, some needs are satisfied outside the relationship, and those satisfied within the relationship are complementary to those satisfied outside of the relationship.

In Winch's hypothesis there is also a problem of changes in needs over time. The needs that might require satisfaction during courtship and early marriage might no longer require satisfaction later in married life. Husbands and wives in college, or starting out in careers, might well need much nurturance and emotional support from their mates during the period of time when they are not confident of their ability to succeed in studies and a career, but after they have become established in a career and feel confident of their competence, they may no longer need or even desire this kind of relationship. If this change takes place in one member of the pair, it is reasonable to hypothesize that the other member must also change, or difficulty will develop in the relationship. Winch provides an example of apparent change in need, but his theory does not really take this phenomenon into account.

Wright (1965) suggested that complementariness might be more apparent than real. That is, people who have certain kinds of needs may be more attractive to all other people. Thus, those who have these characteristics will be attracted to others who are similar to them, while those who lack these characteristics will be attracted to others who are complementary.

The problem of the relationship between a need and overt behavior must also be considered in reviewing Winch. A need is a readiness to act in a certain way. However, for this behavior to appear, the appropriate circumstance must occur. Also, the expression of this need through overt behavior requires certain other personality characteristics. For example, I have worked in psychotherapy with many people who felt a strong need for emotional support, warmth, and nurturance from others, but they never expressed this need to other people because they were afraid they would be rejected or even ridiculed, so the need was not satisfied. Rosow (1957) suggested that a variable which he termed "self-acceptance" intervenes between the need structure and overt behavior. The self-accepting person who feels a need for nurturance will express this need to other people who are likely to meet the need. The person who is not self-accepting is not likely to express the need through fear of embarrassment and rejection, and may even cover the need with a facade of self-sufficiency. This facade may be so well constructed that it not only misleads others, but fools the person who has constructed it. It is from such successful deceptions that marital problems are born.

Another consideration, which harks back to our discussion of the development of the idea of complementary needs early in the chapter is this: The psychoanalysts who noted that certain kinds of men tended to marry women who met their needs were studying married couples who had serious problems. Couples who seek psychoanalytic help for their troubles are no more representative of the general population of married couples than are married undergraduates at Northwestern University. It is conceivable that some people do marry others who complement their needs and that men and women who are attracted to each other on this basis form one kind of relationship, while other men and women who are attracted to each other because of other factors form a different kind of relationship. That is, some couples are attracted to each other because of complementary needs, but not all couples are attracted on such a basis.

It seems that the best conclusion is that there is something to the complementary-needs hypothesis, but that it is not sufficient as it was presented by Winch. Even such a severe critic of Winch as Tharp conceded that "Winch's work contains the ungerminated seed of the theoretical tree which we hope shall fructify in the next section" (1963, p. 108). Tharp then went on to tout role theory, which we shall discuss in Chapter 12. However, the complementary-needs hypothesis should be conceded a role somewhat larger than that of an ungerminated seed. It has some validity—many studies support that. But perhaps even more important is that the hypothesis has had tremendous heuristic affect upon the study of interpersonal relationships. It has stimulated dozens of studies, and beyond the studies themselves, it has stimulated the theoretical thought of many psychologists and sociologists. The complementary-needs hypothesis has value. Perhaps it is too simple an answer for a complex question.

Interpersonal Relations and the Hierarchy of Needs

No chapter that discusses interpersonal relations as a function of needs should neglect the work and speculation of A. H. Maslow. Maslow differs from Winch in several basic respects, although the two points of view should not necessarily be viewed as contradictory to each other. Rather, it might be useful to view Winch as studying intensively the needs operating at a particular stage of life, that stage in which people first meet and form intimate relationships, while Maslow tries to take a view of needs as they operate over the span of a person's life, with the expressed needs changing as the person and circumstances change.

The Basic Needs

Maslow sees needs as arranged in a *hierarchy*. The needs that are lower in the hierarchy must be satisfied before the individual can move on to the satisfaction of the needs that are higher in the hierarchy. Descriptions of the needs in this hierarchy follow.

1. *Physiological Needs:* These needs "are the most prepotent of all needs" (Maslow, 1970, p. 36). They must be satisfied if the body is to be kept functioning. They include the need for food, water, and air, but may also include such things as the need for rest and sleep, or the need for activity and stimulation. Further, physiological research indicates that these needs can be highly specific. For example, an organism might not be just "hungry," but rather hungry for food that supplies a specific bodily need, such as the need for calcium or for certain vitamins. This need is prepotent—that is, it must be satisfied before other needs are expressed. For example, people who are starving but who are also deprived of safety, love, and esteem, will seek to get something to eat before realizing the existence of any other needs. People dying of starvation or thirst do not worry about whether or not their families love them until they have had something to eat and drink.

2. *The Safety Needs:* If the physiological needs are satisfied, the safety needs emerge. These needs include the need for safety from physical harm or threat of harm, the need for security, the need for freedom from fear, the need for structure and order, and the need for stability. Maslow feels that these needs can best be observed in children. Adults have learned to conceal safety needs, while children express them directly. Infants react immediately with fear to such things as loud noises, flashing lights, or the loss of physical support. Small children cry and express the need for physical reassurance when they are sick. Observations of children indicate that they need a "predictable, lawful, orderly world" if they are to feel safe. Unfairness or inconsistency seem to make children feel anxious and unsafe. Children also seem to react with fear to new, strange, and unmanageable situations. From these observations Maslow (1970, p. 40) concludes that both the child and the adult prefer a "safe, orderly, predictable, lawful, organized world" and need to feel that they have powerful protectors to shield them from harm. Since this need is prepotent, it follows that people who live in unpredictable and threatening environments will be more concerned with safety and security than others living in a safe, stable environment. It seems obvious to say that a person who is being shot at is concerned about not getting hit and is giving little thought to wheth-

er or not he is esteemed by his friends. Maslow's elaboration of the safety needs suggests that people who live in unstable and potentially threatening environments are also more likely to worry about their future than about other less immediate things, such as their professional reputation, except as they affect their safety.

3. *The Belongingness and Love Needs:* When the basic needs for food and drink and safety have been satisfied, the person then hungers for love and affection. People need satisfying relationships with other people. Many clinical studies indicate that children must have satisfying relationships with others, first parents and then peers, if they are to develop normally. Maslow suggests that this need extends beyond the more intimate relationships to include relations with one's own neighbors, with others of one's own kind.

4. *The Esteem Needs:* The esteem needs break down into two kinds of need. The first is the need for self-esteem, the need to have a high and stable evaluation of one's own self. People must have self-respect. Self-respect requires a sense of having competence and of being adequate to handle the problems the world is likely to present. The second kind of esteem need is the need to have esteem and recognition, appreciation, or respect from other people. Obviously, this need must be based on reality. Healthy self-esteem is based on a realistic appraisal of a person's own actual performance which earns respect from others. The person who has self-esteem and the respect of others faces problems with confidence, while the person who lacks esteem tends to be hampered or even crippled by a sense of inferiority and helplessness.

5. *The Need for Self-Actualization:* The need for self-actualization is the need for a person to do what he is uniquely fitted for. "A musician must make music, an artist must paint, a poet must write, if he is to be ultimately at peace with himself" (Maslow, 1970, p. 46). This is a need people have to develop and use the potentialities that they uniquely possess. This need will vary widely from person to person in its expression. In one person it might be expressed by being a mother, in another person by gardening, and in a third person by selling life insurance.

6. *The Desire to Know and to Understand:* This need may be related to, or confused with the lower needs in the hierarchy. For example, to satisfy the physiological needs, it is necessary for people to know how to obtain or produce food, drink, and so on. In order to be secure, people must know how to protect themselves from danger or how to obtain protection from danger. But beyond knowledge and understanding as an instrument through which other needs are satisfied, there is a basic need for knowledge and understanding. People are curious about things that have nothing to do with more food, or more security, or receiving love from other people.

Studies of psychologically healthy people indicate that they are, as a defining characteristic, attracted to the mysterious, to the unknown, to the chaotic, unorganized, and unexplained. This seems to be a per se attractiveness; these areas are in themselves and of their own right interesting. The contrasting reaction to the well known is one of boredom (Maslow, 1970, p. 49).

7. *The Aesthetic Needs:* Maslow is convinced that in some individuals, at least, there is a basic need for beauty. "What," he asks, "does it mean when a man feels a strong conscious impulse to straighten the crookedly hung picture on the wall?" (1970, p. 51). This behavior might be the expression of another need, such as the need for self-actualization, but Maslow asserts that people seem to have a need to improve the appearance of things even when it has nothing to do with other needs. No doubt people of past ages felt a strong need for swords primarily to protect themselves, that is to satisfy their safety need, but the elaborate decoration and ornamentation of those swords had nothing to do with safety.

As Maslow views needs, they have certain characteristics which differ from the needs as described by Murray and adopted by Winch. Murray views needs as being essentially an internal state of the organism. This internal-state approach has certain problems, particularly in research, which we have already discussed. The most obvious problem is that a particular need may exist, but to be exhibited through behavior, a particular situation must exist, and beyond that the personality structure of the person within whom the need exists affects the way in which this need is expressed. Maslow recognizes this problem and feels that the best way to study the process of human motivation is through studying goals rather than drives, since drives fluctuate. However, Maslow sees basic needs as being in some sense constitutional or hereditary. Perhaps a correct comparison between Murray and Maslow would be that both recognize needs as being essentially internal, but Maslow places more stress on the goals through which people strive to satisfy needs. Of course, as Winch applied Murray's theory to mate-selection, the mate was the "goal" of the person whose needs that mate could satisfy.

Characteristics of Needs

Basic needs have certain characteristics. One of these characteristics is that needs are a part of a person who functions as a whole. A person does not really "have a hunger need," but rather he is hungry, and if he is hungry enough this need governs his whole outlook on life. People function as a whole, and the need operating within them functions as a whole.

Another characteristic of needs is expressed by Maslow (1970, p. 60) in his "Grumble Theory." This theory holds that the satisfaction of a need leads to only temporary satisfaction, which is shortly followed by a new, higher level, discontent. The alternative to this discontent would be boredom and aimlessness. People generally do not stay bored for long. They look for something new to turn their attention to. In this context, it is interesting to reflect upon the wide variety of games people have devised to play. Obviously these games serve no instrumental function. No one (aside from a professional, which most people aren't) satisfies needs for food, esteem, or love by playing football or chess or bridge; yet most people devote some time during their lives to these pursuits, and some people devote great amounts of time to them. Obviously they must be satisfying some basic human need or needs. Belongingness, self-actualization, and knowledge would seem to be the most likely candidates.

Needs arrange themselves in a hierarchy, which we have described, with the basic and most powerful needs coming first in the hierarchy. This hierarchy, in itself, suggests another characteristic of needs. That is, the lower needs which come first in the hierarchy are stronger than the needs which come later in the hierarchy. The needs for air and water and safety are stronger, more specific, and more urgent than the needs for self-actualization or knowledge. However, for most people in a reasonably stable and modern society, the basic needs are regularly and habitually satisfied, so that they have little effect on the behavior of most people. College students do not typically go to college so they will have something to eat. They go to college to learn more about the world in which they live, to learn to become psychologists because they like to work with people, to learn mathematics because mathematical formulas and relationships have fascinated them since they were children, and so on. In short, they typically go to college to satisfy the needs for self-actualization, knowledge, or beauty. (Of course, we are excepting those rare few who go to college because they can't think of any other way to spend the years between eighteen and twenty-two.) What Maslow is asserting is that most of the decisions made by people are in terms of needs different from the physiological or safety needs. These needs must be met—people living in urban areas do shop for groceries and lock their doors at night—but for most people, the physiological and safety needs are so habitually met that they have a minor effect on people's significant behavior.

This leads us to another characteristic of needs, which is that needs that are habitually met tend to be undervalued. That which we are used to having we take for granted. "Food is," as the hippies say, but to the Amazonian Indian or the ghetto child, food often "isn't." Therefore, teenagers of the American upper middle-class take food for granted and undervalue it. However, a need that is not met is overvalued. The same American teenager who takes food for granted lusts mightily after an electric guitar or a ten-speed bike.

Needs and Interpersonal Relationships

Implicit in the whole concept of a needs hierarchy is the idea that the way one person relates to another will be a function of the needs of the people who are interacting. A person who is starving will relate to another in terms of whether or not that other person can provide something to eat. In fact, if a person is really starving he may even relate to the other person as something to eat. Cannibalism is not unknown among humans. Such a relationship, interpersonally speaking, is not likely to be very happy or long-lasting, however intimate it may become. If we take one step up the needs hierarchy to the safety needs, we would expect a person who feels insecure and threatened to relate to another person primarily in terms of whether or not that other person is a threat or might provide protection.

If the way people relate to others is a function of the unsatisfied needs of the people involved, it then follows that the nature of their relationship will change as their lower, more basic needs are satisfied and as the higher needs emerge. Thus between any two people the relationship will change over a period of time. This fact can most easily be observed in the relationship between parents and children. Young children are quite dependent on their parents and cling to them for sustenance, protection, and love. Adolescents however, who are beginning to develop their own unique talents, try to avoid too close an embrace from their parents, whom they feel might hamper their own unique development. At one stage in life people cling, but at a later stage they withdraw.

This same idea can be generalized to relationships between adults. A husband who arrives home at night tired and hungry is apt to view his wife primarily in terms of the demands she spares him and the food she puts on the table. He is not likely to appreciate the redecorating she has done in the living room or to be very receptive to her declarations of undying devotion. Later in the evening he will probably be in a different mood. The same sequence holds for the wife. She may feel assured of her husband's love, but if his demands interfere with or prevent her from developing her own talents—fulfilling her need for self-actualization—she will feel unhappy with her husband, even though he has many good characteristics.

This brings us to a consideration of the two needs that perhaps most directly affect interpersonal relationships, the need for love and the need for self-actualization. Maslow (1962) divides motivation into two kinds, "D," or *deficiency-motivation*, and "B," or *being-motivation*. When a person behaves because of deficiency-motivation, the behavior is aimed toward making up for the deficiency; but when a person is moved by being-motivation, the behavior flows out of the person as an expression of the person. In applying this concept to interpersonal relationships, Maslow writes that "the deficit-motivated man is far more dependent upon other people than is the man who is predominantly growth-motivated" (1962, p. 33). People's dependency colors their relationships with the other people. They see the other person, in part at least, in terms of the unmet needs which the other person can fulfill. For the person who is being-motivated, however, the other person "is loved because he is love-worthy rather than because he gives out love" (1962, p. 34). The love for the other flows out of a perception of the other person as an "end-in-himself" rather than out of any need that is fulfilled by the other.

If we view Winch's work in this light, those mates who select each other do so out of a deficiency-motivation rather than a being-motivation. They meet each others needs, and these needs are a deficiency that seeks elimination through fulfillment in a relationship with another person. If, however, partners that are first attracted to each other through satisfying mutual needs have those needs satisfied, what then? Maslow's approach to needs would suggest that new needs would emerge which would take center stage in their lives, and necessarily the nature of the relationship between the two would change. But change to what?

The next need in Maslow's hierarchy is self-actualization. The hierarchy suggests that the partners in a relationship would then be concerned with self-actualization. However, Maslow deals with self-actualization as a continuum along which people can be rated. Some people are more self-actualized and some less self-actualized, and there are certain characteristics shared by the more self-actualized people.

Maslow (1970) studied self-actualized people in order to determine their characteristics. He chose the people to be studied on the basis of absence of any neurotic or psychotic symptoms and the presence of "the full use and exploitation of talents, capacities, potentialities, etc. . . . [since] such people seem to be fulfilling themselves and to be doing the best that they are capable of doing . . ." (Maslow, 1970, p. 150). This criterion also implied "gratification, past or present, of the basic needs for safety, belongingness, love, respect, and self-respect, and of the cognitive needs for knowledge and for understanding . . ." (Maslow, 1970, p. 150). Maslow studied these subjects in "the clinical style" and with this process teased out characteristics they had in common, thus sharpening his definition of the concept. Then he chose and studied new groups of subjects to confirm his initial observations. The people he studied included friends and acquaintances, and public and historical figures. Most of the subjects were studied indirectly, through observation and the reports of others (such as biographies and so on) rather than directly, because Maslow found that the subjects tended not to be cooperative when approached directly. Of course some of the figures could not be studied directly, except through personal writings such as autobiographies, since they were dead when the study was conducted. The well-known people he studied included Abraham Lincoln, Thomas Jefferson, Albert Einstein, Eleanor Roosevelt, Jane Addams, William James, and Albert Schweitzer. Of course, many of the people he studied were not famous.

The following are the characteristics Maslow (1970, Ch. 11) found shared by most of his self-actualized people:

1. They are more accurate in their perception of reality and are more comfortable in their relations with reality than the average person. Their predictions of the future from whatever facts are at hand are, more often than not, correct.

2. They are accepting of themselves, of other people, and of nature. This does not mean that they necessarily approve of everything they themselves or other people do or that they like all of the characteristics of themselves or others; rather, they don't fret about these things, but accept themselves, others, and nature for what they are.

3. They are spontaneous, simple, and natural in expressing themselves. This does not mean that they are necessarily unconventional. In fact, most of them are conventional, but they can easily cast this conventionality aside.

4. Their attention is centered on problems outside of themselves. They customarily feel that they have some mission to perform in life and expend much of their attention and energy on it.

5. They are detached and have a greater liking for solitude and privacy than the average person. They find it easy to be aloof and reserved, and also calm and serene.

6. They are autonomous, self-contained, independent of their culture and environment, and stable in the face of frustration. While deficiency-motivated people may *need* other people, the self-actualized may at times actually be hampered by other people.

7. They are able to appreciate the basic experiences of life over and over again with a repeated freshness. They gain the same thrill repeatedly from the simple pleasures of life.

8. It is fairly common for them to have mystical experiences, or what Maslow terms "peak experiences."

9. They have a deep feeling ("Gemeinschaftsgefühl") of identification, sympathy, and affection for other human beings in spite of the occasional disgust or irritation they may feel for the stupidities of the human race.

10. Their interpersonal relationships are deeper and more profound than those of the average person. They are capable of more fu-

sion with other people. They tend to have relatively few people with whom they have close ties, but those ties are deeper. Their circle of friends tends to be rather small. The others they have close relationships with also tend to be self-actualizing people. They tend to attract some admirers or followers, but these admirers are apt to demand more than the self-actualizer is willing to give. They can break off relationships with others if the other behaves in a way to merit disfellowship. When they do break off with another person, it is either deserved by the other person or for the other person's own good. Their hostility to another person is in reaction to something that other person has done.

11. They are democratic in the sense that they can associate on terms of equality with people from all stations in life.

12. They discriminate between right and wrong and have exact moral standards. However, their notions of right and wrong may not necessarily be the conventional ones. Maslow (1970, p. 169) refers to David Levy as saying that "a few centuries ago these would all have been described as men who walk in the path of God or as godly men." In addition to a distinction between right and wrong, these people seem to make a clear distinction between means and ends. Though they aim toward ends, they also seem to enjoy the means.

13. They have a philosophical, unhostile sense of humor.

14. They have a creativeness that is akin to the creativeness of unspoiled children.

15. They resist enculturation and maintain a certain detachment from the culture within which they live. They generally are conventional in such everyday things as dress, food, and manners, but they have an ability to stand off from the culture as though they did not quite belong to it.

16. They may have some imperfections, such as an ability to be ruthless and absent-minded when preoccupied. They may have a callous disregard for the opinions of others, and they may sometimes make mistakes out of misguided kindness.

This rather lengthy description of the self-actualized person is actually a lead-in to a more extended discussion of the ways in which these people relate to others. Item 10 listed above mentions some characteristics of the ways in which self-actualized people relate to others, but there are more characteristics to consider in their love relationships.

First, their love is "B-love," or being-love, rather than "D-love," or deficiency-love. That is, they do not love people because they have a need for the companionship, approval, or support of another person. This means that, theoretically at least, their marriages should not fit into one of the four patterns described by Winch. It should be added that in searching for self-actualized people Maslow was unable to find any among the many college students he studied. And Winch's subjects were all college students, of course. Self-actualization is a level of development or maturity that is achieved only after having lived and grown as a person for a longer time than has been available to most college students. Therefore, the self-actualized person should, if Maslow's contention has some validity, be expected to relate intimately to other people on a basis that is different from those described by Winch. And the nature of their relationships with others should also differ from those described by Winch.

Maslow found that self-actualized people have less tendency than the average person to put their best foot forward in their relationships. There was much less maintenance of distance or concealment in their relationships with others. They are open about themselves rather than secretive. Their relationships improve over time. Self-actualizing people find that their love satisfaction and their sexual satisfaction improve with time in a relationship. Maslow likens this to the finding that good paintings become preferred with increased familiarity and bad paintings become less liked with increased familiarity. He writes that "the better people are, the *more* they will be loved with greater familiarity; the worse people are the *less* they will be liked as familiarity increases" (Maslow, 1970, p. 185).

The self-actualized are described as more loving and more loveable. That is, they know how to express love to others and they know how to receive it from others. However, these subjects use the word "love" rather sparingly in describing their relationships to others. But at any given time they are actively involved in a love relationship with another or others.

Sex and love are fused among the self-actualized. They are not interested in sex for the sake of sex. Their sexual relationships improve with the length of their relationship to the other person, and their enjoyment of sex seems to be deeper and more intense than that of the average person. Although their experience of orgasm may at times be so intense as to be an almost mystical experience, they seem to be more able to tolerate the absence of sex than most people. They seem to have easy, casual relationships with the opposite sex and are attracted to and attractive to the opposite sex, even though they seem to do less about it than the average person. They accept sex, but do not find it necessary. Their easier acceptance of sexuality seems to make it easier for them to be monogamous.

The kinds of people they are attracted to and most likely to form intimate relationships with are others who are also relatively self-actualized. With respect to the personality variable of self-actualization, like appears to attract like, rather than opposites attracting.

In their intimate relationships they seem to pool their needs with the other person, so that the other's needs become their own and are felt as their own. Thus they feel a responsibility and care for the other, and if the other's immediate needs come higher in the pooled hierarchy, then the other's needs are satisfied first.

Their love relationships are characterized by "fun, merriment, elation, feeling of well-being, gaiety" (Maslow, 1970, p. 194). Their relationships are cheerful and full of play. They enjoy themselves. Maslow compares these relationships to the play of small children and puppies. In this ideal kind of love relationship, each affirms the other's individuality. This kind of love acknowledges the other person as independent and autonomous, and entitled to respect and dignity. This holds not only for their relationships to adults, but also for their relationships with children. Even though a child may be dependent on them, self-actualized parents (also nonparents) nonetheless recognize and respect the individuality of the child.

In relationships between the sexes, the self-actualized recognize the equality of all people, men and women, and this sometimes finds itself being expressed in a failure to perform the acknowledged rituals of society, such as opening doors for a woman or arising when greeting a woman.

Before the experience of love, self-actualized people feel awe and see the relationship and its attendant feelings as an end in itself, serving no instrumental purpose. Love, for them, is essentially an expression of the kind of people they are.

An apparent paradox in this kind of relationship is that although the relationship between self-actualizing people is deep and profoundly satisfying, the two do not *need* each other. They are capable of functioning perfectly well when separated and philosophically accept long separation or death. It appears that although theirs is a merging of two personalities into one, in the process the individuality of each is strengthened, so that in the relationship each becomes more sharply and strongly his or her own unique self.

Discussion

This chapter has presented two theories of needs as they relate to interpersonal relationships. One theory, that of Winch, holds that two people are attracted to each other and form an intimate interpersonal relationship because their needs complement each other. Each person provides what the other needs in the interpersonal relationship. The other theory, that of Maslow, holds that needs are arranged in a hierarchy: At the lower end of the hierarchy, the deficit end, people are attracted to each other because they meet each other's needs, while at the higher, or healthy and mature, end of the hierarchy, people are attracted to and love others because they are loving people. These people are self-actualized, and the people they are attracted to are like themselves in emotional health and maturity. Both Winch and Maslow provide some empirical evidence to support their points of view.

Though it might seem that only one of the two views can be correct, there is not necessarily any contradiction between the two views. Winch has taken, so to speak, a cross-sectional view. He has studied the attraction between a man and a woman at the time they are courting and marrying, and also at the time when they are college students. That is, he has studied love relationships at a particular stage of life. Maslow, on the other hand, might be viewed as taking a longitudinal view, looking at various needs as they express themselves in sequence, a process that lasts for a lifetime. The kind of love Maslow describes is that which is *not* likely to be found in youths, but rather is achieved after people have grown as individuals through a fairly large part of their lifetime.

What is most clearly suggested by these two theoretical and research efforts is the need for a thorough study of the development and expression of needs through the course of the normal person's lifetime, and of the ways in which these various strengths of various needs effect and are expressed in the person's intimate relationships with other people. Certainly individuals vary along all of these dimensions at all stages of life. Winch describes the life histories of some of his subjects and relates these to the ways they relate to their spouses in marriage. It seems highly probable that some kinds of childhood and adolescent experiences are more likely to satisfy basic needs and promote or hinder the development of self-actualization and thus profoundly affect the ways a person interacts intimately with others. Clinical experience supports this notion. The woman whose father deserted her mother when she was a child and who was herself jilted by a boyfriend when she was in high school is almost certainly going to have doubts about her lovability, and is therefore likely to have a very strong and unsatisfied deficiency need for love. Any man that she marries will have to devote a fair amount of energy and attention during the early years of marriage to reassure her that she is loved. And her demand for this reassurance is likely to be rather desperate at the times when she feels unsure of herself. However, what happens to her after five or ten years of constant reassurance? If this deficiency need for love is satisfied, she changes, her needs that are seeking satisfaction change, and therefore her relationship with her husband should also change. It seems reasonable to assume, until evidence to the contrary is produced, that if her husband is also "growing," their relationship should change in the general direction of the more healthy kind of love relationship Maslow describes as existing among the self-actualized.

Out of curiosity about the kind of love relationships maintained by people at different levels of self-actualization, I did a small study in 1968. I gave a large sample of students a test to measure levels of self-actualization[4] and then picked out ten subjects at each of three levels of self-actualization. One group was high, one group average, and one group low. I then interviewed these people, asking them to describe their relationships to their closest friend of the same sex and to their closest friend of the opposite sex, or their spouse if they were married. I found that those who had scored highest on the self-actualization test described their relationships rather realistically. They could tell the good things in the relationship, but they could also discuss the conflicts and problems in their relationships. The average self-actualizers glorified and romanticized their relationships. They could describe all sorts of beautiful things about the relationship, but could think of no problems, conflicts, or difficulties. The people who scored low on self-actualization either had had no intimate relationships or else described conflict or broken relationships. This small study, which was only suggestive at best, does seem to indicate that the self-actualizing need dimension is one that is related to interpersonal relationships in an important way. Perhaps additional investigation would have revealed that those in the "average" self-actualization group were originally attracted to each other because of complimentary needs.

In any case, there does not seem to be necessarily any contradiction between the concept of attraction as a function of complementary needs and attraction as a function of similarity, whether it be on the basis of attitudes as Byrne has demonstrated (see Chapter 9), or on the basis of similar levels of self-actualization. Rather, it seems probable that the different types of attraction each play some part in a relationship, but that this part depends on the stage of the relationship and the levels of development, maturity, or need satisfaction of the people involved.

The data base on which the needs view of interpersonal relations depends is essentially clinical, although few of the subjects studied were people with emotional problems. The original observations of Kubie and Mittelmann were made on people who had marriage problems, but the twenty-five students studied by Winch were all normal, and the self-actualized described by Maslow might be considered "supernormal." Thus, the *kinds* of people studied by the needs theorists are more diverse than the *kinds* of people studied by any other theorists. Needs theory is based on patients, normals, and supernormals. However, the *number* of people studied is quite small. Rather than obtaining partial data from a large number of people, Winch and Maslow obtained extensive data from a relatively small number of people. As a consequence, needs theory appears to have a "depth" and complexity

[4]Actually, I used two tests, choosing people at three levels of self-actualization and self-acceptance. The tests were: (1) Shostrom, E. L. *Personal Orientation Inventory.* San Diego: Educational and Industrial Testing Service, 1963; and (2) Fitts, W. H. *Tennessee Self-Concept Scale.* Nashville: Counselor Recordings and Tests, 1964.

that is lacking in some of the other theories discussed. Because the information has been obtained from the people themselves, or from other people with whom they had interacted, needs theory tends to be discussed in terms that are similar to the terms used in the existential approach (see Chapter 6), that is, the terms of life as people experience it.

The situation within which Winch and Maslow obtained data is essentially the clinical situation. That is, the information was obtained from people discussing their relationships with other people. The actual behavior and feelings discussed in these interviews were feelings and behavior that occured in real life. The level studied is both the level of the person and the level of the dyad. The study of needs, themselves, is at the level of the person, while the patterns of marriage interactions are at the level of the dyad. These theories are really theories that relate characteristics of the individual person to the patterns of relationships these people tend to create.

The kinds of data obtained by Winch and Maslow are self-report data, behavior observation data, and psychological test data, including both self-report and apperceptive tests. Thus the data base of these theories tends to be rather broad in the kinds of data used and the kinds of different subjects studied, although it is based on a rather small number of subjects. There is also some experimental research data supporting these theories. However, the experimental research has not contributed so much to the creation of these theories as to the assessment of their validity.

The theories of Winch and Maslow are both broad and narrow. They are broad in the sense that they include two levels, both the personal and the dyadic level, but they are narrow because they are primarily concerned with one aspect of the interpersonal relationship — the relationship as it is affected by the needs of the individuals participating in the relationship.

Summary

In this chapter two approaches to interpersonal relationships as a function of needs have been described. One, that of Winch, attributes interpersonal attraction to *complementary needs* between the pair that is attracted to each other. The second, that of Maslow, describes relationships that differ depending on the *level of need satisfaction* of the people involved.

Winch asserts that two main needs, *nurturance-succorance* and *dominance-submission* operate in the attraction of people to each other. Assertive people tend to be attracted to passive people and vice versa. That is, those who are dominant form intimate relationships with those who are submissive, and those who have a need to nurture others form intimate relationships with others who need succorance. These two dimensions combine to create four different kinds of marriage: Ibsenian, Master-Servant Girl, Thurberian, and Mother-Son. In the Ibsenian marriage the husband is both dominant and nurturant; in the Master-Servant Girl marriage the husband is dominant and the wife is nurturant; in the Thurberian marriage the wife is dominant and the husband succorant; and in the Mother-Son marriage the wife is both dominant and nurturant. The needs may be either *overt* or *covert,* so that the needs that appear to be met overtly may be different from those needs satisfied covertly within the marriage. The subjects studied by Winch were all college students who had been married less than two years, so it may be that the needs expression he found in the dynamics of the intimate interpersonal relationship changes as the relationship progresses through time, or changes because of a change of circumstances for the couple.

Maslow describes a hierarchy of seven needs: *physiological, safety, love, esteem, self-actualization, knowledge,* and *aesthetic.* The basic motivations may be *deficiency-motivations,* which impel a person to seek satisfaction for unmet needs, or *being motivations,* in which a person's behavior is an outward expression of the kind of person he is. People who need love will seek satisfaction from other people because of their unmet needs for companionship, approval, support, and so on. However, the more healthy, more mature, *self-actualized people* relate intimately to others because they are loving people, rather than people trying to satisfy unmet needs. In a relationship the self-actualized person merges his own need hierarchy with that of the other so that the other's needs become his own. In the relationship the other is accepted and respected as a unique, independent individual in his own right, and the relationship is sought and maintained for its own sake rather than for the satisfaction of any particular need. In this kind of relationship, the relationship becomes more satisfying and deeper with the passage of time. Self-actualized people seem to seek intimate relationships with others who are similar to themselves, that is, who are also self-actualized.

References

Banta, T. J., & Hetherington, M. Relations between needs of friends and fiances. *Journal of Abnormal and Social Psychology,* 1963, 66, 401–404.

Barry, W. A. Marriage research and conflict: An integrative review. *Psychological Bulletin,* 1970, 73, 41–54.

Bermann, E., & Miller, D. R. The matching of mates. In R. Jessor & S. Feshbach (Eds.), *Cognition, personality and clinical psychology.* San Francisco: Josey-Bass, 1967.

Bowerman, C. E., & Day, B. A test of the theory of complementary needs as applied to couples during courtship. *American Sociological Review*, 1956, 21, 602–605.

Cattell, R. B. *Factor Analysis*. New York: Harper & Row, 1952.

Fiske, D. W. Some hypotheses concerning test adequacy. *Educational and Psychological Measurement*, 1966, 26, 69–88.

Hilkevitch, R. R. Social interactional processes: a quantitative study. *Psychological Reports*, 1960, 7, 195–201.

Izard, C. Personality similarity and friendship. *Journal of Abnormal and Social Psychology*, 1960, 61, 47–51.

Katz, I., Cohen, M., & Castiglione, L. Effect of one type of need complementarity on marriage partners' conformity to one another's language. *Journal of Abnormal and Social Psychology*, 1963, 67, 8–14.

Katz, I., Glucksberg, S., & Krauss, R. Need satisfaction and Edwards Personal Preference Scale scores in married couples. *Journal of Consulting Psychology*, 1960, 24, 205–208.

Katzell, R. A., & Katzell, M. Development and application of structured tests of personality. *Review of Educational Research*, 1962, 32, 51–63.

Kerchoff, A. C., & Davis, K. I. Value consensus and need complementarity in mate selection. *American Sociological Review*, 1962, 27, 295–303.

Kubie, L. S. Psychoanalysis and marriage; practical and theoretical issues. In V. W. Eisenstein (Ed.), *Neurotic interaction in marriage*. New York: Basic Books, 1956.

Levonian, S. A statistical evaluation of Edwards Personal Preference Schedule. *Journal of Applied Psychology*, 1959, 43, 355–59.

Maslow, A. H. *Toward a psychology of being*. New York: Van Nostrand, 1962.

Maslow, A. H. *Motivation and personality*. (2nd ed.) New York: Harper & Row, 1970.

Mittelmann, B. Analysis of reciprocal neurotic patterns in family relationships. In V. W. Eisenstein (Ed.), *Neurotic interaction in marriage*. New York: Basic Books, 1956.

Murray, H. A. *Explorations in personality*. New York: Oxford University Press, 1938.

Murstein, B. I. The complementary need hypothesis in newlyweds and middle-aged married couples. *Journal of Abnormal and Social Psychology*, 1961, 63, 194–97.

Reilly, M., Commins, W. D., & Stefic, E. C. The complementarity of personality needs in friendship choice. *Journal of Abnormal and Social Psychology*, 1960, 61, 292–94.

Rosow, I. Issues in the concept of need complementarity. *Sociometry*, 1957, 20, 216–33.

Rychlak, J. F. The similarity, compatibility, or incompatibility of needs in interpersonal selection. *Journal of Personality and Social Psychology,* 1965, 2, 334–40.

Sapolsky, A. Relationship between patient-doctor compatibility, mutual perception, and outcome of treatment. *Journal of Abnormal Psychology,* 1965, 1, 70–76.

Schellenberg, J. A., & Bee, L. S. A re-examination of the theory of complementary needs in mate selection. *Marriage and Family,* 1960, 22, 227–32.

Schutz, W. *FIRO: Fundamental interpersonal relations orientation.* New York: Holt, Rinehart, & Winston, 1958.

Swensen, C. H. Psychotherapy as a special case of dyadic interaction: Some suggestions for theory and research. *Psychotherapy: Theory, Research and Practice,* 1967, 4, 7–13.

Tharp, R. G. Psychological patterning in marriage. *Psychological Bulletin,* 1963, 60, 97–117.

Winch, R. F. *Mate-selection: a study of complementary needs.* New York: Harper & Row, 1958.

Wright, P. H. Personality and interpersonal attraction: basic assumptions. *Journal of Individual Psychology,* 1965, 21, 127–36.

Conflict
and
Game Theory

The principal advantage of the game method in psychological research lies in the circumstance that, while the thought processes so tapped are quite rich in psychological content . . . the experimental tool itself is an extremely simple one. . . . Observed regularities can be described in an organized fashion by mathematical models. The parameters of these models can serve as a link between formal rigorous theory . . . and significant psychological content, since these parameters can often be quite naturally interpreted in terms of rich psychological concepts: trust and suspicion, responsiveness and vengefulness, caution and daring, dominance and submission, adherence to principle and opportunism (1961, p. 139).

—A. Rapoport

At first glance a chapter on game theory might seem to be out of place in a book dealing with the interpersonal relationship. Those working with game theory have concerned themselves primarily with such matters as decision making and conflict situations, particularly in the context of business or international relations. It might be fairly said that game theory did not originate in an interest in conflict between persons or parties so much as in a desire to apply mathematics to problems in behavioral science. John Neumann and Oskar Morgenstern, who originated game theory, stated that their "major interest is, of course, in the economic and sociological direction" (1947, p. v). That is, they wanted to apply mathematical methods to the social sciences. In recent years the game approach has been applied to such diverse topics as disarmament, fishing strategy, formation of political coalitions, "bride-price" in an African tribe, and the analysis of ethical systems (Buchler & Nutini, 1969).

However, our more immediate concern is the relationship between individuals, and it is in the application to the interaction between individuals that most game research has been conducted. Specifically, game research has focused on factors relating to cooperation and competition between individuals. But the long-range importance of game theory to the study of the interpersonal relationship is perhaps not so much in the empirical studies it generates as it is in the mathematical methods it provides for research. However primitive these methods may be at the present time and however far removed their basic assumptions may be from the ways people typically behave, they foreshadow the development of a powerful tool for studying what goes on between people.

In addition to the methodological contribution, game theory provides an approach to studying the interpersonal relationship that may be conducted in the laboratory and thus subjected to the controls that are absent in real life. As Rapoport points out, a game may be set up as a model of a situation "abstracted from life" (1969, p. 129).

Thus game theory provides the first steps toward a mathematical analysis of the interpersonal relationship and supplies a paradigm for the laboratory study of interpersonal relationships. The author of the first popular volume on game theory, J. D. Williams, wrote that "it is provocative to speculate on whether game theory will develop a new mathematical discipline destined for a comparable role in analyzing the interactions of men" (1954, p. 7).

Characteristics of Games

Game theory is primarily concerned with the decisions that people make in conflict situations. Obviously games are, by their very nature, situations of conflict contrived by people for their amusement. Most common games, such as checkers or baseball or bridge, are "zero-sum" games. That is, they are games in which one person or one team wins and another person or team loses. The algebraic sum of wins and losses is zero. The game itself is a conflict situation, since if one person wins, his win must necessarily be at the expense of his opponent's loss. The game is a conflict in which one person tries to defeat another.

In a game, the first concern is *strategy*, or how to win and defeat the other fellow. In some games the strategy is quite simple. In tick-tacktoe the objective is simply to get three of your signs, either X or O, in a line and to prevent the opponent from accomplishing this. In more complex games such as chess, the strategy is considerably more compli-cated. In either case the objective is to gain the maximum *payoff*, which is to win.

Games have two basic characteristics:

1. The outcomes of the game are well specified and the players have preferences among the outcomes.
2. The variables that control the possible outcomes are well speci-fied.

In a simple game such as checkers, this means that the players know the outcomes. That is, they know that they will either win or lose and that the loser will be the player who loses all of his checkers first; and the players each know which outcome they prefer. Presumably they each prefer to win, although this might not necessarily be so. (A girl on her first date with a boy she likes might prefer to lose.) Implicit in these assumptions is the understanding that each player knows how to play the game.

There are certain other characteristics of games (Rapoport, 1966):

1. A game must have at least two players.
2. A game begins with one player making a choice among a group of alternatives, this choice being known in some games as a "move."
3. After the first move, a certain situation occurs which determines who moves next and what alternatives are open to him.
4. The moves the players make may or may not be known to the other player.
5. The play of the game ends when a certain termination point is reached.

In a game such as checkers, there are two players. The first player to move has four pieces he can move, with a possible choice of seven moves (see Figure 1). After the first player has made his move, the sec-ond player has seven possible moves, but the consequences of these moves are not the same as they were for the first player since the situa-tion changed when the first player made his move. In checkers, each move is immediately obvious to the other player. (In many card games, such as bridge, the move may be concealed.) The checker players lose pieces when they are jumped, and the game proceeds until one player has lost all his pieces, at which point the game is considered to be at the termination point.

FIGURE 1.   **DIAGRAM OF BEGINNING MOVES IN CHECKERS**

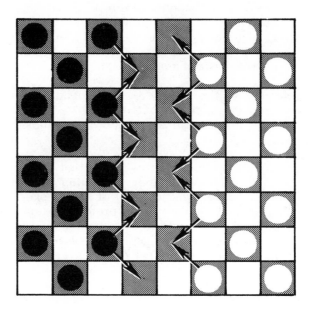

Games and Utility

All games have payoffs, which in game theory are called *utilities.*
The payoff is what you get for playing the game. In simple parlor games
like checkers, the payoff may be nothing more than winning or losing.
Payoff can always be reduced to numbers, the numbers representing
some point on some kind of scale. In the case of checkers, winning
could be represented by +1, losing by −1, and a stalemate by 0. In
sports, the immediate payoff is usually represented by the number of
games listed in the won-and-lost columns. If, for example, a major
league baseball team wins a game, "1" is added to the games-won column of its baseball standing; if a game is lost, "1" is added to the
games-lost column. The standings in the baseball league are based on
the percentage of games won, with the team winning the highest percentage in first place, the team winning the lowest percentage in last
place, and the other teams ranked between them, according to percent-
ages. Of course, for a professional baseball team there are other payoffs
in addition to the number of games listed in the won-and-lost columns.
If the team ends the season in first place, it wins the league pennant,
plays in the World Series, and gets a share of the money paid by customers to see the World Series games.

This last point illustrates some of the difficulties with the concept of payoff, or utility. It is easy enough to see that the player who wins a game may get +1 and the player who loses, −1. The problem arises when we consider the fact that winning or losing a game may well mean many things other than a number added to a won column or a lost column. A man and his son playing checkers in the evening after supper are presumably playing for the fun of the game. Winning or losing isn't even entered in the "standings." However, winning might be very important to the son, since he rarely manages to defeat his father, while winning is probably not nearly so important to the father, who usually wins anyway; winning has more utility to the son than it does to the father. In this case it might be closer to reality to give the son +2 for winning and −2 for losing and to give the father +½ for winning and −½ for losing. As can be seen from this example, there is a subjective element in utility, so that in game theory "it is assumed that magnitudes assigned to the payoffs denote the worth of the payoffs to the respective players" (Rapoport, 1969, p. 28). This subjective difference in the evaluation of payoffs is perhaps best illustrated in sport, particularly college football. If one team is heavily favored over another team, then a tie between the two teams is not equally valuable. In such a situation, the underdog would be jubilant over the tie, and sports fans would say that the underdog had won a "moral victory," which in the terminology of sports means that they didn't win, but they performed much better than expected.

Measuring Scales. We will return to a consideration of utility later and describe methods of determining the value of a payoff for a player. But first we should consider other aspects of utility. We have already said that all games have payoffs and that these payoffs can be reduced to numbers. Numbers generally refer to a quantity of something. That is, in ranking baseball teams, "60" in the won column of the baseball standing means that the team has won sixty games. If two people engaged in a pushup contest and one of them got a "32," it would mean that one of the contestants had done thirty-two pushups. These numbers bring up the problem of scales.

Generally speaking there are four kinds of scales: nominal, ordinal, interval, and ratio. A *nominal scale*, strictly speaking, is not a scale at all, since no quantity is referred to. It is just a list of categories into which things can be sorted. For example, people can be categorized into "male" and "female." There is no quantity underlying that scale, except that presumably those who are classified as "male" are more male than the people classified as "female," and vice versa. Another example would be "married" and "single." Again, no particular quantity is implied, although most people classified as "married" would probably be considered more married than those classified as "single."

Again, there is no quantity which one group possesses more than the other group. A nominal scale, then, is merely a series of categories into which people can be sorted.

An *ordinal scale* is one which orders people or things into some sort of continuum. In the army it is customary for men to line up according to height. The tallest man is at one end of the line, the shortest man is at the opposite end, and all the others are in between according to height. Here the underlying quantity is height, but the men are arranged in order of height, with no reference to the differences in their heights. If the tallest man is six feet four inches, the next tallest six feet, and the third tallest five feet eleven inches, the number two man stands exactly in the middle between the tallest man and the third tallest man, regardless of the fact that the difference in height between the second man and the first man is four inches, while the difference between the second man and the third man is only one inch. The order on height is the important thing, and the actual magnitude of the differences is ignored.

In an *interval scale*, the magnitude of the difference is important. If we order the three men described above according to height by an interval scale, the distance between them would be a function of the difference in their height. The second man, who is six feet tall, would stand closer to the number three man, who is one inch shorter, than to the number one man, who is four inches taller. In an interval scale the intervals are equal. A good example of an interval scale is the Intelligence Quotient (IQ). A person who receives an IQ score of 120 is ten IQ points smarter than a person who receives an IQ score of 110, and a person who receives an IQ score of 110 is ten points smarter than a person who receives an IQ score of 100. The interval from 120 to 110 is equal to the interval from 110 to 100. Though IQ scores differ in measurable intervals, there is no "0" IQ, or in other words, the IQ scale has no true zero point. This is true of all interval scales. If there is a zero point, it is not a "true" zero. Most temperature scales are examples of interval scales with no true zero. Zero degrees Fahrenheit is not a state of "no" heat—it can get much colder than zero.

A *ratio scale* has a "true" zero, which means that equivalent ratios can be constructed from points on the scale. Distance is an example of a ratio scale. There is "zero" distance: Two objects touching each other have no distance between them. And the ratio of two miles to one mile (2:1, or 2/1) is equal to the ratio of ten miles to five miles (10:5, or 10/5). That is, two miles is twice as far as one mile, and ten miles is twice as far as five miles.

Quantification of Utility. The utilities in games—that is, the numbers that the payoffs are reduced to—should be stated in terms of an interval scale, and it is better yet if they can be in terms of a ratio scale. This is so the numbers may be linearly transformed for easier computation. Suppose we return to our checker game between the father and son. We said that a win was worth +1 and a loss −1. But suppose we want to eliminate negative numbers to make our calculations easier. We can do this very simply by adding the same quantity (1) to each payoff, thus maintaining the same interval (2) that existed between the original payoffs. That is, we add 1 to the +1 we get for a win, so that a win equals 2; likewise, we add 1 to the −1 we get for a loss, so that a loss equals 0. Instead of the payoffs being +1 and −1, they are now 2 and 0. In such a way we eliminate the negative numbers and yet maintain the interval (2) of the original payoff in the transformed payoff. Or again, suppose we assume that the son wants to win more than the father does, so that a win for the son is worth +2, while a win for the father is only worth +½, and a loss for the son is −2, while a loss for the father is −½. But fractions are a bother, so we want to get rid of them. We can do this very simply by multiplying the payoffs by 2. Thus the payoff for the son becomes 4 if he wins, and the payoff for the father becomes 1; and a loss for the son becomes −2, while a loss for the father becomes −1. Through this multiplication process, we eliminate the fractions and yet maintain the ratio between the original and transformed payoffs, since the ratio of $2 : \frac{1}{2}$ is the same as the ratio of $4 : 1$, and the ratio of $-2 : -\frac{1}{2}$ is the same as the ratio of $-4 : -1$. Yet in these transformed payoffs we still have negative numbers, so to eliminate them we determine the largest negative payoff (−4) and add its positive counterpart (+4) to each payoff. Then the payoff for the son when he loses is 0 and the father's is 3; and the son's payoff when he wins is 8 and the father's is 5. In these newly transformed payoffs we maintain the interval (3) that was present in the other transformed payoffs, and yet we eliminate the negative numbers. To get rid of the fractions, we multiplied each of the payoffs by 2 (maintaining the ratio), and to get rid of the negative numbers we added 4 to each payoff (maintaining the interval). The payoff matrices for the father-son checker game appear in Table 1.

TABLE 1. **ORIGINAL AND LINEARLY TRANSFORMED PAYOFF TABLES**

Original Payoff				Transformed Payoff (multiplied by 2 and added 4 to already multiplied payoff)		
	Son	Father			Son	Father
Win	+2	+½		Win	+8	+5
Lose	−2	−½		Lose	0	+3

The payoffs are linearly transformed by the following formula: $Y = ax + b$, in which x is the original payoff, a is the number by which the original payoff is multiplied, b is the number added to ax, and Y is the transformed payoff. Through this method the *relationships* remain the same in the transformed payoff matrix as they were in the original payoff matrix. That is, the son wins the most if he wins and loses the most (or gains the least) if he loses.

These mathematical matters may seem rather unrelated to the interpersonal relationship, but they become quite important if relationships are to be manipulated mathematically and if game theory is to provide a means toward the mathematical representation of the interpersonal relationship.

Utility and Rationality. The idea of utility relates to the concept of rationality. In game theory it is assumed that the players are "rational." That is, the players want the outcome that has the greatest utility, and therefore they will certainly choose the strategy that seems most likely to bring them their preferred outcome.

Edwards, Lindman, and Phillips (1965) list four criteria for rationality. The first is *decidability*. That is, given two outcomes, a player should be able to decide which he prefers. In the case of our checker players there are two outcomes, win or lose, and both players prefer to win. Or there may be a third possible outcome in which a player may decide that he is indifferent to the outcome. This could be true in our father/son checker match if the son very much wants to win, and the father has won so many matches that he really doesn't care whether he wins or loses. In any case, decidability means that the player is able to determine that he either prefers one outcome over another, or that he is indifferent to the outcome.

The second criterion of rationality is *transitivity*, which means that among several outcomes, a person is able to compare each outcome with every other outcome, and the ordering of the preferences is linear. If a player has three possible outcomes—x, y, and z—and if he prefers x to y and y to z, then he should prefer x to z. The ordering of his preferences would be first x, then y, and finally z. If his preferences cannot be ordered in this way—that is, if he prefers x to y, and y to z, but prefers z to x—then his preferences are not transitive. If we go back to our checker game for an example, the three possible outcomes might be win, stalemate, and lose. The players would prefer winning to a stalemate and a stalemate to losing. Transitivity seems a rather safe assumption in this case, since it is unlikely that a player who prefers winning to a stalemate and a stalemate to losing would prefer losing to winning. When a player's outcome preferences are not transitive, analysis becomes, obviously, quite difficult.

Dominance is the third criteria for rationality. It means that if for every circumstance choice A produces an outcome that is at least as good as that produced by choice B, and if in addition, for one circumstance A produces an outcome that is superior to the outcome produced by B, then the player would prefer A to B. And finally, the fourth criteria for rationality is the *sure thing principle*, which states that outcomes that do not depend on a player's choice will not affect his choice.

The idea that the chooser, or player, is always rational is, of course, open to argument. How about the masochistic person who gets his joy out of the smallest payoff? Or the father who purposely loses to his son at checkers? Or the girl who deftly manages to let her boyfriend win at tennis? It could be pointed out that these players are also achieving their highest utility, but it is a different coin than that paid out by game theorists. As Rapoport (1969, Ch. 2) points out, real payoffs for real people in real situations are a problem for psychology, not game theory.

Utility and Preference. Having assumed that people should be able to decide whether or not they prefer one outcome over another or whether they are indifferent to the outcome, and having assumed that preferences can be ordered, we now come to the problem of how to establish the order of preferences. One method suggested is that of the *lottery*. The lottery involves the idea of risk, and different people prefer to take different amounts of risk, depending on the situation. A common example of a lottery is what is popularly called the "chance," in which a person buys a ticket for so much money, say one dollar, and if his ticket is drawn, he wins some prize, such as a color television set. Let us assume that the color television set is worth five-hundred dollars and that a thousand tickets are sold. If the person buys the one-dollar ticket he is, by his behavior, saying that he is willing to pay one dollar for a thousand-to-one chance of winning a five-hundred-dollar television set.

In choosing any strategy for winning a game there is a certain amount of risk. Let us return to our checker game for a moment. We said that the player who has the first move in the game has seven possible moves. Which move will he make? Or which strategy will he choose in starting the game? Any strategy has a certain probability of success—that is, of leading to winning the game. This becomes a decision-making situation. In checkers, one player may decide to jump the other's pieces every chance he gets and may seek to gain opportunities to jump. He may seek to avoid being jumped for as long as possible. Or he may choose some other strategy in the game. In any decision-making situation there are four kinds of certainty situations:

1. The situation of certainty, in which choosing a given strategy will always lead to a certain outcome—if you make a choice, you can be sure of what will happen as a consequence;

2. The situation of risk, in which you cannot be sure of what will happen, but you can estimate that certain outcomes may result with a certain probability—in the case of the television lottery you could estimate that there is only 1 chance in 1000 that you would win the television set and 999 chances out of 1000 that you would win nothing;

3. The situation of uncertainty, in which you have no idea of what might happen;

4. The situation of combined risk and uncertainty, in which certain outcomes might result with a certain probability—but there are certain other possible outcomes that are unknown at the present time, or outcomes which are possible, but whose probability of occurring is unknown.

Games are generally played under conditions of risk, or of risk and uncertainty. When you start to play a game of checkers you know that you will either win, lose, or end up in a stalemate. You can estimate, based on past experience with your opponent, what the chances are of winning or losing, with the possibility of a stalemate being quite low, regardless of your opponent.

For any given strategy, the chance that it will be successful must be considered in estimating the payoff for the adoption of that strategy. Let us say, for the son, that his payoff if he wins is +8, as indicated in the payoff matrix represented in Table 1. If he adopts a strategy of trying to conserve his pieces, his chances of winning are, let us say, one out of ten, or .10. On the other hand, if he adopts the strategy of trying to jump at every opportunity, his chances of winning are less, since his father will take advantage of his impetuousity; so let us say that the probability of winning with the jump-every-chance strategy is only one out of twenty, or .05. In this example, we will assume that the chances of a stalemate are so slight that, practically speaking, a stalemate is not worth considering. Now the sum of the probabilities must total 1.00. That is, something must happen as an outcome, so the total probabilities of all things that might happen sum to 1.00. In the case of the checker game, what will happen is that the boy will either win or lose. If his chances of winning with the saving-pieces strategy are .10, then his chances of losing with this strategy are 1.00−.10, which equals .90. His utility is his chances of winning (.10) multiplied by his payoff (+8), which equals .80. His chances of losing are .90, and his payoff if he loses is 0, so his utility for losing is .90 multiplied by 0, which is 0. His total utility for the saving-pieces strategy is going to be the sum of the utilities for the two outcomes, .80 + 0, which equals .80. His utility for the jumping-pieces strategy would be figured in the same way: .05 (+8) + .95 (0) = .40. So his utility for one strategy, saving pieces, is .80 and his utility for the other strategy, jumping pieces, is .40. It would seem obvious that he would prefer the saving-pieces strategy since his utility is higher, or to put it another way, his chances of winning are greater. Over a series of many games the boy would win more games this way than by jumping pieces as rapidly as possible.

Now let us change the situation a little. Suppose that the object of the "human" game between the father and the son is to win, and that winning is more important to the son than to the father. Suppose further that checkers is not the only game they play — they also play Monopoly and "memory." (Memory is a card game easy for children to play well, since all it requires is simple memory, a task which children do as well as, or sometimes better than, their elders.) Now assume that the chances of the son defeating his father at checkers are 1 in 10, of winning at Monopoly, 1 in 5, and of winning at memory, 1 in 2 (which is to say that he is as likely to win at memory as his father). However, winning at memory isn't really as valuable to him as winning the other games, since winning is so much more common; so let us say that the son gets a payoff of +1 for winning and 0 for losing. We have already established that he gets +8 in payoff for winning at checkers and 0 for losing. But what is his payoff for winning at Monopoly? We can establish it by using the lottery approach. This is done by giving the son a choice: Would he prefer to play a game of Monopoly if he were sure to win, or would he prefer to take a chance on playing either memory, in which his chances of winning are p, or playing checkers, in which his chances are $1 - p$? If the lottery were set up so the chances of winning at memory were 1 or close to 1 (therefore the chances of winning at checkers were 0 or close to 0 since the total probabilities must add up to 1), the son would most likely choose to play the sure chance of winning at Monopoly, since winning at memory is not so important to him. On the other hand, if the lottery were such that the chances of winning at memory were 0 or close to 0 (therefore the chances of winning at checkers were 1 or thereabout), he would most likely choose the lottery, since he would rather win at checkers than Monopoly. Suppose we found that when the lottery was a $p = 4/7$, he was indifferent to choosing between the lottery and playing Monopoly. That is, if given 3 chances in 7 of winning a game of checkers with his father, he could not make a choice between the two. He would just as soon risk playing checkers with 3 chances in 7 of winning as playing Monopoly with a sure chance of winning. We could then say that winning at Monopoly was 3/7 as important as winning at checkers. We multiply this probability, 3/7, by the payoff for winning at checkers, +8, which equals 24/7 ($3/7 \times 8 = 24/7$). The chances of winning memory are 4/7, which we multiply by the payoff for winning at memory, +1, which equals 4/7 ($4/7 \times 1 = 4/7$). Adding these two payoffs together, we get a total payoff for playing and winning Monopoly of 28/7, or +4 ($24/7 + 4/7 = 28/7$, or 4). Thus the payoff for winning at Monopoly is +4. We now have a probability and payoff matrix for the boy as shown in Table 2. From this payoff matrix we would assume that the boy would prefer to play either Monopoly or checkers, since both have a higher utility than memory.

It will be noted that in the figuring of utility, the probability of obtaining the payoff, that is, of winning has been included. So utility includes both the value of the payoff and the probability of obtaining it.

Let's stop for a moment and consider how all this arithmetic might be applied to interpersonal relationships. Assume that John is a college student. He wants a date for his fraternity party Saturday night. He would also like to have a date with a girl whose company he enjoys and who is liked or esteemed by his fraternity brothers, since dating high-status girls enhances his own status among his brethren. Now, assume that he knows three girls whom he might ask for a date. The first is Mary, who can't carry on a conversation, who is not frequently asked out, but who is an "A" student in her major, which happens to be mathematics. Since Mary isn't popular, the chances of getting a date with her would be quite high, let us say .95, or 95 chances in a 100. However, the payoff for a date with her would not be much. She would add nothing to his reputation among his brethren. However, she would be better company than no date at all, so let's give her +1 as a payoff. Thus the utility for John for trying to date Mary would be 1 × .95 = .95. The next possibility is Susan. Susan is not particularly attractive, so dating her would not gain John many points with his appearance-minded friends. But Susan is a very charming girl, has a delightful sense of humor (i.e., she laughs at John's jokes), and can discuss anything from international politics to football with knowledge, charm, and wit. In short, she is good company; she is a well-liked "buddy." So she rates more points than Mary, and spending an evening with her is sure to be enjoyable. Let us say that the payoff for her is +5. However, since Susan is good company, it is quite possible that she already has a date for Saturday night—let us say that the chances are only fifty-fifty that she will be available. Thus the utility for Susan is 5 × .50 = 2.50. The third possibility is Desdemona ("Des" for short). She is both beautiful and intelligent. She was the Sweetheart of Sigma Chi and Queen of the Spring Swine Festival. If John dates her, his stock with his brethren

TABLE 2. **WINNING PROBABILITIES, PAYOFF, AND UTILITY FOR THREE GAME EXAMPLES.**

Game	Probability of Winning	Payoff for Winning	Utility
Memory	.50	+1	.50 (1 × .50)
Monopoly	.20	+4	.80
Checkers	.10	+8	.80

will rise substantially. Also, Des is good company—sometimes she laughs at John's jokes. So let us say that a date with her gets +7 for reputation and +3 points for fun, for a total of +10 points payoff. However, Des is a very popular girl. The chances that she is still available for Saturday night are only one in ten, or .10. So the utility for Des is 10 × .10 = 1.00. The matrix of the probabilities, payoffs, and utilities of John's possible dates are represented in Table 3.

For John, the highest utility is for asking Susan for a date, and the next highest is for asking Des. Poor Mary will probably spend another Saturday night in her room working math problems; but most likely she enjoys that, so perhaps her plight is not too sorrowful after all. Thus, by using an elementary aspect of game theory, or decision theory, to be more exact, we have helped John decide whom to ask for a date Saturday night.

Now to return to our discussion of the general characteristics of games. Games may be presented in either extensive or normal forms (Luce & Raiffa, 1957, Ch. 3). Any game specifies a series of well-defined moves. One player makes a move, then the opponent makes a move. Where and how the players move is specified by the rules of the game. In any ordinary game, the play continues through a series of moves until one player finally loses. In the *extensive form* of a game, a player treats each move as a new choice in strategy, while in the *normal form*, a player chooses one strategy for the whole game—that is, in the extensive form, a player considers each move, one at a time, while in the normal form, he treats the whole game as if it consisted of only one basic move.

Most games can be played in their extensive forms. In checkers, for example, a player who treats each move separately, considering all possible strategies for each move, is playing the game in its extensive form. However, games can easily be reduced to their normal form—which is an easier, less-complicated form to study for our psychological purposes. In this form, the game is treated as a one-move proposition. In a checker game, this is done by giving each player a strategy-choice selection that includes all the possible general strategies for a game of checkers. By doing this, we end up with one matrix which lists all the

TABLE 3. **MATRIX OF JOHN'S POSSIBLE DATES**

Girl	Probability of Getting a Date	Payoff	Utility
Mary	.95	+1	.95
Susan	.50	+5	2.50
Desdemona	.10	+10	1.00

checker strategies available to each player. In the cells of the matrix is the payoff, which is the probability that a given player will win the game.

Using the normal form in the matrix in Table 4, we might assume that there are n total strategies in checkers available for player A and m total strategies for player B. The entries in each cell are the utilities for player A (upper left-hand part of each cell) and player B (lower right-hand part of each cell) if each plays the strategy for that cell. For example, let us assume that in strategy 1 each player avoids jumping as much as possible and tries to conserve his pieces for as long as possible. In strategy 2, each tries to jump the other's pieces as often as possible. One stategy is conservative and the other is devil-may-care. In the matrix, if A (the father) uses strategy 1 and B (the son) uses strategy 2, we will assume that the chances of the father winning the match are $+.95$. Since winning at checkers is worth $+5$ for the father (see Table 1), the utility of that strategy for him, assuming that the son adopts strategy 2, is the probability of winning multiplied by the payoff, which is $.95 \times 5 = 4.75$. The utility for the son in this same cell is his chance of winning (.05) multiplied by his payoff ($+8$), which is $.05 \times +8 = .40$.

In this particular matrix, we are assuming that the conservative strategy is more likely to be successful than the impulsive strategy. So in filling in the other four cells of the matrix, we assume that when the

TABLE 4. **MATRIX OF UTILITIES FOR VARIOUS STRATEGIES OF TWO PLAYERS PLAYING CHECKERS**

		Player B (Son) Strategies			
		1	2	• • • • • • • • • •	• m
Player A (Father) Strategies	1	4.50 / .80	4.75 / .40		
	2	3.75 / 2.00	4.50 / .80		
	• • • • • • •				
	n				

players use the same strategy, the probability that the father will win is his probability of winning regardless of strategy. This probability, let us say, is .90, which means that the son's probability of winning is .10. Thus, the payoff for each, when both use either strategy 1 or strategy 2, is .90 × +5 for the father, or 4.50, and .10 × +8 for the son, which is .80. If the father uses the impulsive strategy, strategy 2, and the son uses the conservative strategy, strategy 1, we will assume that the son's chances of winning go up to .25; the son's utility for that combination is .25 × +8 = 2.00, and the father's is .75 × +5 = 3.75.

Strategy in Games

In discussing payoffs, utilities, and rationality, we have necessarily introduced the concept of strategy, since making a "rational" choice naturally assumes that there are some possibilities (as we have already pointed out). In playing games, these possibilities are strategies for winning. So now we come to a consideration of strategy. Actually, the first practical use of game theory was finding the best strategy for getting the highest *utility* from a conflict situation.

The basic objective of strategy is to maximize the payoff—or to maximize the utility. The two main types of strategy are *pure strategy* and *mixed strategy*. A pure strategy is one that would always be adopted in a game, regardless of what the other person did. A mixed strategy would be one in which the person shifted from one strategy to another on some sort of schedule. In applying strategy to a particular game it is generally assumed that, whatever the extensive form of the game, it is reduced to normal form. It is further assumed that the strategy adopted will ultimately produce the highest utility regardless of the strategy the opposing player adopts.

Some basic principles of strategy which have become orthodox in game theory are the concepts of *minimax, maximin,* and the *saddle-point*. A good illustration of these points—good because it is clear and also graphic—is provided by Williams (1954, p. 24). This illustration uses, instead of a game, an interpersonal relationship problem. A married couple, Dotty and Ray, want to camp in the mountains. Unfortunately, they have a conflict. Ray likes to camp at high altitudes while Dotty prefers low altitudes. The area in which they plan to camp is illustrated in Figure 2. The area, as can be seen in the drawing, is crossed by four dividing lines, or roads, running from east to west, and four running from north to south. The four running from east to west are the roads along which Ray may make his choice of camping area, and those running from north to south are those along which Dotty may make her choice. The place they camp will be at the intersection of the roads

FIGURE 2. **DRAWING OF DOTTY AND RAY'S CAMPING AREA**

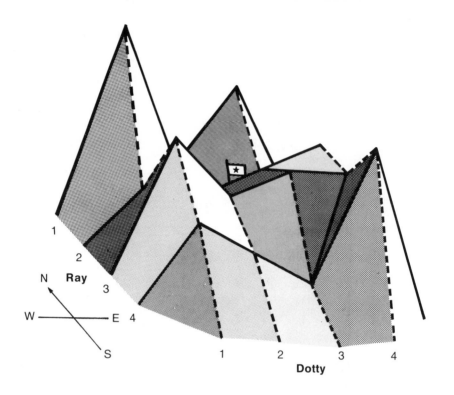

From J. D. Williams, *The compleat strategyst.* New York: McGraw-Hill, 1954, p. 24. Copyright © 1954, 1966 by The Rand Corporation, and reproduced by permission of McGraw-Hill Book Company and The Rand Corporation.

chosen by each. The matrix in Table 5 shows the altitudes of the inter-section points of the roads (in thousands of feet).

Ray's strategy is to pick the road that will give him a camp at the highest possible altitude, while Dotty's strategy is to pick the road that will give her a camp at the lowest possible altitude. How can they ar-range their choices so that they will end up maximizing their satisfac-tion? (They have to camp together.) Off hand, it might appear that Ray would choose the road that has the highest point. That would be road 1. However, if Dotty chooses road 4, Ray will end up camping at the low-est point in the area rather than the highest point. So Ray's strategy should be to choose the *maximin*, that is, the road that has the highest *low* point. This way he guarantees that the lowest point that he could end up on would be as high as possible. That would be road 3, since its lowest point is at three thousand feet. Dotty's problem is the reverse.

TABLE 5. **MATRIX OF INTERSECTION-POINT ALTITUDES FOR DOTTY AND RAY**

Dotty's Roads

	1	2	3	4
1	7	2	5	1
Ray's Roads 2	2	2	3	4
3	5	3	4	4
4	3	2	1	6

She wants the lowest point possible. Therefore, she might choose either road 3 or road 4, since both have points at one thousand feet. However, if she chooses road 3, Ray might choose road 1, thus putting her at five thousand feet instead of one thousand feet. If she chooses road 4, Ray might choose road 4, putting her at six thousand feet instead of one thousand feet. Dotty's best strategy is to choose the *minimax* — that is, the road that has the lowest *high* point. This would be road 2, since the highest she could end up would be at three thousand feet.

As it turns out, the place where Ray's road 3 and Dotty's road 2 intersect forms a "saddle" in the mountains — as you can see in Figure 4. The place where they camp is marked by a flag. That point where the two roads, or strategies, intersect is the *saddle-point*. The strategy each adopted was a pure strategy, since that strategy guaranteed them, over a series of choices, the best utility, regardless of what the other person chose to do. Dotty's strategy used a minimax principle (minimizing the maximum), while Ray's used a maximin principle (maximizing the minimum).

These various types of strategy were taken from economic decision-making situations in which there is typically a buyer and a seller. The person who is buying tries to get the product for the smallest amount of money possible, so he tries to minimize the maximum he will have to pay (adopting the minimax strategy); the seller tries to make as much money as possible, so he tries to maximize the minimum amount of money he will make (adopting the maximin strategy). If the two should happen to intersect, the point of intersection is a saddle-point (called a saddle-point since it is the lowest point on the ridge of the maximums and the highest point in the valley of the minimums); if diagramed, the saddle-point looks as though it is the center of a saddle, as does the point at which Dotty and Ray camped in the mountains.

Another type of strategy which can be selected is a *dominant strategy*, if there is one in the game. A dominant strategy is so named because it dominates every other possible strategy. That is, no matter what happens, the dominant strategy provides a utility that is at least as good as, and usually better than, the outcome provided by any other strategy, regardless of the strategy the opponent adopts. The principle of dominance was mentioned earlier in the discussion of rationality. A rational player chooses the strategy that will guarantee him a utility which in any given circumstance will provide him with at least as high a utility as any other strategy, and most of the time will give him a higher utility.

To illustrate this point, let's use the matrix for the checker game (Table 4) between the father and son. You will recall that in this table, strategy 1 is the conservative strategy in which the player tries to conserve his pieces, while strategy 2 is the impulsive strategy in which the player tries to jump as much as possible, without regard to possible consequences. In that matrix there are two utility figures for each move, one for the father (upper part of each cell) and one for the son (lower part of each cell). To facilitate analysis, we can combine those figures into a single number by subtracting the utility for the son from the utility for the father. (Since the father has the greater chance of winning, regardless of strategy, the father's utility is always the larger, so we will end up with a positive number.) In cell 1–1 (upper left-hand cell) the utility for the father is 4.50 and the utility for the son is .80, so the combined utility obtained by subtracting the son's from the father's is 4.50 − .80, or 3.70. Table 6 shows the matrix of combined utilities for the filled cells.

Since the utility is always in the father's favor (he has the highest probability of winning), it would be to the father's advantage to choose

TABLE 6. **MATRIX OF COMBINED UTILITIES FOR FATHER-SON CHECKER GAME**

		Son's Strategies	
		1	2
Father's Strategies	1	3.70	4.35
	2	1.75	3.70

strategies that lead to utilities that have the highest numbers, while it is to the son's advantage to select strategies that lead to utilities with the lowest numbers. If we look at the matrix we see that for the father the row with the highest numbers is row 1, where the utilities are 3.70 and 4.35. If the father chooses this strategy, the worst utility he can get is 3.70. If the father chooses strategy 2 with utilities of 1.75 and 3.70, the best he can attain is 3.70, which is equal to the worst he can do in strategy 1. For the father, strategy 1 "dominates" strategy 2.

The son's objective is the reverse of his father's. The son wants to choose the strategy that will produce the lowest utilities, since lower utilities mean a reduced chance of losing. If he selects strategy 1, the utilities are 3.70 and 1.75, while if he chooses strategy 2, they are 4.35 and 3.70. Obviously, with strategy 2 his chances of losing are greater, regardless of which strategy his father chooses, so unless he wants to lose, he would be foolish to choose strategy 2. The worst he can do with strategy 1 is equal to the best he can do with strategy 2. Therefore, for the son, strategy 1 also "dominates" strategy 2. If father and son are rational players, both will choose strategy 1; the father will probably win, and it will be a long checker game as these two prudent players cautiously move their pieces around the board.

Rapoport (1966, Ch. 5) points out that games may be classified according to whether or not the players have a dominating strategy, but we will leave this concern until later in the chapter when we discuss particular kinds of experimental games.

Unfortunately, most games—and most decisions or conflicts in life—don't yield to such obviously advantageous solutions as are provided by choosing the dominant strategies or the minimax or maximin strategies. And two people frequently don't find a "saddle-point" in their interaction. When such occasions as these arise, mixed strategies are used. If, in football, the running game isn't working, the passing game is tried, and if that doesn't work, a new quarterback is put in. To illustrate the use of mixed strategies, we will use a matrix borrowed from Williams (1954), presented in Table 7.

TABLE 7. **EXAMPLE OF MIXED STRATEGY SITUATION**

		Red's Strategies	
		1	2
Blue's Strategies	1	3	6
	2	5	4

From J. D. Williams, *The compleat strategyst.* New York: McGraw-Hill, 1954, p. 36. Copyright © 1954, 1966 by The Rand Corporation, and reproduced by permission of McGraw-Hill Book Company and the Rand Corporation.

In this game, as in the earlier checker game, the utility is to the advantage of the player who is listed on the left, and he (in this case, Blue) is trying to obtain the maximum utility, while Red is trying to end up with the minimum utility, since it means he has to pay the least. If Blue follows the maximin principle, he will choose strategy 2, since this would result in the highest minimum utility; if Red follows the minimax principle, he will choose strategy 1, since this contains the lowest maximum utility. However, this solution is not stable. That is, if Blue keeps choosing strategy 2, it is not going to take Red long to realize that Blue is holding to strategy 2, so it would be to Red's advantage to switch to his strategy 2, since this will lower the utility from 5 to 4. If Red switches, Blue will soon realize it and see that it would be to his advantage to switch to strategy 1, since with Red choosing strategy 2, Blue will gain a utility of 6 if he uses strategy 1, which is higher than the utility 4 he is getting by sticking with strategy 2. As soon as Red perceives that Blue has switched to strategy 1, Red should than switch back to strategy 1, since this will lower the utility from 6 to 3. By this time, if both players are rational, each should be trying to determine what the other is planning to do, and what the other thinks *he* is planning to do, and so on. It now becomes a case of who can one-up whom. In situations like this mixed strategies have been devised whereby each player can determine how often he should play each strategy in order to get his own best utility without worrying about what the other player might do. Thus the worry is taken out of the game. (Of course, if a player has serious money involved in the game he will probably do some sweating anyway).

Players can learn ways to work out how much to use which strategies in which mixture; some of the rationale about these ways can be obtained by consulting more extensive discussions of how to mix strategies (e.g., Rapoport, 1966; Luce & Raiffa, 1957; Williams, 1954). To determine a quick and simple solution to the game (or more accurately, to the utility matrix) we have presented here, you would subtract the numbers in the lower row from those in the upper row and switch columns to get the mix for Red; to get the mix for Blue, you would subtract the numbers in the right-hand column from those in the left-hand column and switch rows. (Table 8 illustrates this method.) Thus Red would randomly switch back and forth from strategy 1 to strategy 2, making certain that he used each equally and frequently, while Blue would randomly switch back and forth between strategies 1 and 2 also, but he would use strategy 2 three times for every time he used strategy 1. To average the utility over several plays of this game, you would multiply the number of choices by the utilities for each strategy and divide by the sum of the number of choices. The utility should be the same for each strategy of the other player. In the case of this game, if Blue uses strategy 1, Red's utility works out as follows:

TABLE 8.   METHOD OF DETERMINING PROPORTIONS OF PURE STRATEGIES USED IN MIXED-STRATEGY SITUATIONS

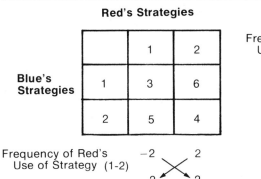

Red's Strategies

		1	2
Blue's Strategies	1	3	6
	2	5	4

Frequency of Blue's
Use of Strategy   (1-2)

3   1

1   3

Frequency of Red's   −2   2
Use of Strategy   (1-2)

2   2

From J. D. Williams, *The compleat strategyst.* New York: McGraw-Hill, 1954, p. 44. Copyright © 1954, 1966 by The Rand Corporation, and reproduced by permission of McGraw-Hill Book Company and The Rand Corporation.

$\dfrac{(3 \times 2) + (6 \times 2)}{4} = \dfrac{6 + 12}{4} = 4\frac{1}{2}$. If Blue uses strategy 2, Red's utility is

$\dfrac{(5 \times 2) + (4 \times 2)}{4} = \dfrac{10 + 8}{4} = 4\frac{1}{2}$. For Blue the utility is found in the

same way. If Red uses strategy 1, Blue's utility is $\dfrac{(1 \times 3) + (3 \times 5)}{4} =$

$\dfrac{3 + 15}{4} = \dfrac{18}{4} = 4\frac{1}{2}$, and if Red should choose strategy 2, Blue's utility is

$\dfrac{(1 \times 6) + (3 \times 4)}{4} = \dfrac{6 + 12}{4} = \dfrac{18}{4} = 4\frac{1}{2}$. So, no matter how it is figured,

the mixed strategy has a utility of $4\frac{1}{2}$, in Blue's favor.

In most games, the strategy will be mixed, since there are few interaction situations in which the most rational strategy is a pure one. Of course, in life itself the obvious strategy to choose differs among individuals, in part because different people see different utility matrices in the same game. But that is another issue.

To summarize, game theorists have generally discussed two kinds of strategy, pure and mixed, and the pure strategy is determined by the minimax and maximin principles or by the dominating principle.

Kinds of Games

There are all kinds of games, but the kinds of games we are primarily interested in are two-person games. Luce and Raiffa (1957) classify two-person games on the basis of whether or not the games are cooperative and whether or not they are zero-sum.

In a *cooperative game* the two players can communicate beforehand to make certain arrangements between themselves. In a *noncooperative game* the players do not communicate with each other prior to the start of the game. Of course, players may communicate to each other through their moves. For example, in our father-son checker game, one player would communicate quite quickly to the other by the moves he made as to whether or not he intended to play a conservative game.

A *zero-sum game* is one in which one player's wins are another player's losses. If two players are flipping quarters, and player 1 wins if the quarter comes up heads while player 2 wins if it comes up tails, the quarter the one wins is paid off by the other player. The game is called a zero-sum game because the algebraic sum of the winnings of the two players comes to zero. That is, if player 1 wins one dollar ($+1$), then player 2 loses one dollar (-1), and the algebraic sum of the winnings of the two players is $(+1) + (-1) = 0$. Most parlor games are zero-sum games. That is, if one player wins a game of checkers, the other player loses. Likewise, in poker what one player wins, some other player or players lose.

A *nonzero-sum game* is one in which what one player wins is not necessarily what another player loses, and it is this type of game on which researchers concentrate their efforts. As Rapoport has pointed out, psychologists are interested in the game "as a model of a situation from life, a replica cut down in size . . ." (1969, p. 129), so it naturally follows that the kinds of games psychologists would be most interested in studying would be those that come closest to providing a replica of life, and life is not usually a zero-sum game. In life, it often happens that when one "player" wins, the other wins, and when one "player" loses, the other also loses. Most of the interest in games, then, centers around nonzero-sum games.

Games may also be classified on the basis of how many strategies each player has available: If one player has 3 strategies available and the other has 5 strategies available, the game is a 3×5 game. If one player has 10 strategies and the other has 100 strategies, it is a 10×100 game. Most common parlor games have a relatively large number of strategies available to each player. However, the problem with using a game that provides each player with a large number of strategies is that it makes research difficult. Therefore, most serious interest in games has involved games with only 2 strategies available to each player — that is, 2×2 games.

In these games, as in other games, each player will try to follow the best strategy. The point, or the cell, at which the best strategy for each player intersects is the equilibrium point. If the game has a stable equilibrium point, it will not be a particularly interesting game from the standpoint of studying interaction between people, since the players will merely select their own best strategies and stick with them. There will be no action. The 2 × 2 games described in this section are interesting because their equilibrium points are not stable. Although there is a maximin strategy for each player and a cell at which each of these strategies intersect, each player can improve his own utility by switching to his alternate strategy. However, by improving his own payoff, he also affects his opponent's payoff. Thus there is within these games a competitive and a cooperative component. By choosing a certain strategy, the player is offering to cooperate with his opponent, and by choosing the other strategy, he is competing. If the players cooperate, they may maximize the utility of the game for each player. If they compete, one player may maximize his payoff, at the expense of the other player. Furthermore, if these games are analyzed by Williams' method for determining mixed strategy (see p. 349), one discovers that the payoff is either zero, or it is positive or negative, depending on the strategy adopted by the other player. In short, that method for determining mixed strategy is useless. Each game provides a positive payoff for each player if the players cooperate. If the players compete with each other, at least one player, and possibly both, will lose. However, the temptation to compete exists, since each player might get a better payoff by competing.

Rapoport (1967) analyzed the 2 × 2 nonzero-sum game and concluded that there are seventy-eight nonequivalent 2 × 2 games, but that of these seventy-eight possible games, only four are interesting. By "interesting," Rapoport means that there is conflict between the players and that the equilibria are not stable. There are two other games that provide for some conflict, but in these two, each player has a dominating strategy that brings him the highest payoff regardless of what the other player does; these games have "strongly stable equilibria," meaning that it is obvious what each player will do if he is rational. That leaves four games that are considered worthy of being researched.

The first of these four games, called Exploiter, or Chicken, provides a payoff matrix as shown in Table 9. (The payoff for Player 1 is always the first number in each cell, and the payoff for Player 2 is the second number.) In this game, the maximin is in the cell in the upper left-hand corner, but the game is not stable, because each player is motivated to switch to get a higher payoff. If player 1 switches to strategy B1 while player 2 retains strategy A2, then player 1 will gain a payoff of 2 instead of only 1. Likewise, if player 2 switches while player 1 retains strategy A1, then player 2 will gain a payoff of 2 instead of 1. The conflict comes in that each player is motivated to switch, but if both switch, both lose more than they would lose otherwise. Thus, each player is motivated to switch, but only if the other player doesn't switch, too.

TABLE 9. **MATRIX FOR** *EXPLOITER,* **OR** *CHICKEN*

		Player 2	
		A_2	B_2
Player 1	A_1	1, 1	−1, 2
	B_1	2, −1	−2, −2

This game has been labeled *Chicken,* since the player who dares to switch, who isn't "chicken," wins the most. Rapoport has also called this game *Exploiter,* since the one who makes the move to switch benefits himself at the expense of the other player. In this game, if one player switches first, the game enters an equilibrium—that is, it is not to the advantage of the other player to switch, because it will just increase his loss.

The next game, which Rapoport has labeled *Leader,* is similar to the first game in that the maximin is in the upper left-hand cell of the payoff matrix, and each player is motivated to switch in order to increase his payoff. This matrix appears in Table 10. As in Chicken, if both players switch, both lose. The first player to switch improves his own payoff, but by switching he also improves the payoff of his opponent. However, he improves his own payoff more, so this game has been dubbed *Leader.* It has also been called the *Battle of the Sexes,* after a game situation in which a husband and wife both want to go out for the evening, but one wants to see a movie, while the other wants to go to a concert. Either would enjoy going out with his or her spouse more than staying at home or going out alone, so the one who gives in to the other gains, but not as much as the one who gets his or her preference.

TABLE 10. **MATRIX FOR** *LEADER,* **OR** *BATTLE OF THE SEXES*

		Player 2	
		A_2	B
Player 1	A_1	−1, −1	1, 2
	B_1	2, 1	−2, −2

TABLE 11. **MATRIX FOR** *HERO,* **OR** *APOLOGY*

		Player 2	
		*A*2	*B*2
Player 1	*A*1	−1, −1	2, 1
	*B*1	1, 2	−2, −2

Reprinted from A. Rapoport, "Exploiter, Leader, Hero, and Martyr: the four archetypes of the 2 × 2 game," in *Behavioral Science*, Volume 12. No. 2, p. 82, 1967, by permission of James G. Miller, M.D., Ph.D., Editor. Copyright © 1967 by James G. Miller, M.D., Editor.

The next game, *Hero*, is similar to the previous two in that the maximin is in the upper left-hand cell, and each player is motivated to switch strategies to improve payoff (see Table 11). In this game, as in the previous game, both players gain if one of the players switches, but the player who switches gains less than the player who sticks with strategy A, so the player who switches becomes a "hero"; he wins, but not as much as the other. Rapoport has suggested that this game might also be called *Apology*, since if one person apologizes, both people gain, but the one who apologizes pays something, in that he loses face. If each goes to the other's house to apologize, they will miss each other, and so both will lose—as is the case in the preceding two games.

The last of these 2 × 2 nonzero-sum games is the best known, since it is the game which has been most extensively researched. It is known as *Prisoner's Dilemma*. In this game the maximin is still in the upper left-hand cell, but the game is different from the preceding three in that neither player is motivated to change strategy, since if he does, he will lose and the other will gain. This game is also different in that if both players switch, both gain rather than lose. The matrix for Prisoner's Dilemma appears in Table 12. This game has also been called *Martyr*, since the player who switches helps the other player, but loses, himself.

TABLE 12. **MATRIX FOR** *PRISONER'S DILEMMA,* **OR** *MARTYR*

		Player 2	
		*A*2	*B*2
Player 1	*A*1	−1, −1	2, −2
	, *B*1	−2, 2	1, 1

Reprinted from A. Rapoport, "Exploiter, Leader, Hero, and Martyr: the four archetypes of the 2 × 2 game," in *Behavioral Science*, Volume 12. No. 2, p. 82, 1967, by permission of James G. Miller, M.D., Ph.D., Editor. Copyright © 1967 by James G. Miller, M.D., Editor.

The name "Prisoner's Dilemma" comes from the story of two criminal suspects who were arrested, taken to jail, and kept separated from each other. The district attorney is certain they are guilty of a serious crime, but lacks the evidence to convict them. He tells each of them that if he confesses he will receive a lighter sentence for having turned state's evidence, but that if he does not confess he will be jailed on some minor, trumped-up charge. Thus the dilemma is this: if neither confesses, both will get off with relatively trivial sentences. However, if the prisoner refuses to confess, he is taking the chance that his partner will confess, so he might end up getting "the book thrown at him," while his partner gets off with a light sentence. On the other hand, if he confesses and his partner does also, they will probably both get sentences that are relatively more severe. Obviously, the maximin in this situation is to confess, since regardless of whether or not his partner confesses, he will have avoided the maximum sentence. However, this situation is unstable, since if he refuses to confess and his partner does likewise, they will both get off with trivial sentences. This game might also be labeled *Do You Trust Your Accomplice?*

The interest in these dilemma games is due mainly to the fact that they are games with unstable equilibria. The games contain a maximin, but each player is motivated to switch from that maximin, since he stands to gain by doing so. The dilemma is that he gains only if his partner does not switch. If his partner also switches, both lose. Prisoner's Dilemma is the exception to this, in that if each switches from his maximin, both gain. The interest in dilemma games centers in the fact that the player must make some sort of judgment of what the other player is likely to do, since this estimate of the other player's behavior is crucial to arriving at his own best strategy. Of course, the players could use the method described earlier for determining how to mix strategies in a game. That method wouldn't be of much help in Prisoner's Dilemma, however, since in that game the result would be the recommendation of a one-to-one strategy in which each player uses one strategy half the time and the other strategy half the time, mixing the strategies in a random fashion; and the result of such a strategy would be that each player frequently loses.

Research on Games

The primary interest in games has not been in games per se, but rather in games as paradigms for real human interaction. As Rapoport states "parameters (of games) can often be quite naturally interpreted in terms of rich psychological concepts: trust and suspicion, responsiveness and vengefulness, caution and daring, dominance and submission, adherence to principle and opportunism" (1969, p. 139). In short, games provide a mathematical model for the interaction between people.

In the research on games, there are several variables that may be manipulated. Vinacke (1969) listed three kinds: *task variables, situation variables,* and *characteristics of the players.* Task variables are the tasks the subject is supposed to perform. Situation variables include the rules under which the game is played and the payoffs each player receives for various outcomes. The people playing the game may vary in some personality characteristic, or in sex, age, or any other dimension along which people vary. In fact, the opponents do not both have to be people — real people really interacting, that is. One of the players may be a stooge who is instructed to choose his strategies in a certain way, or one of the players may even be a computer programmed to respond in a certain way. In this case, the only person variable in the study is the one person responding to some preprogrammed player, be it human or machine.

Of these variables, Rapoport (1969) argues that the variables inherent in the game structure itself should be manipulated, rather than the personality characteristics of the subjects. Most of the manipulation in research with games has been, for obvious reasons, manipulation of personality characteristics of subjects. Psychologists are interested in how different kinds of people will interact with each other in certain kinds of situations. The game offers one kind of experimental situation in which this can be determined. Rapoport's argument carries some weight, particularly in view of the practical and statistical problems involved in manipulating the personality variables of subjects without considering the problem of the validity of the personality measures themselves. However, Rapoport's argument is basically an argument in favor of adapting the research to the instrument, rather than using the instrument as a projective test to study what the psychologist is really interested in, namely people interacting with each other. Both approaches should be taken. Certainly the ways in which people vary along the parameters inherent in the game itself must be studied before it becomes possible to draw accurately the full implications of the ways in which people differ in their behavior in games. But it is too much to expect curious psychologists to delay using a new tool to study the kinds of problems they are interested in, even if the tool is not fully understood. Games are not the first projective test to be put to extensive use before the test is thoroughly understood. In fact, it would be accurate to say that no projective instrument is yet fully understood.

The two games that have been subjected to the most research are Prisoner's Dilemma and Chicken. These two games have already been described, but we will present them again here, both to define them in the generalized game form and to show the most common kinds of payoff matrices used in research on these two games.

In a typical game, there are two players (or there may be two teams of players). Each side has two strategies it may choose, and each player knows what payoff he will get, depending on which strategy the opposing player chooses. The game may be a one-shot affair in which each player makes a choice and either gets paid off if he wins or pays off if he loses. However, more commonly the players will work through a series of plays, with a score being kept and the player collecting his winnings or paying his losses at the end of the series. Each player is aware of his own choices, his opponent's choices, and the payoffs.

Table 13 shows the basic form of the game matrix. In this matrix, R stands for "reward," which is the reward for cooperation; therefore, C_1C_2 is the result of mutual cooperation. S stands for "sucker" or "saint," which is the payoff to the one who cooperates by himself. T stands for "temptation," which is the largest payoff and therefore tempts each player to defect from cooperation. P stands for "punishment," which is what happens to both players if neither cooperates. The "C" in C_1 and C_2 stands for "cooperation" — the C response is the cooperative response. The "D" in the D_1 and D_2 responses stands for "defection," which is what a player does when he leaves the cooperative response in order to gain a greater return for himself or perhaps to punish the other player for his previous defection. In the game of Prisoner's Dilemma, $T > R > P > S$, and $2R > S + T$. In Chicken, P and S are reversed in quantity, so that in Chicken, $T > R > S > P$, and $2R > S + T$.

The most common payoff matrices used in research on games are given in Table 14. In these payoff matrices, Chicken is a rougher game than Prisoner's Dilemma. Each player stands to win less and lose more in this game, particularly if both players compete with each other. In this case, a game of *Let's You and Him Fight* can end up to the advantage of the experimenter. The main difference between these two games is that Prisoner's Dilemma has one equilibrium, D_1D_2, while Chicken has two equilibria, C_2D_1 and C_1D_2. The equilibrium, you will recall, is the point from which a player does not improve, and usually impairs, his outcome by changing his strategy.

TABLE 13. **BASIC FORM OF DILEMMA GAME MATRIX**

		Player 2	
		C_2	D_2
Player 1	C_1	R, R	S, T
	D_1	T, S	P, P

Reprinted from A. Rapoport & A. M. Chammah, "The game of chicken," in *Game theory in the behavioral sciences*, p. 151, Ira Buchler and Hugo Nutini, editors, by permission of the University of Pittsburgh Press. © 1969 by the University of Pittsburgh Press.

TABLE 14.   **COMMON PAYOFF MATRICES FOR PRISONER'S DILEMMA AND CHICKEN**

Prisoner's Dilemma

Player 2

		C_2	D_2
Player 1	C_1	3, 3	0, 5
	D_1	5, 0	1, 1

Chicken

Player 2

		C_2	D_2
Player 1	C_1	1, 1	−1, 2
	D_1	2, −1	−2, −2

From W. E. Vinacke, "Variables in experimental games: toward a field theory," in *Psychological Bulletin,* 1969, 71, p. 294. Copyright © 1969 by the American Psychological Association, and reproduced by permission.

Vinacke (1969) has reviewed the research on these two games and analyzed the results along the dimensions of (1) the game tasks, (2) the rules under which the game is played and the payoffs in the payoff matrix, and (3) the characteristics of the subjects playing the games. The following summary is drawn primarily from Vinacke's article.

Varying the amount of payoff in the matrix appears to have the greatest effect as a function of the differences among the payoffs in the various cells of the matrix, rather than as a function of the size of the payoff itself. That is, what affects whether or not two people will cooperate with each other, or compete with each other, does not seem to be how much payoff they get; rather, it seems to be a function of how each player's payoff *compares* with the other person's payoff. When the differences between the payoffs in the cells are great in favor of cooperating, subjects tend to cooperate with each other, but when the payoffs are differentially in favor of competing, the subjects compete. The results here are not very different from life, in which a person's satisfaction with his pay is not so much a function of the absolute amount he gets as it is a function of how his reward compares with other people's rewards. Studies that presented the payoff in a form different from that of the matrix suggest the same result. That is, the player tends to select the strategy that will give him the best outcome relative to his opponent and avoid the outcome that leaves him relatively worse off than the opponent.

When the game is a lengthy series of choices over a period of time, the cooperation between subjects tends to decline and then rise again. Generally, the longer the game runs, the more cooperation tends to develop.

Various studies have tried to discover strategies that stimulate trust and cooperation. Generally speaking, players were more likely to respond with trust than to initiate responses that would lead to trust. Any procedure that clearly expresses an intention to cooperate increases the likelihood of cooperation occurring. Usually, shifts in strategy have the greatest effect on the opponent's behavior. For example, studies have shown that the opponent is more likely to cooperate if one player is competitive at the beginning and then shifts to a cooperative strategy, than if the player starts the game with a cooperative strategy.

Almost any kind of communication between opponents increases the probability of cooperation between them. Of course, as many researchers have pointed out, the effect of the communication depends on its content. For example, feedback in the form of keeping a cumulative score of the winnings of the two players tends to increase the competition between them.

Studies of whether friends who are playing each other tend to be more cooperative or competitive have obtained contradictory results. In one college, friends cooperated, and the closer the friendship, the greater the cooperation. However, at another college the results were just the opposite, and the closer the friendship, the stronger the competition. Probably the basic meaning of these findings is that friends are more responsive to each other than they are to other people, so that the response tendency of the players — cooperation or competition — will be more pronounced with friends than with other people. This suggests that games might be a valuable method of predicting the probable course of close relationships — such as marriage — or might prove to be a valuable technique for uncovering what goes on between people involved in an intimate relationship.

In general, the results of task and situation variables indicate that these variables do affect what goes on between people in games. But for the psychologist, the most interesting research has investigated those variables that Rapoport questions — the personal characteristics of the subjects. Many studies have reported sex differences, but the studies differ on which sex is the most cooperative and which the most competitive. Most report men as being more cooperative and women as being more competitive, but Vinacke's own studies suggest that men are more exploitive and women more accommodating. Vinacke suggests that the discrepancy in these results may be because women who are more competitive in the games are actually not competing, but merely cooperating with the experimenter who has put them in a competitive situation — to cooperate they have to compete!

The results of studies of age factors have been contradictory. Age differences have been reported, with accommodation staying high for women at all ages as well as declining with age, and with exploitive tendencies increasing with age for men and also decreasing with age.

Cross-cultural studies show that people who live in an accommodating culture tend to be more accommodating, while those who live in an exploitive culture tend to be more exploitive. Likewise, those who come from families in competitive business tend to be more competitive, while those who come from families with a bureaucratic background tend to be more cooperative. Generally, those who are more cooperative come from groups that are free of neuroticism or psychosis, high in ethicality, low in authoritarianism, high in altruism and trustworthiness, and higher in abasement and deference. On the other hand, those who are more competitive tend to have traits that are opposite to those just described.

However, these studies of simple dimensions have not been as suggestive as studies that have attempted to get at more complex interactions among variables. Studies of motivation, in particular, have been suggestive. Ryan and Lakie (1965) had subjects perform in both competitive and cooperative situations and found that subjects who were high in need for achievement and low in manifest anxiety performed best in the competitive situation, while those who were low in need for achievement and high in manifest anxiety performed best in the cooperative situation.

One of the most interesting series of studies was done by Terhune (1968), who was motivated to do his research, in part, because of the equivocal results reported by so many previous studies. He was interested in studying the way "personal predispositions" affect the development of conflict and cooperation between players playing the Prisoner's Dilemma game. He reviewed the research and concluded that the reason for the conflicting results was that in an interaction sequence both players eventually behave alike, so that the eventual behavior is the result of a complex interaction between the two personalities.

Terhune investigated three basic motives thought to be relevant to behavior in the game situation. These motives were: (1) need for achievement, (2) need for affiliation, and (3) need for power. He selected subjects with three patterns of motivation on these three variables. One group was composed of subjects who were high on need for achievement and low on the other two, one group was composed of those high on need for affiliation and low on the others, and one group was high on need for power and low on the others. In effect his three groups were composed of pure personality types. He had three hypotheses: (1) Subjects high on need for affiliation would be mostly cooperative; (2) subjects high on need for power would be mostly competitive; (3) subjects high on need for achievement would vary between cooperation and competition, depending on the situation.

The subjects each played an opponent who was of the same type. Each pair played three game series: (1) a one-play game which was played three times with a payoff matrix that increased the temptation to compete, (2) an extended thirty-play game, and (3) a final thirty-play game in which the pair could communicate. Thus, Terhune had nine basic experimental situations with three different personality types, each playing under three different conditions.

On the first game series of one-play games, his results did not quite agree with his hypotheses. He found: (1) The high-need-for-achievement subjects were the most trusting and trustworthy regardless of the game matrix. As the temptation to defect increased, they defected more, but mainly as a defense against the opponent's defection. Seldom did they try to exploit their opponent; (2) the high-need-for-affiliation subjects were highly cooperative when playing a safe game, but when the game became more risky they became suspicious and defensive, and thus more competitive; (3) the high-need-for-power subjects were consistently uncooperative and tried to exploit their partners.

Terhune asked his subjects after the game what they thought they were trying to accomplish during the game. He found that the high-need-for-power subjects were the most optimistic about expecting cooperation from their partners. They apparently did not see other people as behaving like themselves. He also found that as the temptation to defect was increased by the change in the payoff matrix (and the threat of defection by the opponent also increased), the differences among the three kinds of subjects also decreased. As the situation pressure increased, the differences disappeared. Terhune concluded that "motives do predispose individuals to play the PD (Prisoner's Dilemma game) in different ways, but these differentials tend to be wiped out the more threatening is the situation" (1968, p. 10).

In the second series, consisting of an extended thirty-play game, the differences among the subjects tended to disappear, but the cooperation was highest among those subjects who were high in need for achievement and who had experienced cooperation in the first three games. Terhune concluded that motivation and experience tend to interact.

In the third series of thirty games, in which the subjects could communicate, cooperation increased for all three groups. Terhune analyzed the communication between the subjects and noted that the content of the communication did not seem to affect the cooperation. He concluded that the simple fact of coordination may be more important in cooperation than mistrust or hostility. The high-need-for-power subjects seemed to need a large number of coordinating messages to maintain cooperation. They wanted constant reminders of their opponent's intentions.

When asked to explain what they were doing, many subjects gave competitive reasons for their behavior on the first game series, but on the second series when cooperation prevailed, most explained their behavior in terms of mutual interests. On the first series, most players saw their opponent as a competitor, but on the second series most saw him as a co-worker.

Terhune concluded that: (1) motives do predispose people to behave in different ways in the game situation; (2) situation characteristics can be so dominant that motivational differences are minimized; (3) in extended social interaction, initial experiences have a marked effect on the development of subsequent cooperation or conflict; and (4) prevention of communication inhibits cooperation and minimizes motivational differences.

The most interesting finding in this study is that the high-need-for-achievement subjects were consistently the most cooperative, while the high-need-for-affiliation subjects were cooperative in the low-risk situation, but became defensive and competitive in the high-risk situation. This suggests that defensiveness may lead to as much conflict as aggressiveness.

Games have not yet provided an easy road to research on the effect of personality factors in interpersonal interaction. Indeed, the conflicting results produced by many studies are a repetition of the confusion found in other areas of personality research. However, the investigation of behavior in games in which factors are combined and the situation varied suggests an approach that may be fruitful for the sophisticated investigator.

Discussion

Game theory is promising because it presents a method for mathematically analyzing the interaction between people. Although this use of mathematics has not been fully developed and applied, it does represent the first step toward such a goal. Game research has not yet produced any information that could not have been obtained by other means, or even that has not already been obtained by other means. Any clinical psychologist knows that one defense against fear is aggression and that some of the most vicious fights between people are stimulated by threat, so Terhune's results are not exactly new and different. A growl often hides a trembling hand and a wildly beating heart. The most dangerous rat is a cornered rat. However, the practice of putting interactions into a format that is potentially representable in mathematical terms is a contribution of no small measure. This contribution is more a promise for the future than a performance for today, however.

There are several difficulties inherent in the game theory approach. One of the most basic is the assumption that people will behave in a rational fashion. As Vinacke (1969) points out, the evidence suggests that people do not always behave in a rational fashion and that, in fact, players may vary their strategy just to make the game more interesting, even though it lowers their payoff. Of course, this is no argument that the utility has necessarily been lowered for the subjects. Although they may get less payoff in terms of whatever the payoff numbers in the matrix represent, they may actually get more utility—that is, more personal payoff—by varying their strategy just out of curiosity to see what will happen. That is, the players' personal payoff matrices may be quite different from the payoff matrices provided by the game. We suggested this possibility in our discussion of the checkers game between the father and son. People obviously have very different payoff matrices, or they would not behave in such different ways. Some people get a very high payoff from racing automobiles, even though they may get very little or no monetary return. Other people wouldn't race an automobile for all the gold in the world. In terms of their payoff matrix, the potential gain may be high, but the potential loss—the risk—is too high, so they don't play.

A further difficulty in game theory is that the payoff matrices for people might change from day to day, or even from minute to minute. This is a basic weakness in the game approach to interpersonal interaction: How are payoff matrices to be determined for people? This weakness is not fatal, but it is one that will require a great deal of work to overcome. Earlier in the chapter the discussion of the lottery suggested one way in which payoff matrices might be constructed for people. Another way would be to study how people choose in decision-making situations. Those objectives they choose must have a higher payoff than the objectives ignored or rejected. Studying choice behavior provides a way of determining what people value and how much they value it.

The chapter on exchange theory (Chapter 8) suggests that the values in exchange theory matrices change from moment to moment, depending on what satisfactions people have recently received. Hungry people will value food quite highly—food has a high utility for them—but after they have eaten a large meal, the utility value of food drops substantially. Game-method suggests a mathematical approach to analyzing events, while exchange theory provides a psychological approach that could be easily wedded to the game-method.

Rapoport's suggestion that research should concentrate on the basic dimensions of games is fundamental. How people in general vary in their behavior as the games are varied along various dimensions must be determined before it will be possible to determine how personality factors affect the way people behave in game situations. The "base rate"—how people in general behave—has to be known before anything definite can be established about the ways in which people deviate.

Base-rate research is a methodological necessity, but it is not likely to be the primary focus of interest for psychologists. Psychologists will continue to be interested mostly in the kinds of things that affect the ways real people behave in the real world, and therefore will be interested in games mostly as a way of obtaining information in the laboratory that is useful in understanding and predicting the behavior of people outside the laboratory. A great deal of research on games has centered around conflict resolution and international diplomacy. However, the people who do this research (e.g., Pilisuk, Potter, Rapoport, & Winter, 1965) are not primarily interested in games, but rather in obtaining information that will be useful in bringing about world peace.

The data base of game theory, or to be more exact, the data obtained from research using the game theory approach, is quite narrow. Most of the subjects have been college students studied in the experimental laboratory. Analogies have been made with the real world, but little observational research has been done in real-life settings. There has been little attempt to relate game theory findings to clinical findings or to test clinical observations with game theory methods. The game approach could profit from a broadened base. Little is known about the responses of older people, of children, or of married couples who have various kinds of patterns of marital interaction, and so on. The game-method needs to be related to other methods of inquiry and should be used with a more diverse group of subjects. Further, the cooperative-versus-competitive response needs to be studied in a wider variety of situations and to be related to the results obtained in game research.

The level of data in game theory is at the level of the behavior segment. That is, the essential behavior studied is the competitive response versus the cooperative response. The research of Terhune which attempts to relate the behavior segment to personality factors, which are data at the level of the person, is an example of the kind of research that needs to be pursued. To some extent the individual behavior segments have been related to patterns of interaction. The studies of trends toward cooperation or competition are examples of patterns of interaction. This kind of research that relates the levels to each other needs to be extended.

The data obtained by the game approach to interpersonal relations is, for the most part, behavioral data. There have been occasional attempts to obtain reports in which the subjects explained what they thought they were doing, but these attempts have not been a common tactic. It would be helpful to obtain introspective reports from all sub-jects in game theory research. Then the experience of the individual could be related to the responses he made.

As a theory, game theory is peculiar. In a sense, it might not be considered a theory at all, but rather a research method. To the extent that it is a theory, it is primarily a mathematical theory, rather than a theory of interpersonal relationships. Its unique contribution is an at-tempt to mathematically represent the processes of interpersonal inter-action; in this regard, game theory is a hopeful infant. If those doing game research develop points of interaction with psychology and with the real world, the infant may ultimately deliver on its promise. If those researchers become bemused with the game theory technique as a technique, and if others ignore the gamesters as they play in their labo-ratory, then the infant will become a playboy.

Summary

Game theory began as a method of mathematically analyzing common games, but it was soon recognized as a technique for studying and mathematically representing conflict between people or groups. *Games* deal basically with making decisions within situations of conflict.

The basic assumption in games is that the *player* is rational; that is, he will choose the *strategy* in the game that will provide him with the highest payoff. Strategies may be pure or mixed. A *pure strategy* is one which the player continues to use because it will bring him the highest payoff, regardless of what his opponent does. A *mixed strategy* is composed of two or more pure strategies. In a mixed strategy the player switches from one strategy to another, or to others randomly, in such a way that he is using each strategy for a specified proportion of the plays. A *dominant strategy* is one that will provide a player with a payoff that is at least as high as the payoff that could be obtained by any other strategy in every situation and will provide a higher payoff than the other strategies in most situations. A *maximin strategy* is one in which the player chooses the strategy that will guarantee him at least a minimum payoff of some amount. A *minimax strategy* is one in which the player guarantees that his losses will not rise above a certain maxi-mum amount. In a bargaining situation the seller is generally trying to guarantee that he will get at least a minimum payment for the product he is selling, so he follows a maximin strategy; the buyer is trying to obtain the product for the lowest price, so he follows a minimax strate-gy. Where the strategies of the two players intersect is called the *sad-dle-point*. If the strategies chosen by the two players offer both their best result, the two are then in *equilibrium*. If either player, or both, could obtain a better payoff by switching strategies after both have chosen a strategy, then the solution is not in equilibrium, and the probability is high that one or both will switch.

A group of games that does not have stable equilibrium points is the group of *dilemma games*, in which the players are tempted to switch strategies in order to improve their payoff. The dilemma arises in that one player may gain by switching strategies, but both will lose if both players switch. Most of the research on games has centered on the dilemma games and the variables that dispose players to cooperate or compete on these games.

References

Buchler, I. B., & Nutini, H. G. (Eds.) *Game theory in the behavioral sciences*. Pittsburgh: University of Pittsburgh Press, 1969.

Edwards, W., Lindman, H., & Phillips, L. D. Emerging technologies for making decisions. *New directions in psychology*. Vol. II. New York: Holt, Rinehart & Winston, 1965.

Luce, R. D., & Raiffa, H. *Games and decisions*. New York: McGraw-Hill, 1957.

Pilisuk, M., Potter, P., Rapoport, A., & Winter, J. A. War hawks and peace doves: alternate resolutions of experimental conflicts. *Journal of Conflict Resolution*, 1965, 9, 491–508.

Rapoport, A. *Two-person game theory; the essential ideas*. Ann Arbor, Mich.: University of Michigan Press, 1966.

Rapoport, A. Exploiter, leader, hero, and martyr: the four archetypes of the 2 × 2 game. *Behavioral Science*, 1967, 12, 81–84.

Rapoport, A. Games as tools of psychological research. In I. B. Buchler & H. G. Nutini (Eds.), *Game theory in the behavioral sciences*. Pittsburgh: University of Pittsburgh Press, 1969.

Rapoport, A., & Chammah, A. M. The game of chicken. In I. B. Buchler & H. G. Nutini (Eds.), *Game theory in the behavioral sciences*. Pittsburgh: University of Pittsburgh Press, 1969.

Ryan, E. D., & Lakie, W. L. Competitive and noncompetitive performance in relation to achievement motive and manifest anxiety. *Journal of Personality and Social Psychology*, 1965, 1, 342–45.

Terhune, K. W. Motive, situation, and interpersonal conflict within Prisoner's Dilemma. *Journal of Personality and Social Psychology*, Monograph Supplement, 1968, 8 (3, Pt. 2).

Vinacke, W. E. Variables in experimental games: toward a field theory. *Psychological Bulletin*, 1969, 71, 293–318.

Von Neumann, J., & Morgenstern, O. *Theory of games and economic behavior*. Princeton, N. J.: Princeton University Press, 1947.

Williams, J. D. *The compleat strategyst*. New York: McGraw-Hill, 1954.

Additional Sources

Bales, R. F., & Borgatta (Eds.) *Small groups: studies in social interaction.* New York: Knopf, 1965.

Rapoport, A. *Fights, games, and debates.* Ann Arbor, Mich.: University of Michigan Press, 1960.

Rapoport, A., & Chammah, A. M. *Prisoner's Dilemma: a study in conflict and cooperation.* Ann Arbor, Mich.: University of Michigan Press, 1965.

Seigel, S., & Fouraker, L. E. *Bargaining and group decision making.* New York: McGraw-Hill, 1960.

Role Theory

12

Individuals in society occupy positions, and their role performance in these positions is determined by social norms, demands, and rules; by the role performances of others in their respective positions; by those who observe and react to the performance; and by the individual's particular capabilities and personality. . . . In essence, the role perspective assumes, as does the theater, that performance results from the social prescriptions and behavior of others, and that individual variations in performance, to the extent that they do occur, are expressed within the framework created by these factors (1966, p. 4).
— B. J. Biddle & E. J. Thomas

Perhaps the first point to be made about "role theory" is that there is no such thing as "the" role theory. Rather, role theory is a way of looking at what goes on between people. As Sarbin and Allen (1968) point out, the word "role" is a metaphor, and thus it carries certain implications. Since the concept of role was borrowed from the theater, its implications are theatrical in nature. In the theater a role is a specified part in a play. The words and actions of the part are prescribed by the script. The parts of a particular play remain the same, and the play wends its way to the same conclusion, regardless of the actors who perform the roles. Romeo and Juliet recite the same lines, and both die in the end. However, within the limits of the role, individual actors and actresses who have performed the parts of Romeo and Juliet have portrayed the roles differently. Every Romeo has not portrayed Romeo in the identical manner that all previous actors portrayed the part. So the concept of role implies that certain words and behaviors are required—each actor that plays Romeo does not ad lib his lines—but within the limits prescribed by the script, each individual actor has scope to portray the part in his own way. Romeo may be impassioned or languid, eager or reluctant, self-determined or moved by forces beyond his control.

Role theory (or theories) applies this metaphor to social interaction. In any social interaction there are parts which are being played and also certain prescribed words and actions. Taking a sample of the interactions in which I have engaged today, I can recall the following: (1) husband-wife, in which my wife and I discussed such topics as what we would eat for breakfast, whether or not we could visit her parents over the weekend, and whether or not we should go to the movies this evening; (2) father-son, in which my son and I discussed yesterday's baseball scores and what he had done with a thesis he had been reading; (3) professor-secretary, in which we discussed having some diagrams reproduced and when and how much her salary could be increased; (4) colleague-colleague (with several colleagues), in which we discussed hiring a particular person to fill a vacant faculty position, a variety of different kinds of research, the budgetary problems of universities, and social trends in the United States. In reviewing the interactions described above, it can be seen that the topics vary, depending on the relationship involved. Some of the topics would be appropriate to any of the relationships (e.g., social trends in the United States), while other topics would almost certainly be confined to one or a very few relationships (visiting wife's parents, having diagrams reproduced). That is, the relationship or the role prescribes certain behavior. I am expected to be responsible for supporting my wife and my son. I am not responsible for supporting my secretary or my colleagues. Neither they nor I expect it, and in fact, if I happened to be making private payments toward paying the rent for my secretary or one of my colleagues, other people who discovered this fact would be inclined to suspect that something irregular was going on.

Thus role theory is structured on the observable fact that there are certain kinds of transactions that are prescribed for certain kinds of relationships. The parent in the parent-child relationship is expected to provide for the material needs of the child. The teacher in the teacher-student relationship is expected to teach the student. The secretary in the secretary-boss relationship is expected to type the boss's letters. It is this regularity—more or less prescribed by any social system and observable in relationships between people—that provides the rationale for the application of the concept of role to the study of the interaction between people.

Definitions of Role

Some idea of the nature of the concept *role* may be gleaned from definitions of the term by a variety of writers on the topic. One such definition, that of Biddle and Thomas, was quoted at the beginning of the chapter. Another definition, by Sarbin and Allen, reflects the theatrical origins of the term. They define role in the following way:

> Role, a term borrowed directly from the theater, is a metaphor intended to denote that conduct adheres to certain "parts" (or positions) rather than to the players who read or recite them. In the semantics of the word "role" there is a historical continuity not usually found associated with words in psychological vocabularies. The current term developed out of several earlier forms, *roll, rolle,* and *rowle,* the reference for which is a sheet of parchment turned around a small wooden roller for convenience of handling (1968, p. 489).

Roger Brown's definition of role also reflects its theatrical origins:

> The word *role* is borrowed from the theater, and there is little in its social-psychological sense that is not prefigured in its theatrical sense. A role in a play exists independently of any particular actor, and a social role has also a reality that transcends the individual performer. Shakespeare's *Macbeth* has lasted for about 350 years; very many actors have passed in and out of the role and have proved shorter lived than the role. Actors are human beings; a role is a scenario prescribing certain actions and a script prescribing the lines to be spoken. Roles in society, too, are prescribed actions and words rather than persons (1965, p. 152).

Although a role is a part played, it also serves the function of placing a person in the social order, and thus prescribes to a certain extent how a given person will interact with another person occupying a different place in the social order. Romeo and Juliet played the parts of lovers, but they also were younger members of their own families, the Montagues and the Capulets. Had they been the heads of their respective families (assuming such a thing were possible), they may have been able to end the feud between the families and carry on their courtship in public. Since they occupied a social position that made such a solution impossible, it was necessary for them to interact in the way that led to the inevitable tragedy. Some definitions of role reflect the function of role as a position in a social structure. Lennard and Bernstein define role as follows:

> The concept of role refers to a configuration of acts that accompany status occupancy (for example, husband or therapist). To move up to still more complex levels of description, such as role systems, requires the fitting together of patterns of role behaviors (1969, p. 43).

Sargent and Williamson also reflect role as a concept defining a person's position within a social group:

> The concept of role, well established in sociology and anthropology, aids in describing and interpreting social interaction, especially within clearly defined groups. Role, as the social psychologist defines it, permits individual variation, stresses the perceptual factor and reciprocal nature of the interaction, and includes "situational" roles (1966, p. 415).

The Nature of Role Theory

As was indicated at the beginning of this chapter, there is no particular theory that can be identified and described as role theory. Rather, role theory is a metaphor—that is, a way of looking at the interaction between people—which has been borrowed from the theater. The concept has been used to study the interaction between people in many different contexts. The more common kinds of role interactions studied are the most obvious ones, such as those that occur in the family (husband-wife, father-child, mother-child) or within the contexts of daily life (teacher-student, leader-follower). Different researchers have developed their own vocabulary and their own constructs, so that there is no unified, generally accepted role theory as such. Shaw and Costanzo describe the situation in the following way:

> Role theory is a body of knowledge and principles which at one and the same time constitutes an orientation, a group of theories, loosely linked networks of hypotheses, isolated constructs about human functioning in a social context, and a language system which pervades nearly every social scientist's vocabulary. . . . Roles as the basic data within this "theoretical system" have been considered from many viewpoints: learning, cognitive, field-theoretical, sociocultural, and dynamic points of view. As such, role theory seems to be more of a subject matter than a theoretical framework (1970, p. 326).

It might be argued that role theory is actually a collection of "middle-range" theories that have some loose relationship among themselves, but which are not unified into one comprehensive scheme.

Robert Merton (1968) argues for the use of what he terms "middle-range" theories for maximizing the progress of sociology. By his definition, a middle-range theory is a theory which is applicable to a limited range of phenomena and is tied through empirical research to the phenomena it seeks to explain and describe. Merton uses his own role-set theory as an example of middle-range theory. A *role-set* is a group of interactions tied to one role. A teacher, for example, must interact with people occupying several other roles. The teacher interacts with students, with the school principal, with the superintendent of schools, with the supervisor of his own area of teaching, and with the parents of his students. All of these different interactions compose a role-set. Other examples of middle-range theory suggested by Merton include topics such as purposive action, social perception, reference groups, and social control. All of these topics either directly or tangentially apply to the concept of role and the elaboration of various forms of role theory. Therefore, if we used Merton's description of middle-range theory, role theory would appear to be an example of a collection of related middle-range theories.

As might be expected, the existence of several middle-range role theories creates certain problems. Among the more obvious problems is the matter of definition of terms. Different theorists use different words to apply to the same or very similar concepts, and different theorists also use the same word to mean different things. Also, one term might have both technical and popular meanings. Using different words to mean the same thing and the same word to mean different things leads to confusion. As Biddle and Thomas (1966) point out, role language has two shortcomings: lack of denotative clarity and incompleteness of language. Not every concept has a satisfactory word or phrase by which it may be identified.

In an attempt to bring some order out of semianarchy, Biddle and Thomas (1966) have classified the statements made by role theory into three categories: (1) single hypotheses (e.g., husbands are primarily concerned with supporting the family, while wives are primarily concerned with maintaining harmonious relationships within the family); (2) sets of logically unrelated hypotheses on the same topic (e.g., a series of hypotheses about the relationships between husbands and wives no two of which are directly related to each other); and (3) sets of logically, as well as topically, related hypotheses (e.g., a series of hypotheses about the relationships between husbands and wives, with each hypothesis fitting into a larger structure within which the hypotheses are related).

Two sets of authors, Biddle and Thomas (1966) and Sarbin and Allen (1968), have independently described and ordered the constructs used in role theory. The following discussion will present the main features of the ordering of both pairs of authors.

Role Theory

Biddle and Thomas developed the more abstract and logically consistent scheme for ordering the various concepts of role theory. Their scheme might be described as a step toward an integrated role theory. Since theirs is a larger and more integrated description of role theory, it is, of necessity, more abstract than the description by Sarbin and Allen. As this chapter progresses, we shall move from the more abstract to the more particular, describing first the general outline of Biddle and Thomas. This will be followed by a more extensive discussion of the concepts of role theory, following the outline used by Sarbin and Allen, with some revisions and additions. Sarbin and Allen's description of role concepts stays closer to the data of role research, and more nearly fulfills Merton's description of middle-range theory than does the Biddle and Thomas scheme. Finally, in the last two sections of the chapter, role theory will be discussed as it has been applied to research in two areas of interpersonal interaction, marriage and psychotherapy.

The Four Categories of Role Concepts of Biddle and Thomas

Biddle and Thomas (1966, Ch. 2) classify the phenomena of role into four basic categories:

1. Terms for partitioning persons;
2. Terms for partitioning behaviors;
3. Terms for partitioning sets of persons and behaviors;
4. Terms for relating sets of persons and behaviors.

In the following paragraphs, these categories will be discussed.

1. The first category has to do with classifying people. Within this category would be included all the ways in which role theorists distinguish among the persons they study. The first kind of classification of people, which is so obvious that it is usually not even noted, is the distinction between the people studied and the people not studied. This is the kind of categorization that is generally implied rather than explicitly defined. If, for example, some researchers study the interaction between husbands and wives, they implicitly exclude other people such as children, in-laws, and work colleagues of the husband and wife. Only husbands and wives are studied; everybody else is not studied.

The most common partitioning of people in studying interaction is the distinction between the self and the other person. The one behaving is the self, or the actor, and the person toward whom the behavior is directed is the target, or the other or the alter. Of course, in studying an ongoing interaction between two people, the self and the other alternate as the interaction proceeds.

Another dimension along which people can be partitioned is number. When studying role, researchers may be talking about one person, or a group of persons, or all persons. Or the researchers may study particularized persons. Particularized persons are identifiable kinds of persons such as husbands or wives—that is, persons occupying a particular role. Reference persons and reference groups are individuals or aggregates of individuals who are referred to in some way. They are a group whose judgments or values are a reference to which the person behaving compares his own behavior. However, they are not, strictly speaking, behavers, but rather persons to whom the person behaving refers.

2. Terms for partitioning behaviors refer to specific behaviors which are classified. The first kind of behavior is *action*, which is generally considered to have been learned, and which is voluntary. *Role performance* and *role behavior* are common terms that refer to the action of a person performing a role. In partitioning behavior, evaluation of that behavior or performance is implied. That is, when one performs, one of the implicit aspects of the description of that performance is whether or not the performance included all of the behaviors that are expected to be included in the performance of the role. A mathematics teacher, for example, is supposed to teach mathematics. This is an "expectancy" of that role. If an expectancy, or *role expectation*, is stated overtly, then Biddle and Thomas call it a *role demand*. If the expectancy is covert, they term it a *norm*. Whether overt or covert, every role has prescriptions which specify what behaviors are expected from the person who occupies the role.

In addition to the prescriptions, or expectations, of the behavior that will be performed by people occupying a role, there is also the *evaluation* of how well they performed the role. Mathematics teachers may teach mathematics, but they may teach mathematics well or poorly. Their students may learn how to solve algebra problems, or they may merely gain a vague idea of what algebra is about. Biddle and Thomas term overt evaluation *assessment* and covert evaluation *values*.

Any behavior that is performed may be described, without prescription or evaluation. This *description* of behavior may be overt, which Biddle and Thomas call a *statement*, or the description may be covert, which is termed a *conception*. Biddle and Thomas consider most role descriptions in research literature to be conceptions rather than statements.

Finally, there are *sanctions*, which are the consequences of behavior. Sanctions might be considered behavior in response to behavior. A sanction is behavior that is designed to change the behavior of the other person. Punishment, reward, and incentives are sanctions, as are school grades, pats on the head, jail sentences, salaries, and bonuses.

Biddle and Thomas point out that the five kinds of partitions of behavior described above (action, expectancy, evaluation, description, and sanction) are independent of one another. Some behavior may be partitioned in more than one way. Behavior that is an action can also be a sanction. If someone insults me, and I respond by punching him in the nose, my punching him in the nose is both a role behavior (probably in violation of a norm, since college professors are not generally expected to punch people in the nose) and a sanction (since most people won't utter insults which they expect to bring physical retaliation). Of course, if the person I punched in turn punched me, then his behavior would also be both an action and a sanction—and so on, until one of us altered his behavior in a more adaptive direction.

3. Terms for partitioning persons and their behaviors include positions and roles. A *position* usually refers to a collectively recognized category of persons. This category is one that is distinct in the minds of most people. *Ascribed categories* are categories into which people are born or placed through no effort or behavior of their own. Such categories might be based on age (child, teenager, middle-aged), on sex (male, female), or on ethnic group (Mexican-American, Puerto Rican, Italian-American, Navajo). *Achieved categories* are based on a position people have come to occupy through some behavior. Examples are husband, wife, lawyer, teacher, murderer. This position is a collectively recognized category of persons who all have one characteristic or behavior in common.

The concept of role also falls within partitions for persons and behaviors. The person aspect of the concept applies to particular kinds of people who occupy a particular role. A person occupying the role of "mathematics teacher" falls within certain person categories. A mathematics teacher falls within a certain age group (probably twenty years old or older), within the category of persons having received a certain amount of education (probably a college degree in mathematics or mathematics education), and finally, within the category of the "employed." A mathematics teacher also performs certain behaviors that go with teaching mathematics. Thus the role "mathematics teacher" includes persons falling within certain categories who behave in ways that fall within certain behavior categories.

4. The fourth category for partitioning role phenomena deals with the relationships among the three categories that have already been described. The discussion of the relationship among partitions applies primarily to partitions of behavior or partitions of persons and behavior. Actually, relationships apply mostly to roles—that is, relationships among roles—and roles are classified by Biddle and Thomas as coming under partitions of persons and behaviors.

There are three criteria for relating the categories of persons, behaviors, and persons and behaviors: (1) the degree of similarity or dissimilarity among the partitions; (2) the determination or interdependence among the partitions; and (3) the combined criteria of similarity and determination.

Similarity or dissimilarity in the relationship of partitions is largely in role behavior, role expectation, role evaluation, or sanctions. That is, it is mostly a matter of agreement or disagreement among people on who did what, who should do what, who should be expected to do what, or what should be done about somebody who has done something. If there is agreement (similarity), then there is *consensus*. If there is disagreement (dissimilarity), then there is *dissensus*. There are two kinds of dissensus, polarized and nonpolarized. *Polarized dissensus* is when the persons involved congregate around two poles of opinion, the poles being in opposition to each other: He is guilty or he is not guilty; he should be put in jail or he should be given a medal; we should invest or we should not invest. *Nonpolarized dissensus* is when there is no agreement on anything — everyone has a different opinion.

The second criterion of partition relationship is interdependence. Two roles may be independent, which means that whether or not one person fulfills his role has nothing to do with a second person performing his own role. It is not necessary for third-grade mathematics teachers to do their jobs well in order for the fourth-grade English teachers to perform their roles. However, if the fourth-grade mathematics teachers are to do their jobs, the third-grade mathematics teachers must first have done their jobs. Likewise, it is not necessary for the shortstop to do anything in order for the center fielder to catch a fly ball, but it is essential for the shortstop to field a grounder if the second baseman is to perform his part in a double play. Interdependence, when it occurs, means that one person performing one role may either facilitate the second person in the performance of his role (the shortstop throws accurately to the second baseman) or hinder the second person in the performance of his role (the shortstop makes a bad throw to the second baseman); the first person may even make it impossible for the second person to perform his role (the shortstop throws the ball over the second baseman's head).

The third criteria of relationship is a combination of the first two, similarity and determination. For example, a father and mother would be different in sex and perhaps in function or behavior and yet highly interdependent in playing their roles. As persons they would be different, though their role relationships would be highly interdependent.

Biddle and Thomas represent their classification of the categories of role concept in matrix form in Figure 1. In this figure, the horizontal axis represents the partition for persons, and the vertical axis represents the partition for behaviors. The intersection of the person segment and the behavior segment represents the cell (or cells) of the person-behavior segment. Each column (P_1, P_2, etc.) contains all the behaviors of a given person or group of persons regardless of whether the behavior is or is not a part of the role being studied. Each row (C_1,

FIGURE 1. **THE PERSON-BEHAVIOR MATRIX AND ITS SEGMENTS**

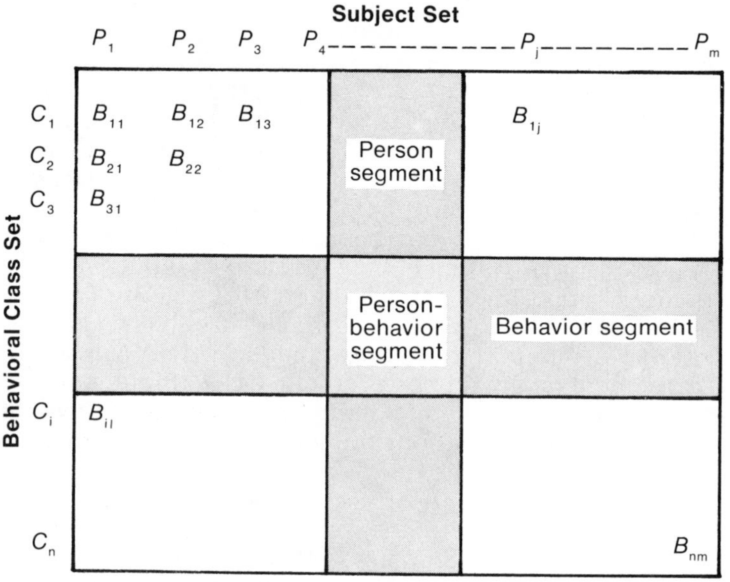

From B. J. Biddle & E. J. Thomas, *Role theory: concepts and research.* New York: John Wiley & Sons, Inc., 1966, p. 30. Copyright © 1966 by John Wiley & Sons, Inc., and reproduced by permission of John Wiley & Sons, Inc.

C_2, etc.) registers all of the persons behaving in a certain way regardless of who those people might be. A particular role is represented by a combination of persons behaving in the ways that go with that role. Therefore, the figure contains a representation of the first three categories of role concept—that is, persons, behaviors, and persons and behaviors combined. Biddle and Thomas do not refer to the fourth category relationships among the first three categories, when discussing their matrix; we might infer, however, that those columns and cells that are closest to each other are the most similar, while those farthest from each other are the most dissimilar.

Sarbin and Allen's Description of the Phenomena Studied in Role Research

In this section we will summarize the Sarbin and Allen (1968) discussion of role theory, more or less following their organization, but with some additions and some reorganization.

Role Enactment. Role enactment is the actual social behavior performed by people in a role. Observations of role enactment lead to judgments of how appropriate the exhibited behavior is for the role being played and how adequately the behavior is performed — whether it is a good performance or a poor performance. Since role enactment is behavior, this category fits into Biddle and Thomas's partitions for behavior.

The dimensions of role enactment are:

1. The number of roles a given actor plays;
2. The degree of organismic involvement of an actor in a given role;
3. The preemptiveness, or amount of time spent in a role.

Within a group there are many roles to be played. Some of these roles are prescribed by certain criteria. That is, in a family there can be the roles of father, mother, son, and daughter. In addition to these roles there are other roles, such as dishwasher, first-aid dispenser, financial manager, comedian, and so on. Within a family, if it is an extended family which includes three generations, a person might play the roles of parent, sibling, and spouse, and in addition, might play the functional roles of breadwinner, financial manager, and first-aid dispenser. One person may play several roles within one social system. Within a marriage a man may play the roles of husband, father, son, and brother in relation to his wife, who in her turn plays wife to his husband, daughter to his father, mother to his son, and sister to his brother. Sarbin and Allen, among others, point out that the more roles people have in their repertoires, the more different kinds of situations they are prepared to handle.

Organismic involvement is a dimension that is concerned with how deeply people are involved in the role they are playing. Sarbin and Allen describe eight levels of involvement (see Figure 2). (Zero) The zero level indicates no involvement, meaning the role is not played. An example of this is the husband who never comes home. (I) Casual role enactment involves the actor in a temporary and off-handed sort of way. A browser in a bookstore is not very involved in the role of customer. (II) Ritual acting is played almost automatically and perhaps mechanically. A checker at the cash register of a supermarket may mark up the items bought by a customer while daydreaming about plans for the evening. In ritual acting the behavior for the role is performed, but the person doing the performing is not really consciously involved in the action. (III) Engrossed acting is performed by a person who is involved in the role being played. A professor giving an important lecture or a student working hard on a term paper are engrossed in the role they are playing. (IV) In classical hypnotic role-taking, the person has a high degree of engrossment in the role being played. An example of

FIGURE 2. SCALE REPRESENTING DIMENSION OF ORGANISMIC INVOLVEMENT

Role and self differentiated Zero involvement Few organic systems No effort	Role and self undifferentiated Maximal involvement Entire organism Much effort

Zero. Noninvolvement

I. Casual role enactment

II. Ritual acting

III. Engrossed acting

IV. Classical hypnotic role-taking

V. Histrionic neurosis

VI. Ecstasy

VII. Object of sorcery and
witchcraft (sometimes
irreversible)

From T. R. Sarbin & V. L. Allen, "Role theory," in *The handbook of social psychology*, Volume I, Second edition, edited by G. Lindzey & E. Aronson. Reading, Mass.: Addison-Wesley, 1968, p. 493. © 1968, Addison-Wesley, Reading, Mass., and reproduced by permission.

this is a person who is in an hypnotic trance and is behaving in accordance with an hypnotist's instructions. (V) Histrionic neurosis overlaps the amount of involvement of the previous two categories, but this role involvement lasts for a longer period of time than does the hypnotic role. In this case, the person undertakes a role that becomes, at least for a time, a way of life. This level can include persons suffering the seizures, anesthesias, or paralyses that are found in hysterics. (VI) In ecstasy there is a suspension of voluntary action; the person is totally under the effect of the role. The mystic in the midst of a mystical experience is in ecstasy. (VII) Bewitchment involves the person to such an extent that the role may be permanent and irreversible. A person undergoing a voodoo death exemplifies this; also, the paranoid schizophrenic who is in a psychotic state approximates bewitchment.

The third dimension of role enactment is preemptiveness, or the amount of time spent in a role. Variability of time is primarily applicable to roles that people have achieved—that is, that they have come into through their own behavior. Ascribed roles, into which people have been placed by birth or circumstance, are usually full-time roles. That is, people born female are female all the time, and people twenty years old are twenty years old all the time for a year. On the other hand, people who are taxicab drivers may drive their cab forty hours of the week, but may spend varying amounts of the remainder of the week playing the roles of parent, sibling, spouse, golfer, etc.

Role enactment is largely learned behavior. As learned behavior, it is learned in all the kinds of ways other behavior is learned, including reinforcement, imitation, and so on. Part of this learning is cognitive. That is, in learning a role a person learns what people in that role do and what people in that role are expected to do (see Hartley, 1966). One aspect of learning a role, the anticipatory aspect of entering a role, is acquiring the values and practicing the behavior that is expected in that role (see Merton, 1966). Sarbin (1964) described a formula which includes the factors involved in effective role enactment. The formula is: Effective Role Enactment = f (accuracy of perception of roles of the other [s] and of role demands, a set of valid role expectations, role-relevant skills or aptitudes, self-role congruence, and reinforcement properties in the social ecology). In the sections that follow, the meaning of the terms contained within this formula will become clear.

Role Expectations. Role expectations are the rights and obligations, duties and privileges that go with a role. The expectations are what people are supposed to do when they play a particular role — a shortstop is supposed to catch ground balls that are hit toward him, a husband is supposed to relate to his wife, and a teacher is supposed to teach. A person who is in a role interacts with other people — a teacher interacts with students, with the principal, and with the students' parents. The role and the others with whom a person in a role interacts make up what is termed a *role-set*. A person who occupies a certain role is expected to perform certain acts in certain ways. The appropriate acts are also expected to be performed at the right time, at the right place, and in the right way.

Role expectations vary along certain dimensions. One dimension is generality or specificity; some roles are very specifically defined, while others are broad and general. The role of airplane pilots on a scheduled airliner is very specifically defined. Their duties and obligations are spelled out in detail. On the other hand, people's expectations as spouses are spelled out only in a general kind of way. The way one pilot flies a particular plane and the way another pilot flies that same plane will be quite similar, since the procedures are specified for them in great detail. Both pilots may be married, and the ways in which they fulfill the role of spouse may be quite different, and yet both could be deemed successful in their roles.

Roles also vary in their scope, or extensiveness. Some roles may occupy much of a person's life. The role of a monk in a monastery is generally a full-time role. However, the role of a customer in a store is short-term and applies to a very narrow segment of a person's life. Roles also vary in their degree of clarity or uncertainty. To return to the airline pilots, their role is highly specified insofar as their behavior while they are flying a plane is concerned. However, if a pilot attends a party which is composed of people with whom he is not acquainted, he would find himself playing the role of guest, with no clear idea of what behavior he is supposed to perform. If it is a party of college students, one set of behavior might be expected; if it is a party held by a religious organization, another set of behavior might be expected. Most people feel self-conscious at social gatherings in which they are strangers. This feeling of uncertainty and self-consciousness is the result of being uncertain of the behavior expected by this group of people. Lack of role clarity results in ineffective instrumental and affective interaction. If people don't know what kind of behavior is expected, they are likely to be ineffective in interacting with other people. Sarbin and Allen describe three kinds of lack of role clarity: (1) ambiguity about role expectations, which is the situation at a party with strangers; (2) lack of agreement among the people occupying the complementary roles in the role-set as to what kind of behavior should be expected of one occupying a given role; (3) lack of agreement between the expectations for the role held by the person performing the role and the people with whom he is interacting.

Role expectations vary in the degree of consensus on the expectations for the role. For some roles there is a high degree of consensus as to what is expected (e.g., a traffic policeman) but for other roles there may be little agreement or even wide disagreement over what is expected (e.g., woman in modern society). For some roles there may even be high agreement about some aspects of the role and high disagreement over other aspects of the role. This state of affairs is probably most likely to be encountered in roles which are in a process of change (e.g., the role of minister or priest.)

Finally, roles vary in the degree of their formality. Some roles are formally a part of society while other roles are informal and no regular or specified part of society. The role of husband or wife or teacher are all formal, specified parts of society and have specified expectations. Other roles—the "life of the party," the village drunk, or the neighborhood gossip—are informal roles and have no specified expectations, although we might easily recognize the town drunk or the neighborhood gossip should we encounter them.

Role expectations have the characteristics of norms. That is, the expectations serve as a kind of measure against which the fulfillment of the role is measured. If the expectations are not fulfilled, then the person holding the expectations is likely to be disturbed by the lack of fulfillment. If people who are performing a role fail to fulfill their own expectations for that role, they will be disappointed in themselves and may even feel guilty about it. If the expectations of the other people in the role-set are not fulfilled, they will be disappointed and dissatisfied. Secord and Backman (1966, Ch. 14) describe five characteristic properties of norms: (1) Norms shape behavior in the direction of the values of the norms. People tend to behave in accordance with their expectations for a role. (2) Norms vary in the degree to which they are related to important values. Some expectations are quite closely tied to values. Bank tellers are expected to give an exact and honest account of the money they handle. If they do not handle money honestly, they will certainly lose their job and be sent to jail. Bank tellers are also expected to be friendly and pleasant to the customers of the bank, but if they fail to smile at customers and engage in small talk with them, no great value is involved. (3) Norms are enforced by the behavior of others. Dishonest bank tellers are discharged; unfriendly bank tellers are not smiled at by customers. (4) Norms vary as to how widely they are shared. Honesty by bank tellers is a norm widely shared; friendliness by bank tellers is less widely shared. (5) Norms vary in the range of behavior they permit. There is little variation in the expectation of accuracy and honesty on the part of bank tellers. There is somewhat wider variation in the expectation of friendliness from bank tellers. Some people might welcome the opportunity to spend the morning gossiping with the teller, while others might prefer to transact their financial business with a minimum of social amenity.

As should be obvious from the discussion thus far, the expectations held for the performance of a role affect the way a role is performed. If two people in a role-set have different expectations about the performance of the role, it follows that one of them will be disappointed in the performance of the role. If a wife expects her husband to give her daily reassurances of his love, but the husband expects that his role requires protestations of love only at appropriate occasions like New Year's Eve and wedding anniversaries, it seems likely that his wife will be disappointed. If a person fails to meet the important expectations others have for his role, he is likely to be removed from the role. His wife may divorce him, or his boss may fire him.

While considering role norms, it might be worthwhile to mention another norm for the interaction between people that has received little attention in research, but which might be of more importance than has thus far been suspected. Gouldner (1966) identifies the existence of what he terms the norm of reciprocity: "Social system stability . . . presumably depends in part on the mutually contingent exchange of gratifications, that is, on reciprocity as exchange" (1966, p. 139). Reciprocity implies that in any relationship each side has rights and obligations, so

> . . . reciprocity has its significance for role systems in that it tends to structure each role so as to include both rights and duties. . . . the norm of reciprocity, in its universal form, makes two interrelated, minimal demands: (a) people should help those who have helped them, and (b) people should not injure those who have helped them (Gouldner, 1966, p. 140).

A final rather interesting note about role norms is that violating minor role norms may not necessarily be a bad thing. Roger Brown observes that "one acquires a 'character,' a perceptible personality, by violating minor role norms" (1965, p. 155). Jones, Davis, and Gergen (1966) found that in playing a role, people who completely met role expectations were judged *not* to have revealed themselves, while people who did violate role expectations were seen as revealing more of themselves. This phenomenon may be observed in the judgment the public makes of public figures. Those figures who meet all social norms are often considered bland or stuffy, while those who violate relatively unimportant norms are seen as more "human" and as having a more clearly definable personality; thus they are better liked by the public. A little eccentricity helps popularity.

Role Location. Role location, or choice of role, is a cognitive process by which people locate themselves and other people in the social system. Back in the days of chivalry, when men gave their seats to women on buses and other public conveyances, this process could often be observed in action. When a woman entered a bus on which all the seats were taken, the men on the bus would look around to see if there were other men on the bus and, if so, whether any of them were rising to give the newly arrived woman passenger a seat. If only one man were on the bus, it became his obvious duty to rise and give the woman a seat.

Sarbin and Allen describe the role placement of others as following a pattern of four steps. The first step is the major premise, which is a proposition that states which cues go with which positions. The second step is the minor premise, which links the current sensory inputs with an individual. The third step is the conclusion, which links the subject of the minor premise with the major premise. The fourth step is the implication, which is the adoption of the appropriate role behavior for one occupying one's own role position. If we apply this process to a woman climbing on a bus, the steps for a man on the bus are: (1) Women are identified by certain cues, such as dresses, long hair, etc.; (2) this person climbing on the bus has a dress on and long hair, etc.; so (3) she is a woman; therefore, (4) if there are no other men present, I should rise and give her my seat. If there are other men present, I will wait for someone else to give her a seat. (Of course, it is easily discernible that this example is a bit archaic. A more appropriate example today would be the circumstance in which a very old person gets on a bus. In this case, any younger person would probably adopt the role of offering his seat to the person.)

Role Demands. Role demands are what lead people to act in certain ways in given situations. These demands are the subtle cues in the environment or from another person that, in effect, prompt a person occupying a role to behave in certain ways. Biddle and Thomas classify norms and demands as partitions of behavior, with norms being covert and demands being overt behavior partitions. Sarbin and Allen consider role demands to be extensions of the folkways and mores of the culture. Aspects of role demands are often revealed when a mistake is made. For example, when a shopper cannot find a certain article, he then searches for a store employee to ask where the sought article might be found. This behavior on the part of the shopper is a role demand. The employee is expected to tell the shopper whether or not the store handles the article and where that article might be found if it is in stock. If another customer is standing around with no apparent purpose, he is likely to be mistaken for an employee of the store, and thus may be the target of the questions of other shoppers. This mistake reveals one of the common role demands of the supermarket employee.

Demands are subtle cues a person puts out to another person, thus "pulling" from the other person the desired behavior. A role norm or expectation is what that other person is expected to do. When that expectation is translated into an action which indicates what is expected from the other person, it has become a demand.

Role Skills. Some people have more of the required skills to play a particular role than others. Sarbin and Allen divide role skills into two components, *cognitive skills* and *motoric skills.* Cognitive skills are those skills with which a person detects his position in the social system, the position of the other people in the social system, and what those other people expect of him in his role. This skill is sometimes referred to as social perceptiveness, social intelligence, sensitivity, or empathy. It is the ability to discern what is going on and what is expected. People who repeatedly make social errors probably lack cognitive skills. Motor skills are those skills that a person exercises in carrying out the appropriate acts for the role or in producing the appropriate facial expressions. Athletics are the most obvious arena for the exercise of motor skills in performing roles. To return to the shortstop, if he lacks the necessary motor skills, he is more likely to fail than to succeed in playing the role of shortstop. This kind of failure can be observed with great frequency in Little-League baseball games. Comedies often utilize lack of motor skill, as in the waiter who spills soup, or the Sunday plumber who can't get the pipes back together.

In the literal playing of roles as roles, some people have greater role-playing skills than others. Coe and Sarbin (1966) demonstrated that drama students, who presumably have both role-playing aptitude and training, perform roles better than science students, who have had no role-playing training and probably less role-playing aptitude as well.

Self-Role Congruence. To play a role satisfactorily, a person must have a self-concept that fits the role. As Sarbin and Allen discuss the problem of self-role fit, they appear to have included within self-concept such variables as values and personality characteristics. They cite, for example, a study involving personality characteristics by Smelser (1961), in which pairs of subjects were given a problem-solving task in which the subjects were to operate two model railroad trains. In the task there were two roles: the dispatcher who was to plan the solutions and the other person who was to carry out the dispatcher's orders. Smelser found that the most productive pairs were composed of one person who was dominant (as determined by prior personality measurement) and who served as the dispatcher, and a second person who was submissive. No other combination of personality types worked as well. That is, people assigned to roles that fit their personality characteristics performed more satisfactorily. Probably the same results would be obtained in relationship to values. Ministers who have no faith in God would probably not serve satisfactorily as ministers. Sales manuals often stress the necessity for good salespeople to believe in their product. A Ford salesperson who really believed that the Chevrolet was a superior automobile would probably not be very successful.

Much of the research on personnel selection and placement might be viewed as an attempt to first assess the ability, aptitude, and personality characteristics required for the satisfactory performance of a role (scientist, teacher, business executive). This research also is concerned with the development of methods of measurement that will detect which people possess the characteristics necessary for the satisfactory performance of the role.

Audience. The audience is whoever watches the role performance. The audience may be a third person who is observing the interaction between two people, it may be the other person to whom the actor's behavior is being directed, it may be the actor himself, it may be a group of people who are observing the action, or it may be a person or a group present only in the mind of the actor.

One kind of group or person who may not be present is the reference group. The reference group is a group whose opinion or values are of importance to the person performing the role. A college professor lecturing a class has both the members of the class and himself as an audience that is present, but the professor probably also has in his mind another audience, his colleagues, against whose values and standards he measures his performance in the role of lecturer. He may, in the lecture, mention by name such colleagues as might support or disagree with the conclusions he presents to the class. References to other people in a lecture might be taken as evidence of the reference group which exists for the lecturer.

Reference groups are important since they are a source of norms for the performance of a role. Ordinarily a reference group is a group to which the performer of a role belongs and whose values are important to the performer. Merton (1969) points out that membership in a group does not necessarily mean passionate devotion to the values of that group, and that a person may use the values of a reference group in all situations or only in a few situations. Most college students belong to a family and have some awareness of the values of their family or their parents (a reference group), but may make decisions that do not agree with their perception of their parents' values. The mention of the fact that "My mother would like that," or "If my father knew this he would be furious," is evidence of the existence of a reference group that is not physically present.

The audience serves several functions in role performance. The audience may apply sanctions to the performance. That is, the audience may reward or punish the performance. In school the teacher, as an audience, applies sanctions by giving grades. Sanctions serve to reward or punish performance, and as such are designed to maintain a particular kind of performance (in the case of reward), or to change the performance (in the case of punishment). A mother who sends her son to bed without supper for coming home late from play is an audience who is applying a sanction (sending the boy to bed without his supper) to the performance (coming home late from play) in order to change the performance (to coming home for supper on time).

The audience supports the performance of a role by accepting the performance as valid. Accepting a performance as valid is a little difficult to discriminate from reinforcing the performance through reward or punishment; it should be apparent, however, that there is a difference between accepting a performance as being the valid enactment of a role, on the one hand, and approving or disapproving of that performance, on the other hand. One may accept Hitler's invasion of Denmark as a valid performance of the Chancellor of the Third Reich, but at the same time disapprove of that action and apply sanctions against it by engaging in war against him.

The audience also provides a cue property to the performer, showing him how to perform the role. If a lecturer is explaining something to another person, and that other person exhibits a quizzical expression or asks "What do you mean?" the lecturer knows that the other person is not getting the message, so he elaborates his explanation. Lecturers, if they are accomplished in the role of lecturer, learn to read the expressions on the faces of their audience in order to tell whether or not the message is being understood—that is, if the role is being played properly. A large number of blank faces is a cue to the lecturer that his audience is not following the lecture. Likewise, saying "Ouch!" to a "painless" dentist is a cue that tells him that he is not playing his role properly.

Finally, an audience serves to maintain role behavior over time. By reinforcement, cue properties, and so on, the audience tends to maintain a person in the same role. Graduate students who stay on to teach at the school at which they studied usually find it difficult to get out of the student role and into the teacher role, because the audience continues to see them as students and to give them the cues and reinforcements that maintain them in the student role. Sarbin and Allen write that "a person desiring to change his role behavior drastically usually finds it difficult, if not impossible, without a geographical change. To change behavior he must escape the previous audiences which helped maintain and sustain role enactment" (1968, p. 534).

Complex Role Phenomena. Complex role phenomena derive from the fact that people play many roles. Sometimes people may play several roles simultaneously, while at other times they may play several roles in sequence. However, this complexity of roles makes for confusion and conflict.

How does a person handle all these roles? Sarbin and Allen cite Linton (1945), who suggests that sometimes only one role is activated, with the other roles being "latent." Second, there may be a merging of two or more roles; or third, multiple roles may alternate, with first one then another role being played. Finally, informal roles may interpenetrate into the formal role system. Take the situation of a man attending dinner with his extended family, which includes his parents, his siblings, his wife, and his children. He may, in sequence, play the role of husband, son, father, and brother. If he alternated roles, depending on the other person with whom he was interacting, he would be following the third alternative mentioned above. However, it is more likely that in a discussion, he would merge the roles of son, husband, and brother into the role of adult—that is, as a peer, interacting with other adults. If his children were still children, he would probably behave as a parent toward them.

A person occupying a particular role interacts with other people who occupy roles that are complementary to him. This situation is termed by Merton (1969) a *role-set*. By role-set Merton means "that complement of role relationships which persons have by virtue of occupying a particular social status" (1969, p. 423). We have already given the example of the teacher who, as a teacher, must interact with students, other teachers, principals, superintendents and parents. The teacher and the persons in the other, interacting roles compose a role-set.

The fact that a person occupies many roles at the same time and also must interact with a variety of people occupying other roles, creates a situation in which conflict may occur. Sarbin and Allen describe two kinds of role conflict, *inter-role conflict* and *intra-role conflict*. Inter-role conflict occurs when one role a person is playing comes into conflict with another, different role he is playing. A teacher who had his own child in his class would have an inter-role conflict between his roles as teacher and parent. Now, let us suppose that this teacher-parent discovered his child cheating on a test. What should he do? Report the child to the principal or lecture him as a parent—or both? Most teachers avoid this problem by not teaching their own children, but this might be difficult if the parent were the only person in town who taught the subject his child wanted to learn. Another example is the man who is a policeman when a tornado strikes his town. Does he remain at his post as a policeman, helping those he is directed to help, or does he revert to his role as a husband and father and run to his own home to help his family?

A more common form of conflict is intra-role conflict. Intra-role conflict is divided into two types by Brown (1965). In the first type, many persons occupying the same role disagree on how a complementary role should be played. The second kind occurs when people occupying different complementary roles disagree on how the complementary role should be played. The teacher can serve as an example of both kinds of intra-role conflict. A class of students disagreeing on how the teacher should teach a subject is an example of the first kind of intra-role conflict. I taught a graduate course in psychotherapy at one time. At the end of each semester I asked the students how the course could be improved. Invariably one group of students expressed a desire for the course to contain more practical material while another group of students expressed a desire for the course to contain more theoretical material. Then there was a third group who opined that the course would be improved if it contained less material, regardless of the content. It was impossible to satisfy everyone; what one wanted more of, another wanted less of. With the teacher again as an example, the second type of intra-role conflict can be demonstrated. The students may think that the teacher gives too much homework, and the parents may feel he gives too little homework; the principal may be indifferent to the homework, but wants the teacher to maintain an orderly classroom (which conflicts with the students' desires that he maintain a free classroom); and finally, the superintendent may be concerned with the teacher keeping the parents happy, even though this may conflict with what the students or the principal want. The teacher cannot satisfy all those occupying different roles complementary to his own.

Beyond this disagreement as to how a role is played, there may also be disagreement among the members of the role-set as to the norms they think are held by other members of the role-set. Biddle and Thomas (1966) studied the norms teachers held for themselves and the norms others thought teachers held for themselves, and found wide disagreement among teachers, students, parents, and school administrators.

Still another kind of intra-role conflict occurs when there is conflict between one person playing one role and another person playing a complementary role. This happens when there is inconsistent role expectation on the part of the complementary person. This kind of conflict is especially observed between adolescents and their parents. The parents complain about the adolescent asking for advice, then when the advice is given, the adolescent insists he wants to make up his own mind and gets tired of being told what to do. The adolescent complains that his parents tell him to "grow up" but that when he tries to make a grown-up decision they tell him he is too young to take such a step. This kind of intra-role conflict occurs when persons occupying complementary roles are inconsistent in their role demands. This last kind of intra-role conflict is most likely to occur when the relationship between the pair is changing. The relationship between a parent and an adolescent is changing from a parent-child relationship to an adult-adult relationship. Secord and Backman (1966) note that role strain is especially likely to occur when new roles are emerging. Lovers' quarrels, for example, serve the function of redefining the respective roles of the two persons. This suggests that when two people who have maintained a harmonious relationship over a period of time begin to have conflict, a change in their role relationship is taking place. And conversely, when a change in role relationship takes place between two people, the possibility of conflict between them rises.

Role conflict raises the problem of how such conflicts are resolved. Sarbin and Allen describe five ways in which role strain may be eliminated.

1. A person may use instrumental acts to solve the situation. This might involve redefining the role so that the conflict is eliminated, it might mean merging roles so that the conflict is eliminated, or it might mean ending the role relationship. An example of the latter is a person who is appointed to an important government office and who is required to end any financial involvement he may have in a business that might possibly profit from decisions he makes as a government official. What is called "conflict of interest" is really a conflict of role.
2. A person may resolve role strain through a change in attention deployment. One role is attended to and the conflicting role ex-

pectation is ignored. There are probably many times when the President of the United States attends to his role as President and ignores his role as father and husband. Politicians often complain that the President (whoever he might be) also pays little attention to his role as the head of his political party.

3. A person caught in role conflict may change his beliefs. A teacher, caught in a conflict between students, parents, principal, and superintendent may decide that the students and the parents are in no position to decide what and how much homework should be given, thus eliminating a substantial amount of conflict. The expectations of some of the members of the role-set are dismissed, either on the basis of expediency or on the basis of principle.

4. A person caught in a role conflict may solve the problem chemically by taking tranquilizers.

5. There may be no solution to the conflict problem. All the unfortunate conflicted soul can do is grin and bear it.

Secord and Backman (1966) point out that people caught in role conflicts are often protected by society which overlooks certain discrepancies in role performance, or which organizes roles so that some discrepancies are low in visibility. The teacher's role, for example, is highly visible to the students and is relatively visible to the school principal, but is not highly visible to the superintendent or the parents. Thus teachers can give relatively short shrift to the expectations of parents and superintendents, just so long as they are not too obvious about it. Parents and superintendents are not in a very good position to see how well or poorly teachers do their job. They depend largely on the information they receive from the principal and student. Thus, teachers who reasonably meet the expectations of their students and principal are not likely to get into trouble with anybody else. Also, people who occupy roles maintain formal and informal associations through which they can provide mutual encouragement and support to each other. If a teacher is caught in a role-conflict bind, it is very likely that other teachers are caught in the same bind, so they can commiserate with each other. Likewise, the overburdened housewife can share stories of travail with other housewives in the neighborhood, and the children can mutually support each other in sympathy over the impossible demands of parents and teachers.

One aspect of role-conflict resolution that falls under the heading of Sarbin and Allen's "instrumental" solution is the factor of power. There is a saying, "He knows which side his bread is buttered on," meaning that a person knows, in cases of conflict, where the power lies, and thus which role expectations had best be honored and which can be safely ignored. If the person occupying the role has enough power of his own, he may ignore all role demands that he does not want to meet. A role conflict, then, may be resolved in the direction desired by the person in the role-set who holds the most power to reward conformity or to punish nonconformity to expectations. In the case of school teachers, the superintendent would presumably have more power to reward or punish them than any other person in the role-set. Teachers might then resolve the conflict in favor of the superintendent's wishes. However, they might decide that what and how they teach their students is a matter of principle, and that they would rather risk loss of their jobs than compromise their principles. That is, in choosing which demands to honor and which demands to ignore, the basis for choice might be relative power in the role-set, or it might be on the basis of principles held by a person occupying the role.

Resolution of role strain as a function of power (or expediency) and principle was the subject of a study by Gross, McEachern, and Mason (1966). They studied the ways school superintendents resolve role conflicts. In this case, the conflict was over the superintendents' recommendations of teachers' salary increases.

A school superintendent is in the center of a role-set that includes teachers, parents, school board members, and various civic and community organizations that might have an interest in the schools and the taxes which must be raised to support the schools. The people occupying roles complementary to a superintendent could have three different expectations as to what his recommendations for salary increases would be: (a) He would recommend the highest possible raises; (b) he would recommend the lowest possible raises; (c) no expectations one way or the other. The superintendents who were studied revealed that they would expect teachers and parents to expect them to recommend the highest possible salary increases, while politicians and taxpayer associations would expect them to recommend the lowest possible increases. That is, the superintendents were in a role for which the expectations were contradictory.

Gross et al. observed that there are two grounds on which a decision can be made by a superintendent—"moral" grounds or "expedient" grounds. Expectations can be viewed by the superintendent as legitimate expectations or as illegitimate expectations. A legitimate expectation is an obligation, while an illegitimate expectation is felt as pressure. A moral decision, in a situation of conflict, is one that is made on the basis of legitimate expectations. If it is a rather poor town and teachers are well paid, then the legitimate expectations might well be that the raises be kept low so that the already overburdened and poverty-stricken taxpayers are not burdened even more. That is, the taxpayers' and politicians' expectations are the legitimate ones, while the rich teachers' expectations of a maximum raise are illegitimate. However, the teachers may be well organized and have substantial power. If the superintendent does not recommend a maximum raise, in accordance with the teachers' expectations, the teachers may exercise their power and relieve him of his job.

Gross et al. hypothesized that different superintendents will have different orientations toward conflict resolution. Some superintendents will have a moral orientation. They will tend to resolve conflicts in terms of the legitimacy of expectations, so that where two expectations are in conflict, they will choose that which they view as legitimate and reject that which they view as illegitimate. If both expectations are viewed as legitimate, they will work out a compromise, and if both are viewed as illegitimate, they will reject both. Other superintendents will have an expedient orientation toward the resolution of conflict. They will act to minimize the negative sanctions exercised against themselves. If there is a conflict in expectations, their decisions will be in favor of the expectations held by those persons in a position to punish them the most severely. If they perceive that both are able to exercise sanctions against them, they will seek a compromise, and if neither can exercise sanctions, they will decide on the basis of legitimacy of the expectations.

A third type of orientation toward resolution of conflict over expectations is called the "moral-expedient," in which both legitimacy and expedience are taken equally into account. If both legitimacy and the power to punish lie with one alternative, that alternative will prevail. If both choices A and B are viewed as legitimate, but greater sanctions are to be incurred by A than by B, then A will be chosen. If A is viewed as legitimate but B has the power to enforce greater sanctions, then the moral-expedient type will seek to compromise the two.

On the basis of the questionnaire, Gross et al. classified the school superintendents into moral types, expedient types, and moral-expedient types; they found that in situations of expectation conflict, they could accurately predict how 91 percent of the superintendents would resolve the conflict.

The importance of this study is that it demonstrates that different people will resolve role conflicts in different ways. The ways in which the conflicts are resolved are partially a function of the person and partially a function of the situation.

Finally, we come to a consideration of social identity. Sarbin and Allen write:

> . . . the point of departure for the analysis of social identity is the role-location variable—the placement of self and other in the various social systems relevant to the individual. As we pointed out before, placement in the social ecology may be thought of as answering the questions: Who is he? Who are you? Who am I? (1968, p. 550).

From the role theory point of view, social identity is built up out of people's interactions with people in complementary roles. That is, people learn who they are from the way others act toward them. Those others are, early in life, parents and siblings; later in life they are peers and colleagues, friends and spouses. From these interactions a self-concept is formed—that is, people learn who they are.

Sarbin and Allen list three dimensions of social identity: (1) status, which tells people where they stand in the social order; (2) value, which evaluates how well people play their role—good mother, poor shortstop, mediocre musician; and (3) involvement, which indicates how active people are in a role. Involvement may be measured in the amount of time spent in a role or the amount of effort put into playing a role.

A person's identity may change, and in fact does change as he moves through various roles in life. A child remains a child in identity only through childhood. Identity may be changed through changes in the knowledge structure, changes in performance, changes in attention deployment, and changes in somatic processes. Identity changes as a person gets older, as a person acquires certain skills, as a person's interests change, and so on. A world record holder in the mile-run at age twenty-one may become a surgeon at age thirty-five and a cabinet minister at age sixty. Social identity—that is, a person's position in the social structure—changes throughout a person's life.

Roles and Marriage

Having plowed through a rather lengthy exposition of the concepts of role theory, it should be apparent that role theory does have something to do with the interaction between people. We have, after all, discussed interaction between selves and others, husbands and wives, and teachers and students, as well as other kinds of social interaction. As we now progress, we will describe some of the ways in which the role approach has been applied to studying particular kinds of social interaction. In this section we will discuss the marriage relationship, and in the next section we will discuss psychotherapy.

After reviewing a number of theories concerning marriage, Roland Tharp (1963) concluded that the best theoretical approach to marriage is the role theory approach, and that the most promising role theory approach to marriage is that of Parsons and Bales (1955). Certainly the Parsons and Bales theory has stimulated more research than any other role theory. It should be noted, however, that the roles which Parsons and Bales define are in a process of change; although these roles were generally accurate and characteristic when first proposed, they are increasingly becoming less rigid and defined. This trend toward change is evidenced in the subsequent studies described after the Parsons and Bales study; marriage roles are progressively less specific as the studies become more recent.

Parsons and Bales' theory asserts that there are two main roles in marriage, the *instrumental* and the *expressive:*

> The marriage relation . . . is a two member system . . . the husband role is specialized *more* in the instrumental direction than the wife's, the wife role, more in the expressive direction . . . the husband specializes in meeting the adaptive exigencies, the wife, the integrative (Parsons & Bales, 1965, p. 163).

By this is meant that the husband's chief role in the family is instrumental, that is, getting things done. He is concerned with earning money, paying bills, planting the garden, and maintaining the outside relationships with the government, the school system, the economic system, and the other external agencies with whom the family must interact in order to function. The wife, on the other hand, is primarily concerned with maintaining satisfactory relationships within the family, and with the expressions of feeling that are a part of intimate relationships. This does not mean to imply that these functions are exclusive. The wife, after all, may shop for groceries and call the school about her children, and the husband may settle quarrels among the children and tell his wife that he loves her. Rather, this theory suggests which person assumes *primary* responsibility for which area. "We would expect, by and large that other things being equal, men would assume more technical, executive, and 'judicial' roles, women more supportive, integrative, and 'tension-managing' roles" (Parson & Bales, 1955, p. 101).

In Parsons and Bales' theory the family has two basic functions. One function is the primary socialization of the children, and the second is the stabilization of the adult personalities of the society. The family is not an independent small society, but an identifiable subsystem of a larger society. This means that the adult members of a family must have roles other than familial roles which occupy important places within their personalities. The most important of these is the occupational role of the father.

> . . . a mature woman can love, sexually, only a man who takes his full place in the masculine world, and above all its occupational aspect, and who takes responsibility for a family; conversely, the mature man can only love a woman who is really an adult, a full wife to him and mother to his children, and an adequate 'person' in her extrafamilial roles (Parsons & Bales, 1955, p. 22).

Within the family are two main role dimensions. The first is the *instrumental-expressive dimension,* with the husband occupying the instrumental pole and the wife the expressive pole. In addition, there is the *superior-inferior dimension,* a power dimension, with the parents occupying the superior pole and the children the inferior pole. This differentiation of role types is presented in Figure 3.

As children are socialized — that is, as they learn their social role — they, in effect, internalize this scheme, so that when they are in an inferior position to another person, they play the child role to the other person's parent, while when they are in the superior position, they play the parent role to the other person's child. This conceptualization is strikingly similar to Eric Berne's transactional analysis concept of representing interpersonal interaction as a function of the interaction between the Parent, Adult, and Child of the people who are interacting (see Chapter 5).

FIGURE 3. **EIGHT-FOLD DIFFERENTIATION OF ROLE-TYPES**

	Instrumental		Expressive	
	Universalistic	Particularistic	Universalistic	Particularistic
Superior +	Instrumental Superior (Father)		Expressive Superior (Mother)	
	Technical Expert	Executive (Instrumental Leader)	Expressive virtuoso and "cultural" expert	Expressive (Charismatic) Leader
Inferior —	Instrumental Inferior (Son)		Expressive Inferior (Daughter)	
	Adequate technical performer	"Cooperator"	Willing and "accommo-dating" person	"Loyal" member

Reprinted with permission of The Macmillan Company and Routledge & Kegan Paul, Ltd. from *Family, socialization and interaction process* by T. Parsons and R. F. Bales. Copyright © 1955 by The Free Press of Glencoe.

It should be noted that for Parsons and Bales the husband and wife occupy positions of equal power. In modern, nuclear marriage the husband and wife are colleagues. The difference between them is one of primary responsibility; the husband is primarily concerned with instrumental functions and secondarily with expressive functions, while for the wife the situation is reversed. "The husband has the primary adaptive responsibilities, relative to the outside situation, and internally he is in the first instance 'giver-of-care,' or pleasure, and secondarily the giver of love, whereas the wife is primarily the giver of love and secondarily the giver of care or pleasure" (Parsons & Bales, p. 151).

Morris Zelditch (1955) reviewed the cross-cultural research on the family and concluded that in both matrilineal families and patrilineal families women were influential in integrative functions of the family rather than in instrumental functions. Thus, anthropological research appears to support the Parsons and Bales theory. Zelditch also made the provocative observation that "the problem of the 'weak, ineffectual' father is more significant than that of the 'weak, ineffectual' mother. (Conversely, of course, and quite as significant, the problem of the 'cold, unyielding' mother is more of a problem than the 'cold, unyielding' father.)" (1955, p. 314).

Tharp in his review of theory and research on marriage, concluded, among other things, "The husband role is the more instrumental, the wife role, the more expressive-integrative" (1963, p. 115). He based this conclusion on the review of several empirical studies, two of which we will briefly review here.

Farber (1957) studied ninety-nine married couples. One of the hypotheses he tested was that wives would rank items relating to the socioemotional aspects of the marital interaction higher than husbands would. The subjects were to rank five values of socioemotional valuation in interaction. These five values were: (1) *companionship*, the family members feeling comfortable with each other; (2) *personality development*, continued increase in family members' ability to understand and get along with other people and to accept responsibility; (3) *satisfaction* among the family members with the amount of affection shown, and satisfaction of the husband and wife with their sex life; (4) *emotional security*, members of the family feeling they needed each other and trusted each other; (5) a *home*, having a place where the family members felt they belonged and were at ease. The husbands and wives were to rank these variables according to their importance. Farber found that the results were in accordance with Parsons and Bales' prediction that the wives would rank the socioemotional aspects of the interaction higher than their husbands did.

A second study reviewed by Tharp was that of Langhorne and Secord (1955) in which they had five thousand male and female college students list those traits that were desirable in a mate. They found significant differences between the sexes in the traits listed. Women were more concerned with receiving affection, love, sympathy, and understanding from a husband, while men were more interested in a wife who would keep a neat home and who would be reasonable and dependable. Women listed for men such traits as being ambitious and getting ahead in his profession, while not one man listed such traits as desirable in a wife.

Couch (1958) studied thirty-two relatively recently married couples. He had the husbands and wives each list the five most important obligations of a wife and the five most important obligations of a husband. After listing these obligations, the husband was to rate his wife on how well she fulfilled hers, and he was to rate himself on how well he fulfilled his. The wife was to do the same for her husband and for herself. Finally, the husband was to list what he thought his wife would list as the most important obligations, and the wife was to do the same. Couch found that wives were more likely to list affectional items, while husbands were more likely to list instrumental items. He also found that husbands and wives were both more likely to give the wife a higher rating on marital performance than the husband. Couch concluded that "There are reasons to believe that women identify more with the family than do men . . ." (1958, p. 357).

Heiss (1962) studied fifty-four dating couples by giving each member of a couple a questionnaire, selecting from the responses to the questionnaire a topic on which the couple disagreed, and then asking the couple to discuss the topic. The discussion was observed from behind a screen. The men did dominate the discussion in the task areas, while the women dominated in positive reactions, as rated by the Bales system (see Chapter 7 for a description of Bales' Interaction Process Analysis). An interesting sidelight to this study was the finding that the more intimate the couple were in their relationship, the less likely each sex was to dominate in its own area (instrumentality for males or expressiveness for females).

A study that clarifies the power dimension of the Parsons and Bales system is one by Walter Emmerich (1966). Emmerich studied 225 children aged six to ten. He showed the children pictures of interactions between mother-girl, father-boy, mother-father, and girl-boy and then asked them questions about the interaction between the people in the pictures. He found that the most common parental behaviors described were dominance and nurturance, thus indicating that children perceive the power relationships in the family as Parsons and Bales described them. They also described the father as having more power.

Several studies report results that do not agree with Parsons and Bales' theory. Goodrich, Ryder, and Raush (1968) studied fifty couples who had been married for four months. They interviewed the couples and observed the couples making decisions; then they gave the couples a variety of questionnaires. They factor-analyzed their data, deriving four main factors: (1) closeness to husband's family; (2) role orientation; (3) marital problems; and (4) closeness to wife's family. The main factor of interest here is role orientation, in which they found that the couples differed widely. The different kinds of role orientation ranged from couples in which the husband was primarily interested in his occupation and was relatively uninvolved in the home, to couples in which the husband was quite involved in the home and the wife was primarily involved in her work.

Kotlar (1965) studied fifty couples who were maritally adjusted and fifty couples who were not maritally adjusted. She had them complete the Interpersonal Checklist (a list of attitudes) twice—once for themselves and again for their spouses. She found that the adjusted husbands rated more highly than the nonadjusted husbands on affection, but that there was no difference between the two on dominance. Husbands and wives of the adjusted couples saw themselves as having more similar attitudes than did the nonadjusted couples. This research might appear to contradict the Parsons and Bales theory, but it should be kept in mind that this theory does not postulate superior dominance for the husband, but rather equality, which is what this study found. In this study both husbands and wives among the maladjusted couples saw their spouses as less affectionate than did the adjusted couples. Further, in both groups wives rated higher than husbands on affection. So this research might be considered tangential support for the Parsons and Bales hypothesis.

Leik (1963) conducted an experiment in which the members of nine families served as the subjects. Each family was composed of a father, mother, and college-age daughter. The subjects met under three conditions: (1) as a homogeneous group of three, in which all members of the group were either fathers or mothers or daughters; (2) as a group of three composed of a father, a mother, and a daughter, with none of the members of the group related to any other member of the group; and (3) as a real family of father, mother, and daughter. These groups were to discuss a question which might result when two students marry while they are still in college: Should the family continue to support the students or not? Leik found that in the nonfamily groups, the father showed more task-oriented behavior and the daughter, more emotional behavior, with the mother's behavior in between the father and the daughter. In the real families, however, the members behaved more equally on both the task and emotional dimensions. Leik found that agreement among real family groups was positively related to instrumental behavior and negatively related to emotional behavior; among nonfamily groups, agreement was positively related to emotionality, but unrelated to instrumental behavior. In short, it appears that in real families the instrumental-emotional dimension tends to disappear among the members.

Levinger (1964) studied sixty married couples; he interviewed them, had them rank their marital goals, and had them describe the real and ideal performance for each spouse in the task and emotional areas of marriage. The results indicated that in the task area either the husband or wife took responsibility, depending on the type of task, except for decisions about buying expensive items or what to do on vacation, in which case both participated in the decision. In social-emotional areas husbands and wives were about equal. Levinger also observed that the more satisfied couples reported more socially supportive activity in their relationship, rejected each other less in the laboratory, and communicated better on more topics than did the less satisfied couples.

In reviewing research applicable to the Parsons and Bales theory, Barry (1970) concluded that

> . . . recent experimental work . . . raise[s] serious questions as to whether the sex role differentiation postulated by Parsons and Bales actually typifies interaction between spouses. These studies, however, . . . do not consider modes of conflict resolution nor the relation of conflict and modes of resolution to marital adjustment. In the absence of empirical research the field is wide open to speculation (1970, p. 49).

Rossi (1968), in a theoretical article, tried to clear up some of the confusion by suggesting that the father-instrumental and mother-expressive role descriptions of Parsons and Bales "lead to more distortion than illumination when applied to the actual functioning of a specific system . . ." (1968, p. 36). She pointed out that a person may play one role at work and another role at home, and that every role requires a person to exercise both the instrumental and integrative functions. "This means that the role of father, husband, wife, or mother each has these two independent dimensions of authority and support, instrumentality and expressiveness, work and love (Rossi, 1968, p. 37). In fairness to Parsons and Bales, it should be pointed out that they don't disagree with this analysis, but they do assert that the husband is more concerned with instrumentality, while the wife is more concerned with expressiveness. It is a relative difference, not an absolute one.

One result does seem to emerge from the marriage role research, however, and that is the conclusion that husbands and wives are more likely to be satisfied with marriage if they are in agreement on what their roles are to be. Ort (1950) studied fifty married couples and asked them questions about twenty-two issues in marriage. He obtained answers from the couples on what they expected in marriage and what actually occurred in their own marriages. He also had each member of each couple rate his happiness with marriage on a ten-point scale. He obtained a correlation of −.83 between conflict on actual and expected marriage behavior and marriage happiness, indicating a very high relationship between marriage happiness and both spouses finding their role expectations fulfilled in marriage. Ort concluded that marriage happiness is a result of the person playing the role he or she expects to play in marriage, and the spouse playing the role expected of him or her.

Jacobson (1966) gave a twenty-eight-item scale of attitudes to one hundred divorced and one hundred happily married couples. He found that the difference between the attitude scores of the divorced couples was four times as great as the difference between the attitude scores of the married couples. This finding is certainly in harmony with Parsons and Bales' opinion that "It is a paramount necessity, if their roles (husband's and wife's) are to be integrated with each other, for them to share common values" (1955, p. 164). For a husband and wife to relate happily to each other they must agree on the role each is to play in their relationship.

Roles and Psychotherapy

There are two aspects to viewing psychotherapy from the role theory point of view. One has to do with the client's problem, and the other has to do with psychotherapy itself. From the role theory point of view, a person who seeks psychotherapy is seeking help because he cannot properly play the roles he is called upon to play in life. Let us take a hypothetical client as an example. Let us suppose the client is a married woman who feels anxious and depressed. Her husband spends much of his time working. When he is at home he is too tired to exert himself beyond reading the newspaper and watching television. He rarely expresses any feeling, positive or negative, for the client. The client feels that something is wrong with her life—she knows she is unhappy and dissatisfied with the life she is now living, but she doesn't know what is wrong and doesn't know what to do about it. Having just read about research that demonstrates that disagreement on marriage roles leads to dissatisfaction in marriage, we might reasonably hypothesize that part of the client's problem lies in unsatisfactory role performance by her as a wife, and unsatisfactory role performance by her husband as well. We might guess that her role performance in other areas is less than satisfactory, too. So, from the role theory point of view, her problem requires that the therapist help her learn how to play the roles of wife and woman more effectively. This brings us to the second aspect of role theory as it applies to psychotherapy. That is, before the client can be taught how to more effectively play the role of wife and woman, she must first effectively play the role of client in psychotherapy.

Lennard and Bernstein (1969) studied the psychotherapeutic interaction as a role system. They listed three kinds of agreement that must be established between the client and the psychotherapist: (1) who is to do what, and when and why he is to do it; (2) what behavior follows what behavior; (3) what attitudes and views participants are to maintain toward each other and the situation. They wrote, "Teaching a person who comes for treatment how to be a patient and what to expect from a therapist is a necessary part of what must transpire during psychotherapy" (Lennard & Bernstein, 1969, p. 147). It might be added that the training of psychotherapists consists of exactly the same kind of training.

Let us pause briefly to consider some of the things the client must learn in psychotherapy. Psychotherapy is a relationship that, like other relationships, involves two people talking to each other. However, this similarity is deceptive since there are important ways in which psychotherapy differs from other relationships. First, the most common misunderstanding that must be cleared up in psychotherapy concerns giving advice. The psychotherapist is a professional person. In other relationships with professionals the client presents the problem and the professional diagnoses the problem and suggests a solution to it. Most kinds of psychotherapy do not proceed in this way. Rather, the client is helped by the therapist to arrive at his own solution. The client must learn that when he asks questions he is not likely to get the kinds of answers he expects. If the client asks, "What do you think is wrong with me?" he is likely to get a reply something like, "What do *you* think is wrong with you?" rather than an explicit answer to the question. A second way in which psychotherapy differs from other relationships is that any kind of thought or feeling is expected to be expressed, even if it is insulting or shocking. In ordinary relationships a person who freely expresses his thoughts and feelings is more likely to get trouble than to get help. Psychotherapists are not likely to be judgmental. Where another person responds to a shocking disclosure with "How awful!" or "You shouldn't have done that!" the therapist is more likely to nod his head or say, "Go on."

In studying the psychotherapy relationship, Lennard and Bernstein (1969, Ch. 6) found that during the first three sessions of psychotherapy 20 percent of the statements by therapists and 15 percent of the statements of the client were communications about their role relationships to each other. That is, they were talking about who was supposed to do what in psychotherapy. They found that as treatment progressed, the percentage of statements about the role relationship within therapy decreased. They found, as did the marriage researchers, that the greater the disagreement between the therapist and the client in their expectations about therapy, the more problems the pair had, which was reflected in a greater proportion of statements about the therapy situation. Overall and Aronson (1966) found that the greater the discrepancy between clients' expectations in therapy and what the clients found in therapy, the more frequently the client quit therapy. Lennard and Bernstein compared active therapists who gave their clients verbal instructions on how to behave in psychotherapy with relatively passive therapists who made few statements relative to therapy roles. They found that at the beginning of therapy, the active therapists made many more statements about the therapy role, but that the number of role-relevant statements declined rather rapidly. Passive therapists made relatively fewer therapy role-relevant statements at the beginning of therapy, but after four months of therapy both the passive therapist and his client were still making role-relevant statements at about the same rate as they were at the beginning of therapy. This finding would suggest that it helps in psychotherapy to teach the client, at the beginning, what is expected of him.

Lennard and Bernstein suggest that therapy clients who have a poor prognosis may have a poor prognosis "precisely . . . because they do not assume the patient role" (1969, p. 153). They suggest that patients with poor prognoses are those who have trouble differentiating role relationships and learning roles. They studied schizophrenic patients, who have poorer psychotherapy prognoses than neurotic patients, and found that therapists made many fewer role references to schizophrenic patients than to other kinds of patients. Lennard and Bernstein suggest that therapists make fewer role teaching responses to schizophrenics because schizophrenics fail to respond to role-relevant statements and thus extinguish the therapists' inclination to teach roles to them.

Still another source of difficulty in psychotherapy with difficult clients might be the therapist's own expectations. Goldstein (1962) found that the therapist's own expectations for change in the client were significantly related to whether or not the client did, in fact, change for the better. Therapists who expected their clients to change in a positive direction were significantly more likely to have clients who changed in a positive direction. There is probably an interaction effect working in this situation, with the client's capacity for learning the appropriate role responses and the therapist's expectations both exerting an influence on the outcome. The therapist's expectations might be considered a case of role demand, with the therapist emitting subtle cues that will tend to nudge the client to move toward emitting behavior that confirms the therapist's expectations.

Lennard and Bernstein suggest that learning in therapy takes place along three dimensions: *behavioral roles, attitudes,* and *properties of the system.* In learning behavioral roles the client learns about activeness: Who should take the initiative in talking? How much talking shall be done by each person? Who is dominant? What topics are important to talk about? The client learns the extent to which the participants are allowed to express their disagreements, the extent to which reciprocity between them holds, and the extent to which the relationship is formal or casual.

The second dimension pertains to attitudes. To what extent can the pair trust each other? How much hope can the client reasonably entertain—will he improve, and if so, how soon? How freely can the client feel to express his thoughts and feelings?

The third dimension pertains to the properties of the system. What are the goals of therapy? How long will therapy take? Are the communications between the therapist and client confidential? How highly structured are the practical arrangements, such as appointment times and fees?

After learning the role of client, the client is in a position to begin psychotherapy. That is, he can now start working on his problem. Rapoport and Rosow (1966) suggest that the client's problem can be viewed as a role failure toward which the treatment can be directed. They suggest three factors involved in role failure: (1) the role in which the failure occurred, (2) the social norms expected in that position, and (3) the personality of the patient. The problem becomes one of analyzing how the client's role performance fails, or how his role expectations conflict with those of the people with whom he interacts, or how his personality fails to fit the role he is called upon to play.

The full range of psychotic, neurotic, and personality disorders can be encompassed within the role framework. Therapy becomes a process of learning more effective role behavior. Sarbin suggests that "changes following psychotherapeutic intervention may be seen as the effects of role enactments over time reinforced by appropriate reinforcements on the part of therapists and other significant audiences" (1964, p. 185). Lennard and Bernstein (1969) suggest that therapy can be viewed as a "metarelationship"—that is, a relationship about relationships.

Within therapy the therapist may teach the client how to play his role more effectively by helping him see more clearly the role expectations of himself and of other people. This would include the expectations the client has for himself about his own role and the expectations others have for the role he is playing. It also would include the expectations the client has for the roles played by other people and what he can learn about the expectations other people have for their own roles from their behavior or their own statements about their own roles. Therapy would reveal conflicts among role expectations. It would reveal conflict between the client's personality or self-concept and the roles he is required to play. By this process of learning, the client would develop a clearer cognitive picture of himself, his expectations, his expectations for others, others' expectations for him, and others' expectations for themselves. The client could then more adaptively change either his expectations or his behavior, or he could change to a role that is more congenial to his own personality and self-concept. Much psychotherapy operates in just such terms as have been described in this paragraph, without specifically labeling the kind of thinking that produces the concepts of role theory.

Finally, it should be noted that research in psychotherapy indicates, as did research on marriage, that when the client and the therapist agree on the role expectations each has for his own role and the role of the other, the relationship is more likely to last. Heine and Trosman (1960) studied forty-six outpatients in psychotherapy and found that those patients whose expectations about treatment were in harmony with the treatment they actually received were significantly more likely to remain in treatment. Heine and Trosman concluded that "the variable which appears to be significant for continuance is that of mutuality of expectation between patient and therapist" (1960, p. 278).

Discussion

Shaw and Costanzo (1970) trace the beginnings of role theory back to early writers in the social sciences, such as William James, William Graham Sumner, Emile Durkheim, and John Dewey. But had they wished, they could have traced the idea many centuries further back than that. With regard to role learning, for example, we could quote Epictetus who wrote, "We see that a carpenter becomes a carpenter by learning certain things; that a pilot, by learning certain things, becomes a pilot" (1909, p. 140). What is that but a description of role learning?

The concept of role is really a common-sense idea. Any ordinary citizen, who hasn't the least idea that such a thing as role theory exists, could tell you what he thinks the President of the United States should do, and he could give you an assessment of the performance of the current incumbent of that office. That is, he could list role norms, and he could give an evaluation of a case of role playing based on those norms. Role is really a common-sense concept that has been adopted by social science, and as such, it has the strengths and the weaknesses that derive from such a concept.

The obvious strength of the concept of role is that it is closely related to observable data. Parents train their children, and what they train their children to do is to perform roles adequately. Schools train students, and what they train students to do is to play roles adequately. Much of the activity of our institutions is devoted to role training. A parent teaches a child to become an adult, with all that being an adult implies, including the ability to take on responsibility, the ability to manage finances, the ability to cope with problems, and the ability to relate to and understand other people. A school system trains one young person to read and write, and ultimately to be a surgeon or a teacher—or along a different line, another person to be a carpenter or automobile mechanic. The young are trained for roles.

The weakness of the concept of role derives from the same source as its strength. Role concepts are close to everyday life. But by the same token they are subject to being contaminated by the definitions of everyday life. That is, a word such as "norm" may have different meanings, depending on who is using the word. It may mean average, or the usual, or it may refer to an absolute minimum. If we say that a norm for wives is cooking the meals for the family, does this mean that the wife usually cooks the meals, or does it mean that a woman who does not cook the meals has failed to fulfill the role of a wife? Further, when we speak of a norm, are we also speaking of an expectation or a value—or both? Shaw and Costanzo reflected this weakness in role theory when they wrote:

> Despite the ubiquity of the concept of role, it is nevertheless a rather ephemeral concept. At one and the same time, its flexibility and generalizability are assets and detriments. The most apparent detriment is that the deceptive similarity in language among the various analysts of role phenomena does not by any means reflect a similarity among them in their conceptual definitions of role phenomena. Therefore, individuals who employ role analysis in examining various sociopsychological phenomena speak similar languages but often do not communicate (1970, p. 344).

However, role theory should be judged as a theory. A theory is a tool. Like any other tool the ultimate criterion is whether or not it is useful—useful in the sense that it orders data in a way that is simple and clear, in the sense that it seems to provide more explanation of behavior than is obvious from the behavior by itself, in the sense that it suggests new and fruitful areas for research, and in the sense that it stimulates useful research. If role theory does this, and at the same time adds a minimum of confusion to the phenomena under study, then it has served a useful purpose. Sarbin reflected this feeling when he wrote:

> I am not under any illusion that this theory is the only road to the truth. The demands that I make on theory are modest ones—that the theory tell me where to look for facts. The test of a theory is its utility; if role theory is useful in pointing to the possible sources of variation in behavior and in organizing facts, then it serves its purpose (1964, p. 219).

So the real question is Has role theory proved useful in pointing people in the proper direction to look for facts? The answer is yes. Let us look at the field of marriage interaction for support for this conclusion. In 1963, Tharp surveyed the research on marriage and concluded that role theory provided the best explanation then available for marriage interaction. Whether or not role theory still provides the "best" framework for marriage research may still be open to question, but the fact is that up to 1963, it provided the main theoretical framework for marriage interaction research; role theory seems to deserve credit for having served to both stimulate and organize the framework for most of the fruitful research on marriage.

Let us consider Tharp's conclusions about marriage, based on a review of the research available in 1963. Tharp concluded that the greater the congruence between the two marriage roles, the greater the marriage satisfaction; that two roles exist in marriage, the husband's role, which is instrumental, and the wife's role, which is expressive; and that the likelihood of marital success is primarily a function of the husband fulfilling the expected role of a husband, that is, the instrumental role. All of these conclusions derive directly from research done within the role theory framework.

Now, let us move forward to 1970, and consider Barry's review of research on marriage. Barry (1970) was not willing to be as firm as Tharp in his support of the instrumental-expressive role theory, but in the review of subsequent research, he confirmed Tharp's observation that marital success is primarily a function of the husband. On the basis of additional research, Barry went on to say that background and personality factors in the husband were the primary sources of marital success because of the support the husband must provide for the wife. His explanation is that the wife must make the greater adjustment in marriage; if she is to make that adjustment successfully, she must have support from her husband; for the husband to provide that necessary support, he must have a stable personality and must adequately fulfill the husband role.

These two research review papers provide an example of research that is progressing. It is providing increasingly more extensive explanations based on sound empirical data. And most of these data were stimulated by and collected within the framework of role theory. Therefore, role theory, despite its shortcomings, is nonetheless serving the function for which theories are designed.

When we assess role theory in terms of the dimensions by which we have been comparing theories, it immediately becomes apparent that role theory is a theory of substance. It has quite a broad and deep data base. The subjects studied have been patients with a variety of emotional problems, as well as people who are emotionally healthy. The situations within which these people have been studied include all of the kinds of situations within which people interact: in the clinic, in real life, and in the experimental laboratory. The data obtained from them have included external observation of behavior and introspective self-report. However, this self-report has concentrated on expectations rather than experiences, although experiential information has been included.

In terms of level, role theory has discussed the interpersonal relationship at all levels, including the behavior segment, the level of the person, and the level of the dyadic (or group) interaction. Thus, role theory is quite broad. This breadth helps to explain why role theory has proved so useful in the study of the interpersonal relationship.

As a theory, role theory is extensive in the phenomena it covers, but limited in the view it brings to the phenomena. It covers phenomena ranging from the behavior segment to the pattern of the interpersonal interaction, and it includes both external behavior observation and introspective self-report, but it views this range of phenomena from the point of view of the performance of specified roles. That is, it views the interpersonal relationship from the point of view of the roles specified, and roles specified are rules described, and rules described are rules learned. Thus, it is the study of the culturally specified and learned behavior which people perform in their interaction with each other. If one assumes, as many do, that some interpersonal behavior is not learned or specified by the culture, but arises from within the person himself, then role theory is inadequate. Role theory sees people purely as a function of their society. It does not see them as individuals who, in however small a measure, have some control of the direction of their own relationships. Thus role theory is narrow in that it is a theory about the learned, socially prescribed factors in interpersonal relationships.

Summary

Role theory is not so much a single theory as it is a collection of middle-range theories. Role theory is derived from the theater, and its sources go back to antiquity, but in more recent years it may be traced to writers in the social science of the late nineteenth and early twentieth centuries.

Biddle and Thomas and Sarbin and Allen have endeavored to bring some order into the realm of role theory by collecting, defining, and relating various role theory concepts to one another.

Biddle and Thomas categorized role theory terms into four categories: (1) *terms for partitioning persons*, (2) *terms for partitioning behaviors*, (3) *terms for partitioning persons and behaviors*, and (4) *terms for relating partitions to one another.*

Sarbin and Allen described and defined the following areas of role phenomena: *role enactment, role expectations, role location, role demands, role skills, self-role congruence, the audience for role performance,* and *complex role phenomena,* including *role-sets* and *role conflict.*

Social roles are learned primarily in the family, but in other institutions of society as well. Much of the training in any society is role training. Some roles, such as *ascribed roles* like age, sex, race, and nationality, are permanent. *Achieved roles,* which people acquire through their own efforts, change through life as people progress or regress in their development of skills.

Role theory has served to stimulate research in many areas of interpersonal interaction. In this chapter two areas, marriage and psychotherapy, have been discussed. The most prominent role theory relative to marriage is that of Parsons and Bales, who hold that there are within the family two role dimensions: power and the instrumental-expressive. They theorize that in the family, the parents are high on power while the children are low on power. The husband's primary role is the instrumental role, while the wife's primary role is the expressive-integrative one. Some research supports this theory, while other research questions it. Role research on marriage does seem to be converging on the husband, who appears to be most responsible for whether or not a marriage is successful. Research on psychotherapy indicates that clients whose therapy is successful learn to play their roles—both their role of therapy client and, through therapy, their roles in real life—more effectively than do clients whose therapy is unsuccessful.

Whatever its ultimate fate may be, role theory, at its present stage of development, appears to have contributed to the advance of social science.

References

Barry, W. A. Marriage research and conflict: an integrative review. *Psychological Bulletin,* 1970, 73, 41–54.

Biddle, B. J., Rosencranz, H. A., Tomich, E., & Twyman, J. P. Shared inaccuracies in the role of the teacher. Selection 37 in B. J. Biddle & E. J. Thomas, *Role theory; concepts and research.* New York: Wiley, 1966.

Biddle, B. J., & Thomas, E. J. *Role theory; concepts and research.* New York: Wiley, 1966.

Brown, R. *Social psychology.* New York: The Free Press, 1965.

Coe, W. C., & Sarbin, T. R. An experimental demonstration of hypnosis as role enactment. *Journal of Abnormal Psychology,* 1966, 71, 400–406.

Couch, C. J. The use of the concept "role" and its derivatives in the study of marriage. *Marriage and Family Living,* 1958, 20, 353–57.

Emmerich, W. Family role concepts of children ages six to nine. Selection 45 in B. J. Biddle & E. J. Thomas, *Role theory; concepts and research.* New York: Wiley, 1966.

Epictetus, *The golden sayings of Epictetus.* New York: Collier, 1909.

Farber, B. An index of marital integration. *Sociometry*, 1957, 20, 117–33.

Goldstein, A. P. *Therapist-patient expectancies in psychotherapy.* New York: Pergamon Press, 1962.

Goodrich, W., Ryder, R. G., & Raush, H. L. Patterns of newlywed marriage. *Journal of Marriage and the Family,* 1968, 30, 383–91.

Gouldner, A. W. The norm of reciprocity: a preliminary statement. Selection 12 in B. J. Biddle & E. J. Thomas, *Role theory; concepts and research.* New York: Wiley, 1966.

Gross, N., McEachern, A. W., & Mason, W. S. Role conflict and its resolution. Selection 35 in B. J. Biddle & E. J. Thomas, *Role theory; concepts and research.* New York: Wiley, 1966.

Hartley, R. A developmental view of female sex-role identification. Selection 44 in B. J. Biddle & E. J. Thomas, *Role theory; concepts and research.* New York: Wiley, 1966.

Heine, R. W., & Trosman, H. Initial expectations of the doctor-patient relationship as a factor in continuance in psychotherapy. *Psychiatry,* 1960, 23, 275–78.

Heiss, J. S. Degree of intimacy and male-female interaction. *Sociometry,* 1962, 25, 197–208.

Jacobson, A. H. Conflict of attitudes toward the roles of the husband and wife in marriage. Selection 36 in B. J. Biddle & E. J. Thomas, *Role theory; concepts and research.* New York: Wiley, 1966.

Jones, E. E., Davis, K. E., & Gergen, K. J. Role playing variations and their informational value for person perception. Selection 17 in B. J. Biddle & E. J. Thomas, *Role theory; concepts and research.* New York: Wiley, 1966.

Kotlar, S. L. Middle-class marital role perceptions and marital adjustment. *Sociology and Social Research,* 1965, 49, 283–92.

Langhorne, M. C., & Secord, P. F. Variations in marital needs with age, sex, marital status, and regional location. *Journal of Social Psychology,* 1955, 41, 19–37.

Leik, R. K. Instrumentality in family interaction. *Sociometry,* 1963, 26, 131–45.

Lennard, H. L., & Bernstein, A. *Patterns in human interaction.* San Francisco: Josey-Bass, 1969.

Levinger, G. Task and social behavior in marriage. *Sociometry,* 1964, 27, 433–48.

Linton, R. *The cultural background of personality.* New York: Appleton-Century-Crofts, 1945.

Merton, R. K. Anticipatory socialization. Selection 42 in B. J. Biddle & E. J. Thomas, *Role theory; concepts and research.* New York: Wiley, 1966.

Merton, R. K. *Social theory and social structure.* New York: The Free Press, 1968.

Ort, R. S. A study of role-conflicts as related to happiness in marriage. *Journal of Abnormal and Social Psychology*, 1950, 45, 691–99.

Overall, B., & Aronson, H. Expectations of psychotherapy in patients of lower socioeconomic class. Selection 19 in B. J. Biddle & E. J. Thomas, *Role theory; concepts and research.* New York: Wiley, 1966.

Parsons, T., & Bales, R. F. *Family, socialization and interaction process.* New York: The Free Press, 1955.

Rapoport, R., & Rosow, I. An approach to family relationships and role performance. Selection 26 in B. J. Biddle & E. J. Thomas, *Role theory; concepts and research.* New York: Wiley, 1966.

Rossi, A. S. Transition to parenthood. *Journal of Marriage and the Family*, 1968, 30, 26–39.

Sarbin, T. R. Role theoretical interpretation of psychological change. In P. Worchel & D. Byrne (Eds.), *Personality change.* New York: Wiley, 1964.

Sarbin, T. R., & Allen, V. L. Role theory. In G. Lindzey & E. Aronson (Eds.), *The handbook of social psychology.* (Vol. 1) Reading, Mass.: Addison-Wesley, 1968.

Sargent, S. S., & Williamson, R. C. *Social psychology.* New York: The Ronald Press, 1966.

Secord, P. F., & Backman, C. W. *Social psychology.* New York: McGraw-Hill, 1964.

Shaw, M. E., & Costanzo, P. R. *Theories of social psychology.* New York: McGraw-Hill, 1970.

Smelser, W. T. Dominance as a factor in achievement and perception in cooperative problem-solving interactions. *Journal of Abnormal and Social Psychology*, 1961, 62, 535–42.

Tharp, R. G. Psychological patterning in marriage. *Psychological Bulletin*, 1963, 60, 97–117.

Zelditch, M. Role differentiation in the nuclear family; a comparative study. In T. Parsons & R. F. Bales, *Family, socialization and interaction process.* New York: The Free Press, 1955.

The Rules of Encounter

13

More than to any family or club, more than to any class or sex, more than to any nation, the individual belongs to gatherings, and he had best show that he is a member in good standing. The ultimate penalty for breaking the rules is harsh. Just as we fill our jails with those who transgress the legal order, so we partly fill asylums with those who act unsuitably—the first kind of institution being used to protect our lives and property; the second, to protect our gatherings and occasions (1963a, p. 248).

—Erving Goffman

Most of the ideas and research discussed in this book have dealt with what goes on between two people in intimate relationships and with the processes and regularities that intimate relationships follow. This chapter, rather than dealing with intimate relationships, deals with ordinary, everyday, casual relationships. And rather than being primarily concerned with what goes on within these relationships, this chapter is concerned with the rules of society that govern all relationships.

Erving Goffman is a sociologist, although it might be more accurate to describe him as a cultural anthropologist who has studied the American scene. He has studied what goes on between people in all sorts of ordinary situations, such as at parties, at meetings, and on the street. He has also studied the way people behave in "total institutions," such as mental hospitals, prisons, and the armed forces. Rather than concerning himself with what goes on inside people to make them behave the way they do, he has looked at the other side of the coin to study the rules of society. He has concluded that these are rules we all obey — most of the time without even being aware of it and, for most of us, without even realizing that such rules exist.

These rules that we follow are not written in any law book or rule manual. To the extent that they exist at all in written form, they are found in books of etiquette and in the columns of newspapers and magazines that advise people — especially young, inexperienced, and untrained people — how to behave in various kinds of situations. As Goffman puts it:

> The rule of behavior that seems to be common to all situations and exclusive to them is the rule obliging participants to "fit in." The words one applied to a child on his first trip to a restaurant presumably hold for everyone all the time: The individual must be "good" and not cause a scene or a disturbance; he must not attract undue attention to himself, either by thrusting himself on the assembled company or by attempting to withdraw too much from their presence. He must keep within the spirit or ethos of the situation; he must not be *de trop* or out of place (1963a, p. 11).

Everyone who has children knows what Goffman means. Much of what is called "child rearing" is a matter of teaching children how to behave, especially toward other people. This was demonstrated for me during a summer vacation trip with the whole family. We stayed in motels, ate in restaurants, and visited all kinds of tourist attractions. This was the first time the younger children had been taken on such a trip. One evening after a particularly trying day I complained to my wife about the way the children behaved. On that particular occasion we had been to a very expensive restaurant. I said that it seemed to me that the kids all had left feet. They held back, wouldn't walk to the table, couldn't find anything to say when they were asked what they wanted to order, and generally acted as though they were either simple schizophrenics or mentally retarded or both. My wife replied that the reason they were acting that way was because they didn't know how to behave, so to avoid scandalous error they froze and did nothing. I might add that the alternative to freezing behavior seems to be its exact opposite: uninhibited, noisy running around, which in places such as motels late at night is also inappropriate.

Goffman (1961a) apparently developed his ideas while working in a mental hospital in which he observed the behavior of all of the people in the institution, including the staff and the patients. He concluded that the reasons people were in mental hospitals was because they had violated social rules:

> Psychotic behavior . . . runs counter to what might be thought of as public order, especially one part of public order, the order governing persons by virtue of their being in one another's immediate physical presence. Much psychotic behavior is . . . a failure to abide by rules established for the conduct of face-to-face interaction. . . . Psychotic behavior is, in many instances, what might be called a situational impropriety (Goffman, 1967, p. 141).

Goffman also pointed out that most of what we call psychotic behavior is perfectly acceptable sometime, somewhere, in some situation.

People are put in mental hospitals because they have upset somebody very much, having done so because they didn't follow the rules for social interaction. This same idea was demonstrated for me in a different context than that of a mental hospital. For several years I did research in a country workhouse. In connection with this research I interviewed dozens of prisoners and conducted group discussions with them over this period of several years. These prisoners were placed in the workhouse to serve relatively short sentences of a year or less. Most prisoners complained they had been unjustly jailed. They based their claim of injustice on the fact that they knew other people who had committed the same offense, but who had never been picked up by the police, much less been tried and sentenced. I became curious as to why these men should have been jailed while others went free, so I inquired in detail into their crimes. What I found was that in every instance the prisoner had behaved in a way that seriously upset another person who then made a complaint. These men did not seem to have much ability to anticipate how other people would react to their behavior. If you borrow a friend's car without telling him, he is not likely to complain to the police if he doesn't need the car at the time. If you borrow his car when you know he will need it, and he then comes to get the car, finds it gone, and calls the police, you should not be too surprised to discover that he is so angry at you when he finds out you took his car that he lets the police throw you in jail.

This chapter, then, will describe the rules that govern the ordinary, everyday, face-to-face interactions between people. The chapter will be more concerned with the rules that govern the interactions between two people rather than groups, but since the rules tend to be general, there will frequently be no distinction made between dyads and larger gatherings.

Self and Identity

Although Goffman is not primarily concerned with the individual personality as such, it is not possible to discuss the interaction between people without some consideration of the way a person functions as an individual. To discuss the individual, then, Goffman (1963b) uses personality constructs that are closely related to the historical concerns of sociology, such as *self, role, identity,* and *character.* But in addition he uses the psychological concepts of *defense* and *projection.*

Each individual is unique, and this uniqueness derives from three sources. A person may be unique by possessing some outstanding personality trait or characteristic. He may be unique because of his own unique pattern of traits. Finally, a person is unique in the basic core of his *self.* For *personal identity,* only an outstanding trait or a unique pattern of traits are important in the social situation. These are the aspects of a person that are visible to other people. Personal identity identifies a person as unique to other people. In addition to personal identity there are two other kinds of identity. A person has a *social identity* which places him in a social class or an occupational category. He also has an *ego identity* which is his own sense of who he is.

A person engages in roles. A *role* is the activity in which a person engages in some situation, and the behavior he performs in that situation is prescribed by the situation. A teacher is expected to communicate new knowledge and skills to his students. He is supposed to evaluate each student's performance and to correct each student's errors. These are the behaviors that are a part of a teacher's role. A person performs a role toward others — a teacher toward pupils, a doctor toward patients, and a salesperson toward customers. However, no person confines himself to one role. A teacher may also be a son or daughter, a spouse, a parent, a customer, a reader, a taxpayer, a cook, and a painter. A person plays many roles, and some of these roles have no relationship to each other, or at times may even come into conflict with each other. The role of parent may come into conflict with the role of teacher when a teacher's child is sick. The more agonizing situations in life occur when two of a person's roles come into conflict.

A person may play a role, or he may play at it. When he is playing a role he is totally engrossed in it. When he is "playing at it" he is aware of the fact that he is playing a role and may ham up his performance as a way of showing observers that he is not altogether engrossed in the role. A surgeon who is in the middle of a serious operation is certainly engrossed in his role. An actor playing the part of a surgeon is playing at being a surgeon. A surgeon may also "play at" being a surgeon when he removes a small splinter from his son's toe or when he removes the tonsils from his daughter's doll (Goffman, 1961b).

A person achieves *role distance* when he can and does perform a role satisfactorily, but with a certain disdain for the role itself. This happens when a person has mastered a role, and it is no longer completely challenging to him. Surgeons in the operating room are not always completely engrossed in their task. Sometimes they crack jokes or discuss the performance of their favorite football team. College professors often demonstrate role distance in lectures by making asides about the foibles of their profession or of the university. Goffman (1961b) argues that it is in demonstrating role distance that each person demonstrates his individuality, and that role distance is an unstudied topic that needs more attention than it has received.

In any situation a person expresses himself. This expression is through every aspect of the person. He expresses himself through his clothing and the style of his hair; he expresses himself through his stance, his movements, and his gestures; he expresses himself through his voice and his choice of words. Everything about a person that can be seen, heard, or smelled tells the other something about him. All of these expressions are considered by other people to be symptomatic of the person.

The expressions a person gives are both *given* and *given off*. What a person "gives" is what he directly and intentionally tries to communicate to other people. What he "gives off" is what other people deduce from every aspect of the person. People are always trying to figure out what another is "really like" or what he is "really after." It is from the expressions "given off" that they try to glean this information (Goffman, 1959).

Literature is full of examples of what happens when there is a discrepancy between the expression "given" and the expression "given off." In *The Prince and the Pauper*, Mark Twain wrote about two boys, one a prince and the other a beggar, who traded places in order to find out how the other lived. The action of the story revolved around the real or potential conflict between the "given" and the "given off."

I had an experience in a mental hospital that was instructive on this point. I was leading a therapy group of inmate schizophrenics which contained a man who claimed to own a string of hotels. He frequently talked of business matters and off-handedly mentioned various expensive items that he owned. However, he was only twenty-four years old, he had not finished high school, his speech was littered with incorrect grammar, and after going through the process of being inducted into the hospital, he looked like a typical twenty-four-year-old semi-literate schizophrenic. There was a marked discrepancy between his "given" and his "given off," so we credited his possessions to paranoia and assumed that his hotels were a part of his grandiose delusion. That is to say, we of the professional staff resolved the discrepancy between his "given" and his "given off" in favor of the "given off." It was not until a visitor came to the hospital to see our patient about some business matters that we discovered we had resolved in the wrong direction. He might be a slovenly, semiliterate, twenty-four-year-old schizophrenic, but he actually did own a string of hotels.

Expressiveness always has a promissory character to it. On the basis of expressiveness other people come to expect certain things from us in the future, and by our expressiveness we randomly give promises to others, without necessarily intending to convey what kind of a person they can expect us to be and how they can expect us to act in some unspecified situation in the future (Goffman, 1959). Expressiveness is a promise that we randomly distribute to those around us.

In every situation a person takes a *line*, or he projects a definition of the situation. He also projects a definition of himself in the situation, and this projection of himself is his *face*. A person has an investment in his projection of the situation and in his face, and it is around trying to protect it that the intrapsychic operations of the person in the social situation revolve (Goffman, 1959, 1967).

A person tries to protect his projection of his face and his projection of the situation. His attempts to protect his own projection of the situation are *defenses*. These are techniques he uses to protect the impression he makes on others. Some of the aspects of what Goffman calls *face-work* and the dynamics of the interaction between people trying to protect their own face and the face of others will be discussed later in the chapter. Let it suffice for now to say that disruption of a person's projections is a serious matter which lies at the heart of what is most upsetting to people in their personal relationships.

A person presents a *front*, which is what he wants other people to see and think of him. However, there is also a *back*, which is where all the work goes on that is inconsistent with the front (Goffman, 1959). When the front is being presented, but the back threatens to break through and be exposed or is exposed, then defensive repair work must be carried out. The "front" is the dress of the glamorous woman, while the "back" is the garter that breaks. As Goffman (1967) suggests, the self that is presented is, among other things, a ceremonial object; therefore a person owes it to himself and to others to maintain a proper self.

The fact that a person presents a certain face or front to others does not necessarily mean that he is cynical or hypocritical about it. He is presenting himself to others partly out of consideration for them. In fact, the social occasion (or more specifically, other people) demand it. In a sense, it is what other people think he owes them and what they think he owes himself. Witness the case of Jacqueline Kennedy who was seen as a certain kind of a person, based on her appearance and her public behavior. When she broke this image by marrying a wealthy Greek shipowner of indifferent reputation, the public outrage was intense.

A person may be taken in by his own front. He may really believe he is what he presents himself as being. Actually, any person goes through cycles of belief and disbelief in his own front. Today a mother thinks she is a good mother and tomorrow, or next week at the latest, she is sure she should never have been allowed to have children. Martin Buber (1961, p. 32) illustrates this point in discussing the Holy Teacher: When a great teacher has reached the place in his own development where he has no teacher of his own and has no colleagues, he finds himself wondering at times who he really is and what his teaching is or should be. He alternates between being and wondering what it is that he really is and really is presenting. So it is for everyone. We present a face. Sometimes we are convinced that we honestly are what we portray to the world; at other times we wonder if we aren't fooling ourselves. Perhaps both conclusions are true.

The disruption of a person's projection has consequences on three levels. It disrupts the social interaction going on. Things may come to an embarrassed halt. The person risks losing, perhaps permanently, his reputation. But perhaps most important, the person's image of himself is disrupted or changed. Therefore a person engages in defensive maneuvers to maintain his front, and if others want to continue the interaction with him, they help him repair his front (Goffman, 1959).

A special kind of threat to a person's front is *stigma* (Goffman, 1963b). A stigma is something about a person that would damage the front he is trying to maintain. It is something about his life or his past history that would damage his reputation if it became known. Stigma management is a matter of information control if the stigma is not known, or of tension control if it is known. Generally a person tries to keep the skeletons hidden in closets, as a way of maintaining a front. But a stigma that escapes from the closet disrupts the front and brings into play a whole host of defensive maneuvers that will be discussed later in the chapter.

A final aspect of the personality that should be discussed is *character*. Character is a person's self, but it is also the part a person plays (Goffman, 1959). That is, using some earlier concepts, character is both the social identity or the face that is presented, and also the unique person himself or the ego identity of the person. These two concepts often get equated or confused, but actually they are different. Popularly, character is often defined as that which a person "really" is. But in considering what a person "really" is it becomes necessary to use Goffman's two categories. His social identity is what other people think he "really" is, while his ego identity is what the person himself thinks he "really" is. If a person is taken in by his own front (which we all are part of the time), then the two are approximately identical.

There are two more aspects of character that are of importance. First, the concept of character is basically a moral one. When we discuss a person's character we are essentially making a moral evaluation of him. Second, character is something that can be gained or lost. That is, apparently the person has it within his own power to improve or degrade his character. If a person performs a despicable act, he has ruined his character, or his character has broken. If he performs some worthy, self-sacrificing act, he may redeem his character.

An example of a person who experienced this loss and redemption of character is Nathan Leopold. As a young University of Chicago student in 1924, he, with a friend, killed a boy and dismembered his body primarily as an idle prank to see if they could commit the perfect murder. This grisly crime horrified the country and resulted in a classic court trial in which Leopold was sentenced to life imprisonment. The case created such an outcry that it was used as an example of the horrors that could be expected to come from atheism and modern philosophy. This conclusion was drawn from the fact that Leopold was a devotee of the philosopher Friedrich Nietzsche. Leopold's character was ruined, and Nietzsche's character certainly suffered. While serving his sentence, Leopold became involved in medical experiments in which he not only contributed intellectually to the success of the research, but he also served as a human subject at some risk to himself. As a consequence of his performance in medical research, in which he risked his own life and health in order to help others, Leopold was deemed both by the public and the State to have redeemed himself. He was subsequently paroled.

Encounters, Transactions, and Interactions

An encounter is a face-to-face interaction between two or more people and is governed by rules peculiar to the encounter itself. These rules are internal to the encounter; rules from the external world do not apply, although some rules from the external world may intrude into the encounter. When external rules intrude, they are transformed in some way (Goffman, 1961b). For example, in a bridge game the players may be two married couples. Each person in the encounter has a special relationship, that of husband or wife, to one other person in the encounter. Within the bridge game, this relationship might be transformed by some rule within the encounter to the effect that spouses do not play as partners. This factor from the external world would then be transformed by the rules of this particular encounter in such a way that each husband might be paired with the other's wife as his partner in the game.

Each encounter, then, runs according to the rules for the encounter. The rules and relationships from the external world may intrude, but they will be transformed in the encounter by the rules of the encounter.

The Setting

Encounters occur in *settings*. There are many aspects to the setting in which an encounter between or among people occurs, but two are the most important. There is the *physical setting,* which Goffman terms the *situation,* and there is the *social occasion,* which is whatever it is that is supposed to be going on between the people that brought them together in that particular place, at that particular time. Both of these factors have an effect on what goes on between the people.

Since we are concerned here with what happens between people when they meet in the ordinary course of their lives, it follows that the situations, or physical settings, in which they encounter each other will be wherever two or more people can be found. The settings can be on the street, in a store, in an office, in a factory, at the beach, or even at the bottom of the sea. Any place qualifies as long as two or more people happen to run into each other there.

Since there are so many possible settings for people to encounter each other, for the purposes of exposition, Goffman (1959; 1961b) has discussed the game and the theater as paradigms for the setting. In the theater there is a frontstage and a backstage. The frontstage is where the audience sees what it is supposed to see. That is where the performance is carried on. The backstage is where all the props are kept, where the actors put on their costumes and makeup and generally make the preparations for the performance. Actually, the "front" and "back" of the setting include more than the physical setting. The rehearsals are likewise a part of the back, since even though they are conducted on the frontstage with the curtains open, they are conducted long before any audience arrives. "Back" is where all of the activities that support or are preparatory to the performance in the face-to-face encounter with another person are carried on.

In everyday life all kinds of encounters have a back of some sort. "Back" is usually an idea rather than a place. For insurance agents "back" is mental practicing of their sales pitch before approaching a potential customer. For lovers "back" might be thinking about how they feel toward their beloved before they meet, and it could also include the purchasing of gifts for the beloved. Every encounter, for Goffman, might be considered a performance, and backstage is where each of those who engage in the encounter prepares for it.

When the backstage intrudes into the frontstage it may threaten to disrupt the performance. It threatens the image created by the frontstage performance. Therefore a person who is engaged in an encounter generally tries to keep his back and front separated. Sometimes, however, it may serve the purposes of the front to reveal the back. Perhaps the point at which a person engaging in an encounter decides to reveal the back is the point at which an encounter moves from being a routine one to an unusual, possibly intimate one.

An encounter might be viewed as having a kind of membrane around it which surrounds it and separates it from the rest of the world (Goffman, 1961b). However, this membrane is permeable if the encounter occurs in a situation that is *accessible* — that is, where there are bystanders present. If two people carry on their encounter in a room full of other people, their encounter is accessible to the others present (Goffman, 1963a). The others generally will not intrude in the encounter, but there are certain rules the encounter must follow if it is to continue in this setting without interruption. The participants will probably space themselves away from the other people in the room in such a way that another person is not between them. They will keep the general excitement level of their encounter down so as not to draw the attention of the others. They will avoid topics that involve bystanders.

People who are engaging in encounters in public places can sometimes be observed pulling the membrane of their encounter a little tighter around themselves by glancing around the room to see who is present and possibly eavesdropping. Perhaps a good place to study the care and tending of encounter membranes in public places would be the spy movie.

Unfocused Encounters

There are two kinds of face-to-face interactions, focused and unfocused. An *unfocused interaction* is when two people just happen to be in the same place at the same time, and their behavior affects each other. A *focused interaction* is when two people are cognitively concentrated on each other, as in a conversation. Two people sitting in the waiting room of a bus station and having a conversation are in a focused interaction. Two unacquainted people sitting in the waiting room of a bus station are in an unfocused interaction. A handsome boy and an attractive girl who are unacquainted with each other can carry on quite an unfocused interaction in such a situation.

An unfocused interaction is really an interaction between two people who do not acknowledge to each other or to anybody else that such an interaction is occuring. People communicate to each other through their dress, their grooming, their posture, their movements, and their glances every time they come into one another's presence (Goffman, 1963a, p. 33). This communication goes on whether or not either of the participants is aware of it; and even if they both are aware of it, they do not acknowledge it to each other. A certain amount of dissimulation goes on. The boy mentioned in the previous paragraph might be ostensibly reading the newspaper, when in fact he is concentrating on the girl. The girl might be presumably studying the bus schedule, when in fact she is primarily involved in her interaction with the boy. Both participants in such an unfocused interaction are primarily involved with each other.

In an encounter people have differing involvements which apply to both unfocused and focused encounters (Goffman, 1963a, p. 46). There are *main involvements* and *side involvements*. A main involvement is a person's activity of primary attention, while a side involvement is something else he is doing at the same time. In the bus-station example above, the boy's main involvement is the girl, while his side involvement is the paper he is reading. There are also *dominant involvements* and *subordinate involvements*. When the station announcer announces the bus that the boy has been waiting for, the boy gets up and leaves, thus revealing that his dominant involvement all the time has been catching the bus, while the girl has been a subordinate involvement to the bus. A person may also be *underinvolved* or *overinvolved*. If he is underinvolved, he is not paying as much attention to the encounter as the encounter has a right to demand of him. If he is overinvolved, he is so involved that he is tense and upset about the situation to the extent that it disrupts his performance in the encounter.

A final type of involvement is *dissimulation*. Perhaps dissimulation is especially apparent in the unfocused encounter. In the unfocused encounter two people are presumably carrying on another activity while they are also interacting with each other. Their main involvement appears to be one thing, when in fact it is another. They hide behind an "involvement shield." Likewise, their dominant involvement may also not be what it appears to be. The typical master burglar at a formal ball is apparently engaged in socializing as both his main and dominant involvement, while we know he is really mainly involved in casing the joint for an imminent theft.

A type of unfocused interaction that has always fascinated me is that between some unacquainted men and women in public places. The man eyes the woman, while ostensibly reading his newspaper or feeding the pigeons, while the woman preens and struts or otherwise plays the model who is receiving a kind of applause for her efforts at personal grooming. The thing that has interested me about this interaction is the expression that sometimes appears on the woman's face in this kind of situation; it is a sort of Mona Lisa hemi-demi-semi-smile. There is room for photographic research into this phenomenon.

There are certain rules that people appear to observe in unfocused interactions. For example, for one person to stare at another is generally against the rules, unless the other has behaved in some unseemly way, in which case staring is a kind of punishment for the misdeed. On the street there is a certain kind of "civil inattention" that people are supposed to give to each other. If two unacquainted people pass each other on the street they will usually glance at each other, then when they are about eight feet from each other their glances will veer off from each other, just as two motorists dim their headlights at night when they pass (Goffman, 1963a, p. 84).

Focused Interaction

An unfocused interaction may lead into a focused interaction, or it may not. In any case, one of the rules of society is that people are supposed to make themselves accessible to encounters. People make themselves accessible to encounters because, in part, it may be to their advantage to do so. A stranger who approaches a person may be coming to return the wallet he dropped without knowing it, or to warn him that the British are coming, or to bring some other message that will be helpful to him.

However, in being accessible to encounters people are also taking risks, since they may have something to lose in an encounter. In an extreme case, the stranger who hails a person may take his life or rob him. Or he may make a request that the person does not want to meet, or he may merely waste the person's time. Nonetheless, most of us usually follow the general rule that we should be accessible to encounters, and we make ourselves accessible to all people who do not give off by their looks or bearing a message that tells us that we possibly have more to lose than gain by the impending encounter (Goffman, 1963a, p. 107).

The initiation of encounters follows certain rules. When two people who are acquainted meet, they are expected to initiate an encounter with each other. On the other hand, when two people who are not acquainted happen to find themselves in the same situation, they require a special reason to initiate an encounter. Some people, by their roles or situations in life, are always open to encounters with strangers. Policemen are open to encounters; clerks in stores are open to encounters. Generally the very old and the very young are open to encounters by strangers. People who are put out of their role by some unusual event, such as tripping and falling on the street or by dropping a package, are available to be encountered by an unacquainted person, who may help them to their feet or pick up their package for them.

There are certain situations in which people are open to initiate encounters with strangers. When two people from the same country meet in a foreign land, they will generally initiate an encounter, as will two people from the same state when they meet in another part of the United States. Two people who accidently bump into each other on the sidewalk should initiate an encounter, if only to exchange apologies. And two motorists who run into each other on the highway are obliged by law to initiate an encounter to exchange names, addresses, and insurance companies. People involved in a common disaster are open to the initiation of encounters. There are certain areas and situations, such as parties and parks, where people are more-or-less open to the initiation of encounters by others. There are certain cocktail lounges where men and women go to pick up other people or be picked up by others, and certain roller skating rinks where younger persons go for the same purpose. In small towns, everybody, by virtue of being an inhabitant of a place where everybody is supposed to know everyone else, is open to the initiation of an encounter (Goffman, 1963a).

An encounter is typically initiated with a glance. First the person who is initiating the encounter catches the eye of the person whom he wishes to encounter, then after a slight pause, he begins to speak. If the other answers back with a glance and responds to the verbal overture, the encounter begins.

When one person has taken the first step toward initiating an encounter, the person who has been approached may accept the initiative or reject it. This is the risk that a person always takes when he initiates an encounter—he may be rejected. The techniques of rejection are several. The approach may be ignored, it may be rejected, or it may be parried by what Goffman (1963a, p. 146) calls the "terminal squirm," in which the person turns away and makes some not completely audible remark of rejection. Of course the person who is trying to initiate the encounter may counter the rejection by pursuing the person and trying to "get a rise" out of him.

People who are acquainted are obliged to initiate a focused encounter when they meet. Acquaintanceship, per se, is generally not very important to relationships, but it does oblige us to be accessible to encounters with those with whom we are acquainted. People may become acquainted informally, by working at the same plant or by participating jointly in some event, such as traveling on the same train. Or people may become acquainted formally by being introduced to each other by a third person. However, some kinds of introduction do not really constitute an acquaintanceship. When, for example, two people are walking down the street and run into a third person who is known to one of the pair but not to the other, the one will probably introduce the stranger as a courtesy, but this kind of introduction is not generally held to form the basis for claiming acquaintanceship. In fact, it is possible for two people to run in overlapping circles and as a consequence be introduced to each other several times without ever forming the basis for an acquaintanceship. This sort of thing is quite likely to happen to people who attend the same conventions (Goffman, 1963a, p. 112).

There are several different kinds of focused encounter. If two people are cognitively, fully engaged in an interaction—which is to say they are paying attention to each other—then it is a *fully focused encounter*. If there are more than three people present, with two people fully engaged with each other, and if next to them within the same gathering another couple is also fully focused on each other, then it is a *multifocused encounter*. If there are three people involved, with two fully focused on each other, and if the third standing idly by is not engaged in the encounter, then it is a *partly focused encounter*.

A focused encounter has all the involvements that are found in an unfocused encounter. It has main and side involvements, and dominant and subordinate involvements. A participant may be underinvolved or overinvolved. In addition, there is another aspect of involvement that becomes of some importance in the focused encounter. A person may be "away"—that is, he may withdraw into his own thoughts or fantasies. This kind of involvement does not seem to be really applicable to an unfocused encounter, since if a person were "away" in an unfocused encounter, the encounter would not occur. This would, in effect, constitute a refusal to become involved in the encounter. However, in a focused encounter situation—for example, at a party—a person is expected to be accessible to and involved in encounters, and if he is away in his own fantasies, then he has a noticeable main involvement that is not with the person with whom he is ostensibly interacting. Also there are what Goffman (1963a) calls *occult involvements* such as baying at the moon or bobbing for apples, which if engaged in alone are likely to result in the neighbors talking, but when engaged in while in an encounter with another are generally looked upon as fun, or as understandable high-spiritedness.

Every conversation is a focused encounter, and getting into it is a touchy business. Essentially it requires the person initiating the encounter to scale down his self-expression, and the person to whom the opening is directed must scale up his interest (Goffman, 1967). The encounter itself may be viewed as a performance in which both participants are trying to maintain a front before each other (Goffman, 1959). Each person tries to present his best front in an idealized performance. This generally results in the performer giving the impression that he is reasonably successful in his business or profession, that he is happily married, and that his children are doing tolerably well in school. He gives the impression that he is versed on the topic of conversation, or if he is not familiar with the topic, he is then fascinated with the other's demonstration of his own knowledge in the area. If, in the middle of the other's peroration on American Asian policy, the listener should happen to yawn, he has broken a rule by inadvertently exposing his back (his fatigue) when he should have been keeping his front up (his mouth shut).

One of the main objectives of a focused encounter is for each person to present his front and to have it confirmed by the other person. As Goffman puts it, "The elements of a social encounter, then, consist of effectively projected claims to an acceptable self and the confirmation of like claims on the part of others" (1967, p. 105). However, beyond the desire to have an audience before whom one can perform, and who can confirm the act that a person projects, there is also in each person in the encounter a desire for a more intimate relationship. This leads people to feel each other out cautiously as a way of seeing whether or not the front may be let down. After all, it is not onstage but backstage that an actor relaxes. It is with those with whom we can release our inhibitions that we engage in our most relaxed and enjoyable encounters. So two people engaged in an encounter gradually feel each other out, letting down the front a little to reveal what they really think, how they really feel, and how they really managed to build the house they live in, sew the dress they are wearing, or get the job they now have. Each move is made in such an ambiguous conversational way that it can be disavowed without difficulty if the other person should react in the wrong way. Although few encounters reach real intimacy, presumably that is the desired goal. As Goffman puts it, "Whatever it is that generates the human want for social contact and for companionship, the effect seems to take two forms: a need for teammates with whom to enter into collusive intimacies and backstage relaxation" (1959, p. 206).

In addition to being fully engaged in an encounter, two people may also be engaged in a focused encounter that procedes in an intermittent fashion. This is what Goffman (1963a, p. 102) calls *copresence*, as when two people are lying on the beach and exchange comments from time to time, or are walking down the street and occasionally say something to each other.

Instead of becoming engaged in an encounter, a participant may also become alienated. People are expected to be spontaneously interested in the encounters in which they engage. If they have to feign interest, the pleasure of the encounter is killed, and they become alienated from it. This alienation may take several forms. A person may be alienated because he is preoccupied with something else; his main involvement is elsewhere. Or he may be self-conscious, which is to say that his main involvement is with his own performance rather than with the encounter itself. Or he may be overly conscious of the interaction process itself rather than the encounter with the other person. Or he may be overinvolved with the other person, so that he is overly concerned with what the other person is thinking or feeling rather than with the encounter per se. Or he may be distracted by the mannerisms of the other person who might, for example, speak with an unusual accent or have an unusual appearance.

Some of these kinds of alienation are common sources of social discussion and concern. A person who is self-conscious in an interaction is overinvolved with himself and underinvolved with the encounter. An affected person is primarily concerned with the image he is projecting and is only secondarily involved in the encounter. In a sense, he is mainly involved with himself without being overinvolved with himself. The insincere person is mainly involved with what the others think of his opinions, and therefore is also mainly involved in not revealing opinions he may hold of which he thinks the others might disapprove (Goffman, 1967). People who cannot maintain at least the appearance of spontaneous involvement in encounters are killjoys, wet-blankets, and faulty interacters. They don't live up to the rules, and their punishment is exclusion from parties in the future.

How long a focused encounter lasts depends on the situation. Encounters can be as short as a brief glance, or they may consist of a greeting, or they may develop into conversations that last for hours (Goffman, 1963a, p. 101). Two acquaintances who meet again just five minutes after they have spent some time talking to each other will probably only exchange friendly glances. On the other hand, two old friends who see each other after several months of separation will be expected to spend some time chatting together. Generally speaking, each encounter lasts a period of time that is appropriate to how close the participants are to each other and to how long it has been since last they saw each other. The length of the encounter is positively related to their closeness and to the length of time since last they met.

Finally, a person makes himself known to others by the focused encounters he engages in. A person is known by the company he keeps. Further, a person may be known by the encounters he does *not* engage in. It is not unusual for a person to eat breakfast alone while he reads his paper. However, if he is seen every night in the same restaurant eating supper alone, others are likely to conclude that he is a recluse. There are certain times and places when one is supposed to be engaged in an encounter, and if he is not, others debit that to his social reputation (Goffman, 1963a, p. 104).

Face and Face-Work

The concept of face was discussed briefly earlier in the chapter in the section entitled *Self and Identity.* The main exposition of the topic was delayed for inclusion in this section on interaction because face is mostly concerned with what one presents to another in a focused, face-to-face interaction, and because face-work is concerned more with the interaction between people than with the intrapsychic dynamics of an individual (Goffman, 1967, p. 5).

Face is the positive social value a person assumes for himself. It is that "good Joe" face he presents to the world in which he portrays himself as capable, kind, wise, or whatever positive line it is he takes for himself in public. Face is established by what other people assume his line to be. It is what he wants others to think he is, and what others think he wants them to think about him. It is the image of himself that he tries to project to the public.

Since a person puts out, or on, a face, he has a vested interest in the face that he has projected and tries to protect or enhance his face. Face-work revolves around the project of protecting and enhancing face. When a person takes a line in an encounter, he, in effect, is making promises to other people that he will perform in certain ways in the future. A person who passes himself off as an expert in mathematics is promising, without saying so in so many words, that he will be able to explain the method by which the paths of space vehicles can be plotted. His face as a math expert has, in an unspecified and implicit way, promised others that he understands and can explain mathematical problems. Should someone ask him to explain how it is that a computer can compute so rapidly and he is unable to explain this, he will then fail to fulfill his promise and will lose face.

Perhaps the most common example of this kind of public operation of promise, face, failure to fulfill promise, and loss of face is exhibited in sports. A great batter like Ted Williams was booed frequently by baseball fans. This kind of reaction does not seem to make sense, since Ted Williams was the greatest hitter of his time. But because he frequently made base hits, people expected him to make a hit every time he came to bat. His high batting average projected a face that implicitly promised a hit. Therefore, if he came to bat with the bases loaded and his team two runs behind, the fans expected him to get a hit and knock in two or three runs. If he failed, he had failed to deliver on the promise implicit in his batting average, and thus he lost face.

A given face often suggests other attributes about a person that have not been exhibited at all in public. For example, marriage counselors presumably know how to help husbands and wives get along well in marriage, so people will expect them to be happily married themselves, without knowing anything about the marriage counselor's spouse or their relationship. I once knew a marriage counselor who was the director of a marriage counseling clinic and had quite a thriving practice. The community considered him an expert at helping people solve their marriage problems. One day he left his wife. This created quite a shock for the people in the community, since they expected him to be able to solve his own marriage problems. As a consequence, he lost substantial face, as well as most of his clients, and was subsequently forced to ply his trade elsewhere, since he did not have enough business to support himself in the community in which he had lost face.

Therefore, the line a person takes has a promissory quality which leads other people to expect certain kinds of performance from the person in future situations, even though the person's line has revealed nothing about how he is likely to perform in such a situation. In fact, the whole business of aptitude testing is built upon the idea that answering a lot of multiple-choice questions correctly and logically leads to the expectation that a person will get good grades in school. A person who does well on aptitude tests and entrance examinations is taking the line that he is a good student.

A person is in *wrong face* when information comes out that is not consistent with the face he has presented. He is *out of face* when he doesn't have a line available that others would ordinarily expect him to be able to maintain in a situation. *Saving face* is the process by which a person gives the impression that he has not lost face. *Giving face* is what a person does to give the impression that another person has not lost face. *Face-work* is what a person does to maintain face. In encounters the rules call for a person to maintain his own face and to help other people maintain their face. A person has two points of view: a defensive orientation toward saving his own face and a protective orientation toward helping other people save theirs. Great skill at saving one's own face is generally known as *savoir-faire*, while skill at helping others maintain their face is tact.

There are many kinds of loss-of-face situations. The best way to avoid loss of face is to avoid the situations in which face might be lost. This can be accomplished by avoiding topics or persons who might lead to loss of face. It can be done by treating a situation as a joke. Or it can be accomplished by interpreting the information that threatens face as meaning something entirely different from what was implied.

Face is lost through the action of a person, and the repair of face depends on how it was lost. Face may have been lost because a person acted innocently. In this case it can be repaired by a simple apology, or in certain situations by going on as though nothing happened. An ice skater who falls down in the middle of a performance has lost face, but there is not much he can do but get up as gracefully as possible and continue the act. A person who inadvertantly lets slip to another that a party is planned in the honor of the other, and then learns that the party was supposed to be a surprise, can't do much more than apologize. Or an offense may have been a simple accident or inadvertancy. Again a simple apology may suffice. If the offense was malicious, a whole new set of rules apply.

The sequence of acts set into motion when face has been lost is an *interchange.* The four moves of an interchange are: (1) the challenge, by which the other person or persons call attention to the misconduct; (2) the offering, where the offender has a chance to correct his mistake and offers to correct it; (3) the acceptance of the offender's offering by the person who has been offended; (4) the expression of gratitude by the offender for having been allowed off the hook.

If the original offense was intentional and malicious, the offender may refuse to accept the challenge, in which case the offended one must take another course of action. He has several alternatives: (1) fight, in which he then returns an offense; (2) flight, in which he leaves the field; (3) he may ignore the whole thing; or (4) he may divert attention to another topic.

One problem that arises as a consequence of face-work is that every face-saving practice that is introduced to save the situation raises the possibility that threats to face may be introduced in the future in order to take advantage of the face-saving procedures. For example, a husband and wife may entertain occasional face-destroying spats because they enjoy the face-saving procedures that follow—that is, the loving apologies.

When face-work is not treated as something that everyone must perform, then an encounter may become a game in which the participants each try to accumulate as many points as possible. Points are gained through snubs, digs, one-upmanship, and so on. In some circles the participants may even chalk up imaginary points on imaginary blackboards when someone has scored a point. Such an encounter becomes a game, and usually the participants recognize the game character of the encounter. This type of encounter is often clearly illustrated when two comedians get together on an unrehearsed television talk show in which each tries to top the other.

Deference and Demeanor

Deference is what one person shows to another, while *demeanor* is a person's dress, bearing, and so on (Goffman, 1967, p. 47). Both deference and demeanor are governed by rules of conduct. These rules have two aspects, a moral aspect, in which the rule is an obligation, and an aspect of expectation as to how others will act toward one. There are two main classes of rules of conduct, symmetrical rules and asymmetrical rules. A *symmetrical rule* is one which leads people to act toward each other in the same way. An *asymmetrical rule* is one which prescribes that one person will treat the other in one way, while the other will act in a different way. The relationship between two colleagues is governed by symmetrical rules, while the relationship between a teacher and a student is governed by asymmetrical rules. There are also rules of substance and rules of ceremony. *Substantive rules* guide conduct that is important in its own right, such as not physically abusing another person. *Ceremonial rules* govern conduct in which the act in itself is not important, but it is important in what it communicates, such as an expression of the person's character or an expression of appreciation for another person. Gift-giving is governed by ceremonial rules.

Deference is what one person shows to another. It serves two main functions: to express regard and appreciation to another person and to keep another person at a distance. Deference may be shown by a subordinate to a superordinate, as by an employee to an employer, and it may also be shown between equals, as by one ballplayer to another who has just hit a home run. It does not necessarily have to contain an element of awe, but it must contain an expression of regard or respect.

Society is governed by rules that keep people at a distance from each other. Goffman ties this into the sacred character of the human personality which must not be violated, but must be protected. Rules protect others from penetrating the reserve that protects the personality, and deference is one of these protective means. Deference that keeps a superior at a distance may protect the personality of the superior, but perhaps it protects the personality of the subordinate even more, since a superior has rights to penetrate the private reserve of a subordinate, while the subordinate does not have rights to penetrate the reserve of a superior. Parents have the right to ask personal questions of their children, but children do not often ask personal questions of their parents. Teachers ask questions of pupils, but pupils don't often ask personal questions of their teachers, and when they do, it is with a certain amount of trepidation.

Demeanor is also governed by rules that are symmetrical and asymmetrical. By his dress and bearing a person presents himself as having certain qualities. In compliance with the symmetrical rule of demeanor, people will expect, implicitly or explicitly, a sloppy dresser to perform sloppily in other areas of life. When a sloppy dresser appears neatly attired, or a neat dresser shows up a mess, others assume something of importance has happened in each of their lives. The asymmetrical character of demeanor is usually in evidence on a university campus, where many students dress in T-shirts and jeans, while professors usually dress a little more formally.

Deference and demeanor are also a means of communication. When a person does not exhibit deference to one to whom he would be expected to show deference, it is not only a violation of a social rule, but it also may signal the beginning of a rebellion. Blacks who began the movement toward full participation in the life of their communities were sometimes described as "uppity," which meant that they weren't showing the deference and demeanor that was expected of them. Of course, when a person fails to show the deference and demeanor which others expect, he can assume that sanctions will be applied. It is at this point that a shift in the social relationship is signaled.

Dynamics of an Encounter

Encounters have *dynamics*, which means that an encounter is not static, but rather a moving, changing phenomenon. Things go on between people in an encounter, and the encounter as a total phenomenon may move in particular directions.

In his book, *Encounters* (1961b), Goffman discusses the dynamics of the encounter within the paradigm of the game. The basic activity in the game is the move, which is made, or taken. In a move a person commits himself to a position which must be chosen, usually, from a rather small range of possibilities. At any given point in a given game there are a limited number of moves open to a player. The dynamics of the game are in the moves back and forth between players.

The purpose of a game, ostensibly, is to win. However, for most games winning in and of itself is not the real objective. Witness the lackadaisical attitude of both players and spectators, or even kibitzers, toward a one-sided game. Obviously, the primary purpose of a game is the pleasure the participants get out of it, and that pleasure is maximized when the game is a very close one. So the real purpose of an encounter is *euphoria,* which is enjoyable engrossment. Euphoria is maximized in a game or an encounter when the outcome is in doubt until the very end, when the stakes in the game are high enough to arouse interest but not so high that external reality intrudes into the encounter, and when the play is somewhat removed from reality but close enough so that real rivalry intrudes into the play. In a conversation the participants should be personally close enough to each other so that they can talk with ease, but not so close that everything between them has already been said and they are bored.

Dysphoria, or tension, may be produced in an encounter if the participants are not fully engaged—they are pretending to an involvement that they don't feel. Carrying on the pretense of being interested in the monologue of a bore is a very wearying experience. People try to eliminate tension by introducing incidents such as jokes, puns, or whatever as an intrusion into the encounter. These incidents may produce a *flooding out*—when a person breaks out laughing or crying. When a person floods out, his personal reaction overwhelms the encounter, and he is removed from immediate play.

Embarrassment may be a kind of flooding out. It occurs when a person is out of balance—that is, when the front a person is presenting to others is not what he wishes it were—and is usually a sign of weakness or feeling of inferiority. For example, a person who puts forth claims about himself and fails to live up to them becomes embarrassed. Or a person who inadvertantly accepts two dinner invitations for the same evening becomes embarrassed upon realizing his mistake, because he cannot possibly deliver for both invitations what he promised—his promise for one, at least, will have to remain unfulfilled.

Embarrassment can come from role confusion. When we display one role in a situation that calls for another role, we are embarrassed. A story from World War II illustrates this point. A pilot radioed an airfield asking for clearance to land. The radio operator gave him the clearance. The pilot answered the operator's response by saying, "Roger dodger." The operator responded with, "You say 'Roger, sir' to me. I'm a major." The pilot responded, "Roger dodger, you old codger. I'm a major, too."

Embarrassment does serve a useful social function. For example, by becoming embarrassed because he can fulfill neither of two possible roles, a person may leave open the possibility that he can fill either of them. That is, if a person accepts two invitations for the same time, then by being embarrassed, he is saving face for the other people involved. They are not being rejected or put down; rather the error and shame are all his. And he can say either "I'm so sorry, I can't come" or "I'll see if I can work it out so I can come." In both cases, face is saved, and a satisfactory solution for all parties involved is likely. Through embarrassment the "social structure gains elasticity; the individual merely loses composure" (Goffman, 1967, p. 112).

Encounters have a tendency to drift away from the original purpose of the meeting or the original topic of discussion. This "drift" is perhaps most apparent on occasions that call for a particular mood. People at funeral homes generally speak in lowered tones out of deference to the bereaved family, but the conversations among the people drift away from the dead person to more immediate considerations. If the dead person left a widow, the discussion may start with a discussion of the widow's emotional reaction to the death, then move on to a consideration of how well-off her husband left her financially. If the discussants have known the widow for a long time they might then speculate on how much better off she might have been had she married another man she dated during her maiden days, a fellow who is now wealthy and still alive. From this they might speculate on whether or not she will take a job, and mention a place at which she has worked part-time, let us say a real-estate office. This then might lead into a discussion of houses and the real-estate market and how the participants are planning to re-do their own homes. What started out as a discussion of concern for a widow has become a conversation on interior decorating.

Ending an Encounter

An encounter is usually ended with some kind of ritual that will assure the participants that the relationship will continue even though the encounter has come to an end. If relationships are in the process of change, the ending will be managed in such a way as to insure that the development of the relationship will not be altered. The enthusiasm of the farewell is designed to compensate the relationship for any harm that is about to come to it from the impending separation (Goffman, 1967, p. 41).

Stigma

Some people have special problems in social interaction. These people are disqualified from social acceptance by a given group because of some stigma (Goffman, 1963b). *Stigma* is a blemish or flaw (as defined by the particular group). There are three kinds of stigma: physical disability; membership in some stigmatized group, such as a specific religious body or social class; and character defects, which are usually manifested by some discrediting event in a person's past, such as giving birth to an illegitimate child or serving a prison sentence.

When a "normal" person and a stigmatized person meet in a face-to-face encounter, the latter is faced with several problems. If the stigma becomes known, it might discredit him before other people. Therefore should he keep it a secret, or should he make it known? If he keeps it a secret, he himself knows that he is discreditable; yet if he makes it known, others may discredit him. His main problem, then, becomes one of *information control*, or information management. In addition, another problem arises if he discloses the stigma. In this case he has the problem of *tension control*, since once the stigma is disclosed, he cannot be sure what other people "really" think about the stigma, and because of this he may experience tension. The most typical pattern of stigma management in face-to-face relationships is to disclose the stigma to a very few close friends and to keep it a secret from everyone else.

As Goffman (1963b, p. 137) points out, the problem of stigma control is not really a case of a few who are stigmatized and a majority who are not. Rather, it is a perspective. A person who is stigmatized in one situation may be perfectly normal in another situation. A person who has a prison record would be normal among the Black Muslims, since they have several prisoner rehabilitation programs, but abnormal among the FBI. Conversely, a member of the FBI would be abnormal among the Black Muslims. All people in our society suffer some discrepancy between their virtual identity and their actual identity and thus are faced in some situations with the problem of information management or tension management.

The problem of information management versus tension management has been demonstrated to me repeatedly by graduate students in clinical psychology. The typical graduate program in clinical psychology is generally loaded with generous amounts of "hard," behavioristic psychology, based on the measurement of segments of peripheral, observed behavior. Most clinical psychology graduate students are interested in "soft," phenomenological kinds of data and problems. They want to study love and hate, or hope and fear, or the purposes which people try to achieve in life. These are rather difficult subjects to relate to courses that study the learning curve of a rat in a maze or the behavior of a psychotic patient in a token economy. So many graduate students feel that they have to bootleg their interests by undertaking extracurricular reading and discussion. Their problem is, Should they disclose their "real" interests to their professors and risk being discredited as serious graduate students by the psychology faculty? We all share this problem in some context.

Action and Fateful Activity

Action is taking a risk. "Wheresoever action is found, chance-taking is sure to be" (Goffman, 1967, p. 149). *Fateful activity* is activity that is both problematic and consequential. The outcome of a risk-taking venture is its consequentiality, or its consequences. *Problematic activity* is activity in which what to do is a problem. What people do when they are at work or in school is not likely to be a problem. That activity is prescribed. What they do during their free time may be a problem; it is up to them to decide. By "action" Goffman (1967, p. 185) means activities that are consequential, problematic, and done for their own sake.

Face-to-face interactions may involve fateful activity. Certainly courtship falls into this category—it has consequences that can last for a lifetime, it is problematic since it is up to the people involved to decide what to do, and it is undertaken for its own sake.

The most important risk in interpersonal action is the risk of the self. In every encounter people take the risk that their self might be confirmed or disconfirmed; their face might be lifted, enhanced, lost, or totally destroyed. For that matter, their character might be redeemed or lost.

Any encounter might become a character contest—a dispute between the participants over the boundaries of their selves. "When the contest occurs over whose treatment of the other is to prevail, each individual is engaged in providing evidence to establish a definition of himself at the expense of what can remain for the other" (Goffman, 1967, p. 241). An encounter, then, can become something approaching a zero-sum game. Both people may lose, one may lose and the other gain, or both may emerge from the combat with honor. Perhaps it would be worthwhile to do research, as a kind of diagnostic technique, on the personal gains and losses that occur in a person's interpersonal encounters with others. In any case, some aspects of interpersonal encounters are much like those of a high-stakes game, or even a war. Fiction is full of examples of this sort of fateful action. The main character of Saul Bellow's *Herzog* is a kind of constant loser on the field of interpersonal encounters. Dr. Hudson in Lloyd Douglas's *Magnificent Obsession* arranges his encounters so that everybody usually wins. Ian Fleming's character James Bond usually ends his encounters with him winning and his evil adversary losing. Perhaps unwittingly, Goffman has provided us with a method for classifying fiction.

Discussion

Goffman's approach to interpersonal relations makes a unique contribution to understanding what goes on between people, but also contains one marked weakness. The contribution is the view of the interpersonal interaction, not from what is going on within the people participating in the engagement, nor even primarily from the point of view of what goes on between the people, but rather from the point of view of the rules of society the participants follow in their interaction with each other. The rules people follow when they interact with each other have not been so extensively delineated by any other researcher studying the interpersonal interaction. Nor has anyone else devoted himself to what goes on between people in ordinary, everyday interactions.

Paradoxically, this unique contribution contains within it the weakness in Goffman's approach. He seems to view most of what goes on between people as a function of the rules society has taught them: "Universal human nature is not a very human thing. By acquiring it, the person becomes a kind of construct, built up not from inner psychic propensities but from moral rules that are impressed upon him without" (Goffman, 1967, p. 45). But where do these rules come from, and what is this impersonal, inhuman "something" that impresses these rules from without? Rules are not impressed upon a person by an impersonal society. They are taught to people by people. And where did these rules come from? Did they drop from the sky, or were they developed by people over centuries as a way of dealing with unhappy interpersonal encounters and of preventing unhappy interpersonal events from occurring in the future? We might raise the question, What would happen if these rules ran counter to the "inner psychic propensities" of humanity? They would probably die in a hurry. The moral upheavals of the twentieth century are an example of what happens to moral principles that become inharmonious with the ongoing dynamic of life. When the moral principles become more of a hindrance than a help, they are changed.

The more accurate way to look at these rules, which Goffman has described well, is the same way that we look at the performance of a person in a role. The observation of a rule, as well as the playing of a role, emerges out of a dynamic interaction between the person and the requirement. When the inner dynamics or the needs of the person come into conflict with either the rule or the role, the rule (or role) goes.

In a sense, Goffman's observations have a very narrow data base, although in another sense they have the best data base of all. His data are his observations of the behavior of people in everyday life. He is, in a sense, a naturalist who studies human beings—his subjects are normal human beings observed in their native habitat. The level of his study is at the level of the person and the level of the dyad or group. His data are composed entirely of overt, observed behavior. In his assertion that people are built up out of the rules impressed upon them, he implies that the experiences of people are of no value and are therefore not worth studying. In this sense he is in direct opposition to introspectionists such as Laing and Maslow.

As a theory, Goffman's is a rather broad one. He provides useful metaphors for describing how people function and how they interact with each other. He accounts for the development of patterns of behavior. The content of his theory is composed of those phenomena that are observable by the man-on-the-street. However, whereas the average man-on-the-street is content to observe and perhaps develop a few unconnected conclusions about how people behave in public places, Goffman has created a structure within which his observations may be related to one another. Goffman is a people-watcher's theorist. Goffman hasn't done any experimental research to validate his conclusions, but it is likely that when the experimental research is done, it will confirm his observations of what people do in ordinary situations: They follow rules.

Summary

Goffman seeks to describe the *rules* that govern the encounters between people. He is not primarily concerned with the internal personal needs of people as they effect the interaction between people, nor is he concerned primarily with what goes on between people as an expression of needs; rather, he is concerned with the rules people observe in their interaction with each other. These rules are prescribed by the society in which people live. Thus, what goes on between people is described as a function of the rules which people have learned to observe in their interaction with each other.

There are two kinds of encounters, focused and unfocused. A *focused encounter* is one in which the people involved are cognitively engaged with each other; they are overtly paying attention to each other. An *unfocused encounter* is one in which the people involved are interacting, but they are not ostensibly engaged with each other. Two strangers waiting for the same bus, though not speaking to each other, are engaged in an unfocused encounter.

Within an encounter the objective is to gain *euphoria*, or involved enjoyment. In an encounter people are always taking *interpersonal risks*. These risks are that they might suffer loss of *face*, or diminution of their selves, or embarrassment. Therefore, much of what goes on between people in an encounter is designed to help people enhance themselves. *Defenses* serve to prevent a person from suffering a loss to his own face, while *tact* is what a person displays when he helps another person maintain that person's face.

One aspect of people that requires special handling in order to maintain face is stigma. *Stigma* is some blemish, which, if known, would cause loss of reputation or loss of face. We all suffer some discrepancy between the self we present to others and the self we really are, so we all are faced in some situations with problems of stigma management.

Finally, encounters may be fateful action. *Action* is any situation in which there is risk. *Fateful action* is action in which there is some risk, in which the activity has consequences that extend beyond the immediate situation, and in which it is up to the engaged people to decide what to do. In encounters, what we risk is confirmation or disconfirmation of the self.

References

Buber, M. *Two kinds of faith.* New York: Harper & Row, 1961.

Goffman, E. *The presentation of self in everyday life.* Garden City, N.Y.: Doubleday Anchor Books, 1959.

Goffman, E. *Asylums.* Chicago: Aldine Publishing Co., 1961. (a)

Goffman, E. *Encounters.* Indianapolis: Bobbs-Merrill, 1961. (b)

Goffman, E. *Behavior in public places.* New York: The Free Press, 1963. (a)

Goffman, E. *Stigma.* Englewood Cliffs, N.J.: Prentice-Hall, 1963. (b)

Goffman, E. *Interaction ritual.* Garden City, N.Y.: Doubleday Anchor Books, 1967.

A Summing Up

14

History suggests that the road to a firm research consensus is extraordinarily arduous (1969, p. 16).

—T. Kuhn

In the first chapter of this book, I suggested that certainty was not possible in the study of interpersonal relationships, but that probabilities were probable. By that statement I meant that from the effort devoted to studying interpersonal relationships should come information that ought to provide some tentative conclusions concerning their nature. These tentative conclusions ought to include such things as the basic kinds of concepts that are of importance in interpersonal relationships, the variables that operate, the instruments and units by which these variables might be measured, and the relationships among these variables. In addition, the summary of these conclusions ought to give some idea of the stage of development of the study of interpersonal relations.

In this final chapter I will endeavor to fulfill this mission. The first section of the chapter will attempt to describe the current stage of development of the field of interpersonal relations. The second section will summarize the more important generalities that seem to emerge from the wide variety of methods by which interpersonal relationships have been studied.

Stage of Development of the Field of Interpersonal Relations

I have attempted to gain an overview of the field of interpersonal relations in two ways. First, I have summarized the kinds of people studied by the various researchers, the kinds of research they have conducted (that is, the means by which the data have been collected), and the theoretical background out of which the particular kind of study developed. This summary appears in Table 1. Second, I have attempted to locate the various methods of studying interpersonal relationships on a graph (see Figure 1) containing two dimensions describing the kinds of data on which a particular approach to the study of interpersonal relationships is based. One dimension is the *level*. Level can vary from a behavior segment, such as a gesture, a word, or some other piece of individual, identifiable behavior to a group of people acting in concert, like a football team in action. The behavior segment is the lowest level presented on the graph. The next level is at the level of the person. Ordinarily this level would refer to behavior of the whole person and would include the measurement of somewhat more global variables, such as personality traits like dominance or defense mechanisms like obsessionalism. The group or dyad level consists of concepts that require two or more people if it is to be applicable. Variables such as competition, cooperation, rejection, and acceptance all require two or more people. The second dimension is the *type of data,* ranging from introspection on one end of the continuum to overt behavior at the other end. Introspection is the subject's report of what he thought, how he felt, or what he was planning to do. Overt behavior is action that is observable by another person and includes such things as overt choices among several alternatives, and specifically observable movements, such as smiling, walking, embracing, or hitting.

If you look at Table 1, some conclusions become obvious. First, it is apparent that research has been conducted on two kinds of subjects: patients, or people with emotional problems, and normals, or people who, so far as the researchers knew, had no emotional problems beyond those of the average person. Second, research data have been obtained from three kinds of situations: psychotherapy, field observation, and laboratory experimentation. Third, the theoretical sources of the study of interpersonal relationships have been various, including among others, psychiatry, existentialism, behaviorism, communications, social psychology, Gestalt psychology, linguistics, and decision theory. "Empiricism" refers to research that has collected data without proceeding from any explicit theoretical assumptions and has attempted to make some sense out of the data collected.

If you look at Figure 1, you can see that the various methods of studying interpersonal relationships are scattered throughout the space

TABLE 1. **VARIOUS APPROACHES TO THE STUDY OF**
INTERPERSONAL RELATIONS

Approach	Chapter	Kind of Subjects	Research Situation	Theoretical Source
SULLIVANIAN	2	Psychiatric patients	Psychotherapy	Social psychology Psychiatry
VERBAL COMMUNICATIONS	3	Patients Normals	Observation Laboratory	Psychiatry Communications
NONVERBAL COMMUNICATIONS		Patients Normals	Psychotherapy Observation Laboratory	Linguistics Personality theory Empiricism
TRANSACTIONAL ANALYSIS	5	Patients	Psychotherapy	Psychiatry
EXISTENTIAL PHENOMENOLOGY	6	Patients Normals	Psychotherapy Laboratory	Existentialism
PSYCHOLOGICAL MEASUREMENT	7	Patients Normals	Laboratory Observation	Psychometrics Empiricism
SOCIAL EXCHANGE	8	Normals	Laboratory	Behaviorism Economics
ATTITUDES AND ATTRACTION	9	Normals	Laboratory	Gestalt psychology Behaviorism
NEEDS	10	Normals Supernormals	Observation Laboratory	Personality theory
GAMES	11	Normals	Laboratory	Decision theory Economics
ROLE	12	Patients Normals	Observation Laboratory Psychotherapy	Social psychology
ENCOUNTERS	13	Normals	Observation	Empiricism

described by the two dimensions. There appears to be some approach
to the study of the interpersonal relationship in every part of the graph
except the lower center, the lower left-hand corner, and the upper left-
hand corner. This may suggest that some creative souls might advance
the study of interpersonal relationships by devising some method for
studying them by data that are either introspective or a combination of
introspection and overt behavior at the level of the behavior segment.
Or they might devise a method of studying the interpersonal relation-

FIGURE 1.   **LOCATION GRAPH OF VARIOUS APPROACHES TO STUDYING INTERPERSONAL RELATIONS BASED ON LEVEL (CONTENT) OF THEORY AND TYPE OF DATA COLLECTED**

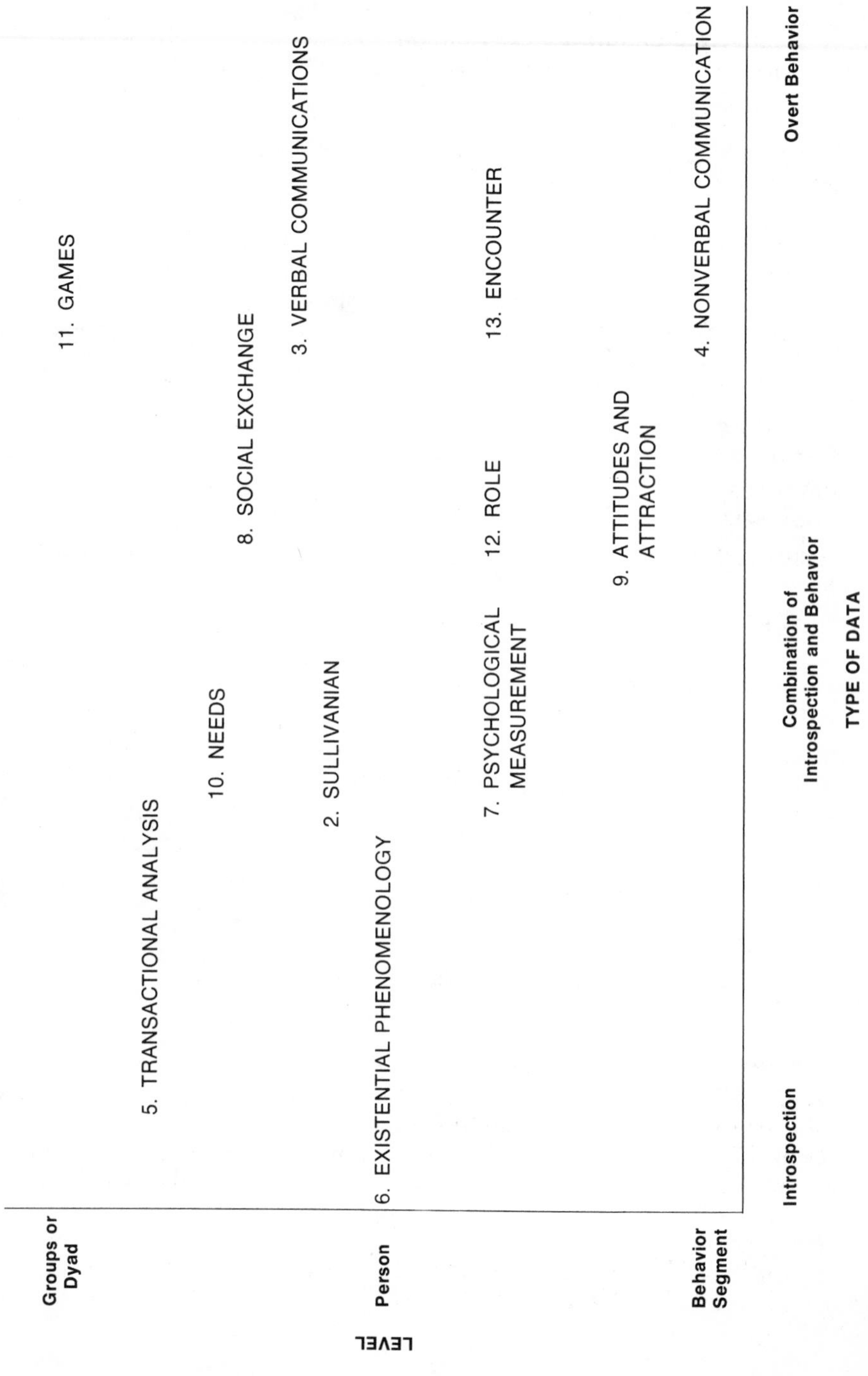

	Introspection	Combination of Introspection and Behavior	Overt Behavior
Groups or Dyad	5. TRANSACTIONAL ANALYSIS	11. GAMES 10. NEEDS 8. SOCIAL EXCHANGE	3. VERBAL COMMUNICATIONS
Person	6. EXISTENTIAL PHENOMENOLOGY	2. SULLIVANIAN 7. PSYCHOLOGICAL MEASUREMENT 12. ROLE 9. ATTITUDES AND ATTRACTION	13. ENCOUNTER
Behavior Segment			4. NONVERBAL COMMUNICATION

LEVEL

TYPE OF DATA

ship that uses introspective data at the level of the dyad. This location chart is not meant to imply that any of the particular approaches to the study of the interpersonal relationship rely exclusively on the kind of data described by the point on the chart at which a particular approach has been placed. Rather, the placement represents a kind of central tendency, or mean, or average of the kinds of methods typically used by a particular approach.

I did not compile Table 1 and Figure 1 as a definitive summary of the current status of interpersonal relations. Rather, I compiled them as a way of summarizing, roughly, the current status of the field of interpersonal relations. One conclusion that is clear from this summary is that currently the study of interpersonal relationships is highly diverse. It is diverse in the kinds of subjects it uses, the kinds of research methods it uses, the kinds of theoretical sources from which it has developed, and the kinds of data it collects. This diversity can tell us something about where interpersonal relations now stands as a field of research — that is, the stage of development the field has reached. If we use the model of scientific development described by Thomas Kuhn (1969), the situation in the study of interpersonal relationships described above appears to fit neatly into one of the stages of scientific development described by Kuhn.

Kuhn describes science as progressing via the mechanism of the paradigm. A *paradigm* is "an accepted model or pattern" (Kuhn, 1969, p. 23) for a field of study. A paradigm contains concepts, and these concepts contain the variables that should be studied and measured if the field is to progress. One of the main tasks of a field of study is to determine how these variables relate to each other. To take an example from the field of electricity, there is a simple equation, Ohm's Law, which states that in a direct current electrical circuit, the important variables are current (I, measured in amperes), electromotive force (E, measured in volts), and resistance (R, measured in ohms). The relationship among these variables is described by the equation $I = E/R$. That is, in an electrical circuit the amount of direct current flowing through the circuit is equal to the amount of electromotive force divided by the amount of resistance in the circuit. The paradigm provides the basic variables to be studied, and in the course of this study, the relationships among the variables are worked out. Thus, science progresses. But before the relationships among these variables can be worked out, some model must have been accepted which states which variables are important to measure. A paradigm is a model of how things work, and science normally progresses most rapidly when there is a single model that is generally accepted by all of the people working in the field. Having just one model to work on, researchers can each relate their work to the work of others in the field, and thus with maximum speed, work out the relationships among the variables in a particular field of study. Of course, paradigms change, because as workers investigate a field they inevitably find that some aspects of the model are incorrect, or they discover phenomena that cannot be contained within the model. This situation creates a crisis in science that continues and worsens until a new paradigm is developed which accounts for the inaccuracies in the old model and accounts for the new phenomena discovered. This is the process of scientific progress as described by Kuhn.

However, before a paradigm is developed that is generally accepted by most of the workers in a field of research, the field is in a stage Kuhn terms the *preparadigm stage*. This stage is characterized by a number of schools, each school more-or-less competing with the other schools of thought. Each school has its own model, contains its own concepts, stresses its own group of variables as being the important ones to study, and has its own measuring instruments and research methods. Of course, if the people involved in studying a particular phenomenon are all studying approximately the same thing, there should be some overlap among the concepts they use and the measuring they do, and there should be considerable similarity among the variables studied by these competing schools.

Kuhn describes how the preparadigm stage comes about. In the absence of any paradigm that determines which facts are the important ones to study, the people involved in a field of study use whatever facts happen to be available. The facts that are most likely to be available are the facts obtained in everyday experience. These are the kinds of facts ordinary people could gather if they observed what was happening around them. The next most obvious category of facts that are gathered are those gathered by professionals working in a particular field. Farmers and sailors were probably the first professionals to observe the weather because it is a crucial variable in the success of their craft. Those working in a craft make observations which may be written down, but which are certainly passed down verbally from the old masters to the apprentices in the trade. However, Kuhn observes that this sort of fact gathering produces a plethora of varying data. Out of these emerge different schools of thought concerning the topic being studied. The situation in which there are many different competing schools of thought characterizes the early stages of a science's development. If we now return to Table 1 and Figure 1, it would appear that this is where the field of interpersonal relations stands today. If we use Kuhn's system of scientific development as a basis for diagnosing the status of interpersonal relations, it appears that it is in the preparadigmatic stage of development.

How does a field get out of this preparadigmatic stage of development? Kuhn describes the process as one in which one of the preparadigmatic schools gradually wins out over the other schools and becomes accepted as the basic paradigm for the field by most of the people working in the field. So, if Kuhn's analysis is correct, the next stage in the development of the field of interpersonal relations would appear to be one in which one of the models described in this book (or some more highly developed variant of it) would ultimately become accepted by most of the people engaged in studying interpersonal relationships. Kuhn states that "to be accepted as a paradigm, a theory must seem better than its competitors, but it need not, and in fact never does, explain all the facts with which it can be confronted" (1969, p. 17). Kuhn suggests that the way a paradigm comes to be accepted is that it appears more attractive to the young people entering the field. Thus, if we are to try to determine which of the approaches to the study of interpersonal relationships is the most likely to emerge as *the* paradigm for the field, we must make a judgment as to which is likely to appeal most to those people entering the field. It seems likely that the maturation of interpersonal relations into the paradigmatic stage is still a long way off, but we might make a brief detour to speculate on which of the current methods of studying interpersonal relationships seems the most likely to develop into a generally accepted paradigm.

A school which becomes a more generally accepted paradigm in interpersonal relations will have to have enough breadth to account for a wide range of phenomena in the field; it will have to stimulate research that adds to the understanding of the phenomena; and it will have to have "aesthetic" appeal, which is to say that it will have to appeal to the young researchers entering the field. By young researchers I think we have to include clinicians as well as those who do their research by experimentation and field observation, since much of the early and current information being collected has either been collected by clinical observations or by research stimulated by interpersonal behavior observed in the clinic.

Using these as the criteria, I suggest that the most likely paradigm candidates for interpersonal relations are the Sullivanian approach, role theory, and the psychological measurement tradition, probably in some combination with exchange theory. If you observe Figure 1, you will notice that all three of these approaches to the study of interpersonal relationships are located toward the center of the two-dimensional space.

Starting with the last of these three, psychological measurement in combination with social exchange theory, it can be observed that this combination has the advantage of developing from a long and honored tradition in research psychology. Both have stimulated a large amount of empirical research; and Foa (described in Chapter 7) has published two papers (Foa & Foa, 1971; Turner, Foa, & Foa, 1971) that point out the possibility of a rapprochement between the two. Foa has studied the resources, or rewards, or payoffs exchanged in interpersonal relations and has concluded that the payoff concept used in both social exchange theory and game theory does not take into account that the same kind of payoff, whether in money, or a kiss, or a kind word, does not mean the same thing to all people in all situations. To give an example, a complementary word to a person for having done a good job at designing a building means one thing if it comes from a panel of architects and a different thing if it comes from his spouse. Likewise, a kiss from his spouse means something quite different from a kiss from a member of the panel of architects. Foa suggests that the commodities exchanged to provide the payoff can be ordered on two dimensions: *particularism* and *concreteness*. The order of the commodities exchanged on these two dimensions is presented in Figure 2.

Particularism refers to the extent that the value of a particular reward is influenced by the particular person who gives the reward. Love from a spouse has more value than love from an acquaintance or a colleague, so the value of love is highly particular to the person who gives it. Money, on the other hand, has the same value regardless of who gives it. Concreteness refers to how concrete or symbolic a reward is. Specific services like shining shoes, and specific goods like shoes are highly concrete. Information and status, on the other hand, are symbolic. Love and money have both concrete and symbolic aspects. With this scheme Foa feels that it is possible to fix more precisely the value of a payoff in either the social exchange system or the game theory system. Thus it is a step toward more precisely determining the value of payoff, a problem in those systems which were discussed in Chapters 8 and 11. This scheme was developed by Foa by applying his psychometric way of thinking about things to a problem in the social exchange and game theory systems. This example is cited here to illustrate the possibility of the development of a more extensive and widely applicable paradigm from a productive interaction between the psychometric and social exchange approaches.

The continuation of such a development is also made more prob-

FIGURE 2. **CLASSIFICATION OF RESOURCES BY PARTICULARISM AND CONCRETENESS**

	Concreteness	
	More	Less
More		
	Love	
	Services	*Status*
Particularism		
	Goods	*Information*
Less		
	Money	

able and more useful by the fact that the psychometric approach in combination with the social exchange approach ties in with the other reinforcement or reward systems that have developed in other areas of behavioral science, particularly learning theory. However, this approach seems to suffer from two disadvantages. First, it suffers from the extensive philosophical, social, and ethical criticisms levelled against behavioristic theory (see Wann, 1964). Many people seem to be against behavioristic theory for one reason or another. And this ties in with the second weakness, which is that behavioristic theory is not very popular with young people these days. If Kuhn is right about a paradigm becoming generally accepted because, among other reasons, it appeals to the young people entering the field and gradually gains general acceptance as the young take over and the old die off, then any behavioristic theory will probably suffer in the competition. This, of course, is a debatable point, in view of the present popularity of behavior therapy. It seems to me that whether or not it is just, or rational, or desirable for a theory to be accepted because it has aesthetic appeal to the young, nonetheless this is probably a factor of significance in the acceptance of a paradigm, and that, because of this, the combination of the psychometric and social exchange approaches probably will not be the ultimate paradigm that is accepted. However, much useful research has been produced by these two approaches to the study of interpersonal relationships, much additional information will be gathered by these approaches, and this body of knowledge will have to be incorporated into any paradigm that does eventually gain authority in the field.

The next paradigm candidate to the field of interpersonal relations, role theory, probably holds more general sway in the field than any other approach today. It has a fairly long history and a secure place in sociology and social psychology and has stimulated more research than any other theory. Generally, as was indicated in Chapter 12, it seems to be the most useful theory in studying some kinds of interpersonal relationships, particularly the marriage relationship. However, role theory suffers from a certain lack of generality. It is not really a theory, but rather, a collection of hypotheses. There is no generally accepted role theory. Furthermore, it does not stimulate any great excitement. It is a battered, trusty old tool that has been used over and over again, and like a good screwdriver or hammer, it will continue to be used without arousing any particular affection or stimulating any scintillating deeds of interpersonal investigation. I suggest that if role theory were likely to evolve into a generally accepted paradigm, it would probably have begun to do so by now, and in any case, it does not seem likely to excite the imaginations of the young. However, role theory, like the psychometric and social exchange approaches, has stimulated the collection of masses of information that will have to be incorporated into any system that does become a generally accepted paradigm.

This brings us to Sullivanian theory. Sullivanian theory has an honored history. It is in a direct line of descent tracing back through Mead and Cooley to earlier moral philosophers. It has the widest generality of any of three approaches we have discussed here. Carson (1969) has demonstrated that Sullivanian theory can be expanded and revised to incorporate much of the information accumulated by other approaches to interpersonal relationships, including the concepts of role and reinforcement. And, in most applied areas at least, Sullivanian theory has demonstrated considerable capacity to attract the young. Thus, my candidate for a future, generally accepted paradigm for the field of interpersonal relations is one that has a general structure similar to that contained in Sullivanian theory, and which incorporates the content of most of the other approaches to the study of interpersonal relationships. I believe that Sullivanian theory, more nearly than any other approach, has the capacity to lend itself to other theories. Let me illustrate this point. Laing, in his existential phenomenology makes many of the same observations as Sullivan. Laing has observed that the symptoms of the patient are a product of the social situation within which the patient is living. Sullivan began from the same observation. Laing has developed a conceptualization of the schizophrenic that is not too different from that of Sullivan (compare Chapter 2 and Chapter 6). So the existential-phenomenological approach can surely be incorporated within the structure of a Sullivanian-derived system. Sullivan included the concept of needs, so needs theory can be accommodated within his system. Sullivan stressed both verbal and nonverbal communications, so the communications approaches can be incorporated. Sullivan discussed the role of learning and included concepts of learning that are based on reinforcement, so there is a point of entree for social exchange theory and game theory. Finally, the psychometric approach can be applied to any conceptual system — since any set of variables needs to be measured if research is to progress — so the psychological measurement approach has a point of entree.

To summarize, Sullivanian theory seems to have more potential generality than any other approach to interpersonal relations. However, this potentiality has not yet been realized, nor is it likely to be realized for some time to come. But if I were forced to bet, my bet would be that when a generally accepted paradigm for the study of interpersonal relations comes, it will be a direct lineal descendant of Sullivanian theory.

Some General Conclusions

At the beginning of this chapter, I stated that I would attempt to summarize the general conclusions that emerge from the material discussed in this book. I will endeavor to fulfill this task in this section by including the concepts that seem to have emerged repeatedly in the various approaches to the study of the interpersonal relationship and summarizing the conclusions that seem to emerge from the facts collected in the various and sundry studies, whether clinical, observational, or experimental. The topics discussed are in descending order of their generality. For example, the first topic, communications, is one in which there is the widest agreement concerning its importance and its nature. Presumably the more people agree on something, the more probable their conclusion is one that will stand the test of time. Therefore, the order in which these topics are discussed should approximate the degree of confidence that can be placed in the conclusions.

Communications

Clearly the single most important topic on which there is the widest agreement is that communication is an essential, integral part of the interpersonal relationship. Communications includes everything that goes on between two or more people, including the words uttered, the manner of utterance, the facial expressions, gestures, and body movements made by the people involved.

Communication goes on at more than one level. One message may be sent verbally, but another message may be sent by tone of voice, facial expression, or gesture. The messages that are sent simultaneously may agree with each other, they may conflict with each other, or they may deal with separate topics. When the messages conflict, difficulty is apt to occur in the relationship.

Communication has a corrective characteristic. That is, as two people communicate, their communications tend to clear up misunderstandings. The more communications that occur, the more likely two people are to cooperate with each other.

There is some indication that verbal communications tend to communicate information, or cognitive content, while nonverbal communications tend to communicate feelings, or emotional content. Also, there is some evidence to suggest that there are three basic dimensions to communications: potency or dominance, liking or attraction, and responsivity or activity or amount. That is, what is communicated is who is in control, who likes whom, and how strong these feelings are.

Importance of Parental Teaching

People interact with other people in the same ways that they have observed their parents interact with other people. This is indicated by research that shows that a person in an interpersonal interaction is described in the same way by those others as the person describes his own parents. People who grow up in families in competitive business tend to be competitive, while people who grow up in families in which their parents are engaged in a cooperative kind of occupation are more likely to cooperate in a game situation. The families in which people who become schizophrenic are raised usually have a father who is passive, a mother who is dominating, and a psychological split between the mother and father.

Generally, it is agreed that people behave like their parents because they have learned how to behave from their parents. There is no general conclusion as to the processes of learning by which this interpersonal behavior is taught by parents to their children, but it seems safe to say that there is more than one process of learning involved.

The self-concept is learned in interaction with other people, and the most important other people that a person interacts with in the most important years of his development are his parents. A person develops his concept of himself largely from his perception of his parent's perception of him. "Just as the twig is bent the tree's inclined."

Needs

There is general agreement within psychology that people have needs. One of these needs is the need for satisfying relationships with other people. This need is described in different terms, such as a need for teammates, or a need for human contact, or a need to be significant to another person. However, just contact with another person is not enough. It must be a contact in which the person feels secure, in which his self-esteem is not injured — a contact with a person whom he feels knows and approves of him as a person. Laing suggests that we have a need to have a relationship with another person who sees us as we see ourselves — and accepts us as we are.

Other needs are also suggested as having importance to the interpersonal relationship, including such needs as dominance, submission, nurturance, succorance, love, esteem, self-actualization, achievement, power, and affiliation. About the function of these other needs there is some dispute; but there is agreement that "people need people."

Self and Identity

The two most common categories of people that keep appearing in the study of interpersonal relationships are the "self" and the "other." The concept of self has had a long and checkered history in psychology, but it has had staying power. There is a general need for a concept such as "self" in the study of interpersonal relationships. However, the kinds of selves that are described vary considerably. Thus, perhaps the most that can be concluded is that some such concept of self as viewed by others, or social identity — that is, how others see us and behave toward us — is essential. The self, as a social phenomenon, develops out of interaction with other people. The self-concept, the conception we have of ourselves, develops in substantial part from our perception of how others perceive us. Beyond these statements, there is little consensus, but there are many provocative observations.

Basis of Attraction

People are attracted to other people. That is obvious. One clear basis for attraction is similarity. We are attracted to those who are like us. As to why, there is some dispute. Perhaps it is safe to say that we are attracted to other people who reward us in some way, whether this is in terms of net payoff in social-exchange-theory terms, or satisfying our needs in needs-theory terms, or in meeting our need to be seen by another person in a way that is similar to the way we see ourselves. Those who are like us are attractive to us. Those who reward us or meet our needs are attractive to us. Those whom we think will be like us or will reward us are attractive to us. Whether the mechanism by which this works is cognitive balance or reward or self-confirmation or some combination of the three is a matter of dispute.

Factors in Interpersonal Relationships

A substantial amount of research on different kinds of interpersonal relationships suggests that there are at least two basic dimensions in the dyadic relationship. These dimensions are called by different names, but they have to do with dominance versus submission and acceptance versus rejection. In groups, a third dimension seems to appear—a dimension that has to do with whether or not a person helps the group progress toward its goal. Interestingly, research on voice quality and facial expressions indicates that similar dimensions can be discriminated in those phenomena.

Other kinds of dimensions have been suggested, such as stability versus instability, satisfaction versus dissatisfaction, and competitive versus cooperative. However, they do not have the generality of acceptance, empirical support, or general usefulness that exist for dominance-submission and acceptance-rejection.

Types of Relationships

When people start to study a field, one of the first tasks they set for themselves is categorizing the phenomena they are studying. People classify things before they do anything else. Interpersonal relationships is no exceptance to this rule. However, there is little agreement among the various kinds of categories proposed. Perhaps the categorization that might come closest to achieving general acceptance is the categorization of relationships into symmetrical, complementary, and parallel ones, or some variant of that categorization. That is, people either relate to other people as equals, or they relate to them in a superior-subordinate relationship, or their relationship is one that oscillates between equality and superiority-subordination. There is, of course, general agreement that relationships can be categorized. The disagreement is over which categories to use.

Reward

There is substantial disagreement as to the role reward should play in the study of interpersonal relationships, but there is agreement that behavior rewarded is behavior repeated. There is also disagreement as to what a reward is and what is rewarding, but again, agreement that people are attracted to those who reward them and are more likely to compete or cooperate, depending on which behavior promises the greater reward. Reward is a potent variable, but it is also a concept about which there is substantial dispute.

Norms and Rules

Regularities occur in interpersonal behavior, and these regularities are evidence for the existence of norms or rules which people follow. Norms serve the function of reducing the uncertainty or cost involved in interacting with another person. There is evidence to suggest that people have a need for predictability in their relationships, and this predictability is provided by norms that other people can be expected to follow. When the norms, or expectations are met, relationships proceed more harmoniously. Marriages are more likely to be happy if the husband and wife meet each other's expectations of the culture for a husband and wife. That is, husbands and wives are happier in their relationship to each other if they comply with the norms. The important factor here seems to be agreement between the people involved on what the norms are, and then on meeting those norms.

To the extent that there has been research on this topic, there seems to be agreement. However, except for the role theorists, this seems to be an important topic that has been relatively ignored by others studying interpersonal relationships.

Reciprocity

There is some evidence that there is a rule of reciprocity in interpersonal relationships. We tend to treat other people the way they treat us. Role theorists suggest that reciprocity is a rule or norm. Empirical observations indicate that over a period of time, people in interaction with each other come to behave about the same way toward each other. There seems to be a need in people to maintain some sort of balance or equity in relationships. This is another topic that seems to be of importance, but on which there has been little research.

Social Intelligence

Among the more provocative conclusions that seem to have emerged from research is one that has relatively little data to support it; yet the data that do exist, though they come from diverse backgrounds, seem to point to one conclusion: that ability to be sensitive to other people and to relate harmoniously to them is a function of a kind of social intelligence. Studies of role performance and nonverbal communications indicate that those who are more sensitive to others and who are more perceptive of the requirements of a role are those who have the cognitive ability to detect the cues in the environment that indicate what another person feels or expects. That is, there is a kind of social intelligence that should be measurable, and those who are high in this intelligence have more satisfying interpersonal relationships than those who are low.

The results of studies indicate that self-actualized persons may be exemplary of persons with social intelligence. They perceive reality more clearly, and they have more satisfying relationships than people who are less self-actualized.

The idea of social intelligence appears to be another topic in which the evidence is thin, but such evidence as exists strongly suggests that it would be profitable to pursue research that has as its goal the development of a test of social intelligence. This intelligence would appear to be a kind of cognitive intelligence in which the person who has it detects accurately such things as pitch, timbre, and rhythm of sounds, small movements in facial expression and gesture, and similar kinds of sensory cues.

Stages of Relationships

There is evidence that indicates that relationships progress through stages. However, the surprising thing about this topic is the relative dearth of empirical information on it. It seems reasonable to conclude, on the basis of common-sense observation and personal experience, that relationships do, in fact, proceed through stages, but comparatively little attention has been given to determining these stages. Social exchange theory suggests that these stages are sampling, bargaining, commitment, and institutionalization.

Other evidence suggests that relationships change as the needs of the people involved change. Social exchange theory would predict that if a relationship lasted long enough, it would tend to be satisfying to the people involved, regardless of how the relationship started out. Game theory research tends to support this conclusion, with the finding that the longer two people engage in a game, the more they tend to cooperate with each other.

But the main conclusion suggested by this review is that there is need for extensive research on the normal course of development of various kinds of interpersonal relationships.

The Situation

Every interaction occurs in some kind of situation or setting, and the situation or setting within which the interaction occurs affects the kind of interaction that occurs. This is another topic that has been relatively ignored, although it is perhaps more understandable. The kinds of relationships that people studying interpersonal relationships are most likely to be interested in are either the sort of relationships, like marriage, that occur in a variety of settings and situations — so that the situation tends to cancel itself out — or else it is a relationship, like psychotherapy, that occurs in the same or similar settings and situations — so that the situation is not one of apparent importance. Another factor is that when the setting or situation is of substantial importance, it overrides interpersonal considerations, so that the potency of the situation swamps the relationship. Two lovers in a riot behave in terms dictated by the riot, not by their relationship to each other. A husband and wife with a critically ill child behave toward each other in ways dictated by the illness of the child.

However, the effect of the setting and the situation is another aspect of interpersonal relations that has received rather sparse attention.

Basic Units

Back when we were considering one of the important variables in the development of a field of study, general agreement on the basic units of measurement was mentioned as one of the variables of critical importance to unity and speed of progress within a field. There has been a lot of argument about the basic units in the interpersonal interaction, but not much agreement. Perhaps the closest thing to a unit is the action-reaction unit, which is composed of one person's action and another person's reaction to it. As Carson (1969) points out, in an ongoing interaction between two or more people it is often difficult to know how to discriminate these units. One person's action may start the interaction, but the other person's reaction also serves as the stimulus to the first person's next action, and so on. Where should the units be divided? As a consequence, the basic units used tend to be arrived at mostly by fiat and the arbitrary judgment of the people doing the research. And when people make arbitrary judgments, others who consider themselves as expert as the person making the initial judgment are likely to disagree.

*   *   *

It should be pointed out that the conclusions suggested above all derive from more than one source. These are the conclusions that seem to have some basis in more than one school of thought. Each approach to the field of interpersonal relations can suggest many additional conclusions that seem secure when based on the information derived from that particular tradition.

One broad conclusion clearly emerges from this survey of the field: The study of interpersonal relations is a vital, lively field of endeavor that is producing a continuous and growing stream of information, hypotheses, theories, and controversies. Such a dynamic field of endeavor is also one that is in a state of constant change, so that any overview is out of date as soon as it is produced. And that is true of this survey. The picture presented in this book is the picture of a situation that has already passed.

One, final, grand conclusion returns us to the point at which we started. That conclusion is that "human nature is something social through and through . . ." (Mead, 1934, p. 229).

Summary

The field of interpersonal relations appears to be at the preparadigmatic stage of development. It is characterized by many competing schools of thought rather than by one model or paradigm that is accepted by most of those working within the field. When one generally accepted paradigm emerges, it will probably be one that has developed out of the Sullivanian framework.

Certain general conclusions about interpersonal relations are suggested. They are: Communications is an integral part of the interpersonal interaction—communications is verbal and nonverbal, and in communications more than one message is sent at the same time; the way a person interacts with other people is learned primarily from parents; needs affect relationships with others; the self is an important concept, and the view we have of our self develops from our perception of how other people perceive us; people are attracted to others who agree with them and reward them; dominance-submission and acceptance-rejection are basic dimensions in the interpersonal relationship;

relationships can be classified into relationships between equals, relationships between superiors and subordinates, and relationships that oscillate between equality and superiority; rules develop in any relationship; relationships tend to be reciprocal; sensitivity to other people is a kind of cognitive intelligence; relationships go through stages of development; relationships are affected by the situation within which they occur; and there is no agreement on the basic units within interpersonal relationships.

Finally, it is concluded that human nature is basically social.

References

Carson, R. C. *Interaction concepts of personality.* Chicago: Aldine, 1969.

Foa, U. G., & Foa, E. B. Resource exchange: toward a structural theory of interpersonal communication. In A. W. Siegman & B. Pope (Eds.), *Studies in dyadic communication.* New York: Pergamon Press, 1971.

Kuhn, T. S. *The structure of scientific revolutions.* (2nd ed.) Chicago: The University of Chicago Press, 1969.

Mead, G. H. *Mind, self and society.* Chicago: The University of Chicago Press, 1934.

Turner, J. L., Foa, E. B., & Foa, U. G. Interpersonal reinforcers: classification, interrelationship, and some differential properties. *Journal of Personality and Social Psychology,* 1971, 19, 168–80.

Wann, T. W. (Ed.) *Behaviorism and phenomenology.* Chicago: University of Chicago Press, 1964.

Index